THE BEST OF BIBLE PATHWAY

THROUGH THE BIBLE IN ONE YEAR BY READING 15 MINUTES A DAY

366 Daily Devotional Commentaries

7TH EDITION

Presented to

_____

on this _____ day of _____

*We . . . do not cease to pray for you, and to desire
that ye might be filled with the knowledge of His will
in all wisdom and spiritual understanding;
That ye might walk worthy of the Lord
unto all pleasing, being fruitful in every good work,
and increasing in the knowledge of God*

(Col. 1:9-10)

_____
_____

By

_____
_____
_____

The Heart of Our Government:
"In God We Trust"

The anticipation of the crowd was contagious! All eyes were riveted on **Gen. George Washington**. The man was legendary – the hero of the decade! He approached the outdoor balcony of Federal Hall in New York City on April 30, 1789; viewed the podium; paused; then asked for a Bible. Stepping onto the balcony, the General placed his right hand on the open Book and took the oath of office, becoming **the 1st President of the United States of America, 1789-1797**.

It is impossible to account for the creation of the universe without the agency of a Supreme Being. And it is impossible to govern the universe without the aid of a Supreme Being.

Bible Pathway is a Christ-centered through-the-Bible
devotional commentary and not a theological exposition.

The devotional thought reveals how each day's Bible reading relates to our personal relationship with God and our fellowman, as well as our own spiritual needs.

The world's most-widely-read through-the-Bible devotional commentary

Endorsed by leaders in all major denominations.

Scripture quotations are from the *KJV*

The text of the *KJV* may be quoted in any form (written, visual, audio, or electronic).

Any portion of this devotional guide may be reprinted without revision by adding the following: Reprinted from *The Best of Bible Pathway* – devotional guide; Murfreesboro, Tennessee

PRINTED IN CANADA

THE BEST OF BIBLE PATHWAY
7TH EDITION

THROUGH THE BIBLE IN ONE YEAR BY READING 15 MINUTES A DAY

366 Daily Devotional Commentaries

Published By

Bible Pathway Ministries
INTERNATIONAL
P.O. Box 20123
Murfreesboro, Tennessee 37129

TABLE OF CONTENTS

Presentation Page	I
The Heart of our Government/George Washington	II
Title Page	III
Table of Contents	IV-V
Foreward	VI
Introduction	VII
The One True God vs Idolatry	VIII-X
Life's Most Consequential Decision	XI
Life's Foremost Opportunity	XI-XII
The Power of God's Word	XIII
Annual Bible-Reading Check List	XIV-XV
The Privilege of Prayer	XVI

Index of Old Testament Book Introductions as well as
Maps, Charts, and Other Helps

Genesis	1
Journeys of Abraham, Sarah, & Lot	6
Jewish Calendar	19
Exodus	20
Tabernacle Encampment, Arrangement of Tabernacle Furniture	29-32
Leviticus	41
Five Major Offerings	44
3 Annual Pilgrimages to Jerusalem Required of All Men	51
Numbers	55
Israel's Unbelief	64
Exodus Out of Egypt & Route to the Promised Land	68-69
Deuteronomy	77
Joshua	90
Joshua's Conquest of Canaan	92-93
Judges	102
Twelve Tribes of Israel & The Six Cities of Refuge	104
Judges of the Israelites & The Six Cities of Refuge	105
Ruth	114
Kings & Prophets of Israel	116-117
I & II Samuel	118
David's Kingdom	129
I & II Kings	140
I & II Chronicles	161
Divided Kingdom	175
Ezra	184
Exiles & Return	186
Nehemiah	191
Esther	198
Job	202
Psalms	214
Proverbs	239
Ecclesiastes	248
Song of Solomon	252
Isaiah	254
Names & Titles of Christ in Isaiah	255
Isaiah's Prophecies	268
Jeremiah's Prophecies	269
Jeremiah	271
Lamentations	288
Ezekiel	291
Daniel	306
Two Views of Governments That Rule During "The Times of The Gentiles"	307
Hosea	312
Joel	315
Amos & Obadiah	317
Jonah	320
Micah	322
Nahum & Habakkuk	324
Zephaniah, Haggai, & Zechariah	326
Malachi	330

Index of New Testament Book Introductions as well as *Maps, Charts, and Other Helps*

Distance from Jerusalem
  to Major Places 332
Matthew 333
Old Testament Quoted by Christ 336
Israel At The Time of Christ 347
Mark 348
Luke 356
John 369
Appearances of Jesus
  After His Resurrection 377
Acts 379
Paul's Missionary Journeys 385-386
Events in The Life of
  The Apostle Paul 387-390
Romans 396
I & II Corinthians 402
Galatians 410
Map 410
Ephesians 413
Victory Over Satan Assured
  The Whole Armour of God 416-419
Philippians & Colossians 420
I & II Thessalonians 423
I & II Timothy 426
Titus & Philemon 429
Hebrews 431
James 436
I & II Peter 438
I John 442
II & III John & Jude 445
Revelation 447
The 7 Churches of Asia 448
The Isle of Patmos 448

For those wishing to pursue more in depth topical and word studies, a special section of Bible Reading Helps has been added.

Dictionary of Archaic Words 458-470

A partial list of hard-to-understand words will help Bible readers and students better understand various passages of Scripture.

Topical Index References 471-480

It is designed to cover specific topics such as faith, love, redemption, etc. Devotions dealing with the various subjects are listed for easy access.

- The Scripture references given in the devotions often include more verses than the ones actually quoted.

- When consecutive Scripture references from the same book are given, the name of the book is only mentioned with the first reference.

- **Upon completion of reading through the entire Bible**, send $2 for shipping and handling, along with your name as you wish it to appear/address/city/state/zip along with the following statement to receive your 8-1/2" x 11" **Certificate of Acknowledgement**. I have finished reading through the entire Bible on _____ (date) for the _____ (1st, 2nd, 3rd, etc.) time.

Foreword

God gives every generation of believers a select group of saints whose unique gifts and insights help keep His people on the right track. During the past half century, the Body of Christ has been blessed by the energetic yet unassuming work of Dr. John Hash.

I was still a boy when, the year after the close of World War II, Pastor Hash began a brilliant work among the people the Lord had given into his charge. Because knowing God's Word is the key to life for any Christian, Dr. Hash made it his top ministry priority. He developed a reading plan to guide people through the entire Bible each year.

Years later, after Dr. Hash's faithful daily devotions blossomed into Bible Pathway Ministries, I had the privilege of meeting him personally. At the time, I was serving as president of the Southern Baptist Convention and so was in a position to see a remarkable variety of approaches faithful pastors and teachers could take to help people draw nearer to God. But I said to Dr. Hash, in all sincerity, that there is nothing more valuable anyone can do than to establish a daily commitment simply to read the Word of God itself. For that reason, I cannot praise highly enough the vision and purpose of Bible Pathway. Its sole focus is to encourage believers to read the Bible and facilitate their understanding of Scripture.

As I reviewed the manuscript for this book, it was everything I would have expected from Dr. Hash – and a great deal more! It's ripe with some of the most helpful charts, maps, and illustrations available, and Dr. Hash offers sensitive insights into pressing issues that face today's church. Yet he always keeps foremost in mind the need of individual believers to maintain a vital, growing relationship with Jesus Christ.

If you've never read the Bible through in a year, you're in for a wonderful experience, and if you have, then you know the richness that awaits you as you do it again.

The Lord promised in Matt. 5:6 – *Blessed are they which do hunger and thirst after righteousness: for they shall be filled.* There is truly no better way to be filled with the righteousness for which you thirst than to read through the Word of God each year.

May God bless your journey on your Pathway with Him!

– **James T. Draper, Jr.,
President Emeritus, LifeWay Christian Resources**

Our prayer is *that the God of our Lord Jesus Christ . . . may give unto you the spirit of wisdom and revelation in the knowledge of Him: The eyes of your understanding being enlightened; that ye may know . . . the hope of His calling, and . . . the riches of the glory of His inheritance in the saints*
(Eph. 1:17-18)

The One True God vs Idolatry

You have often heard it said: "It really doesn't matter what a person believes as long as he is sincere." – But, what if he is sincerely wrong?

Throughout the Bible we learn that it matters enormously what or who is actually Lord (in control) of our lives.

There is a great deal in the Bible about idolatry. Even today, many are deceived and assume that they may have several man-made gods (though they do not call them such) in their lives. These "gods" are objects of their hearts' real desire and preoccupation. Although they haven't rejected the One True God, His importance above all gods continues to diminish.

Thou shalt have no other gods before Me (Ex. 20:3) is the first of the Ten Commandments from God. The Old Testament idols were images representing a deity, such as "the golden calf" (32:1-4) and the Israelites willingly gave their gold to Aaron to achieve that "god." It is written that they worshiped ***the works of their*** (own) ***hands*** (II Kin. 22:17).

The Lord Jesus Christ quoted from Deuteronomy, the command: ***Thou shalt worship the Lord thy God, and Him only shalt thou serve*** (Matt. 4:10; see Deut. 6:13). On another occasion, Jesus said: ***The first of all the commandments is, Hear, O Israel; The Lord our God is one Lord: And thou shalt love the Lord thy God with all thy heart, and with all thy soul, and with all thy mind, and with all thy strength: this is the first commandment. And the second is like, namely this, Thou shalt love thy neighbour as thyself. There is none other commandment greater than these*** (Mark 12:29-31).

When you know what it is that takes first place in a person's thoughts concerning material things and desires, what he looks forward to, and what he is willing to sacrifice for above all other things, you know what his god – his "golden calf" – is.

A person's real god is what he finds the most satisfaction in his heart thinking and talking about. These things or persons could become his idols.

In contrast, if we acknowledge our real God is the One True God expressed in three Persons as Father, Son (Jesus, born of the Virgin Mary), and Holy Spirit, we will find great pleasure in sharing Scripture from Genesis through Revelation and our experiences about the Lord Jesus with others. In every decision He will be our first consideration. A true Christian will ***seek . . . first the Kingdom of God, and His righteousness*** (Matt.

6:33). This means our first consideration is to know the will of God as revealed in the Bible in regard to all decisions: Our loyalty to Christ and His Church will be our first consideration. All else will be of less importance, such as employment, hobbies, sports, friends, etc.

As God's children, it is of utmost importance that our loyalty, love, and devotion to the One Living and True God be first in all earthly considerations. We will desire to have Christ as Lord (Ruler) over our lives.

We cannot have two supreme loyalties. As Jesus said: *No servant can serve two masters: for either he will hate the one, and love the other; or else he will hold to the one, and despise the other. Ye cannot serve God and mammon* (material things) (Luke 16:13). *But they that will be* (desire to be) *rich* (in material things) *fall into temptation and a snare, and into many foolish and hurtful lusts, which drown men in destruction and perdition* (ruin, downfall) (I Tim. 6:9). These Scriptures suggest that the word "idolatry" stands for whatever secular activity or persons become more important than our submission to Christ as Lord of our lives.

The Apostle Paul was led to warn that *covetousness . . . is idolatry* (Col. 3:5). Covetousness is self-concern and self-interest, as well as devotion to a person or material things, that interfere with our opportunities to serve the Lord. This means giving to self that loyalty and devotion which belongs to Jesus as Lord of our lives.

A true believer in the One True God is not deceived by the theory of "situation ethics" which assumes there is no absolute standard of right and wrong but rather that right or wrong depend upon circumstances.

The Apostle Paul was led by the Holy Spirit to describe true Christian conversion as turning *from idols to serve the living and True God* (I Thess. 1:9). Turning from idols is far more than merely professing that we are a Christian. The Lord Jesus Christ proclaims: *Thou shalt worship the Lord thy God, and Him only shalt thou serve* (Matt. 4:10). Jesus warned that the way of eternal life is a *narrow . . . way, which leadeth unto life, and few there be that find it* (7:14). *Not every one that saith unto Me, Lord, Lord, shall enter into the Kingdom of Heaven; but he that doeth the will of My Father which is in heaven* (7:21). In contrast to the world, Jesus demonstrated by His life and death that doing *the will of My Father which is in heaven* involves a willing subordination of our wills and way of doing things to the will of God. Each of us gives allegiance to someone or something; we're made that way. We do have a God in which we find life's satisfaction.

Paul was also led by the Holy Spirit to write of some *whose end is destruction, whose God is their belly, and whose glory is in their shame, who mind earthly things* (Phil. 3:19).

But he also wrote: *Present your bodies a living sacrifice, holy, acceptable unto God, which is your reasonable service. And be not conformed to this world: but be ye transformed by the renewing of your mind, that ye may prove what is that good, and acceptable, and perfect, will of God* (Rom. 12:1-2). If we are committed to Jesus being Lord of our lives, then we will bring *into captivity every thought to the obedience of Christ* (II Cor. 10:5).

We . . . do not cease to pray for you, and to desire that ye might be filled with the knowledge of His will in all wisdom and spiritual understanding; That ye might walk worthy of the Lord unto all pleasing, being fruitful in every good work, and increasing in the knowledge of God; Strengthened with all might, according to His glorious power, unto all patience and longsuffering with joyfulness (Col. 1:9-11).

Giving thanks unto the Father, which hath made us meet (qualified us) *to be partakers of the inheritance of the saints in light: Who hath delivered us from the power of darkness, and hath translated us into the kingdom of His dear Son* (Jesus our Savior): *In whom we have redemption through His blood, even the forgiveness of sins: Who is the image of the invisible God, the firstborn of every creature* (1:12-15).

For by Him were all things created, that are in heaven, and that are in earth, visible and invisible, whether they be thrones, or dominions, or principalities, or powers: all things were created by Him, and for Him: And He is before all things, and by Him all things consist. And He is the Head of the body, the Church: who is the beginning, the firstborn from the dead; that in all things He might have the preeminence (1:16-18).

That I may know Him, and the power of His resurrection, and the fellowship of His sufferings, being made conformable unto His death; If by any means I might attain unto the resurrection of the dead. Not as though I had already attained, either were already perfect: but I follow after, if that I may apprehend that for which also I am apprehended of Christ Jesus. Brethren, I count not myself to have apprehended: but this one thing I do, forgetting those things which are behind, and reaching forth unto those things which are before, I press toward the mark for the prize of the high calling of God in Christ Jesus (Phil. 3:10-14).

Life's Foremost Opportunity

We have one supreme reason for living. The question that needs to be addressed is: Will we read the Bible to see how we must live to please our Creator, or suffer the consequences? Pity the person who is wasting the few short years of life chasing earthly goals to obtain material success, but failing to achieve the purpose for which God created them. God has allotted just one short lifetime with a fourfold responsibility:

[1] **That we may know the One True God.** There is but One Living God expressed in three Persons, ***the Father . . . the Son*** (Jesus born in Bethlehem), ***and . . . the Holy Ghost*** (Spirit) (Matt. 28:18-20), who dwells within every true Christian. ***For there is One God, and One Mediator between God and men, the Man Christ Jesus*** (I Tim. 2:5; also John 14:16-17; 16:13-15; I John 5:7). All other gods are false counterfeits that can save no one from eternal hell fire, where there is ***weeping and gnashing of teeth*** forever (Matt. 22:13). They cannot provide for our needs, protect us from enemies, or answer our prayers. We are ***looking for that blessed hope, and the glorious appearing of the great God and our Saviour Jesus Christ*** (Titus 2:13). ***The only wise God our Saviour, be glory and majesty, dominion and power, both now and ever*** (Jude 1:25).

[2] **That we may know what God planned for us and how to be prepared for eternity** by reading His only-inspired Guide from Gen. 1:1 through Rev. 22:21. **God has said that** *the Holy Scriptures* (Old Testament) *. . . are able to make thee wise unto salvation through faith which is in Christ Jesus. All Scripture is given by inspiration of God, and is profitable for doctrine, for reproof, for correction, for instruction in righteousness* (in holy living, in conformity to God's will in thought, purpose, and action)*: That the man of God may be perfect* (adequate), *throughly furnished* (efficient, well prepared) *unto all good works* (II Tim. 3:15-17). We are all dependent upon the Holy Spirit to reveal His will as we read His Word. But the Holy Spirit will not reveal what we refuse or neglect to read. God has said: ***Desire the . . . Word*** (the Bible), ***that ye may grow thereby*** (I Pet. 2:2). *Then said Jesus to those . . . which believed on Him, If ye continue in My Word, then are ye My disciples indeed; And ye shall know the Truth, and the Truth shall make you free. . . . If ye keep My Commandments, ye shall abide in My love; even as I have kept My Father's Commandments, and abide in His love* (John 8:31-32; 15:10). Jesus said: *Heaven and earth shall pass away, but My words shall not pass away* (Matt. 24:35).

[3] **To be fully prepared to face eternity with confidence.** Jesus said: ***Man shall not live by bread alone, but by every Word that proceedeth out of the mouth of God*** (Matt. 4:4). ***Bread*** refers to our daily food; but, ***every Word that proceedeth out of the mouth of God*** is vitally important to our eternal destiny. ***Every Word*** begins with Gen. 1:1 and ends with Rev. 22:21. If we fail to read ***all Scripture***, we will be something less than what God planned for us to be. The Bible is beyond compare because it is your Creator's only Guide to prepare you to be the person He expects you to be in order to accomplish

the purpose for which He created you and to prepare you for eternal life with Him.

[4] We have a responsibility to provide this message to the world. Jesus said: *Go . . . teach all nations . . . to observe ALL THINGS . . . I have commanded you* (Matt. 28:19-20). We must *be . . . doers of the Word, and not hearers only, deceiving your own selves* (James 1:22).

I pray as I write each day's devotion *that ye might be filled with the knowledge of His will in all wisdom and spiritual understanding; That ye might walk worthy of the Lord unto all pleasing, being fruitful in every good work, and increasing in the knowledge of God* (Col. 1:9-10; also II Pet. 3:18).

THE POWER OF THE WORD OF GOD

Jesus Christ set the example of how important the Old Testament was to Him and should be to us. His emphasis started with the first recorded words of our Lord following His baptism. After 40 days of fasting, He was tempted of the Devil, who said: *If Thou be* (Since You are) *the Son of God, command that these stones be made bread. But He answered and said, It is written, Man shall not live by bread alone* (physical necessities), *but by every Word that proceedeth out of the mouth of God* (spiritual necessities) (Matt. 4:3-4; comp. Deut. 8:3). By quoting this Old Testament Scripture, our Lord revealed the "Key to Victory" over satanic deceptions.

All Scripture is given by inspiration of God, and is profitable for doctrine, for reproof, for correction, for instruction in righteousness: That the man of God may be perfect, throughly furnished unto all good works (II Tim. 3:16-17).

Study (Be diligent) *to shew thyself approved unto God, a workman that needeth not to be ashamed, rightly dividing the Word of Truth* (II Tim. 2:15).

My people are destroyed for lack of knowledge: because thou hast rejected knowledge, I will also reject thee, that thou shalt be no priest to Me: seeing thou hast forgotten the Law of thy God, I will also forget thy children (Hos. 4:6).

So then faith cometh by hearing, and hearing by the Word of God (Rom. 10:17).

Jesus said: *Sanctify them* (Make them holy) *through Thy Truth: Thy Word is Truth* (John 17:17).

Seeing ye have purified (cleansed) *your souls in obeying the Truth through the Spirit unto unfeigned* (sincere, genuine) *love of the brethren, see that ye love one another with a pure heart fervently* (I Pet. 1:22).

This Book of the Law shall not depart out of thy mouth; but thou shalt meditate therein day and night, that thou mayest observe to do according to all that is written therein: for then thou shalt make thy way prosperous, and then thou shalt have good success (Josh. 1:8).

Holding forth the Word of Life; that I may rejoice in the day of Christ, that I have not run in vain, neither laboured in vain (Phil. 2:16).

JANUARY – VOLUME 1

Date	Day	Reading	Check as you read each day
1	1	Genesis 1 - 3	
2	2	Genesis 4 - 6	
3	3	Genesis 7 - 9	
4	4	Genesis 10 - 12	
5	5	Genesis 13 - 15	
6	6	Genesis 16 - 18	
7	7	Genesis 19 - 21	
8	8	Genesis 22 - 24	
9	9	Genesis 25 - 27	
10	10	Genesis 28 - 30	
11	11	Genesis 31 - 33	
12	12	Genesis 34 - 36	
13	13	Genesis 37 - 39	
14	14	Genesis 40 - 42	
15	15	Genesis 43 - 45	
16	16	Genesis 46 - 48	
17	17	Genesis 49 – Ex. 1	
18	18	Exodus 2 - 4	
19	19	Exodus 5 - 7	
20	20	Exodus 8 - 10	
21	21	Exodus 11 - 13	
22	22	Exodus 14 - 16	
23	23	Exodus 17 - 19	
24	24	Exodus 20 - 22	
25	25	Exodus 23 - 25	
26	26	Exodus 26 - 28	
27	27	Exodus 29 - 31	
28	28	Exodus 32 - 34	
29	29	Exodus 35 - 37	
30	30	Exodus 38 - 39	
31	31	Exodus 40	

FEBRUARY – VOLUME 2

Date	Day	Reading	Check as you read each day
1	32	Leviticus 1 - 3	
2	33	Leviticus 4 - 6	
3	34	Leviticus 7 - 8	
4	35	Leviticus 9 - 10	
5	36	Leviticus 11 - 13	
6	37	Leviticus 14 - 15	
7	38	Leviticus 16 - 18	
8	39	Leviticus 19 - 21	
9	40	Leviticus 22 - 23	
10	41	Leviticus 24 - 25	
11	42	Leviticus 26 - 27	
12	43	Numbers 1 - 2	
13	44	Numbers 3 - 4	
14	45	Numbers 5 - 6	
15	46	Numbers 7	
16	47	Numbers 8 - 9	
17	48	Numbers 10 - 11	
18	49	Numbers 12 - 13	
19	50	Numbers 14 - 15	
20	51	Numbers 16 - 18	
21	52	Numbers 19 - 20	
22	53	Numbers 21 - 22	
23	54	Numbers 23 - 25	
24	55	Numbers 26 - 27	
25	56	Numbers 28 - 29	
26	57	Numbers 30 - 31	
27	58	Numbers 32 - 33	
28	59	Numbers 34 - 35	
29	60	Numbers 36	

MARCH – VOLUME 3

Date	Day	Reading	Check as you read each day
1	61	Deuteronomy 1 - 2	
2	62	Deuteronomy 3 - 4	
3	63	Deuteronomy 5 - 7	
4	64	Deuteronomy 8 - 10	
5	65	Deuteronomy 11 - 13	
6	66	Deuteronomy 14 - 16	
7	67	Deuteronomy 17 - 20	
8	68	Deuteronomy 21 - 23	
9	69	Deuteronomy 24 - 27	
10	70	Deuteronomy 28	
11	71	Deuteronomy 29 - 31	
12	72	Deuteronomy 32 - 34	
13	73	Joshua 1 – 3	
14	74	Joshua 4 – 6	
15	75	Joshua 7 – 8	
16	76	Joshua 9 – 10	
17	77	Joshua 11 – 13	
18	78	Joshua 14 – 16	
19	79	Joshua 17 – 19	
20	80	Joshua 20 – 21	
21	81	Joshua 22 – 24	
22	82	Judges 1 – 2	
23	83	Judges 3 - 5	
24	84	Judges 6 - 7	
25	85	Judges 8 - 9	
26	86	Judges 10 - 11	
27	87	Judges 12 - 14	
28	88	Judges 15 - 17	
29	89	Judges 18 - 19	
30	90	Judges 20 - 21	
31	91	Ruth 1 – 4	

APRIL – VOLUME 4

Date	Day	Reading	Check as you read each day
1	92	I Samuel 1 – 3	
2	93	I Samuel 4 – 7	
3	94	I Samuel 8 – 11	
4	95	I Samuel 12 – 14:23	
5	96	I Samuel 14:24 – 16	
6	97	I Samuel 17 – 18	
7	98	I Samuel 19 – 21	
8	99	I Samuel 22 – 24	
9	100	I Samuel 25 – 27	
10	101	I Samuel 28 – 31	
11	102	II Samuel 1 – 2	
12	103	II Samuel 3 – 5	
13	104	II Samuel 6 – 9	
14	105	II Samuel 10 – 12	
15	106	II Samuel 13 – 14	
16	107	II Samuel 15 – 16	
17	108	II Samuel 17 – 18	
18	109	II Samuel 19 – 20	
19	110	II Samuel 21 – 22	
20	111	II Samuel 23 – 24	
21	112	I Kings 1 – 2:25	
22	113	I Kings 2:26 – 4	
23	114	I Kings 5 – 7	
24	115	I Kings 8	
25	116	I Kings 9 – 11	
26	117	I Kings 12 – 13	
27	118	I Kings 14 – 15	
28	119	I Kings 16 – 18	
29	120	I Kings 19 – 20	
30	121	I Kings 21 – 22	

MAY – VOLUME 5

Date	Day	Reading	Check as you read each day
1	122	II Kings 1 - 3	
2	123	II Kings 4 - 5	
3	124	II Kings 6 - 8	
4	125	II Kings 9 - 10	
5	126	II Kings 11 - 13	
6	127	II Kings 14 - 15	
7	128	II Kings 16 - 17	
8	129	II Kings 18 - 20	
9	130	II Kings 21 - 23:20	
10	131	II Kings 23:21 - 25	
11	132	I Chronicles 1 - 2	
12	133	I Chronicles 3 - 5	
13	134	I Chronicles 6 - 7	
14	135	I Chronicles 8 - 10	
15	136	I Chronicles 11 - 13	
16	137	I Chronicles 14 - 16	
17	138	I Chronicles 17 - 20	
18	139	I Chronicles 21 - 23	
19	140	I Chronicles 24 - 26	
20	141	I Chronicles 27 - 29	
21	142	II Chronicles 1 - 3	
22	143	II Chronicles 4 - 6	
23	144	II Chronicles 7 - 9	
24	145	II Chronicles 10 - 13	
25	146	II Chronicles 14 - 17	
26	147	II Chronicles 18 - 20	
27	148	II Chronicles 21 - 24	
28	149	II Chronicles 25 - 27	
29	150	II Chronicles 28 - 30	
30	151	II Chronicles 31 - 33	
31	152	II Chronicles 34 - 36	

JUNE – VOLUME 6

Date	Day	Reading	Check as you read each day
1	153	Ezra 1 – 2	
2	154	Ezra 3 – 5	
3	155	Ezra 6 – 7	
4	156	Ezra 8 – 9	
5	157	Ezra 10	
6	158	Nehemiah 1 – 3	
7	159	Nehemiah 4 – 6	
8	160	Nehemiah 7 – 8	
9	161	Nehemiah 9 – 10	
10	162	Nehemiah 11 – 12	
11	163	Nehemiah 13	
12	164	Esther 1 – 3	
13	165	Esther 4 – 7	
14	166	Esther 8 – 10	
15	167	Job 1 – 4	
16	168	Job 5 – 8	
17	169	Job 9 – 12	
18	170	Job 13 – 16	
19	171	Job 17 – 20	
20	172	Job 21 – 24	
21	173	Job 25 – 29	
22	174	Job 30 – 33	
23	175	Job 34 – 37	
24	176	Job 38 – 40	
25	177	Job 41 – 42	
26	178	Psalms 1 – 9	
27	179	Psalms 10 – 17	
28	180	Psalms 18 – 22	
29	181	Psalms 23 – 30	
30	182	Psalms 31 – 35	

JULY – VOLUME 7

Date	Day	Reading	Check as you read each day
1	183	Psalms 36 – 39	
2	184	Psalms 40 – 45	
3	185	Psalms 46 – 51	
4	186	Psalms 52 – 59	
5	187	Psalms 60 – 66	
6	188	Psalms 67 – 71	
7	189	Psalms 72 – 77	
8	190	Psalms 78 – 80	
9	191	Psalms 81 – 87	
10	192	Psalms 88 – 91	
11	193	Psalms 92 – 100	
12	194	Psalms 101 – 105	
13	195	Psalms 106 – 107	
14	196	Psalms 108 – 118	
15	197	Psalm 119	
16	198	Psalms 120 – 131	
17	199	Psalms 132 – 138	
18	200	Psalms 139 – 143	
19	201	Psalms 144 – 150	
20	202	Proverbs 1 – 3	
21	203	Proverbs 4 – 7	
22	204	Proverbs 8 – 11	
23	205	Proverbs 12 – 15	
24	206	Proverbs 16 – 19	
25	207	Proverbs 20 – 22	
26	208	Proverbs 23 – 26	
27	209	Proverbs 27 – 31	
28	210	Ecclesiastes 1 – 4	
29	211	Ecclesiastes 5 – 8	
30	212	Ecclesiastes 9 – 12	
31	213	Song of Sol. 1 – 8	

SEPTEMBER – VOLUME 9

Date	Day	Reading	Check as you read each day
1	245	Ezekiel 1 – 4	
2	246	Ezekiel 5 – 9	
3	247	Ezekiel 10 – 13	
4	248	Ezekiel 14 – 16	
5	249	Ezekiel 17 – 19	
6	250	Ezekiel 20 – 21	
7	251	Ezekiel 22 – 24	
8	252	Ezekiel 25 – 28	
9	253	Ezekiel 29 – 32	
10	254	Ezekiel 33 – 36	
11	255	Ezekiel 37 – 39	
12	256	Ezekiel 40 – 42	
13	257	Ezekiel 43 – 45	
14	258	Ezekiel 46 – 48	
15	259	Daniel 1 – 3	
16	260	Daniel 4 – 6	
17	261	Daniel 7 – 9	
18	262	Daniel 10 – 12	
19	263	Hosea 1 – 6	
20	264	Hosea 7 – 14	
21	265	Joel 1 – 3	
22	266	Amos 1 – 5	
23	267	Amos 6 – 9 / Obadiah 1	
24	268	Jonah 1 – 4	
25	269	Micah 1 – 7	
26	270	Nahum 1 – 3 / Habakkuk 1 – 3	
27	271	Zephaniah 1 – 3 / Haggai 1 – 2	
28	272	Zechariah 1 – 7	
29	273	Zechariah 8 – 14	
30	274	Malachi 1 – 4	

NOVEMBER – VOLUME 11

Date	Day	Reading	Check as you read each day
1	306	John 1 – 3	
2	307	John 4 – 5	
3	308	John 6 – 8	
4	309	John 9 – 10	
5	310	John 11 – 12	
6	311	John 13 – 16	
7	312	John 17 – 18	
8	313	John 19 – 21	
9	314	Acts 1 – 3	
10	315	Acts 4 – 6	
11	316	Acts 7 – 8	
12	317	Acts 9 – 10	
13	318	Acts 11 – 13	
14	319	Acts 14 – 16	
15	320	Acts 17 – 19	
16	321	Acts 20 – 22	
17	322	Acts 23 – 25	
18	323	Acts 26 – 28	
19	324	Romans 1 – 3	
20	325	Romans 4 – 7	
21	326	Romans 8 – 10	
22	327	Romans 11 – 13	
23	328	Romans 14 – 16	
24	329	I Corinthians 1 – 4	
25	330	I Corinthians 5 – 9	
26	331	I Corinthians 10 – 13	
27	332	I Corinthians 14 – 16	
28	333	II Corinthians 1 – 4	
29	334	II Corinthians 5 – 8	
30	335	II Corinthians 9 – 13	

AUGUST – VOLUME 8

Date	Day	Reading	Check as you read each day
1	214	Isaiah 1 – 4	
2	215	Isaiah 5 – 9	
3	216	Isaiah 10 – 14	
4	217	Isaiah 15 – 21	
5	218	Isaiah 22 – 26	
6	219	Isaiah 27 – 31	
7	220	Isaiah 32 – 37	
8	221	Isaiah 38 – 42	
9	222	Isaiah 43 – 46	
10	223	Isaiah 47 – 51	
11	224	Isaiah 52 – 57	
12	225	Isaiah 58 – 63	
13	226	Isaiah 64 – 66	
14	227	Jeremiah 1 – 3	
15	228	Jeremiah 4 – 6	
16	229	Jeremiah 7 – 10	
17	230	Jeremiah 11 – 14	
18	231	Jeremiah 15 – 18	
19	232	Jeremiah 19 – 22	
20	233	Jeremiah 23 – 25	
21	234	Jeremiah 26 – 28	
22	235	Jeremiah 29 – 31	
23	236	Jeremiah 32 – 33	
24	237	Jeremiah 34 – 36	
25	238	Jeremiah 37 – 40	
26	239	Jeremiah 41 – 44	
27	240	Jeremiah 45 – 48	
28	241	Jeremiah 49 – 50	
29	242	Jeremiah 51 – 52	
30	243	Lamentations 1 – 2	
31	244	Lamentations 3 – 5	

OCTOBER – VOLUME 10

Date	Day	Reading	Check as you read each day
1	275	Matthew 1 – 3	
2	276	Matthew 4 – 6	
3	277	Matthew 7 – 9	
4	278	Matthew 10 – 11	
5	279	Matthew 12	
6	280	Matthew 13 – 14	
7	281	Matthew 15 – 17	
8	282	Matthew 18 – 20	
9	283	Matthew 21 – 22	
10	284	Matthew 23 – 24	
11	285	Matthew 25 – 26	
12	286	Matthew 27 – 28	
13	287	Mark 1 – 3	
14	288	Mark 4 – 5	
15	289	Mark 6 – 7	
16	290	Mark 8 – 9	
17	291	Mark 10 – 11	
18	292	Mark 12 – 13	
19	293	Mark 14 – 16	
20	294	Luke 1	
21	295	Luke 2 – 3	
22	296	Luke 4 – 5	
23	297	Luke 6 – 7	
24	298	Luke 8 – 9	
25	299	Luke 10 – 11	
26	300	Luke 12 – 13	
27	301	Luke 14 – 16	
28	302	Luke 17 – 18	
29	303	Luke 19 – 20	
30	304	Luke 21 – 22	
31	305	Luke 23 – 24	

DECEMBER – VOLUME 12

Date	Day	Reading	Check as you read each day
1	336	Galatians 1 – 3	
2	337	Galatians 4 – 6	
3	338	Ephesians 1 – 3	
4	339	Ephesians 4 – 6	
5	340	Philippians 1 – 4	
6	341	Colossians 1 – 4	
7	342	I Thessalonians 1 – 5	
8	343	II Thessalonians 1 – 3	
9	344	I Timothy 1 – 6	
10	345	II Timothy 1 – 4	
11	346	Titus 1 – 3 / Philemon 1	
12	347	Hebrews 1 – 4	
13	348	Hebrews 5 – 7	
14	349	Hebrews 8 – 10	
15	350	Hebrews 11 – 13	
16	351	James 1 – 5	
17	352	I Peter 1 – 2	
18	353	I Peter 3 – 5	
19	354	II Peter 1 – 3	
20	355	I John 1 – 3	
21	356	I John 4 – 5	
22	357	II John 1 / III John 1 / Jude 1	
23	358	Revelation 1 – 2	
24	359	Revelation 3 – 5	
25	360	Revelation 6 – 8	
26	361	Revelation 9 – 11	
27	362	Revelation 12 – 13	
28	363	Revelation 14 – 16	
29	364	Revelation 17 – 18	
30	365	Revelation 19 – 20	
31	366	Revelation 21 – 22	

Introduction To The Book Of GENESIS

The Book of Genesis is the first of the five books that God inspired Moses to write, except for the Ten Commandments which were written on **two tables... of stone, written with the finger of God** (Ex. 31:18). This points out how exceedingly important the Ten Commandments are and how ignoring them is an offense to God.

Genesis is an accurate account of the origin of the universe, the creation of man, marriage, the family, sin, and the origin of the Hebrew nation. The first sentence in the Bible states: **In the beginning God created the heaven and the earth** (Gen. 1:1). This makes it clear that God is a living, personal Being who is the Creator of all things and is the unlimited Sovereign over all things (John 1:1-3; Col. 1:16-17).

The word **God** used here in Genesis 1 is the Hebrew plural noun **Elohim**, even though the singular noun **Eloah** could have been used if God had so chosen (Deut. 32:15,17; Hab. 3:3). The first chapter of Genesis also states: **Let Us make man in Our image, after Our likeness** (Gen. 1:26). By recognizing the plurality of the Hebrew noun **Elohim** and the plural Hebrew words translated as **Us** and **Our**, as well as the reference to **the Spirit of God** (1:2), we have a clear revelation that the One True God is Triune (three Persons in One) and exists as God the Father, God the Son, and God the Holy Spirit.

Jesus also made the Trinity clear when He said: **When the Comforter** (Holy Spirit) **is come, whom I will send unto you... the Spirit of Truth... He shall testify of Me.... He shall not speak of Himself.... I came forth from the Father, and... I leave the world, and go to the Father** (John 15:26; 16:13,28).

The Lord Jesus Christ is coequal and coeternal with God the Father and God the Holy Spirit. Consequently, we give Jesus Christ His rightful exalted place as Lord and Savior.

All things were made by Him; and without Him was not any thing made that was made (1:3). John was speaking of Jesus, as did Paul, who declared that **by Him were all things created, that are in heaven, and that are in earth, visible and invisible, whether they be thrones, or dominions, or principalities, or powers: all things were created by Him, and for Him: And He is before all things, and by Him all things consist** (Col. 1:16-17). It was the creative power of God the Father, God the Son, and God the Holy Spirit.

The historical reliability of Genesis also becomes apparent in the Gospel of Matthew when Jesus referred to Sodom and Gomorrah as actual cities that were destroyed by fire because of sodomy and to

Noah as a righteous man who lived at the time of the Flood (Matt. 10:15; 24:37-38; Gen. 6:5,13; 7:6-23; 19:24-25). Furthermore, when Jesus was questioned by His critics concerning divorce, He confirmed the validity of creation when He said: **Have ye not read, that He which made them at the beginning made them male and female . . . a man . . . shall cleave to his wife: and they twain** (two) **shall be one flesh** (Matt. 19:4-6; Gen. 1:27; 2:24)**?**

Of all creation, only man has a **spirit . . . soul and body** joined together for all eternity (I Thess. 5:23). It is in the image of God that Adam was created. **God is a Spirit: and they that worship Him must worship Him in spirit and in truth** (John 4:24). No animal has a spirit, a God consciousness, or the ability to worship God.

Genesis explains how Satan deceived Eve, who then, with Adam, decided not to obey their Creator God. Because Adam sinned, mankind inherited a sin nature – a disobedient nature – and became destined for both physical and spiritual death (Gen. 3:1-7,16-19). **For as in Adam all die, even so in Christ shall all be made alive** (I Cor. 15:22). In the first promise of God of a Savior (Gen. 3:15), He prepared the way for repentant sinners to receive eternal life. The woman would have a Son (descendant) (Luke 3:38). That Son (Jesus Christ) would defeat Satan and provide eternal life for **as many as** (that) **received Him** (John 1:12). **Jesus . . . said . . . Except a man be born again** (anew)**, he cannot see the Kingdom of God** (3:3). The Lord Jesus also said: **I am The Way, The Truth, and The Life: no man cometh unto the Father, but by Me** (14:6).

Genesis Chapters 1 – 11 record the first 2,000 years* of man's history. During that time, six major events took place: (1) the creation of all things; (2) the sin of Adam and Eve; (3) some 1600 years* later, the building of an ark by Noah; (4) the great Flood; (5) 200 years* after that, the building of the Tower of Babel; and (6) the diversification of tongues and scattering of people across the earth.

Chapters 12 – 50 cover the next 500 years* and focus on four men – Abraham, Isaac, Jacob, and Joseph. Through these men we see the love of God for His creation and His willingness to protect and to provide for those who are obedient to His revealed Word.

*Note: **Dates are approximate time periods.**

> As we read through His Word our desire should be that we *walk worthy of the Lord unto all pleasing, being fruitful in every good work, and increasing in the knowledge of God* (Colossians 1:10).

JANUARY 1   Read Genesis 1 – 3

Highlights: You will be thrilled today as you read: ***God said. . . . God saw. . . . God made***, describing creation. Read what God did in six days (chap. 1). Seventh day blessed and sanctified (Gen. 2:1-3). A ***help meet*** (2:18). Adam and Eve chose to believe Satan and forfeit the Garden of Eden. SIN, punishment.

Creation, as recorded in Genesis, is the testimony of our Creator God who made man in His own image. Man was made distinctly different from any animal in that God breathed into him ***the breath of life*** (Gen. 2:7).

The L<small>ORD</small> God took the man (Adam)***, and put him into the garden of Eden to dress it and to keep it*** (2:15). Man's responsibility was to obey the Word of God. Yet, God allowed man's love, loyalty, and obedience to be tested. In Eden, we are introduced to Satan, the one who came in the guise of ***the serpent*** (3:1). He is also called ***the dragon, that old serpent . . . the Devil*** (Rev. 20:2; Is. 14:12; Matt. 13:39; I Pet. 5:8; Rev. 12:10). Satan did not reveal himself as the enemy of God or as a wicked deceiver intent on destroying every enjoyment of mankind (John 8:44). His intent was, and still is, to prevent man from obeying his Creator.

Adam and Eve were created to enjoy fellowship with God. However, He also gave them the right to choose either to be their own "god" and do what they wanted to do, or by faith to believe, without exception, that everything God told them to do was in their best interest. By choosing the fruit from ***the tree of knowledge of good and evil*** (Gen. 2:9), Adam and Eve foolishly listened to Satan, rather than rely on the Word of God.

Just as Adam and Eve's fellowship with God was dependent upon their obedience to what He had said, our fellowship with Him is also dependent upon our obedience to His Word. If we are to receive His blessing and enjoy His abundant life, we must choose to obey His Word – which is to obey the Lord Himself (John 1:14).

Those who receive Christ as their personal Savior, receive a new spiritual life – the nature of God. As the children of God, we ***were born, not of blood, nor of the will of the flesh, nor of the will of man, but of God*** (1:13). As Christians read the Bible, the indwelling Holy Spirit of God ***will guide*** (them) ***into all Truth*** (John 16:13; comp. 1:12-13).

Thought for Today: The only means to heaven is through Jesus Christ (John 14:6).

Christ Revealed: As Creator (Gen. 1:1; comp. John 1:1-4; Col. 1:15-17; Heb. 11:3). As the Seed of woman (Gen. 3:15; Is. 7:14; 9:6-7). ***God sent forth His Son, made of a woman*** (Gal. 4:4).

JANUARY 2 — Read Genesis 4 – 6

Highlights: The Lord contrasts the worldly sacrifice of Cain with the godly sacrifice of Abel. About 1600 years later, universal corruption brings about the third great event of history – the flood in Noah's day. Worship of God revived (Gen. 4:25-26).

Cain had become jealous of his brother Abel and angry with God, because Abel's sacrifice was accepted while his was rejected (Gen. 4:4-5). The Lord reproached Cain in love and offered him an opportunity to repent of his sin: **If thou doest well, shalt thou not be accepted? and if thou doest not well, sin lieth at the door** (4:7). Cain's offering of the firstfruits of the ground recognized God as Creator, but it was not a sacrifice for his sin. **Without shedding of blood is no remission** (forgiveness of sin) (Heb. 9:22). **By faith Abel offered unto God a more excellent sacrifice than Cain, by which he obtained witness that he was righteous** (11:4). Since Abel recognized himself as a sinner, he **brought ... the firstlings of his flock**, meaning he offered a lamb as a blood sacrifice to atone for his sins (Gen. 4:4; Heb. 11:4). In anger **Cain rose up against Abel his brother, and slew him** (Gen. 4:8).

From the time of Cain and his family (4:26), mankind became increasingly sinful, and eventually, a godly witness was reduced to just one family. Consequently mankind's rebellion resulted in the flood. It was the greatest catastrophe ever experienced upon the earth (Matt. 24:37-39; Heb. 11:7; I Pet. 3:20; and II Pet. 2:5; 3:3-7). **And God saw ... only evil continually.... But Noah found grace in the eyes of the LORD .... Noah was a just man and perfect in his generations, and Noah walked with God** (Gen. 6:5-9). The word **grace** reveals the love and mercy of God for mankind.

The genealogy of **the sons of God** (6:2,4) continued through Noah from whom Jesus came (Luke 3:38). What often happens today is exactly what happened then: **The sons of God saw the daughters of men that they were fair; and they took them wives** (Gen. 6:2). Marriage of believers (**the sons of God**) with nonbelievers (**the daughters of men**) has always been contrary to the biblical principle: **Be ye not unequally yoked together with unbelievers ... what part hath he that believeth with an infidel** (unbeliever)**? And what agreement hath the Temple of God with idols? for ye are the Temple of the Living God** (II Cor. 6:14-16).

Thought for Today: Jesus is the Way that leads us to where God is.

Christ Revealed: Through Abel's blood sacrifice (Gen. 4:4-7). Christ is **the Lamb of God,** sacrificed for man's sin (John 1:29; Heb. 9:22; 11:4). Man's best achievements can never take the place of Christ's atonement made through His own sinless blood.

JANUARY 3   Read Genesis 7 – 9

Highlights: Noah enters the ark. The great flood wiped out all but eight that lived in Noah's day (Gen. 7:23)! Noah's assignment (9:1,7; see 1:28). The rainbow, the sign of the Covenant of God (9:11-17). Noah's prophecy concerning his three sons.

Noah was able to save his family and preserve mankind because of his faith in the spoken Word of God which led him to build the ark. During the many years spent in constructing the ark, he was also known as *a preacher of righteousness* in an ungodly world (II Pet. 2:5). This illustrates the New Testament Truth that *faith without works is dead* (James 2:26). The ark was a secure refuge from certain death; it was also a type of Christ, who provides refuge from spiritual death for all believers. Christ, our spiritual Ark, continues to call the lost: *Come unto Me . . . and I will give you rest* (Matt. 11:28).

For Noah and his family, there came a day, prior to the flood when *the LORD said unto Noah, Come thou and all thy house into the ark. . . . and the LORD shut him in* (Gen. 7:1,16). This shows the special attention and personal care that God gives to all who are faithful to Him. All who wait for a more convenient time to be saved need to realize that it is an insult to God who said: *Now is the accepted time . . . now is the day of salvation* (II Cor. 6:2). *Let us therefore fear, lest, a promise being left us of entering into His rest, any of you should seem to come short of it* (Heb. 4:1).

Just as Noah was able to rest within the ark, secure from the waters of death, Christians can be assured of spiritual rest, for our lives are *hid with Christ in God* (Col. 3:3). As soon as he was once more on dry land, *Noah builded an altar unto the LORD . . . and offered burnt offerings on the altar* (Gen. 8:20). Our obedience of faith and our worship of God go hand in hand. Just as Noah was not given an exact day when the flood would come, neither do we know the day we will face the Lord, either through death or at His Coming.

Of that day and hour knoweth no man, no, not the angels (messengers) *of heaven, but My Father only. But as the days of Noe were, so shall also the coming of the Son of Man be. . . . before the flood they were eating and drinking, marrying and giving in marriage, until the day that Noe entered into the ark, And knew* (understood) *not until the flood came, and took them all away. . . . Therefore be . . . ready* (Matt. 24:36-39,44).

Thought for Today: We don't know the day that our lives will end, so be prepared.

Christ Revealed: Through the Ark (Gen. 7:1,7; Acts 4:12; I Pet. 3:12,20). Christ is our Ark of safety. *Jesus . . . delivered us from the wrath to come* (I Thess. 1:10).

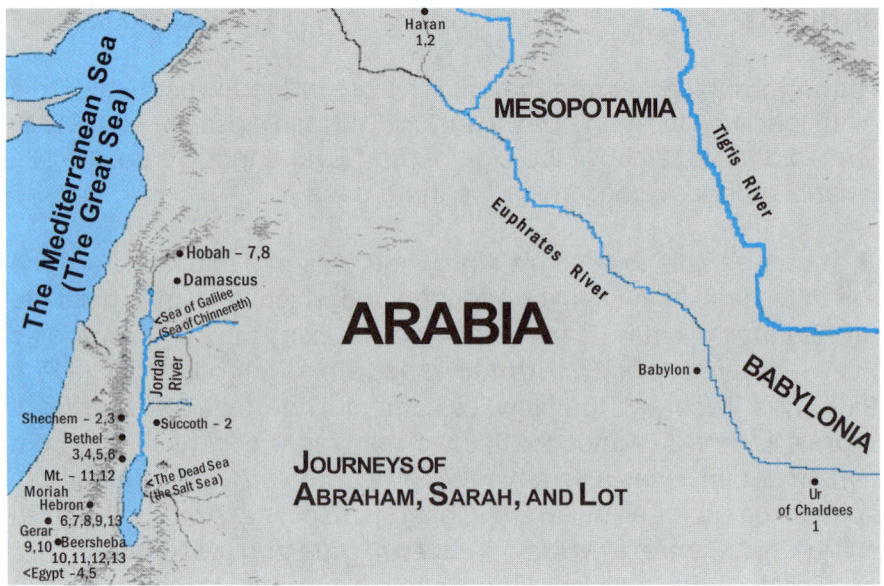

1. Ur of Chaldees (150 miles south of Babylon) **To Haran** (Genesis 11:27-31)
Distance: 600 miles
Reason for leaving Ur: Called of God
(Acts 7:2-4; Hebrews 11:8)
Death of Abram's father (Gen. 11:32)

2. Haran to Shechem (12:1-7)
(crossing Jordan)
Distance: about 400 miles; Age: 75
First altar built; Abram worships God

3. Shechem to near Bethel (12:8)
Distance: 20 miles
Second altar built; prayer offered;
famine in Canaan

4. Bethel to Egypt (12:9-20)
Distance: about 225 miles south
Abram denies that Sarai is his wife;
She was taken into Pharaoh's house

5. Egypt to Bethel (13:1-4)
Abram called on the Name of the Lord
Lot's selfish decision and separation
from Abram (13:5-13)

6. Bethel to Mamre (Hebron) (13:14-18)
Distance: 35 miles
Third altar built
Abram promised the whole land by God

7. Hebron to Hobah (North of
Damascus) (14:1-17)
Distance: 160 miles
Battle of the Canaanite Kings
Lot taken captive (14:1-12)
Abram rescues Lot

8. Hobah to Mamre (Hebron) (14:18-20)
Abram gives tithes to Melchizedek and
is blessed by Him
Promise of a son renewed (15:1-5)

Covenant renewed (15:6-18)
Ishmael born
Abram 86 years old (16:15-16)
Everlasting covenant and sign of
circumcision at age 99 (17:1-27)
Abram and Sarai names changed to
Abraham and Sarah (17:5-15)
Isaac, the heir to the Covenant promised
(18:1-19)
Intercession for Sodom (18:20-32)
Sodom destroyed, Lot rescued (19:1-38)

9. Hebron to Gerar (20:1)
Distance: 40 miles
Isaac born when Abraham was 100
(21:1-8; Hebrews 11:11)
Hagar and Ishmael cast out (21:9-21)

10. Gerar to Beersheba (21:27-34)
Covenant with Abimelech
Abraham called on the name of the Lord

11. Beersheba to Mount Moriah
(Jerusalem) (22:1-14 Hebrews 11:17-19)
Distance: about 54 miles
Abraham built altar
Isaac prepared to be offered as a sacrifice – a type of God offering Jesus,
His only Son, on same site 2,000 years
later God renews covenant (22:15-18)

12. Mount Moriah to Beersheba (22:19)
Death of Sarah (23:1-20)
Abraham sends servant to Mesopotamia
to get wife for Isaac (24:1-67)

13. Beersheba to Hebron (25:1-4)
Distance: about 30 miles
Abraham marries Keturah
Abraham's death and burial in cave of
Machpelah at age 175 (25:7-9)

JANUARY 4 — Read Genesis 10 – 12

Highlights: What a time to be alive! Note lineage from Shem, Ham, and Japheth. From Shem came the Savior. Seeking personal fame, the descendants make a **monumental** error (Gen. 11:4). In contrast, God introduces the Hebrew race beginning with Abram.

More than four hundred years had passed since the last recorded communication from heaven. Because of the sinful tendency of mankind, God spoke to Abram (Abraham), asking him to submit himself to Him and fully trust His leading. ***Now the LORD had said unto Abram, Get thee out of thy country*** (in Mesopotamia), ***and from thy kindred, and from thy father's house, unto a land that I will shew thee. . . . So Abram departed, as the LORD had spoken unto him; and Lot went with him*** (Gen. 12:1,4). Abram, by faith, obeyed God, committing himself to an unknown future. He could not have known that it was more than a thousand miles to the promised land. Abram's nephew Lot, like many today, was more concerned over material advantages and eventually ***pitched his tent toward Sodom*** (13:12). In contrast, Abraham remained faithful.

Many have started out in the right direction with the people of God, but when faced with worldly opportunities and self-interests, they eventually are drawn into worldly affairs. Lot never recovered from his disastrous decision to choose the well-watered plains of Sodom and forsake the godly influence of Abraham (13:10).

Abraham endured many years of severe testing, and God found him to be a man who would remain faithful and obey His Word regardless of the circumstances. The call of God demands that we make a choice. Even the closest ties of human loyalty or affection must be cut when they conflict with our submission to Christ and what is written in His Word.

Abraham's life was one of building altars and communicating with God. Every Christian has the privilege to be known of God as one who consistently reads His Word and prays with a desire to understand His will with a willingness to walk in it.

And the Scripture was fulfilled which saith, Abraham believed God, and it was imputed (regarded) ***unto him for righteousness: and he was called the Friend of God. Ye see then how that by works a man is justified, and not by faith only*** (James 2:23-24).

Thought for Today: Nothing is more important than obeying the Word of God.

Christ Revealed: As the Promised Seed of Abraham (Gen. 12:3; Matt. 1:1; Acts 3:25-26; Gal. 3:16). Abraham was a type of Christ who leads the way to a far better promised land (John 14:2-4,6; Heb. 11:8-10). ***He took on Him the seed (offspring) of Abraham*** (Heb. 2:16).

JANUARY 5 — Read Genesis 13 – 15

Highlights: Don't miss the life-changing message in today's reading. Lot chooses to be greedy (Gen. 13:10-12). See the blessings increase as Abram allows Lot to take advantage of him. Abram's act of faith was reaffirmed (13:14-17); Abram and Lot separate; Abram moves to Hebron; Abram rescues Lot; Melchizedek blesses Abram; the Covenant of God with Abram.

Abraham reached the age 80 but had no children. Humanly speaking it seemed unlikely that the promise of God, *I will make of thee a great nation* (Gen. 12:2), could be fulfilled. *After these things the Word of the LORD came unto Abram in a vision, saying, Fear not, Abram: I am thy shield, and thy exceeding great reward. And Abram said, Lord GOD, what wilt Thou give me, seeing I go childless, and the steward of my house is this Eliezer of Damascus? . . . And he believed in the LORD; and He counted it to him for righteousness* (15:1-2,6). Abram confessed his fears: *Lord GOD, what wilt Thou give me, seeing I go childless?* This was not a prayer of unbelief in the power of God but rather asking how He would fulfill His promise. God knew Abram's thoughts and revealed Himself to him for the fifth time, encouraging him to *fear not*.

The Lord assured Abram that Eliezer of Damascus would not be his heir but that his own son would be born. Even though there was no prospect of a child, the Scripture says that Abram *believed in the LORD.* To *believe in the LORD* means so much more than to merely believe in His existence. We may believe the Bible is the inspired Word of God, yet this may be nothing more than acknowledging its existence. When we say we believe that the Lord exists, it is one thing; but when we say that we *believe in the LORD,* the real meaning is eternally different and deeper. *If thou shalt confess with thy mouth the Lord Jesus, and shalt believe in thine heart that God hath raised Him from the dead, thou shalt be saved* (Rom. 10:9). Faith grows even when circumstances look impossible if we simply take God at His Word and remain faithful.

For what saith the Scripture? Abraham believed God, and it was counted unto him for righteousness. Now to him that worketh is the reward not reckoned of grace, but of debt. But to him that worketh not (to gain salvation)*, but believeth on Him that justifieth the ungodly, his faith is counted for righteousness* (Rom. 4:3-5).

Thought for Today: The trials we face now will one day seem insignificant compared to what God was able to accomplish through them.

Christ Portrayed: By the high priest, Melchizedek (Gen. 14:18-20; Heb. 4:15-16; 5:5-10; 7:1-4). Christ is our High Priest today who is interceding in prayer for us and who is deserving of our gifts and service to Him.

JANUARY 6 — Read Genesis 16 – 18

Highlights: What dynamic chapters of Scripture! Birth of Ishmael. Abram's name changed to Abraham. Circumcision seals the Covenant between God, Abraham, and his descendants (Gen. 17:9-14,23-27). God tells Abraham at 99: *Sarah thy wife shall have a son* (18:10). Who laughed? Why (18:1-15)? Abraham takes his heavy heart straight to God (18:16-33).

Abram and Sarai were childless. God had promised Abram a son (Gen. 15:2-4), but 10 years had passed and now he was 85 years old. At that time, *Sarai said unto Abram . . . the Lord hath restrained me from bearing . . . go in unto my maid; it may be that I may obtain children* (have a family) *by her* (16:2). At age 86, Abram fathered a son, Ishmael, by Hagar.

Thirteen years after the birth of Ishmael (16:16; 17:1), God again spoke to Abram: *I am the Almighty God. . . . thy name shall be Abraham. . . . I will establish My Covenant* (Agreement) *between Me and thee and thy seed* (descendants). *. . . My Covenant will I establish with Isaac, which Sarah shall bear unto thee at this set time . . . next year* (17:1-21).

Abraham was now 99 years old and Sarah was 90, an age when it was humanly impossible for her to have a child. But God revealed to Abraham: *I am the Almighty God* (One who is All-Sufficient), and said: *I know him . . . he will command his children . . . and they shall keep the way of the Lord, to do justice and judgment; that the Lord may bring upon Abraham that which He hath spoken of him* (18:19).

One of the great tests of our faith is patiently waiting upon the Lord. It may take two weeks, two years, or, as in Abraham's situation, 25 years for our prayers to be answered. Abraham was *fully persuaded that, what He* (God) *had promised, He was able also to perform. . . . therefore it was imputed* (credited) *to him* (Abraham) *for righteousness* (Rom. 4:21-22).

God had said to Abraham: *Walk before Me, and be . . . perfect* (remain faithful) (Gen. 17:1). We too have a responsibility in our covenant relationship with God. Jesus said: *Be ye therefore perfect, even as your Father which is in heaven is perfect* (Matt. 5:48). In biblical language it means: *It is required in stewards, that a man be found faithful* (perfect) (I Cor. 4:2).

Thought for Today: The greatest test of our faith is waiting upon the Lord, but the outcome is always His best.

Christ Revealed: As the Seed of Isaac (Gen. 17:19). Christ was a descendant of Isaac. *Jesus . . . Which was the Son of Jacob, which was the son of Isaac* (Luke 3:23-34; Heb. 11:18).

JANUARY 7 — Read Genesis 19 – 21

Highlights: The cities of Sodom and Gomorrah destroyed by fire; Lot and his daughters escape; Abraham's lie and covenant with Abimelech; birth of Isaac; Hagar and Ishmael sent away.

Sodom was known for homosexuality. Our Creator has said: ***Thou shalt not lie with mankind, as with womankind: it is abomination.... Defile not ye yourselves in any of these things: for in all these the nations are defiled which I cast out before you.... I am the L*ORD** *your God*** (Lev. 18:22,24,30). ***The L*ORD** *rained upon Sodom ... brimstone and fire*** (Gen. 19:24). Since homosexuality is so detestable in the eyes of God, we in our day should pray that those involved will repent and forsake this sin (I Cor. 6:9-11).

After the story of Sodom, we read: ***Sarah ... bare Abraham a son in his old age, at the set time of which God had spoken to him*** (Gen. 21:2). Isaac, the miracle child God had promised, entered the family life of Abraham, Sarah, Ishmael, and Hagar the bondwoman. Ishmael soon revealed his contempt for Isaac. In the New Testament we read *that Abraham had two sons, the one by a bondmaid, the other by a freewoman.... these are the two covenants* (agreements); *the one from the Mount Sinai, which gendereth* (leads) *to bondage, which is Agar* (Hagar).... *But as then he that was born after the flesh persecuted him that was born after the Spirit, even so it is now* (Gal. 4:22,24,28-29).

Ishmael and Isaac illustrate the dual nature of our lives. We are first **born of the flesh** (through human parents) (John 3:6), symbolized by Ishmael. But the moment a sinner believes in his heart that Jesus Christ died on the cross for his sins, repents of them, and confesses Christ as Savior and Lord of his life, he becomes a child of God (1:12). This is symbolized by Isaac, the child of faith.

On the Day of Pentecost, Peter answered the people by saying: **Repent, and be baptized ... and ye shall receive the gift of the Holy Ghost** (Spirit) (Acts 2:38; Rom. 10:9-10; I John 3:1-2; 4:15). We do not become sinless, but we are freed from the power of sin (Rom. 6:7). **They that are Christ's have crucified the flesh with the affections** (passions) **and lusts. If we live in the Spirit, let us also walk in the Spirit** (Gal. 5:24-25).

Thought for Today: God will guide those who read His Word.

Christ Revealed: By Isaac, the promised Son of the Covenant of God (Gen. 21:12). Faith in Christ sets us free from bondage of the Law because God made a new Covenant through Christ (Matt. 26:28; Mark 14:24; Luke 22:20; I Cor. 11:25; also Heb. 12:24).

JANUARY 8

Read Genesis 22 – 24

Highlights: Miraculous intervention because of obedience to God. Abraham faces the greatest test of his life. How would we respond (Gen. 22:2)? Trust Him: ***God will provide.... Jehovah-jireh*** (22:8,13-14). God answers prayer for a wife (24:48).

Abraham was called of God and is known for his remarkable faithfulness to Him. However, he experienced one severe trial after another. It was a test of faith when he left his father's house and the security of his home country to seek the land of promise. It was a test of faith when he arrived and there was a famine in the land and he felt it was necessary to go to Egypt to survive. It was a test of faith when Lot chose all the well-watered plains and left Abraham nothing but barren hills for grazing his herds. It was a test of faith when, as an old man, Abraham could not understand why God had not answered his prayer for a son to be his heir. It was ***after these things, that God did tempt*** (test the faith of) ***Abraham, and said unto him, Abraham: and he said, Behold, here I am. And He said, Take now thy son, thine only son Isaac, whom thou lovest, and get thee into the land of Moriah; and offer him there for a burnt offering*** (Gen. 22:1-2).

The intention of God was not to sanction human sacrifices, but to test Abraham's willingness to surrender to His will and His Word. Abraham obeyed that call with unwavering trust in God because he was convinced that God would be faithful to His promise that ***in Isaac shall thy seed be called*** (21:12).

We read of this incident, knowing the outcome, and could easily overlook the deep distress of heart of this godly man. Every time Abraham looked upon Isaac, he was reminded that Isaac was a special gift in answer to prayer. ***Thine only son Isaac.*** We cannot conceive of a greater test than this heartbreaking command by which God chose to test Abraham's faith (James 1:3).

It was a three-day journey of about 50 miles to Mount Moriah – uphill the whole way. It is always "uphill" for those who walk by faith. It takes self-denial to gain the best blessings of God. The man of faith is not searching for an oasis on the way. His only concern will be to please God – to sacrifice even life itself.

By faith Abraham, when he was tried, offered up Isaac: and he that had received the promises offered up his only begotten son (Heb. 11:17).

Thought for Today: Our faith is strengthened through stressful situations, even though they are painful.

Christ Revealed: Through Isaac's submission to his father and his willingness to be offered (Gen. 22:7-10). Jesus willingly offered His life. ***I lay down*** (give up) ***My life.... No man taketh it from Me, but I lay it down of Myself*** (John 10:11-18).

JANUARY 9   **Read Genesis 25 – 27**

Highlights: Abraham dies. We meet Isaac's family: wife Rebekah and twin sons, Jacob and Esau. God reveals His plan for: (1) His people; (2) salvation (Gen. 25:23). ***Esau despised his birthright*** (25:32-34). God said: ***I loved Jacob, And I hated Esau*** (Mal. 1:2-3).

Esau was born before his twin brother Jacob and thereby became legal heir to the family birthright, which included the Covenant between God and Abraham. This birthright was a link in the line of descent through which the Promised Messiah was to come (Num. 24:17-19). In contrast with Esau, ***Jacob was a plain man, dwelling in tents*** (Gen. 25:27). The Hebrew word for ***plain*** is the same word translated in other Scripture as ***perfect, upright, undefiled***. So the word ***plain*** refers to Jacob's character as a man of God. God records His highest praise and blessing for Jacob: ***The Lord hath chosen Jacob unto Himself*** (Ps. 135:4).

    Esau came from the field, and he was faint: And Esau said to Jacob, Feed me . . . with that same red pottage (stew)***; for I am faint*** (Gen. 25:29-30). Knowing the character of his brother, Jacob replied: ***Sell me this day thy birthright*** (25:31). Esau had no interest in spiritual things so he agreed, saying: ***I am at the point*** (about) ***to die: and what profit shall this birthright do to me*** (25:32-34)***?*** Esau was not about to die by missing one meal, but he revealed how worthless the birthright was to him.

    It appears that Isaac's admiration for his worldly-minded son Esau caused him to ignore the prophecy that God had revealed to Rebekah before the twins' birth (25:23). Furthermore, Isaac chose to disregard Esau's sale of his birthright to Jacob (25:33-34).

    After Isaac had conferred the Abrahamic Covenant on Jacob, Esau later came to receive a blessing. Isaac realized then that Rebekah had thwarted his evil scheme. There is no hint Isaac thought Rebekah did wrong. A short time later, he sent Jacob to seek a wife with his blessing (28:1-4). The Hebrew word **Jacob** is often translated "supplanter." One of the definitions of **supplant** is "to take the place of and serve as a substitute for, especially by reason of superior excellence." To speak evil of Jacob's actions is to misinterpret the Word of God. ***Looking diligently lest any man fail of the grace of God . . . Lest there be any . . . profane*** (godless) ***person, as Esau, who for one morsel . . . sold his birthright*** (Heb. 12:15-16).

Thought for Today: How prone we are to blame others for our failures.

Christ Revealed: As the promised spiritual Seed (Gen. 26:4). ***Now to Abraham and his Seed were the promises made. . . . which is Christ*** (Gal. 3:16).

JANUARY 10   Read Genesis 28 – 30

Highlights: Be sure to grasp the incredible Truth found in the mighty Abrahamic Covenant (one of the greatest honors God has ever given). The Abrahamic Covenant confirmed to Jacob; vision of Jacob's ladder; journey to Haran; Jacob's marriage to Leah and to Rachel.

When Isaac realized that God had overruled his scheme to confer the God-ordained Abrahamic Covenant on Esau, who forfeited his birthright, *Isaac trembled very exceedingly* (Gen. 27:33). He conferred with Rebekah, not to accuse her of wrongdoing, but to follow her God-inspired plan for Jacob's future (27:26–28:1-2).

If Jacob were to marry an idol-worshiping woman, as Esau had done, Rebekah knew they would have failed God and said: *What good shall my life do me* (27:46)*?* Then *Isaac called Jacob, and blessed him, and charged him . . . Thou shalt not take a wife of the daughters of Canaan. . . . Go to Padan-aram . . . take . . . a wife from . . . the daughters of Laban thy mother's brother. And God Almighty . . . give thee the blessing of Abraham, to thee, and to thy seed with thee; that thou mayest inherit the land wherein thou art a stranger, which God gave unto Abraham* (28:1-4).

The remarkable blessings of God upon Jacob began on his first night away from home. Without map or companion, but according to the exact plan of God, Jacob journeyed more than 500 miles to Padan-aram. God marvelously guided him to Rachel and the home of his *mother's father; and* (to) *take thee a wife from . . . the daughters of Laban thy mother's brother* (28:2-3). Jacob received a warm welcome when he arrived.

You may, like Jacob, experience many hardships in life. But all who live to do the will of God will choose marriage partners, activities, and workplace in order to please Him.

This can be seen in Jacob's beloved son Joseph, who was sold as a slave by his brothers and suffered much for 20 years, but later he confidently said to them: *Ye thought evil against me; but God meant it unto* (for) *good* (50:20).

One of the greatest comforts all of us will ever have is the assurance that: *All things work together for good to them that love God, to them who are the called according to His purpose* (Rom. 8:28).

Thought for Today: Eternal treasures are reserved for those who forsake earthly pleasures to do the will of God.

Christ Portrayed: By Joseph who was born (Gen. 30:23-24) in order to save and preserve his people (50:20). Jesus was born in order to offer salvation to all mankind. *For God so loved the world, that He gave His only begotten Son, that whosoever believeth in Him should not perish, but have everlasting life* (John 3:16).

JANUARY 11   Read Genesis 31 – 33

Highlights: An exciting climax to the personal problems and struggles of Jacob. Laban and his sons are jealous of Jacob's blessings. Jacob flees; the covenant between Laban and Jacob; Jacob's intense wrestling in prayer; God changes Jacob's name to Israel. Esau and 400 men come to meet Jacob (Gen. 32:3-21; 33:1).

Laban and his sons eventually became hostile and envious of Jacob's prosperity. They assumed that Jacob had employed unfair manipulation to gain their father's riches. However, Jacob said to his wives: **And ye know that with all my power I have served your father** (Gen. 31:6; comp. 31:7,14,16). Jacob foresaw the coming conflict and, in prayer, **the LORD said unto Jacob, Return unto the land of thy fathers . . . and I will be with thee** (31:3). When Jacob was returning to the land of his fathers, he learned that his brother, Esau, was coming to meet him with 400 men. Jacob could see no visible hope of survival for himself and his family.

Fearing the upcoming meeting with Esau, this godly and humble servant of the Lord spent the night earnestly praying to God for His mercy to deliver him and his family from the overwhelming odds of 400 armed men. God not only answered his prayer, but He conferred on Jacob the highest honor of any man in Old Testament history: **Thy name shall be called no more Jacob, but Israel** (Prince of God)**: for as a prince hast thou power with God and with men, and hast prevailed** (overcome) (32:28). Through the centuries, the people of God would be called by his name – Israelites. No one in Hebrew history has received such a distinguished name. Jacob's descendants **cannot be numbered** (32:12). Through his son Judah, Jesus the Messiah was promised (49:10).

Jacob's prayer is a model prayer. He was honest and specific with the Lord and claimed the promise of God, even as he wrestled with the angel (32:9-12,24; Hos. 12:4). Jacob prayed for deliverance, and God answered his prayer. As he had been delivered from Laban, he was also delivered from Esau and his 400 men. Jacob illustrates the power available to a diligent intercessor.

Through Jacob's life we learn that God will develop our faith in Him in the school of difficulties and tragedies. Let us be conscious of His presence because He **is able to do exceeding abundantly above all that we ask or think** (Eph. 3:20).

Thought for Today: The more we love the Word of God, the more we will love the God of the Word.

Christ Revealed: As **the Angel** (Messenger) **of God** who guides (Gen. 31:11-13). The Angel speaks not merely in the Name of God but as God, leaving no doubt that He is the Lord Jesus in his pre-incarnate state. **I and My Father are One** (John 10:30).

JANUARY 12   Read Genesis 34 – 36

Highlights: Don't miss the real reason Dinah was disgraced. Abrahamic Covenant renewed with Jacob; Jacob told to return to Bethel (the House of God), but stops at Succoth. When we're out of the perfect will of God we're susceptible to sinful harm (chap. 34); The household "cleans up," throws out **strange gods**, heads home, and worships God (Gen. 35:1-7). Rachel's death.

After Jacob had made peace with Laban and then with Esau, he continued on his journey to Bethel and completed the vows (promises) which he had made with God twenty years earlier (Gen. 28:20-22). But just three miles from the promised land, he arrived at the well-watered plains of Succoth with the convenient markets of Shechem nearby. He **built him an house. . . . And he erected there an altar** (33:17,20). Ten years passed swiftly. Jacob's neglect to do the will of God led to Dinah's encountering Shechem, the prince of this Canaanite country where a series of sinful events transpired.

Jacob realized that drastic changes were needed in his family and he again looked to God. **And God said unto Jacob, Arise, go up to Bethel, and dwell <u>there</u>: and make <u>there</u> an altar unto God. . . . Then Jacob said unto his household, and to all that were with him, Put away the strange gods that are among you, and be clean, and change your garments: And let us arise, and go up to Bethel** (35:1-3).

Three things that Jacob said to his family have a parallel for Christians. First he said: **Put away the strange gods** – a reminder that the old habits of sin must be forsaken. Then he said: **Be clean, and change your garments**. This was a reminder to **follow . . . holiness, without which no man shall see the Lord** (Heb. 12:14). Thirdly, he worshiped God. We are to worship only God: **Thou shalt worship the Lord thy God, and Him only shalt thou serve** (Luke 4:8).

Our priority must be to do His will. As we consider our earthly needs, there is a great danger of neglecting the wil of God. This often results in worldly attractions controlling our families' hearts and often leads to heartbreaking outcomes. Difficult circumstances should lead us to renew our relationship with God on His terms. **For the love of money** (even for necessities) **is the root of all evil: which while some coveted after, they have erred from the faith, and pierced themselves . . . with many sorrows** (I Tim. 6:10).

Thought for Today: Compromise always results in disappointments.

Christ Revealed: As **God Almighty**, El Shaddai, the All-Sufficient One (Gen. 35:11). Jesus is **the Lord . . . which is . . . the Almighty** (Rev. 1:8).

JANUARY 13   **Read Genesis 37 – 39**

Highlights: You may weep as you read about Joseph who foreshadows Christ. Both are loved by their fathers. Joseph's dreams result in his brothers hating him and selling him into slavery. Because of the lies of Potiphar's wife, Joseph is imprisoned, but God accompanied him (Gen. 39:2-3,21-23).

Joseph, the only one of Jacob's 12 sons who showed an interest in spiritual things, was deeply troubled about his older brothers' evil conduct. At age 17, **Joseph . . . was feeding the flock with his brethren** and reported to his father the evil things they were doing (Gen. 37:2). Because Joseph **was the son of his old age** (37:3) and the son of his favorite wife, Rachel, and possibly because of Joseph's concern for his brothers' spiritual well-being, Jacob loved him **more than all his brethren** (37:4).

Some people discourage exposing others' wrongdoing. But Joseph possessed spiritual integrity and was willing to face abuse from his brothers for revealing their evil ways. When Joseph shared his prophetic dreams with them (37:5-7), they scoffed him, saying: **Shalt thou indeed reign over us? . . . they hated him yet the more for his dreams** (37:8). After this, Joseph's brothers **went to feed their father's flock in Shechem**, a considerable distance from their home (37:12). Some time later, Jacob, concerned about his sons' welfare, sent Joseph, who found his brothers near Dothan (37:17).

They stript (stripped) **Joseph out of his coat . . . of many colours . . . and cast him into a pit** (37:23-24). They sold Joseph as a slave to traveling Ishmaelites, who, in turn, sold him in the Egyptian slave market to Potiphar, the captain of Pharaoh's royal guard (37:27-28,36; 39:1). Their last memories of their terrified younger brother were of him pleading for his life (42:21).

The Christian life as foreshadowed by Joseph's ordeal is illustrated in these words: **Beloved, think it not strange concerning the fiery trial which is to try you, as though some strange thing happened unto you** (I Pet. 4:12).

God used Joseph's difficulties in Egypt to prepare him as the preserver of the people of God and, thus, the lineage of the coming Messiah, Jesus Christ. Joseph's experiences remind us that our Lord promises: **I will answer him: I will be with him in trouble; I will deliver him, and honour him** (Ps. 91:15).

Thought for Today: Faith is strengthened when trials are accepted with patience, **knowing that tribulation** (troubles) **worketh** patience (Rom. 5:3).

Christ Portrayed: By Joseph whose brothers sold him to the Gentiles for 20 pieces of silver, but who eventually became their savior (Gen. 37:28; 41:39-40). Jesus was sold for 30 pieces of silver. He became our Savior who soon will return to rule the world (Rev. 19:11-16; 22:3).

JANUARY 14   Read Genesis 40 – 42

Highlights: Thrilling as well as horrifying events follow Joseph's God-given gift of dream interpretation. For example, the lives of Joseph's brothers are preserved. Forced to buy corn (grain) in Egypt, his brothers bow down to him, not knowing Joseph is their brother.

Thirteen years had passed since Joseph had been sold by his brothers into slavery and taken to Egypt. As a slave, Joseph's character and self-control were tested again and again. Although Joseph was innocent, he was later imprisoned and endured all the shame and punishment of the dungeon. During that horrifying ordeal, Joseph experienced many lonely nights suffering as a prisoner, *whose feet they hurt with fetters: he was laid in iron* (Ps. 105:18). He never became bitter, but remained faithful to God, believing that *the LORD was with him* (Gen. 39:23). Joseph realized that earthly recognition cannot compare to the honor of being faithful to God. Even though Joseph was eventually highly exalted, his true reward was unseen by the world. Joseph stands as an example that God has a much greater reward to bestow upon His faithful servants than the elusive, soon-vanishing satisfactions of this world.

At the age of 30, Joseph was called to interpret Pharaoh's dreams. *Joseph answered Pharaoh . . . God shall give Pharaoh an answer of peace* (41:16). Because the Lord interpreted the dreams through Joseph, Pharaoh acknowledged him as the wisest man in Egypt. This former outcast then received Pharaoh's own ring, designating him second ruler over all the land of Egypt (41:39-44). Joseph's dreams from many years before were now reality.

We may endure our circumstances for months, or even years, when it appears that God does not care about us or cannot do anything. However, God has amazing ways of developing our talents and maturing us spiritually through difficult times when we remain faithful to Him. God *worketh all things after the counsel of His own will* (Eph. 1:11). How foolish to judge the wisdom or love of God by present circumstances!

For who hath known the mind of the Lord? or who hath been His counseller? Or who hath first given to Him, and it shall be recompensed unto him again? For of Him, and through Him, and to Him, are all things: to whom be glory for ever. Amen (Rom. 11:34-36). *We shall reap, if we faint not* (persist) (Gal. 6:9).

Thought for Today: Adverse circumstances will not defeat the faithful.

Christ Revealed: By the wisdom of Joseph (Gen. 41:39). *Christ; In whom are hid all the treasures of wisdom and knowledge* (Col. 2:2-3).

JANUARY 15   Read Genesis 43 – 45

Highlights: Jacob's sons, including Benjamin, return to Egypt for food. Can you imagine the emotions flowing through the minds of Joseph's brothers as he reveals himself to them? Jacob is informed that Joseph is still alive and is the governor of Egypt.

Because of the great famine, Jacob was forced to send his sons to Egypt to buy food again. Joseph, the second most powerful ruler of Egypt, spoke to his brothers through an interpreter. As he spoke, they were unaware the ruler was their brother whom they had sold into slavery about 20 years earlier. ***Joseph said . . . I am Joseph; doth my father yet live*** (Gen. 45:3)? Joseph's brothers had deceived their father and escaped accountability for their cruel sin against him. Now in shame, Joseph's brothers were face to face with him, ***and his brethren could not answer him; for they were troubled at his presence***. Imagine their shock when he said, in their own Hebrew language: ***I am Joseph your brother, whom ye sold into Egypt*** (45:4).

The words ***I am Joseph*** struck fear in the hearts of his brothers. They were speechless as thoughts of Joseph's revenge and their execution appeared imminent. To their amazement, he lovingly added: ***Be not . . . angry with yourselves, that ye sold me hither: for God did send me before you to preserve life*** (45:5). He did not hold a grudge or denounce them for heartlessly abandoning him in a pit, and then wickedly selling him as a slave to the Ishmaelites. ***Moreover he kissed all his brethren, and wept upon them*** (45:15).

Christians need to demonstrate the spirit of Joseph. When we are misunderstood, unjustly maligned, or cruelly abused, do we react in **the spirit of Joseph**? With a heart filled with love, we can say: ***As for you, ye thought evil against me; but God meant it unto good*** (50:20). What a spirit of love and mercy! Here the offended one showed willing forgiveness towards the guilty. The love of God is still the same today toward all who, like Joseph, express this forgiving mercy toward those who mistreat them.

In His Sermon on the Mount, Jesus taught us: ***Love your enemies, bless them that curse you, do good to them that hate you, and pray for them which despitefully use you, and persecute you; That ye may be the children of your Father which is in heaven*** (Matt. 5:44-45).

Thought for Today: Don't wait until difficulty is past to praise God.

Christ Revealed: Through Joseph's dealings with his brothers. Christ deals with us in such a way as to bring about our confession of sin and a recognition of His forgiving love. In a similar way, He reveals His sovereignty over the affairs of life (Gen. 45:5-8,15; comp. Rom. 5:8; Eph. 1:17,20-22).

The Jewish Calendar

Civil Calendar – Official calendar of kings, childbirth, and contracts

Month Sacred/Civil	Days in Month	Pre-Exile Name	Post Exile Name	Present-day Equivalent	Biblical References
1/7	30	Abib	Nisan	March/April	Exodus 12:2; 13:4; 23:15; 34:18; Deut. 16:1; Nehemiah 2:1
2/8	29	Zif (Ziv)	Iyyar	April/May	I Kings 6:1,37
3/9	30		Sivan	May/June	Esther 8:9
4/10	29		Tammuz	June/July	
5/11	30		Ab (Av)	July/August	
6/12	29		Elul	August/September	Nehemiah 6:15
7/1	30	Ethanim	Tishri	September/October	I Kings 8:2
8/2	29	Bul	Cheshvan or Marcheshvan	October/November	I Kings 6:38
9/3	30		Chisleu (Chislev or Kisleu)	November/December	Nehemiah 1:1 Zechariah 7:1
10/4	29		Tebeth (Tevet)	December/January	Esther 2:16
11/5	30		Sebat (Shebat, Shevat)	January/February	Zechariah 1:7
12/6	29		Adar	February/March	Ezra 6:15 Esther 3:7; 8:12; 9:1,15,17,19,21

Sacred Calendar – Used to compute festivals

Season	Day	Feasts (Festivals)
Spring, Latter rains, Barley harvest	14th 15-21st	Feast of Passover (Exodus 12:18; Lev. 23:5) Feast of Unleavened Bread (Lev. 23:6-8) Feast of Firstfruits (Lev. 23:10-14)
Dry season begins		
Wheat harvest, Early figs ripen		Feast of Weeks/Harvest (Pentecost) (Lev. 23:15-21)
Hot season; Grape harvest		
Olive harvest	9th	Fast, Destruction of Temple
Dates & Summer figs		
Early (former) rains, plowing time	1st 10th 15-21st 22nd	Feast of Trumpets (Lev. 23:24; Num. 29:1) Day of Atonement (Lev. 23:27-28) Feast of Tabernacles (Lev. 23:34) Solemn Assembly (Lev. 23:36)
Wheat & Barley sown, Winter figs		
Winter rains, sowing	25th	8-Day Feast of Dedication (John 10:22) added in between Old & New Testaments
Winter rains		
Almond trees blossom		
Latter rains, citrus harvest	14th	Feast of Purim - began with Queen Esther (Esther 9:15-19)

The Jewish day was from sunset to sunset, in 8 equal parts:

FIRST WATCH .... SUNSET TO 9 P.M.		FIRST HOUR .... SUNRISE TO 9 A.M.	
SECOND WATCH ... 9 P.M. TO MIDNIGHT		THIRD HOUR .... 9 A.M. TO NOON	
THIRD WATCH ...... MIDNIGHT TO 3 A.M.		SIXTH HOUR .... NOON TO 3 P.M.	
FOURTH WATCH ... 3 A.M. TO SUNRISE		NINTH HOUR .... 3 P.M. TO SUNSET	

[3 watches in Old Testament (Exodus 14:24; Judges 7:19)
4 watches in New Testament (Matthew 25:6; Acts 20:7)]

The Jewish calendar is a lunar one established by God at creation: *And the evening and the morning were the first day* (Genesis 1:5). Feasts or holy days began at *even* (Leviticus 23:5). The Hebrew year has 354 days based on a lunar cycle. Months are alternately 30 and 29 days long. An extra 29-day month, Vadar, is added between Adar and Nisan about every 3 years.

JANUARY 16   Read Genesis 46 – 48

Highlights: Jacob's vision at Beersheba; journey to Egypt; best land given to Jacob; Joseph and the famine; Joseph's sons blessed. God uses Joseph to save the small Israelite family from extinction.

Knowing that God had planned for his people to live in Canaan (the Promised Land), not in Egypt (a symbol of worldly and sinful living), Jacob did not rush to Egypt for a grand reunion with his precious son Joseph. Since the will of God was uppermost in Jacob's heart, he prayed to God concerning his journey to Egypt. Jacob left Hebron, journeyed about 25 miles **to Beersheba, and offered sacrifices unto the God of his father Isaac. And God spake unto . . . Jacob. . . . fear not to go down into Egypt; for I will there make of thee a great nation . . . I will also surely bring thee up again** (Gen. 46:1-4). For many years, Jacob's family enjoyed Egypt's prosperity, but they eventually became involved in its sin of idol worship and lost sight of the covenant promise of God. God said He would bless them, if they would live in obedience to Him. The nation that had once welcomed Jacob and his sons eventually enslaved them.

Egypt was symbolic of the world with its many "good things" that often keep us from doing the will of God. Satan directs all his deceptive efforts to keep us from being devoted to the Lord. Jesus said: **Seek ye first the Kingdom of God, and His righteousness; and all these things shall be added unto you** (Matt. 6:33).

We are warned: **Love not the world, neither the things that are in the world. If any man love the world, the love of the Father is not in him. For all that is in the world, the lust of the flesh, and the lust of the eyes, and the pride of life, is not of the Father, but is of the world** (I John 2:15-16). It is essential that we not become sidetracked by materialism, but live to serve the Lord. **The whole world lieth in wickedness. . . . Little children, keep yourselves from idols** (5:19,21).

But godliness with contentment is great gain. . . . And having food and raiment let us be therewith content. But they that will be rich fall into temptation and a snare . . . which drown men in destruction and perdition. For the love of money is the root of all evil: which while some coveted after, they have erred from the faith. . . . But thou, O man of God, flee these things; and follow after righteousness (I Tim. 6:6-11).

Thought for Today: Christians are to forgive regardless of circumstances.

Christ Portrayed: By Joseph, who was placed second only to Pharaoh (Gen. 41:39-40) to sustain life and give provision (47:15-17). Jesus said: **For the Bread of God is He which cometh down from heaven, and giveth life unto the world** (John 6:33).

Introduction To The Book Of EXODUS

Exodus means "exit, departure, the way out" (Heb. 11:22). This book continues the history of the descendants of Jacob's 12 sons.

Chapters 1:1 – 11:10 cover the period when the Israelites settled in the most fertile land in Egypt until the time they became slaves to the Egyptians. God had foretold to Abraham: ***Know of a surety that thy seed*** (descendants) ***shall be a stranger*** (temporary residents) ***in a land that is not theirs*** (Egypt)***, and shall serve them; and they shall afflict them four hundred years*** (Gen. 15:13; Acts 7:6). The Word of God was fulfilled, and the time had come for the Israelites to be set free and to prepare for their journey to the promised land.

Chapters 12:1 – 14:18 relate the Passover instructions, judgment on the firstborn, the Israelites' departure from Egypt, and their journey to the Red Sea. At the time chosen by God, He said: ***Against all the gods of Egypt I will execute judgment: I am the L***ORD (Ex. 12:12). The Israelites' miraculous deliverance from slavery and bondage in Egypt was made possible by their obedience to the Word of God as they, by faith, applied the blood of an innocent lamb to their doorposts. God had also required them to ***eat the flesh in that night, roast with fire, and unleavened*** (yeast-free) ***bread. . . . with your loins girded, your shoes on your feet, and your staff in your hand*** (12:7-11). Only after they obeyed all that God commanded were they prepared to leave Egypt. This was the beginning of a new life as a nation (12:2). It also was the beginning of a new liberty from Egyptian bondage (13:3). But, best of all, it meant a new relationship with God through the Feasts (Festivals) and sacrificial offerings (13:6).

Chapters 14:19 – 15:27 detail Israel's victorious deliverance from Pharaoh, and Moses' song of praise to the Lord for redeeming them. It is estimated that at the time they were delivered from slavery, there were about 2 million people. There were approximately 600,000 Israelite men in addition to the women and children and a mixed multitude who were probably the result of intermarriage (12:37-38).

Chapters 16:1 – 18:27 provide an account of the Israelites' 3-month journey from Elim, along the Red Sea to Mount Sinai.

Chapters 19:1 – 40:38 begin in the third month of the Exodus and record the Israelites' 11-month stay at Mount Sinai, when the covenant relationship between God and the Israelites as a nation was established. God said to ***the children of Israel . . . if ye will obey My voice indeed, and keep My Covenant, then ye shall be a peculiar*** (select, special) ***treasure unto Me above all people*** (Ex. 19:3-5).

JANUARY 17   Read Genesis 49 – Exodus 1

Highlights: Jacob's prophecies concerning his twelve sons; Judah to be an ancestor of the Messiah; deaths of Jacob and Joseph; Hebrew people oppressed in Egypt. The chosen people of God begin a new era as the Lord leads them out of Egypt to the promised land.

Although Judah was not the firstborn, God chose him to be part of the Abrahamic Covenant with its promise of the Messiah (Gen. 22:18). ***Judah is a ... lion. ... The sceptre shall not depart from Judah, nor a lawgiver from between his feet, until Shiloh come; and unto Him shall the gathering of the people be*** (49:9-10). Judah's tribe emerged as the powerful leader of Israel and one who was feared by his enemies ***as a lion***. Added to this, he was to hold ***the sceptre*** of legislative control over the other tribes ***until Shiloh come. Shiloh*** means the "Peacemaker" and is commonly accepted to be a name or title for the Messiah.

Throughout Scripture, God reveals His wonderful plan of salvation through Christ, our Savior; as we look forward to His glorious return our hearts are thrilled. His coming is good news to all who love Him ***and keep His Commandments. . . . For whatsoever is born of God overcometh the world: and this is the victory that overcometh the world, even our faith*** (I John 5:2,4).

We may face situations that leave us feeling as powerless as the baby Moses in a homemade ark floating in the Nile River. It could be that death has left us without a parent, a child, or a spouse. Some may feel defeated following a divorce. Others may have received a terminal diagnosis from a doctor. God has revealed that throughout life all of us will face unforeseen and unavoidable sorrows.

In spite of all life's difficulties, **every** Christian, regardless of circumstances, can say with the Apostle Paul: ***I am persuaded*** (convinced)***, that neither death, nor life, nor angels, nor principalities, nor powers, nor things present, nor things to come ... nor any other creature, shall be able to separate us from the love of God, which is in Christ Jesus our Lord*** (Rom. 8:38-39).

When our King ***is come, He will reprove the world of sin ... and of judgment ... because the prince of this world*** (Satan, whose demonic power has oppressed the world with hate and suffering) ***is judged*** (John 16:8,11). Oh, the freedom of that day! ***Even so, come, Lord Jesus*** (Rev. 22:20).

Thought for Today: The All-Sufficient God doesn't show favoritism.

Christ Revealed: As the Messiah who would come through the tribe of Judah. ***The sceptre shall not depart from Judah ... until Shiloh*** (Peacemaker) ***come*** (Gen. 49:10). ***Jesus ... the son*** (descendant) ***of Juda*** (Luke 3:23-33).

JANUARY 18 — Read Exodus 2 – 4

Highlights: Moses' flight into Midian; the burning bush; his commission to free the nation of Israel; his return to Egypt. Moses was a type of Christ. Both were endangered in infancy. Both were deliverers and mediators.

Moses was only a peasant shepherd when God said to him: *I will send thee unto Pharaoh, that thou mayest bring forth My people the children of Israel out of Egypt. And Moses said unto God, Who am I, that I should go unto Pharaoh* (Ex. 3:10-11)?

The Israelite slaves were controlled by the most powerful nation on earth. Moses had forfeited his influence in Egypt forty years earlier. Added to that, he felt he was not a fluent speaker. Moses' response could be expected. However, the Almighty Creator rules and overrules the affairs of life. *Who am I* was not important. It was of much greater significance that Moses had faith in the One who said *I will send thee unto Pharaoh.*

At one time Moses could have been the next Pharaoh. But *he ... refused to be called the son of Pharaoh's daughter; Choosing rather to suffer affliction with the people of God, than to enjoy the pleasures of sin for a season; Esteeming the reproach of Christ greater riches than the treasures in Egypt* (Heb. 11:24-26). Moses now acknowledged his insufficiency and had to accept, by faith, the Word of God. God gave Moses the assurance: *I will be with thee* (Ex. 3:12), and He still promises to be with every Christian: *I am with you alway* (Matt. 28:20; Heb. 13:5).

We are sometimes in a hurry to produce results with our abilities. But God is more concerned with our learning to trust Him, even when faced with difficulties.

Note the familiar phrase: *Moses ... did as the LORD commanded* (Ex. 7:6,20; 16:34; 17:6; 39:1,5,7,21,26,29,31,32; 40:16,19,21,23,25,27,29,32). As a result, he became a great leader.

We too can experience Christ as Lord of our lives. Obedience means that day by day we personally listen to the whole counsel of God as it is revealed in His Word (I Sam. 15:22).

As obedient children, not fashioning yourselves according to the former lusts in your ignorance: But as He which hath called you is holy, so be ye holy in all manner of conversation (behavior) (I Pet. 1:14-15).

Thought for Today: You are a vital part of the plan of God to reach others.

Christ Revealed: As the *I AM THAT I AM* who commissioned Moses (Ex. 3:13-14; comp. Heb. 13:8). *Jesus said unto them, Verily, verily* (Truly, truly), *I say unto you, Before Abraham was, I am* (John 8:58).

JANUARY 19

Read Exodus 5 – 7

Highlights: The battle intensifies as Pharaoh brashly questions: ***Who is the LORD, that I should obey His voice*** (Ex. 5:2)***?*** Aaron speaks for Moses; Moses' rod turned into a snake; the plague of blood.

God commanded Moses to face the Pharaoh of Egypt, who referred to himself as a god, and say: ***Thus saith the LORD God of Israel, Let My people go, that they may hold*** (celebrate) ***a feast unto Me in the wilderness. And Pharaoh said, Who is the LORD, that I should obey His voice? . . . I know not the LORD, neither will I let Israel go*** (Ex. 5:1-2). Moses' immediate reaction was to blame God, saying: ***Wherefore hast Thou so evil entreated*** (brought harm to) ***this people? why is it that Thou hast sent me? For since I came to Pharaoh to speak in Thy Name, he hath done evil to this people; neither hast Thou delivered Thy people*** (5:22-23).

How often in life our questions far outnumber our answers: "Why do I have cancer? Why did my husband divorce me? Why did my child become a drug addict? Why was my child born with handicaps? Why did I lose my job? Why me?" God didn't answer Moses' questions, and seldom does He answer us in the way we expect.

When Moses cried out: "Why, Lord?," God first reminded him of who He is: ***I am the LORD*** (6:2), meaning: "I am the only Self-Existent God and the One who knows what is best. I am altogether sufficient to meet your needs." What is important for us to know is that God is the unchangeable, loving, Almighty, all-wise God of Truth. He promised Moses: ***I will bring you out from under the burdens of the Egyptians, and I will rid you out of their bondage . . . I will take you to Me for a people, and I will be to you . . . your God*** (6:6-8).

Everyone is important to God. He ***is no respecter of persons*** (Acts 10:34). After His seventh ***I will***, He repeated for emphasis: ***I am the LORD*** (Ex. 6:8). God has never once failed to keep His Word. His promises are always fulfilled, but seldom come as soon as we expect, and almost never in the way we think best.

Pharaoh persisted in tyrannizing the Israelites. However, as had been foretold, the judgment of God was poured forth on each false Egyptian deity, and, eventually, on Pharaoh himself and his armies. ***To day . . . hear His voice, Harden not your hearts, as in the provocation*** (provoking Me)***, in the day of temptation*** (testing) ***in the wilderness. . . . I was grieved with that generation*** (Heb. 3:7-8,10).

Thought for Today: Some people are more concerned over present problems than being submissive to the will of God.

Christ Revealed: As the Redeemer from the bondage of sin. ***I will bring you out . . . I will redeem you*** (Ex. 6:6). ***Forasmuch as ye know that ye were not redeemed with corruptible things . . . But with the precious blood of Christ*** (I Pet. 1:18-19).

JANUARY 20 **Read Exodus 8 – 10**

Highlights: Plagues of frogs, lice, flies, dying cattle, boils, hail, locusts, and the utter darkness. If you think these eight plagues are bad, wait until you see what happens in tomorrow's reading.

Pharaoh gave permission for the Israelite men to go with Moses to sacrifice to God (Ex. 10:10-11), but the little ones, the women, and the aged were to remain in bondage. Moses, as the servant of God, would not yield to Pharaoh's offer to compromise. **Moses said** (to Pharaoh), **We will go with our young and with our old, with our sons and with our daughters, with our flocks and with our herds will we go; for we must hold a feast unto the LORD. . . .** (But Pharaoh said) **Not so: go now ye that are men, and serve the LORD; for that ye did desire. And they were driven out from Pharaoh's presence** (10:9,11). The commands of God are not negotiable. We too have but one ultimate Authority.

Like the Israelites, we also must be delivered from the power of the enemy. When we are determined to make a complete break from the world, we will, by faith, forsake our sins and trust the Risen Savior for cleansing and the power to overcome. The power that raised Christ from the dead now enables the believer to live a new life with Christ. **Therefore we are buried with Him by baptism into death: that like as Christ was raised up from the dead by the glory of the Father, even so we also should walk in newness of life** (Rom. 6:4; II Cor. 5:17).

There are some who desire to worship God on the Lord's day, but never forsake their sins throughout the week. Instead, they conform to contemporary, questionable worldly activities.

If our worship and life are to please our Savior and Lord, there can be no compromise. **If any man will come after Me, let him deny himself, and take up his cross daily, and follow Me** (Luke 9:23). The cross is a symbol of death to self-will and self-pleasing – of separation from the old life of sin to be a true disciple of Christ. The criminal in Roman times who was forced to pick up his cross and start down the road for crucifixion had already said goodbye to his friends. He was not coming back – there would be no return. Jesus said: **He that taketh not his cross, and followeth after Me, is not worthy of Me** (Matt. 10:38).

Thought for Today: The real issue is: "Who is in control of your life?"

Christ Revealed: As the Light to His people. **There was a thick darkness in all the land of Egypt . . . but all the children of Israel had light in their dwellings** (Ex. 10:22-23). Jesus said: **I am the Light of the world: he that followeth Me shall not walk in darkness** (John 8:12).

JANUARY 21   **Read Exodus 11 – 13**

Highlights: Death of the firstborn; Passover instructions; departure from Egypt; firstborn to be set apart; pillar of cloud and pillar of fire; journey to the promised land begins.

God had only one plan for sparing the lives of the Israelites: *I . . . will smite all the firstborn in the land of Egypt. . . . and when I see the blood, I will pass over you, and the plague shall not be upon you to destroy you, when I smite the land of Egypt* (Ex. 12:12-13). Not one family was so good that it did not require the blood to be applied – no, not even Moses' or Aaron's. This was their only hope of deliverance. The divine Command of God had to be obeyed.

Just as the blood of an innocent lamb was the only appointed means to preserve the Hebrews from death, so also **we have redemption through His** (Christ's) **blood, the forgiveness of sins, according to the riches of His grace** (Eph. 1:7). One may assume that he is sincere or good enough, thus some means would satisfy God, but that assumption can cause him to be eternally lost.

Later instruction regarding sacrifices states: **They shall eat those things wherewith the atonement was made** (Ex. 29:33). The Hebrew word translated **atonement** carries the idea of covering something, removing it from the sight of God, and assuring His forgiveness. This points out that an innocent lamb made only a temporary atonement – sin was not fully eradicated. Even though there were numerous sin offerings, the Israelites were still required to observe a full Day of Atonement annually. The New Testament reveals: **We also joy in God through our Lord Jesus Christ, by whom we have now received the atonement** (Rom. 5:11). The Greek word for **atonement** means: We have **now** obtained complete reconciliation.

God sent His only Son to die on the cross to save us from eternal death and adopt us into His family. Our security from this eternal death is through trusting Christ as our personal Savior. He alone can satisfy God and save the repentant sinner.

    Being justified freely by His grace through the redemption that is in Christ Jesus: Whom God hath set forth to be a propitiation (a means of reconciliation, redemption) **through faith in His blood, to declare His righteousness for the remission of sins that are past. . . . Therefore we conclude that a man is justified by faith without the deeds of the Law** (Rom. 3:24-25,28).

Thought for Today: The cross that ended the earthly life of Jesus forever ended the power of Satan to control the Christian.

Christ Revealed: Through the sacrifice of lambs without blemish. Not one of the lambs' bones was to be broken (Ex. 12:5,46). We were redeemed **with the precious blood of Christ, as of a lamb without blemish and without spot** (I Pet. 1:19).

JANUARY 22   Read Exodus 14 – 16

Highlights: Miracle after miracle fills the chapters of this Book; a reminder of the power of God. Crossing the Red Sea; song of Moses; the waters of Marah; murmurings, manna, and quail.

The will of God was revealed to the Israelites in Egypt, and **the people believed** and **they bowed their heads and worshipped** (Ex. 4:31). God was in the process of fulfilling His promise to Abraham, Isaac, and Jacob. He would deliver His chosen people from slavery and lead them to the promised land. After **four hundred years** (Acts 7:6), a victory for Israel had been accomplished that freed them from Egyptian oppression! The song of Moses was sung to celebrate deliverance from Egypt.

    Moses brought Israel from the Red Sea, and they went . . . three days in the wilderness, and found no water. . . . when they came to Marah, they probably were excited to find water, however, **they could not drink of the waters of Marah, for they were bitter: therefore the name of it was called Marah** (Ex. 15:22-23). The Israelites' joy and thankfulness turned to disappointment and then anger. This unexpected trouble was an opportunity for Israel to trust in the Word of God alone, but **they waited not for His Counsel** (Ps. 106:13).

    God had clearly revealed His will to lead them to the promised land, yet ten times they expressed their unbelief (Ex. 14:10-12; 15:22-24; 16:2-3,7-9,12,19-20,25-29; 17:3,8-16; 32:7-10). Their faith in the Word of God never went beyond the next obstacle. **They believed not His Word** (Ps. 106:24).

    The Lord still leads His faithful children through circumstances of apparent defeat, but it is here they learn the futility of human reasoning and how to wait upon Him for direction. Our disappointments are His appointments to develop our faith.

    As soon as the child of God is persuaded of the will of God, Satan, the enemy of man's soul, will attempt to prevent it from being accomplished. Seek the Lord's guidance (Prov. 3:5-7) and **wait upon the LORD. For evildoers shall be cut off: but those that wait upon the LORD, they shall inherit the earth** (Ps. 37:9). Don't depend upon your own changing emotions or the uncertain circumstances around you. **Without faith it is impossible to please Him . . . he that cometh to God must believe that He is, and that He is a rewarder of them that <u>diligently seek Him</u>** (Heb. 11:6).

Thought for Today: A heart filled with faith in God has no room for fear.

Christ Revealed: Through the **bread** (manna) **from heaven** (Ex. 16:4,15). Jesus said: **I am the Living Bread which came down from heaven** (John 6:51; also 6:32-48).

JANUARY 23   Read Exodus 17 – 19

Highlights: The Israelites are called *a peculiar treasure* (Ex. 19:5), which means they are precious to the Lord. Thirst causes murmuring against Moses; water from the rock; Amalek defeated; Jethro's advice accepted; God speaks on Mount Sinai.

The Israelites faced another test of their dependence upon God. *All the congregation . . . journeyed . . . according to the Commandment of the LORD, and pitched* (encamped) *in Rephidim: and there was no water for the people to drink. . . . And the people thirsted there for water; and the people murmured* (grumbled) *against Moses, and said, Wherefore* (Why) *is this that thou hast brought us up out of Egypt, to kill us . . . with thirst? . . . And he called the name of the place Massah* (Tempting God), *and Meribah* (Contention, Complaint), *because of the chiding* (faultfinding) *of the children of Israel, and because they tempted the LORD, saying, Is the LORD among us, or not* (Ex. 17:1,3,7)?

Again and again, the wilderness exposed the Israelites' refusal to trust the Lord. God has warned us: *Harden not your hearts, as in the provocation* (rebellion), *in the day of temptation* (testing) *in the wilderness: When your fathers tempted Me, proved Me, and saw My works forty years. . . . I was grieved with that generation, and said, They do alway err* (disobey) *in their heart* (Heb. 3:8-10).

Israel's release from bondage and their wilderness journey illustrate the Christian's pilgrimage through life. We should learn from their experiences to trust God even when anticipated resources are not available. Often we are tempted to blame others for our problems and failures. Frustration on the job, emotional stress, discontent, finding fault, hatred, jealousy, fits of anger – these are all evidence of the self-centered life demanding its own way. Even more serious, it is an expression of unbelief in the wisdom, competence, and goodness of God. *But let patience have her perfect work, that ye may be perfect and entire* (mature), *wanting* (lacking) *nothing* (James 1:4).

The key to peace of mind and overcoming all life's problems is confidence in God and in His Word. The Christian is admonished to express faith when *ye are in heaviness through manifold temptations* (various testings): *That the trial of your faith, being much more precious than of gold that perisheth, though it be tried with fire, might be found unto praise and honour and glory at the appearing of Jesus Christ* (I Pet. 1:6-7).

Thought for Today: To complain exposes a lack of faith in God.

Christ Revealed: As the Rock and the Water that came forth from it (Ex. 17:6). *They drank of that spiritual Rock* (*Petras* in Greek) *that followed* (accompanied) *them: and that Rock was Christ* (I Cor. 10:4; comp. John 7:38).

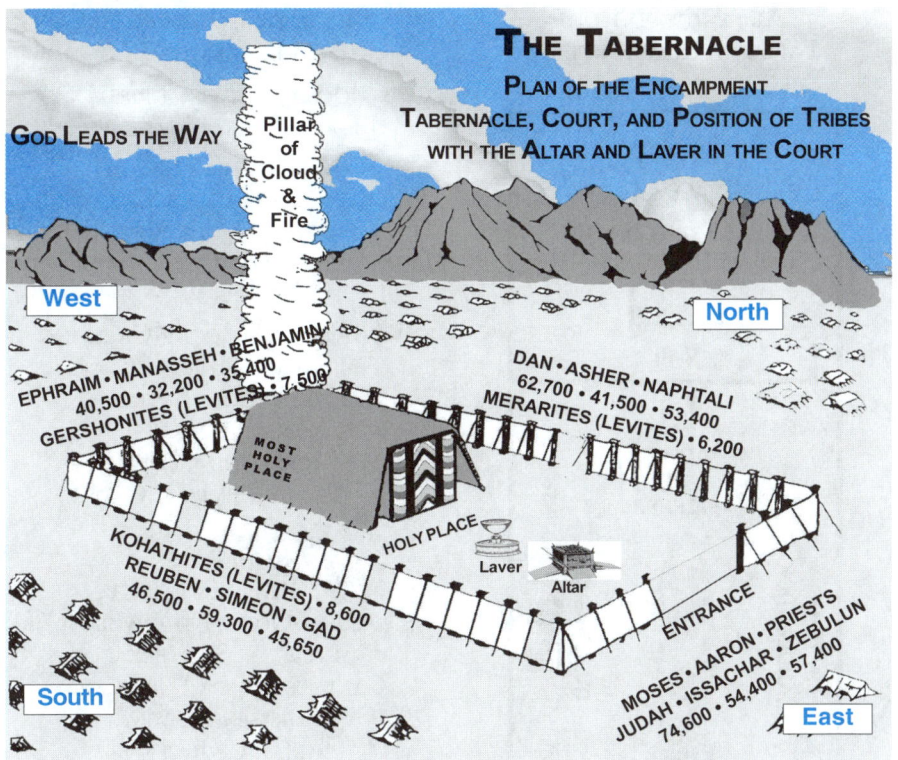

Look that thou make them after their pattern, which was shewed thee in the mount (Exodus 25:40).

Shadow of heavenly things, as Moses was admonished of God . . . make all things according to the pattern (Hebrews 8:5).

THE TABERNACLE

The Tabernacle was a rectangular structure, about 45 feet long and 15 feet wide, and was set up in the center of the encampment of the 12 tribes. It was protected by an outer court that was about 150 feet long and 75 feet wide. All items were based on a pattern the Lord had shown Moses. Nothing was left to human opinion.

Sixty posts, 7½ feet high, were equally spaced around the Tabernacle. This wall separated the unbeliever from the worshiper and was symbolic of the righteousness of God that bars the sinner from His presence.

There was only one door through which sinful man could approach God (Exodus 26:36). It was symbolic of Christ, who said: *I am The Door: by Me if any man enter in, he shall be saved, and shall go in and out, and find pasture* (John 10:9).

ARRANGEMENT OF TABERNACLE FURNITURE

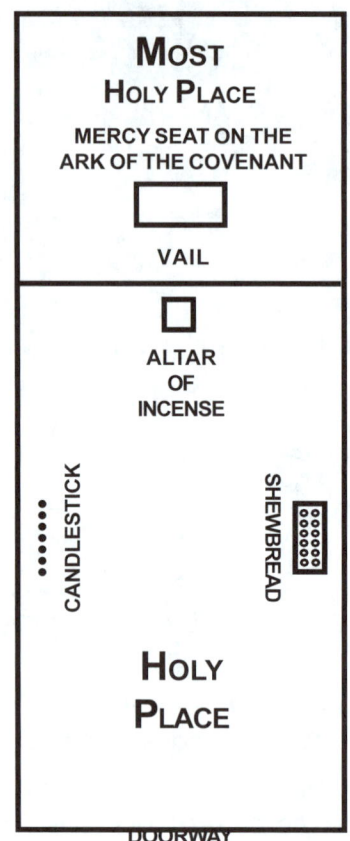

PILLAR OF CLOUD & FIRE
GOD LEADS THE WAY

MOSES, AARON, PRIESTS
JUDAH, ISSACHAR, ZEBULUN

GERSHONITES
WITH TWO WAGONS CARRYING
THE TABERNACLE, CURTAINS, COVERS,
HANGINGS, GATE, DOOR AND CORDS

MERARITES
WITH FOUR WAGONS CARRYING
THE BOARDS, BARS, PILLARS,
SOCKETS, COURT PILLARS,
COURT SOCKETS,
PINS, AND CORDS
REUBEN, SIMEON, GAD

KOHATHITES
BEARING THE
ARK – GOD IN THE MIDST
TABLE OF SHEWBREAD
CANDLESTICK OF PURE GOLD
BRASEN ALTAR
ALTAR OF INCENSE
VESSELS
LAVER OF BRASS

EPHRAIM, MANASSEH, BENJAMIN,
DAN, ASHER, NAPHTALI

THE BRASEN ALTAR
(Exodus 38:1-7)

After passing through the gate into the fenced court, the worshiper was confronted with the Brasen Altar (Altar of Burnt Offering).

This altar of sacrifice was the only God-ordained means to atone for sin. Sin had to be punished by the death of the sinner or an acceptable substitute of an unblemished animal so its death would allow God to forgive the sinner. All the sacrifices, the Altar, and the Officiating Priest illustrated the Sinless Savior Jesus Christ who died for our sins. The sacrifice represented the sinner who had to enter **The Door** (John 10:9), present his sacrifice, and, by faith, believe that God had forgiven his sin. The sacrifice symbolized the end of the old life and the beginning of the new life. *Old things are passed away; behold, all things are become new* (II Corinthians 5:17).

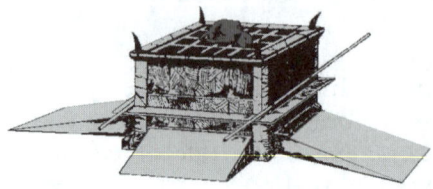

Our Lord was both *the Lamb of God, which taketh away the sin of the world* (John 1:29; Ephesians 2:13; I Peter 2:24), and also our High Priest. *We have such an High Priest . . . on the right hand of the throne of the Majesty in the heavens* (Hebrews 8:1; 9:11-14).

THE LAVER of BRASS
(Exodus 29:4; 30:18-21; 38:8)

Before a priest officiated in the Tabernacle, he approached the Laver of Brass that contained water to cleanse his hands and feet (Exodus 30:18-20). The Laver was symbolic of the Word of God that both reveals our sins and is the cleansing power in our lives (John 15:3; Titus 3:5; James 1:23-25).

THE TABLE of SHEWBREAD
(Exodus 25:23-30; 37:10-16)

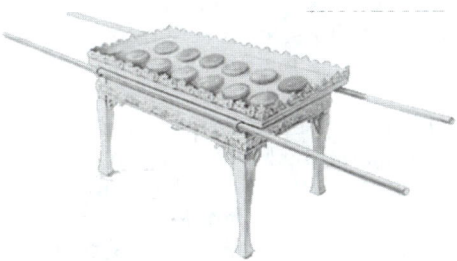

After the priest washed his hands and feet at the Laver of Brass, he proceeded toward the Tabernacle, passing through the linen vail, the only door to the Holy Place. Inside the Holy Place on the right was the Table of Shewbread, made of shittim (acacia) wood and overlaid with pure gold. It measured 3 feet by 1½ feet by 2 1/4 feet. Twelve loaves of unleavened bread sprinkled with incense were placed in two rows of six upon the Table. They were eaten only by the priests *in the Court of the Tabernacle* (Leviticus 6:16). Its name "Bread of the Presence" meant more than physical nourishment; it indicated gaining spiritual insight that was not obtainable in any other way. The Holy Spirit is able to do something beyond our ability to explain. He enlightens, empowers, and then transforms the lives of those who prayerfully continue to read the Word of God with a desire to do His will. Jesus said: *I am the living Bread which came down from heaven: if any man eat of this bread, he shall live for ever* (John 6:51; also 6:29-38; 12:24-33).

THE CANDLESTICK of PURE GOLD

(Exodus 37:17-24)

Inside the Holy Place on the left was the seven-branched Candlestick of pure gold that provided the only source of light. Without this light, the room would have been in total darkness. The Candlestick represented Christ, *the Light of the world*, who makes Himself known through His Word (John 8:12).

THE ALTAR of INCENSE
(Exodus 30:1-10; 37:25-28; 40:5; Leviticus 16:12-13)

Just in front of the vail leading to the Holy of Holies was a Golden Altar called the Altar of Incense (I Kings 6:22; Hebrews 9:4). This Altar was about 3 feet high, 1½ feet wide, and 1½ feet deep, made of shittim (acacia) wood overlaid with pure gold.

The Altar of Incense was used exclusively to burn incense morning and evening. A coal of fire from the Brasen Altar was placed on this Altar each morning and incense put on it. Only the high priest was permitted to offer incense, a type of intercessory prayer that ascended toward heaven day and night.

The Altar of Incense was the smallest piece of furniture in the Tabernacle and, as such, may seem insignificant. But it was symbolic of Christ as our Intercessor (John 17:1-26; Hebrews 7:25). It is through Him that the praise as well as the prayers of undeserving people become precious to God (Hebrews 13:15).

THE ARK OF THE COVENANT with THE MERCY SEAT
(Exodus 37:1-9; Numbers 10:33)

The Ark of the Covenant measured 3 3/4 feet by 2 1/4 feet by 2 1/4 feet and it was made of shittim (acacia) wood covered within and without with pure gold. The Ark contained Aaron's rod that budded, a golden pot of manna, and the two tables of stone on which were written the Ten Commandments (Exodus 16:33; 31:18; 34: 1,29; Numbers 17:10; Deuteronomy 10:5; Hebrews 9:4).

The Mercy Seat, or lid of the Ark, was made of pure gold and measured 3 3/4 feet by 2 1/4 feet. On its top were two golden cherubim with outstretched wings, facing each other, but looking down on the Mercy Seat. Between the cherubim dwelt the manifestation of the presence of God, which lighted the Holy of Holies.

Only one man, the high priest, symbolic of Christ, could enter the Most Holy Place (Holy of Holies) once each year. On the Day of Atonement, he sprinkled the blood of the sacrificed animal on the Mercy Seat and then before it seven times, symbolic of the perfect and complete salvation and forgiveness of sins to be made possible by Jesus Christ.

Christ, our High Priest, presented His blood as His sacrifice that we might be acceptable to God (Hebrews 9:11-15; 10:19).

Devotions continued from page 28

JANUARY 24   Read Exodus 20 – 22

Highlights: Ten Commandments and other laws and regulations given. The Law is a mirror that reveals with absolute accuracy and authority what we are and what we should be. God provided His perfect standard for His people to live by.

The Ten Commandments were **written with the finger of God** (Ex. 31:18), and are of utmost importance. **God spake all these words, saying, I am the LORD thy God. . . . Thou shalt have no other gods before Me. Thou shalt not make unto thee any graven image, or any likeness of any thing . . . in heaven above, or . . . the earth. . . . Thou shalt not take the Name of the LORD thy God in vain; for the LORD will not hold him guiltless that taketh His Name in vain. Remember the Sabbath day, to keep it holy. . . . Honour thy father and thy mother. . . . Thou shalt not kill. . . . commit adultery. . . . steal. . . . bear false witness against thy neighbour. . . . covet** (20:1-4,7-17). The Ten Commandments are essential, basic principles for the spiritual and moral conduct of mankind. Without them we have no standard of right and wrong. **The heart is deceitful above all things, and desperately wicked** (Jer. 17:9).

It is wrong to steal – whether it is done by shoplifting, cheating on income tax, failing to give an employer a full day's work, or to tithe one's income to God. If I love my neighbor, I will not steal his property, or commit adultery with his wife. I will protect and respect his loved ones because they belong to God, who commanded: **Love thy neighbour as thyself** (Matt. 22:39).

Christ revealed that: **By the deeds of the Law there shall no flesh be justified in His sight: for by the Law is the knowledge of sin. But now the righteousness of God without the Law is manifested, being witnessed by the Law and the prophets; Even the righteousness of God which is by faith of Jesus Christ unto all and upon all them that believe** (Rom. 3:20-22).

Many people think they can get to heaven by being good; but they are unwilling to recognize that **all have sinned, and come short of the glory of God** (3:23). **If we confess our sins, He is faithful and just to forgive us our sins, and to cleanse us from all unrighteousness** (I John 1:9). Jesus said: **If a man love Me, he will keep My words: and My Father will love him, and We will come unto him, and make Our abode with him** (John 14:23).

Thought for Today: We enjoy the peace of God when our desire is: "Whatever pleases You, Lord, pleases me."

Christ Revealed: The perfection of Christ is revealed through the Ten Commandments, for He kept them (Ex. 20:1-17). He was perfect and **without sin** (Heb. 4:15).

JANUARY 25   Read Exodus 23 – 25

Highlights: Laws instituted; three annual Feasts (Festivals) required and must be kept; angel promised for a guide; instructions for Tabernacle furnishings. Confirming the Covenant (Ex. 24:4-8). God desires to **dwell** with His children, to commune with them (25:8,22).

How easy but sinful it is to spread gossip! Of all sins, some of the vilest are committed with the tongue. **Thou shalt not raise a false report: put not thine hand with the wicked to be an unrighteous witness. Thou shalt not follow a multitude to do evil; neither shalt thou speak in a cause to decline after many to wrest** (pervert) **judgment** (Ex. 23:1-2). The Hebrew word also means that a person should refuse to even listen to slander. **A talebearer revealeth secrets: but he that is of a faithful spirit concealeth the matter** (Prov. 11:13).

God has determined and revealed what conduct and worship is acceptable to Him. God says that anyone who **uttereth a slander** (repeats an ill report or accusation), **is a fool** (10:18), and the one who **repeateth a matter separateth very** (close) **friends** (17:9).

Slander is perhaps the easiest, most subtle sin a person commits; yet, it is so wicked that it is listed with the seven most abominable sins that God hates: **These six things doth the Lord hate: yea, seven are an abomination unto Him: A proud look, a lying tongue, and hands that shed innocent blood, An heart that deviseth wicked imaginations, feet that be swift in running to mischief, A false witness that speaketh lies, and he that soweth discord among brethren** (6:16-19).

By gossiping, some not only have destroyed the good reputation of others but their own usefulness to God as well. The Bible says: **If any man among you seem to be religious, and bridleth not his tongue, but deceiveth his own heart, this man's religion is vain. ... The tongue is a fire, a world of iniquity ... it defileth the whole body ... and it is set on fire of** (from) **hell. ... it is an unruly evil, full of deadly poison. ... Who is a wise man and endued with knowledge among you? let him shew out of a good conversation his works with meekness of wisdom. ... the wisdom that is from above is first pure, then peaceable, gentle, and easy to be intreated, full of mercy and good fruits, without partiality, and without hypocrisy** (James 1:26; 3:6,8,13,17).

Thought for Today: If you don't have something good to say about someone, say nothing.

Christ Revealed: As the Ark of the Covenant (Testimony). The wood demonstrates His humanity; the gold overlay represents His deity. Only through the blood sprinkled on the Ark could one receive forgiveness. **Neither by the blood of goats and calves, but by His own blood He ... obtained eternal redemption for us** (Heb. 9:12).

JANUARY 26 — Read Exodus 26 – 28

Highlights: Directions given for constructing the Tabernacle, court, furniture, and enclosure. Plans for: the Altar; Aaron's priestly garments; the ephod. Notice the progression from suffering, blood, and death – to beauty, holiness, and the glory of God in these chapters.

The high priest was anointed as the mediator between God and the nation of Israel to make atonement for them so that they could be reconciled to God. He took the atoning sacrificial blood of animals before the Lord into the Holy of Holies and sprinkled it on the Mercy Seat. Thus, he foreshadowed **the blood of Jesus Christ His Son** (the Son of God that) **cleanseth us from all sin** (I John 1:7). **God was in Christ, reconciling the world unto Himself** (II Cor. 5:17-19). Just think! His blood alone (representing His life) washed away sins.

The inscription on the high priest's forehead was: **HOLINESS TO THE LORD** (Ex. 28:36-38; 39:30). It reminded the people that their Creator was a Holy God who loved them (the sinners) and provided a way for them to enjoy continuing fellowship with Him. Before the priests could intercede on behalf of the people, they had to put on the clothing that was specially made for them according to the instructions of God. Only then was Moses told: **Thou ... shalt anoint ... and consecrate them** (Aaron and his sons) **... that they may minister unto Me** (28:41). They were representatives of God.

Every person except Jesus has a sinful nature and is therefore imperfect, even the high priest. **But Christ being come an High Priest of good things to come, by a greater and more perfect Tabernacle, not made with hands, that is to say, not of this building; Neither by the blood of goats and calves, but by His own blood He entered in once into the Holy Place, having obtained eternal redemption for us** (Heb. 9:11-12). In Christ, our High Priest, we see the Perfect, Absolutely Sinless One (7:25-27).

In writing to **my little children** (the teachable Christians) (I John 2:1), the Apostle John said: **If we walk in the light, as He is in the light, we have fellowship one with another, and the blood of Jesus Christ His Son cleanseth us from all sin. If we say that we have no sin, we deceive ourselves. ... If we confess our sins, He is faithful and just to forgive us our sins, and to cleanse us from all unrighteousness. If we say that we have not sinned, we make Him a liar, and His Word is not in us** (I John 1:7-10).

Thought for Today: What will I do today to honor the Lord?

Christ Revealed: Through the Brasen Altar, upon which the Sin Offering was burned (Ex. 27:1-8; Lev. 4:1-35). Jesus' offering of Himself as the final sacrifice was the fulfillment of all Old Testament altars as well as all sacrificial offerings. **Jesus Christ ... In whom we have redemption through His blood** (Eph. 1:5-7; John 1:29,36; Col. 1:14; Heb. 9:12).

JANUARY 27   Read Exodus 29 – 31

Highlights: Notice how precisely each detail is given of the Tabernacle and the clothes of the high priest. The Lord is also concerned with each detail of our lives. The rules and sacrifices for consecrating the priests; continual Burnt Offering; Altar of Incense; the ransom of souls; the holy anointing oil; Sabbath regulations. Moses receives *two tables . . . of stone, written with the finger of God* (Ex. 31:18).

The priests who ministered in the Tabernacle had to be cleansed before entering. *The LORD spake unto Moses . . . make a Laver* (tub, basin) *of Brass, and his foot* (base) *also of brass . . . put it between the Tabernacle . . . and the Altar, and . . . put water therein. For Aaron and his sons shall wash their hands and their feet thereat* (Ex. 30:17-19). This signified cleansing from the activities of life. They were then qualified to enter the Tabernacle through a heavy linen veil – the only entrance into the Holy Place.

On the right was the Table of Shewbread with its 12 loaves of unleavened bread sprinkled with incense. The Shewbread signifies spiritual insight that is not obtainable anywhere else. It is symbolic of Christ, who said: *I am that Bread of Life. . . . the Living Bread which came down from heaven: if any man eat of this Bread, he shall live for ever* (John 6:48,51; 6:29-38; 12:24). Just as physical food is assimilated to sustain our physical lives, so too, as we continue to read the Word of God which is the Bread of Life, the Holy Spirit uses it to enlighten and then transform our lives. *Laying aside all malice, and all guile* (deceit)*, and hypocrisies, and envies, and all evil speakings, As newborn babes, desire the sincere* (unadulterated, pure) *milk of the Word, that ye may grow thereby* (I Pet. 2:1-2).

On the left was the seven-branched Candlestick made of solid beaten gold. Its seven lamps burned continually with pure olive oil. It was the only source of light in the Holy Place, and that light fell on the Shewbread, the only other item in the Holy Place (Lev. 24:2-4).

God has provided just one Book – the Holy Bible – as the source of *Light* for understanding His will. It is written: *Thy Word is a Lamp unto my feet, and a Light unto my path. . . . The entrance of Thy words giveth Light; it giveth understanding unto the simple* (Ps. 119:105,130; Prov. 6:23). Christ declared: *I am The Light of the World: he that followeth Me shall not walk in darkness, but shall have The Light of Life* (John 8:12).

Thought for Today: Ignoring the Word of God always leads to deception or misconception.

Christ Revealed: Through the Laver, Christ is revealed as both the container and the dispenser of *Living Water* (Ex. 30:18; John 4:10). *Jesus . . . cried, saying, If any man thirst, let him come unto Me, and drink. . . . ye are clean through the Word which I have spoken unto you* (John 7:37; 15:3; comp. I Cor. 10:4).

JANUARY 28   Read Exodus 32 – 34

Highlights: Moses delayed on Mount Sinai; Aaron's golden calf; its destruction; death of 3,000 Israelites; the Law renewed; the Covenant of God; three Feasts.

Moses was on Mount Sinai when God gave him the ***two Tables of Testimony, Tables of stone, written with the finger of God*** (Ex. 31:18). Tragically, ***when the people saw that Moses delayed to come down out of the mount, the people gathered themselves together unto Aaron, and said unto him, Up, make us gods, which shall go before us; for as for this Moses, the man that brought us up out of the land of Egypt, we wot*** (know) ***not what is become of him*** (32:1). It didn't take Aaron long to submit to their sinful demands and to make a golden calf. Then ***he built an altar before it. . . . And they rose up early on the morrow, and offered burnt offerings, and brought peace offerings*** (32:2-6).

A true Burnt Offering was a delight to the Lord since it symbolized full surrender to Him; but these idolatrous sacrifices were an abomination. The people were attempting to combine worship of the True God with the worship of idols.

Returning to the camp, Moses saw how quickly the Israelites had **corrupted themselves** (become apostate) (32:7). Did they think it was better to worship a golden calf, which they could see, than the invisible, yet ever-present God? Had they turned to Apis, an Egyptian god in the form of a bull? Only six weeks earlier, the whole congregation had sworn: ***All that the Lord hath spoken we will do*** (19:8).

The worship of false gods – the impulse of human desires – leads to irresponsible, immoral conduct. Most Christians would reject man-made idols. But, think about how easily money, possessions, talents, hobbies, and success become an obsession or idol for many. Centuries later, the Apostle Paul spoke of those who, although ***they knew God, they glorified Him not as God, neither were thankful; but*** (their worship) ***became vain*** (foolish, worthless) ***in their imaginations, and their foolish heart was darkened*** (Rom. 1:21).

The golden calf stands as a symbol of human intellect that devises its own system of worship excluding, or added to, the Word of God. The world admires the independent person who controls his own behavior. We must not be like the Israelites who ***rejoiced in the works of their own hands*** (Acts 7:41-43).

Thought for Today: Following the opinions of people, instead of listening to God, results in disaster.

Christ Revealed: As the One who is ever-present. ***My Presence shall go with thee, and I will give thee rest*** (peace) (Ex. 33:14). ***He hath said, I will never leave thee, nor forsake thee*** (Heb. 13:5; comp. Matt. 11:28; John 14:27).

JANUARY 29   Read Exodus 35 – 37

Highlights: Freewill offerings; the Tabernacle; the Ark; Mercy Seat; Table of Shewbread; Candlestick (Lampstand); Altar of Incense.

The Tabernacle and all its furniture were constructed *according to the fashion thereof which was shewed thee in the mount* (Ex. 26:30). Nothing was added, altered, or left out. *And every wise hearted among you shall come, and make all that the LORD hath commanded* (35:10-11).

The Tabernacle was more than a worship center. Its design and order of worship were meant to teach Israel the meaning of the Covenant made at Sinai. Furthermore, it was a means whereby the Holy God could fellowship with sinful man through its sacrificial system. It was further designed to lead the believer into the Lord's presence undefiled, with a heart, thoughts, and motives to please Him. The Tabernacle and every item were symbolic of Jesus Christ's life, ministry, and our relationship with Him.

The Altar of Incense was *made ... of shittim* (acacia) *wood. ... and. ... a crown* (moulding) *of gold round about. ... And he* (Bezaleel) *made the holy anointing oil, and the pure incense* (37:25-26,29). Moses was told to *put it before the vail* (veil) *that is by the Ark of the Testimony* (Covenant)*, before the Mercy Seat that is over the Testimony, where I will meet with thee. ... Aaron shall burn thereon sweet incense every morning. ... a perpetual incense before the LORD throughout your generations* (30:6-8).

The Altar of Incense was also symbolic of Christ our High Priest, who is constantly interceding for us not only when we pray but also by His constant watchful care (John 17:1-26; Heb. 7:25).

Each morning, Aaron the high priest would refill the lamps with pure olive oil. He would take a coal of fire from the Brasen Altar, place it on the Altar of Incense, and then add the incense for a sweet fragrance that ascended toward heaven day and night. God alone was the source of fire on both of the Altars (Lev. 9:24).

None of the "mixed multitude" could enter the one gate to this enclosure – only a true Israelite. Jesus, our Savior, said: *I am The Door: by Me if any man enter in, he shall be saved. ... I am The Way, The Truth, and The Life: no man cometh unto the Father, but by Me* (John 10:9; 14:6).

Thought for Today: It is through Christ that the prayers of sinful, undeserving people become precious to God.

Christ Revealed: Through *The Candlestick* (Ex. 35:14). Christ is *The Light of the World* (John 1:6-9; 8:12; 9:5; comp. Luke 1:78-79).

JANUARY 30   Read Exodus 38 – 39

Highlights: Altar of Burnt Offering; the Tabernacle courtyard; all priests' garments.

The Tabernacle was completed according to all the instructions the Lord commanded Moses: ***Thus was all the work of the Tabernacle . . . finished. . . . and all his furniture . . . The Ark of the Testimony . . . and the Mercy Seat*** (Ex. 39:32-35). ***The Ark of the Testimony*** (25:22) is also called the ***Ark of the Covenant*** (Num. 10:33). It contained the Ten Commandments, and later the ***Book of the Law*** recorded by Moses (Deut. 31:9-26). This was the Covenant between God and Israel. The Ark was a wooden chest overlaid with gold, both inside and out. It was a type of Jesus the Messiah, the Son of God, who alone can atone for sin. The wood – acacia wood which grew in the deserts, symbolic of the barren world system – represented His human nature, as foretold by Isaiah: ***He shall grow up before Him as a tender plant, and as a root out of a dry ground*** (Is. 53:2). The gold represented His divine nature, for He is both fully God and fully man (John 1:1,14).

The pure gold ***Mercy Seat*** – the "lid" of the Ark – covered the Law that had been placed in the Ark. Although ***all have sinned, and come short of the glory of God*** (Rom. 3:23), Christ, the sinless Son of God, offered Himself as the only acceptable substitute, providing a perfect atonement for our sins. The ***Mercy Seat*** represents His perfect atonement. Jesus also became our ***High Priest, that is passed into the heavens, Jesus the Son of God*** (Heb. 4:14).

The Ark was behind the veil inside the Holy of Holies. Without the Presence of the Lord above the Ark, all the services of the Tabernacle would have been meaningless.

On the Day of Atonement, the high priest sprinkled the blood of an innocent goat on the Mercy Seat, then in front of it seven times (Lev. 16:14). The number seven is symbolic of the perfect salvation and forgiveness of sins which Jesus would later provide.

As you prayerfully read the Word of God daily and worship the Lord, His indwelling presence will bring meaning to your life. The Law provides the "knowledge" of sin, but it cannot provide the "forgiveness" of sin (Gal. 2:16; 3:11). ***The Law was given by Moses, but grace and Truth came by Jesus Christ*** (John 1:17). Jesus is the One ***in whom we have redemption through His blood, even the forgiveness of sins*** (Col. 1:14).

Thought for Today: The more we recognize our unworthiness, the more we will appreciate the Lord's mercy in saving us.

Christ Revealed: Through the ***Golden Altar*** and its incense – representing prayers going up to heaven (Ex. 39:38; Rev. 5:8; 8:3-4). Christ prayed for us. ***Neither pray I for these alone, but for them also which shall believe on Me through their word*** (John 17:20).

JANUARY 31 — Read Exodus 40

Highlights: Tabernacle completed and erected; furnishings arranged; consecration of Aaron and his sons; the glory of the Lord fills the Tabernacle.

After the Sin Offering had been sacrificed, the priests approached the Laver of Brass (Ex. 38:8), containing water for their cleansing before they entered the Holy Place. The first room of the Tabernacle was known as the Holy Place (26:35; 40:22-23). **And he** (Moses) **brought the Ark into the Tabernacle . . . as the LORD commanded. . . . And he put the Table in the Tent . . . northward, without** (outside but near) **the vail** (veil). **And he set the bread in order . . . as the LORD had commanded Moses. And he put the Candlestick . . . over against** (opposite) **the Table . . . southward. . . . lighted the lamps** (seven bowls filled with oil atop the candlestick). **. . . And . . . put the Golden Altar in the Tent of the congregation before** (in front of) **the vail** (just outside the Holy of Holies) (40:21-26). The Golden Altar illustrates the privilege of prayer.

Bread was set on the Table of Shewbread (25:23-30) in the presence of Jehovah, one loaf for each tribe of Israel. It reminded the Israelites of their dependence upon Jehovah for their daily sustenance (Ezek. 16:19; Hos. 2:8). It also was symbolic of Christ who said: *I am the Bread of Life: he that cometh to Me shall never hunger; and he that believeth on Me shall never thirst* (John 6:35).

The Candlestick's light portrayed guidance by the Holy Spirit: *He will guide you into all Truth* (John 16:13). Israel was guided at night by the presence of the Lord *in a pillar of fire, to give them light* (Ex. 13:21). The Candlestick's flame was fueled with oil, which illustrates the Spirit of God. The Candlestick also stood as a symbol foreshadowing Christ, who declared: *I am the Light of the World: he that followeth Me shall not walk in darkness, but shall have the Light of Life* (John 8:12).

The Word of God and His Holy Spirit provide all of the wisdom, spiritual guidance, and strength necessary to live obediently and victoriously for Him. He has revealed *that ye are the Temple of God, and that the Spirit of God dwelleth in you? If any man defile the Temple of God, him shall God destroy; for the Temple of God is holy, which Temple ye are* (I Cor. 3:16-17; 6:18-19). *Rejoice in the Lord alway: and again I say, Rejoice* (Phil. 4:4).

Thought for Today: Allow Christ to take charge of the affairs of your life. You will be so glad you did.

Christ Portrayed: By Aaron as the high priest (Ex. 40:13). *Christ being come an High Priest. . . . to appear in the Presence of God for us* (Heb. 9:7-24).

INTRODUCTION TO THE BOOK OF LEVITICUS

Leviticus was written to teach the Israelites how to live as a holy people with a personal relationship with God. Equally important for Christians are the sacrifices and the appointed feasts that illustrate the various aspects of the character, conduct, and purpose of the life, death, and resurrection of Jesus who alone can atone for our sins. Without Leviticus, we would have an incomplete knowledge of our Savior. Consequently, it is vital that we prayerfully read and understand Leviticus. In AD 70 the Temple, along with its sacrificial system, was destroyed. However, the principles of the old system show how to have a fellowship with God – a sacrifice is required because sin separates man from God who is holy. By His death on the cross, Jesus **offered one sacrifice for sins for ever** (Heb. 10:12); therefore, He is now **The** (only) **Way** to God (John 14:6).

Chapters 1 – 7 of Leviticus deal with the five primary sacrifices, which were essential for a fuller understanding of the death of **our Lord Jesus Christ, Who gave Himself for our sins, that He might deliver us from this present evil world** (Gal. 1:3-4). **And every man that hath this hope in Him purifieth himself, even as He is pure** (I John 3:3).

Chapters 8 – 10 cover the priesthood; chapters 11 – 16 express the qualifications for sanctification (being set apart to a sacred purpose) and explain the Day of Atonement; and chapter 17 emphasizes the Brasen Altar as the place where sacrifices were to be offered.

Chapters 18 – 27 reveal how fellowship with God is maintained. The New Testament reveals that the basic principle is the same today, **because it is written, Be ye holy; for I am holy** (I Pet. 1:16). **Follow peace with all men, and holiness, without which no man shall see the Lord** (Heb. 12:14; also Lev. 11:44-45; 19:2; 20:7).

Chapters 18 – 22 express the Lord's standard of holiness for all the people and the regulations of sanctification for the priests. Chapters 23 – 27 give instructions for **the feasts of the LORD** (23:44) and the requirements for the Israelites to maintain fellowship with the Holy God, including the making of vows and paying of tithes. **Three times in the year all thy males shall appear before the Lord GOD** (Ex. 23:17) for the feasts.

The Sabbaths, **holy convocations**, and **feasts** were occasions free from work. They were times to teach the Word of God and worship the Lord (Lev. 23:2-4,7-8,21,24-25,27-28,35-37).

FEBRUARY 1   Read Leviticus 1 – 3

Highlights: God told Moses: *Speak unto the children of Israel* (Lev. 1:2). How to approach God and maintain fellowship with Him.

God emphasized that if a person offered a Burnt Sacrifice, he should *offer it of his own voluntary will . . . before the LORD*. It is stated three times in chapter 1 that such an offering was *a sweet savour unto the LORD* (Lev. 1:3,17). But the Sin Offering and the Trespass Offering were never a *sweet savour*; they were required to restore one's relationship with God. Only then could the worshiper present the *sweet savour* offerings that truly satisfied God.

For the successful farmer, the *Burnt Offering* was often an ox that plowed in a field or pulled a cart. The most valuable of all clean animals, it was killed, burned outside the gate, and reduced to ashes. (After this it ascended to God as *a sweet savour unto the LORD*.)

Like the "powerful oxen," our talents and abilities must be "reduced to ashes" (fully dedicated to God for His glory) for us to become a sweet savor – a satisfaction to God. This means that in all our activities we will ask: "What would Jesus have me do?" He has said: *It is good neither to eat flesh, nor to drink wine, nor any thing whereby thy brother stumbleth, or is offended, or is made weak* (Rom. 14:21). If it were possible for Christians to drink alcohol with a clear conscience, we would never know how many people we might influence to become alcoholics. We are to *present your* (our) *bodies a living sacrifice* (not just on Sunday)*, holy, acceptable unto God. . . . And be not conformed to this world: but be ye transformed by the renewing of your mind, that ye may prove what is that good, and acceptable, and perfect, will of God* (12:1-2). To offer God less than our best may hinder or influence another from being fully devoted to serving the Lord.

A *Burnt Offering* illustrates the basic requirements of a Christian's life regarding both the inward cleansing and external conduct such as: *Be not drunk with wine . . . but be filled with the* (Holy) *Spirit* (Eph. 5:18). Obviously, either wine or the Holy Spirit can control. *The works of the flesh are manifest . . . Adultery* (sexual perversions) *. . . drunkenness . . . and such like . . . they which do such things shall not inherit the Kingdom of God* (Gal. 5:19-24). *If ye live after the flesh, ye shall die: but if ye through the Spirit do mortify the deeds of the body, ye shall live* (Rom. 8:13).

Thought for Today: It's the spirit of giving that counts most.

Christ Revealed: Through the Meat (Meal, Grain) Offering which was made without leaven (symbolic of sin) (Lev. 2:11). Christ was *without sin* (Heb. 4:15).

FEBRUARY 2   Read Leviticus 4 – 6

Highlights: Again, God told Moses: ***Speak unto the children of Israel*** (Lev. 4:2). Sinners can approach the Holy Creator God who provides forgiveness for all sin and gives eternal life through Christ!

God gave specific requirements for the Sin Offering: ***If a soul shall sin through ignorance against any of the Commandments of the Lord . . . let him bring for his sin . . . a young bullock without blemish unto the Lord for a Sin Offering. . . . Even the whole bullock shall he carry forth without the camp unto a clean place, where the ashes are poured out*** (Lev. 4:2-3,12). All sacrifices must be ***without blemish*** (Lev. 4:3). Every man had to also bring his own sacrifice to God. The worshiper had to offer it willingly and take a personal part by laying his hands on the head of his sacrifice to make it representative of his sins. Then he killed the animal, and the body of this Sin Offering was burned ***without*** (outside) ***the camp***. The camp must not be defiled, because the Lord dwelt in its midst (Num. 5:3). But only the priest could offer the blood sacrifice.

In other offerings, the offerer came as a worshiper, but here he came as a convicted sinner. The Sin Offering was a distinct witness to the fact that sin exists within the heart of all mankind (Jer. 17:9; Rom. 3:23; 5:12). God has provided just one Sacrifice for sin under the New Covenant by which to redeem and restore a sinner. ***He*** (God) ***hath made Him*** (Jesus) ***to be sin for us, who knew no sin; that we might be made the righteousness of God in Him*** (II Cor. 5:21).

To demonstrate its seriousness, if a priest sinned, his sacrifice was the same as that of the whole congregation (Lev. 4:14,23). Christians are ***a royal priesthood*** (I Pet. 2:9) and have a similar influence and an obligation to ***abstain from fleshly lusts*** (2:11).

The Sin Offering typified Christ who would die in the sinner's place. Animal sacrifices served their purpose until Christ shed His sinless blood on the cross for man's sins (Heb. 10:10). Today, by faith, the sinner believes that Jesus died in his place and receives Christ as Savior and Lord of his life. Then, the believer is urged to ***present your*** (our) ***bodies a living sacrifice, holy, acceptable unto God, which is your*** (our) ***reasonable service*** (Rom. 12:1).

Without shedding of blood is no remission (of sin) (Heb. 9:22). True repentance will result in obedience to the Word of God, and will be evidenced by our daily conduct. ***Faith without works is dead*** (James 2:20).

Thought for Today: Loyalty and dependability are of far more value than outstanding abilities.

Christ Revealed: Through the body of the young bull which was burned ***without the camp*** (Lev. 4:12). This pictures Jesus as He ***suffered without the gate*** (Heb. 13:11-12).

The Five Major Offerings

The Offering	Purpose	Meaning for Today
Sin Offering (Required First) Lev. 4:1-35; 6:24-30 Bulls, goats, or lambs were acceptable. The poor could bring two young pigeons or turtledoves.	This was the first offering, because *all have sinned, and come short of the glory of God* (Rom. 3:23); no one was exempt. It was offered for all the people on feast days.	Providing reconciliation with God for all who accept Christ as their Savior and Lord (John 1:12; II Cor. 5:20-21; Gal. 1:4; Heb. 10:3-4; 13:12).
Trespass Offering (Required) Similar to Sin Offering Lev. 5:1-19; 6:1-7; 7:1-10; 14:12-18	The sinner was required to *make amends for the harm that he hath done* (Lev. 5:16), whether the sin was against another or against God. A lamb or a ram was sacrificed for these sins.	The injured person was compensated. Fellowship with the wronged person and with God also was restored.
Meat Offering (Voluntary) Lev. 2:1-16; 6:14-23; 7:9-10 "Fine" flour, unleavened bread and grain were offered – always with salt and oil, and with frankincense. This always followed the morning and evening burned offerings.	Meat is an old English word for food in general. This freewill offering was an expression of thanksgiving: *A sweet savour* (pleasing aroma) *unto the LORD* (Lev. 2:2). Grain ground into fine flour signifies Christ's crucifixion on our behalf. *Christ . . . hath given Himself for us an offering and a sacrifice to God for a sweetsmelling savour* (pleasing aroma) (Eph. 5:2).	The individual grains being ground into fine flour and mixed with oil symbolize our need to lose our identity to become part of the Body of Christ. *For we are unto God a sweet savour of Christ, in them that are saved* (II Cor. 2:15).
Burnt Offering (Voluntary) Lev. 1:1-17; 5:7; 6:8-13 Based on financial ability: bull for rich; two turtledoves or young pigeons for the poor.	After sin and trespass offerings, the offerer was reconciled to God and came to worship Him. A bull, ram, goat, turtledoves, or young pigeons were completely burned to ashes on the altar. This was a freewill offering.	This offering illustrates complete surrender (Matt. 22:37). To present our bodies as *a living sacrifice* (Rom. 12:1-2) – this means we are to give the best of our time, talents, and possessions.
Peace Offering (Voluntary, Last) Lev. 3:1-17; 7:11-36 *Of the herd. . . . flock. . . . a goat. . . . the priest shall burn them upon the altar* (3:1,6,12,16).	The only offering shared in fellowship with God, the priests, and families expressing praise to God. It symbolized peace with God and with others – always a joyful occasion (Eph. 2:14-15; 5:2; also 1:2; Col. 1:20; 3:12-16).	Christ is "our peace offering." He alone makes possible true peace with God and other believers. His prayer was: *That they may be one* (John 17:22). Jesus promised: *My peace I give unto you* (14:27).

FEBRUARY 3   Read Leviticus 7 – 8

Highlights: Consecration and 10 steps to cleansing. How do priesthood requirements parallel the Christian walk? See the parallel between Aaron, the **high priest** (Lev. 21:10), and Christ, the **Great High Priest** (Heb. 4:14).

The Peace Offering was a sacrifice to express thanksgiving and praise, and was presented for some special blessing or vow of dedication. It could also be a freewill offering, simply because the worshiper desired to express his praise, love, and thanksgiving to the One True Holy God. **And this is the Law of the sacrifice of Peace Offerings, which he shall offer unto the LORD** (Lev. 7:11). The Peace Offering required that "unleavened bread" be offered as a part of the sacrifice. The absence of leaven represented the absence of sin and foreshadowed the perfect Lord Jesus Christ. Yeast, or leaven, was a symbol of corruption, for it caused fermentation.

The Peace Offering was the last one to be offered because there could be no peace or fellowship with God until all the regulations of the Sin and Trespass offerings had first been obeyed.

The special feature of the Peace Offering was the sacrificial meal wherein the priest and the worshiper shared together what was offered, and part of the offering was presented to God upon His Altar, as though it were being consumed by Him. It was a joyful, fellowship feast celebrating restored peace and communication with God. What joy there is in knowing **the peace of God, which passeth all understanding** (Phil. 4:7).

Jesus promised: **My peace I give unto you: not as the world giveth, give I unto you. Let not your heart be troubled, neither let it be afraid** (John 14:27). The Lord's peace is imparted to every Christian who submits his will to the will of God.

If our heart condemn us not, then have we confidence toward God. And whatsoever we ask, we receive of Him, because we keep His Commandments, and do those things that are pleasing in His sight (I John 3:21-22). **Let** (Allow) **the peace of God rule in your hearts, to the which also ye are called in one body; and be ye thankful** (Col. 3:15). **God was in Christ, reconciling the world unto Himself, not imputing their trespasses unto them; and hath committed unto us the word of reconciliation. Now then we are ambassadors for Christ** (II Cor. 5:19-20).

Thought for Today: Pride and jealousy are deadly to health, happiness, fellowship with others, and peace with God.

Christ Portrayed: By Moses as he consecrated the priests who were called for the work (Lev. 8:1-24). Christ is the One who sets the believer apart for service. **Ye have not chosen Me, but I have chosen you, and ordained** (appointed) **you** (John 15:16).

FEBRUARY 4   Read Leviticus 9 – 10

Highlights: We begin with "strange" fire! What is the difference between holy and unholy; clean and unclean (Lev. 10:10-11)? Discover why God demands that we be holy.

Nadab and Abihu were sons of Aaron, the high priest. They were anointed to serve as priests, assisting him in conducting sacrifices and worship services. ***Nadab and Abihu . . . offered strange fire before the LORD. . . . And there went out fire from the Lord, and devoured them, and they died before the LORD*** (Lev. 10:1-2). Apparently, they took fire for the altar sacrifice as if it did not matter where it came from or how it was administered. They failed to recognize the importance of obedience to the authority of the Word of God.

What a fearful report of Nadab and Abihu being struck dead while "serving the Lord"! God had chosen Aaron to be the first high priest, and the anointing oil was poured upon his sons' heads as a sign of consecration. ***That ye may put*** (a) ***difference between holy and unholy, and between unclean and clean; And that ye may teach the children of Israel all the Statutes which the LORD hath spoken unto them by the hand of Moses*** (10:10-11).

We are commanded: ***As obedient children, not fashioning yourselves according to the former lusts in your ignorance: But as He which hath called you is holy, so be ye holy in all manner of conversation*** (conduct)***; Because it is written, Be ye holy; for I am holy*** (I Pet. 1:14-16). God has also said ***that we should be holy and without blame before Him in love*** (Eph. 1:4).

How often zeal for God and activities are mixed by showing a proud spirit and seeking personal recognition! Christians are often willing to do the will of God when it coincides with their desires to get attention. Mixed motives and pride are great hindrances to humility. The basic principle of a successful life is for us to recognize that we are nothing in ourselves, as Jesus said: ***As the branch cannot bear fruit of itself, except it abide in the vine; no more can ye, except ye abide in Me. . . . Without Me, ye can do nothing. If a man abide not in Me, he is cast forth as a branch, and is withered; and . . . burned*** (John 15:4-6). Christ alone must be exalted.

Let us have grace, whereby we may serve God acceptably with reverence and godly fear: For our God is a consuming fire (Heb. 12:28-29).

Thought for Today: We cheat ourselves when we give less than our best to the Lord.

Christ Revealed: Through the sacrifice of a lamb without defect (Lev. 9:3). ***Behold the Lamb of God, which*** (who) ***taketh away the sin of the world*** (John 1:29).

FEBRUARY 5   Read Leviticus 11 – 13

Highlights: Requirements of God to cleanse sin. Laws about clean and unclean animals, childbirth, and leprosy (symbolic of sin).

Numerous times God said: *I am the Lord your God: ye shall therefore sanctify yourselves, and ye shall be holy; for I am holy: neither shall ye defile yourselves. . . . make a difference between the unclean and the clean* (Lev. 11:44-47). The people of God must be a morally clean people, inwardly and outwardly, in order to be in a right relationship with God. Every Christian should conduct his life as a *purchased possession* (of Christ), *unto the praise of His glory* (Eph. 1:14). The Holy Spirit warned concerning this first generation of slaves that had left Egypt, *that . . . all passed through the sea . . . And did all drink the same spiritual drink . . . of that spiritual Rock . . . and that Rock was Christ. But with many of them God was not well pleased: for they were overthrown* (died) *in the wilderness. Now these things were our examples, to the intent we should not lust after evil things. . . . let him that thinketh he standeth take heed lest he fall* (I Cor. 10:1-12).

As believers read through the Bible with a desire to do the will of God, we will realize the importance of allowing His Holy Spirit to guide our thoughts and conduct. *Whether therefore ye eat, or drink, or whatsoever ye do, do all to the glory* (honor) *of God* (10:31).

The Holy Spirit led the Apostle Paul to also write: *Know ye not that ye are the Temple of God, and that the Spirit of God dwelleth in you? If any man defile the Temple of God, him shall God destroy; for the Temple of God is holy, which Temple ye are* (3:16-17). *For God hath not called us unto uncleanness, but unto holiness* (set apart to live as children of the One True God) (I Thess. 4:7).

God left nothing to human opinions or contemporary trends. It is our responsibility to learn how God expects us to live. We are to *study to shew thyself approved unto God, a workman that needeth not to be ashamed* (II Tim. 2:15). If we neglect reading His Word, then it will become easy to substitute human opinion for the Holy Spirit's guidance. *My thoughts are not your thoughts, neither are your ways My ways, saith the Lord* (Is. 55:8). As we compare our ways with the Word, we discover the *will of God* (Rom. 12:2).

If any man be in Christ, he is a new creature: old things are passed away; behold, all things are become new (II Cor. 5:17).

Thought for Today: The worldly-minded person never perceives what God reveals to those who are *pure in heart* (Matt. 5:8).

Christ Revealed: Through the clean food of the believer (Lev. 11:47). Our Lord is the *Bread of Life* (John 6:35), supplies *living water* 4:10,14), and His Father's will was His *meat* (food, nourishment) (4:34).

FEBRUARY 6   Read Leviticus 14 – 15

Highlights: After reading these chapters, you will discover how detestable sin is in the eyes of God. Separation from sin is of utmost importance to have fellowship with God. Be "clean" in mind, thought, and deed.

All lepers would surely defile everything they touched. *And the leper in whom the plague is, his clothes shall be rent, and his head bare, and he shall put a covering upon his upper lip, and shall cry, Unclean, unclean. . . . he shall dwell alone; without the camp shall his habitation be* (Lev. 13:45-46).

The word "leprosy" struck terror in the heart of an Israelite for two reasons. First, the person who had leprosy became an outcast from society. When anyone went near him, the leper had to cry out the warning: *Unclean, unclean.* But perhaps the most horrifying reason leprosy was so feared was that there was no known cure for it.

Leprosy often appears as just a small, harmless, pink spot; but how dreadful, loathsome, and fatal it eventually becomes! Leprosy illustrates how detestable sin is to God. It may first appear as insignificant. Like leprosy, sin immediately separates us from God and makes us *unclean*. People controlled by sin exist in a state of living death, and only Christ can cleanse a sinner. *Not by works of righteousness which we have done, but according to His mercy He saved us . . . through Jesus Christ our Saviour* (Titus 3:5-6). When we turn to Christ, truly repent, and forsake our sins, *the blood of Jesus Christ His Son cleanseth us from all sin. . . . If we confess our sins, He* (God) *is faithful and just to forgive us our sins, and to cleanse us from all unrighteousness* (I John 1:7,9).

This illustrates how only Christ could touch a leper and the leper be instantly healed. The leper typifies how Christ reaches out *to seek and to save that which was lost* (Luke 19:10).

For by grace are ye saved through faith; and that not of yourselves: it is the gift of God: Not of works, lest any man should boast (Eph. 2:8-9). All the "good works" we could do in a lifetime cannot save us. But once we are saved, we should become known for our dedication to the Lord through our good works. *Whoso looketh into the perfect Law of Liberty, and continueth therein, he being not a forgetful hearer, but a doer of the work, this man shall be blessed in his deed* (James 1:25).

Thought for Today: The lust of the flesh and the eye are never satisfied.

Christ Portrayed: By the priest who made atonement for the leper (Lev. 14:20). *Our Lord Jesus Christ, by whom we have now received the atonement* (reconciliation) (Rom. 5:11).

FEBRUARY 7   Read Leviticus 16 – 18

Highlights: Three spiritual Truths stand out – Atonement, Sacrifice, and Holiness; learn how Jesus fulfills them all. Praise the Lord! Warnings against various defilements (listed in chapters 18-19).

The Day of Atonement was the most important day in the Hebrew calendar. **On that day shall the priest make an atonement for you, to cleanse you, that ye may be clean from all your sins before the LORD. It shall be a Sabbath of rest unto you, and ye shall afflict your souls, by a Statute for ever** (Lev. 16: 30-32).

On this day, two goats were brought for the **Sin Offering** (16:9) for the sins of the people. The high priest received the goats at the Tabernacle Door, where he cast lots to determine which one would be sacrificed and which one would be released into the desert. The first was sacrificed as a **Sin Offering**; the second was **the scapegoat** (16:8,10,26). The people's sins for the past year were transferred to this scapegoat by the high priest laying his hands on the goat. It was then led into the wilderness where it departed from human view, symbolically carrying away the sins of the congregation.

The sacrificed goat represents the sufficiency of a blood sacrifice, **for it is the blood that maketh an atonement** (17:11). **Without shedding of blood is no remission** (of sin) (Heb. 9:22). The scapegoat represents the fact that all our sins are forgiven and forever removed. **For as the heaven is high above the earth, so great is His mercy toward them that fear Him. As far as the east is from the west, so far hath He removed our transgressions from us** (Ps. 103:11-12). We can thank God that **the blood of Jesus Christ His Son cleanseth us from all sin** (I John 1:7).

Not realizing this, many Christians pray again and again for God to forgive them; they continue to carry the unbearable guilt of past sins. God does not want us to carry the guilt of past confessions; to do so would infer that we do not really believe He has forgiven us.

The two goats represent the twofold purpose of our Lord's death on the cross: (1) Our sins are forgiven and are forever removed from the sight of God. (2) Our peace and fellowship with God are restored by the blood of Christ. We can confidently believe His Word. **If we confess our sins, He is faithful and just to forgive us our sins, and to cleanse us from all unrighteousness** (I John 1:9).

Thought for Today: We should never condemn ourselves or others over sins confessed and forsaken – because God has forgiven them.

Christ Revealed: Through two goats used on the Day of Atonement (Lev. 16:8). The slaying of the first goat typifies that our peace with God was restored by the blood of Christ (Rev. 5:9). The second goat represents the precious mercy of God in forever removing from His sight the sins of His people – **As far as the east is from the west** (Ps. 103:12). **Their sins and iniquities will I remember no more** (Heb. 10:17).

FEBRUARY 8   **Read Leviticus 19 – 21**

Highlights: God again instructs Moses: *Speak unto all the congregation of the children of Israel* (Lev. 19:2). Count how many times, just in today's reading, God reminds us: *I am the Lord*.

The Law and all the Ordinances were given to the nation of Israel as a means of revealing to the world the wisdom and lovingkindness of our Heavenly Father. *I am the Lord your God, which brought you out of the land of Egypt. Therefore shall ye observe all My Statutes . . . and do them: I am the Lord. . . . Sanctify yourselves therefore, and be ye holy* (Lev. 19:36-37; 20:7).

The instructions against fraud, hatred, an unforgiving attitude, and immorality are summed up in one Commandment: *Thou shalt love thy neighbour as thyself* (19:18). Other Commandments call for reverence for parents and the aged, and compassion for the suffering and the weak. All of these reveal the loving concern of the Creator God who cares for all people.

Love in the heart of God is the source of everything that is good (Gen. 1:10,12,18,21,25). *God saw every thing that He had made, and, behold, it was very good* (1:31). God has chosen Christians to express His love to the world. *By this shall all men know that ye are My disciples, if ye have love one to another* (John 13:35).

Most of us, have at times thought: *How can I possibly love some people I know – that rude egotist at the office who deliberately puts me down, or that smooth liar who has deceived me, or that one-time friend who took advantage of my trust?* The list continues.

To love those we consider "unlovable" takes a Christian who, from his heart, seeks to manifest the nature of Christ his Savior who has forgiven his sins. Jesus said: *Love your enemies, bless them that curse you, do good to them that hate you, and pray for them which despitefully use you, and persecute you . . . For if ye love them which love you, what reward have ye? do not even the publicans the same? And if ye salute your brethren only, what do ye more than others? do not even the publicans so? Be ye therefore perfect, even as your Father which is in heaven is perfect* (Matt. 5:44-48). It is of utmost importance that we sincerely express His love and compassion without exception.

Be kindly affectioned one to another with brotherly love; in honour preferring one another (Rom. 12:10).

Thought for Today: A Christian represents the Lord God at all times.

Christ Revealed: As a source of true guidance, in contrast to evil guidance (Lev. 20:6-8). Jesus, who is *The Truth* (John 14:6) also sent us *the Spirit of Truth* who guides us *into all Truth* (16:13).

THE 3 ANNUAL PILGRIMAGES TO JERUSALEM REQUIRED OF ALL MEN (Ex. 23:17; Deut. 16:16)

FEASTS	SIGNIFICANCE TO ISRAEL	MEANING TODAY
PASSOVER NISAN 14 (MARCH/APRIL) THE FIRST MONTH OF THE RELIGIOUS YEAR (LEV. 23:5-8)	The Passover commemorated the deliverance of the Jews from death by placing a lamb's blood on the door post, eating the lamb, and preparing for the Exodus out of Egypt.	Our deliverance from eternal death by Christ, the Lamb of God, who died for our sins (John 1:29; I Cor. 5:7; I Pet. 1:18-19).
UNLEAVENED BREAD NISAN 15-21 (MARCH/APRIL)	Leaven is symbolic of sin and was prohibited during this week. This feast involved careful house cleaning. It was a reminder that they were a holy people separated unto the Lord.	Unleavened bread is a type of the sinlessness of Christ, the *Bread of Life* (John 6:35; Ex. 23:16; Lev. 23:34-36; Num. 29:12-34; Deut. 16:13-15).
FIRSTFRUITS (DAY AFTER SABBATH OF PASSOVER WEEK)	One sheaf of the firstfruits of the barley harvest was presented as a wave offering (Leviticus 23:5-10).	Jesus arose on Firstfruits. *Now is Christ risen from the dead, and become the Firstfruits of them that slept* (died) (I Cor. 15:20).
FEAST OF PENTECOST (FEAST OF HARVEST) 6TH DAY OF THE THIRD MONTH (MAY/JUNE) SIVAN	Celebrated seven weeks (50 days) after Firstfruits, it marked the completion of the harvest (Firstfruits) (Lev. 23:15-22; Deut. 16:9-12). It included the offering and waving of two loaves of leavened bread commemorating the end of the summer harvest.	The outpouring of the Holy Spirit took place at Pentecost, 50 days after the resurrection of Christ (Acts 2). Pentecost means 50th in Greek. Two loaves of leavened bread illustrate the sinful nature of both Jew and Gentile.
FEAST OF TRUMPETS 1 DAY – TISHRI 1 (SEPT/OCT)	Held on the first day of the seventh month. Beginning of the civil year. Trumpets were blown from morning to evening (Lev. 23:23-25; Num. 29:1-6). Symbolic of the voice of God.	The trumpets were symbolic of the Word of God preached to all nations (Acts 1:8; II Tim. 4:1-2; Rev. 4:1).
DAY OF ATONEMENT 1 DAY – TISHRI 10 (SEP/OCT) A DAY OF FASTING	The high priest made atonement for the nation's sins of the past year and then once a year entered the Most Holy Place and sprinkled the blood on the Mercy Seat for all the people (Lev. 16:6,11-22; 23:26-32).	Christ, our High Priest, gave Himself as the perfect sacrifice. He did this not only by dying on the cross for our sins but also by removing the guilt and consequences of sin (Heb. 7:27; 8:12; 10:17; I John 1:7-9).
TABERNACLES (OR BOOTHS OR FEAST OF INGATHERING) 7 DAYS TISHRI 15-21 (SEPT/OCT)	Began 5 days after the Day of Atonement. During this feast they lived in temporary shelters in commemoration of the gracious provisions of God during the 40 years in the wilderness.	Jesus revealed Himself as the source of Living Water at this feast (John 7:37-39). *The Word was made flesh, and dwelt* (tabernacled) *among us* (1:14).

FEBRUARY 9   Read Leviticus 22 – 23

Highlights: These two chapters outline the holy days of Feasts and fasts God required. Every Christian should learn how they all foreshadowed our relationship with Christ who was crucified on Passover (Lev. 23:5; John 19:14).

On the annual Day of Atonement the high priest had to offer sacrifices for himself and then for the sins of the nation. He was then prepared to offer incense (symbolic of prayer) before the Lord (see Ex. 6:3). He passed beyond the veil, where he was alone with our Creator. ***There shall be a Day of Atonement . . . ye shall afflict your souls, and offer an offering made by fire unto the L***ORD***. And ye shall do no. . . . manner of work. . . . It shall be unto you a Sabbath of rest*** (Lev. 23:27-32).

The priests . . . shall come near to Me to minister unto Me, and they shall stand before Me . . . saith the Lord GOD***. . . . when they enter in at the gates of the inner court, they shall be clothed with linen garments; and no wool shall come upon them, whiles they minister. . . . they shall not gird themselves with any thing that causeth sweat*** (Ezek. 44:15-18). Fleshly "sweat" in many of our activities causes the blessings of God to be withheld.

Individual Israelites under the Old Covenant did not have the privilege of going into the presence of God. But under the New Covenant, Jesus made a way for us to come into His presence at any time, day or night, and eventually to see Him visibly and to be with Him for eternity. Jesus will make all Christian believers His priests. ***Blessed and holy is he that hath part in the first resurrection . . . they shall be priests of God and of Christ*** (Rev. 20:6; see 1:6; 5:10). ***Seeing then that we have a Great High Priest, that is passed into the heavens, Jesus the Son of God, let us hold fast our profession. For we have not an High Priest which cannot be touched with the feeling of our infirmities; but was in all points tempted like as we are, yet without sin. Let us therefore come boldly unto the throne of grace*** (with our prayers)***, that we may obtain mercy, and find grace to help in time of need*** (Heb. 4:14-16).

Only a few take time to pray and fast as did the early believers. ***As they ministered to the Lord, and fasted, the Holy Ghost*** (Spirit) ***said, Separate Me Barnabas and Saul for the work whereunto I have called them*** (Acts 13:2).

Thought for Today: Christians desire to please the Lord, be clean in mind and body.

Christ Revealed: Leviticus 23 – in the seven great feasts of the Lord: Passover, Feast of Unleavened Bread, Feast of Firstfruits, Feast of Pentecost, Feast of Trumpets, Day of Atonement, Feast of Tabernacles (Booths) – all of which typified Jesus Christ. ***Christ our Passover*** (I Cor. 5:7); ***Bread of Life*** (John 6:35); ***Christ . . . the Firstfruits of them that slept*** (died) (I Cor. 15:20).

FEBRUARY 10   Read Leviticus 24 – 25

Highlights: A rebellious son **blasphemed the Name of the Lord** (Lev. 24:11,16). The Lord **commanded** to stone him (24:23). Note the number of perfection (seven) and its eventual climax in **the year of Jubile** (25:8-55).

One of the Ten Commandments written by the finger of God states: **Thou shalt not take the Name of the Lord thy God in vain** (Ex. 20:7). It's a very serious sin to **take the Name of the Lord ... in vain**, but, even worse, **the Israelitish woman's son blasphemed the Name of the Lord, and cursed** (Lev. 24:11). This was much more serious because it showed active rebellion and discredited the Name of the Lord.

Every 50th year in Israel was to be proclaimed as a year of **Jubile ... ye shall not sow, neither reap** (25:9-11). The land was to rest while the people lived on whatever grew on its own. The **Jubile** reminded the nation of their total dependence upon God and acknowledged, **the earth is the Lord's, and the fulness thereof** (Ps. 24:1).

As the trumpet announced the **Jubile** year, a sacrifice for atonement was made. This informed the people that an acceptable offering had been presented for their sins. In this year every downtrodden Hebrew who lost his ancestral property because of debts, or who had become a slave through poverty or misfortune, regained his freedom and all his former property rights and privileges. All debts were to be forgiven. This is a foreshadowing of the Gospel (Good News) which Christ came to reveal. **If the Son therefore shall make you free, ye shall be free indeed** (John 8:36).

Jesus' death on the cross is the sinner's **Jubile**. He sets us free from the power of sin and Satan and forgives all sins as well as provides us equal access to all the blessings of God. We, in turn, are to forgive everyone even as God forgives us because His forgiving Spirit indwells our lives. **And when ye stand praying, forgive, if ye have ought against any: that your Father also which is in heaven may forgive you your trespasses** (Mark 11:25).

In the Synagogue, Jesus read: **The Spirit of the Lord is upon Me, because He hath anointed Me to preach the Gospel to the poor; He hath sent Me to heal the brokenhearted, to preach deliverance to the captives, and recovering of sight to the blind, to set at liberty them that are bruised** (Luke 4:18; compare Is. 61:1-2).

Thought for Today: Everything we possess is a gift from God.

Christ Portrayed: By the kinsman-redeemer (Lev. 25:47-55). Christ is our Savior and Redeemer (Is. 60:16) who made us His kinsmen: **The Spirit Itself** (Himself) **beareth witness with our spirit, that we are the children of God** (Rom. 8:16).

FEBRUARY 11   Read Leviticus 26 – 27

Highlights: The marvelous blessings of walking on the "straight and narrow." Contrast the horrific results of disobedience. The fear of the Lord plus three things that are absolutely of the Lord.

Israel's success could not be explained by natural causes; the supernatural power of God was in control. The Israelites were reminded that God had brought them out of Egypt, and they were His people. Therefore, in loving gratitude, they should live to please Him.

If ye walk in My Statutes, and keep My Commandments, and do them; Then I will give you rain . . . and the land shall yield her increase. . . . And ye shall chase your enemies, and they shall fall before you by the sword. And five of you shall chase an hundred, and an hundred of you shall put ten thousand to flight: and your enemies shall fall before you by the sword (Lev. 26:3-4,7-8). If they would keep His Commandments He promised them blessings beyond compare: *I will walk among you, and will be your God, and ye shall be My people* (26:12).

God also graciously warned: *If ye will not hearken unto Me, and will not do all these Commandments. . . . I will break the pride of your power; and I will make your heaven as iron, and your earth as brass. . . . and ye shall have no power to stand before your enemies. And ye shall perish among the heathen, and the land of your enemies shall eat you up* (26:14,19,37-38). The continual complaining and dissatisfaction of the adults who were delivered from Egyptian slavery prevented them from possessing the promised land (I Cor. 10:1-11; Heb. 3:7-19).

This should be a warning to Christians today. Just as the blessings of God were dependent upon the Israelites' obedience and gratitude, we, too, must obey His Word and be grateful to the Lord if we are to receive His blessings.

We have the privilege and highest honor of being soldiers in the army of the King of kings. Victory to the Israelites was not dependent on their strength but upon God who promised: *Not by might, nor by power, but by My Spirit, saith the LORD of Hosts* (Zech. 4:6).

To Christians, Jesus still says: *I am The Vine, ye are the branches: He that abideth in Me, and I in him, the same bringeth forth much fruit: for without Me ye can do nothing* (John 15:5).

Blessed are they that hear the Word of God, and keep it (Luke 11:28)!

Thought for Today: The tragic losses of a wasted lifetime cannot be relived or restored, but the sins can be forgiven.

Christ Revealed: As the Tabernacle to be sent to dwell among us (Lev. 26:11). *The Word was made* (became) *flesh, and dwelt* (tabernacled) *among us* (John 1:14; Rev. 21:3).

INTRODUCTION TO THE BOOK OF NUMBERS

The Book of Numbers continues the history of the Israelites where the Book of Exodus left off. Just one month had passed between the completion of the Tabernacle (Ex. 40:17) and the Command of God to number the people (Num. 1:1-2). During that time, the Instructions in the Book of Leviticus were given. The first census of all men age 20 and older records that 603,550 men were qualified to serve in the army of Israel (1:1-46).

And it came to pass on the twentieth day of the second month, in the second year, that the cloud was taken up from off the Tabernacle of the Testimony (10:11), and the Israelites followed the cloud as it moved toward Kadesh-barnea. But soon the people complained and then rebelled against God (10:11 – 14:45).

After the Israelites arrived at Kadesh-barnea, 12 spies were sent out to investigate the land (Num. 13 – 14; Deut. 1:22-40). When they returned 40 days later, *Caleb stilled the people before Moses, and said, Let us go up at once, and possess it; for we are well able to overcome it* (Num. 13:30). Ten of the spies strongly protested, saying: *We be not able to go up against the people; for they are stronger than we* (13:31). However, Joshua and Caleb pleaded: *The LORD is with us: fear them not* (14:9). But the people agreed with the ten disbelieving spies (14:1-45). Consequently, God pronounced His judgment of death upon that generation (14:22-37). Thus, they wasted 38 years wandering in the wilderness until all the people from that first generation, who were 20 years of age or older at the first census, had died (15:1 – 21:35; 26:63-65).

Later, the Lord commanded Moses and Eleazar, Aaron's son and successor, to take a second census of the new generation of men age 20 and older, whose parents had left Egypt (26:1-65). This second numbering took place almost 40 years after the first census, in the 11th month of the 40th year (1:19; 26:1-4; comp. Ex. 1:1-5; Deut. 1:3).

Only Joshua and Caleb, the two men of faith from the first generation of Israelites, lived to enter the promised land. The new generation was estimated to be more than two million people. They gathered on the Plains of Moab, east of the Jordan River, across from Jericho, ready to take the land their parents, in unbelief, had rejected.

One of the greatest illustrations of New Testament doctrine is found in this Book. *These things were our examples, to the intent we should not lust after evil things, as they ... lusted* (I Cor. 10:6).

FEBRUARY 12   **Read Numbers 1 – 2**

Highlights: God organizes the people in preparation to inherit the promised land. He speaks to Moses over 85 times, and **Moses did as the L**ORD **commanded** (Num. 20:27).

The Israelites had been camped near Mount Sinai for more than a year. It took about 30 days to receive all the laws and regulations recorded in the Book of Leviticus. It was just one month after the erection of the Tabernacle **on the first day of the second month, in the second year after they were come out of the land of Egypt** (Num.1:1). They were now ready to move toward the promised land.

As long as they were at Mount Sinai but not yet required to go forward, **the children of Israel did according to all that the L**ORD **commanded Moses** (2:34). But months earlier, during their journey from the Red Sea to the promised land, it was far different. When they saw the Egyptian chariots led by Pharaoh coming toward them, their faith of living in the promised land completely failed. The Israelites murmured against Moses saying it would have been better to stay in Egypt (Ex. 14:10-12). After numerous times of refusing to trust God on their way to the promised land, He would declare: **All those men which have seen My glory, and My miracles . . . and have tempted Me now these ten times, and have not hearkened to My voice; Surely they shall not see the land which I sware unto their fathers** (Num. 14:20-23).

Yes, as Moses said: **We went through all that great and terrible wilderness** (Deut. 1:19). But if the children of Israel had believed God and had entered the land when Caleb said: **Let us go up at once, and possess it** (Num. 13:30), they would have been in Canaan within less than two years after they left Egypt. Consequently, very little is said about the 38 years of wandering in the wilderness, for it was a time of failure. They would not trust God, even after all He had done for them. Instead, they **murmured against Moses. . . . And they said . . . Let us make a captain, and let us return into Egypt** (Num. 14:2-4).

The people of God should always live by faith, obey His Word, and trust in His promises. Fulfillment in life becomes a reality when we realize that **we are His workmanship, created in Christ Jesus unto good works, which God hath before ordained that we should walk in them** (Eph. 2:10).

Thought for Today: Don't disqualify yourself from the Lord's best blessings because of faultfinding and dissatisfaction with your circumstances.

Christ Portrayed: By Moses as he led the people (Num. 1:54). Jesus said: **I am the Good Shepherd, and know My sheep. . . . My sheep . . . follow Me** (John 10:14,27).

FEBRUARY 13   Read Numbers 3 – 4

Highlights: The census, duties, and order of God. The details required for transporting the Tabernacle. Are you allowing God to bring His order and detail into **your** life? Redemption of the firstborn!

It was essential that the Tabernacle workers (Levites) remain faithful and loyal if the priests were to perform their sacred responsibilities. **All that enter in to perform the service, to do the work in the Tabernacle. . . . so shall they serve** (Num. 4:23,26).

The words **to perform the service** occur again and again. They refer to the Levites' ordinary hard work of disassembling the Tabernacle and carrying the curtains, poles, furniture, and everything pertaining to the Tabernacle worship throughout the dangerous, difficult wilderness journey (Deut. 1:19).

Just as the priests at that time were dependent upon the faithfulness of the workers, the outreach of the Word of God throughout the world today is dependent upon the faithfulness of the people of God. Every Christian is called upon to **perform the service** – to faithfully help make it possible for others to know about Jesus Christ who alone can set souls free from sin and hell.

God has first claim on the lives of all His people, for all were created and sustained by Him (Col. 1:15-17). Salvation is more than a doctrine. It takes place when a person fully gives himself to the Lord. Christ expects not only to be our Savior but to be our Guide through life, **that Christ may dwell in your hearts by faith . . . that ye might be filled with all the fullness of God** (Eph. 3:17,19). It is of utmost importance that we allow Him to be Lord of our lives. **Jesus Christ, who . . . washed us from our sins in His own blood, And hath made us kings and priests unto God and His Father; to Him be glory and dominion for ever and ever. Amen** (Rev. 1:5-6).

Everything is changed when the believer submits to the Lordship of Christ and realizes that everything of eternal value does have its source in Him. It is then that Bible reading and prayers become the means of discovering His will and living daily to please the Lord.

Satan continually seeks to hinder every believer from serving the Lord. We must be on guard against the more subtle temptations of using the Lord's day and His tithes for personal pleasure. **Let us not be weary in well doing: for in due season** (at the proper time) **we shall reap, if we faint not** (don't give up) (Gal. 6:9).

Thought for Today: No Christian is worthy, but we have been accepted by our Savior because of the forgiving love and grace of God.

Christ Portrayed: By Aaron, the high priest, who was served by the Levites (Num. 3:6). As a **holy** and **a royal priesthood**, we serve Christ, our **great High Priest** (John 12:16; I Pet. 2:5,9; Heb. 4:14).

FEBRUARY 14   Read Numbers 5 – 6

Highlights: Read the laws of cleansing, recompense, jealousy; the Nazarite vow; the threefold blessing of the Lord. The Lord bestows an abundant blessing on all who dedicate their lives inwardly and outwardly to Him.

Taking the vow of a Nazarite meant separating oneself to God for a specific period of time – a month to a lifetime. **When either man or woman shall separate themselves to vow a vow of a Nazarite, to separate themselves unto the LORD. . . . All the days of his separation he is holy unto the LORD** (Num. 6:2-8).

During that period of time, the Nazarite was not to go near or touch a dead body or drink wine. God has warned: **Wine is a mocker, strong drink is raging: and whosoever is deceived thereby is not wise. . . . He that loveth wine and oil shall not be rich. . . . Look not thou upon the wine, when it is red** (alcoholic)**. . . . At the last it biteth like a serpent. . . . It is not for kings to drink** (alcoholic) **wine; nor for princes strong drink** (Prov. 20:1; 21:17; 23:31-32; 31:4). The Nazarite willingly gave up physical satisfaction – even his total being. His personal consecration to God was to **serve Him with a perfect heart and with a willing mind** (I Chr. 28:9) at all times.

In contrast to a Nazarite, the self-absorbed exhibit: **Pride**, exalted sense of self-worth due to appearance or abilities; **independence**, refusing to submit to authority; **discouragement**, expressing a negative attitude; **anger** and **impatience**, resentment and retaliation when others excel or things don't go one's way; **self-will**, having a stubborn and unteachable spirit; **love of praise**, seeking to be noticed; and **deceit**, evading and covering up the truth or exaggerating. All of these are signs of spiritual **deadness** (lack of love for God) or not possessing inward light. This results in an indifference to the written Word of God and His will for one's life.

Like the Nazarite, one should desire to go beyond just being called a Christian, but should recognize the value of a personal relationship with Jesus Christ. Christians should also be willing to give up anything that keeps them from being their best to serve and worship the Lord. As you read His Word, pray: **Search me, O God, and know my heart: try me, and know my thoughts: And see if there be any wicked way in me, and lead me in the way everlasting** (Ps. 139:23-24).

Thought for Today: Accomplishing the will of God often requires self-denial, even of things which in themselves may not be sinful.

Christ Revealed: Nazarite is the transliteration of a Hebrew term meaning "dedication by separation" (Num. 6:1-8). Jesus dedicated Himself to do only the will of His Father even unto death: **Thy will be done** (Matt. 26:39,42).

FEBRUARY 15   Read Numbers 7

Highlights: Picture the awesome, overwhelming parade of animals, tribal leaders, and offerings. Where were they all going? Why such huge offerings? Does God give attention to our individual offerings?

The princes recognized the needs of the Levites and desired to help them carry out their duties. ***The princes of Israel* (the tribes) . . . *brought their offering before the* L**ORD**, *six covered wagons, and twelve oxen; a wagon for two of the princes, and for each one an ox: and they brought them before the Tabernacle. And the* L**ORD** *spake unto Moses, saying, Take it of them . . . and thou shalt give them unto the Levites, to every man according to his service*** (Num. 7:2-5).

The princes (leaders) of the tribes could not participate in the duties of the Tabernacle; but through their offerings, they were able to assist the Levites in their God-appointed responsibilities. Since the leaders did not have a prominent spiritual position, as did the Levites, they could have expressed a spirit of jealousy and given little or nothing. But, rather, they willingly brought generous, sacrificial gifts to supply the needs of the Levites. This generosity was an extra blessing and God continued His presence among His people (7:89).

When the Levites moved previously, they had to carry upon their shoulders the things belonging to the Tabernacle, but now they would be eased from this burden by these generous gifts.

What a thrilling experience to observe this harmony in the people of God working together and caring for one another! The offering of the princes of the tribes manifested a thoughtfulness which only the Spirit of God can create in the hearts of His people when they are dedicated to God. The Levites, no doubt, were encouraged by others willing to share in the burden of their load.

Since all the offerings were exactly the same, it may seem monotonous to read all the details that were given for each one. But the repetition reveals the significance God places on every sacrifice given to support His ministry. Our individual offerings may seem small to us, but everyone and every gift is important to God. Those who receive the gifts are to use them for the glory of the Giver.

Let nothing be done through strife or vainglory; but in lowliness of mind let each esteem other better than themselves (Phil. 2:3).

Thought for Today: When our thoughts are to please God, not self, we enjoy peace of mind.

Christ Revealed: Through the voluntary offerings of the leaders which were sufficient to meet the needs (Num. 7). Jesus gave His life to meet our very need. ***My God shall supply all your need according to His riches in glory by Christ Jesus*** (Phil. 4:19).

FEBRUARY 16   Read Numbers 8 – 9

Highlights: How much time has passed since the Exodus (Num. 9:1)? The Second Passover. It was vital to remember the One who freed them. Cloud of protection by day and pillar of fire by night.

The Passover was a memorial of the historic deliverance from hopeless slavery in Egypt (Ex. 12:41-42). *In the first month of the second year after they were come out of the land of Egypt. . . . . they kept the Passover . . . according to all that the LORD commanded Moses* (Num. 9:1,5).

The Israelites' only hope of deliverance from Egypt was to *take . . . a lamb. . . . And . . . take of the blood, and strike it on the two side posts and on the upper door post. . . . And they shall eat the flesh. . . . And . . . let nothing of it remain. . . . and ye shall eat it in haste: it is the LORD's Passover. . . . and when I see the blood* (on your doorposts), *I will pass over you. . . . And . . . at midnight the LORD smote all the firstborn in the land of Egypt* (Ex. 12:3,7-8,10-11,13,29). God protected Israel from the **destroyer** (12:23) and the Passover lamb strengthened the family as they left Egypt. The Lord commanded that there be **nothing left** of the Passover meal (12:10; Num. 9:12). It was not meant for those who would settle down in Egypt. It provided strength for the journey to the promised land. Today the believer's daily strength comes through obedience to **ALL** the Word of God. *Man shall not live by bread alone, but by every word that proceedeth out of the mouth of God* (Matt. 4:4).

Egyptian slavery would have kept Israel in bondage until physical death. Similarly, sin can keep men and women in bondage (Rev. 20:15). Since Christ died for us to deliver us from eternal death, we must receive Him as our Savior and Lord. Jesus warned eight times that the destiny of the lost is eternal hell (Matt.10:28; 11:23; 18:9; 23:15,33; Mark 9:43; Luke 12:5; 16:22-23). Jesus also let us know that hell was much more than separation from God. Six times He states that it is a place of **outer darkness: there shall be weeping and gnashing of teeth** (Matt. 8:12; 13:42,50; 22:13; 24:51; 25:30).

Ye were not redeemed with corruptible things . . . But with the precious blood of Christ, as of a Lamb without blemish and without spot (I Pet. 1:18-19).

Have no fellowship with the unfruitful works of darkness, but rather reprove them (Eph. 5:11).

Thought for Today: Our objective in life should be to accomplish the purpose of God for creating us, which is to let the life of God be lived through us.

Christ Revealed: The Passover serves as a beautiful illustration of the redemption Christ accomplished at Calvary as *the Lamb of God* (Num. 9:2; John 1:29; I Cor. 5:7).

FEBRUARY 17

Read Numbers 10 – 11

Highlights: Canaan is in sight! All Israel has to do is trust God and move forward in conquest of Canaan. But, lusting for **flesh** (meat) to eat, once again they murmur, and failure is inevitable (Num. 11:4-34).

On their way to the promised land, the Israelites were always complaining about something. They failed to see that every problem, every disappointment, and every difficulty was a test of their faith and an opportunity for them to trust God to supply their every need. **My God shall supply all your need according to His riches in glory by Christ Jesus** (Phil. 4:19). Thanksgiving and praise should have been their response. **In every thing give thanks: for this is the will of God in Christ Jesus concerning you** (I Thess. 5:18). **Be filled with the Spirit . . . Giving thanks always for all things unto God and the Father in the Name of our Lord Jesus Christ** (Eph. 5:18-20). But, instead, they complained about the manna.

When the people complained, it displeased the Lord. . . . And the mixt multitude that was among them fell a lusting: and the children of Israel also wept again, and said. . . . We remember the fish, which we did eat in Egypt freely . . . But now . . . there is nothing at all (Num. 11:1,4-6). God answered their prayer for meat (11:31,33). **He gave them their request; but sent** (it resulted in) **leanness into their soul** (Ps. 106:15).

God sends trials to test our faith and provide an opportunity to reveal Himself as the All-Sufficient One. We must come to that place where we discover that our feelings are not trustworthy, and truly say, **we . . . have no confidence in the flesh** (Phil. 3:3).

As believers, we will discover satisfaction and pleasure as we read and believe all of the Word of God and leave the outcome of our situations to Him. Although we do not understand all the things God permits in our lives, we know that **all things** (do) **work together for good to them that love God, to them who are the called according to His purpose** (Rom. 8:28). We should be content with what Christ has chosen for us, knowing that, without exception, it is always in our best interest. Paul wrote: **I have learned, in whatsoever state I am, therewith to be content** (Phil. 4:11). We also need to pray as Jesus did: **Not My will, but Thine, be done** (Luke 22:42).

For it is God which worketh in you both to will and to do of His good pleasure (Phil. 2:13).

Thought for Today: The most insignificant person in man's eye is important to Christ.

Christ Revealed: The two trumpets were made of silver (Num. 10:2). Silver in the Bible stands for truth. Christ is **The Way, The Truth, and The Life** (John 14:6).

FEBRUARY 18   Read Numbers 12 – 13

Highlights: A valuable lesson on the dangers of not believing the Lord, resulting in His having to withhold His blessing; report from the 12 men who spied out Canaan.

As the Israelites neared the promised land, **the LORD spake unto Moses, saying, Send thou men, that they may search the land of Canaan, which I give unto the children of Israel.... So they went up, and searched the land.... and came unto Hebron** (Num. 13:1-2,21-22). The spies stood on the very site where Abraham had **built... an altar unto the LORD** (Gen. 13:18). It was at Hebron that Abraham had pleaded with God not to destroy Sodom (18:23) and where he later bought the cave of Machpelah and buried his wife Sarah (23:17). But the thrill of standing here did not enter into their report. **They returned** (and reported)**.... the people be strong... and the cities are walled, and very great** (Num. 13:25,28). As unbelievers, the 10 spies could see only the high walls and the giants. Had they recognized that God is Almighty, as Joshua and Caleb did, they could have conquered and possessed this promised land.

Caleb had a heavenly view of the giants in the land. He knew God was able to subdue every enemy. Caleb had learned to trust his God. **Caleb... said, Let us go up at once, and possess it; for we are well able to overcome it** (13:30).

Satan is always present to discourage and try to defeat every desire of the believer to trust in the Lord. Spiritual victories are assured when we place our faith in God, as did Caleb, who said: **Let us go up at once**. The high walls and the giants were a test, revealing the spies' lack of faith. Those who trust in God have no need to fear the giants and high walls regardless of what they represent in their lives. The believer should learn to rely on God and to trust Him for every outcome. We can inherit the promised land. The enemies without and within the heart will fall, as did the walls of Jericho, when we have faith to believe the promises of God.

We dare not presume to possess the promises of God by worldly means or schemes, as did the Israelites when they decided they would enter the promised land (14:44-45). Later they unsuccessfully attempted to take Ai without asking directions from God (Josh. 7:4). **The weapons of our warfare are not carnal** (worldly)**, but mighty through God to the pulling down of strong holds** (II Cor. 10:4).

Thought for Today: Covetous people never get enough money, proud people never get enough praise, and self-centered people never get enough attention.

Christ Portrayed: By Moses, who **was very meek** (humble)**, above all the men which were upon the face of the earth** (Num. 12:3). Jesus said: **I am meek** (gentle, mild) **and lowly in heart** (Matt. 11:29).

FEBRUARY 19   Read Numbers 14 – 15

Highlights: The turning point of the nation of Israel is their rebellion at Kadesh; they choose wasted lives rather than conquest. The reward of the faithful and judgment of the faithless (Num. 14:22-23,34).

It seems incredible that the children of Israel would cry out in foolish rebellion: ***Were it not better for us to return into Egypt*** (Num. 14:3)***? All the children of Israel murmured against Moses and against Aaron. . . . Let us make a captain, and let us return into Egypt*** (14:2,4). How could they forget that God had answered their prayer? When their suffering had become unbearable, God had spared them from continued slavery and had miraculously opened the Red Sea and delivered them from Egypt.

Let us make a captain. It appears from Nehemiah 9:17 that they actually did. The One True Guide had been rejected! Could they expect God to lead, defend, and provide for them on a journey which was entirely opposed to His will? Did they expect that God would again open the Red Sea and allow them to return to Egypt? The very root of their self-destructive unbelief was rebellion, which refuses to accept the ability and integrity of God to fulfill His promises.

In bold opposition to the majority opinion, Caleb shouted his faith in the promises of God: ***Let us go up at once . . . we are well able to overcome*** (13:30). Caleb had faith to recognize the vital importance of obeying the Word of God, regardless of circumstances. It appears that the Israelites were ready to stone Caleb and Joshua, who were willing to die for their faith, trusting in the promises of God. God rewarded the faithfulness of Caleb who later asked if he could possess Hebron as his inheritance in the promised land.

One of the greatest tests of sincerity is found in the willingness to remain faithful to Christ when it seems like everyone is against you. It is no surprise that God declared: ***My servant Caleb, because he had another spirit with him, and hath followed Me fully, him will I bring into the land whereinto he went; and his seed shall possess it*** (14:24). Our usefulness to God lies in obedience, and the measure of our usefulness is determined by our faith in the Word of God and the degree of our discipline and submission to the will of God. ***By faith Abraham . . . obeyed. . . . Through faith also Sara . . . was delivered of a child when she was past age, because she judged Him faithful who had promised*** (Heb. 11:8,11).

Thought for Today: *Faithful is He that calleth you, who also will do it* (I Thess. 5:24).

Christ Revealed: As the glory of God (Num. 14:22). Jesus Christ is ***the brightness of His glory*** (the glory of God)***, and the express image of His person*** (Heb. 1:3).

ISRAEL'S UNBELIEF

The LORD said. . . . all those men which have seen My glory, and My miracles, which I did in Egypt and in the wilderness, and have tempted Me now these ten times, and have not hearkened to My voice; Surely they shall not see the land which I sware unto their fathers (Num. 14:20-23).

PLACE	REBELLION	THE MERCY OF GOD REVEALED	KEY THOUGHT
RED SEA Ex. 14:10-12	Israelites murmuring against Moses at the sight of Egyptian chariots	In destroying their enemies and providing a way of deliverance (14:21-31)	There is a great temptation for a person to desire the things of his sinful past (I John 2:15-17).
MARAH Ex. 15:23-24	Grumbling because God took them to bitter water	By sweetening the water (15:25-26)	Disappointments provide opportunities to exercise faith (II Cor. 4:16-17).
DESERT Ex. 16:2-3	Grumbling – they feared starvation	By providing manna (16:14-15)	God supplies all our needs *according to His riches in glory* (Phil. 4:19).
DESERT Ex. 16:20	Disbelieving God by keeping manna overnight	Provision continued for 40 years (16:35)	The Word of God is essential and must be obeyed (II Tim. 3:16-17).
DESERT Ex. 16:26-27	Ignoring God and searching for manna on the Sabbath	In still providing a day of rest (16:28-30)	We must show proper respect for the Lord's day (Heb. 10:25).
REPHIDIM Ex. 17:1-3	Quarreling with Moses over the lack of water	In providing water from the rock (17:6)	Christians must depend on God (Matt. 6:33).
HOREB Ex. 32:1-10	Worshiping the golden calf	In sparing those who did not sin (32:32-33)	Satan will provide opportunities for us to return to sin (II Tim. 4:10).
TABERAH Num. 11:1	Complaining against God about adversity	Answering Moses' prayer (11:2-3)	Remedy for sin is loving obedience (John 14:21).
KIBROTH-HATTAAVAH Num. 11:10-15,34	Weeping for the variety of food left behind in Egypt	By providing quail in abundance (11:31-32)	Discontentment is a lack of trust in the love of God (I Tim. 6:8; Phil. 4:11; Heb. 13:5).
KADESH-BARNEA Num. 14:2-10	Refusing to believe God and enter the promised land	In sparing Joshua, Caleb, and the children (14:20-31)	God always rewards the faithful (Heb. 11:6).

FEBRUARY 20   Read Numbers 16 – 18

Highlights: See how jealousy, discontent, and failure to cooperate with God-ordained leadership can destroy the usefulness of "good" people. God will reveal His will to anyone who desires to follow it.

Once again, Moses was confronted with opposition, this time from his own cousins (Ex. 6:18-21) and key leaders of the 12 tribes. ***Korah, (and) the ... sons of Reuben ... rose up before Moses, with certain of the children of Israel, two hundred and fifty princes of the assembly, famous in the congregation ... And they gathered themselves together against Moses and against Aaron.... And Korah gathered all the congregation against them*** (Num. 16:1-3,19). Korah and his followers believed that the majority should rule the nation. They accused Moses and Aaron of assuming too much authority: ***Ye take*** (assume) ***too much upon you, seeing all the congregation are holy, every one of them, and the L<small>ORD</small> is among them: wherefore then lift ye up yourselves above the congregation of the L<small>ORD</small>*** (16:3)***?*** They refused to recognize that Moses and Aaron were appointed by God to lead the people and that the rebels were actually ***gathered together against the L<small>ORD</small>*** and His anointed servants (16:11).

Korah did not just make a mistake; he committed a serious sin, as recorded by Jude, who wrote: ***I will therefore put you in remembrance ... how that the Lord, having saved the people out of the land of Egypt, afterward destroyed them that believed not.... Woe unto them! for they ... perished in the gainsaying*** (rebellion) ***of Core*** (Korah) (Jude 1:5,11).

Perhaps Korah was a believer in God from the priestly tribe of Levi through Kohath. The Kohathites were responsible for bearing the Sanctuary ***upon their shoulders*** (Num. 7:9) and later would be ***set over the service of song in the House of the L<small>ORD</small>*** (I Chr. 6:22,31) and ***over the Shewbread, to prepare it every Sabbath*** (9:31-32). However, it appears that Korah would serve the Lord only if it would bring recognition to himself. Self-willed people need to recognize that ***the wrath of God is revealed from heaven against all ungodliness and unrighteousness of men, who hold the truth in unrighteousness*** (Rom. 1:18). They will not believe the Truth or teach it to others. ***It is a fearful thing to fall into the hands of the Living God*** (Heb. 10:31).

Thought for Today: It is the life of God living in us rather than our decision to live as we choose.

Christ Portrayed: By Aaron and his sons who were responsible for making proper atonement for all the iniquity of Israel (Num. 18:1). Jesus ***was wounded for our transgressions, He was bruised for our iniquities*** (Is. 53:5). He ***gave Himself for us, that He might redeem us from all iniquity*** (lawlessness) (Titus 2:14).

FEBRUARY 21   Read Numbers 19 – 20

Highlights: God puts the disobedient sons of the high priest, to death. A nation seals its own fate by refusing to help the people of God. How gloriously Christ is typified twice in today's reading!

Moses took the rod as the Lord commanded him, but from that point on there was a mixture of Moses' feelings and the will of God. ***The Lord spake unto Moses, saying . . . speak ye unto the rock . . . and it shall give forth his water. . . . And Moses . . . said unto them, Hear now, ye rebels; must we fetch you water out of this rock? And Moses lifted up his hand, and with his rod he smote the rock twice: and the water came out abundantly.*** The people – and even Moses – were pleasantly satisfied until ***the Lord spake unto Moses and Aaron, Because ye believed Me not, to sanctify Me*** (regard My Word as sufficient) ***in the eyes of the children of Israel . . . ye shall not bring this congregation into the land which I have given them*** (Num. 20:7-12). Anger and self-will destroy much, much more than at first appears.

Moses was satisfied when the water came forth and the people's needs were met. Undoubtedly the people were delighted and impressed by Moses' ability to provide for their thirst, but God was not satisfied. Today much attention is placed on man's ability to meet our needs, but few seem concerned about whether Christ is satisfied.

Moses was not "obedient" when he angrily shouted: ***Must we fetch you water out of this rock?*** Nor was he obedient when ***he smote the rock twice*** even though he knew that only the power of God could bring forth water.

Many believers know that ***all Scripture is given by inspiration of God, and is profitable for doctrine, for reproof, for correction, for instruction in righteousness: That the man of God may be perfect*** (well-prepared to be) ***throughly furnished*** (adequately equipped) ***unto all good works*** (II Tim. 3:16-17), yet they foolishly rely on their own "good judgment" and keep "too busy" to read ***all Scripture.*** The fearful warning from God is that ***the time will come when they will not endure sound doctrine; but after their own lusts shall they heap to themselves teachers, having itching ears; And they shall turn away their ears from the Truth, and shall be turned*** (from biblical Truth) ***unto fables*** (man-inspired religious fiction) (II Tim. 4:3-4).

Thought for Today: When we try to impress others with our importance, the Lord will not be glorified.

Christ Revealed: Through ***the rock*** that Moses struck (Ex. 17:6; Num. 20:8-11). Christ, our Rock, who was struck once through His death on the cross, does not need to be struck again. ***That spiritual Rock*** (Petra) ***that followed*** (accompanied) ***them . . . was Christ*** (I Cor. 10:4). ***For in that He died, He died unto sin once*** (Rom. 6:10).

FEBRUARY 22   Read Numbers 21 – 22

Highlights: Fiery serpents kill; brass serpent typifies Christ who heals! Failures, blessings, and victories. Refugees near destination. A donkey speaks to save a prophet (Num. 22:28).

Balak was aware that Israel's God had conquered the Egyptian armies and he knew *all that Israel had done to the Amorites*. He probably feared that he was to be destroyed next (Num. 22:2-4). *He sent messengers therefore unto Balaam* (22:5), the prophet, to persuade him to prophesy against the Israelites.

Balaam received marvelous prophetic revelations and inspiration that came from God. He was endowed with far more than ordinary knowledge of the One True God. He was aware of the relationship of Israel to God, and he knew he could not curse those whom God had blessed. However, the wealth and prominence that King Balak had offered him, enticed Balaam to eventually compromise what he knew was the will of God. He should have refused Balak, but he coveted the rewards that were offered him. He *loved the wages of unrighteousness* (II Pet. 2:15).

Balaam belonged to that great number of people who know the right doctrine and can even quote the Scriptures, but they deceive themselves and choose error over what they know the Word of God instructs them to do. They too love *the wages of unrighteousness*. Like Balaam, they expect to *die the death of the righteous* (Num. 23:10), yet they are unwilling to live the life of the righteous.

Covetousness comes in a variety of forms, such as: Christ and biblical values not being their first concern. Their concern may not be evil or mere personal pleasure. But they have forsaken the Lord's day, tithing, participation in the Lord's Supper, and the support of the local church that Christ died to establish. They have no personal heart interest in what God has said concerning *Christ* (who) *also loved the Church, and gave Himself for it* (Eph. 5:25) and *not forsaking the assembling of ourselves together, as the manner of some is; but exhorting one another* (Heb. 10:25). They may "serve" God in their "own way" while they live to please themselves. *If any man will come after Me, let him deny himself, and take up his cross, and follow Me. For ... whosoever will lose his life for My sake shall find it* (Matt. 16:24-25). *Take heed, and beware of covetousness: for a man's life consisteth not in the abundance of the things which he possesseth* (Luke 12:15).

Thought for Today: It is impossible to have a right attitude toward God while maintaining a wrong attitude toward delegated authority.

Christ Portrayed: By Moses who was faithful to pray to God for the people (Num. 21:7). *Christ Jesus; Who was faithful to Him that appointed Him, as also Moses was faithful in all his house* (family, i.e. the Israelites) (Heb. 3:1-2).

The Exodus Out of Egypt & Route to the Promised Land

Scholars do not agree on the route, but the "traditional" route is located near the vicinities shown
(Also Ex. 12:37 – 19:1 for Exodus from Egypt to Sinai)

1. **Rameses** – (Num. 33:3)
2. **Succoth** – (Num. 33:5)
3. **Etham** – (Num. 33:6)
4. **Migdol / Pi-Hahiroth** – (Num. 33:7-8)

5. **Marah** – (Num. 33:8)
6. **Elim** – (Num. 33:9)
7. **Wilderness of Sin** – (Num. 33:11-12)
8. **Rephidim** – (Num. 33:14) – People complain of thirst, Moses smites the rock in Horeb and brings forth water (Ex. 17:1-7); Victory over Amalekites (17:8-16)
9. **Wilderness at the base of Mount Sinai** – (Num. 33:15; Ex. 19:1 – 40:38) – Moses receives 10 Commandments (Exodus 20:1-17); Golden calf worshiped; Moses receives instructions for building the Tabernacle (25:1 – 31:18); Moses intercedes; People repent; Moses prays; Second Tables of the Law are given; Covenant is renewed (32:1 – 34:35); Tabernacle is built (35:1 – 40:38); Passover observed at Sinai (Num. 9:1-14)
10. **Taberah/Kibroth-hattaavah** – 3 days' journey from Mount Sinai (Num. 10:33; 33:16-17); People murmur and then die from eating too much quail (11:31-35)
11. **Hazeroth** – (Num. 33:17) – Miriam and Aaron rebel against Moses; Miriam becomes a leper; Moses intercedes for Miriam and she is restored (12:1-16)
12. **Wilderness of Paran** (Num. 12:16)/**Kadesh-barnea** (Rithmah?) – Num. 13:26; 33:18) – Spies sent out from Kadesh-barnea and they explore: A. Rehob (North end of Jordan Valley); B. Hebron; C. Valley of Eshcol; The people refuse to believe Joshua and Caleb's good report (14:6-10); Rebellion against God; God's judgment was that the unbelieving adults would die in the wilderness (14:11-38)
13. **Arad** *top of the mountain* – People attempt to enter the promised land without the Lord (Num. 14:40-45)
14. **Hormah** – Amalekites and Canaanites defeat Israel *even unto Hormah* (Num. 14:44-45); Israelites return to Kadesh-barnea

WILDERNESS WANDERINGS FOR 38 YEARS – Miriam dies at Kadesh-barnea (20:1)

15. **Meribah** – No water; People complain; Moses sins by striking rock (Num. 20:2-13); Refused passage through Edom (20:14-21); Aaron dies on Mount Hor in 40th year (20:22-29; 33:38-39); Victory over king of Arad at Hormah (21:1-3)
16. **Oboth** – Between Kadesh-barnea and Oboth, sin results in *fiery serpents*; God has Moses make a brass serpent to save those who would look upon it (Num. 21:4-10)

VARIOUS OTHER UNIDENTIFIED LOCATIONS – (Num. 33:12-47; 21:10-20)

17. **Plains of Moab** – From Kadesh-barnea to the plains of Moab via Elath and Ezion-geber (Num. 33:37-49; Deut. 2:8)
18. **Jahaz** – The Amorite king, Sihon, refuses Israel passage through his territory; Israel defeats him at Jahaz (Num. 21:21-32)
19. **Edrei** – After defeating the Amorites, they defeat Og, the king of Bashan (Num. 21:33-35); King Balak, a Moabite, hires Balaam to curse Israel (22:1 – 24:25)
20. **Peor (near Shittim)** – (Num. 25:1-18) – Israelites' apostasy with the Moabites and Midianites; Second Census (26:1-65)
21. **Mount Nebo** (Pisgah in Abarim mountain range) – (Num. 27:12-23; Deut. 34:1-4) - Moses appoints Joshua his successor (Num. 27:12-23); Israelites defeat Midianites and kill 5 kings and the prophet Balaam (31:1-8); Moses ascends to the top of Mount Pisgah (Mount Nebo) and views the promised land; Moses dies there and God Himself buries Moses (Deut. 34:5-6)

JOSHUA ASSUMES LEADERSHIP OF THE ISRAELITES – (Deut. 34:8-9; Josh. 1:1-2)

FEBRUARY 23   Read Numbers 23 – 25

Highlights: Balaam prophesies blessings on Israel and yet thousands die. We learn why Phinehas is given the highest priestly honor recorded in the Old Testament. *A Star out of Jacob* (Messianic prophecy) (Num. 24:15-19).

All the sacrifices offered by Balak, the Moabite king, and all the clever schemes of Balaam could not hinder the blessing God had promised earlier to Abraham, Isaac, and Jacob. Balaam told Balak: *I have received commandment to bless: and He hath blessed; and I cannot reverse it* (Num. 23:20).

Furthermore, God used this self-centered prophet to reveal his own awful fate as well as remarkably foretell the coming of the Savior. *I shall see Him* (Jesus Christ)*, but not now: I shall behold Him, but not nigh: there shall come a Star* (Christ) *out of Jacob, and a Sceptre* (Ruler) *shall rise out of Israel. . . . Out of Jacob shall come He that* (who) *shall have dominion* (24:17,19).

It seems incredible that the wealth Balak was offering him was so important to Balaam that he advised the Midianites to seduce the Israelites to join them in "worship of Baal-peor" (25:1-3; Rev. 2:14)! This led the Israelite men to commit fornication and adultery with the Midianite women, resulting in a plague of death, and *those that died in the plague were twenty and four thousand* (Num. 25:9). Balaam was still with them at the time God led Moses to go to war *against the Midianites. . . . And they slew the kings of Midian . . . Balaam also . . . they slew with the sword* (31:5-9,15-17).

It is pathetic to read that Balaam, who had once confessed: *I cannot go beyond the Word of the Lord my God* (Num. 22:18,38) and: *All that the Lord speaketh, that I must do* (23:26; 24:13), sinned against the people of God to gain worldly rewards (Jude 1:11).

We are warned to beware of going astray in *the way of Balaam* (II Pet. 2:15). *Likewise also these . . . despise dominion. . . . Woe unto them! for they . . . ran greedily after the error of Balaam for reward. . . . These are spots in your feasts of charity* (Jude 1:8,11-12). We are further warned: *The love of money is the root of all evil: which while some coveted after, they have erred from the faith, and pierced themselves through with many sorrows. But thou, O man of God, flee these things; and follow after righteousness, godliness, faith, love* (I Tim. 6:10-11).

Thought for Today: Covetousness is always self-defeating.

Christ Revealed: As the prophesied *Star* and *Sceptre* (Num. 24:17). Christ is coming to reign in great glory, not only over Israel, but over all men (Rev. 19:15-16). *Unto the Son He saith, Thy throne, O God, is for ever and ever: a Sceptre of righteousness is the Sceptre of Thy Kingdom* (Heb. 1:8). *I Jesus. . . . am the Root and Offspring of David, and the Bright and Morning Star* (Rev. 22:16).

FEBRUARY 24   Read Numbers 26 – 27

Highlights: The new generation prepares to enter the promised land. A generation lost – except for Caleb and Joshua; Moses to die; Joshua the new commander-in-chief.

Why must Moses die before entering the promised land? Certainly it was not because he was physically or mentally feeble. *His eye was not dim, nor his natural force abated* (Deut. 34:7). Moses prayed that he could *go over, and see the good land that is beyond Jordan* (3:25). *The LORD said unto Moses, Get thee up into this mount Abarim, and see the land which I have given unto the children of Israel. And when thou hast seen it, thou also shalt be gathered unto thy people, as Aaron thy brother was gathered. For ye rebelled against My Commandment... to sanctify Me at the water before their eyes* (Num. 27:12-14).

Although his request was denied, the meekness in Moses is demonstrated when he does not complain.

David is another illustration that, regardless of how influential a person may be, God cannot permit a chosen one to live above the Law. *David said... I have sinned.... Nathan said... The LORD also hath put away thy sin.... Howbeit, because by this deed thou hast given great occasion to the enemies of the LORD to blaspheme, the child also that is born unto thee shall surely die* (II Sam. 12:13-14). *Thus saith the LORD... the sword shall never depart from thine house; because thou hast despised Me, and hast taken the wife of Uriah the Hittite to be thy wife* (12:7-10). The believer was *bought with a price: therefore* (he is instructed) *glorify God in your body, and in your spirit, which are God's* (I Cor. 6:20). When we glorify God in this way, we can no longer regard personal abilities and possessions as our own.

We need to recognize that since we are set apart to magnify the Lord, we must live righteously before an unholy world as those saved from eternal hell. *Be not deceived: neither fornicators... nor adulterers, nor effeminate, nor abusers of themselves with mankind, Nor thieves, nor covetous... nor revilers, nor extortioners, shall inherit the Kingdom of God. And such were some of you: but ye are washed, but ye are sanctified* (6:9-11). Praise the Lord for His forgiveness. *Whether therefore ye eat, or drink, or whatsoever ye do, do all to the glory of God* (I Cor. 10:31).

Thought for Today: Remain faithful to serving the Lord – even when you must step down and release your position.

Christ Portrayed: By the man (Joshua) who would lead the people like a shepherd (Num. 27:17). Jesus said: *I am the Good Shepherd.... My sheep... follow Me* (John 10:11,27).

FEBRUARY 25   Read Numbers 28 – 29

Highlights: Fascinating details of Israel's great Feasts (Festivals), which reveal the many aspects of the love of Christ. After 40 years a second generation prepares to enter the promised land.

All sacrifices, offerings, and ceremonies detailed in Numbers 28 and 29 were designed to cause the children of Israel to gratefully acknowledge the mercies of God. **The LORD spake unto Moses, saying, Command the children of Israel, and say unto them, My offering, and My bread for My sacrifices made by fire, for a sweet savour unto Me, shall ye observe to offer unto Me in their due season** (appointed time) (Num. 28:1-2). Worshipers were led to express their appreciation to the Lord for protection and victory over their enemies, and for supplying their needs. Furthermore, the worshiper experienced the joy of fellowship with God.

Note the precious care which causes God to involve Himself with His people: **My offering, and My bread for My sacrifices . . . for a sweet savour unto Me.** God reveals the value He places upon acceptable gifts brought by those who love Him. Believers recognize that an acceptable gift is not primarily something we *do* for God, but foremost, it is that we *be* the person He created us to be.

The purposes of the sacrifice at the Feast of Tabernacles still remain. The trees that were used for these tabernacles (temporary dwellings) had symbolic meanings. The fig tree would provide shade, as well as remind them of the Lord's protection and provision. The palm tree was the emblem of victory; and the olive tree was a symbol of peace and the presence of God (Neh. 8:15). The willow tree of the brook signified a thriving and blessed people **planted by the rivers of water** (Ps. 1:3).

The Feast of Pentecost (Num. 28:26-31) acknowledged His faithfulness to Israel, to whom He gave **rain from heaven, and fruitful seasons, filling our** (their) **hearts with food and gladness** (Acts 14:17). This Feast was set apart for joyful acknowledgment of the love of God. **The LORD thy God hath blessed thee: And thou shalt rejoice before the LORD thy God** (Deut. 16:10-11).

Blessed is the man that walketh not in the counsel of the ungodly, nor standeth in the way of sinners, nor sitteth in the seat of the scornful. But his delight is in the Law of the LORD (Ps. 1:1-2).

Thought for Today: It is impossible to gain His best when our hearts are obsessed with gaining more and more things of the world.

Christ Revealed: By the Tabernacles (Booths) (Num. 29:12-39; Lev. 23:34). **The Word** (logos, i.e. the sayings of God) **was made** (became) **flesh, and dwelt among us** (John 1:14). The Greek word translated **dwelt** means to "tabernacle or live in a tent temporarily."

FEBRUARY 26   Read Numbers 30 – 31

Highlights: Note the vital principles in today's reading. Integrity *(If a man vow a vow* – Num. 30:2); Vengeance (The Lord is the only One qualified to take vengeance – Heb. 10:30).

When Pharaoh sought to kill Moses, Moses fled Egypt and went to Midian, where he married Zipporah, one of the daughters of Jethro the priest (Gen. 25:2; Ex. 18:1; Num. 10:29; Judg. 1:16). Later, after the Israelites had been in the wilderness for nearly 40 years, the Midianite women and girls, through Balaam's influence, were able to seduce the men of Israel. *The LORD spake unto Moses, saying, Avenge the children of Israel of the Midianites. . . . And Moses spake . . . Arm some of yourselves unto the war, and let them go against the Midianites, and avenge the LORD of Midian. . . . And they slew the kings of Midian . . . Balaam also the son of Beor they slew with the sword* (Num. 31:1-3,8).

Yes, it is the same Balaam who chose to settle in Midian to enjoy his reward. It is doubtful that he intended to stay there long. Listen to his earlier testimony: *Let me die the death of the righteous, and let my last end be like his* (Jacob's) (23:10)! What a sad example of a double minded man who disobeyed the will of God!

Balaam still has many followers today with reputations as spiritual leaders, who believe they can ignore the will of God and still be, eventually, welcomed into heaven. Like Balaam, many may believe in the love, mercy, and patience of God, but forget that He is also a righteous and Holy God who must judge sin.

There are spiritual laws that are just as absolute as natural laws. *Be not deceived; God is not mocked: for whatsoever a man soweth, that shall he also reap* (Gal. 6:7). Sin results in consequences that affect generations to come that often include sorrow, suffering, and a wasted life. God has graciously provided His Word to guide us to the true values of life. To help us set our priorities straight, the Apostle Paul wrote: *Set your affection on things above, not on things on the earth* (Col. 3:2).

When Christ, who is our life, shall appear, then shall ye also appear with Him in glory. Mortify (put to death) *therefore . . . evil concupiscence* (lusts)*, and covetousness, which is idolatry: For which things' sake the wrath of God cometh on the children of disobedience* (Col. 3:4-6).

Thought for Today: All earthly treasures cannot compare to an eternal inheritance.

Christ Revealed: As the Ruling One who will righteously judge all sinners (Num. 31:1-17). *In righteousness He doth judge* (Rev. 19:11; II Thess. 1:7-9; Jude 1:14-15).

FEBRUARY 27   Read Numbers 32 – 33

Highlights: The Amorites and the rest of the Canaanites were to be expelled so Israel could possess the promised land. Sad summary of the wilderness journeys – 38 wasted years.

Reuben, Gad, and Manasseh asked for permission to settle in the territory recently captured on the east side of Jordan – just across the Jordan River, but outside the promised land. ***The children of Reuben and the children of Gad had a very great multitude of cattle: and when they saw the land . . . behold, the place was a place for cattle . . . Wherefore, said they . . . bring us not over Jordan. And Moses said . . . Shall your brethren go to war, and shall ye sit here? And wherefore discourage ye the heart of the children of Israel from going over into the land which the L<small>ORD</small> hath given them? . . . be sure your sin will find you out*** (Num. 32:1-23). Their reasoning for wanting to settle outside the promised land may have been good from a financial point of view, but it was one of compromise. Only one judge or deliverer came from these tribes – Jephthah the Gileadite.

The God-appointed territory for all the tribes **was inside Canaan**, not nearby. The two and one-half tribes were willing to give up their birthright in the promised land for what appeared to be material gain. The unity of the nation, their nearness to the Tabernacle, and the presence of God should have been uppermost in their desires.

We have no record that the Reubenites or the Gadites ever rejected Jehovah as their God. They still expected the blessings and security of God, but did not want to give up the lush grasslands to fulfill His will. Their association with heathen neighbors on the east side of Jordan eventually led them into idolatry, and they were the first of the tribes to be taken captive (I Chr. 5:25-26).

Like the Reubenites and the Gadites, many Christians today make decisions that are influenced by material advantages. Business, social advancement or an atmosphere of prominence often are chosen rather than the will of God. A worldly policy often overrules spiritual separation, but it is self-deceiving and self-defeating. We cannot ***serve two masters*** (Matt. 6:24). People who are faithful and obedient always find ways to please God; others will make excuses. ***They that are Christ's have crucified the flesh with the affections and lusts*** (Gal. 5:24).

Thought for Today: Men of faith find ways to obey God – others settle for excuses.

Christ Revealed: Through the promised land – filled with abundance, as well as protection, for those who live in harmony with His Word (Num. 33:50-54). *I am come that they might have life, and that they might have it more abundantly* (John 10:10).

FEBRUARY 28   Read Numbers 34 – 35

Highlights: God lays out the boundaries of the land He gave His people after they fought for it. He provides for those dedicated to His service. God reveals how to deal with manslaughter and murder.

God provided cities of refuge to protect those who had accidentally killed someone. ***Among the cities which ye shall give unto the Levites there shall be six cities for refuge, which ye shall appoint for the manslayer*** (Num. 35:6).

Even if the act was proven to be accidental, the manslayer was required to remain in the city of refuge until the death of the high priest. As long as he was there, he was protected from the avenger (the nearest male relative of the victim). The death of the high priest "atoned" for the manslayer and portrayed Christ's death to atone for our sins. The manslayer could then leave as a free person with no fear of being put to death.

However, if the incident was proven to be deliberate murder, ***the murderer shall be put to death. . . . ye shall take no satisfaction for the life of a murderer . . . but he shall be surely put to death. . . . So ye shall not pollute the land wherein ye are: for blood it defileth the land: and the land cannot be cleansed of the blood that is shed therein, but by the blood of him that shed it. Defile not therefore the land which ye shall inhabit*** (35:30-34). There was to be no consideration of time in prison, the possibility of reform, or a financial settlement. The guilty person was immediately delivered to the avenger of blood to be put to death. God said that to spare the life of a murderer would defile the nation, for the murderer not only had destroyed one created ***in the image of God*** (Gen. 1:26-27), but also had intentionally taken from God His authority over that life.

Murder does not mean the taking of another's life in self-defense or in time of war. The Lord often commanded the Israelites to defend their country and themselves, and directed them to bring judgment on ungodly nations through war.

In the New Testament, Christ revealed that hate and anger are sinful since they often lead to murder (Matt. 5:21-22). God expects more from His followers, who have been saved by the blood of His Son, than merely refraining from murder. God demands the highest respect for human life, for man was created in His image. He commanded: ***Love one another; as I have loved you*** (John 13:34).

Thought for Today: God demands the highest respect for human life, for He created man in His image.

Christ Revealed: By the cities of refuge. Christ is our Refuge from the judgment of God and the curse of the Law. ***We . . . have fled for refuge to lay hold upon the hope set before us . . . even Jesus*** (Heb. 6:18-20).

FEBRUARY 29 — Numbers 36

Highlights: Laws concerning female inheritance within their patriarchal tribe.

Five *daughters of Zelophehad... of the families of Manasseh the son of Joseph.... stood before Moses, and before Eleazar the priest, and before the princes and all the congregation, by the door of the Tabernacle* (Num. 27:1-2), awaiting a decision concerning their tribal territory after they married. *Moses brought their cause before the L*ORD (27:5). The Lord declared through Moses: *Let them marry to whom they think best; only to the family of the tribe of their father shall they marry.... for every one of the children of Israel shall keep himself to the inheritance of the tribe of his fathers* (36:6-7).

Although they had the legal right to marry anyone they chose, they were to consider the responsibility that rested on their actions. To marry someone from another tribe would forfeit their father's inheritance. The decision involved an important principle of denying one's own personal satisfaction and remaining faithful to fulfilling the will of God. *Even as the L*ORD *commanded Moses, so did the daughters of Zelophehad* (36:10).

No one should overlook how perfectly the request of the five *daughters of Zelophehad* corresponds to our relationship with Christ. We are often faced with personal satisfaction that is not sinful but which can cause us to relinquish other spiritual opportunities.

In contrast, no one who remains true to Christ forfeits the best in life. A commitment to the Word of God preserves and enhances, rather than hinders, the enjoyment of one's life. Our enemy Satan often appears as an angel of light, seeking our consent to yield, just once, so that he can gain a foothold. If we continue to yield to his deceptions, we may eventually turn away from the Lord.

The Book of Hebrews continues the warning of God: *Harden not your hearts, as in the provocation, in the day of temptation* (testing) *in the wilderness.... Take heed, brethren, lest there be in any of you an evil heart of unbelief, in departing* (turning away) *from the Living God* (Heb. 3:8,12-13; Ps. 95:8).

Thought for Today: We always miss the Lord's best when we neglect His Word.

Christ Revealed: As *the inheritance of the children of Israel* (Num. 36:7). While they were given an inheritance of the land that will pass away, we have been given a greater inheritance, one that will not pass away. *Blessed be the God and Father of our Lord Jesus Christ, which according to His abundant mercy hath begotten* (i.e. through spiritual birth) *us again unto a lively* (living) *hope by the resurrection of Jesus Christ from the dead, To an inheritance incorruptible* (imperishable)*, and undefiled, and that fadeth not away, reserved in heaven for you* (I Pet. 1:3-4).

Introduction To The Book Of DEUTERONOMY

The events of the Book of Deuteronomy took place in the 40th year after the Israelites left Egypt and during the final weeks of Moses' life. At that time, the new generation of Israelites was camped on the Plains of Moab, about to enter the promised land (Deut. 29:1-5).

From Genesis through Numbers, the love of God was never mentioned; but now, four times, Moses revealed: *He loved thy fathers. ... and redeemed you out of the house of bondmen* (slavery) (4:37; 7:7-8; 10:15; 23:5). *And He brought us out ... that He might bring us in, to give us the land which He sware unto our fathers* (6:23).

Moses stated that the Lord had made a Covenant with their parents at Horeb (Mount Sinai), but they had continually failed to keep it. After giving the Mosaic Law to the new generation, Moses stressed the importance of obeying the Word of God: *Love the Lord thy God with all thine heart.... diligently keep the Commandments of the Lord your God* (6:5,17). He reminded them of the importance of being loyal to God: *What doth the Lord thy God require of thee, but to fear the Lord thy God, to walk in all His ways, and to love Him, and to serve the Lord thy God ... for thy good* (10:12-13; 27:1 – 29:1; 30:20). The two key words *for thy good* are *obey* and *do*, which occur more than 170 times in this Book. The central message of Deuteronomy as well as the entire Bible is to *love the Lord thy God with all thine heart*.

Jesus said: *He that hath My Commandments, and keepeth them, he it is that loveth Me. . . . Ye are My friends, if ye do whatsoever I command you* (John 14:21,24; 15:14). The beloved Apostle John was led to write: *Hereby we do know that we know Him, if we keep His Commandments. He that saith, I know Him, and keepeth not His Commandments, is a liar, and the truth is not in Him* (I John 2:3-4). *Blessed are they that do His Commandments, that they may have right to the tree of life* (Rev. 22:14).

Moses prophesied that *the Lord thy God will raise up unto thee a Prophet from the midst of thee, of thy brethren, like unto me; unto Him ye shall hearken* (Deut. 18:15,18-19). Almost 1500 years later, this prophecy was applied to Jesus (Acts 3:20-23; 7:37).

The Book of Deuteronomy ends with the death of Moses after his commission of Joshua, a man *full of the spirit of wisdom,* to lead the Israelites into the promised land (Deut. 34:1-9).

MARCH 1   Read Deuteronomy 1 – 2

Highlights: Moses' review of Israel's 40 years after leaving Egypt; commanded to leave Mount Sinai; commanded to enter the promised land *but* (they) **rebelled against the Commandment of the LORD** (Deut. 1:43); 38 years of wanderings.

Despite their miraculous deliverance from Egypt, the provision of manna and water every day, and the cloud by day and fire by night to guide them, the adult generation of Israelites that left Egypt continually complained and found fault. They refused to enter the promised land and trust God for victory over the Canaanites.

Consequently, the first generation rejected the will of God and wasted their lives wandering in the wilderness until they all had died except Joshua and Caleb, who had said: **Let us go up at once, and possess it** (Num. 13:30).

Some today are like the Israelites who found excuses for their disobedience to God, but others choose to be like Caleb and Joshua, whose faith led them to be faithful servants regardless of dangers and adversities. After the older generation died, Moses began **to declare** (Deut. 1:5) the original message God had given the Israelites nearly 40 years earlier. **To declare this Law** meant more than to merely rehearse it; it meant to go into the Word of God to get a fuller understanding of what God meant. Four times, Moses spoke a new revelation of the love of God for His people (4:37; 7:7-8; 10:15; 23:5). This realization strengthened the new generation's faith in Him for whatever lay ahead. Christians can rejoice that, by faith in the Word of God, they can overcome the "giants" in their lives: **The lust of the flesh, and the lust of the eyes, and the pride of life** (I John 2:15-17). It is our privilege as Christians to be **doers of the Word, and not hearers only** (James 1:22).

Regardless of adverse circumstances, loving submission to the Lord develops our faith in His ability to guide, protect, and provide for our every need. We should **live . . . to** (do) **the will of God. For the time past of our life** (lives) **may suffice us to have wrought the will of the Gentiles** (unbelievers)**, when we walked in lasciviousness** (sensuality, indecency)**, lusts, excess of wine, revellings, banquetings, and abominable idolatries** (I Pet. 4:2-3).

Thought for Today: In the midst of "giant" problems, strength to be an overcomer through the Holy Spirit is available to all who trust in Him.

Christ Portrayed: By Moses, who **spake unto the children of Israel, according unto all that the LORD had given him in commandment unto them** (Deut. 1:3). Jesus faithfully told others everything God told Him to say. **I do nothing of Myself; but as My Father hath taught Me, I speak these things** (John 8:28).

MARCH 2 — Read Deuteronomy 3 – 4

Highlights: Still on the east side of the Jordan River outside Canaan, the Israelites defeat a giant king; division of land east of the Jordan; Moses not allowed to enter the promised land – emphasizing the importance of doing the will of God and not claiming credit for what God is doing; cities of refuge established east of the Jordan.

Moses reminded the new generation of Israelites that living according to the Word of God would bring lasting fulfillment. He began to explain his first message which highlighted the importance of keeping all the Word of God that was given to their parents nearly 40 years earlier at Mount Sinai (Deut. 1:3-5).

That ye may live (4:1) meant that the Israelites would enjoy the best in life. The one essential requirement for remaining in the land of promise was **obedience** to the Word of God. Moses warned them: *When thou shalt . . . do evil in the sight of the LORD thy God . . . ye shall soon utterly perish. . . .* (God desires that you) *seek Him with all thy heart* (4:25-29).

We too need a daily reminder to *take heed to thyself, and keep thy soul* (inner thoughts) *diligently, lest thou forget the things which thine eyes have seen, and lest they depart from thy heart . . . teach them thy sons* (children) (4:9).

Unfortunately, unless children are taught to respect their parents, they seldom learn to respect and obey God, who has promised: *Train up a child in the way he should go: and when he is old, he will not depart from it* (Prov. 22:6).

The Bible provides our only true source for knowing the will and character of our Creator. As we read the Bible with a desire to obey it, the Holy Spirit makes the Word *quick, and powerful* (Heb. 4:12) so that it becomes a reality in our lives.

The people of God often face seemingly impossible situations. But the Lord has provided the Christian with His Word, which is the *sword of the Spirit* (Eph. 6:17) and the *shield of faith* (6:16). Since *faith cometh by hearing, and hearing by the Word of God* (Rom. 10:17), we should *keep therefore . . . His Commandments . . . that it may go well with thee, and with thy children after thee* (Deut. 4:40).

Thought for Today: It is our faith in God – not our strength or wisdom – that leads to victory.

Christ Portrayed: By Joshua, who led the Israelites into their inheritance (Deut. 3:28). Through Jesus we receive His promised *inheritance among them which are sanctified* (set apart) *by faith that is in Me* (Acts 26:18).

MARCH 3   Read Deuteronomy 5 – 7

Highlights: The Ten Commandments are the foundation of the moral laws for all mankind; they are the one portion of our Bible written by *the finger of God* (Ex. 31:18).

The Hebrew word translated **our God** is **Elohenu**, meaning "our" Gods." This, then, is what Moses said: **Hear, O Israel: The LORD our God**(s) **is one LORD** (Deut. 6:4). The word **one** (*'echad*) expresses "one" in the collective sense and signifies a compound unity. Thus, **one LORD** reveals the One True God as being one yet expressed in three distinct persons: Father, Son, and Holy Spirit.

Consider these revelations: **Let Us make man in Our image** (Gen. 1:26); **as one of Us** (3:22); **let Us go** (11:7); and **who will go for Us** (Is. 6:8)? The same Hebrew word *'echad* is used in Genesis 2:24 where man and woman become **one flesh**. Even with numerous children, they are still "one" family.

The Hebrew word **yacheed** is "one" in the sense of absolute one. But, God accurately referred to Himself by the word *'echad*, meaning a compound unity. Those who reject Jesus as fully God, as well as fully Man, are rejecting the true revelation of God the Father, God the Son, and God the Holy Spirit. **For ye are all the children of God by faith in Christ Jesus** (Gal. 3:26). **In whom we have redemption through His blood, the forgiveness of sins** (Eph. 1:7). **God... created all things by Jesus Christ** (3:9). **And that every tongue should confess that Jesus Christ is Lord, to the glory of God the Father** (Phil. 2:11). **For there is one God, and one Mediator between God and men, the Man Christ Jesus** (I Tim. 2:5).

In the beginning was the Word (**Logos**, i.e., Divine Expression of God)**, and the Word was with God, and the Word was God. ... And the Word was made** (became) **flesh, and dwelt among us** (John 1:1,14).

The real reason some insist on believing the false theory of evolution is that if they acknowledge that God created all things, they must submit to Him as Lord of their lives.

There are a thousand voices clamoring for our attention. But, when we realize that there is only One True God and He has provided one Guide to live by, we must **be still, and know that I am God** (Ps. 46:10). Notice that He does not say merely: **Be still**, but He tells us something so awesome: **I am God**.

Thought for Today: Rejoice! Jesus will soon return to rule the world as King of kings.

Christ Revealed: Through the land flowing **with milk and honey** (Deut. 6:3). This pictures Christ who provides for our needs. **Seek ye first the Kingdom of God, and His righteousness; and all these things shall be added unto you** (Matt. 6:33).

MARCH 4 — Read Deuteronomy 8 – 10

Highlights: Discover "gems" from our Heavenly Father in these three chapters. The purpose of God is given for all His Commandments (Deut. 8:1). There's a divine promise included (9:3). Reminder of the result of rebellion.

Jesus began His earthly ministry by quoting from Deuteronomy: ***Man shall not live by bread alone, but by <u>every</u> <u>word</u> that proceedeth out of the mouth of God*** (Deut. 8:3; Matt. 4:4). This was His response to Satan when he tempted Jesus to make bread for Himself from stones after His 40-day fast in the desert: ***If Thou be the Son of God, command that these stones be made bread*** (4:3), meaning: "If You are the Son of God, why should You, of all people, need to remain hungry?"

Satan attempted to lure Jesus into using His Deity to satisfy His physical need. But, Jesus quoted Scripture: ***It is written again, Thou shalt not tempt the Lord thy God*** (4:7; Deut. 6:16). He again told Satan: ***It is written, Thou shalt worship the Lord thy God, and Him only shalt thou serve*** (Matt. 4:10; Deut. 6:13-14).

Throughout His ministry, Jesus quoted Scripture when answering His critics and set an example for us to whom He also said: ***He that hath My Commandments, and keepeth them*** (guards with his life and obeys)***, he it is that loveth Me.... If a man love Me, he will keep My words*** (John 14:21-23).

For the Word of God is quick (living)***, and powerful*** (Heb. 4:12), and it is the only means Jesus used to defeat Satan. As we continue reading all of the Word of God, then the Holy Spirit is able to bring it to our minds when we need it.

We need to remember Moses' warning to Israel: ***Beware that thou forget not the Lord thy God, in not keeping His Commandments... And thou say in thine heart*** (to yourself)***, My power and the might of mine hand hath gotten me this wealth. But thou shalt remember*** (and praise) ***the Lord thy God: for it is He that giveth thee power to get wealth.... serve the Lord thy God with all thy heart and with all thy soul, To keep the Commandments of the Lord... for thy good*** (benefit) (Deut. 8:11,17-18; 10:12-13).

Thought for Today: Does Jesus get all the credit for your achievements?

Christ Revealed: Through the ***shittim*** (acacia) ***wood*** used to make the Ark of the Covenant (Deut. 10:3). Acacia wood, a desert growth, is symbolic of Christ in His human form.

MARCH 5   **Read Deuteronomy 11 – 13**

Highlights: Warning against false gods and adding to or taking away anything from His Word. Just think! We are to cleave (hold fast) to the Lord (Deut. 11:22)! We must choose between loyalty to and love for the Word of God and enjoying His blessing, or conforming to worldly standards that are inspired by Satan (12:28).

At Sinai, God had directed Moses to tell the people: *If ye will obey My voice indeed, and keep My Covenant, then ye shall be a peculiar treasure unto Me above all people* (Ex. 19:5). The importance of obedience was emphasized 19 times in the instructions concerning the building of the Tabernacle (chap. 38 through 40). Moses repeated to the new generation what the Lord had said to their parents and reminded them of how important it is to *diligently keep all these Commandments which I command you, to do them, to love the LORD your God, to walk in all His ways, and to cleave* (hold fast) *unto Him* (Deut. 11:22).

To perpetuate loyalty and love for God in future generations, every Israelite was to live in subjection to the Word of God and also to teach it to their children. As Christians, we too should love the Lord and be obedient to Him. We also are responsible to teach our children to truly love God their Heavenly Father and obey Him.

Moses stood in sight of the promised land and said: *I set before you this day a blessing and a curse; A blessing, if ye obey . . . and a curse, if ye will not obey* (11:26-28). Let's not be so concerned about praying for blessings as we are with being obedient to His Word; then, God will take care of the blessings. Another fundamental principle for pleasing God is to *rejoice in all that ye put your hand unto, ye and your households, wherein the LORD thy God hath blessed thee* (12:7).

What our children will become is often influenced by what they learn from us about our values in life. That is why parents need to devote time to developing the minds of their young children. It is of utmost importance that parents guide even the youngest child to reverence God, to worship Him, to pray, and to recognize the Bible as the voice of God speaking directly to them.

It is vital in this time of moral chaos to provide our children with a strong spiritual home environment that includes prayer at meal times and family Bible reading and devotions every day.

Thought for Today: Christian parents are responsible to teach their children the way they should live (Prov. 22:6).

Christ Revealed: Through the *burnt offerings* which were totally consumed. These typified Christ's total offering of Himself to death (Deut. 12:6; Heb. 10:5-7). *For the bodies of those beasts, whose blood is brought into the Sanctuary* (Holy Place) *by the high priest for sin, are burned without the camp. Wherefore Jesus also, that He might sanctify* (make holy) *the people with His own blood, suffered without the gate* (Heb. 13:11-12).

MARCH 6   Read Deuteronomy 14 – 16

Highlights: Clean and unclean food; the Law of the tithe; dedication of the firstborn; three Feasts to be observed; Passover celebrated, foreshadowing Christ's redemptive work on the cross as the ultimate Sacrificial Lamb; judges and justice.

The prosperity of the Israelites in the promised land did not depend on advanced agricultural techniques but on their obedience to the Word of God (Deut. 11:10-15).

Tithing reminded the Israelites that they, as well as the land, belonged to the Lord. Before all other considerations, tithes to the Lord were to be given first. Furthermore, no Israelite could come before the Lord without an offering commensurate with his income (16:16-17).

The Israelites were to "rejoice" with a heartfelt appreciation for the privilege of honoring God with their tithes and offerings, **that the LORD thy God may bless thee** (14:29).

Giving to the poor was recognition that all our possessions actually belong to the Lord. We are merely stewards of the love of God, distributing to the less fortunate.

When we give to someone who needs our help, we are loaning to the Lord. **He that hath pity upon the poor lendeth unto the LORD; and that which he hath given will He pay him again** (Prov. 19:17). Giving a cup of cold water in His Name is the same as giving to the Lord. **But whoso hath this world's good, and seeth his brother have need, and shutteth up his bowels of compassion from him, how dwelleth the love of God in him** (I John 3:17)?

Over 630 years before the Law was given to Moses, Abraham – father of the faithful (Rom. 4:11) – paid a tenth (tithe) to **Melchizedek ... priest of the Most High God** as an acceptable offering to the Lord (Gen. 14:18-20). Both tithing (Luke 18:12) and the giving of offerings (21:4; Acts 24:17) were still being practiced by the Israelites during New Testament times. Today, the Lord's ministries, missionaries, churches, and Bible schools are being sustained through the tithes and offerings of His people. Jesus said: **Render** (Give) **therefore unto Caesar the things which are Caesar's; and unto God the things that are God's** (Matt. 22:21).

Thought for Today: Tithing is acknowledgment of the Lord's ownership of everything!

Christ Revealed: Through the year of release, which typifies Christ's forgiveness of our sins (Deut. 15:1). This should teach us to forgive others, even as He has forgiven us (Matt. 6:14-15). **Be ye kind one to another, tenderhearted, forgiving one another, even as God for Christ's sake hath forgiven you** (Eph. 4:32).

MARCH 7 — Read Deuteronomy 17 – 20

Highlights: Even kings must obey the Laws of God and His Word. Every Israelite king was commanded to read the Law of God (the Books of Moses) *all the days of his life* (Deut. 17:19). Learn how to recognize the difference between a true prophet and a false prophet (18:22).

Many centuries after Moses foretold of the Prophet (Jesus – Deut. 18:15-19), the prophet Jeremiah foretold that, at Christ's return, God *will make a new Covenant with* His people who will hearken (Jer. 31:31-34). In conversation with His critics, Jesus said that both Moses and the Scriptures bore witness of Him: *For had ye believed Moses, ye would have believed Me: for he wrote of Me. But if ye believe not his writings* (Genesis – Deuteronomy), *how shall ye believe My words* (John 5:46-47)?

Jesus declared to Pilate: *My Kingdom is not of this world*, meaning it has no earthly origin but is a spiritual Kingdom (18:36). On the Day of Pentecost, Peter quoted Moses' prophecy and boldly proclaimed that Jesus had fulfilled that prophecy: *A Prophet shall the Lord your God raise up unto you of your brethren, like unto me; Him shall ye hear in all things whatsoever He shall say unto you. . . . Yea, and all the prophets from Samuel and those that follow after . . . have likewise foretold of these days* (Acts 3:22-24; comp. Deut. 18:18-19). While the Jews sought both the promised Prophet and the Messiah (John 1:25), they failed to recognize Jesus as being both the Prophet and Messiah whom Moses foretold. Christ has the sovereign right *as a Son over His own House* (Heb. 3:6) to be Master in His House (the Church). The keys belong to Him, and He must have control. He dwells within *His own House*, as a life within a life.

The writer of the Book of Hebrews wrote: *He that despised* (rejected) *Moses' Law died without mercy . . . how much sorer* (more severe) *punishment, suppose ye, shall he be thought worthy, who hath trodden under foot the Son of God, and hath counted the blood of the Covenant* (Agreement), *wherewith he was sanctified, an unholy thing, and hath done despite unto* (insulted) *the Spirit of grace* (Heb. 10:28-29)?

Thought for Today: Christ makes intercession for all who come to the Father through Him.

Christ Revealed: Through the Old Testament sacrifices which were made without blemish or defect (Deut. 17:1). Christ was perfectly pure from all sin and all appearance of evil. *Christ . . . without blemish and without spot* (I Pet. 1:19).

MARCH 8   **Read Deuteronomy 21 – 23**

Highlights: Read about laws, rules, regulations, and responsibilities to fulfull the purpose of God to preserve the cleanliness and holiness of the promised land.

The Israelites had been taught that, because God had created all things, everything belonged to Him and they were only caretakers of His possessions. Because of their Covenant relationship with the Lord, they were even responsible for the welfare of their neighbor's property.

The person we help may or may not appreciate or even deserve the kindness we express. Our responsibility, however, is not as much to the person who needs our help as it is to the Lord, who is the true Owner of all creation, and who provides us with the opportunities to express His love to the lost and unloved.

Under the laws of most countries, one is not held legally responsible for failing to help prevent someone else's financial loss. But, as the people of God, our loving concern should cause us to respond to another's needs in a spirit of Christlike love.

Jesus illustrated this by saying: **A certain man went down from Jerusalem to Jericho, and fell among thieves, which . . . wounded him . . . leaving him half dead. . . . a certain priest. . . . And likewise a Levite . . . looked on him, and passed by on the other side** (Luke 10:30-32). Perhaps they had completed their religious responsibilities in Jerusalem and were on their way home to Jericho, the city of palm trees, where many of the Temple priests lived. To stop and help this man could have "defiled" them according to their traditions and made them ceremonially unclean; or, perhaps, they felt he was undeserving. **But a certain Samaritan . . . had compassion on him** (10:33). He wasn't looking for excuses to avoid giving aid or questioning whether the hurting man was deserving of help. Instead, this outcast from Samaria, who was much despised by the religious Jews, demonstrated a Christlike love by providing for his care.

Our Lord taught His followers to go far beyond merely helping to care for the property of a friend or neighbor. Jesus commanded His followers: **Love your enemies, bless them that curse you, do good to them that hate you, and pray for them which despitefully use you, and persecute you; That ye may be the children of your Father which is in heaven** (Matt. 5:44-45).

Thought for Today: We should take advantage of opportunities to express Christ' love.

Christ Revealed: Christ died on the cross in our place, submitting to the penalty of death imposed by the Law for our sins (Deut. 21:23). In the evening He was taken down from the cross, signifying the Law had been satisfied (John 19:31). **Christ hath redeemed us from the curse of the Law, being made a curse for us** (Gal. 3:13).

MARCH 9   Read Deuteronomy 24 – 27

Highlights: God speaks of His blessings at Mount Gerizim; curses are pronounced at Mount Ebal. The blessings result from obedience and faithfulness. The curses result from disobeying the Word of God! Take note of the Law of the offering of firstfruits.

Moses, the lawgiver and prophet, placed great emphasis on the necessity of honesty and truthfulness in all areas of life. When presenting the Law, he warned against two sets of weights and measures – one for buying and the other for selling (Deut. 25:13-16). It is of utmost importance in our business dealings with others not to take advantage of them or misrepresent the facts. We must conduct our business transactions in a true Christian way that conforms to the character of our Heavenly Father. It is cruel to neglect to pay what one owes. God hates lying and thievery. We choose whether to exercise the principles of justice and equity or to take advantage of others. Dishonesty is expressed in various ways: wasting time on the job, taking what doesn't belong to us, unethically conducting business, and lying. These are greatly displeasing to God.

Our conduct with others goes much deeper than either word or deed; it goes to the hidden motives of our hearts and reveals what we truly are. Jesus taught: **From within, out of the heart of men, proceed ... All ... evil things ... and defile the man** (Mark 7:21-23; comp. Matt. 15:19-20). This means that the thoughts and actions of a Christian should always express what Jesus would think and do.

The attitude of fairness and consideration for others' well-being applies to a Christian's daily relationships with others. It is possible to have bitter thoughts while doing kind deeds and to say loving words while having wrong attitudes and motives. But, our Adamic nature and its self-serving conduct can be overcome by the Christ-centered nature that He has bestowed within us. The self-centered "I" must give way to Christ and His control.

We do not war after the flesh: (For the weapons of our warfare are not carnal (fleshly)**, but mighty through God to the pulling down of strong holds;) ... bringing into captivity every thought to the obedience of Christ** (II Cor. 10:3-5).

Thought for Today: A Christian should resist all temptation to lie, cheat, or steal. These evils will result in the judgment of God.

Christ Revealed: Through the deliverance of the Israelites from Egypt and Pharaoh (Deut. 26:8). **Our Lord Jesus Christ, Who gave Himself for our sins, that He might deliver us from this present evil world** (Gal. 1:3-4).

MARCH 10   Read Deuteronomy 28

Highlights: This powerful chapter has been used by the Holy Spirit to bring many to receive Christ as their Savior as well as to warn of the destruction of those who ignore Him.

The Israelites' enjoyment of **His good treasure** (Deut. 28:12) was inseparably linked with obedience to the Word of God. God bestows **His good treasure** of blessings on all who read His Word with a desire to know His will – that we **might walk worthy of the Lord unto all pleasing, being fruitful in every good work, and increasing in the knowledge of God** (Col. 1:10). When we delight in His ways and pray: **Open Thou mine eyes, that I may behold wondrous things out of Thy Law** (Ps. 119:18), we will experience great satisfaction.

Moses further warned: **If thou wilt not hearken unto the voice of the LORD thy God, to observe to do all His Commandments. ... The LORD shall make the pestilence** (disease) **cleave unto thee. ... The LORD shall smite thee .... thou shalt not prosper in thy ways** (Deut. 28:15,21-22,29).

Almost four times as many verses warn of the consequences of disobedience than of the blessings for obedience. The obvious conclusion of the Word of God is that each sin has a consequence – and it definitely does. However, this fact can also be misapplied, as in the case when Jesus' **disciples asked Him, saying, Master, who did sin, this man, or his parents, that he was born blind? Jesus answered, Neither hath this man sinned, nor his parents: but that the works of God should be made manifest** (revealed) **in him** (John 9:2-3). What seemed to be a curse became a blessing, for it brought this man to his Savior. This points out that not all suffering is the result of sin and not all wealth and good health are necessarily a blessing from God. Consider the rich young ruler who chose to keep his wealth; it kept him from denying self and becoming a follower of Jesus (Matt. 19:16-22).

Victory over our present-day "Canaanite" giants – **the lust of the flesh, and the lust of the eyes, and the pride of life** (I John 2:16) – is achieved, not because of our abilities or lack of them but because of our desire to do the will of God. Overcoming power is found in cooperating with the Holy Spirit, who dwells within us. We too can say: **I can do all things** (that He calls me to do) **through Christ which strengtheneth me** (Phil. 4:13).

Thought for Today: God takes note of every thought of the heart.

Christ Revealed: As the One from whom our blessings come (Deut. 28:1-2). *Blessed be the God ... who hath blessed us with all spiritual blessings ... in Christ* (Eph. 1:3).

MARCH 11   Read Deuteronomy 29 – 31

Highlights: Moses begins his last words to Israel. He reviews their past, once again clearly emphasizing the blessings of obedience. He pleads with them: ***Choose life*** (Deut. 30:19).

The Creator chose the small Israelite nation through whom He would reveal Himself as the One True God. Moses continued to warn the people of the consequences of disregarding their Covenant responsibilities to the One True God: ***Lest there should be among you man, or woman, or family, or tribe, whose heart turneth away this day from the L<small>ORD</small> our God, to go and serve the gods of these nations . . . And the anger of the L<small>ORD</small> was kindled against this land, to bring upon it all the curses that are written in this Book*** (Deut. 29:18-27).

The chosen people of God confirmed their Covenant with God by promising to keep it. The Covenant was for a lifetime ***to love the L<small>ORD</small> thy God, to walk in His ways, and to keep His Commandments . . . the L<small>ORD</small> thy God shall bless thee. . . . I have set before you life and death . . . therefore choose life*** (30:16-19).

When the Israelites entered the promised land, they were surrounded by influences that would test their loyalty to the One True God. They were faced with people who seemed to have "advantages" such as chariots for war and an "attractive" religious system with images they could see and touch. The Israelites would be tempted to depart from loyalty to God. In one of Joshua's last messages, he proclaimed: ***When ye . . . have gone and served other gods . . . then shall the anger of the L<small>ORD</small> be kindled against you, and ye shall perish quickly from off the good land*** (Josh. 23:16). Israel's One True God is our God. There is no other. Israel's Messiah is our Savior. There is no other. Christians are also the people of God by a far more precious ***Covenant*** (Heb. 8:6) than that of Abraham, and we too are tempted by the many false gods that surround us.

As the nations of the world become our near neighbors, some people are deceived into assuming that the false gods of these nations are the One True God who is called by another name, and that their religions are some of the many ways to worship the Almighty God. But all worshipers of these false gods reject ***that blessed hope, and the glorious appearing of the great God and our Saviour Jesus Christ*** (Titus 2:13).

Thought for Today: Our love for the Lord is the same as our love for the Word of God.

Christ Revealed: As *life* (Deut. 30:15). Jesus is ***The Resurrection, and The Life*** (John 11:25).

MARCH 12 — Read Deuteronomy 32 – 34

Highlights: The prophetic Song of Moses (Deut. 32:1-43). Don't miss "the Words of Life" and how to **prolong your days** (32:46-47)! Moses blesses the 12 tribes; death of Moses on Mount Nebo; Joshua succeeds Moses.

Moses foretold the blessings and happiness the Israelites would have if they lived in obedience to the Word of God (33:6-29). After conferring spiritual blessings upon each of the tribes, Moses concluded with praise to God: **The eternal God is thy refuge, and underneath are the everlasting arms: and He shall thrust out the enemy from before thee** (33:27). Although it is written: **There arose not a prophet since in Israel like unto Moses, whom the Lord knew face to face** (34:10), he forfeited the privilege of leading Israel into Canaan because of his sin (32:48-52; comp. Num. 20:1-13). Thus he became an example for all Israel that God is Holy and cannot allow His Word to be broken without consequences.

Moses' life had been almost perfect. Just before his death, Moses was all alone, climbing one of the most prominent mountain peaks in Moab from which he could view the promised land though he could not personally enter it. Even though he had been the Lord's lawgiver, he sinned by striking the rock instead of speaking to it as God had told him to do, and the Law did not permit one exception. Moses' penalty illustrates that even forgiveness of sin does not remove its earthly consequences. **For whosoever shall keep the whole Law, and yet offend in one point, he is guilty of all** (James 2:10).

Centuries later, Moses, symbolizing the Law of God, stood on Mount Hermon in the promised land with Elijah, who symbolized the prophets of God. Together they talked with Jesus as He **was transfigured before them: and His face did shine as the sun, and His raiment was white as the light. And, behold, there appeared unto them Moses and Elias** (Elijah) **talking with Him. Then answered Peter, and said ... let us make here three tabernacles; one for Thee, and one for Moses, and one for Elias** (Elijah)**. While he yet spake, behold, a bright cloud overshadowed them: and behold a voice out of the cloud ... said, This is My beloved Son, in whom I am well pleased; hear ye Him** (Matt. 17:2-5).

Thought for Today: Express the same patience to others that you expect to receive from the Lord.

Christ Portrayed: As **our Rock** (Deut. 32:31). Christ was **that spiritual Rock** (Petra) **that followed** (accompanied) **them** (I Cor. 10:4).

Introduction To The Book Of JOSHUA

The Book of Joshua covers a period of about 25 years and is a continuation of the history of Israel recorded in Numbers.

God spoke to Joshua, saying: **This Book of the Law shall not depart out of thy mouth; but thou shalt meditate therein day and night, that thou mayest observe to do according to all that is written therein: for then thou shalt make thy way prosperous, and then thou shalt have good success** (Josh. 1:8).

Major events in the Book of Joshua:

1. Two men spy out the land and make a covenant with Rahab (2:1-24).

2. The Israelites move from Shittim to the eastern bank of the Jordan River and remain three days to **sanctify** themselves (3:1-5).

3. The flood waters of the Jordan are miraculously parted (3:9-17). The Israelites cross the Jordan. **Joshua set up twelve stones in the midst of Jordan** (4:9-24).

4. In the promised land, the Israelites first camp at Gilgal where **the LORD said unto Joshua, Make thee sharp knives, and circumcise again the children** (all males of the new generation) **of Israel the second time** (5:2,5). A second memorial is built at Gilgal (4:20).

5. The first Passover in the promised land is observed (5:10). Jericho and Ai are conquered (6:1 – 8:29).

6. Joshua offered a Burnt Sacrifice and Peace Offering on Mount Ebal, near Jacob's Well. **He wrote there upon the stones a copy of the Law of Moses** (8:32).

7. Deception by the Gibeonites is followed by a peace treaty (9:1-27). War is declared by kings in the south. Joshua conquers them through the miraculous intervention of the Lord (10:1-43).

8. The remaining kings in the land, and their armies, are defeated (11:1-23). The key to conquering the Canaanites is clear: **As the LORD commanded Moses His servant, so did Moses command Joshua, and so did Joshua; he left nothing undone** (11:15).

9. Territory is assigned to the tribes (13:1 – 22:34), except to the tribe of Levi (21:41) which is given 48 cities throughout all the tribes. **There failed not ought of any good thing which the LORD had spoken unto the House of Israel** (21:43-45; see also 1:1-6).

10. Joshua's farewell message is clear: **Be ... very courageous to keep and to do all that is written in the Book of the Law of Moses, that ye turn not aside** (23:6).

MARCH 13   Read Joshua 1 – 3

Highlights: Moses is dead! God chooses Joshua, the servant of Moses, to lead this great multitude. See the miracles as, by faith, the feet of the priests touch the water. At last, after 40 years, the two million children of the adults who were delivered from Egypt enter their promised land.

Joshua was born in Egyptian slavery. While the majority complained and found fault with Moses during their desert trials, Joshua remained a faithful coworker with Moses. In fact, his faith in God almost caused him to be stoned to death by the former generation when he urged them to go into Canaan (see Num. 14:6-10).

To be **brought out** of Egypt was one thing, but it was altogether another to **go over this Jordan** (Josh. 1:2) and thus become committed to fighting against the power of the Canaanites with their **chariots of iron** (17:16) and their armies of giants (Num. 13:33). To do this was to commit themselves to a course which 10 out of 12 spies who reported on the land 38 years earlier had opposed. The crossing of **this Jordan** was a major step of faith which the former generation had refused to take. To the natural eye, they risked losing everything – even their very lives.

By faith, Rahab the harlot decided to put her trust in the One True God and protect the spies. She eventually had the honor of being in the Messianic Line. Christians face a similar choice of faith – whether or not there will be a once-and-for-all abandonment of self to the will of God, so that He is truly first in one's life.

It is one thing to trust Christ as Savior from our sins, but it is another to allow Him to be Master of our will and life. It is one thing to join the people redeemed by God and live by faith; but it is another thing to "cross over Jordan" and **present your bodies a living sacrifice . . . and be not conformed to this world** (Rom. 12:1-2).

When the Lord is leading the way, we will conquer the "giants" in our lives. Victory is assured – whether it is overcoming a Pharaoh, a Red Sea, the wilderness, or other "giants" in our lives, such as fear, lust, jealousy or envy. His grace is sufficient.

But without faith it is impossible to please Him: for he that cometh to God must believe that He is, and that He is a rewarder of them that diligently seek Him (Heb. 11:6).

Thought for Today: Most of us will pass into eternity with unfinished goals; but if our life's work is of God, it will continue to bless others.

Christ Revealed: Through **the scarlet line in the window** that saved Rahab and her household – symbolic of the blood of Christ (Josh. 2:21; Heb. 11:31; James 2:25). **The blood of Jesus Christ His Son cleanseth us from all sin** (I John 1:7).

Joshua's Conquest of Canaan

For hundreds of years Israel had hoped to occupy the land promised to Abraham; now that time had come. The Israelites were encamped at Shittim (Acacia) where Moses had delivered his farewell address, and Joshua had taken command. The qualifications of his success were very clear for the Lord commanded and promised: *This Book of the Law shall not depart out of thy mouth; but thou shalt meditate therein day and night, that thou mayest observe to do according to all that is written therein: for then thou shalt make thy way prosperous, and then thou shalt have good success* (Josh. 1:8). Outline for this map:

1. **Crossing the Jordan** (chap. 3:1 – 5:1)

The priests bearing the Ark of the Covenant led the way as the nation followed at a distance. As their feet touched the water at flood stage, it ceased to flow and they walked across *on dry land* (4:22). This was a repetition of the Exodus miracle.

2. **Preparation that preceded any battle – circumcision and Passover** (chap. 5:2-15)

The nation of Israel then encamped at Gilgal, a site which remained their base of operation for about seven years during the conquest. *The Captain of the LORD's host* reminded Joshua that this new land was holy ground and that He (Christ Pre-incarnate) was leading Israel (5:15).

3. **The Central Campaign** (chap. 6:1 – 8:35)

In obedience to the Word of God, the walls of Jericho fell (6:20). Because of Achan's sin, the Israelites were at first defeated at Ai, but after obeying God's command in dealing with the sin, the city of Ai was reduced to a ruin and the king hanged (8:18-29). Then Israel assembled together at the ancient site of Shechem, between Mount Ebal and Mount Gerizim. An altar was built as the Lord had commanded through Moses and the Law was recorded on stones in Mount Ebal (Deut. 27:1-8; Josh. 8:30-35).

4. **The Southern Campaign** (chap. 9:1 – 10:43)

The Gibeonites decided the only wise course was to join their enemy Israel (9:3-27). The Amorite kings of Jerusalem, Hebron, Jarmuth, Lachish, and Eglon were next to fall (10:1-5). The Lord sent giant hailstones from heaven and the sun and moon stood still to help the Israelites in battle (10:10-14). These five kings fled to Makkedah, where they were found hidden in a cave. Later Joshua slew them, hanged their bodies on trees, and then buried them in the same cave (10:17-27). Joshua next struck deep into the south and west and conquered all the towns of any importance (10:40-42).

5. **The Northern Campaign** (chap. 11:1-15)

With the central and southern parts of the land under Israel's control, a northern coalition made up of the Canaanite, Amorite, Hittite, Perizzite, Jebusite, and Hivite kings united in a vast federation led by Jabin, king of Hazor. Jabin enlisted the kings and their soldiers from as far north as Lake Huleh and as far east as Damascus in Syria, all the kingdoms east of Jordan as far south as the Dead Sea and from the Jezreel Valley on the west bank of the Jordan. He united his armies at the waters of Merom, with all their chariots awaiting the Israelite invasion. In this last and final battle of the conquest, Hazor was burned to the ground; 31 kings had been defeated without one horse or one chariot to aid the Israelites. All of the promised land was now under the control of the Israelites, although pockets of resistance would continue for centuries.

6. **Summary of Israel's wars** (chap. 11:16 – 12:24)

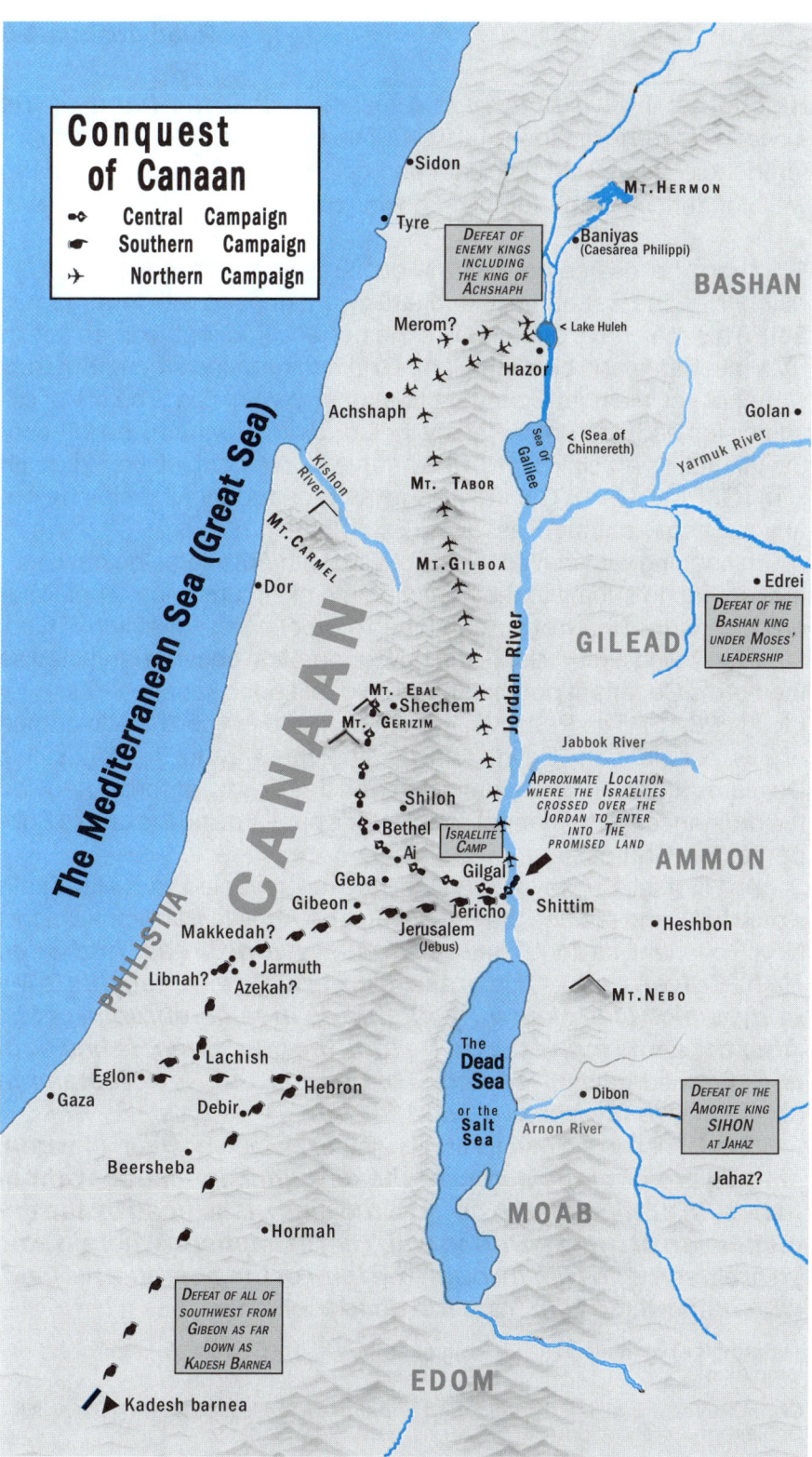

MARCH 14   Read Joshua 4-6

Highlights: Twelve stones are a testimony that ***the hand of the LORD ... is mighty*** (Josh. 4:20-24). The Israelites enter a new chapter in their lives by circumcision and celebrating Passover. Then the walls of Jericho come tumbling down (chap. 6)!

When the estimated two million Israelites crossed the Jordan River, the Canaanite inhabitants were gripped with terror (Josh. 2:9). This may have seemed like the perfect time for the Israelites to rush into battle and claim the land God had promised them. But they were not yet in a right Covenant relationship with God. The rite of circumcision had been instituted by the Lord with Abraham, the father of the faithful, as a visible sign of the people's Covenant relationship with Him (Gen. 17:9-14). Circumcision was required by all males before anyone could eat the Passover (Ex. 12:48).

In keeping with the Covenant of God with Abraham, the new generation had to submit to the humbling rite of circumcision. Their obedience ensured them of the continued protection and direction of God.

After being circumcised, the new generation became identified as the Lord's Covenant people and were qualified to keep the Passover (Josh. 5:8,10). The Passover commemorated the Lord's deliverance of His people from Egypt and pointed the way to the Messianic Deliverer (I Cor. 5:7). Circumcision and the Passover foreshadowed the ordinances (commands) of believer's baptism and the Lord's Supper for the Church.

At His last Passover, our Lord Jesus revealed that His death would fulfill and replace the Passover. The Apostle Paul spoke of this New Covenant, saying: ***The Lord Jesus ... took bread: And when He had given thanks, He brake it, and said, Take, eat: this is My body, which is broken for you: this do in remembrance of Me. After the same manner also He took the cup, when He had supped*** (finished eating), ***saying, This cup is the New Testament*** (Covenant) ***in My blood*** (I Cor. 11:23-25).

The Christian's circumcision is also explained by Paul: ***In whom also ye are circumcised with the circumcision made without hands, in putting off the body of the sins of the flesh by the circumcision of Christ: Buried with Him in baptism, wherein also ye are risen with Him through the faith of the operation of God, who hath raised Him from the dead*** (Col. 2:11-12).

Thought for Today: The Holy Spirit through the Word of God enables us to rise above temptations.

Christ Revealed: As the ***Captain of the host of the LORD*** (Josh. 5:14). Christ is the Captain of our salvation (Heb. 2:10).

MARCH 15   Read Joshua 7 – 8

Highlights: Sin of Achan; Israel defeated at Ai; judgment of Achan; Ai defeated; altar on Mount Ebal; Covenant renewed. What was read to Israel is **very** important for us to know.

After Jericho was destroyed by God, Joshua commanded: ***All the silver, and gold, and vessels of brass and iron, are consecrated unto the L***ORD***: they shall come into the treasury of the L***ORD (Josh. 6:19). Achan was a soldier in the Lord's army, privileged to gather silver and gold from the ruins of Jericho for ***the treasury of the L***ORD. But he buried some of it in his tent.

Perhaps he thought that a few extra shekels would be nice to have. He assumed that no one would know. Apart from believing the Word of God, it's easy to allow our selfish greed to deceive us. Achan's sin of coveting was detestable to God and was revealed by His fierce anger.

Nine times in the first six chapters of the Book of Joshua it is said that the Lord had spoken and directed Joshua (1:1; 3:7; 4:1, 8,10,15; 5:2,15; 6:2). Without consulting the Lord, Israel went to war with Ai, and was soundly defeated (7:2-5). Joshua had momentarily failed to consider that the Lord Himself was their Commander-in-Chief.

The fierceness of the Lord's anger reveals how detestable to God is the sin of coveting, and Achan had to be judged.

We are all selfish by nature and, unless we submit to the indwelling Holy Spirit, the smallest temptation can at times prove too powerful for us. To covet is dishonest. Honesty includes refusal to lie, steal, cheat, or deceive.

It is recorded that Judas coveted and stole money entrusted to him by the Lord (John 12:4-6). Christians will ***provide things honest in the sight of all men. . . . Let us walk honestly, as in the day. . . . In all things willing to live honestly*** (Rom. 12:17; 13:13; Heb. 13:18).

Honesty is a test of character. Our motives and our attitudes are revealed in our character and conduct. If we are not "honest" in all our dealings with God and man, we need to repent (I John 1:9) and ***do that which is honest*** (II Cor. 13:7).

Thought for Today: Any of our accomplishments that are worthwhile are the result of God working through us.

Christ Revealed: Through the uncut stones of the altar (Josh. 8:31). Daniel saw Christ as a Stone which was not cut by human hands (Dan. 2:34,45). Jesus is our **Chief Corner Stone** (I Pet. 2:6-8).

MARCH 16 — Read Joshua 9 – 10

Highlights: Israel's treaty with Gibeon. Just as we are gullible when we don't seek the Lord's guidance, the Israelites are deceived by a heathen nation (Josh. 9:3-5). Years later their past comes back to haunt them (II Sam. 21:1-9). Joshua battles five kings and their armies. He prays for a miracle and God grants it (Josh. 10:12-13).

After Joshua's victories over Jericho and Ai, five kings (10:3) united to fight the Israelites. However, the Gibeonites, located between the land of the Canaanite kings and the encampment of Israel (9:17), decided their chances of survival would be greater by making a league with the Israelites than by joining with the Canaanite kings in their war against Israel. They deceptively told Joshua: ***From a very far country thy servants are come because of the Name*** (awesome Reputation) ***of the L***ORD ***thy God: for we have heard the fame of Him. . . . Wherefore our elders and all the inhabitants of our country spake to us, saying, Take victuals*** (provisions, food) ***with you for the journey, and go to meet them, and say unto them, We are your servants: therefore now make ye a league*** (treaty) ***with us. . . . And the men*** (of Israel) ***took of their victuals, and asked not counsel at the mouth of the L***ORD***. And Joshua made peace . . . and . . . a league with them, to let them live*** (9:9-11,14-15). This league with the Gibeonites reveals the enemy's skill in deception and how fallible our human reasoning can be. Had Joshua prayed to the Lord, he would never have made this league.

The Israelites did not break their oath, even though the Gibeonites had deceived them. However, over 400 years later, Israel suffered a 3-year famine because King Saul broke this covenant (II Sam. 21:1). One sin never justifies another. As children of God, what distinguishes us from all other people is that we ***overcome evil with good*** (Rom. 12:21). God wants us to learn from the Gibeonites' covenant, even though wrongly made, the importance of having personal integrity and keeping our commitments.

The moldy bread and worn clothing seemed to be visible proof of the strangers' words (Josh. 9:12-13). Too often we make decisions based on what we see or think instead of asking guidance from God. ***Trust in the L***ORD ***with all thine heart; and lean not unto thine own understanding. In all thy ways acknowledge Him, and He shall direct thy paths*** (Prov. 3:5-6).

Thought for Today: Faith dispels fear of the future (I John 4:18-19).

Christ Revealed: As the One through whom we have victory (Josh. 10:25). ***Thanks be to God, which giveth us the victory through our Lord Jesus Christ*** (I Cor. 15:57)..

MARCH 17 Read Joshua 11 – 13

Highlights: In Joshua 1:3, the Lord said to Joshua: *Every place that the sole of your foot shall tread upon, that have I given unto you.* All the Canaanite kings mobilize their armies to defeat Israel. Joshua and the Israelites win every battle. God promises to "give" them the land; which meant for them to put forth all their strength and God would guide, protect, and give victory. The key to their victory is the same for us.

Everyone in Jericho knew the reputation of Israel's God, as Rahab confessed: *Our hearts did melt, neither did there remain any more courage in any man, because of you: for the Lord your God, He is God in heaven above, and in earth beneath* (Josh. 2:11). Rahab put her faith in the God of the Hebrews and was not only saved but became an ancestor of Jesus (Matt. 1:5; Heb. 11:31; James 2:25). The Canaanite kings knew what Rahab knew but they decided to fight against the Israelites and their God.

News of Joshua's invasion spread throughout Canaan. Jabin, King of Hazor in the north, enlisted the kings and their soldiers from far into the mountains (Josh. 11:1-2,8).

Joshua's small army heard that they were facing *much people ... with horses and chariots. ... the Lord said unto Joshua, Be not afraid because of them: for to morrow ... will I deliver them up all slain. ... and. ... they smote them* (11:4-8).

So Joshua took the whole land, according to all that the Lord said unto Moses. ... And the land rested from war (11:23). Thirty-one kings (12:24) had been defeated, and Joshua established military control over all of the promised land. However, the individual tribes were each to complete the destruction of the Canaanites in their own territories (Ex. 23:29-30; Deut. 7:22).

History and Scripture alike join in saying to everyone: *Whatsoever thy hand findeth to do, do it with thy might* (Eccl. 9:10). The Lord never promised anyone an easy time in serving Him or told anyone they were not qualified. Christ has said: *The night cometh, when no man can work* (John 9:4).

Only one life, 'twill soon be past. Only what's done for Christ will last (is eternal). All worldly achievements are temporary. *Wherefore ... Awake thou that sleepest, and arise from the dead, and Christ shall give thee light* (Eph. 5:14).

Thought for Today: Obedience to the Word of God is the key to victory.

Christ Portrayed: By *Moses the servant of the Lord* (Josh. 12:6). Jesus was the servant of God. *Behold My Servant, whom I have chosen* (Matt. 12:18).

MARCH 18   Read Joshua 14 – 16

Highlights: Canaan territories divided among the tribes. Caleb gets his mountain (Josh. 14:6-12). Note his age! As the tribes receive their inheritance, notice how precisely the boundaries are laid out.

The tribe of Ephraim was powerful enough to dominate the Canaanites, so they allowed the idol-worshiping Canaanites to live under their control. Apparently their financial gain from these Canaanites was more important to them than being obedient to God. It is no surprise that the Ephraimites soon became idolators.

The Anakim (giants) had been driven out of Hebron by Joshua, perhaps five years before this time (Josh. 10:2-11; 11:21-22). Now they were back and in control of the territory – undoubtedly, with a much greater determination to retain the land promised to Caleb. But God always honors the faith of men like Caleb who rely upon Him and His Word. Consequently, he defeated the Anakim.

At Caleb's "retirement" age of 85, he recounted to Joshua how God had faithfully brought him that far: ***Forty years old was I when Moses the servant of the LORD sent me from Kadesh-barnea to espy*** (spy) ***out the land; and I brought him word again as it was in mine heart. Nevertheless my brethren that went up with me made the heart of the people melt: but I wholly*** (wholeheartedly) ***followed the LORD my God*** (14:7-8).

Caleb's unshakable faith can be seen in his report 38 years earlier as a spy: ***I brought him word again as it was in mine heart***. As he faced the opposition of the other spies and the people, he spoke his convictions, saying: ***Let us go up at once, and possess it*** (Num. 13:30).

Caleb and Joshua were willing to believe God. We are sometimes afraid to speak about spiritual and moral issues when our convictions are unpopular; but the person blessed of God, like Caleb, is unaffected by what others say or do; they courageously move forward to accomplish the Lord's will.

Surely our faith ought to even exceed Caleb's, inasmuch as ***it is Christ . . . at the right hand of God, who also maketh intercession for us*** (Rom. 8:34).

Thought for Today: God honors faith that is established in His Word.

Christ Portrayed: By Caleb, who ***followed the LORD*** (Josh. 14:8,14). Our Savior said: ***Lo, I come . . . to do Thy will, O God*** (Heb. 10:7,9).

MARCH 19   **Read Joshua 17 – 19**

Highlights: Canaan under the control of the Israelites; the Tabernacle set up in a central location at Shiloh; Joshua's inheritance. As they reap the rewards of the promise given on the other side of the Jordan River, the land is divided among all the tribes by lot; but some tribes fail to claim their territory.

The conquest of Canaan was completed and the land was divided among them by the Lord. **The whole congregation of the children of Israel assembled together at Shiloh, and set up the Tabernacle. . . . the land was subdued before them. . . . Joshua cast lots for them in Shiloh before the LORD: and there Joshua** (under the direction of God) **divided the land unto the children of Israel** (18:1,10).

Although they had received some of the best territory in the promised land, the tribes of Manasseh and Ephraim complained that they should have more territory given to them because of their great numbers and what they perceived as their prominent position among the tribes (17:14-18). The Ephraimites were proud of their history as descendants of Joseph and the fact that Joshua, the victorious commander who had led in the conquest of Canaan, was also from their tribe. (See Num. 13:8,16. Joshua is also called "Oshea" and "Jehoshua."

Sadly, these two tribes chose to compromise with the Canaanites (Josh. 16:10; 17:12-13). Faithfulness is built on faith, which they greatly lacked. The blessings of God often depend upon faith but **faith without works is dead** (James 2:20).

In a striking contrast to the tribes of Manasseh and Ephraim, Joshua chose to be the last to lay claim to any territory (Josh. 19:49). As captain, we could expect him to choose first and to take the best for himself. Instead, he chose last. His choice was a very small area near Shiloh where the Tabernacle was erected and where he could best worship and serve the Lord. It was there, in the nearness of the Lord's presence, that Joshua built his small city of **Timnath-serah in Mount Ephraim** (Josh. 19:50). Joshua illustrates the importance of being **fervent in spirit; serving the Lord. . . . Submit yourselves therefore to God. Resist the devil, and he will flee from you. . . . Humble yourselves in the sight of the Lord, and He shall lift you up** (Rom. 12:11; James 4:7,10).

Thought for Today: Meekness is not weakness. It is trusting God.

Christ Revealed: Through Shiloh. **The children of Israel assembled together at Shiloh, and set up the Tabernacle** (Josh. 18:1). Shiloh was the dwelling place of the presence of God which was prophetic of Jesus. **The Word** (Jesus) **. . . dwelt** (tabernacled) **among us** (John 1:14).

MARCH 20   **Read Joshua 20 – 21**

Highlights: Six cities appointed as places of refuge; forty-eight cities given to the Levites. The responsibility for their support belonged to all the tribes (Josh. 21:44-45).

Unlike all the other tribes of Israel, the priestly tribe of Levi was not given separate territory (Josh. 14:3). **Unto the tribe of Levi Moses gave not any inheritance: the LORD God of Israel was their inheritance, as He said unto them** (13:33). **But the Levites have no part among you; for the priesthood of the LORD is their inheritance** (18:7).

The Levites were divided into three groups according to the descendants of Levi's three sons, Gershon, Kohath, and Merari. But only the descendants of Levi through Kohath's grandson Aaron could be priests and serve in the Tabernacle (Ex. 6:16-20; Num. 3:10). However, some of these descendants were physically disqualified to be ministers at the altar because of disabilities and defects, and some were spiritually disqualified because they violated one or more of the Commandments (Lev. 21:1-23). The priests were responsible for preserving, transcribing, teaching, and interpreting the Law. They were also the civil officers responsible for the administration of the Law (Deut. 17:9-12; 31:9,11-12,26). All the Levites, not merely the ones who were responsible for the worship at the Tabernacle, were to receive an equal share of the tithes from the other tribes (Num. 18:21-24). Each tribe was to provide for the physical welfare of the priests within its own territory. This was not left up to the goodwill of the people but was a responsibility commanded by God.

God devoted 42 of the 45 verses in Joshua 21 to emphasize the Israelites' obligation to support the ministers of His Word. No one was too poor or exempt from giving his tithe (a tenth of his income) which was proportionately equal for all. When Israel was faithful in this, God mightily blessed them. When they failed to tithe, they suffered.

The Apostle Paul illustrated this: **It is written ... Thou shalt not muzzle the mouth of the ox that treadeth out the corn. Doth God take care for oxen? Or saith He it altogether for our sakes? For our sakes, no doubt, this is written. ... If we have sown unto you spiritual things, is it a great thing if we shall reap your carnal** (financial) **things? ... the Lord ordained that they which preach the Gospel should live of the Gospel** (I Cor. 9:9-11,14).

Thought for Today: Nothing is too hard for God (Jer. 32:17)!

Christ Portrayed: By Eleazar, the chief priest (Josh. 21:1). Christ is our High Priest. **The ... High Priest of our profession** (confession), **Christ Jesus** (Heb. 3:1).

MARCH 21   Read Joshua 22 – 24

Highlights: Two and one-half tribes build an altar near the Jordan River on the west side of Jordan (Josh. 22:10), then return home on the east side of the Jordan; civil war averted. Joshua's final proclamation to the Israelites to live holy lives and not accept or be friends with the Canaanites.

When God told Joshua: ***Every place that the sole of your foot shall tread upon, that have I given unto you, as I said unto Moses*** (Josh. 1:3), he did not merely "trust" that the Lord would force the Canaanites to voluntarily give up their land. The fact is, the Israelites received their inheritance by faith as God helped them conquer every foot of land that He had promised them (see the Key to Success in 1:8). After about seven years under the leadership of Joshua the Israelites had conquered Canaan. ***And the L̲o̲r̲d̲ gave them rest round about, according to all that He sware unto their fathers . . . the L̲o̲r̲d̲ delivered all their enemies into their hand*** (21:44).

The Israelites' greatest danger was yet to be faced. ***Joshua said unto the people. . . . If ye forsake the L̲o̲r̲d̲, and serve strange*** (foreign) ***gods, then He will . . . do you hurt*** (bring disaster), ***and consume*** (destroy) ***you, after that He hath done you good. . . . Now therefore put away . . . the strange gods which are among you, and incline*** (yield) ***your heart unto the L̲o̲r̲d̲ God of Israel*** (24:19-20,23). Jesus (a name that means "Joshua" in Hebrew) freed us from the penalty of death for our sins by His substitutionary death on the cross and His triumphant physical resurrection.

We too need to be reminded daily to ***incline*** (our) ***heart unto the L̲o̲r̲d̲***. What a tragedy that so many assume that, once a person has accepted Jesus Christ as Savior, he has nothing to do but "just leave everything up to the Lord." But the Lord has left it up to us. ***Wherefore take unto you the whole armour of God, that ye may be able to withstand in the evil day. . . . Stand therefore, having your loins girt*** (belted) ***about with Truth, and having on the breastplate of righteousness; And your feet shod with the preparation of the Gospel of peace; Above all, taking the shield of faith, wherewith ye shall be able to quench all the fiery darts*** (arrows, shots) ***of the wicked. And take the helmet of salvation, and the Sword of the Spirit, which is the Word of God*** (Eph. 6:13-17).

Thought for Today: Every day serve only the Lord.

Christ Revealed: Through the peace offering (Josh. 22:27). Our Lord offered Himself to God as our means of peace with the Father. ***Being justified by faith, we have peace with God through our Lord Jesus Christ*** (Rom. 5:1).

Introduction To The Book Of JUDGES

The Book of Judges covers about 450 years of Israel's history in the promised land. It relates scattered events that took place from the death of Joshua to the beginning of Samuel's ministry.

The key to the conquest of Canaan is clear: **And the people served the Lord all of the days of Joshua, and all the days of the elders that outlived Joshua, who had seen all the great works of the Lord, that He did for Israel** (Judg. 2:7).

After Joshua's death there was no God-appointed national leader, so each tribe acted independently (1:1 – 2:23). Most of them disregarded the Lord's command to drive out all the Canaanites who remained in their territories. Instead, they compromised by gradually enslaving them. This compromise led to intermarriage with the Canaanites and, ultimately, to Israel's idol worship of their false gods.

The reason for this failure is obvious: **Also all that generation were gathered unto their fathers** (died): **and there arose another generation after them, which knew not the Lord, nor yet the works which He had done for Israel. . . . And they forsook the Lord, and served Baal** (the chief god of the Canaanites) **and Ashtaroth** (2:10,13). Spiritual failure and confusion resulted.

Because of their sins, surrounding nations and tribes, including the Philistines, Moabites, and Midianites were used of God to defeat them and cause them to realize why they had lost their freedom.

Seven major apostasies are recorded when **the children of Israel did evil in the sight of the Lord, and served Baalim** (false gods) (2:11; 3:7,12; 4:1; 6:1; 10:6; 13:1). In each case, the Israelites were overcome by their enemies, enslaved, and were greatly impoverished; but, when the people prayed, God appointed judges to deliver them from their oppressors. As each successive judge acted in submission to the Lord, a period of peace and prosperity would follow.

Chapters 17 – 21 contain insight into the Israelites' moral and spiritual degradation that prevailed preceding the time when Samuel became a prophet of God and their judge. The Book of Judges illustrates that we can never enjoy freedom, peace of mind, and the blessings of God for long if we are only partially obedient to His Word. When we become involved in questionable acts or relationships which may seem harmless, just like the Israelites we will soon find ourselves overcome by the ungodly desires of fleshly interests.

MARCH 22   Read Judges 1 – 2

Highlights: Joshua and the elders die. The Israelites live in the mountains because they did not attack the Canaanites in the valleys with their chariots of iron. The Israelites sin by befriending the Canaanites and they stop serving God (Judg. 2:10-11).

The Israelites were chosen by the One True God to reveal Him to the heathen nations and to glorify Him by being obedient to His Word. The first few verses of Judges give us a sense of high hope for the total conquest of the land as begun by Joshua: **Judah went with Simeon his brother, and they slew the Canaanites that inhabited Zephath, and utterly destroyed it** (Judg. 1:17). One by one, Canaanite cities, then Philistine cities fell to the Israelites (1:10-11,13, 17-18). **And the people served the LORD all the days of Joshua, and all the days of the elders that outlived Joshua, who had seen all the great works of the LORD, that He did for Israel** (2:7).

A new era in the history of the 12 tribes began soon after the death of Joshua. The Lord's command to complete the conquest of Canaan was not fulfilled because of the people's compromise with the pagan inhabitants of the land. It is disappointing to read: **There arose another generation after them, which knew not the LORD.... And the children of Israel did evil in the sight of the LORD, and served Baalim: And they forsook the LORD.... And the anger of the LORD was hot against Israel; and He said, Because... this people hath transgressed My Covenant... I also will not henceforth drive out any from before them** (2:10-21).

The Israelites chose to do what they thought was more "humanitarian" by deciding to allow peaceful coexistence with the enemies of God. Perhaps they argued: "How could a God of love destroy 'innocent' people?"

This is the same argument many people use to justify their disobedience to the Word of God. After all, God is a God of love, isn't He? Yes, God is a God of love, and He wants to bless mankind.

People are being deceived into accepting false gods – things and actions that result in eternal separation from God. Without Christ, people will be eternally lost and will be cast into hell. **And whosoever was not found written in the Book of Life was cast into the lake of fire** (Rev. 20:15).

Thought for Today: Considering our guilt the mercy of God is amazing.

Christ Revealed: As *the Angel of the LORD* (Judg. 2:1,4). *The Angel of the LORD* is understood to be the Lord Jesus Himself pre-incarnate, for He speaks as God Himself (*I made you... I sware... I said, I will*). *Jesus said unto them, Verily, verily, I say unto you, Before Abraham was, I am* (John 8:58).

Judges of The Israelites (Judg. – I Sam. 7)

Judge	From the Tribe of	Text	Oppressor	Oppressed Years	Peace Years
Othniel	Judah	Judg. 3:7-11	Mesopotamians	8	40
Ehud	Benjamin	Judg. 3:12-30	Moabites, Ammonites, Amalekites	18	80
Shamgar	Naphtali	Judg. 3:31; 5:6	Philistines		
Deborah/Barak	Ephraim	Judg. 4:1 – 5:31	Canaanites	20	40
Gideon	Manasseh	Judg. 6:1 – 8:32	Midianites, Amalekites	7	40
Abimelech (A Usurper)	Ephraim	Judg. 8:30 – 9:57	No Peace, Only chaos		
Tola	Issachar	Judg. 10:1-2			23
Jair	Manasseh	Judg. 10:3-5			22
Jephthah	Manasseh (East of Jordan River)	Judg. 10:6 – 12:7	Ammonites, Philistines	18	6
Ibzan	Judah	Judg. 12:8-10			7
Elon	Zebulun	Judg. 12:11-12			10
Abdon	Ephraim	Judg. 12:13-15			8
Samson	Dan	Judg. 13:24-16:31	Philistines	40	20
Eli	Ephraim	I Sam. 4:18	Philistines	40	
Samuel	Ephraim	I Sam. 1:20-7:17	Philistines		About 40

The Six Cities of Refuge (See Map on opposite page)

Kedesh – located about 15 miles north of the Sea of Galilee in the mountains bordering the west side of the Huleh Valley in the territory of Naphtali

Shechem - located in the valley between Mount Ebal and Mount Gerizim in the mountains of Ephraim

Hebron (Kiriath-arba) – located in Judah about 20 miles south of Jerusalem

Bezer – located east of the Jordan River in the tribe of Reuben

Ramoth-gilead – located about 50 miles north of Bezer in the highlands of Gilead in the tribe of Gad

Golan – located in the highlands of the tribe of Manasseh, east of the Jordan River

Since the Law required a near relative of the one killed to become an *avenger of blood* (Deuteronomy 19:6,12), the cities of refuge provided a sanctuary for those who had killed by accident. Under the Law, the slayers had to remain in the city until after the death of the high priest (Numbers 35:25).

The Law did not provide for any sacrifice for the manslayer. The guilt of the man who killed accidentally was removed only by the death of the high priest. He could not pay a fine or be set free any sooner.

There is a sharp distinction between an accidental death and a willful murder. The Levites and the elders in each city were designated to investigate to determine if a death were an accident or a willful murder. God still demands that a murderer be put to death.

MARCH 23   Read Judges 3 – 5

Highlights: The Lord uses other nations to test Israel's loyalty (Judg. 3:1,4). Notice the sequence. First servitude was to Mesopotamia; 1st judge, Othniel. Second servitude was to Moab; 2nd judge, Ehud. Third servitude was to Philistia; 3rd judge, Shamgar (3:8-31). Fourth servitude was to Canaan; 4th judge, Deborah (Barak).

Deborah was the messenger of God to bring His Word of deliverance to His people and free them from oppression. She called for Barak and gave him a message from God: *Go and draw toward mount Tabor, and take with thee ten thousand men ... And I will draw unto thee to the river Kishon Sisera, the captain of Jabin's army, with his chariots and his multitude; and I will deliver him into thine hand* (Judg. 4:6-7).

But Barak refused to go to battle unless Deborah (Israel's judge, and therefore a representative of God, at that time) agreed to go with him. But she told him *the LORD shall sell Sisera into the hand of a woman* (4:49). We read in verse 15 that *the LORD discomfited Sisera, and all his chariots, and all his host, with the edge of the sword before Barak; so that Sisera ... fled away on his feet.*

Sisera sought refuge from Jael, but Jael was a believer in God. After giving Sisera a drink and a place to rest, she *took a nail of the tent, and took an hammer in her hand, and went softly unto him, and smote the nail into his temples, and fastened it into the ground. ... So he* (Sisera) *died* (4:21). *So God subdued on that day Jabin the king of Canaan before the children of Israel. ... Then sang Deborah and Barak the son of Abinoam on that day ... Praise ye the LORD for the avenging of Israel, when the people willingly offered themselves* (4:23-24; 5:1-2). Through Deborah's spiritual leadership, God brought peace to the land for 40 years (5:31).

It is obedience by faith in the Word of God and intercessory prayer that enables us to be victorious. The Lord is seeking Christians today who will intercede in prayer on behalf of others.

And I sought for a man among them, that should make up the hedge, and stand in the gap before Me for the land, that I should not destroy it: but I found none (Ezek. 22:30). *And He saw that there was no ... intercessor* (Is. 59:16).

Thought for Today: Wealth and pleasures can be deceptive snares to keep the believer from accomplishing the eternal purposes of God.

Christ Portrayed: By Othniel, a deliverer upon whom *the Spirit of the LORD* rested (Judg. 3:9-11). *The Spirit of God* was also upon Christ, our Deliverer (Matt. 3:16). *There shall come out of Sion the Deliverer, and shall turn away ungodliness from Jacob* (Rom. 11:26). Jesus declared: *The Spirit of the Lord is upon Me, because He hath anointed Me ... to preach deliverance to the captives* (Luke 4:18).

MARCH 24

Read Judges 6 – 7

Highlights: Israel's repetitious disobedience results in their defeat and domination by Midian. Gideon takes a stand against his father's Baal worship. They battle the Midianites. How did the Lord select Gideon's army (Judg. 7:2-6)?

Once more the Israelites were enslaved, this time by the Midianites. *And the children of Israel did evil* (sinned) *in the sight of the LORD: and the LORD delivered them into the hand* (under the control) *of Midian seven years. . . . Israel was greatly impoverished . . . and the children of Israel cried unto the LORD* (Judg. 6:1,6). The answer to their prayers began with reproof: *The LORD sent a prophet . . . which said unto them, Thus saith the LORD God of Israel, I brought you up from Egypt . . . out of the hand of all that oppressed you . . . and gave you their land . . . but ye have not obeyed My voice* (6:8-10). There was no word of comfort, only reproof. They needed to recognize that their miserable suffering was the direct result of their disregarding the Word of God.

It would appear that this unnamed prophet may have had only one convert – Gideon: *And the Angel of the LORD appeared unto him, and said . . . The LORD is with thee, thou mighty man of valour. . . . Go in this thy might, and thou shalt save Israel from the hand of the Midianites* (6:12,14).

Gideon was deeply conscious of his poverty and his own limited ability, and he confessed: *Oh my LORD, wherewith shall I save Israel? behold, my family is poor in Manasseh, and I am the least in my father's house* (6:15). We tend to think that the only people God can use are those who have influence in their communities. But, often, these people are too busy, want to do it their way, or would rather compromise than lose their popularity.

Gideon was truly a man of inexperience and uncertainty, but he unconditionally obeyed the Lord without fear of the opposition. Gideon was ready to worship the God of Israel and *built an altar there unto the LORD, and called it Jehovah(Yahweh)-Shalom* (the *Lord* is peace) (6:24). We too must get our eyes off circumstances and fix our faith on the Word of God. *Hearken* (listen)*, my beloved brethren, Hath not God chosen the poor of this world rich in faith, and heirs of the Kingdom which He hath promised to them that love Him* (James 2:5)*?*

Thought for Today: Faith in God, not in our own wisdom, brings success.

Christ Revealed: As *The Sword of the LORD* (Judg. 7:20). In the Apostle John's revelation of Jesus, *out of His mouth went a sharp two-edged sword* (Rev. 1:16). We know that the sword *is the Word of God* (Eph. 6:17) and that Jesus is the *Word* of God *made* (became) *flesh* (John 1:14).

MARCH 25   Read Judges 8 – 9

Highlights: Jealousy rises up. Why (Judg. 8:1)? After Gideon's death one son conspires against his brothers and murders all but one. Are we surprised at whom God uses to remove the wicked son? Abimelech's "accident" and death.

Gideon was called of God to deliver the Israelites from the Midianites (see 6:14-16). Thirty-two thousand men responded to Gideon's call to war, but only 300 men qualified. With only 300 men, God used Gideon to defeat 135,000 Midianite soldiers. **And the country was in quietness forty years in the days of Gideon** (8:28). This illustrates a basic biblical principle: **According to your faith be it unto you** (Matt. 9:29). God acts with man's cooperation, but man cannot overcome without the wisdom and power of God. Then the Israelites urged Gideon to be their king. But Gideon knew that it was not he, but God, the True King, who had saved His people. **And Gideon said unto them, I will not rule over you . . . the LORD shall rule over you** (Judg. 8:23).

After Gideon's death, the Israelites soon forgot that God was the One who had miraculously delivered them from the Midianites. With an evil ambition for power, one of Gideon's sons, Abimelech, negotiated a large sum of money from the Baal temple treasury to pay men to murder his 70 brothers. **Jotham the youngest son of Jerubbaal** (Gideon) **was left; for he hid himself** (9:5). Following the execution of Abimelech's competition, **all the men of Shechem . . . made Abimelech king** (9:6).

Jotham, who had escaped execution, warned the people that they would soon discover that this self-made king would bring suffering and death upon them as well as upon himself (9:7-21). As Jotham foretold, within a few short years, they brought about their own destruction in choosing Abimelech (9:22-57).

Abimelech is an example of a person controlled by the deceptive and destructive forces of pride and selfishness. He was determined to gain his evil ends by whatever means regardless of whom he hurt. He is a reminder that **whatsoever a man soweth, that shall he also reap. For he that soweth to his flesh shall of the flesh reap corruption** (destruction); **but he that soweth to the Spirit shall of the Spirit reap life everlasting** (Gal. 6:7-8).

Thought for Today: Surrender to God ensures victory.

Christ Revealed: By Gideon, who delivered the Israelites from Midian (Judg. 8:22-23). The Lord Jesus has delivered us out of the hands of our spiritual enemies, and it is fitting that He should rule over us. **Our Lord Jesus Christ, Who gave Himself for our sins, that He might deliver us from this present evil world** (Gal. 1:3-4; II Pet. 2:9; Rom. 11:26).

MARCH 26   Read Judges 10 – 11

Highlights: Israel forsakes the Lord and worships idols; Israel oppressed by Ammonites for 18 years; Ammonites defeated. Don't miss Jephthah's remarkable loyalty to God. Read about his vow and victory and the depth of dedication of his only child. Why God could be so pleased with her and Jephthah.

After years of suffering, **the children of Israel said unto the LORD, We have sinned. . . . And they put away the strange** (foreign) **gods . . . and served the LORD** (10:15-16). **And . . . the elders . . . said unto Jephthah . . . be our captain, that we may fight with the children of Ammon** (11:5-6).

Jephthah prayed: **If Thou shalt without fail deliver the children of Ammon into mine hands, Then . . . whatsoever cometh forth of the doors of my house to meet me . . . shall surely be the LORD'S, and I will offer it up for a Burnt Offering** (11:30-31). Jephthah could not know what a sacrifice he would make. **And we know that all things work together for good to them that love God, to them who are the called according to His purpose** (Rom. 8:28).

In testing Jephthah's prayer, God arranged that Jephthah's daughter should be the first to meet him. Jephthah knew the Scriptures well, and human sacrifices were condemned by God (Lev. 20:2-5; Deut. 12:29-31; 18:10-12). How could one imagine that this man of God would cut the throat of his daughter to offer her as a burnt offering? To do that would have made God, as well as this man of faith, responsible for a vile murder, since it was **the Spirit of the LORD** who gave Jephthah his victory (Judg. 11:29,32).

How he fulfilled his vow is obvious: **She was his only child; beside her he had neither son nor daughter** (11:34). The Lord had declared that the firstborn were to be "sanctified" – not sacrificed: **It is Mine** (Ex. 13:2; Num. 3:13). And his daughter's response made the outcome unmistakably clear. She asked for **two months . . .** (to) **go up and down upon the mountains . . .** (to) **bewail my virginity** (mourn that I will never marry and will have no children) (Judg. 11:37). Undoubtedly she had the honor to be a servant of God in the Tabernacle in lifelong chastity.

God highly honored Jephthah as one of the heroes of faith: **Of Jephthae; of David also, and Samuel, and of the prophets: Who through faith subdued kingdoms, wrought righteousness, obtained promises** (Heb. 11:32-33).

Thought for Today: Trust and obey . . . for there's no other way.

Christ Revealed: By Jephthah's only child as she wholly submitted to her father's will even as Jesus wholly submitted to His Father's will (Judg. 11:34-40). On the night He was betrayed, Jesus prayed: **Not as I will, but as Thou wilt** (Matt. 26:39).

MARCH 27   Read Judges 12 – 14

Highlights: Ephraimites quarrel with Jephthah; he judges for six years of peace. Three more judges appear in the chapters 10, 11, and 12. It is important to learn how their lives teach us. The 7th servitude is to the Philistines; the Lord raises up Samson.

Each time *the children of Israel cried unto the L*ORD (3:9,15; 4:3; 6:6; 10:10), God provided a deliverer. But this time, there was no mention of prayer for deliverance, although they had been slaves of *the Philistines for forty years* (13:1).

Israel had forsaken Jehovah, but God in mercy *began to move* upon Samson (13:25) who could have delivered them, but the people remained powerless under the control of the Philistines.

Samson was not an idol worshiper, but he was more concerned with satisfying himself than with pleasing God. This was evident when he insisted on having an idol-worshiping Philistine wife, saying to his parents: *Get her for me; for she pleaseth me well* (14:1-3).

Samson's undisciplined life typified the spiritual condition of Israel during that period of the Judges and revealed how a self-willed life results in sorrow and suffering for self as well as others.

The three women in Samson's life represent the attractions of the pleasure-loving world which kept the people of God from the blessings He wanted them to enjoy. All of us are tempted to please ourselves and fail both to pray and to live the will of God. Self-pleasing is expressed in many forms: pride, jealousy, theft, using the tithe for self (robbing God), hate, irresponsibility, using wine, and a host of other fleshly desires. Every day that we fail to deny ourselves and take up our cross, our opportunity of serving the Lord is weakened. Perhaps the greatest failure is that of not presenting our *bodies a living sacrifice* (Rom. 12:1), expecting that the mercy and longsuffering of God will continue indefinitely.

As a Nazarite, Samson could have been an example before all the world to this day of the power of faithful commitment to God as he delivered Israel from Philistine bondage. We too are called upon to be separated from the world with a desire to fulfill the Lord's will.

The night is far spent, the day is at hand: let us therefore cast off the works of darkness, and let us put on the armour of light (Rom. 13:12).

Thought for Today: A person's conscience can only be a safe guide when it is guided by the Word of God.

Christ Portrayed: By Samson, who, as a Nazarite, was to be separated or consecrated *to God from the womb* (birth) *to the day of his death* (Judg. 13:7). Jesus was also set apart and consecrated to God from the womb to the day of His death on the cross. Unlike Samson, who failed God, Jesus totally fulfilled the plan of God as He said He would do when He left heaven saying: *Lo, I come . . . to do Thy will, O God* (Heb. 10:7).

MARCH 28   Read Judges 15 – 17

Highlights: Samson loses his wife; in revenge, he destroys their crops and kills 1,000 Philistines. His escapade with Delilah results in the Philistines capturing and blinding him; his prayer is answered. Chapter 17 warning; Micah's idols.

The Israelites were set apart as a holy nation under the leadership of God. But they ignored the Laws given on Mount Sinai by their True King and ignored His daily direction.

What was wrong with Samson was wrong with the nation. It is recorded in the Book of Judges that everyone **did that which was right in his own eyes** (17:6). They were not concerned with knowing or doing the will of God.

There is no record that Samson ever expressed a desire to be used by the Lord to deliver the Israelites from the Philistine **rulers over** (15:11) them.

Early in life, Samson disregarded the spiritual significance of his Nazarite dedication by marrying a Philistine woman. He sinned greatly with Delilah. When Samson saw Delilah, he should have considered his Nazarite vow and high calling as judge of the people of God. As so often happens with everyone who presumptuously believes that the mercy of God will continue indefinitely, when Delilah **said, The Philistines be upon thee, Samson. . . . he awoke . . . and said, I will go out as at other times . . . And he wist not that the LORD was departed from him** (16:20).

Consequently, **the Philistines took him, and put out his eyes . . . and bound him with fetters of brass; and he did grind in the prison house** (16:21).

Samson's story should remind every Christian who is misusing his God-given abilities (talents) to **seek . . . first the Kingdom of God, and His righteousness** (Matt. 6:33). In contrast, **Moses** chose **to suffer affliction with the people of God,** (rather) **than to enjoy the pleasures of sin for a season** (Heb. 11:24-25).

There are just two walks in life, either the broad (majority) way or the narrow way (living to advance His Kingdom). The narrow way leads to life eternal. Jesus warned: **Beware of covetousness** (of material things and fleshly desires)**: for a man's life consisteth not in the abundance of the things which he possesseth** (Luke 12:15). Christ does not say: "You ought not;" but He says: "You cannot **serve God and mammon** (two masters) (Matt. 6:24)."

Thought for Today: Oh, the high cost of lust and its treachery.

Christ Revealed: Through the strength God gave to Samson for his last victory over the Philistines (Judg. 16:28-30). **I can do all things through Christ which strengtheneth me** (Phil. 4:13).

MARCH 29   Read Judges 18 –19

Highlights: Danites force Micah's Levite to be their priest. They attack, then occupy Laish; a concubine is victimized. Most Israelites choose lust and self-interest instead of the will of God.

The last few chapters represent what life was like among the Israelites during the final period when the judges ruled. Idolatry and sin prevailed in the land and the Word of God was ignored. And yet His Name was used as though He approved their sins.

To illustrate the deplorable moral condition that existed at that time, a Levite, representing "spiritual leadership," and his concubine are introduced. We are disappointed to read of the Levite's violation of the Law through his relationship with his concubine (Lev. 21:7) who *played the whore against him, and went away from him unto her father's house to Bethlehem-judah* (Judg. 19:2). After *four . . . months*, the Levite decided that he wanted her back, so he went to her father's house. *When the father of the damsel saw him, he rejoiced* (19:2-3).

When the Levite decided to return home several days later, it was too late to complete their journey before nightfall, so they stopped in Gibeah (19:14). An old man offered them hospitality in his house, which they accepted, *The men of the city, certain sons of Belial* (homosexuals), *beset the house round about, and beat at the door, and spake to the master . . . saying, Bring forth the man that came into thine house, that we may know* (have sex with) *him. And the man . . . said . . . do not so wickedly. . . . Behold, here is my daughter a maiden . . . but unto this man do not so vile a thing* (rape him) (19:22-24). When the men of the city would not listen to the old man, the Levite *took his concubine, and brought her forth unto them* (19:25).

The vileness of rape, as well as homosexuality, is confirmed in the New Testament where we read: *For this cause God gave them up unto vile affections* (degrading passions): *for even their women did change the natural use into that which is against nature: And likewise also the men, leaving the natural use of the woman, burned in their lust one toward another; men with men working that which is unseemly, and receiving in themselves that recompence* (penalty) *of their error which was meet* (fitting) (Rom. 1:26-27).

Thought for Today: The morally perverted need our prayers.

Christ Revealed: *In those days there was no king in Israel* (Judg. 18:1). Christ was the rejected King of Israel. *Pilate saith unto them, Shall I crucify your King? The chief priests answered, We have no king but Caesar* (John 19:15).

MARCH 30   **Read Judges 20 – 21**

Highlights: Civil war between Benjamites and other tribes; Benjamites defeated; the results.

The tribe of Benjamin refused to allow justice to be done to the homosexual mob that gang-raped a defenseless Israelite woman, causing her death (Judg. 19:25-28; 20:13). All the other tribes of Israel united to execute judgment against them and *came unto the House of God, and wept, and sat there before the LORD, and fasted that day until even, and offered Burnt Offerings and Peace Offerings before the LORD* (20:26). In deep humility, they committed themselves to the Lord.

It was only after they had built an altar and offered the sacrifices for their own sins that *the Lord said, Go up; for to morrow I will deliver them into thine hand* (20:28). The tribe of Benjamin was almost destroyed as the consequence of this wicked sin and their refusal to allow justice to be done to the guilty rapists.

There is a growing indifference to immorality in our society, similar to what existed in the tribe of Benjamin. Many have redefined sin. **Adultery** is now called "having an affair." **Homosexuality** is called "gay and lesbian" or "alternative lifestyles." **Fornication** is referred to as "live-in lovers." Their purpose is to remove the sense of guilt for violating the moral Law of God and to make the sinner not to feel guilty, as they did when *every man did that which was right in his own eyes* (21:25). We must exercise caution, however, while hating and exposing sin; we must also show mercy and kindness as we pray for and lovingly urge sinners to receive Christ as Savior and Lord.

All sin is abominable to our holy God; however, all sin that is truly repented of and forsaken is forgiven through the atoning blood of Jesus Christ (I John 1:9). The Apostle Paul reminded the Corinthians that some of them had been delivered from sexual sins when he wrote: *Be not deceived: neither fornicators, nor idolaters, nor adulterers, nor effeminate, nor abusers of themselves with mankind . . . shall inherit the Kingdom of God. And such were some of you: but ye are washed, but ye are sanctified* (set apart), *but ye are justified in the Name of the Lord Jesus, and by the Spirit of our God* (I Cor. 6:9-11).

Thought for Today: We cheat ourselves when withholding what we should give to God.

Christ Revealed: As our Deliverer (Judg. 20:26-28). As we pray and seek the Lord's will, He delivers us from all evil forces. *Our Lord Jesus Christ, Who gave Himself for our sins, that He might deliver us from this present evil world* (Gal. 1:3-4).

INTRODUCTION TO THE BOOK OF RUTH

The events of the Book of Ruth occurred **when the judges ruled** (Ruth 1:1). **In those days there was no king in Israel: every man did that which was right in his own eyes** (Judg. 21:25). The Book of Ruth provides insight on faithfulness to God during the lawless period of the judges. The Book of Ruth reveals the mercy and providence of God to both Jew and Gentile.

The Book of Ruth highlights our Lord's loving-kindness in selecting a Moabite woman to be included in His Covenant with Israel and to be one of only two women after whom books of the Bible are named. Ruth was one of only four women, other than Mary, mentioned in the genealogy of Jesus (Matt. 1:3,5-6,16), demonstrating the love of God for all people.

The Law provided for Boaz, as a kinsman-redeemer, to buy the deceased Elimelech's inheritance, to marry Ruth, and to raise a child in the lineage of Elimelech. An unnamed near kinsman (symbolic of the Law) refused by saying that to marry Ruth, a Moabite, would **mar** (endanger) **mine own inheritance... I cannot redeem it** (Ruth 4:6). The Law stated: **An Ammonite or Moabite shall not enter into the congregation** (assembly) **of the Lord; even to their tenth generation** (Deut. 23:3). The Law cannot forgive or make exceptions; it exposes and condemns us. But, Ruth had forsaken her false gods by confessing her faith in the one God of Israel who also said: **And now, Israel, what doth the Lord thy God require of thee, but to fear the Lord thy God, to walk in all His ways, and to love Him** (Deut. 10:12-16; Jer. 4:4; Rom. 2:29; Gal. 3:29; Phil. 3:3; Col. 3:11).

Boaz, a type of Christ became the "kinsman-redeemer," purchased the property of Naomi and took Ruth as his wife. After making the necessary arrangements, **Boaz said unto the elders ... Ye are witnesses this day, that I have bought all that was Elimelech's. ... Moreover Ruth the Moabitess, the wife of Mahlon, have I purchased to be my wife, to raise up the name of the dead upon his inheritance** (Ruth 4:9-10; Lev. 25:25-34,47-48; Deut. 25:5-10).

Through the marriage of Boaz and Ruth, for the third time God united both Jew and Gentile in the ancestry of David and of our Lord Jesus, the Messiah (Matt. 1:3,5; Luke 3:32-33). **There is neither Jew nor Greek, there is neither bond nor free, there is neither male nor female: for ye are all one in Christ Jesus. And if ye be Christ's, then are ye Abraham's seed** (offspring)**, and heirs according to the promise** (Gal. 3:28-29).

MARCH 31   Read Ruth 1 – 4

Highlights: Famine; Elimelech and Naomi move down from Bethlehem to Moab; Naomi and Ruth return to Bethlehem; marriage of Boaz and Ruth.

Bethlehem, in the land of promise, was experiencing a severe famine. Israel knew that God had said: *If... ye will not do all My Commandments. ... your land shall not yield her increase, neither shall the trees of the land yield their fruits* (Lev. 26:15,20).

Perhaps, while standing in their unproductive fields in the Judean hills, Elimelech, his wife Naomi, and their sons Mahlon and Chilion looked down on the fertile, prosperous valley of Moab and decided to abandon their God-given inheritance in Bethlehem *to sojourn in the country of Moab* (Ruth 1:1-2), a place God had cursed (Num. 24:17; Amos 2:1-3). What they thought would be a temporary stay from starvation extended to about 10 years (Ruth 1:1-14).

However, unforeseen tragedy struck in the idol-worshiping country of Moab. Elimelech died, then his sons ignored their Covenant relationship with God and married Moabite women, Ruth and Orpah. Later, Mahlon and Chilion also died (1:3-5). The three childless widows were left without a means of support. *Then she* (Naomi) *arose with her daughters in law. ... and they went on the way to return unto the land of Judah* (1:6-7).

Soon Orpah returned *back unto her people, and unto her gods* (1:15). But Ruth had forsaken the gods of Moab and confessed her loyalty to the God of Israel by saying to Naomi: *Thy people shall be my people, and thy God my God* (1:16).

Ruth and Naomi arrived in Bethlehem where Ruth married Boaz. Ruth became the mother of *Obed: he is the father of Jesse, the father of David* (4:17). The Book of Ruth shows our Lord's lovingkindness to Gentiles in selecting a Moabite to become the great-grandmother of King David. Ruth is one of three Gentile women mentioned in the genealogy of Jesus (Matt. 1:3,5-6). This account shows the love of God for all lost mankind.

He is not a Jew, which is one outwardly ... But he is a Jew, which is one inwardly; and circumcision is that of the heart, in the Spirit, and not in the letter; whose praise is not of men, but of God (Rom. 2:28-29).

Thought for Today: We cheat ourselves if we fail to give God our best.

Christ Revealed: Through Bethlehem (Ruth 1:1), which means *House of Bread*. Jesus, the *Bread of Life*, satisfies the spiritual hunger of all who come to Him. *Then Jesus said unto them. ... I am the Bread of Life: he that cometh to Me shall never hunger* (John 6:32-35).

KINGS AND PROPHETS OF ISRAEL

UNITED KINGDOM ABOUT 1051 BC

KING	REIGN	PROPHET
Saul	40 Years	Samuel I Sam. 3:20; 9:15-27; 10:16-27;11:7-12
David	40 Years Note: Kingdom divided first 7 1/2 years as David reigned over Judah at Hebron I Kin. 2:10-11 II Sam. 5:5	Samuel I Sam. 16:11-13; 19:8 Nathan II Sam. 7:2-17; 12:1-25 Gad I Sam 22:5; II Sam 24:11-19
Solomon	40 Years	Ahijah the Shilonite I Kin. 11:29-39 Iddo II Chron. 9:29

THE DIVIDED KINGDOM ABOUT 933 BC

SOUTHERN KINGDOM (Judah)   NORTHERN KINGDOM (Israel)

KING	REIGN	PROPHET	KING	REIGN	PROPHET
Rehoboam	17 Years	Shemaiah I Kin. 12:22-24 II Chr. 11:1-4; 12:5-8 Iddo II Chr. 12:15	Jeroboam I	22 Years	Ahijah I Kin. 11:29-39; 12:15; 14:1-18 15:29; II Chr. 9:29; 10:15 A man of God from Judah I Kin. 13:1-32
Abijam (Abijah)	3 Years	Iddo II Chr. 13:22			
Asa	41 Years	Azariah II Chr. 15:1-7 Hanani II Chr. 16:7-10	Nadab	2 Years	
			Baasha	24 Years	Jehu I Kin. 16:1-4,7,12
			Elah	2 Years	
			Zimri	7 Days	
			Omri [& Tibni] I Kin. 16:21-28	12 Years	
Jehoshaphat	25 Years	Jehu II Chr. 19:1-3; 20:34 Jahaziel II Chr. 20:14-17 Eliezer II Chr. 20:35-37	Ahab	22 Years	Elijah I Kin. 17 – II Kin. 2 Micaiah I Kin. 22:8-28 II Chr. 18:7-27
			Ahaziah	2 Years	Elijah II Kin. 1:1-18
Joram (Jehoram)	8 Years	Elijah II Chr. 21:12-15	Jehoram (Joram)	12 Years	Elisha
Ahaziah	1 Year		Jehu	28 Years	Elisha II Kin. 9 – 10
Queen Athaliah [Usurper]	6 Years				
Joash (Jehoash)	40 Years	Joel ? **Zechariah (1) II Chr. 24:20-22	Jehoahaz	17 Years	Elisha

KINGS AND PROPHETS OF ISRAEL

SOUTHERN KINGDOM (Judah)

KING	REIGN	PROPHET
Joash (cont'd)		
Amaziah	29 Years	
Uzziah (Azariah)	52 Years	**Zech. (2) II Chr. 26:5 Isa. 1:1 Mic. 1:1
Jotham	16 Years	Isa. 1:1 Mic. 1:1
Ahaz	16 Years	Isa. 1:1 Mic. 1:1
Hezekiah	29 Years	Isa. 1:3 II Kin. 19:1 – 20:19; II Chr. 32:20-32; Isa. 37:5-35; 38:1-8; 39:3-8 Mic. 1:1
Manasseh	55 Years	The Lord's Servants II Kin. 21:10-15
Amon	2 Years	
Josiah	31 Years	Jer. 1:1-2 Zeph. 1:1 Nah./Hab.? Prophetess Huldah II Kin. 22:14-20

NORTHERN KINGDOM (Israel)

KING	REIGN	PROPHET
Jehoash (Joash)	16 Years	Elisha II Kin. 13:10-20
Jeroboam II	41 Years	Jon. II Kin. 14:25 Hos. 1:1 *Amos 1:1; 2:6 – 9:10
Zechariah	6 Months	
Shallum	1 Month	
Menahem	10 Years	
Pekahiah	2 Years	
Pekah	20 Years	Oded II Chr. 28:9-11
Hoshea	9 Years	

The Northern Kingdom ended when its people were taken captive by Assyria under Shalmaneser in 723/722 BC.

RISE OF BABYLONIA-CHALDEAN DYNASTY ABOUT 625 BC

KING OF JUDAH	REIGN	PROPHET
Jehoahaz (Shallum)	3 Months	Jer. 22:10-12
Jehoiakim	11 Years "Puppet-king" under Egypt & then Babylon	Jer. 1:3; 22:13-19; 25:1; 27:1; 35:1; 36:11,32; 45:1 Urijah (Uriah) Jer. 26:20-23 Hab. ?

FALL OF ASSYRIA ABOUT 612-607 BC
by Nabopolassar, king of Babylon & father of Nebuchadnezzar

KING OF JUDAH	REIGN	PROPHET
Jehoiachin (Jeconiah/Coniah)	3 Months	Jer. 1:3; 22:24-30 Hab. ?
Zedekiah	11 Years	Jer. 1:3; 21:1 – 22:9 Oba. ?

Note: Dates are approximate; scholars vary. There are difficulties in the chronology which may, in part, be accounted for by "overlapping reigns," "associated sovereignty," and "part of year as years."
* Amos was from Judah but prophesied in Israel.
** Zechariah (1) & Zechariah (2) are not the same as Zechariah the prophet after the Exile.

Introduction To The Books Of I & II SAMUEL

The Book of I Samuel covers about 125 years from the birth of Samuel, the last judge of Israel, through most of King Saul's reign. It goes beyond the Book of Judges during the transition from a federation of the 12 tribes ruled by judges to a kingdom.

Samuel grew up in the home of Eli, judge and high priest of Israel and over the Tabernacle at Shiloh, where Israel worshiped. **And all Israel from Dan even to Beersheba knew that Samuel was established** (confirmed) **to be a prophet of the LORD** (I Sam. 3:20; Acts 3:24). At the time Samuel assumed both civil and spiritual leadership, the Israelites were deeply rooted in apostasy and were politically fragmented. Through his loyalty to God and His Word, Samuel restored the nation's moral and spiritual condition to the highest level since the days of godly Joshua.

Samuel founded the first school of the prophets and faithfully taught the Word of God (I Sam. 10:5; 19:20). Because Samuel was a man of prayer and was obedient to the Word of God (7:5-9; 8:6; 12:17-18,23; 15:11), he was able to unite the tribes into one nation. But, as he grew old, the people rejected God and insisted on a king like the other nations. God directed Samuel to anoint as king **Saul, a choice young man** (9:2), and Saul reigned for 40 years.

The Book of II Samuel opens with a brief account of the death of Saul and David's eventual rise to power. The tribe of Judah immediately anointed David as their king. However, Abner, captain of Saul's army, influenced the other ten tribes to accept Ish-bosheth, Saul's surviving son, as their king (II Sam. 2:8-9).

After seven years, Joab, David's military commander, killed Abner, and Ish-bosheth was assassinated by two of his own captains (4:5-6). **So all ... Israel ... anointed David king over Israel** (5:3). **David ... reigned forty years. In Hebron ... over Judah seven years and six months: and in Jerusalem he reigned thirty and three years** (5:4-5) and built the most powerful nation on earth.

David's first conquest as king was the fortress of the Jebusites. **David took the strong hold of Zion** (Jerusalem)**: the same is the city of David** (5:7). There the Messianic Covenant was foretold to David by the prophet Nathan: **I will stablish the throne of his kingdom for ever** (7:13). Much later the prophet Isaiah foretold: **Of the increase of His government and peace there shall be no end, upon the throne of David ... to establish it with judgment and with justice from henceforth even for ever** (Is. 9:7; 11:1; Jer. 23:5-6; Ezek. 37:25).

APRIL 1   Read I Samuel 1 – 3

Highlights: Wow!! We learn three powerful truths. **1.** Hannah *prays* earnestly (perhaps wiser than most). **2.** God rewards her vow to dedicate her son. Consequently, God mightily uses Samuel as the first prominent prophet after Moses and the last judge of Israel (I Sam. 3:19-21; 7:15). **3.** God **requires** parents to discipline their children in love as He does us (2:12-17,23-25; 3:12-13).

Near the end of the period of the judges, we are introduced to Hannah, a godly woman who had lived many years in deep sorrow and humiliation because she could not have children.

While attending the annual Festival at the Tabernacle, *it came to pass, as she continued praying before the L*ORD*, that Eli* (the priest) *marked* (noticed) *her mouth. Now Hannah ... spake in her heart; only her lips moved ... therefore Eli thought she had been drunken. And Eli said unto her, How long wilt thou be drunken* (I Sam. 1:12-14)*?*

Although Hannah was wrongfully accused, she respectfully answered Eli: *No, my lord, I am a woman of a sorrowful spirit: I have drunk neither wine nor strong drink, but have poured out my soul before the L*ORD (1:15). Had she reacted in anger toward Eli for misjudging her, she would have gone away with only a bitter attitude. Instead of being angry, she entreated Eli, telling him that her desire was to have a son to dedicate to the Lord. *Then Eli ... said, Go in peace: and the God of Israel grant thee thy petition* (1:17). God answered Hannah's prayer, and Samuel became perhaps the greatest and most spiritual judge during the period of the judges, which lasted *about ... four hundred and fifty years* (Acts 13:20).

In the hectic pace of twenty-first-century America, countless thousands of words fill our minds every day from printed and broadcast media. But there is a serious neglect of reading the Bible – the only Written Word from God to mankind.

May we have the wisdom to remember that when our first desire is to allow God to use our lives to fulfill His will, He will provide the necessities of life. *Seek ye first the Kingdom of God, and His righteousness; and all these things shall be added unto you* (Matt. 6:33). The one who is intent on living for physical satisfaction is never satisfied, but our Creator's intent is to let Christ be Lord of our lives.

Thought for Today: When parents are living to please God their children are likely to do the same.

Christ Portrayed: By Samuel who grew in favor with God and men (I Sam. 2:26). *And Jesus increased in wisdom and stature, and in favour with God and man* (Luke 2:52).

APRIL 2   Read I Samuel 4 – 7

Highlights: What a shocking surprise! Ninety-eight-year-old Eli the priest hears that they lost the war, his two sons were killed, ***and the Ark of God*** (was) ***taken*** (I Sam. 4:17,22). A reminder of the judgment of God (2:27-34). What did God do to the Philistines (5:1-12)? They plan to get rid of ***the Ark*** (6:2-9).

The hostile Philistines lived on the coastal plains of the Mediterranean Sea, on the southwestern border of Israel. As the Israelites marched into battle against the Philistines, they were confident of victory. Imagine their surprise ***when . . . Israel was smitten*** (defeated) ***before the Philistines*** (I Sam. 4:2). In desperation, ***the elders of Israel said, Wherefore hath the LORD smitten us to day before the Philistines? Let us fetch the Ark of the Covenant of the LORD . . . that . . . it may save us out of the hand of our enemies*** (4:3). ***And when the Ark of the Covenant of the LORD came into the camp, all Israel shouted with a great shout*** (4:5). The Israelites expected God to give them victory; however, sin was in the camp. The two evil sons of Eli who carried the Ark ***knew not the LORD*** (2:12).

Eli, the old and blind judge, sat near the Tabernacle, anxious to hear the outcome of the battle. A ***messenger*** reported: ***Israel is fled before the Philistines, and there hath been . . . a great slaughter . . . thy two sons . . . Hophni and Phinehas, are dead, and the Ark of God is taken. . . . when he*** (the messenger) ***made mention of the Ark of God . . . he*** (Eli) ***fell . . . backward . . . and he died*** (4:17-18).

When Israel was again threatened by war with the Philistines, ***Samuel spake unto all . . . Israel . . . prepare your hearts unto the LORD, and serve Him only: and He will deliver you out of the hand of the Philistines. . . . And Samuel said . . . I will pray for you unto the LORD. . . . they . . . said . . . We have sinned against the LORD*** (7:3,5-6). When the Philistines learned that the Israelites were worshiping God, they assumed it was time to attack them. ***And as Samuel was offering up the Burnt Offering, the Philistines*** (attacked) ***. . . Israel: but the LORD thundered with a great thunder . . . upon the Philistines, and . . .*** (overcame) ***them*** (7:10-13).

God protects and provides for anyone who is obedient to His Word.

Thought for Today: The most profitable part of our day is the time we spend in God's presence, praying, reading, and obeying His Word.

Christ Revealed: Through the rock called ***Ebenezer*** which means the stone of help (I Sam. 7:12). Jesus is our Rock of salvation; our help comes from Him (Ps. 18:2, 121:2). ***I can do all things through Christ which strengtheneth me*** (Phil. 4:13).

APRIL 3   Read I Samuel 8 – 11

Highlights: The people demand a king and ignore the true King (I Sam. 8:5). God directed Samuel to anoint Saul (9:27 – 10:1). King Saul is challenged and Israel defeats the Ammonites (11:1-11).

During the four-hundred-fifty-year history of the judges (Acts 13:20), Samuel accomplished more as a spiritual leader than any other judge. Repeatedly, the Israelites had turned away from the Lord; but when they repented, God sent a deliverer – a judge. Eventually, when Samuel was old, the people rejected God as their king and told Samuel: ***Make us a king to judge us like all the nations*** (I Sam. 8:5).

God instructed Samuel to do what the people asked, but God reminded Samuel: ***They have not rejected thee, but they have rejected Me, that I should not reign over them*** (8:7). Samuel anointed Saul king in Ramah as the Lord had directed him. After a brief time, ***Samuel called the people together unto the L*****ORD*** **to Mizpeh; And said ... ye have ... rejected your God, who Himself saved you out of all your adversities and your tribulations*** (10:17-19). He then presented Saul to them as the man ***whom the L*****ORD*** **hath chosen.... And all the people shouted ... God save*** (long live) ***the king*** (10:24). Saul's external appearance pleased the people, but he was a symbol of the spiritual weakness of the nation.

The first test of King Saul came when he was told that ***Nahash the Ammonite*** king had put his army in position to attack (11:1). The Ammonites had not attacked the Israelites since Jephthah, a hero of faith (Heb. 11:32), had defeated them about half a century earlier (Judg. 11). Saul called together men from all the tribes to be his soldiers. Saul led the Israelites in a spectacular victory. As he finished his first battle, he gave credit to the Lord as he shouted: ***To day the L*****ORD*** **hath wrought salvation in Israel*** (11:13).

Saul had a good beginning and never worshiped idols. But pride and self-will soon became his way of life, resulting in a succession of failures. This illustrates the deception and temptation that often follow success. Pride inevitably leads to a self-centered life where Christ is Lord in Name only (Matt. 16:24-27). When we assume that we have the ability to make decisions as to what is best for our lives and no longer see the need to read His Word for guidance, we should remember what Jesus said: ***I am the Vine, ye are the branches ... without Me ye can do nothing*** (that has eternal value) (John 15:5).

Thought for Today: There are many ways in which God works in our lives, but most often it is through ordinary circumstances as we allow God to live through us.

Christ Portrayed: Through Samuel who faithfully served Israel as judge, prophet, and priest. Jesus was the Prophet promised through Moses (Deut. 18:15). He is our **High Priest** (Heb. 4:14); and one day He will judge all mankind: ***For the Father judgeth no man, but hath committed all judgment unto the Son*** (John 5:22).

APRIL 4 — Read I Samuel 12 – 14:23

Highlights: Samuel gives the king and the nation serious warnings (I Sam. 12:14-15,24-25). We should all take heed (12:23). Saul reveals his failure when he usurps the office of the priesthood. He loses the kingdom (13:8-14). Saul's son Jonathan trusts God, leads a bold thrust into enemy territory, and Israel is victorious (14:1-23).

Saul, the first king of Israel, was a popular man with great ability, but he had a fatal flaw. Perhaps three years after Saul became king, his first great failure occurred when he trusted his own judgment and not the Lord. **The Philistines gathered... to fight with Israel, thirty thousand chariots, and six thousand horsemen, and people as the sand which is on the sea shore in multitude** (I Sam. 13:5).

In fear of the mighty Philistines, many in Saul's army hid **themselves in caves** (13:6). Saul realized that their only hope was in God. **He tarried seven days... but Samuel came not.... And Saul... offered the Burnt Offering. And... as soon as he had made an end of offering the Burnt Offering... Samuel came** (13:8-10). When assuming the role of a priest, Saul disobeyed the Word of God. Saul's excuse: **Because I saw that the people were scattered from me... Therefore, said I, The Philistines will come down now upon me... and I... offered a Burnt Offering** (13:11-12).

The Burnt Offering symbolized surrender to God; but, when Saul presumed to take the God-ordained position of a priest, the sacrifice became an abomination to the Lord (15:22-23; comp. Num. 16:1-40; Prov. 21:27). What seemed to Saul a tardiness in Samuel's arrival was, in reality, a test by God of Saul's obedience to Him. Samuel spoke bluntly to Saul: **Thou hast done foolishly: thou hast not kept the Commandment of the Lord thy God, which He commanded thee** (I Sam. 13:13).

Saul was not as concerned about God having authority over him as he was with God making him successful. In spite of not waiting on God and disobediently offering a sacrifice to Him, Saul assumed he could bring victory to Israel.

Some may consider Saul's disobedience of little consequence, but disobeying the Word of God is always a serious sin.

We may be tempted at times to disregard what the Bible states is sin, assuming that circumstances justify disobedience. But presumption can never be a substitute for obeying the Word of God.

Thought for Today: A true servant of the Lord willingly follows his Master's instructions without exception.

Christ Portrayed: By Samuel the intercessor (I Sam. 12:23). Right now Jesus is interceding for believers. **It is Christ that died, yea rather, that is risen again, who is even at the right hand of God, who also maketh intercession for us** (Rom. 8:34; Heb. 7:25).

APRIL 5   **Read I Samuel 14:24 – 16**

Highlights: Saul makes a foolish vow (I Sam. 14:24-30). Then he disobeys the direct command of God. First we read of Eli the priest, then Samuel the prophet, and Saul the king. Next enters David, the shepherd boy who becomes the God-anointed king of Israel. His Seed (Descendant) later became our promised Savior, High Priest, Prophet, and King of kings. Don't miss the "rags to riches" account of this shepherd boy.

Saul was influenced by the godly prophet Samuel at the beginning of his reign, and served the people as the servant of God. But it wasn't long before his decisions were calculated to maintain popularity with the people. Saul wanted Samuel's blessing but, when he had to make a choice between obedience to God, he chose to please the people. **And Samuel said, When thou wast little in thine own sight, wast thou not made the head of the tribes of Israel, and the LORD anointed thee king over Israel** (I Sam. 15:17)**?**

We can see that pleasing the people was more important to Saul than having God rule his life. Saul confessed to Samuel: **I have sinned: for I have transgressed the Commandment of the LORD . . . because I feared the people, and obeyed their voice** (15:24).

We need to always remind ourselves of Samuel's inspired Word of God to Saul: **Hath the LORD as great delight in Burnt Offerings and sacrifices, as in obeying the voice of the LORD? Behold, to obey is better than sacrifice. . . . For rebellion is as the sin of witchcraft, and stubbornness is as iniquity and idolatry** (15:22-23). The Israelites were suffering from the misrule of a king who would not be ruled by God, and God used Samuel to bring about a change.

Few things are so subtle and destructive to our spiritual lives as pride. Our unconditional motive needs to be a desire to know and do the will of God as revealed in His Word. The Word of God exposes the deceitfulness and dangers of pride. **Every one that is proud in heart is an abomination to the LORD. . . . Pride goeth before destruction, and an haughty spirit before a fall** (Prov. 16:5,18). The person that is truly pleasing to God will recognize that his ability to fulfill the will of God comes only from the Lord and His Word.

Thought for Today: We form opinions about people, but only God knows their hearts.

Christ Portrayed: Through David's name (I Sam. 16:13) which means "beloved." David is a type of Jesus, whom the Heavenly Father called: **My beloved Son** (Matt. 3:17; 17:5; Mark 1:11; 9:7; Luke 3:22; 9:35).

APRIL 6   Read I Samuel 17 – 18

Highlights: A point to consider: God used both Samuel and David, as youths, to fulfill His will. David gives Saul his résumé, his objective, and why he will fight Goliath (I Sam. 17:26,34-37,47). Check out David's weapon (17:45). David gains the heart of **all Israel and Judah** (18:16), including Saul's son and daughter (18:1,20). Hearing others praise David, Saul becomes jealous of him (18:9-11).

Early in Saul's reign, the giant Philistine warrior Goliath challenged the Israelite army to send a man to fight him and let the outcome of their fight decide which nation won the war. Apparently neither Saul nor anyone in his army were willing to accept his challenge.

But, when young David came into the camp and heard Goliath's taunts, he offered to fight him. He boldly said **to the Philistine, Thou comest to me with a sword, and with a spear, and with a shield: but I come to thee in the Name of the LORD of hosts, the God of the armies of Israel, whom thou hast defied. This day will the LORD deliver thee into mine hand; and I will smite thee** (strike you down) **. . . that all the earth may know that there is a God in Israel** (I Sam. 17:45-46).

Faith in the God of Israel gave David his spectacular victory over Goliath. David was welcomed into the palace of King Saul, made his trusted captain of the guard (18:5), and married his daughter Michal (18:27). We are not told how much time passed after David was welcomed into the king's court before Saul heard women singing David's praises, and he became exceedingly jealous. Saul even attempted to kill David (18:10-11).

David fled and escaped with the help of his wife Michal. He **came to Samuel to Ramah, and told him all that Saul had done to him** (19:12,18). He had enjoyed acceptance in the king's palace, but now he was reduced to hiding in caves. Difficulties, handicaps, and suffering in life are permitted by the Lord to develop godly character and to enable us to accomplish His purposes. Like David, we are put to the test to see if we will remain faithful and prove worthy of our high calling. Each of us is accountable for the effect which trials, suffering, or handicaps will have on us. We can allow them to develop our faith in the Lord, or we can become bitter and resentful, blaming God and others for our troubles.

Thought for Today: Faith is developed as we trust the Lord when we face difficult disappointments, **knowing that tribulation worketh patience** (Rom. 5:3-5).

Christ Portrayed: By Jonathan, who knew the will of God was to make David king and **stripped himself** of his royal robes and **made a covenant** promising all that he had to David (I Sam. 18:3-4). Jesus, knowing the will of God, cast off His heavenly robes **and took upon Him the form of a servant . . . and became obedient unto death, even the death of the cross** (Phil. 2:5-8).

APRIL 7   Read I Samuel 19 – 21

Highlights: Powerful reading! A gigantic "battle" rages between God and Satan – **inside Saul**. Has this ever happened to you? Check chapter 19! Saul is jealous, rebellious, disobedient, and confused. David displays wisdom and confident faith in God.

David became a national hero but, as time passed, King Saul became increasingly jealous of his popularity. Saul had manipulated circumstances to expose David to the Philistines, hoping they would kill him (I Sam. 18:25). **Jonathan spake good of David unto Saul his father, and said . . . Let not the king sin against his servant. . . . For he did put his life in his hand, and slew the Philistine, and the LORD wrought a great salvation for all Israel: thou sawest it . . . wherefore then wilt thou sin against innocent blood, to slay David without a cause? . . . and Saul sware, As the LORD liveth, he shall not be slain** (19:4-6).

Saul's temper had become violent and uncontrolled. Jonathan revealed remarkable spiritual insight and courage when he confronted his father the king in defense of David. In a fit of rage, Saul denounced his son. He even attempted to kill Jonathan. **Saul's anger was kindled against Jonathan, and he said unto him . . . send and fetch him** (David) **. . . for he shall surely die. And Jonathan answered Saul his father, and said unto him, Wherefore shall he be slain? what hath he done? And Saul cast a javelin at him to smite him** (20:30-33).

Jonathan could have avoided any risk to himself if he had decided not to get involved in defending David. But Jonathan had great integrity, and he risked his life to protect David. To defend an innocent person from slander or harm's way, whatever the cost, is to remain faithful to biblical principles by doing what is right.

We too may find ourselves in situations where a person is being accused, intimidated, or taken advantage of. We are then faced with the decision of whether or not to get involved. We should not be an accomplice to evil by remaining silent, but should respond as Jonathan did. There is a direct connection between what we truly believe and how we behave. The Apostle James urged believers: **Be . . . doers of the Word, and not hearers only, deceiving your own selves** (James 1:22).

Thought for Today: The Bible was not given just to inform us but to transform us.

Christ Portrayed: By David, who, as a servant of Saul, suffered at the hands of the one whom he chose to serve (I Sam. 19:1;10-11). Jesus suffered at the hands of the ones He came to serve and to save. **From that time forth began Jesus to shew unto His disciples, how that He must go unto Jerusalem, and suffer many things of the elders and chief priests and scribes, and be killed, and be raised again the third day** (Matt. 16:21).

APRIL 8 — Read I Samuel 22 – 24

Highlights: Saul orders the inexcusable act of murdering all the priests and their families at Nob. A warning to all who allow pride and self-will to get out of control. David's escape; protection of the Lord for David, who trusts God (I Sam. 23:2,4,10-12). David protects the Israelites in Keilah. Although he could, David will not kill Saul since he is the anointed king.

Since the destruction of Shiloh, the priests had kept the sacred vessels at Nob, just northeast and within sight of Jerusalem (Is. 10:32). When David requested, Ahimelech the priest gave him food and the sword that had belonged to Goliath. This was reported to Saul in Gibeah by Doeg, an Edomite servant. (Edomites were descendants of Esau. Traditionally, they hated the Jews, who were descendants of Jacob.) In a fit of anger, Saul accused Ahimelech of conspiracy. **Ahimelech answered the king, and said, And who is so faithful among all thy servants as David, which is the king's son in law, and goeth at thy bidding, and is honourable in thine house** (I Sam. 22:14)**?**

Blinded by jealousy and hatred, Saul ordered the execution of all the priests and their families (22:16,19). **But the servants of the king would not put forth their hand to fall upon the priests of the LORD** (22:17). But without hesitation, **Doeg the Edomite . . . slew on that day fourscore and five** (85) **persons that did wear a linen ephod** (priestly garment). **Both men and women, children . . . with the edge of the sword** (22:18-19).

One of the sons of Ahimelech . . . (a priest) **named Abiathar, escaped, and fled after David** (22:20). David knew Saul was determined to kill him, but he continued to pray for guidance (23:10-12).

There are times in the lives of most Christians when everything seems hopeless and we need encouragement about ourselves, our talents, our children, or even our relationship with the Lord. This was also true of David, who received spiritual direction and comfort from Abiathar and prophets such as Gad (22:5).

Like David, we can be confident in the unchanging, eternal Word of God. Our all-wise Heavenly Father often allows us to experience times of deep distress in order to develop in us a greater faith in Him. He does care, and He stands ready to answer our call for help when we are in submission to Him.

Thought for Today: Loving our enemies means sharing the Word of God with those who need it most.

Christ Revealed: By David's refusal to take the kingdom by force or before the appointed time set by God (I Sam. 24:10-13). Christ refused to become King of Israel. **When Jesus . . . perceived** (knew) **that they would come and take Him by force, to make Him a king, He departed . . . into a mountain Himself alone** (John 6:15).

APRIL 9   **Read I Samuel 25 – 27**

Highlights: Don't miss today's reading! We learn we can receive direction from God, as David did (I Sam. 25:32-33,39; 26:22-24), when we stay faithful and respect biblical principles (26:8-12). Nabal, a wicked landowner, dies; David marries his widow Abigail; Saul continues to pursue David.

Samuel was one of the greatest spiritual giants in Israel's history and is listed as one of the heroes of the faith (Heb. 11:32), but just one sentence (I Sam. 25:1) records the death of this grand, old prophet at this treacherous time in Israel's history. Because of Saul, David could not attend the funeral; instead he **went down to the wilderness of Paran** (25:1). The Israelites were now without spiritual leadership. But the all-wise God, who controls the universe, always knows and does what is best.

We are tempted at times to think that death has come at tshe wrong time, especially when a child is left without a mother, or when children die at a young age. Familiar as we are with death, the ways of God regarding death often seem hard to accept. But, without a doubt, God never abandons His children. He leads us to look beyond our grief by faith and trust in His wisdom and His tender love to comfort our broken spirit. **Wherefore comfort one another with these words** (I Thess. 4:18).

Death for the Christian is a promotion from this world's suffering to a welcome home by our wonderful Lord. Soon, **God shall wipe away all tears from their eyes; and there shall be no more death, neither sorrow, nor crying, neither shall there be any more pain: for the former things are passed away** (Rev. 21:4).

At times we all need comfort. This is especially true during experiences of distress and grief when a loved one dies. Those of us who have lost loved ones know what a word of compassion can mean. As we see others suffering, let us also remember that our Heavenly Father has commanded: **Comfort ... My people** (Is. 40:1).

Last, but not least, the death of loved ones makes heaven all the more precious for we who remain. **Precious in the sight of the LORD is the death of His saints** (Ps. 116:15). The words of our Savior are most comforting: **Let not your heart be troubled. . . . I will come again, and receive you unto Myself; that where I am, there ye may be also** (John 14:1,3).

Thought for Today: Comfort and pray for someone you know who seems discouraged.

Christ Portrayed: By Abigail's efforts to make peace between David and Nabal (I Sam. 25:21-28). **God was in Christ, reconciling the world unto Himself** (II Cor. 5:19).

APRIL 10   **Read I Samuel 28 – 31**

Highlights: The Philistines declare war. Is David caught on the wrong side (I Sam. 28:1-2)? See chapter 29. Saul consults a witch (28:7-20). Saul's death foretold (28:19). Israel is defeated, and Saul and his sons die tragically (31:2-6).

After Samuel became judge, the Philistines were so badly defeated because of his prayer meeting at Mizpeh that **they came no more into the coast** (territory) **of Israel: and the hand of the Lord was against the Philistines all the days of Samuel** (I Sam. 7:13). But, **there was sore** (severe) **war against the Philistines all the days of Saul** (14:52).

God had given Saul the unique privilege of being the first king to reign over His people. But he misused this privilege because of his continual disobedience.

In the final year of Saul's reign, **the Philistines gathered together all their armies to Aphek** (29:1). Saul panicked when he realized the size of the Philistine armies that were ready to attack. Could Saul forget Samuel's words: **Because thou hast rejected the Word of the Lord, He hath also rejected thee from being king** (15:23)? In desperation, **Saul inquired of the Lord** (28:6). After murdering all the priests of God, how could he expect an answer? Saul frantically sought counsel from a witch in Endor. Saul knew that all mediums, witches, and fortune-tellers **are an abomination unto the Lord** (Deut. 18:10-12). Earlier Saul had banished them from the land (I Sam. 28:3). This fortune-teller was no help. Instead, Saul's fears were increased after seeing Samuel, who said: **Wherefore then dost thou ask of me, seeing the Lord is departed from thee, and is become thine enemy** (28:16)? The next day Saul and three of his sons died in battle. Saul reaped what he had sown. He was his own worst enemy. He lived to serve self. Power, wealth, popularity, and talents are often great hindrances to a spiritual life.

All who reject the Truth of God can easily become victims of false prophets, fortune-tellers, and astrologers, and God shall send **strong delusion that they should believe a lie** (II Thess. 2:11; Matt. 24:24; I John 4:1).

Astrology columns, palm readers, and fortune-tellers violate the Word of God, and expose people to satanic forces. In contrast, true success comes from seeking the Lord's will through reading His Word and praying to the Lord for guidance.

Thought for Today: Ignoring the Word of God leads to deception.

Christ Revealed: Through the Urim (I Sam. 28:6), which was used to determine the will of God. Today Christ speaks to us through His Spirit when we read His Word. **God . . . Hath in these last days spoken unto us by His Son** (Heb. 1:1-2). **When He, the Spirit of Truth, is come, He will guide you** (John 16:13).

APRIL 11 — Read II Samuel 1 – 2

Highlights: Saul killed in battle; David mourns the deaths of Saul and Jonathan; David crowned king of the tribe of Judah; Ish-bosheth, son of Saul, made king of 10 tribes of Israel.

Now that Saul was dead, Israel was without a king. Who would reign in his place? David had been anointed long ago by Samuel the prophet to be the next king of all Israel (I Sam. 16:13). Abner, Saul's cousin and the powerful commander of Saul's army (14:50), was determined to retain his position. He persuaded the elders of Israel to put Saul's son Ish-bosheth on the throne over the 10 tribes.

Saul and David had many similarities: both were anointed king of Israel; both reigned about 40 years; both had the loyal support of Samuel, the prophet of God. But they were very different. Saul was a miserable failure; David a successful king.

Saul was a self-willed man who made decisions without waiting for God to direct him. David never lost sight of his need to pray and wait upon the Lord to fulfull **His** promises at **His** appointed time. David could have felt justified to face Abner in battle for his right as the God-anointed king of Israel.

Even after Saul was dead, David made no effort to claim his right to be king. Instead, **David inquired of the Lord, saying, Shall I go up into any of the cities of Judah? And the Lord said unto him, Go up. And David said, Whither shall I go up? And He said, Unto Hebron. . . . the men of Judah came, and there they anointed David king over . . . Judah** (II Sam. 2:1,4).

One of David's greatest desires was to worship the Lord in Jerusalem. With this in mind, we can better appreciate his patience in waiting for the time God appointed (see Ps. 27:4).

Every child of God is more precious to our Heavenly Father than His home in Solomon's Temple, for **ye** (we) **are the Temple of God. . . . His workmanship, created in Christ Jesus. . . . built upon the foundation of the apostles and prophets . . . In whom all the building fitly framed together groweth unto an holy Temple in the Lord** (I Cor. 3:16; Eph. 2:10,20-21).

How many there are who jump at opportunities for personal advancement rather than seek God and His plan for their lives! But we need not fight for our rights. David prayed for the will of God to be done in His way and at His time. There is a peaceful rest for those who wait patiently for the Lord's timing.

Thought for Today: Spiritual victory is not dependent on human strength or reasoning but on submission to the Holy Spirit.

Christ Revealed: In David's noble poem of sorrow (II Sam. 1:17-27). David forgot all his years of suffering at the hand of Saul and considered only the pleasant things. Here David typifies Christ, who **for the joy that was set before Him endured the cross** (Heb. 12:2).

APRIL 12   **Read II Samuel 3 – 5**

Highlights: Satan hates the will of God. The house of Saul continues to war against the house of David (II Sam. 3:1). Abner deserts Ish-bosheth to join David; Abner murdered by Joab; Ish-bosheth murdered; David declared king of all Israel; the city of Jebus (Jerusalem) is captured.

While David was still a sheepherder, he was anointed king over Israel. David endured many hardships and faced many difficulties through his lifetime. During the years Saul was seeking to kill him, David once became discouraged and cried out in despair: *I shall now perish one day by the hand of Saul* (I Sam. 27:1). Through those hopeless years, God was preparing him to be His faithful shepherd – *a captain over Israel* (II Sam. 5:2). David experienced the loving protection and provision of the Great Shepherd for His children and could say: *He is my refuge and my for-tress: my God; in Him will I trust* (Ps. 91:2).

After Saul's death, David was anointed king over Judah. 7½ years later, *all the elders of Israel came to the king to Hebron . . . and they anointed David king over Israel* (II Sam. 5:3,5).

The time had come for David to move his capital from Hebron to a more central location in the heart of the promised land. The Jebusites held a stronghold in the central position of the promised land, which God had chosen for His dwelling place, the Temple. *The king and his men went to Jerusalem. . . . David took the strong hold of Zion: the same is the city of David* (5:6-7).

This *strong hold of Zion* is symbolic of strongholds which lie deep within our minds and hearts and which may not be known to anyone by our conduct. They depict secret motives and desires that keep us from allowing Christ to be Lord of our lives.

Few are willing to accept and endure the Lord's discipline because they often do not recognize the hand of God in their difficulties. They only see people opposing them and they cry out as David once did: *I shall now perish* (I Sam. 27:1).

The greatest obstacle to being used of God is self. Only when we are willing to die to self can we be an expression of His life.

For we which live are alway delivered unto death for Jesus' sake, that the life also of Jesus might be made manifest in our mortal flesh (II Cor. 4:11).

Thought for Today: Genuine devotion to God brings eternal rewards.

Christ Portrayed: By David, the anointed *king over Israel* (II Sam. 5:3). Christ is the Lord's Anointed. "Christ" is Greek for the Hebrew word *Messiah,* "Anointed One" (Ps. 2:2; John 1:41). Jesus is the world's rightful King. *Pilate wrote a title, and put it on the cross. And the writing was, JESUS OF NAZARETH THE KING OF THE JEWS. . . . and it was written in Hebrew, and Greek, and Latin* (John 19:18-20).

APRIL 13   Read II Samuel 6 – 9

Highlights: David's intentions to bring the Ark to its proper place in Jerusalem result in a man's death. (Learn the real reason.) God forbids David to build the Temple, but God builds David an eternal "house" – meaning royal lineage (II Sam. 7:1-11).

For about 75 years, during most of Samuel's leadership, Saul's 40-year reign, and David's 7½-year reign, the Ark had remained with Abinadab at Kirjath-jearim. David desired to honor God by bringing the Ark of the Covenant, the dwelling place of God on earth, to Jerusalem, the religious and political capital of David's kingdom. But David did not read or pray about what was <u>required</u> to move the Ark. ***David gathered together all the chosen men of Israel, thirty thousand. . . . to bring up from thence*** (to Jerusalem) ***the Ark of God. . . . they set the Ark of God upon a new cart*** (II Sam. 6:1-3) as <u>the</u> Philistines had done many years earlier when they captured it, and proceeded toward Jerusalem with great rejoicing. ***Uzzah and Ahio, the sons of Abinadab, drave*** (drove) ***the new cart*** (6:3). David made the procession a national day of rejoicing, putting God in the center of their nation.

Attempting to keep the Ark from toppling off the cart, ***Uzzah put forth his hand to the Ark of God, and took hold of it; for the oxen shook it. . . . and God smote him there for his error; and there he died by the Ark of God*** (6:6-7). David was humiliated and ***displeased*** (6:8). He was sincerely seeking to honor God but had overlooked two very important instructions in the Word of God: The Ark (which contained the original Word of God) had to be carried by poles on the shoulders of the priests. The penalty for touching the Ark (representing the presence of God) was death (Ex. 25:10-15; Num. 4:15; 7:9).

It is a serious error to believe that, as long as a person is sincere, it makes no difference what he believes. It should also teach us the importance of knowing the Word of God.

Study to shew thyself approved unto God, a workman that needeth not to be ashamed, rightly dividing the Word of Truth (II Tim. 2:15; John 6:63).

Thought for Today: Is your chief concern that God be honored? Then tell your friends to read His directions.

Christ Revealed: By the Ark of the Covenant which ***they . . . set . . . in the midst of the Tabernacle*** (II Sam. 6:17). The Ark contained the Word of God given to Moses (Deut. 10:1-5). Christ is the Living Word (John 1:1) and dwells within us. ***Christ in you, the hope of glory*** (Col. 1:27).

APRIL 14   Read II Samuel 10 – 12

Highlights: We're given a never-ending lesson here. Like David, whenever we experience victories in life, we must never forget that Satan will tempt us to sin as he tempted David. Nathan's parable and David's repentance; birth of Solomon.

David, king of Israel, had never lost a war and had grown accustomed to getting what he wanted. ***And it came to pass ... at the time when kings go forth to battle, that David sent Joab, and his servants ... But David tarried still at Jerusalem*** (II Sam. 11:1). Satan always has something or someone to attract us when we are in a position to gratify our desires instead of doing what we should be doing. For David, his defeat began with a look of lust at the beautiful Bathsheba. David was a man of exceptional character – a man after the Lord's ***own heart*** (I Sam. 13:14). But on this occasion, David inquired about the beautiful woman he saw bathing. He learned that she was the wife of one of his very best soldiers in battle. David knew that adultery was a wicked sin against God. But instead of turning from temptation, ***David sent messengers, and took her; and she came in unto him, and he lay with her ... and she returned unto her house*** (II Sam. 11:4).

There seemingly was not one adverse circumstance from the moment David first lusted after this woman until their marriage. But, about one year later, Nathan the prophet boldly confronted David: ***Wherefore hast thou despised the Commandment of the Lord, to do evil in His sight*** (12:9)? Because of David's adultery, Nathan foretold: ***Now therefore the sword shall never depart from thine house; because thou hast despised Me, and hast taken the wife of Uriah the Hittite to be thy wife. Thus saith the Lord, Behold, I will raise up evil against thee out of thine own house*** (12:10-11). Deeply grieved and repentant, David confessed: ***I have sinned against the Lord. And Nathan said unto David, The Lord also hath put away thy sin*** (12:13). Although forgiven, the next twenty years, the entire last half of his reign, until his death, David's sorrows and sufferings never ceased from that one night of yielding to his lust. Because of David's sincere repentance, as recorded in Psalm 51, God forgave him as He will anyone who truly repents and forsakes their sin, but the bitter consequences are inevitable.

Thought for Today: We must live in the world, but we don't have to live by its standards.

Christ Revealed: In the prophet Nathan giving Solomon the name Jedidiah, which means beloved of the Lord (II Sam. 12:24-25). Christ was greatly loved by the Father. Jesus prayed: ***Thou lovedst Me before the foundation of the world*** (John 17:24).

APRIL 15   **Read II Samuel 13 – 14**

Highlights: The consequences of David's sin begin to hit home (II Sam. 12:9-12), first with Amnon's rape and incest, which turns to hate, revenge, and eventually murder as Absalom kills his brother Amnon and flees to Geshur. David and Absalom reconcile (14:28-33). But Absalom's treachery has only begun.

After David's great sin, he was filled with remorse and was seldom seen in public. Other than rare occasions such as when Joab specifically called upon him to take Rabbah (II Sam. 12:26-31), his palace became his place of seclusion – a prison.

David had lived a godly life except for this sin, but his older sons chose to follow his one great sin instead of following David's otherwise godly example. The eldest, Amnon, cruelly raped his half-sister Tamar. When David learned of Amnon's deception and wicked sin against his daughter, **he was very wroth** (13:21). Amnon was the firstborn son and legal heir to the throne, and David ignored that the Law required death for the sin Amnon had committed (Lev. 20:17). **And ... Absalom hated Amnon** for having raped his sister (II Sam. 13:21-22). Then, motivated by a selfish ambition to become king, and by hatred toward Amnon for raping his sister, Absalom determined to carry out "justice" by murdering his half-brother Amnon, who was heir to the throne.

As Christians, we disapprove of Absalom's cold-blooded murder of Amnon. No one is justified in taking the law into his own hands (Rom. 12:19).

The crimes of David's two sons must have reminded him of his own sins – adultery with Bathsheba and placing her husband on the front lines of battle. His sorrow for his sins continued to plague him as two other sons attempted to take over his throne.

A parent suffers greatly to see his own sin copied in his children's lives. Sin always produces unforeseen evil consequences which go far beyond all expectation. We can be thankful that God **always** forgives when we truly repent and forsake our sins.

Forgetting those things which are behind, and reaching forth unto those things which are before, I press toward the mark for the prize of the high calling of God in Christ Jesus (since God has fully forgiven) (Phil. 3:13-14).

Thought for Today: *Sin is a reproach to any people* (Prov. 14:34).

Christ Revealed: Through David's restoration of Absalom (II Sam. 14:33). If an earthly father's compassion reconciles him to his estranged son, how much more will our loving Heavenly Father reconcile us to HImself when we confess our sins. *God was in Christ, reconciling the world unto Himself, not imputing* (counting, crediting) *their trespasses unto them; and hath committed unto us the word of reconciliation* (II Cor. 5:19).

APRIL 16   Read II Samuel 15 – 16

Highlights: The handsome and popular Absalom (II Sam. 14:25) wins over national leaders, including David's most trusted counselor Ahithophel. Absalom leads a revolt and attempts to overthrow and murder his father, King David.

After Absalom had been in exile **three years** (13:38), Joab, David's nephew and commander-in-chief of his army (I Chr. 2:15-16), initiated a clever plot which persuaded David to bring Absalom home.

About two years after Absalom had returned from exile (II Sam. 14:28), with an arrogant, shameless, and defiant attitude, he demanded that Joab arrange to have the king see him (14:29-32). David promptly forgave Absalom, who then began an ambitious conspiracy to overthrow his father and declare himself king of Israel. Soon the shocking news reached David that **the hearts of the men of Israel are after** (with) **Absalom** (15:13).

One of the most pitiful passages in the Bible is of brokenhearted King David, running barefoot down the rocky hills, weeping and fleeing Jerusalem in fear of his own beloved son (15:30). During this time, he had no thought of self-pity or revenge. David's great concern was to avoid bloodshed in Jerusalem, the City of God.

Shimei, one of Saul's relatives (16:5), followed David as he fled from Jerusalem, cursing him and throwing stones at him. He accused David of being responsible for Saul's death and **all the blood of the house of Saul** (16:8). This accusation was not true, and Abishai asked David for permission to kill Shimei. David refused, saying: **Let him curse, because the Lord hath said unto him, Curse David** (16:10).

Too often, when someone treats us unjustly, we have a tendency to retaliate, fight back, or seek revenge instead of looking to God in our sufferings. But once we realize that God has a purpose for everything He allows to come into our lives, and we repent, we can experience the peace of being in His will. The highest privilege Christians have is to yield our will to His ways. May God teach us the precious privilege of accepting and loving His ways!

Thought for Today: In contrast to the accepted immoral principles of the world, the Word of God reveals the vileness of sin.

Christ Portrayed: By David as he rebuked his followers when they wanted to execute his enemies (II Sam. 16:10-11; comp. I Sam. 26:8-9). When Jesus' disciples wanted to do the same, He **rebuked them**, saying: **Ye know not what manner of spirit ye are of. For the Son of Man is not come to destroy men's lives, but to save them** (Luke 9:54-56).

APRIL 17   Read II Samuel 17 – 18

Highlights: Here's an important life lesson: Always compare your desires with the Word of God. Absalom didn't, and his rebellion against God destroyed him (II Sam. 18:9).

The majority of Israel's leaders and many of the people joined Absalom in a rebellion to overthrow King David. Absalom was then declared king and entered Jerusalem without resistance.

Up to this point, all his plans had been successful. But Absalom was determined to pursue and murder his father David. However, in the ensuing battle, **there was . . . a great slaughter that day of twenty thousand men. . . . And Absalom rode upon a mule, and the mule went under the thick boughs of a great oak, and his head** (hair) **caught hold of the oak** (limbs)**, and he was taken up between the heaven and the earth; and the mule that was under him went away** (II Sam. 18:7,9).

There were many who had once stayed by Absalom; but now, with his hair caught in the limbs of the oak tree, he didn't have a friend to help him escape. Everyone rushed past him, concerned only about saving their own lives.

Absalom's rebellion against David is typical of those who **take counsel together, against the LORD, and against His Anointed** (Ps. 2:2). But God allows the wicked to be "successful" only until His purposes have been fulfilled. God provided an insignificant branch of a tree to hold Absalom by his hair until he was killed by Joab. **Pride goeth before destruction, and an haughty spirit before a fall** (Prov. 16:18).

Many people have died an untimely death after having taken an open stand against a God-appointed leader. It is so important that we pray for those in authority instead of taking matters into our own hands without seeking direction from God. **Let every soul be subject unto the higher powers. For there is no power but of God: the powers that be are ordained of God** (Rom. 13:1).

Pity the ignorant who are unaware of the "Unseen Presence" of God, who defends those who trust in Him (Heb. 4:13; Ps. 40:17)! **For promotion cometh neither from the east, nor from the west, nor from the south. But God is the judge: He putteth down one, and setteth up another** (Ps. 75:6-7). **All things work together for good to them that love God** (Rom. 8:28).

Thought for Today: No one can defeat the purposes of God for you.

Christ Revealed: Through Mahanaim, a city of refuge where David went when he was fleeing from Absalom (II Sam. 17:27). Christ is our Refuge. **We . . . have fled for refuge to lay hold upon the hope set before us . . . even Jesus** (Heb. 6:18-20).

APRIL 18   **Read II Samuel 19 – 20**

Highlights: Joab, David's nephew (I Chr. 2:13-16), feels justified as he kills Abner (II Sam. 3:27), his cousin Absalom (18:14), and his cousin Amasa (20:10; I Chr. 2:16-17). Yet he sensibly reproves David twice (II Sam. 19:5-7; 24:1-3). Sheba leads one last revolt before David's kingdom is restored in chapter 20.

Absalom was a traitor who was determined to destroy his father, so that he could be king. The battle ended when Joab killed Absalom.

David's soldiers returned expecting a celebration; instead they heard the king weeping: *O Absalom, my son, my son* (II Sam. 19:4)*!* David had faced many sorrows throughout his life. When Bathsheba's first child became sick, David had prayed and fasted. Then, when he received word the child had died, David confidently said: *I shall go to him, but he shall not return to me* (12:23). David knew heaven would be all the more precious because his child was with the Lord. But David expressed no hope that he would see Absalom in heaven. David may have felt that if Joab had only given Absalom one more chance perhaps he would have turned from his wicked ways. But, had he lived, Absalom would have been in fierce competition with Solomon, the choice of God to take David's place as king.

All of us, at times, are responsible for the adversities and sorrows which we experience. It is also natural to condemn ourselves for our faults and failures, or even to blame others for the things that disappoint us. Like David, we can grieve too long over what might have been. If we are out of the will of God, we need to repent of our sins, ask God to forgive us, and be like the Apostle Paul, who proclaimed: *Forgetting those things which are behind, and reaching forth unto those things which are before, I press toward the mark* (goal) *for the prize of the high calling of God in Christ Jesus* (Phil. 3:13-14).

In our darkest moments, we all need friends to remind us to trust the Lord. In turn, we need to be a friend who can share comforting words with a despondent sufferer. By God's grace, we should encourage them to become involved in a local church where others can help deepen and nurture their faith in the love of God, *for we are members of His body. . . . This is a great mystery* (hidden truth)*: but I speak concerning Christ and the Church* (Eph. 5:30,32).

Thought for Today: Christ heals the brokenhearted who trust Him.

Christ Portrayed: By David, who wished to be invited back as king (II Sam. 19:11). Our Lord Jesus wanted to be invited into the hearts of all mankind. He only comes in by our invitation. *Behold, I stand at the door, and knock: if any man hear My voice, and open the door, I will come in to him* (Rev. 3:20).

APRIL 19   **Read II Samuel 21 – 22**

Highlights: We receive another principle of life: Be careful when you make a vow. God punishes Israel with a 3-year famine as a result of King Saul's breaking a vow. Seven members of Saul's family are put to death. To make a vow as a Christian is also sacred. Read Joshua 9:14-18! Breaking a promise can be serious (II Sam. 21:1-6). Don't miss Chapter 22 for David's inspiring tribute to God.

The days of harvest had come once again (II Sam. 21:10), but there was not much to gather because **there was a famine** (21:1). The famine was the judgment of God. He had told the Israelites: **If thou wilt not hearken** (listen) **unto the voice of the LORD thy God, to observe to do all His Commandments. . . . thy heaven . . . shall be brass, and the earth . . . shall be iron** (unproductive) (Deut. 28:15,23).

As David prayed, God revealed to him that Saul had violated the covenant that Israel had made with the Gibeonites about 400 years earlier. That treaty was still sacred because the covenant had been sworn to in the Name of God (Josh. 9:3,15-19).

God has stated: **When thou shalt vow a vow unto the LORD thy God, thou shalt not slack to pay it: for the LORD thy God will surely require it of thee** (Deut. 23:21; Num. 30:2).

The surviving Gibeonites did not ask David for money or property (II Sam. 21:4). They surely knew the Commandment of God: **Moreover ye shall take no satisfaction for the life of a murderer, which is guilty of death: but he shall be . . . put to death** (Num. 35:31). Since Saul disregarded this command, the Gibeonites requested permission to hang seven men who were descendants of Saul (II Sam. 21:5-6).

Therefore, David was responsible before God to deliver them to the Gibeonites. Because of his covenant with Jonathan, David spared Jonathan's crippled son Mephibosheth (II Sam. 21:7; I Sam. 20:14-17; 23:16-18).

The three years of famine that resulted from a broken vow reveal the importance of keeping one's word. Can people depend upon what you say, or are your vows meaningless? Do you say only what others want to hear? Some Christians may have good intentions, but they allow circumstances to sway their convictions; consequently, their word is unreliable. **That which is gone out of thy lips thou shalt keep and perform** (Deut. 23:23).

Thought for Today: God expects us to keep our promises. Can you be trusted to fulfill what you said you would do?

Christ Portrayed: As the One we call upon for salvation (II Sam. 22:4). **Neither is there salvation in any other: for there is none other Name under heaven given among men, whereby we must be saved** (Acts 4:12).

APRIL 20   Read II Samuel 23 – 24

Highlights: David's last words are a tribute to his ***mighty men*** (II Sam. 23:8-17). First he names the top "three" of his honor roll of 37 (23:18-39). David sins (a census) (24:1-10). Three-day plague; David builds an altar; his sacrifice (24:11-14).

Satan, the instigator of pride, ***stood up against Israel, and provoked David to number Israel*** (I Chr. 21:1). From the standpoint of the absolute sovereignty of God over everything, including Satan, we read: ***The anger of the Lord was kindled against Israel, and He moved*** (allowed) ***David against them to say, Go, number Israel and Judah*** (II Sam. 24:1). David's desire to take a census of his army obviously was not based on any threat by invaders at this time. He had never lost a war or been defeated. When we feel proud of our accomplishments, Satan is quick to suggest thoughts of pride as he did with David. ***When pride cometh, then cometh shame*** (Prov. 11:2; 16:18; 29:23).

David's decision, prompted by pride, reminds us of how easily a person can become a victim of his success and lose sight of who is responsible for all our blessings. In this moment of pride, David seems to have forgotten that he once said: ***Some trust in chariots, and some in horses: but we will remember the Name of the Lord our God*** (Ps. 20:7). He ignored the Law that said when a soldier is numbered, he must pay a half shekel, the price of a sin offering, as ***a ransom for his soul . . . that there be no plague among them, when thou numberest them*** (Ex. 30:12-15).

God gives special talents and abilities. There is a tendency to become proud of "our" accomplishments and no longer depend on Him. No one in himself is good enough to serve the Lord. The silver shekel is symbolic of Truth, and Christ alone is ***The Way, The Truth, and The Life*** (John 14:6). His atonement alone qualifies us to serve the Lord. This needs to be a first consideration when people are chosen to lead in worship, to teach, or to entertain our congregations without regard to their personal relationships to Christ. Even answers to prayer can become dramatic exhibitions wherein we subtly give ourselves the credit for "our" great faith and power in prayer.

Oh, how sensitive we must be to say from our hearts: ***God forbid that I should glory, save in the cross of our Lord Jesus Christ*** (Gal. 6:14)! We must always give our Lord the glory and praise for anything worthwhile.

Thought for Today: The weapons of our spiritual warfare are mighty.

Christ Revealed: Through the silver which David used to purchase ***the threshingfloor*** upon which he built ***an Altar unto the Lord*** (II Sam. 24:24-25). Silver symbolizes Christ's redemption offered for all. Judas ***said unto them, What will ye give me. . . . And they covenanted*** (agreed) ***with him for thirty pieces of silver*** (Matt. 26:15).

INTRODUCTION TO THE BOOKS OF I & II KINGS

All the kings of Judah and Israel are recorded in I & II Kings except for Saul. The purpose of I & II Kings is twofold: (1) to illustrate the blessings that result from faithfulness and obedience to the Lord and (2) His judgment upon unfaithfulness and disobedience. The first 11 chapters of I Kings focus primarily on the reign of Solomon. Chapters 12 – 22 cover the first 80-100 years of the divided kingdom. During that time, four kings reigned over the Southern Kingdom and eight over the Northern Kingdom.

David's final words to Solomon were: **Keep the charge** (requirements) ***of the Lord thy God, to walk in His ways, to keep . . . His Commandments . . . that thou mayest prosper in all that thou doest*** (I Kin. 2:3; Josh. 1:7). But Solomon ignored David's advice.

The first 17 chapters of II Kings focus on the prophets Elijah and Elisha and on the spiritual decline of both the Southern and Northern Kingdoms. Nineteen kings ruled the Northern Kingdom of Israel during its approximately 210-year history as a divided kingdom. Chapter 17 ends with the conquest and removal of the people of Israel by the Assyrians. Most of those Israelites were scattered throughout the Assyrian Empire, while captives from other nations were brought into Samaria. These pagans intermarried with the few remaining Israelites. Their descendants became known as Samaritans, a people despised by the Jews for being impure.

The smaller Southern Kingdom of Judah remained independent for another 135 years, existing for a total of about 465 years. After the 120 years of the United Kingdom (approximately 40 years each by Saul, David, and Solomon), Judah had 19 legitimate kings and one usurper, Queen Athaliah (I Kin. 11:42 – II Kin. 25:30). The closing eight chapters of II Kings are devoted to the Southern Kingdom of Judah.

By the end of the last chapter, we read that Jerusalem was destroyed and Solomon's Temple burned by the Babylonians. Most of Judah's population then was taken captive and dispersed throughout Babylonia.

The prophets Elijah and Elisha prophesied in Israel, as did Amos, Hosea, and Jonah. Obadiah, Joel, Isaiah, Micah, Nahum, Habakkuk, Zephaniah, and Jeremiah prophesied during this time in Judah. These servants of God exposed the nation's sins and appealed to the people to reject their idols and repent or experience defeat and the judgment of God.

APRIL 21   Read I Kings 1 – 2:25

Highlights: King David at death's door. Adonijah, Absalom's younger brother, organizes another revolt! But nothing thwarts the sovereign purpose of God. Look who stops the coup (I Kin. 1:11-53). David charges Solomon to walk with God (2:1-4).

David's last words to Solomon revealed his greatest desire for his son. He stressed the importance of keeping the Commandments of God so that he would live to please God.

Material blessings are incidental and may or may not be obtained by those who *prosper* in the eyes of God. Although Stephen and Paul did not "prosper" in the eyes of the world, their true prosperity cannot be measured.

So shall My Word be that goeth forth out of My mouth: it shall not return unto Me void, but it shall <u>accomplish</u> <u>that</u> <u>which</u> <u>I</u> <u>please</u>, and it shall <u>prosper</u> (progress, succeed) *in the thing whereto I sent it* (Is. 55:11). Thus, we prosper as we <u>follow</u> His Word.

David... charged Solomon... be thou strong... and shew thyself a man (I Kin. 2:1-2). Like Solomon, we cannot **keep the charge of the Lord** (2:3) unless we read and understand what **the charge of the Lord** is. David did not urge Solomon to show himself a man by conquering more kingdoms but by personally seeking the Lord's will through His Word and living it.

David did not use vain repetitions when he spoke of the Lord's **Statutes, and His Commandments, and His Judgments, and His Testimonies** (2:3), for the whole Law, not just the portion that may seem pleasing to one's interests, was to be observed.

We are all tempted to only "partial obedience" – but neglecting some is disobedience.

How irresponsible it is to own a Bible and yet disregard it as if it were not worth spending time to know the Creator's plan for our lives. In it we possess the only Revelation of the One True God, the Creator of all things.

Therefore, let us be **strong** to read it for its own supreme value that we might know the One True God who provided it. What a privilege we have to know our Creator and be in fellowship with Him!

Thought for Today: You are precious to the Lord.

Christ Revealed: Through the oil used to anoint Solomon (I Kin. 1:39). Christos (Greek) and Messiah (Hebrew) mean "The Anointed One." Oil, symbolic of the Holy Spirit, was poured out upon those chosen by God for special service. Jesus is the Anointed One of God: *The Spirit of the Lord is upon Me, because He hath anointed Me to preach the Gospel to the poor* (needy) (Luke 4:18).

APRIL 22   **Read I Kings 2:26 – 4**

Highlights: The prophecy against Eli is fulfilled (I Kin. 2:26-27; see I Sam. 2:27-36). Abiathar banished from the priesthood. Solomon carries out David's instructions concerning Joab and Shimei (2:28-46; see 2:5-9). Solomon's marriage to Pharaoh's daughter; his dream; his kingdom is established (2:12,46).

At the beginning of his reign, Solomon loved the Lord. But early in his reign Solomon compromised his responsibility *to walk in His ways, to keep . . . His Commandments* (I Kin. 2:3). He established a relationship with Egypt for the first time since Israel's Exodus from Egypt 480 years earlier.

Solomon may have thought that marrying Pharaoh's daughter would prevent future wars with Egypt, increase his prestige among the surrounding nations, and give him a better price on the thousands of horses he purchased from Pharaoh (9:16). Solomon's goal was to become famous and popular in the world. In doing this, he ignored the Word of God concerning the responsibilities of the kings of Israel: *He shall not multiply horses to himself, nor . . . return to Egypt, to the end that he should multiply horses. . . . Neither shall he multiply wives to himself, that his heart turn not away: neither shall he greatly multiply to himself silver and gold* (Deut. 17:16-17).

Solomon's most serious neglect was the command to *write him a copy of this Law. . . . and he shall read therein all the days of his life: that he may learn to fear the LORD his God, to keep all the words of this Law and these Statutes, to do them: That his heart be not lifted up above his brethren, and that he turn not aside from the Commandment* (Deut. 17:18-20).

Solomon is typical of overconfident, multitalented, and even very successful people who become too busy to read through the Bible. They believe they can run with the wrong crowd and compromise godly values, and still receive the blessings of obedience.

However, like Solomon they forget Moses' plea to the children of Israel: *I call heaven and earth to record this day against you, that I have set before you life and death, blessing and cursing: therefore choose life, that both thou and thy seed may live: That thou mayest love the LORD thy God, and that thou mayest obey His voice, and that thou mayest cleave unto Him: for He is thy life* (Deut. 30:19-20).

Thought for Today: Surely the highest of all wisdom is to obey the Lord.

Christ Revealed: Through the wisdom which God gave Solomon (I Kin. 3:12). We are *in Christ Jesus, who of God is made unto us wisdom, and righteousness, and sanctification, and redemption* (I Cor. 1:30). *Wonderful, Counseller* and justice will be distinguishing characteristics of the Messianic King and His rule (Is. 9:6-7).

APRIL 23   Read I Kings 5 – 7

Highlights: Solomon plans for the construction of the Temple. Check out how many years it took before Solomon began to build the Temple of God and how long before he began accumulating horses (I Kin. 4:26; 6:1).

Solomon's Temple was twice the size of the wilderness Tabernacle. It was 90 feet long, 30 feet wide, and 45 feet tall (I Kin. 6:2). The interior was divided into two rooms. The first room was called the Holy Place and was 60 by 30 feet; the second room was called the Holy of Holies and was a 30 x 30 x 30 foot cube.

In the four hundred and eightieth year after the children of Israel were come out of the land of Egypt, in the fourth year of Solomon's reign . . . he began to build the House of the LORD (6:1). No other building in the world compared with Solomon's Temple. Before Solomon's father David died, he had spent much time accumulating costly materials and treasures to be used in building the Temple. Its true glory was the Shekinah Glory – the presence of God who dwelt within the Holy of Holies.

This is also true of the Christian, who is *the temple of God* (I Cor. 3:16). The miracle of the new birth resulting in the indwelling Holy Spirit make the difference between the Christian and the unsaved of all other religions. Jesus said: *I am The Way, The Truth, and The Life: no man cometh unto the Father, but by Me* (John 14:6). The Apostle Peter affirmed: *Neither is there salvation in any other: for there is none other Name . . . whereby we must be saved* (Acts 4:12).

Every day is a sacred trust that becomes more meaningful with the awareness that the God of heaven lives within every true believer in Jesus Christ. *Ye . . . are built upon the foundation of the apostles and prophets, Jesus Christ Himself being the Chief Corner Stone; In whom all the building fitly framed together groweth unto an holy temple in the Lord: In whom ye also are builded together for an habitation of God through the Spirit* (Eph. 2:19-22).

For ye are bought with a price (redeemed through the blood of Jesus and now belong to God)*: therefore glorify God in your body, and in your spirit* (I Cor. 6:20).

Thought for Today: The true beauty of a Christian is the presence of God who dwells within and radiates without for our bodies truly belong to Him.

Christ Revealed: Through the Temple (I Kin. 6). Christ is the true Temple (John 2:21). Through Christ all may have access to God (Rom. 5:12-21). *For through Him we . . . have access by one Spirit unto the Father* (Eph. 2:18).

APRIL 24   Read I Kings 8

Highlights: What an inspiring chapter! The Temple is finally finished. The priests carry in the Ark of the Covenant and other sacred items and Solomon prays. The cloud of the glory of the Lord fills the House as trumpet players, and singers with ***cymbals . . . psalteries and harps . . . were as one*** (II Chr. 5:12-13). WOW! You will love it!

The day had arrived for the dedication of the glorious Temple in Jerusalem. ***Then Solomon assembled the elders of Israel . . . in Jerusalem, that they might bring up the Ark of the Covenant of the LORD out of the city of David, which is Zion. . . . the priests brought in the Ark of the Covenant of the LORD unto . . . the Most Holy Place*** (I Kin. 8:1,6). The Ark is where the presence of God dwelt above the Mercy Seat. ***When the priests were come out of the Holy Place . . . the glory of the LORD . . . filled the House of the LORD*** (8:10-11). The people stood and worshiped the Lord at the dedication of the Temple.

    Solomon offered a sacrifice . . . unto the LORD, two and twenty thousand oxen, and an hundred and twenty thousand sheep. So the king and all the children of Israel dedicated the House of the LORD (8:63). The word "sacrifice" does not mean "a great loss." A sacrifice to the Lord is something dedicated to the Lord. Solomon prayed the longest prayer recorded in the Bible as he praised God for His faithfulness as the One ***who keepest Covenant and mercy with Thy servants that walk before Thee with all their heart*** (8:22-23).

    The Israelites were chosen to let the world know there is only One True God: ***That all people of the earth may know Thy Name, to fear Thee, as do Thy people Israel*** (8:43).

    Eventually, Solomon's pride and his love for power, luxury, and physical pleasures brought the judgment of God upon him (11:1,3,9,11). What a difference the outcome would have been if Solomon had lived the truths he expressed in prayer that day! The Lord knows whether our prayers are mere passing emotion or are truly an expression of our innermost worship and obedience to His Word. The amount of emphasis we place on the things of this world – ***The lust of the flesh, and the lust of the eyes, and the pride of life*** (I John 2:16) – reveal the true depth of our sincerity and loyalty to God.

Thought for Today: The holiness of God reveals the vileness of sin.

Christ Portrayed: As the perfect Temple of God before whom all kings of the earth one day must bow (I Kin. 8:54; John 2:19-21). ***Wherefore God also hath highly exalted Him, and given Him a Name which is above every name*** (Phil. 2:9-10).

APRIL 25   **Read I Kings 9 – 11**

Highlights: God visits Solomon again and explains the two paths before him and their consequences (I Kin. 9:2-9). Solomon's fame spreads but, sadly, chapters 10 & 11 explain his shame. Solomon ignores all qualifications for Israel's kings (Deut. 17:14-20). He gradually forsakes the Lord and worships idols (I Kin. 11:4-10). He is an example of one who has *left thy* (his) *first love* (Rev. 2:4).

The Lord gave Solomon privileges that exceeded the privileges of other kings. But the Lord's continued blessings are conditional. Did Solomon deceive himself into thinking that, as king, he could ignore the Word of God in his personal life?

There is no indication that Solomon made an effort to encourage any of his wives to worship the One True God. The horrifying fact is *when Solomon was old ... his wives turned away his heart after other gods* (I Kin. 11:4).

The Lord created us to first fulfill His will in us as well as use our talents (abilities) to extend His Kingdom throughout the world. His righteousness is our first concern: *Wherefore laying aside all malice, and all guile, and hypocrisies, and envies, and all evil speakings, As newborn babes, desire the sincere milk of the Word, that ye may grow thereby* (I Pet. 2:1-2).

Whereby are given unto us exceeding great and precious promises: that by these ye might be partakers of the divine nature, having escaped the corruption that is in the world through lust. And beside this, giving all diligence, add to your faith virtue; and to virtue knowledge; And to knowledge temperance; and to temperance patience; and to patience godliness; And to godliness brotherly kindness; and to brotherly kindness charity (the love of God). *For if these things be in you, and abound, they make you that ye shall neither be barren nor unfruitful in the knowledge of our Lord Jesus Christ. But he that lacketh these things ... hath forgotten that he was purged from his old sins. Wherefore the rather, brethren, give diligence to make your calling and election sure: for if ye do these things, ye shall never fall* (II Pet. 1:4-10).

Thought for Today: The Word of God has solutions to all life's problems.

Christ Portrayed: By David who walked before the Lord *in integrity of heart* (I Kin. 9:4). *Jesus increased in wisdom and stature, and in favour with God and man* Luke 2:52).

APRIL 26   **Read I Kings 12 – 13**

Highlights: Rehoboam follows advice of foolish friends. Selfish ambition in Jeroboam and Rehoboam leads the nation to split into the Northern and Southern Kingdoms. We learn the consequences of not obeying the commands of God (I Kin. 13:11-32).

King Solomon *was buried in the city of David his father* (I Kin. 11:43). His son Rehoboam inherited power and a treasury full of wealth; however, Solomon left the kingdom morally and spiritually bankrupt. *Jeroboam and all the congregation of Israel came, and spake unto Rehoboam, saying, Thy father made our yoke grievous* (harsh, hard)*: now therefore make . . . his heavy yoke which he put upon us, lighter, and we will serve thee* (12:3-4).

Note that Rehoboam said to his newly-appointed cabinet of young friends: *What counsel give ye that we may answer this people* (12:9)*?* Taking the young men's counsel, Rehoboam foolishly threatened the nation with additional taxes and even more cruel treatment. This blunder in judgment resulted in the people rebelling.

Jeroboam successfully led a revolt that divided the kingdom and gained the support of the 10 northern tribes. The tribe of Judah, as well as the tribe of Benjamin and most of the Levites, remained faithful to the worship of God in Jerusalem.

Jeroboam provided his new Northern Kingdom with two "more convenient" places of worship at Bethel in the south and Dan in the north. The Word of God clearly commanded that all worship sacrifices were to be made at the Temple in Jerusalem (Deut. 12:13-14). *And He shall give Israel up because of the sins of Jeroboam . . . who made Israel to sin* (I Kin. 14:16).

A similar departure from the fundamental doctrines of the Word of God is prevalent today. Pitiful as this is, many Christians neglect to to read the Bible; instead, they read numerous other popular books. Consequently, they do not know the Truth of God. *Beware of false prophets, which come to you in sheep's clothing, but inwardly they are ravening* (greedy) *wolves* (Matt. 7:15).

Thought for Today: Pity the one who compromises the Word of God.

Christ Portrayed: Through **Shemaiah** who spoke for the Lord (I Kin. 12:22). Jesus spoke only what the Father told Him. *All things that I have heard of My Father I have made known unto you* (John 15:15).

APRIL 27   **Read I Kings 14 – 15**

Highlights: Jeroboam pays dearly for his sins (I Kin. 13:33-34) by the death of his son (14:1-16). From here on we see one king follow another, leaving a legacy of *evil in the sight of the L*ORD (15:26,34).

During the first three years after the division of the kingdom of Israel, the Southern Kingdom of Judah, ruled by Rehoboam, was greatly influenced to worship the Lord. *For the Levites left their suburbs and their possession, and came to Judah and Jerusalem. ... So they strengthened the Kingdom of Judah, and made Rehoboam the son of Solomon strong* (II Chr. 11:14,17). Most of the priests and Levites from the ten tribes migrated south into Jerusalem as a protest against the two worship centers of King Jeroboam in Dan and Bethel, as well as a new group of idol-serving priests.

    *When Rehoboam had established the kingdom, and had strengthened himself, he forsook the Law of the L*ORD*, and all Israel with him* (12:1). *Judah* (the Southern Kingdom) *did evil in the sight of the L*ORD *... above all that their fathers had done. For they also built them high places, and* (idolatrous) *images, and groves* (idol centers). *... And there were also sodomites in the land; and they did according to all the abominations of the nations* (I Kin. 14:22-24). It is no surprise then that God withdrew His blessings and protection from Judah.

    After Shishak, king of Eygpt, defeated Jerusalem and took away the Temple treasures, including the shields of gold, Rehoboam made shields of brass (bronze) and continued as though nothing had happened. These shields should have reminded the Israelites that their worship was worthless because of their unfaithfulness to God.

    Pity the poor soul that gives the appearance of worshiping God but does not worship Him from the heart in obedience to His Word! That person's worship is worthless. Jesus said: *Not every one that saith unto Me, Lord, Lord, shall enter into the Kingdom of Heaven; but he that doeth the will of My Father which is in heaven* (Matt. 7:21).

    The wrath of God is revealed from heaven against all ... unrighteousness of men, who hold (repress) *the Truth in unrighteousness* (Rom. 1:18).

Thought for Today: *Blessed* (Divinely favored) *are the pure in heart* (Matt. 5:8).

Christ Portrayed: In Asa's ridding the land of idols and sodomites (I Kin. 15:11-14). Christ cleansed the Temple (Matt. 21:12-13; John 2:13-16). As Christians, we are the temples of God, bought with His own blood (I Cor. 6:19-20; II Cor. 6:6-17), and are cleansed of all unrighteousness when *we confess our sins* (I John 1:9).

APRIL 28   **Read I Kings 16 – 18**

Highlights: The prophecy of Jehu against Baasha – what you sow, you shall reap (I Kin. 16:1-7; comp. Gal. 6:7). More evil kings follow until Omri, who *wrought evil . . . worse than all that were before him* (16:25). Ahab and his evil wife Jezebel. Elijah's prophecy of drought; Elijah fed by ravens, and then by a poor widow whose son he raises from the dead. Read about the thrilling battle between a man of God and a nation of evil men (chap. 17 – 18).

Ahab promoted Baal worship as a result of his marriage to Jezebel. During his reign, Israelite worshipers of God hid in caves in fear for their lives. After Elijah *prayed earnestly that it might not rain* (James 5:17), he declared to Ahab that no rain would fall except it be *according to my* (Elijah's) *word* (I Kin. 17:1). Elijah's faith was in God, who had said: *Take heed to yourselves, that . . . ye turn* (not) *aside, and serve other gods . . . And . . . He shut up the heaven, that there be no rain* (Deut. 11:16-17).

After 3½ years without rain (James 5:17), Elijah again informed the king that Israel's drought was the result of rejecting *the Commandments of the L*ORD*. . . . Now therefore send, and gather to me all Israel unto Mount Carmel, and the prophets of Baal four hundred and fifty, and the prophets of the groves four hundred* (I Kin. 18:18-19).

Elijah challenged the 850 false prophets to *call on the name of your* (their) *gods* to consume their sacrifice (18:25). They prayed frantically for a full day, but to no avail. Then Elijah called the people to *come near unto me. . . . And he repaired the Altar of the L*ORD *that was broken down* (18:30). He prayed: *L*ORD *God . . . let it be known this day that Thou art God in Israel, and that I am Thy servant, and that I have done all these things at Thy Word. . . . Then the fire of the L*ORD *fell, and consumed the Burnt Sacrifice. . . . And when all the people saw it, they fell on their faces: and they said, The L*ORD*, He is the God; the L*ORD*, He is the God* (18:36-39).

The false prophets of Baal were then executed (18:40; see Deut. 13:1-5). Afterwards, *Elijah said unto Ahab . . . there is a sound of abundance of rain* (I Kin. 18:41; see James 5:17-18).

Like Elijah we should pray earnestly – and keep on praying, trusting in the grace and promises of God to meet our needs.

Thought for Today: Through difficulties, exercise your faith in the Lord.

Christ Portrayed: By Elijah, whom God used to provide flour and oil to the needy widow at Zarephath (I Kin. 17:13-16). Christ is our Provider, who supplies all our needs *according to His riches in glory* (Phil. 4:19).

APRIL 29 — Read I Kings 19 – 20

Highlights: Wicked Queen Jezebel threatens the life of Elijah *to morrow* (I Kin. 19:2). He is miraculously sustained by angels (19:9-12). Read the plan of God to provide a successor for Elijah (19:15-19). God uses wicked Ahab and proves to him *that I am the LORD* (20:28-34). Ahab's death foretold.

Apparently, Elijah believed that the miraculous fire from heaven and end of the drought would prove Baal to be a false god, and it would result in Ahab and Jezebel's conversion to the One True God.

Ahab headed toward his palace to tell Jezebel what had happened. Responding immediately, *Jezebel sent a messenger unto Elijah, saying, So let the gods do to me, and more also, if I make not thy life as the life of one of them by to morrow about this time. And when he saw that, he arose, and went* (ran) *for his life* (I Kin. 19:2-3). Avoiding the ruthless Jezebel was not weakness but wisdom. However, feeling defeated and discouraged, he prayed: *O LORD, take away my life; for I am not better than my fathers* (19:4).

There is no indication that Elijah contemplated suicide; he believed that God was the Creator and Lord of his life and only God had the right to take a person's life. What he meant was: "I'm a failure. I have not achieved my mission, and there seems to be no hope of restoring the nation to worship You as the One True God." However, God lovingly sent an angel to provide for Elijah's physical needs after his long journey (19:5-6).

Often our mountaintop spiritual victories are followed by moments of disappointment when it seems we have failed. Our estimation of what we hoped to achieve and the value God attributes to our efforts are much more. We are not called to be successful, but to *be . . . faithful unto death, and I* (Jesus) *will give thee a crown of life* (Rev. 2:10).

Although he did not know it, Elijah did accomplish what God wanted him to do. All the Israelites (I Kin. 18:18-20) in Ahab's kingdom went home with a renewed conviction that: *The LORD, He is the God* (18:39). Elijah has given encouragement to millions of believers.

Thought for Today: God has a purpose for the disappointments we face.

Christ Portrayed: By the unnamed prophet who prophesied victory to King Ahab to that he would know his destiny was controlled by God: *Thou shalt know that I am the LORD* (I Kin. 20:13,28). *Thanks be to God, which giveth us the victory* (I Cor. 15:57).

APRIL 30   **Read I Kings 21 – 22**

Highlights: Jezebel murders Naboth to satisfy Ahab's covetousness of the poor man's vineyard; Elijah foretells the deaths of Ahab and Jezebel (I Kin. 21:17-24) and they come to pass (22:37-38). Jehoshaphat does *right in the eyes of the LORD. . . . the sodomites . . . he took out of the land* (22:43,46).

Ahab ruled the Northern Kingdom of Israel in Samaria. Just a few words describe his life: *But there was none like . . . Ahab, which did sell himself to work wickedness in the sight of the LORD, whom Jezebel his wife stirred up* (incited). *And he did very abominably* (behaved in a very vile, detestable manner) *in following idols* (I Kin. 21:25-26).

Ahab invited Jehoshaphat, king of Judah and his daughter's father-in-law (II Kin. 8:16-18), to join him in a war to retake Ramoth-gilead from Syria, and Jehoshaphat agreed. About 400 of Ahab's paid prophets unanimously assured the two kings of a great victory. But godly Jehoshaphat asked Ahab: *Is there not here a prophet of the LORD besides, that we might inquire of him* (I Kin. 22:7)? Reluctantly, Ahab replied: *There is yet one man, Micaiah . . . by whom we may inquire of the LORD: but I hate him; for he doth not prophesy good concerning me, but evil* (22:8).

The messenger who was sent to bring Micaiah from prison *spake unto him, saying . . . let thy word, I pray thee, be like the word of one of them. . . . And Micaiah said, As the LORD liveth, what the LORD saith unto me, that will I speak* (22:13-14). Obedience to God was far more important than freedom to Micaiah, and he courageously proclaimed: *I saw all Israel scattered upon the hills, as sheep that have not a shepherd. . . . And the king of Israel said unto Jehoshaphat, Did I not tell thee that he would prophesy no good concerning me, but evil* (22:17-18)? He then ordered Micaiah returned to prison. *For this is thankworthy, if a man for conscience toward God endure grief, suffering wrongfully* (I Pet. 2:19). Micaiah was right; Ahab died on the first day of battle (I Kin. 22:34,37).

Ahab's disregard for the Word of God should be a warning to all who are making the same fatal mistake. In contrast, a follower of Christ can express unlimited peace of mind with the psalmist: *I have set the LORD always before me: because He is at my right hand, I shall not be moved* (Ps. 16:8).

Thought for Today: All who do the will of God will receive eternal rewards.

Christ Portrayed: By Micaiah, who would say only what God instructed him to say (I Kin. 22:14). Jesus faithfully told others everything God told Him to say. *Then said Jesus unto them . . . I do nothing of Myself; but as My Father hath taught Me, I speak these things* (John 8:28; 12:49-50).

MAY 1   Read II Kings 1 – 3

Highlights: Death of Ahaziah king of Israel; Elijah taken up by a whirlwind; Elisha purifies Jericho's water; Elisha ridiculed. History records one important question in the life of each king: Did he keep the Commandments of God, or ignore them? All of us will face this review: Do our actions and prayers indicate *there is a God* whom we desire to control our lives (II Kin. 1:3)?

Ahaziah king of Israel was on the rooftop patio of his palace when he accidentally fell through a lattice to the marble floor below, gravely wounded. *He sent messengers and said unto them, Go, enquire of Baal-zebub the god of Ekron whether I shall recover of this disease* (injury). *But the angel of the L*ORD *said to Elijah . . . meet* (intercept) *the messengers . . . and say unto them, Is* (there) *not . . . a God in Israel, that ye go to enquire of Baal-zebub the god of Ekron? Now therefore thus saith the L*ORD*, thou* (Ahaziah) *. . . shalt surely die* (II Kin. 1:2-4).

Ahaziah's servants gave this answer to the king. Hating the prophet as his mother Jezebel had, Ahaziah sent 50 soldiers to arrest Elijah. His unfaithfulness to God had hardened his heart, and he failed to see the hand of God in everything – first the death of his father, Ahab; then his mother Jezebel's violent death; and now his "accident." Because he did not turn to the Lord, Ahaziah *died according to the Word of the L*ORD (1:17).

The providential circumstances of God have placed each of us exactly where we are, and the Lord is with us in every circumstance. *Not that we are sufficent of ourselves to think any thing as of ourselves; but our sufficiency is of God* (II Cor. 3:5). Yes, <u>**His grace**</u> (loving-kindess, good will, mercy, compassion) is sufficient to meet every situation.

We may or may not be responsible for the circumstances in which we find ourselves, but we are responsible for the way we react to them. We can become angry with the people or things that God allows or brings into our lives, or we can yield to the Lord, who seeks to use our circumstances to change us into His likeness.

We have had fathers . . . which corrected us, and we gave them reverence: shall we not much rather be in subjection unto the Father of spirits, and live? . . . He (corrects us) *for our profit, that we might be partakers of His holiness* (Heb. 12:9-10).

Thought for Today: The Lord is present in every circumstance. Paul wrote: *He said unto Me, My grace is sifficient. . . . Therefore I take pleasure* (comfort) *in infirmities* (II Cor. 12:9-10).

Christ Revealed: In the taking up of Elijah in the whirlwind and the dropping of the mantle (II Kin. 2:8-15). This is a type of ascension of Jesus Christ and sending the Holy Spirit to indwell believers, giving us power to evanglize the world. *He was parted from them, and carried up into heaven* (Luke 24:51-53; Acts 1 – 2).

MAY 2   **Read II Kings 4 – 5**

Highlights: A widow's oil; her two sons are delivered from slavery (II Kin. 4:1-7). A childless couple have a son (4:8-37). Elisha sustains life (typifying Jesus, the Bread of Life) (4:38-44). Naaman is miraculously healed of his incurable leprosy (5:1-19) – symbolic of Christians who are restored from an incurable life of sin.

Desperate to be healed of his leprosy, Naaman appeared before King Jehoram in Israel with **ten talents of silver, and six thousand pieces of gold, and ten changes of raiment. And . . . the letter** (from King Ben-hadad of Syria that read) **. . . I have therewith sent Naaman my servant to thee, that thou mayest recover** (heal) **him of his leprosy. And it came to pass, when the king of Israel had read the letter, that he rent his clothes, and said, Am I God . . . that this man doth send unto me to recover a man of his leprosy? . . . see how he seeketh a quarrel against me . . . when Elisha the man of God had heard** (it) **. . . he sent to the king, saying, Wherefore hast thou rent** (torn) **thy clothes** (a sign of distress or grief)**? let him come now to me, and he shall know that there is a prophet in Israel** (II Kin. 5:5-8). When Naaman obeyed the words of the prophet, he was miraculously healed.

Like his brother Ahaziah, Jehoram failed to recognize the hand of God in his circumstances. However, he did not consult Baal-zebub, as his brother did (1:2); neither did he attempt to destroy the prophet of God, as his mother Jezebel had done (I Kin. 19:1-2). Nevertheless, the king of Israel did not turn to God – even after Naaman was miraculously healed.

Pity the unbelievers who, like Jehoram, believe their conflicts are merely the arrangements of men who threaten them. How different are the "Elishas" who know the Living God and know that He has arranged our conflicts, adversities, and distresses according to His own will! (See Eph. 1:11.)

It is not necessary to understand the reason God has for our trials and sufferings, but it is of utmost importance that we have faith in Him. He is able to perfect His plan for our lives. God often arranges our circumstances in such a way that we may realize how helpless we are. The Apostle Paul was inspired of God to write: **My God shall supply all your need according to His riches in glory by Christ Jesus** (Phil. 4:19).

Thought for Today: Remain faithful in your trials; God has His purposes.

Christ Revealed: By the meal that took the poison out of the pot (II Kin. 4:40-41). Meal, made of crushed corn, speaks of Christ, who **was wounded for our transgressions, He was bruised** (crushed) **for our iniquities** (Is. 53:5) thereby removing the poison of our sins.

MAY 3   Read II Kings 6 – 8

Highlights: Can you imagine being so in tune with God that you hear and do all His Commandments (II Kin. 6:15)? The ax head made to float; the king of Syria attacks Israel (6:8); famine in Samaria; Elisha's prophecy fulfilled; the Holy Spirit guides them. God uses the most "unlikely" person to satisfy the prophet's hunger (6:24 – 7:20).

The Syrian soldiers had been miraculously blinded and were then led by Elisha inside the walls of the capital city of Samaria. Once trapped there, the soldiers had been at the mercy of the king of Israel. However, God restored their sight and, at Elisha's command, the king *prepared great provision* (a great feast) *for them: and when they had eaten and drunk, he sent them away, and they went to their master. So the bands of Syria came no more into the land of Israel. . . . after this . . . Ben-hadad king of Syria gathered all his host . . . and besieged Samaria* (II Kin. 6:23-25).

The once-powerful, luxurious, fortress city of Samaria was faced with all the horrors of an extended famine. To surrender to Syria meant death for King Jehoram (Joram) and slavery for his people. But, remaining within the walls eventually reduced the people to starvation; some even resorted to cannibalism, as one woman confessed: *We boiled my son and did eat him* (6:29). Because the Israelites had rejected the Word of God, they were helpless before the Syrians as God had forewarned (Lev. 26:14-29; Deut. 28:15,53).

But God, in mercy, once again intervened: *Elisha said, Hear ye the Word of the LORD . . . To morrow about this time shall a measure of fine flour be sold for a shekel, and two measures of barley for a shekel, in the gate of Samaria* (II Kin. 7:1). One of the king's officials ridiculed Elisha: *Behold, if the LORD would make windows in heaven, might this thing be?* Elisha replied: *Behold, thou shalt see it with thine eyes, but shalt not eat thereof* (7:2).

The prophecy was miraculously fulfilled when God, in His marvelous mercy, sent fear into the hearts of the Syrian soldiers and they hurriedly abandoned their camp, leaving their food. The king's official was trampled to death in the rush for food (7:17).

God has provided an abundance of spiritual food for all who will accept it. Obedient Christians can rejoice in the fact that God *is able to do exceeding abundantly above all that we ask or think, according to the power that worketh in us* (Eph. 3:20).

Thought for Today: The answers to our prayers are sometimes posponed because God has a better plan.

Christ Portrayed: By Elisha, who wept when he realized what Hazael would do to Israel and its people (II Kin. 8:11-12). We are reminded of Jesus as He wept over Jerusalem. *O Jerusalem, Jerusalem . . . how often would I have gathered thy children together . . . and ye would not* (Matt. 23:37-38)*!*

MAY 4   **Read II Kings 9 – 10**

Highlights: God calls *the young man the prophet* (II Kin. 9:4) to anoint Jehu king of Israel. Jehu kills Joram and Ahaziah. Prophecy of Jezebel's death is fulfilled and Baal worshipers are executed. Jehu's 28-year reign ends (10:34-36).

After Ahab's death, his son Ahaziah reigned over Israel for two years, followed by the 12-year reign of another son, Jehoram (known also as Joram). Due to the influence of their wicked mother Jezebel, these two kings zealously promoted Baal worship. Baal worship also became popular in Judah because its king, also named Jehoram, had married Athaliah, daughter of Ahab and Jezebel.

During this time of spiritual decline, the Lord selected Jehu, commander of Israel's armies, as His instrument of judgment and king of Israel as God had earlier revealed to Elijah (I Kin. 19:16). After perhaps 20 years the Lord directed Elisha to send a young prophet to Ramoth-gilead, where Jehu was stationed with his army. The prophet anointed Jehu as king of Israel and the God-appointed executioner of Jehoram and all the descendants of Ahab (II Kin. 9:6-7).

Jehu drove his chariot *furiously* (9:20) to Jezreel where he executed Joram (Jehoram), and then Ahaziah, king of Judah. Then Jehu had Jezebel thrown out of a window and he trampled her with his horse. Dogs ate her body (9:33-37) in the field of Naboth, thus fulfilling the Word of God by Elijah against Ahab (I Kin. 21:19-23). The violent deaths of Jezebel, King Ahab, and King Jehoram confirm the limitation of earthly power. Many have died because of disobedience to God.

Jehu zealously executed all the family of Ahab in Samaria (I Kin. 21:17-24). However, his daughter Athaliah, as queen of Judah, promoted Baal worship. Jehu had bragged: **See my zeal for the LORD** (II Kin. 10:16). But he did not execute Athaliah. Jehu's **zeal for the LORD** was just enough to achieve his own selfish ends. **Jehu took no heed to walk in the Law of the LORD God of Israel with all his heart ... he departed not from the sins of Jeroboam, which made Israel to sin** (10:31). It is possible for a person to be used by God and yet never submit to Christ as Lord of one's life. How sad to be so near to and yet so far from eternal reward! **This is the will of God ... That every one of you should know how to possess his vessel** (control his body) **in sanctification and honour.... For God hath not called us unto uncleanness, but unto holiness** (I Thess. 4:3-4,7).

Thought for Today: God may cut short a life that is disobedient to Him.

Christ Portrayed: By Elisha who sent one of the sons of the prophets with oil to anoint Jehu (II Kin. 9:1-6). Oil symbolizes the Holy Spirit, and the Lord sent the Holy Spirit to anoint believers (John 14:16-17; 6:13; Acts 1:8; comp. I Sam. 16:13). **The anointing which ye have received of Him abideth** (lives) **in you** (I John 2:27).

MAY 5   Read II Kings 11 – 13

Highlights: Athaliah murders all of the king's sons – or so she thought. God protects Baby Joash, who eventually is crowned king of Judah. He repairs the Temple and restores worship; evil reign of Jehoahaz, king of Israel.

Joash, king of Israel, had often ignored the prophet Elisha's counsel, for **he did that which was evil in the sight of the Lord; he departed not from all the sins of Jeroboam the son of Nebat, who made Israel sin: but he walked therein** (II Kin. 13:11). Out of respect for the dying prophet, King Joash went to visit him. Though Joash was the king, he recognized that Elisha had been the stabilizing force in Israel, and he **wept over his** (Elisha's) **face, and said, O my father . . . the chariot of Israel, and the horsemen thereof** (13:14).

Israel was at war with Syria. As a sign that God intended to give victory to the Israelites, **Elisha said unto him** (Joash)**, Take bow and arrows. And he took unto him bow and arrows. And he said to the king of Israel, Put thine hand upon the bow. And he put his hand upon it. Elisha** (as the representative of God) **put his hands upon the king's hands. And he said, Open the window eastward. And he opened it. Then Elisha said, Shoot. And he shot. And he said, The arrow of the Lord's deliverance . . . from Syria: for thou shalt smite the Syrians in Aphek, till thou have consumed them. And he said . . . Take the arrows. And he took them. And he said unto the king of Israel, Smite upon the ground. And he smote thrice, and stayed. And the man of God was wroth** (angry) **with him, and said, Thou shouldest have smitten five or six times; then hadst thou smitten Syria till thou hadst consumed it . . . now thou shalt smite Syria but thrice** (13:15-19). Elisha was angry at Joash's halfheartedness.

God desires not only that we serve Him, but that we do so with all our heart. There is a tendency for some Christians to be halfhearted and **lukewarm** (Rev. 3:16) in their service for the Lord, or to have such zeal in doing a work that they fail to wait for God to give direction. Both of these weaknesses can hinder the work of Christ. It is of utmost importance that we pray for the Spirit of God to direct us. **Whatsoever thy hand findeth to do, do it with thy might; for there is no work, nor device, nor knowledge, nor wisdom, in the grave, whither thou goest** (Eccl. 9:10).

Thought for Today: What a privilege to trust God for His guidance.

Christ Portrayed: By Jehoiada, who protected Joash and, in holy judgment, had Athaliah slain (II Kin. 11:4-16). Christ keeps us safe to fulfill His will and will return to judge all who *obey not the Gospel of our Lord Jesus Christ* (II Thess. 1:8).

MAY 6 — Read II Kings 14 – 15

Highlights: Compare the kings of Israel and Judah. Some of the kings of Judah **did . . . that which was right in the sight of the Lord** (II Kin. 14:3), but none of the kings of Israel did. Some not only disobeyed the Word of God but promoted idol worship.

King Jeroboam II (son of Jehoash) was very successful in all his battles and brought material prosperity to the nation. **He restored the coast of Israel from the entering of Hamath unto the sea of the plain, according to the Word of the Lord God of Israel, which He spake by the hand of His servant Jonah, the son of Amittai, the prophet. . . . For the Lord saw the affliction of Israel, that it was very bitter. . . . And the Lord . . . saved them by the hand of Jeroboam the son of Joash** (II Kin. 14:25-27).

But this recognition did not lead Jeroboam to worship God. Instead, **he did that which was evil in the sight of the Lord: he departed not from all the sins of Jeroboam the son of Nebat, who made Israel to sin** (14:24). Immorality and idolatry flourished.

Amos, Hosea, Joel, and Jonah all prophesied during his reign. None were successful in turning Jeroboam toward God. The Israelites seemed to believe that because they prospered materially, God approved of their idol worship. More and more, they placed their confidence in Baal rather than the One True God. Finally, God sent Amos to Bethel to prophesy the destruction of the kingdom (Amos 7:9).

Often, a Christian's greatest tests of loyalty and humility before God come during times of material blessing. While we are enjoying prosperity, we are often less concerned about prayerfully seeking the Lord's guidance and will for our lives.

After Jeroboam's death, anarchy prevailed and Israel rapidly degenerated. Jeroboam was succeeded by his son Zachariah (II Kin. 14:29) who reigned only six months (15:8). This was the fourth and last generation of the house of Jehu (15:12).

About 30 years after Jeroboam's death, the words of the prophets were fulfilled. The Northern Kingdom was destroyed and its people were taken captive by the Assyrians (17:1-18).

Surely the goodness of God should lead us, in gratitude, to do the will of Jesus Christ our Lord. He (the Father) **hath delivered us from the power of darkness, and hath translated us into the Kingdom of His dear Son** (Col. 1:13).

Thought for Today: We forfeit His best when we fail to keep and obey His Word.

Christ Revealed: When the Lord struck King Azariah with leprosy and thrust him out from being king (II Kin. 15:5-7). This foreshadows the time when all who ignore the merciful gift of salvation shall be *cast into the lake of fire* (Rev. 20:15).

MAY 7   Read II Kings 16 – 17

Highlights: Both Israel and Judah are under evil control. Ahaz reigns in Judah, defiles the Temple and gives silver and gold found in the House of the Lord to the king of Assyria. Hoshea reigns in Israel until the captivity and deportation of Israel by the king of Assyria.

The defeat of the ten northern tribes first involved the tribes of Reuben, Gad, and the half tribe of Manasseh on the east side of Jordan, where they chose to settle just outside the promised land. As should be expected, the Assyrians conquered them first. They were among the more powerful tribes, but, rather than live in the promised land that God had chosen for them, they chose what was best for their cattle. When they rejected the one true place of worship, they were soon unfaithful to their covenant with the One True God, and they accepted the gods and conduct of the Canaanites.

Hoshea, the last king of the Northern Kingdom, paid tribute (money in exchange for peace and protection) to the king of Assyria. While pretending loyalty to him, he made a secret agreement with the king of Egypt, hoping to receive help from the Egyptians and freedom from Assyrian control.

The king of Assyria learned about Hoshea's agreement, and Egypt made no attempt to help Hoshea. **In the ninth year of Hoshea, the king of Assyria took** (defeated) **Samaria and carried Israel away.... the LORD was very angry with Israel, and removed them out His sight: there was none left but the tribe of Judah only** (II Kin. 17:6,18). This happened because **they left all the Commandments of the LORD their God.... For the children of Israel walked in all the sins of Jeroboam** (17:16-22). What a warning against unfaithfulness to God!

Some today are making the same mistake. They attend church and call themselves Christians, but they are like people of whom Jesus said: **This people ... honoreth Me with their lips; but their heart is far from Me** (Matt. 15:8).

The Israelites disregarded the Word of God and suffered the consequences. Whoever or whatever receives our loyalty more than God does, is our idol – whether it be a person, purpose, or possession. God warned: **Thou shalt not make thee any graven image ... Thou shalt not bow down thyself unto them, nor serve them: for I the LORD thy God am a jealous God** (Deut. 5:9).

Thought for Today: Compromise is a characteristic of a doubleminded person.

Christ Revealed: Through the Brasen (brass) Altar made by Solomon (II Kin. 16:14; II Chr. 4:1). The Brasen Altar is a type of the cross on which Christ, our whole burnt offering, offered Himself to God (Heb. 9:14). Unlike the necessary daily sacrifices on the Brasen Altar, on the cross, *this He did* (once for all)*, when He offered up Himself* (Heb. 7:27).

MAY 8 Read II Kings 18 – 20

Highlights: Revival comes with the new king of Judah (II Kin. 18:5-7)! Hezekiah's life and death; discover the reason for the Lord's favor in his life (18:5-6). You will want to avoid his foolish error (19:3).

The prophet Isaiah went to King Hezekiah who was *sick unto death. . . . and said unto him, Thus saith the Lord, Set thine house in order; for thou shalt die . . . Then he* (King Hezekiah) *turned his face to the wall, and prayed . . . I beseech Thee, O Lord, remember now how I have walked before Thee in truth and . . . the Word of the Lord came to him* (Isaiah) *. . . tell Hezekiah . . . . I will add unto thy days fifteen years* (20:1-6; comp. 19:15).

Hezekiah had reigned nearly 15 years and had no son at this time to continue his posterity.

Throughout the Gospels it becomes obvious that there is not a cry nor a tear, a sickness nor death by which the compassionate heart of Christ is not touched. Did God announce Hezekiah's death in order to bless him as well as the nation?

The ambassadors from Babylon came with a present to congratulate Hezekiah for his recovery. It's disappointing that he gave no glory to God who had healed him in answer to his prayers. He proudly impressed the ambassadors with his *exceeding much riches* (II Chr. 32:27). By exposing his treasures he was unknowingly encouraging the Babylonians to covet his wealth (32:28; II Kin. 20:17). We need to ask ourselves: "What spiritual good did his boasting to the enemies of God accomplish?"

Hezekiah's additional 15 years also provided him with his son who became an evil king. As we consider the results of Hezekiah's prayer, we realize how little we know of what is best for us. Would Hezekiah have been a greater blessing if he had prayed as our Master prayed: *Not My will, but Thine, be done* (Luke 22:42)?

When there seems to be no hope that an unsaved person will recover from his illness, is it kind to offer hope of a quick recovery when there is little hope? Giving false hope may deprive him of the motivation to turn his *face to the wall* and earnestly pray for God to forgive his sins. It could be that God allowed his sickness to cause him to see his need to receive Christ as Savior and Lord.

Seek the Lord while He may be found; call on Him while He is near (Is. 55:6).

Thought for Today: It is not enough merely to be walking through life; we must be on the narrow road that leads to heaven.

Christ Portrayed: By Hezekiah, who was faithful in leading the kingdom of Judah back to the Word of God (II Kin. 19) – a foreshadowing of Jesus' words to the Pharisees in His attempt to awaken their need to see themselves as sinners and recognize Him as their Savior (Mark 2:17).

MAY 9   **Read II Kings 21 – 23:20**

Highlights: The Book of the Law discovered; true worship restored; idolatry destroyed by Hezekiah's great-grandson, who was one of the most godly of all the kings. Don't miss his covenant with the Lord (II Kin. 23:3).

Though little is known of Huldah the prophetess, she had great influence in Jerusalem. The high priest and the king recognized her prophetic gift and sought her spiritual guidance. Only two other prophetesses are mentioned in the long history of the Old Testament – Miriam (Ex. 15:20), who sang spiritual songs, and Deborah (Judg. 4:4), who aroused the people's enthusiasm to win a war. But neither prophesied like Huldah: ***Thus saith the Lord*** (II Kin. 22:15-16,18-19). God is no respecter of persons or gender in distributiing His spiritual gifts to all who ***seek . . . first the Kingdom of God*** (Matt. 6:33).

When Josiah heard the Lord's words of impending judgment spoken by Huldah, he rent his clothes and could not rest until the House of God had been restored (II Kin. 22:3-6,19,23:4-7). The command was the king's, the oversight was the high priest's, the execution was the workmen's. When the laborers are faithful in doing their work, spiritual leaders in directing it spiritually, and the government leaders in upholding The Commandments of God, a nation cannot fail to receive the blessings of God (22:11-13). ***Huldah the prophetess. . . . said . . . to the king of Judah . . . Because . . . thou hast humbled thyself before the Lord . . . I also have heard thee, saith the Lord*** (II Kin. 22:14-19).

The discovery of the Word of God evidenced the indestructibility of the only inspired revelation of God. In this instance, Huldah acknowledged the authority of the Scriptures which were found.

Unlike religions which disregard the equality of women, the Bible reveals: ***As many of you as have been baptized into Christ have put on Christ. There is neither Jew nor Greek . . . bond nor free . . . male nor female: for ye are all one in Christ Jesus*** (Gal. 3:27-28). This is evidenced by Hulda in the Old Testament as well as in the New Testament by Philip the evangelist's four daughters, who also prophesied (Acts 21:8-9). God has promised: ***Your daughters shall prophesy*** (2:17; Joel 2:28).

Thought for Today: The measure of a person's surrender determines his usefulness to God.

Christ Portrayed: By the prophets (II Kin. 21:10). ***God, who . . . spake in time past unto the fathers by the prophets, Hath in these last days spoken unto us by His Son*** (Heb. 1:1-2).

MAY 10 Read II Kings 23:21 – 25

Highlights: Spiritual insight of King Josiah as he reinstates the Passover. The four final kings fail to serve the Lord; the Kingdom of Judah is taken captive; and the Temple is destroyed by the king of Babylon.

Just twenty-three years after the death of Josiah, the Southern Kingdom of Judah was defeated, and Jerusalem and the Temple were destroyed. *The LORD turned not from the fierceness of His great wrath . . . against Judah, because of all the provocations that Manasseh had provoked Him withal. And the LORD said, I will remove Judah also out of My sight, as I have removed Israel, and will cast off this city Jerusalem which I have chosen, and the House of which I said, My Name shall be there* (II Kin. 23:26-27). Under the reigns of its last four kings, who were mere puppets of Egypt and then Babylon, the Kingdom of Judah was trodden down by successive conquests and its inhabitants deported into heathen lands. Jerusalem was invincible while its people obeyed the Word of God. But eventually it became powerless because of continued disobedience to the Word of God and its people were reduced to suffering and loss of everything.

Nebuchadnezzar, with an immense army, besieged Jerusalem, reducing it to starvation. King Zedekiah, with his wives, children, and guards, fled through an opening in the wall (II Kin. 25:4; Ezek. 12:12), only to be captured near Jericho. Zedekiah watched the horrifying death of his family; then his own eyes were gouged out and he was forced to walk more than 800 miles in chains to Babylon (II Kin. 25:7). The agonizing ordeal fulfilled two prophecies that had appeared contradictory: Zedekiah would be taken to Babylon, but he would not see it (Jer. 32:5; 34:3; Ezek. 12:13; 17:16-17). How pathetic was the fall of the once God-blessed Kingdom of Judah!

We need to see the handwriting on the wall. The world once recognized the United States as a Christian nation – worshipers of the One True God. But our continued sins and rebellion against the Commandments of God reveal our disloyal hearts. America's sins remind us of Judah before its destruction. Oh, how we need to heed the Word of God! *If my people which are called by My Name, shall humble themselves, and pray, and seek My face, and turn from their wicked ways; then will I hear from heaven, and will forgive their sin, and will heal their land* (II Chr. 7:14).

Thought for Today: A nation is successful when it is faithful to the Word of God.

Christ Revealed: Through the Passover (II Kin. 23:21-23), which was a type foreshadowing how Jesus Christ, our Redeemer will keep us from spiritual death. *I am He that liveth, and was dead; and, behold, I am alive for evermore, Amen; and have the keys of hell and of death* (Rev. 1:18).

Introduction To The Books Of I & II CHRONICLES

The Books of I & II Chronicles cover about the same period in Israel's history as II Samuel and I & II Kings. The Books of Kings primarily focus on the political history of Israel and Judah, while the Chronicles primarily present the religious history of Judah, Jerusalem, and the Temple as it relates to the Davidic Covenant. The northern tribes are of little significance in Chronicles. At the time the Chronicles were written, few were alive whom Nebuchadnezzar had taken as captives after he destroyed their kingdoms. With no central place of worship and their long captivity, only a few would have been familiar with the Word of God and how to worship Him.

The Book of I Chronicles opens with the longest genealogical history in the Bible and covers about 4000 years (chapters 1 – 9). Because the promised Messiah would descend from Judah, the second chapter is devoted to its descendants (Genesis 49:8-12). The record begins with Adam (I Chr. 1:1); then to Abraham, Isaac, and Jacob; then Judah; and on to David, through whom the Messiah would come. These families are the vital links connecting the legal genealogy of Christ through Joseph (husband of Mary, mother of Jesus), who was His legal, but not His biological, father (Matt. 1:1-17; II Sam. 7:12-13; Ps. 89:3-4; 132:11; Is. 11:1; Jer. 23:5). The rightful Heir to the throne of David is the Messiah Jesus, born through the virgin Mary, as recorded in Luke 2:7,11; 3:23-38. The legal lineage passed from David to Nathan, Solomon's brother (II Sam. 5:14; I Chr. 3:5; 14:4; Luke 3:31). The line of Solomon was cut off from sitting on the throne (Jer. 22:20-30).

Saul's last battle and death are mentioned in chapter ten of I Chronicles. Chapters 11 – 29 cover the 40-year reign of David.

II Chronicles records the reign of Solomon, the division of the kingdom, and covers the history of Judah until their exile to Babylon. In the last verses the Persian King Cyrus announces their freedom to return to Jerusalem, as prophesied by Jeremiah (II Chr. 36:22-23; Jer. 29:10-14).

The first seven chapters of II Chronicles record the building of the Temple on Mount Moriah in Jerusalem pattern of the Tabernacle. The Temple was completed and dedicated to God in the 11th year of Solomon's reign (chapter 5; I Kin. 6:38). The Book of II Chronicles ends with the fall of Jerusalem and the destruction of Solomon's Temple in 586 B.C. (chapters 10 – 36).

MAY 11 — Read I Chronicles 1 – 2

Highlights: Begin tracing the genealogy of Jesus today from Adam down through Noah, Abraham, Isaac, Jacob, and Judah. But don't stop there, tomorrow we pick up with King David.

These two chapters begin highlighting both the physical and spiritual ancestors of Jesus who, although He was the Second Person of the Godhead, left heaven and came to earth to enter His creation and die on the cross for our sins. Names listed here can also be found in Matthew's and Luke's accounts of His lineage: **Adam . . . Noah . . . Abraham. . . . Isaac . . . Israel. . . . Judah. . . . David. . . . Jesus, who is called the Christ** (I Chr. 1 – 2; Matt 1:1-16; Luke 3:23-28).

The primary purpose of the Chronicles is to emphasize the importance of worship and a right relationship of the believer with the One True God the Father, Jesus the Son, and the Holy Spirit.

The Chronicles focus on Judah and Temple worship and the prophetic promises of the Messiah centered on them. God decided who would be included in the genealogy of Christ. He is personally involved in every Christian's life, desiring to guide us through every detail. God is saying: **Trust in the LORD with all thine heart; and lean not unto thine own understanding. In all thy ways acknowledge Him, and He shall direct thy paths** (Prov. 3:5-6).

Although we cannot understand many of the things He brings into our lives, by faith we can be sure that **all things work together for good to them that love God, to them who are the called according to His purpose** (Rom. 8:28).

Things that happen to believers are not "accidents"; they either are allowed or sent by our Father, the Master Engineer. **He worketh all things after the counsel of His own will** (Eph. 1:11). Therefore, recognize that He is allowing the circumstances of your life today, now – this very moment.

Like the names in the genealogies given in Chronicles and the birth of Jesus, we can be assured we are not "accidents" for God **hath chosen us in Him before the foundation of the world** (Eph. 1:4). And, like Peter we are **elect according to the foreknowledge of God the Father** (I Pet. 1:20) for **we are His workmanship, created in Christ Jesus unto good works, which God hath before ordained that we should walk in them** (Eph. 2:10).

Thought for Today: There are no "accidents" with the children of God. He is in charge.

Christ Portrayed: By the first Adam (I Chr. 1:1). Christ is the last Adam. We have eternal life because **the last Adam was made a living** (life-giving) **soul** (spirit) (I Cor. 15:45,47).

MAY 12   **Read I Chronicles 3 – 5**

Highlights: David's children born in Hebron and Jerusalem; Solomon to Zedekiah; Judah's descendants. The conquest and captivity of the tribes of Reuben, Gad, and half tribe of Manasseh.

Reuben was the firstborn son of Jacob. *But, forasmuch as he defiled his father's bed, his birthright was given unto the sons of Joseph . . . and the genealogy is not to be reckoned after the birthright* (I Chr. 5:1). Thereafter the descendants of Reuben settled for less than the best.

When the time came for the Israelites to settle in the promised land, the tribe of Reuben preferred to live in the fertile area just outside the promised land (Num. 32). They chose what appeared would bring them a better life. However, with the river separating them from their kindred in the promised land, the Reubenites were among the first tribes to be taken as slaves to Assyria. *The God of Israel stirred up the spirit of . . . Tilgath-pilneser king of Assyria, and he carried them away, even the Reubenites* (5:26). Jacob's prophecy, *thou shalt not excel* (Gen. 49:4), truly came to pass; no one from the tribe of Reuben ever became a judge or a prophet.

How satisfying it is to yield oneself to God who uses the men and women who have prepared themselves to serve the Lord. Whatever God has chosen for us, in faith, we should *rejoice in the Lord alway: and again I say, Rejoice* (Phil. 4:4).

It is of utmost importance that we *in every thing give thanks: for this is the will of God in Christ Jesus concerning you* (I Thess. 5:18). There could be nothing more tragic than to come to life's end knowing we chose a self-serving agenda. We have only one life to live, it will soon be past, and only what's done for Christ will last.

Today God wants you to place Him first in your life. Pray for the opportunity to use your talents and time in the ministry of the Gospel. God is always ready *to do exceeding abundantly above all that we ask or think* (Eph. 3:20).

All who *seek . . . first the Kingdom of God, and His righteousness* (Matt. 6:33) can say with the Apostle Paul: *I have fought a good fight, I have finished my course, I have kept the faith: Henceforth there is laid up for me a crown of righteousness, which the Lord, the righteous Judge, shall give . . . them . . . that love His appearing* (II Tim. 4:7-8).

Thought for Today: Those who commit their all to God receive His best.

Christ Revealed: Through the genealogy of David (I Chr. 3:1-24). Christ the Son of God was also called the Son of David. *The book of the generation of Jesus Christ, the Son of David* (Matt. 1:1; Luke 3;23-38; Rom. 1:3).

MAY 13   **Read I Chronicles 6 – 7**

Highlights: Levites' priestly line includes Moses and Aaron. Lists of all the priestly services; the homes of the Levites.

Chapter six is given wholly to the tribe of Levi, whom God appointed to serve as His priests. Observe the striking differences in the character of the men who were set apart for sacred service. Some were wholeheartedly devoted to their God-given responsibilities while others profaned their holy calling. From Aaron, the first high priest, until the Babylonian captivity, the names of the priests are documented in detail. Aaron was devoted to his God-given responsibilities, but two of his sons were hypocrites (Lev. 10:1-2; Num. 3:4). Eli was a faithful prophet but his sons were unworthy, immoral reprobates. Samuel was a godly judge, priest and prophet, but his sons were unscrupulous and took bribes. For years, Zadok (I Chr. 6:8) shared the High Priest position with Abiathar (I Kin. 2:26-35), but by participating in Adonijah's plot to seize the throne from David, Abiathar became a traitor (1:7).

Moreover it is required in stewards, that a man be found (remain) ***faithful*** (I Cor. 4:2). The sons of Levi represented a sacred office – not a political appointment or popular vote of the people – so there was to be submissive obedience to their God-given call. ***Let your light so shine before men, that they may see your good works, and glorify your Father which is in heaven*** (Matt. 5:16).

Every true Christian today has the privilege of being a faithful servant of Christ. ***But wilt thou know . . . that faith without*** (that does not result in) ***works is dead? Was not Abraham our father justified by works, when he had offered Isaac his son upon the altar? Seest thou how . . . by works was faith made perfect*** (proven to be true faith) (James 2:20-22)***?***

People are prone to measure approval by God in the light of sensational success. However, the person who satisfies God is one who gives the best of himself – his time, talents, and thoughts – fulfilling the will of God. Jesus illustrated this by observing a widow who gave only two mites in the Temple offering. She was not in competition with anyone; she was just doing the best she could for the Lord with what she had. ***This poor widow hath cast in more than they all*** (Luke 21:3).

Thought for Today: Your name is recorded in the Book of LIfe when you receive Christ as your Savior.

Christ Revealed: By the *cities . . . of refuge* (I Chr. 6:57,67,71-72,78,80). For a person to have protection from the avenger of blood, he had to flee to a city of refuges. God provided His only begotten Son Jesus Christ to be our Refuge from His judgment against sin (Compare John 3:14-18; 10:24-30; Gal. 2:16; 3:1-14; Heb. 10:1-18; I John 2:2; Rev. 1:5.) When, by faith, in obedience to His Word, we come to Christ, He becomes our Refuge (Heb. 6:18).

MAY 14 — Read I Chronicles 8 – 10

Highlights: We see who dwells in Jerusalem and their duties (I Chr. 9:2-3; Neh. 11:3). Tragic deaths of Saul and his sons; David's great loyalty (I Chr. 10:11-12).

The Israelites had been captives for 70 years when Babylon fell and the victor, Cyrus, king of Persia, proclaimed their freedom. This fulfilled Isaiah's prophecy 200 years earlier that **Cyrus. . . . shall let go My captives** (Is. 45:1,13). Every devout Jew must have been assured beyond all doubt that Jehovah was with them in their return to Judah.

About 80 years after this first group of Jews, about 1,800 more Jews left Babylon with Ezra the priest to rebuild the Temple in Jerusalem. The Chronicles were especially written to encourage these Jews in Judea. **Their brethren, heads of the house of their fathers, a thousand and seven hundred and threescore;** (were) **very able men for the work of the service of the House of God** (I Chr. 9:13). They needed assurance of the presence of God and His prophetic promises for the future. Therefore, this Book centers around the Temple, the priests, and proper worship.

The return was at a critical time and exposed every volunteer to many dangers. The reconstruction required courage and **able men for the work of the service**. Being **able men** meant perseverance and working long hours. In fact, they volunteered to be available day and night and stayed a week at a time (9:25,33).

The Chronicles encouraged new loyalty among the Israelites then and all the people of God. Likewise, we are encouraged: **As ye have therefore received Christ Jesus the Lord, so walk ye in Him: Rooted and built up in Him, and stablished in the faith, as ye have been taught, abounding therein with thanksgiving** (Col. 2:6-7).

Oh, that we might awaken to the seriousness of our opportunities, the urgency of the need around us, and the fleeting nature of time! Let us as faithful men and women give ourselves to provide Bibles and teaching material to the spiritually needy and dying throughout the world today while we still have the opportunity.

Pray ye therefore the Lord of the harvest, that He will send forth labourers into His harvest (Matt. 9:38).

Thought for Today: Faith becomes stronger as we read and obey the Word of God.

Christ Revealed: By Jerusalem, which means "foundation of peace" (I Chr. 9:3). Christ is the only foundation of peace upon which man can stand before God. Jesus said: **My peace I give unto you** (John 14:27; II Cor. 5:18; Eph. 2:14).

MAY 15   Read I Chronicles 11 – 13

Highlights: A new era in the life of David begins as he is finally anointed king by both Judah and Israel. Don't miss the "honor roll" of David's mighty men and their achievements. Note how the men of Israel gather with David to present a united front.

Many years of trial, suffering, and patient waiting preceded the promised reign of David over all the tribes of Israel. After Saul and his sons were killed and Abner and Ishbosheth were both dead: **Then all Israel gathered themselves to David unto Hebron, saying . . . The LORD thy God said unto thee, Thou shalt feed My people Israel . . . and David made a covenant with them in Hebron before the LORD** (I Chr. 11:1-3).

Early in his life, David recognized the sovereignty of God and the futility of human ability. Throughout his life, David never lost sight of his youthful conviction that he expressed before King Saul: **The LORD that delivered me out of the paw of the lion, and out of the paw of the bear, He will deliver me out of the hand of this Philistine** (I Sam. 17:37).

Anyone who recognizes and yields to the authority of God will see that all personal influence and abilities of every kind are gifts of the sovereign God, bestowed lovingly by Him for His eternal purposes. For David it meant waiting patiently for long years and going through many difficult circumstances.

In many respects, David's problems parallel situations that we may face today. Just as surely as the Lord gives us an opportunity to accomplish something for His honor, obstacles will also appear to test our faith. Even though it may seem as impossible to overcome difficulties as it did for David to become king, just remember, **they that wait upon the LORD shall renew their strength** (Is. 40:31). The Lord never promised an easy road for any of His followers. In fact, Jesus said: **If any man will come after Me, let him deny himself, and take up his cross daily, and follow Me** (Luke 9:23). The way of the cross sometimes means intense suffering and often long and lonely days. But once we submit to the authority of Christ as Lord over our lives, we will patiently look to Him in faith for direction and strength.

    I will praise Thee, O LORD, with my whole heart; I will shew forth all thy marvellous works (Ps. 9:1).

Thought for Today: We never build ourselves up by putting others down.

Christ Portrayed: By David, the anointed king (I Chr. 11:3). Christ is the Anointed One who will soon reign as **KING OF KINGS, AND LORD OF LORDS** (Rev. 19:16).

MAY 16 — Read I Chronicles 14 – 16

Highlights: David is blessed by God and his reign prospers. Ark of the Covenant brought to Jerusalem with much thanksgiving. See how our sacrifices are vital to our worship (I Chr. 15:16-24).

During the forty years that Saul reigned over Israel (Acts 13:21), the Ark was ignored. When David became king, he was deeply concerned that the Ark have a central place in his kingdom. He knew that the nation's success depended upon the presence of God being in their midst, so he said: **Let us bring again the Ark of our God to us: for we inquired not at it in the days of Saul** (I Chr. 13:3).

David first attempted to bring the Ark to Jerusalem on a new cart drawn by oxen, which violated the Law of God (Ex. 25:13-15; Num. 4:15; 7:9). As Uzzah reached out to steady the tilting Ark on the cart, he was struck dead (II Sam. 6:1-8).

On the second occasion **David gathered all Israel together to Jerusalem, to bring up the Ark of the Lord unto his place, which he had prepared for it** (I Chr. 15:3). David carefully obeyed the Word of God, telling the priests to sanctify themselves and bear the Ark of God upon their shoulders **as Moses commanded according to the Word of the Lord** (15:11-15).

For that day, David was inspired to write a psalm for his choir to sing. David proclaimed to the world: **Give thanks unto the Lord, call upon His Name; make known His deeds among the people. . . . sing psalms unto Him. . . . rejoice. . . . Be ye mindful always of His Covenant** (Agreement)**; the Word which He commanded to a thousand generations. . . . Declare His glory among the heathen. . . . For great is the Lord, and greatly to be praised. . . . bring an offering, and come before Him: worship the Lord in the beauty of holiness. . . . the Lord reigneth** (16:8-31).

Is it any surprise that God called David **a man after Mine own heart** (Acts 13:22; I Sam. 13:14)? Yes, our Creator is still in control, and the world still needs to hear us praise the Lord and talk of all His wonderful blessings.

The work of God must be done His way if He is to be glorified. As we serve the Lord according to His Word we receive His blessing. **Wherefore we receiving a kingdom which cannot be moved, let us have grace, whereby we may serve God acceptably with reverence and godly fear** (Heb. 12:28).

Thought for Today: People who complain can't sing praises to the Lord.

Christ Revealed: Through David's fame and exaltation (I Chr. 14:17). God highly exalted Christ, our Redeemer, and gave **Him a Name which is above every name** (Phil 2:9-11).

MAY 17   **Read I Chronicles 17 – 20**

Highlights: King David and the Ark of the Covenant. David learns that God does not overlook ignorance of His Word. The Covenant with David. David's kingdom is fully established. A misunderstood kindness leads to a battle and the Ammonites and Syrians are defeated.

It is of utmost importance that we recognize the often-recorded phrase, **David inquired of the LORD** (I Sam. 23:2,4; 30:8; II Sam. 2:1; 5:19,23; 21:1; I Chr. 14:10,14). All of us need to follow his example. Although he was a powerful king who never lost one battle, he opened his prayer with a deep sense of humility and dependence on God: **Who am I, O LORD God** (17:16)**?** Then he magnifies the Lord: **O LORD, there is none like Thee** (17:20).

His love for the Word of God and his prayer life were keys to his greatness. In fact, knowing the Word of God is the foundation to anyone's true wisdom, **that we might know the things that are freely given to us of God** (I Cor. 2:12).

That is why we are told what we need to do to be prepared for prayer: **Put on the whole armour of God, that ye may be able to stand against the wiles of the devil. For we wrestle not against flesh and blood, but against principalities, against powers, against the rulers of the darkness of this world, against spiritual wickedness in high places. Wherefore take unto you the whole armour of God, that ye may be able to withstand in the evil day, and having done all, to stand. Stand therefore, having your loins girt about with Truth, and having on the breastplate of righteousness; And your feet shod with the preparation of the Gospel of peace; Above all, taking the shield of faith, wherewith ye shall be able to quench all the fiery darts of the wicked. And take the helmet of salvation, and the Sword of the Spirit, which is the Word of God:** (THEN) **Praying always with all prayer and supplication in the Spirit, and watching thereunto with all perseverance and supplication for all saints** (Eph. 6:11-18).

Numerous things may interfere with our intent to pray. These seeming coincidences may be Satan's strategy to keep Christians so busy doing "good" things that they fail to allow Christ to be Lord of their lives. Or they may be sent by God to test our devotion to give ourselves to prayer and reading His Word. We need the discernment of the Holy Spirit to know what the Lord's will is.

Thought for Today: Do you have a problem? Pray, then trust God for the outcome!

Christ Portrayed: By David, the shepherd-king (I Chr. 17:7; Matt. 1:1-2; Rom. 1:3), symbolic of Christ as **the Good Shepherd** (John 10:11) and **King of saints** (all believers) (Rev. 15:3).

MAY 18   Read I Chronicles 21 – 23

Highlights: King David, beloved of the Lord, is enticed by Satan and sins; as a result 70,000 people die (I Chr. 21:14). What does the king do to stop the plague (21:26)? David continues gathering material for Solomon to build the Temple.

We could reason, "Why was it a sin to number the people? Did not the Lord command that a census be taken in the wilderness (Num. 1:1-3; 26:2)?" Then, too, wasn't census-taking customary with other kings in order to know the size of their army in case of war? In spite of all our questions, the Bible reveals: **Satan stood up against Israel, and provoked David to number Israel. And David said to Joab and to the rulers of the people, Go, number Israel ... and bring the number of them to me, that I may know it** (I Chr. 21:1). Man has a choice in whether or not he will sin, but a righteous God judges every sin.

Did David want to know so he could boast of his army's power? Did he momentarily lose sight of his true Source of strength? Did thoughts of pride or praise from others entice David to overlook the requirements of God for a census (Ex. 30:12-15)?

David's sin was that of yielding to human nature; he failed to pray as he often did before making a decision. Few are conscious that Satan is so powerful in prompting sin which appears on the surface to be human nature. Be assured that wherever there is a ministry being done for Christ, Satan will tempt us to "humbly" brag what God does through us. But **it is not in man that walketh to direct his steps** (Jer. 10:23). Jesus said: **Without Me ye can do nothing** (John 15:5). On the other hand, we are assured: **I can do all things through Christ which strengtheneth me** (Phil. 4:13). It is of utmost importance that we read the Lord's directions in the Bible, which alone is **the Sword of the Spirit** (Eph. 6:17). Christ withstood Satan, **the tempter** (Matt. 4:3), without wavering by quoting Scripture. Then, **the devil leaveth Him** (4:3-11). We are assured **the devil ... will flee from you. ...** (If you) **draw nigh to God** (James 4:7-8).

Our Lord said Satan **was a murderer from the beginning, and abode not in the Truth ... a liar. ... the prince of this world** (John 8:44; 12:31; 14:30), revealing our adversary as possessing the skill of a mastermind, directing, with executive ability, his work **in the children of disobedience** (Eph. 2:2).

Thought for Today: Satan will tempt you to sin, but by the grace of God you can resist him.

Christ Revealed: Through the altar David built to sacrifice unto the Lord so that Israel might be restored to a right relationship with God (I Chr. 21:18,26). Only through Christ can we be restored to a right relationship with God. We are **justified freely by His grace through the redemption that is in Christ Jesus** (Rom. 3:24).

MAY 19   Read I Chronicles 24 – 26

Highlights: Duties assigned to priests; musicians and singers; divisions of the porters (gatekeepers); treasurers and other officials.

D*avid ... separated* (set apart) **to the service**, Levites, singers, porters (gatekeepers), treasurers, and other workers (I Chr. 25:1; 9:22-29) of the Temple who were entrusted with responsibilities for worship in the Temple. The gatekeepers were called **able men for strength for the service** (26:8). They were the Korahites and Merarites, descendants of Levi (Gen. 46:11). Twenty-four gatekeepers guarded the entrances day and night lest an unqualified person attempt to enter (I Chr. 26:17-18).

Every position was equally important to maintain worship as required by the Lord. Likewise, today, there are no unimportant tasks in the Church (the Body of Christ). All ministries dedicated to fulfilling the great commission are a sacred responsibility from God.

Earlier, David had planned to make Jerusalem the religious center of Israel by bringing the Ark of the Covenant there. After Uzzah was struck dead for touching the Ark, it was taken to the home of Obed-edom. When he received the Ark containing the Word of God in the form of the Ten Commandments on stone, he also received the very presence of God who dwelt above the Mercy Seat (Ex. 25:22; I Sam. 4:4; II Sam. 6:2). The presence of the Lord brought blessing on the home of Obed-edom. In like manner, the presence of the Lord which indwells every believer (Rom. 8:11) will also bless our families and homes and we will want the Word of God prominent in our lives.

Some Christians ignore the Master's ownership rights to their lives and do not recognize their position as His managers of their talents, time, and even the Lord's tithe. All these are meant to be used for His purposes rather than for our own personal interests. Each day is given to us as a trust from God that we may glorify Him. What God has entrusted to us can become multiplied blessings to others or when kept for selfish purposes, can become a curse.

In our daily lives, let us never forget that as a disciple of Jesus Christ each of us has been given an assignment that is not for the clergy alone but us as His followers. **Go ye therefore, and teach all nations, baptizing them in the name of the Father, and of the Son, and of the Holy Ghost: Teaching them to observe all things whatsoever I have commanded you: and, lo!, I am with you alway, even unto the end of the world. Amen** (Matt. 28:19-20).

Thought for Today: Uppermost in our thoughts should be Christ and His Word.

Christ Revealed: Through the Temple treasures (I Chr. 26:20-28). **Christ; In whom are hid all the treasures of wisdom and knowledge** (Col. 2:2-3). In Christ are treasures of wisdom, knowledge, and riches to supply all a believer needs (Phil. 4:19).

MAY 20   Read I Chronicles 27 – 29

Highlights: David assigns twelve captains and twelve chief officers (one from each tribe) to be overseers and counselors. He charges Solomon to build the Temple according to the pattern from God. David's gifts for the Temple; his thanks and prayer; Solomon made king; David's death.

David reigned over Israel **forty years; seven years ... in Hebron, and thirty and three years ... in Jerusalem** (I Chr. 29:27). In his last year, David assembled all the tribal princes and military captains. He told them how God had chosen Solomon to build His Temple and reminded them that their greatest concern should be obedience to **all the Commandments of ... God** (28:8). Then David charged Solomon: **Know ... the God of thy father, and serve Him with a perfect heart and with a willing mind: for the LORD searcheth all hearts, and understandeth all the imaginations of the thoughts: if thou seek Him, He will be found of thee; but if thou forsake Him, He will cast thee off for ever** (28:9).

David then offered one of the most inspiring prayers recorded in the Scriptures: **Blessed be Thou, LORD God of Israel our father, for ... Thine ... is the greatness, and the power, and the glory, and the victory, and the majesty ... Thou art exalted as Head above all. ... we ... praise Thy glorious Name** (29:10-13).

David's heartfelt prayer is a reminder to all of us that prayer should be a time of praising and worshiping God with thanksgiving for who He is. **Now unto the King eternal, immortal, invisible, the only wise God, be honour and glory for ever and ever** (I Tim. 1:17). Even when we face difficult times, our hearts also should overflow with thanksgiving for what He has given us and what He has chosen us to do, **for we are His workmanship, created in Christ Jesus unto good works** (Eph. 2:10). As we recognize our total dependence upon God for everything, we will praise Him. **All things are possible to him that believeth** (Mark 9:23). What a privilege we have to give **thanks for all things unto God and the Father in the name of our Lord Jesus Christ** (Eph. 5:20)!

The Holy Spirit inspired David to write: **Lift up your hands in the Sanctuary, and bless the LORD** (Ps. 134:2). And He inspired the Apostle Paul to write: **I will therefore that men pray every where, lifting up holy hands, without wrath and doubting** (I Tim. 2:8).

Thought for Today: Let us freely offer praise to God *today*.

Christ Revealed: Through the gold offered for the Temple by David from his personal wealth (I Chr. 29:3-5). Gold is the purest metal (Rev. 21:21) and represents the preciousness and great worth of Christ. **He is pure** (undefiled) (I John 3:2-3).

MAY 21   **Read II Chronicles 1 – 3**

Highlights: Solomon began his reign with a humble attitude. But he then *gathered . . . a thousand and four hundred chariots, and. . . . made silver and gold . . . plenteous* (II Chr. 1:14-15). Finally, *Solomon . . . began to build the House of the LORD* (I Kin. 6:1; II Chr. 3:1).

Solomon's kingdom was unequaled in wealth and splendor: *Solomon the son of David was strengthened in his kingdom, and the LORD his God was with him, and magnified him exceedingly* (II Chr. 1:1). It may seem strange for Solomon to possess such wealth and wisdom and still not desire to please the Lord. But possessions can give a false sense of security and self-sufficiency which robs many – even those who otherwise have spiritual insight – of the true values of life.

The prophet Jeremiah confessed: *O LORD . . . it is not in man that walketh to direct his steps* (Jer. 10:23). The Word of God is the Source of true wisdom for daily direction. All of us need to realize the need to: *Trust in the LORD with all thine heart. . . . Be not wise in thine own eyes* (Prov. 3:5,7). When we have a desire to do His will more than our own, the Spirit of Christ – the Living Word – guides our thoughts and actions. *Of Him are ye in Christ Jesus, who of God is made unto us wisdom, and righteousness, and sanctification, and redemption: That, according as it is written, He that glorieth, let him glory in the Lord. . . . For the wisdom of this world is foolishness with God* (I Cor. 1:30-31; 3:19).

Eventually, as *Solomon loved many strange women. . . . For it came to pass . . . that his wives turned away his heart after other gods* (I Kin. 11:1,4). Then the wisest and most wealthy man on earth *did evil in the sight of the LORD . . . and turned from the LORD God of Israel* (11:6-9).

Jesus told of a successful farmer who said: *I will say to my soul . . . take thine ease, eat, drink, and be merry. But God said unto him, Thou fool, this night thy soul shall be required of thee: then whose shall those things be* (Luke 12:19-20)*?*

Whether it is riches or other people which influence our decisions, anything we put in place of God as first place in our lives is a sin. Jesus warned: *A good man out of the good treasure of his heart bringeth forth that which is good* (Luke 6:45).

Thought for Today: God is the True and Only Source of wisdom.

Christ Revealed: By the *thousand burnt offerings* of Solomon (II Chr. 1:6). Wed can be thankful that the one perfect offering of Christ on the cross did away with the need for many and continual individual offerings. *He died unto sin once* (for all) (Rom. 6:10; Heb. 10:10-12;14).

MAY 22   Read II Chronicles 4 – 6

Highlights: The Altar and golden furnishings. The House of the Lord is finished. The Ark brought into the Temple; cloud of the Lord's presence fills the Temple; Solomon's prayer of dedication.

When the Temple was completed, Solomon assembled the leaders of Israel to bring up the Ark of the Covenant of the Lord, and the priests set it in its place within the Holy of Holies. Perhaps no dedication has ever equaled this momentous occasion. *It came even to pass, as the trumpeters and singers were as one, to make one sound to be heard in praising and thanking the Lord . . . saying, for He is good; for His mercy endureth for ever: that then the House was filled with a cloud, even the House of the Lord* (II Chr. 5:13). Then Solomon prayed: *Now therefore arise, O Lord God, into Thy resting place, Thou, and the Ark of Thy strength . . . let Thy saints rejoice in goodness* (6:41).

This awe-inspiring Ark contained the original Ten Commandments. These were to be a constant reminder of the Covenant of God with Israel to make of them a holy nation. The first four Commandments are about man's relationship to God. All ten were summarized by our Lord in two: *Thou shalt love the Lord thy God with all thy heart, and with all thy soul, and with all thy strength, and with all thy mind, and thy neighbour as thyself* (Luke 10:27).

After Adam and Eve sinned, all mankind was born with a sinful human nature. *But as many as received Him* (Jesus)*, to them gave He power to become the sons of God, even to them that believe on His Name: Which were born* (again)*, not of blood* (physical birth)*, nor of the will of the flesh* (efforts to be good enough)*, nor of the will of man, but of God* (John 1:12-13). As Jesus said to Nicodemus (a very good religious leader): *Except a man be born again, he cannot . . . enter into the Kingdom of God. That which is born of the flesh is flesh; and that which is born of the Spirit is spirit* (3:3,5-6).

When a person is born of God he is indwelt with the Spirit of God and becomes *the Temple of God* (I Cor. 3:16). As we meditate daily upon His Word (II Tim. 2:15; 3:16-17), the Holy Spirit of God imparts the strength and understanding we need in order to do His will. *The life which I now live in the flesh I live by the faith of the Son of God, who loved me, and gave Himself for me* (Gal. 2:20).

Thought for Today: Are we so occupied expecting recognition, we fail to praise God?

Christ Revealed: Through Solomon's prayer (II Chr. 6:14). Jesus is that God: *For there is One God, and One Mediator* (Arbitrator, Negotiator) *between God and men, the Man Christ Jesus* (I Tim. 2:5).

MAY 23   **Read II Chronicles 7 – 9**

Highlights: The confirmation of acceptance from God was fire from heaven, consuming the sacrifice. The people bow in reverence! A seven-day feast follows with innumerable sacrifices. Then God appears again. Note the qualification for answered prayer (II Chr. 7:14) and the consequences of sin if Israel ignores the Lord's Commandments (7:19-22).

The fame and wisdom of Solomon attracted the attention of people all over the world. From far away, *the queen of Sheba came to prove* (test) *Solomon with hard questions* (II Chr. 9:1). There was something beyond herself that her wealth and position could not satisfy. Her restless spirit led her on a long and difficult journey. She was astonished at Solomon's profound discernment and declared: *Blessed be the LORD thy God, which delighted in thee to set thee on His throne, to be a king for the LORD thy God: because thy God loved Israel, to establish them for ever, therefore made He thee king over them, to do judgment and justice* (9:8).

Christ commended the queen for her desire for Truth that led her to come from the *uttermost parts of the earth* (Matt. 12:42). Her reception by Solomon illustrates the welcome all receive when they come to the KING OF KINGS for He gives us *according to the riches of His glory, to be strengthened with might by His Spirit in the inner man; That Christ may dwell in your hearts by faith; that ye, being rooted and grounded in love. . . . might be filled with all the fulness of God* (Eph. 3:16-19). Those who receive Christ and His Word are never disappointed by His presence, His wisdom, or His care of His people. There are wonders of His grace and depths of experience beyond all natural comprehension to be discovered in the *love of Christ, which passeth knowledge* (3:19).

To the honest doubter, our appeal is that of Philip to Nathanel: *We have found Him, of whom Moses in the Law, and the prophets, did write, Jesus of Nazareth. . . . Come and see* (John 1:45-47). To all who come with a searching heart and read all His Word, the Bible, all doubt will be removed. They too will say: *Now we believe, not because of thy saying: for we have heard Him ourselves, and know that this is indeed the Christ, the Saviour of the world* (John 4:42).

Thought for Today: *The Lord is nigh* (means near) *unto all . . . that call upon Him* (Ps. 145:18).

Christ Revealed: Through the glory of Solomon's kingdom (II Chr. 9:1-28). Even though Solomon had a rich and glorious kingdom, it cannot begin to compare to Christ's coming kingdom. *The throne of God and of hte Lamb shall be in it* (Rev. 22:1-5).

The Divided Kingdom
(During the ministries of Elijah & Elisha)

MAY 24   Read II Chronicles 10 – 13

Highlights: Rehoboam succeeds Solomon. Jeroboam leads a revolt and becomes king over northern Israel; continuous war between the north and the south; apostasy and judgment. Rehoboam dies; his son Abijah (known also as Abijam) becomes king of Judah; war continues; Jeroboam dies; After a three-year reign, Abijah dies.

We are saddened to read: *Rehoboam . . . forsook the Law of the LORD* (II Chr. 12:1). This was a critical downward step into apostasy. Rehoboam, the grandson of godly King David, promoted then the worship of Ashtoreth, images of Baal, and other abominations in the Kingdom of Judah. *So Shishak king of Egypt . . . took away the treasures of the House of the LORD . . . he took all: he carried away also the shields of gold which Solomon had made* (12:9). This was the price Rehoboam paid when *he forsook the Law of the LORD* (12:1) for the Lord said: *Ye have forsaken Me, and therefore have I also left you in the hand of Shishak* (12:5). For the first time since the Exodus more than 500 years earlier, the Israelites were once again in bondage to Egypt (12:6-8).

The splendor of the gold shields was the symbol of the nation's pride and power which, like the treasures of the Temple and the king's house, were removed by Shishak (12:9). Rehoboam then replaced them with shields made of much less costly brass. He was desperate not to appear before his people disgraced by the absence of the gold shields, his wealth, and freedom.

The loving-kindness of God desires that His people return to Him and once again enjoy His freedom, the peace that only God can provide. If a believer foolishly turns his back on what he knows God has said, he will expose himself to ungodly influences, and will be unable to resist sin. And although a believer cannot be possessed by Satan, he can be greatly influenced to do evil.

We do know there is a satanic power that controls this present world system. *In times past ye walked according to the course of this world, according to the prince of the power of the air, the spirit that now worketh in the children of disobedience* (Eph. 2:2). Rehoboam's life can be summed up as one who lived in disobedience instead of one who sought counsel from Jehovah. In striking contrast to King David, who followed the Lord, Rehoboam *prepared not his heart to seek the LORD* (II Chr. 12:14).

Thought for Today: Without God, the most clever strategy of the wisest counselors is worthless.

Christ Revealed: Through the gold candlestick (lampstand) (II Chr. 13:11). Jesus is **the Light of the world** (John 9:5).

MAY 25   **Read II Chronicles 14 – 17**

Highlights: Asa follows Abijam as king of Judah; King Asa's reforms; his covenant with God and doing right in the eyes of the Lord; then he turns away from God and is warned by the prophet Azariah (II Chr. 15:7); rebuked by Hanani. Asa dies (16:13) and his son Jehoshaphat **reigned in his stead** (17:1).

When Zerah, the Ethiopian king, declared war on the Southern Kingdom of Judah, King Asa and the nation were faced with a million soldiers and 300 chariots – the largest army recorded in the Old Testament (II Chr. 14:9). Asa had to make a choice. He could become fearful and submit himself and the nation to Zerah, or he could pray and trust the God of heaven to help. He chose to pray: *L*ORD*, it is nothing with Thee to help, whether with many, or with them that have no power: help us, O L*ORD *our God; for we rest on Thee, and in Thy Name we go against this multitude. O L*ORD*, Thou art our God; let not man prevail against Thee. So the* L*ORD *smote the Ethiopians before Asa, and before Judah; and the Ethiopians fled* (14:11-12).

Asa then led the people to renew their covenant and *to seek the* L*ORD *God of their fathers with all their heart and with all their soul; That whosoever would not seek the* L*ORD *God of Israel should be put to death.... And all Judah rejoiced at the oath... and sought Him with their whole desire; and He was found of them: and the* L*ORD *gave them rest round about* (15:12,15).

Asa and the Kingdom of Judah enjoyed many years of prosperity. Later when Baasha, king of Israel, became a threat to his border cities, Asa should have prayed once again. Instead, he gave **silver and gold out of the treasures of the House of the L**ORD (16:2) to Ben-hadad, king of Syria, to declare war on Israel. This marked a spiritual decline in Asa's life (16:10-13). His wealth became his weakness when he no longer felt a need to rely on God.

Asa's example serves as a warning. Too often we tend to rely on material things or influence with other people instead of depending on God. An attitude of self-sufficiency has its root in pride and can destroy our trust in the Lord. *Trust in the* L*ORD *with all thine heart; and lean not unto thine own understanding. In all thy ways acknowledge Him, and He shall direct thy paths* (Prov. 3:5-6).

Thought for Today: Only the unsaved are powerless against Satan.

Christ Revealed: Through the rest that God gave Judah (II Chr. 14:7). Jesus declared: *Take My yoke* (yoke of burden) *upon you... and ye shall find rest unto your souls* (Matt. 11:29).

MAY 26   **Read II Chronicles 18 – 20**

Highlights: King Jehoshaphat relies on God, but his association with wicked Ahab, and later Ahaziah, lead to serious mistakes. Bad choices and compromise have serious consequences

Surrounded by vast enemy nations, the people of Judah hastened to Jerusalem, bowed before God, confessed their sins, and prayed earnestly for His protection. They trusted in God when the prophet Jahaziel said: *Be not afraid . . . for the battle is not yours, but God's. . . . Believe in the L*ORD *your God, so shall ye be established* (II Chr. 20:15,20). Then they sang and praised the Lord.

Jehoshaphat was one of the few godly kings in the 500-year history of Judah. He appointed Levites throughout the land to read and instruct the people in the Law of God. He forced the Baal and Ashtoreth cult followers, as well as the male cult prostitutes, out of the Kingdom of Judah (I Kin. 22:46; II Chr. 17:3-9).

But Jehoshaphat made a serious mistake when he associated with Ahab, the Baal-worshiping king of the Northern Kingdom of Israel. The marriage of Jehoshaphat's son Jehoram to Athaliah, daughter of Ahab and Jezebel (18:1; 21:1,6), opened the door to Baal worship in Judah and the eventual massacre of all of Jehoshaphat's grandsons, except for one-year-old Jehoash (Joash), who was hidden by his uncle the high priest Jehoiada for six years (22:10-12).

Some do not agree that fellowship with the ungodly and marriage with the unsaved are not wise; they foolishly assume themselves to be exceptions to the wisdom of God.

All of our relationships should be guided by the Scriptures: *Be not unequally yoked together with unbelievers: for what fellowship hath righteousness with unrighteousness? and what communion hath light with darkness? And what concord hath Christ with Belial? or what part hath he that believeth with an infidel? And what agreement hath the Temple of God with idols? for ye are the temple of the living God; as God hath said, I will dwell in them, and walk in them; and I will be their God, and they shall be My people. Wherefore come out from among them, and be ye separate, saith the Lord, and touch not the unclean thing; and I will receive you* (II Cor. 6:14-17).

Thought for Today: A marvelous transformation takes place when anyone – even the most wretched sinner – prays for mercy. The prayer for mercy covers everything needed in our lives.

Christ Portrayed: By Micaiah, who told the truth even though it was unpopular with his listeners (II Chr. 18:12-27). We are reminded of Christ when He spoke the unpopular Truth to the Pharisees (Matt. 12:1-4). Jesus responded: *Now ye seek to kill Me, a Man that hath told you the Truth, which I have heard of God* (John 8:40).

MAY 27   **Read II Chronicles 21 – 24**

Highlights: Jehoram's evil reign over Judah. *The L*ORD *smote him. . . . he . . . departed without being desired* (II Chr. 21:18,20). Don't overlook I Chr. 24:21-22. King Ahaziah *also walked in the ways of the house of Ahab . . . to do wickedly* (22:3). Athaliah takes over the throne of Judah, murders all her grandchildren except one child that (unknown to Athaliah) was destined to be in the genealogy of Jesus; Joash's reign is influenced by Jehoiada the priest; the Temple is repaired; revival in the land. After Jehoiada dies, Joash does evil.

Jehoshaphat was a successful ruler and his Kingdom of Judah flourished, but he foolishly put policy before principle in arranging the marriage of his son Jehoram to Ahab's wicked daughter Athaliah. As is often the case, Jehoram was influenced more by his idol-worshiping wife than by his father's godliness. After the death of Jehoshaphat, his son Jehoram proceeded to destroy all the godly influence of his father's reign. He also *slew all his brethren with the sword. . . . And he walked in the way of the kings of Israel . . . for he had the daughter of Ahab to wife: and he wrought* (did) *that which was evil in the eyes of the L*ORD*. . . . Moreover he . . . caused the inhabitants of Jerusalem to commit fornication* (worship false gods), *and . . . Judah thereto* (II Chr. 21:4,6,11).

Jehoram is a solemn warning to all parents of the importance of their children marrying a godly person. Can a couple stand before God and take their wedding vows to be united with each other in everything except spiritual things? Can they have interests in common except the most vital of all – Jesus as head of their family? Can they talk with open-hearted confidence about everyone except for the most precious and personal of all – the Lord Jesus Christ? One is preparing for an *inheritance incorruptible* (I Pet. 1:4) and the other *treasureth up . . . wrath against the day of wrath* (Rom. 2:5).

An *unequally yoked* marriage usually results in many conflicts and a lifetime of regret. It openly violates the Word of God that states: *Be ye not unequally yoked together with unbelievers* (II Cor. 6:14). Even to consider marriage to someone with whom you agree in everything except your relationship with Christ is to question the authority and wisdom of the Word of God. God still asks: *What concord hath Christ with Belial? or what part hath he that believeth with an infidel* (unbeliever) (II Cor. 6:15)*?*

Thought for Today: Neglecting the Bible and ceasing to obey it has caused many to lose their spiritual direction.

Christ Portrayed: By Jehoiada, the high priest, who faithfully hid and protected Joash (II Chr. 23:1-11). Jesus is our High Priest (Heb. 5:5-10); we are *hid with Christ in God* (Col. 3:3).

MAY 28 — Read II Chronicles 25 – 27

Highlights: Three kings in today's reading all began doing right in the eyes of the Lord. But, from a great spiritual beginning Amaziah turned to idols and God destroyed him. Uzziah ***did that which was right in the sight of the LORD*** (II Chr. 26:4) and became a powerful king, but he presumed to take to himself the position of priest. Consequently, the Lord struck him with leprosy. Then his son Jotham reigned as king and ***became mighty, because he prepared his ways before the LORD his God*** (27:6).

Amaziah, king of Judah ***did that which was right in the sight of the LORD, but not with a perfect heart*** (II Chr. 25:2). When threatened by war with the Edomites, ***he hired ... an hundred thousand mighty men of valour out of Israel*** (25:6) to join his army in battle. A prophet of God told him: ***O king, let not the army of Israel go with thee, for the LORD is not with Israel*** (25:7). Amaziah expressed concern: ***But what shall we do for the hundred talents which I have given*** (he had already paid) ***to the army of Israel*** (25:9)? The prophet assured him that God was able to give him victory if he would put his trust in God. Amaziah had a great victory without Israel's army ***and took much spoil*** (25:13).

But it is shocking to read that he also ***brought the*** (their) ***gods ... and bowed down himself before them, and burned incense unto them. Wherefore the anger of the LORD was kindled against Amaziah, and He sent unto him a prophet, which said unto him, Why hast thou sought after the gods of the people, which could not deliver their own people out of thine hand*** (25:14-15)?

Like Amaziah, some, when confronted with a crisis, seek help from worldly resources rather than pray for the will of God.

The Bible was provided by our Creator and is the One True Source of wisdom for daily decisions and direction. As we read the Word of God desiring to do His will, the Spirit of Christ – the Living Word – guides our thoughts and actions (John 16:13). ***Every man*** (person) ***that hath this hope in Him purifieth himself, even as He is pure*** (I John 3:3).

Thought for Today: You glorify Jesus when saying: "Praise the Lord."

Christ Portrayed: By Azariah the high priest who stood between Uzziah and the altar, because there was only one proper way to approach the Lord God of Israel and that was through the service of the priests (II Chr. 26:17-18). Jesus, our great High Priest (Heb. 4:14), is the only way for anyone to come to God. ***Jesus saith unto him, I am The Way, The Truth, and The Life: no man cometh unto the Father, but by Me*** (John 14:6).

MAY 29 — Read II Chronicles 28 – 30

Highlights: Another era of wickedness begins with King Ahaz spiritually defiling the whole nation. The consequences (28:19). Revival comes with godly King Hezekiah. Worship is restored in the Temple; the Passover is kept; confession is made to the Lord (II Chr. 30:27).

In striking contrast to the ungodly example of his wicked father, Hezekiah. . . . **did that which was right in the sight of the LORD, according to all that David . . . had done** (II Chr. 29:1-2). He proclaimed a national Passover that exceeded all Passover observances since the time of Solomon. He even sent special letters to the Northern Kingdom of Israel, inviting them to keep this Passover.

The secret of his zeal and power lay in the fact that he **clave to the LORD** and **the LORD was with him** (II Kin. 18:6-7). **In every work that he began in the service of the House of God, and in the Law, and in the Commandments, to seek his God, he did it with all his heart, and prospered** (II Chr. 31:21). Hezekiah repaired and cleansed the Temple. Under extreme difficulty and danger, he was determined to do the will of God: **It is in mine heart** (29:10). No compromise, no half-measures, no delay.

A lawyer once asked Jesus: **Master, which is the great Commandment in the Law? Jesus said unto him, Thou shalt love the Lord thy God with all thy soul, and with all thy mind** (Matt. 22:35-40). There is a strong spiritual tie between what we think of God and what we think is important in our life. Christ calls us to a life of faith and dependence, because it is the life He Himself led. Every Christian should **seek . . . first the kingdom of God, and His righteousness; and all these things** (natural necessities of life) **shall be added unto you** (Matt. 6:33).

When God says: **Seek My face** (II Chr. 7:14), He means for us daily to seek His will in His Word that we may know the true values in life and what He expects us to do. As we read His Word, the Holy Spirit not only enlightens our understanding of how to know His will, but He empowers us to live it and assures us that **the Spirit Itself** (Himself) **maketh intercession for us. . . . according to the will of God** (Rom. 8:26-27).

If we truly love the Lord Jesus Christ, we will be diligent to tell others about Him. Christ's command is clear: **As My Father hath sent Me, even so send I you** (John 20:21) – into all nations.

Thought for Today: Someone today needs to hear how the Lord answers prayers.

Christ Portrayed: By King Hezekiah who offered an intercessory prayer for **every one That prepareth his heart to seek God** (Ii Chr. 30:18-19). Jesus Christ our King, now seated **at the right hand of God**, intercedes in prayer for all who continue to seek Him (Rom. 8:34). **Seek those things which are above, where Christ sitteth on the right hand of God** (Col. 3:1).

MAY 30   **Read II Chronicles 31 – 33**

Highlights: Hezekiah seeks to destroy all idols. He inspires the people, renewing **Burnt Offerings . . . and . . . the set feasts** (II Chr. 31:3). **Hezekiah . . . wrought that which was good and right and Truth . . . in every work . . . and in the Law, and in the Commandments, to seek his God, he did it with all his heart, and prospered** (31:20-21). A powerful enemy threatens Israel. Hezekiah and the prophet Isaiah pray for the Lord's protection (32:20-22).

After Jerusalem was cleansed of idolatry, Hezekiah appealed to the people to supply the physical need **of the priests and the Levites, that they might be encouraged in the Law of the L**ORD**. . . . the children of Israel brought in abundance the firstfruits . . . and the tithe of all things. . . . for the L**ORD **hath blessed His people** (II Chr. 31:4-5,10). The king was amazed at the overabundance when the people were in a right relationship with God. Faith in the ever-present God inspires worship, and **faith cometh by hearing, and hearing by the Word of God** (Rom. 10:17).

After Hezekiah's death, his son Manasseh reigned and committed more evil acts than any king before him. After being captured, bound, chained and imprisoned in Babylon, **when he was in affliction, he besought the L**ORD **his God, and humbled himself . . . and prayed unto Him** (33:12-13). Manassah repented, was miraculously set free, and regained his throne. **He repaired the Altar of the L**ORD **. . . and commanded Judah to serve the L**ORD (33:16); but, it was too late for him to restore the nation to worship the One True God. Upon his death, his evil son Amon reigned but then was murdered, and **the people . . . made Josiah his son king** (33:25) when he was only eight years old.

Repentance and cleansing from sin should always be followed by a desire for fellowship with God. This inevitably results in various offerings and worship since all offerings are directly related to the basic principle of love. God knows that if you love Him with all your heart, you will give faithfully – self first, then offerings. In your giving, recognize that you are giving to the Lord what belongs to Him. Tithes and offerings are His perfect plan to provide for the ministry of His Word. Paul wrote: **Upon the first day of the week let every one of you lay by him in store, as God hath prospered him** (I Cor. 16:2).

Thought for Today: Don't give up. Even the vilest sinner can be saved.

Christ Revealed: By Hezekiah's offering of **the king's portion** (share) **of his substance for the Burnt Offerings** (II Chr. 31:3). The Burnt Offerings were wholly consumed, symbolic of total surrender, and offered as a **sweet savour** to the Lord (Lev. 8:28; Num. 15:3). God offered his King's portion in Jesus Christ who, in total surrender on the cross, was wholly consumed, even unto death. **Christ . . . hath given HImself for us an offering and a sacrifice to God for a sweetsmelling savour** (Eph. 5:2).

MAY 31   Read II Chronicles 34 – 36

Highlights: The Temple is repaired and what Treasure do they find (II Chr. 34:14-16)? Don't miss the promise of God to the king and the king's covenant with the Lord. Josiah's godliness is precious (II Chr. 35:24-25) but, after his death, the nation's sins result in their destruction. Decree of Cyrus to rebuild the Temple.

Josiah *walked in the ways of David. . . . while he was yet young, he began to seek after the God of David* (II Chr. 34:2-3) He reigned on David's throne for thirty-one years. Josiah's reign was the last surge of political independence and spiritual revival before the disintegration of the Southern Kingdom, which ended with the destruction of Jerusalem in 586 B.C.

Josiah's leadership ranked him with David, Jehoshaphat, and Hezekiah as an outstanding godly king. He took a firm stand against idol worship and evils that had permeated the Israelite kingdom (34:1-7). *Moreover Josiah kept a Passover unto the LORD in Jerusalem. . . . And said unto the Levites . . . sanctify yourselves, and prepare your brethren, that they may do according to the Word of the LORD. . . . And there was no Passover like to that kept in Israel from the days of Samuel the prophet* (35:1,3,6,18). But the nation did not follow Josiah's love for God and his righteous example.

Josiah's leadership ended when he attempted to stop Pharaoh Necho's plans to go through *the valley of Megiddo* (35:22) to attack the Assyrians. Josiah did not believe that Necho, a worshiper of many false gods, had received a message from the One True God.

Josiah was a godly man. If God had wanted to stop Josiah, He could have spoken to him, not to Pharaoh Necho. There is *a time to die* (Eccl. 3:2). It is a fact that *all things work together for good to them that love God* (Rom. 8:28). Furthermore, there was no reason to believe that God was displeased with Josiah. Compare his continued dedication with that of Solomon's lack of it (I Kin. 11:9-11). Josiah died a young man, as did Stephen and Jesus. The thirty-nine-year-old king was fatally wounded at Megiddo. He fulfilled the will of God, who spared him from the tragedies that were soon to come upon Jerusalem and the Temple because of the nation's sins (II Chr. 34:28). There are few people during biblical history of whom it is said: *He did that which was right in the sight of the LORD . . . and declined neither to the right hand, nor to the left* (II Chr. 34:2).

Thought for Today: Can others always depend on what you say?

Christ Revealed: Through the messengers of God who were rejected by His people (II Chr. 36:15-16); Is. 53:3; Mark 9:12). Jesus *Came unto His own* (own people), *and His own received Him not* (John 1:11; Matt. 21:42; Mark 8:31; 12:10; Luke 9:22; 17:25; 20:17).

Introduction To The Book Of EZRA

The Book of Ezra begins with the history of the Jews from the time Cyrus, king of Persia, released them from Babylonian exile. He permitted them to return to Jerusalem to rebuild the Temple under the leadership of Zerubbabel, a descendant of King David and the great-grandson of Jehoiakim. Zerubbabel (also called Sheshbazzar) was considered a prince of Judah by Cyrus (Ezra 1:8,11; 2:1-2). Cyrus was not a believer in the One True God; he thought he was just promoting goodwill for his own newly-won empire.

Most of the older Israelites, who had been taken into captivity by Nebuchadnezzar, had died; and the majority of the new generation did not desire to go to a homeland they had never seen.

Ezra records that the first expedition of 42,360 Jews and 7,337 servants (2:64-65) was led by Zerubbabel, appointed governor of Jerusalem by King Cyrus (5:14; Hag. 1:1,14; 2:2,21).

The original Temple, built by King Solomon, had been destroyed by King Nebuchadnezzar of Babylon in 586 B.C. After arriving in Jerusalem with Zerubbabel, the returned exiles built an altar and observed the Feast (Festival) of Tabernacles (Booths) which commemorated the Israelites' 40 years in the wilderness. Ezra records that **in the second year of their coming unto the House of God at Jerusalem, in the second month, began Zerubbabel ... to set forward** (oversee) **the work of the House of the LORD** (Ezra 3:8; 5:16). It took about two years to complete the foundation, after which time the work ceased because of opposition from surrounding adversaries (chapters 3 – 4). About 15 years later, stirred by the preaching of the Word of God by the prophets Haggai and Zechariah, the Israelites **began to build the House of God** (5:2). They completed it in about five years despite intense opposition (chapters 5 – 6). Between chapters 6 and 7 there is an interval of about 60 years. During this time, Zerubbabel, Haggai, and Zechariah died, and the events in the Book of Esther probably took place.

Perhaps 80 years after Zerubbabel's expedition, Ezra, a descendant of Aaron, the first high priest, received authority in a letter from the king to lead another expedition to Jerusalem **according to the Law of thy God. . . . Whatsoever is commanded by the God of heaven, let it be diligently** (zealously) **done** (7:11-14,23). Ezra led about 5,000 men, women, and children from the Persian capital to Jerusalem (7:28 – 8:32). The Book of Ezra reveals how God controls the destiny of His children and, thus, the Book of Ezra is a message of the continuing Covenant grace of God.

JUNE 1 — Read Ezra 1 – 2

Highlights: God stirs the hearts of (1) King Cyrus to send the Israelites to rebuild the Temple and return its *vessels* that had been confiscated by Nebuchadnezzar (Ezra 1:1-3,7-11); (2) the priests, Levites, tribal leaders, and others to willingly return to Jerusalem (1:5); (3) those who are left to help pay the expenses (1:6).

About 200 years before the time of Ezra, Isaiah had prophesied that Babylon would be overthrown by a man named Cyrus. The Lord said of this heathen king of Persia: *He ... shall perform all My pleasure: even saying to Jerusalem, Thou shalt be built; and to the Temple, Thy foundation shall be laid. ... and he shall let go My captives* (Is. 44:28; 45:13). These prophecies reassured the Israelites that, following the judgment foretold by Jeremiah of 70 years of captivity due to their sins, God would restore them once again to the promised land (Jer. 25:11-12).

To fulfill that prophecy, *Cyrus king of Persia ... made a proclamation. ... Who is there among you of all His people? his God be with him, and let him go up to Jerusalem, which is in Judah, and build the House of the LORD God of Israel, (He is the God,) which is in Jerusalem. ... Then rose up the chief of the fathers of Judah and Benjamin, and the priests, and the Levites, with all them whose spirit God had raised, to go up to build the House of the LORD which is in Jerusalem* (Ezra 1:1,3,5).

Ezra and his followers had neither a pillar of fire by night nor a cloud by day to guide the way from Babylon to Jerusalem. No manna fell from heaven as it did many years earlier for their ancestors (Num. 9:15-16,22-23). Yet, not one complaint is recorded. This is in sharp contrast to the continual complaints of their ancestors, who had been miraculously released from Egypt (20:24; 27:14; Deut. 1:26,43; 9:23).

When we recognize that our Creator is Soverign over our lives, we can truly enjoy the peace of God, knowing that *all things work together for good to them that love God* (Rom. 8:28). Believing this promise from God will remove all fear, depression, and discouragement, as well as fault-finding, anger, and strife. Our loving Lord will use whatever happens in our lives to our ultimate good. Because of this, we can *live in peace; and the God of love and peace shall be with you* (us) (II Cor. 13:11).

Thought for Today: *Rejoice in the LORD, ye righteous, and give thanks at the remembrance of His holiness* (Ps. 97:12).

Christ Portrayed: By Sheshbazzar, another name for Zerubbabel, the prince (governor) of Judah (Ezra 1:8). Christ is both **The Prince of Peace** (Is. 9:6) and **the Lion of the tribe of Juda** (Rev. 5:5).

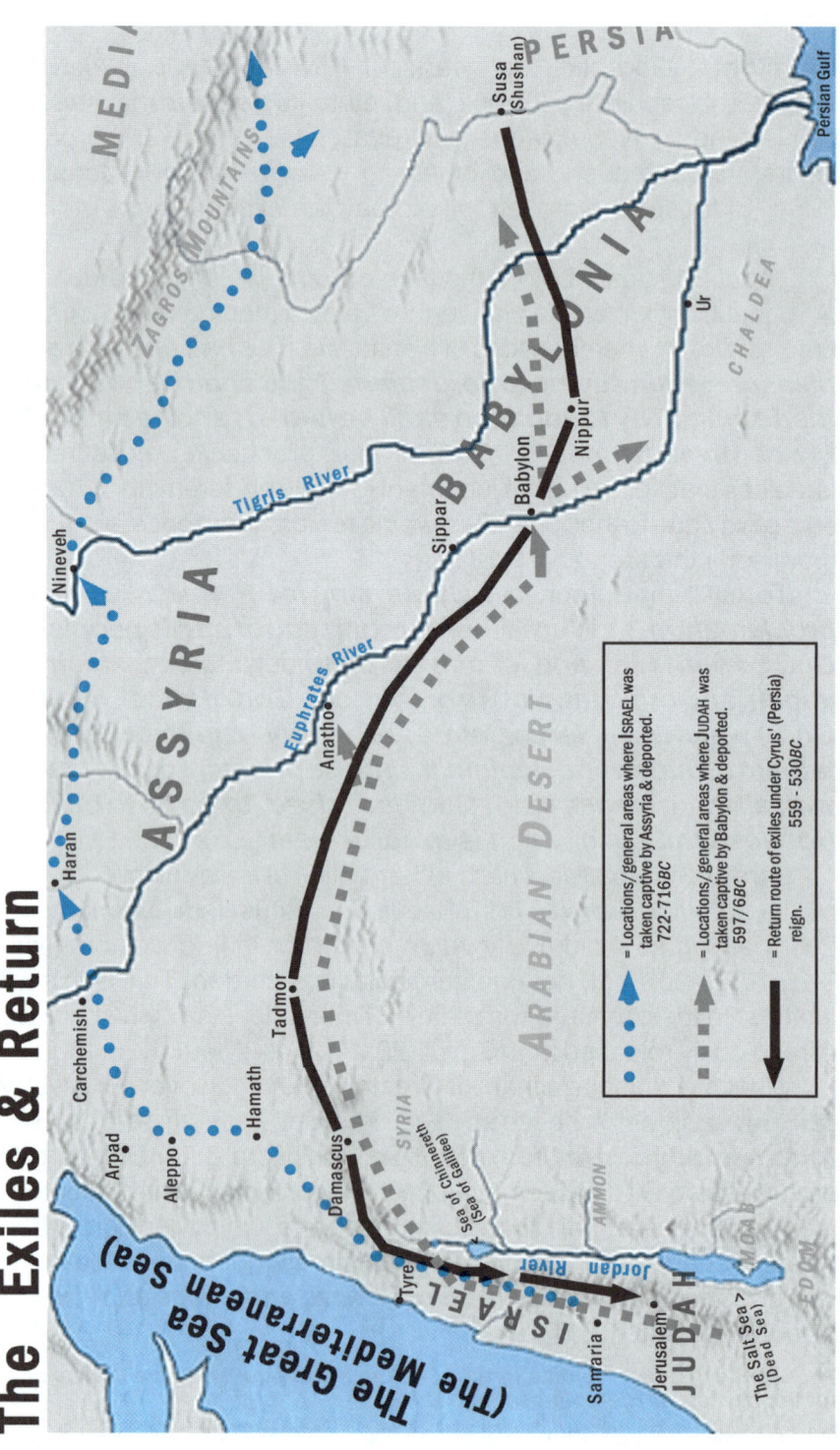

JUNE 2   Read Ezra 3 – 5

Highlights: The work begins! Check their priorities – the altar is rebuilt and then burnt offerings are offered (Ezra 3:2-3). The foundation is finished (3:10-13); their enemies slander them and complain to Darius the king (5:8).

After returning to Jerusalem, ***fear was upon them because of the people of those countries. . . .*** (who) ***troubled them in building, And hired counselors against them to frustrate their purpose*** (Ezra 3:2-3; 4:4-5). ***And they offered burnt offerings . . . morning and evening. They kept also the Feast of Tabernacles, as it is written. . . . But the foundation of the Temple of the LORD was not yet laid. . . . and when the builders laid the foundation of the Temple of the LORD . . . the priests . . . and the Levites. . . . sang . . . praising and giving thanks unto the LORD*** (3:3-11).

It is recorded that many men, ***when the foundation of this House was laid before their eyes, wept with a loud voice; and many shouted aloud for joy*** (3:12). Perhaps they were weeping over what might have been had they not ignored the prophets' warnings that continued sin would result in their destruction. Perhaps others rejoiced as they looked forward to the day when the Temple would be rebuilt.

It is right for us to sorrow over our past sins but, after repenting of and forsaking our sins, we can rejoice for ***He is faithful and just to forgive us our sins*** (I John 1:9). We should not continue to grieve over past losses that blur opportunities for the present and the future but should thank Him for His mercy and grace. Nor should we glory in our past achievements and successes. Daily we need to move on with our lives. The Apostle Paul reminds us: ***Forgetting those things which are behind, and reaching forth unto those things which are before, I press toward the mark*** (goal) ***for the prize of the high calling of God in Christ Jesus*** (Phil. 3:13-14).

A lesson we gain from these devout Jews is that, as we seek to serve the Lord, we will face opposition. Therefore, let us look ahead with confidence – not in ourselves, but in God ***and in the power of His might*** (Eph. 6:10).

Thought for Today: Winners never quit and quitters never win.

Christ Portrayed: Through the ***great*** (huge) ***stones*** used in building the Temple of God (Ezra 5:8). Christ is the Stone which ***the builders refused*** (rejected) and He has become the Cornerstone of our faith (Ps. 118:22; Matt. 21:42).

JUNE 3 — Read Ezra 6 – 7

Highlights: The flesh, the devil, and the world hinder the rebuilding of the Temple, but God overrules (Ezra 6:1-15). Joyously, Passover is celebrated (6:22)! Then comes Ezra, a scribe and priest (7:6). Ezra is well-favored. Know why (7:10)?

The prophets Haggai and Zechariah reminded the Israelites in Jerusalem that the real reason the Lord's work went unfinished was because their first interest was in building their own houses. These anointed men boldly preached the Word of God and inspired the people to rebuild the Temple: **And the elders of the Jews builded, and they prospered through the prophesying of Haggai the prophet and Zechariah ... according to the Commandment of the God of Israel** (Ezra 6:14).

Nothing is recorded about the Jews in Jerusalem between the time of Haggai and Zechariah's ministry and the coming of Ezra from Persia about 60 years later. Zerubbabel, Haggai, and Zechariah had all died, leaving the next generation to grow without spiritual leadership.

Ezra was born during the Babylonian captivity. His geneaology went back many generations to Aaron, Israel's first high priest (7:1-5; I Chr. 6:3-15). The key to Ezra's great effectiveness in accomplishing the will of God is clear: **For Ezra had prepared his heart to seek** (study) **the Law of the LORD, and to do it, and to teach in Israel statutes** (laws) **and judgments** (what God declares is right and wrong) (Ezra 7:10). Note carefully the threefold key to Ezra's great success: Ezra **had prepared his heart to seek the Law of the LORD.** The word **prepared** implies a steadfast effort to know all of the Word of God. The second qualification for the Lord's blessings upon his life was that Ezra committed himself **to do it** (obey the Law). Third, he planned to teach its **statutes and judgments** to the people.

Ezra was committed to seeking, doing, and teaching His Word. This should be a reminder that, if we want the Lord's blessings, we too must set our hearts upon the whole counsel of God. **Above all, taking the shield of faith, wherewith ye shall be able to quench** (put out, extinguish) **all the fiery darts** (arrows, shots) **of the wicked. And take ... the Sword of the Spirit, which is the Word of God** (Eph. 6:16-17). Ezra is an example of how God will use anyone who will take His Word seriously, **rightly dividing the Word of Truth** (II Tim. 2:15).

Thought for Today: Living to please the Lord will encourage others to be obedient to Him.

Christ Revealed: Through **the Feast of Unleavened** (Yeast-free) **Bread** (Ezra 6:22). Jesus is the **Bread of Life** (John 6:35), and He was **without sin** (Heb. 4:15). Leaven is symbolic of sin.

JUNE 4   Read Ezra 8 – 9

Highlights: Ezra documents the journey. The priests are entrusted with the treasure (Ezra 8:24-30,33-34). Discover the Source of strength to stand against sin (9:6-14).

Ezra knew the Scriptures and decided to be responsible for leading perhaps 5,000 men, women, and children on the treacherous, possibly 800 to 1,000 mile journey from Babylon to Jerusalem. Added to this was the responsibility for priceless treasures of **silver ... gold, and the vessels ... of the House of our God, which the king ... had offered** (Ezra 8:25). Ezra was also aware of the danger of bandits who could murder and plunder. The people would face physical and emotional hardships as well.

It would have been easier to remain in Babylon and just pray for the people in Jerusalem. But Ezra decided to do what he could. Furthermore, he did not ask the king for a protective military guard; rather it is recorded that Ezra **proclaimed a fast ... that we might afflict** (humble) **ourselves before our God, to seek of Him a right way. ... I was ashamed to require of the king a band of soldiers ... to help us against the enemy ... because we had spoken unto the king, saying, The hand of our God is upon all them for good that seek Him** (8:21-22).

Ezra and all his followers arrived safely in Jerusalem about four months after leaving Babylon (7:8-9; 8:31). However, Ezra was grief stricken when he heard about the low moral and spiritual state of affairs in Jerusalem since the Temple had been rebuilt. Ezra was told: **The people of Israel, and the priests, and the Levites, have not separated themselves from the people of the lands, doing according to their abominations** (detestable practices) (9:1). Again, he did not say: "It's not my problem, so I'll leave it up to someone else." Instead, he became involved and **every one that trembled at the words of the God of Israel** (9:4) assembled before him. At the evening sacrifice, he fell on his knees and spread out his hands to the Lord as he prayed: **O my God, I am ashamed ... for our iniquities .... for we have forsaken Thy Commandments** (9:6,10).

When the Word of God is neglected today, we too need to be as concerned as Ezra. **If My people ... shall humble themselves, and pray ... and turn from their wicked ways; then will I ... forgive their sin, and will heal their land** (II Chr. 7:14).

Thought for Today: *Faith without works is dead* (James 2:20).

Christ Portrayed: By Ezra, who mourned over the sins of the people of Jerusalem (Ezra 9:5). Twice it is recorded that, when Jesus looked upon Jerusalem, He also mourned for the people (Luke 19:41; 13:34).

JUNE 5   Read Ezra 10

Highlights: Confession of the sin of **holy seed** (Israelites) (Ezra 9:2) intermarrying with idol-worshipping Canaanites (10:1-2). Cleansing begins (10:3-5). Transgressors are warned (10:7-8). Look how long it takes (10:16-17). Note Ezra's infamous list after he finally cleans house (10:18-44).

The Israelites had married Canaanites. Consequently, many were worshiping their idols. The Law of God had warned: **Neither shalt thou make marriages with them.... For they will turn away thy son from following Me... so will the anger of the LORD... destroy thee** (Deut. 7:3-4). As the Israelites listened to Ezra proclaim the Word of God, they were convicted of their sins. Shechaniah, spokesman for the offenders, said to Ezra: **We have trespassed against** (been unfaithful to) **our God, and have taken strange** (foreign, Gentile) **wives.... therefore let us make a covenant** (agreement) **with our God to put away all the** (idol-worshiping) **wives** (Ezra 10:2-3). Each man who had married a Canaanite had to present himself with his wife and children before a court of **the elders of every city, and the judges thereof** (10:14) to determine if they were involved in idol worship or were worshipers of the True God of Israel.

If the only consideration had been the excommunication of all Canaanite wives, it would have been a simple, immediate decision. But, something more than simple separation was being considered in their courts. Each family was examined to determine if the Canaanite wives had forsaken their idols and converted to the One True God of Israel. If these men had led their wives to reject their idols and worship the One True God, their wives would have become Israelites and would not have been called **strange wives**. This precedent had been set by Joshua when he welcomed and protected Rahab, the harlot of Jericho, who had rejected her idols and sinful life to place her trust in the One True God of Israel. Much later, Ruth, a Moabitess, joined with Naomi, confessing: **Thy God** will be **my God** (Ruth 1:16). Ruth rejected her people's idols and became an Israelite. In the providence of God, both she and Rahab became a part of the genealogy of Jesus.

We are prone to underestimate the heartbreak and suffering that results from disobedience to the Word of God. The price of sin is much greater than anyone suspects! **He that soweth to his flesh shall of the flesh reap corruption** (is doomed to destruction); **but he that soweth to the Spirit shall of the Spirit reap life everlasting** (Gal. 6:8).

Thought for Today: Self-denial honors Christ and the outcome is peace and satisfaction beyond corruption.

Christ Revealed: Through the ram (male sheep) offered for the offenses of the sons of the priests (Ezra 10:19). Christ offered Himself up for the sins and offenses of all mankind. **He is able also to save them to the uttermost that come unto God by Him, seeing He ever liveth to make intercession for them** (Heb. 7:25).

Introduction To The Book Of NEHEMIAH

The Book of Nehemiah is a continuation of the history recorded in the Book of Ezra. Nehemiah grew up in Persia among the Jews who had been exiles in Babylon before Cyrus restored their freedom. Nehemiah had the honored position of cupbearer to King Artaxerxes, son of Xerxes, also known as Ahasuerus in the Book of Esther. Nehemiah's position was one of great trust and responsibility (I Kin. 10:5; II Chr. 9:4).

Nehemiah was heartbroken when he received news of the spiritual and physical poverty that existed in Jerusalem. Upon learning of Nehemiah's great concern, the Persian king appointed him governor of Judah and gave him the authority to return to his homeland to rebuild the walls of Jerusalem (Neh. 2:5-7; 5:14). This was about 100 years after Zerubbabel had arrived in Jerusalem to rebuild the Temple (Ezra 1:5) and about 14 years after Ezra had gone to Jerusalem to restore worship (7:6). After much opposition, the work had ceased. Darius issued the second decree to rebuild the Temple in 519 B.C. In 458 B.C., Ezra dedicated the completed Temple (6:6).

The walls had remained in ruins since Nebuchadnezzar had completely destroyed Jerusalem about 140 years earlier (II Kin. 25:8-11). The Jewish remnant had no protection against surrounding nations. In 444 B.C. Artaxerxes issued the third decree, permitting Nehemiah to rebuild the wall. Restoring the broken-down walls which had once protected Jerusalem from its enemies was Nehemiah's first major project. Yet some of the leading citizens of Jerusalem who would benefit from those walls refused to cooperate (Neh. 2:19; 3:5; 4:1-12).

Although faced with many problems (4:12-23; 6:2-4,10-13), by continual prayer, fasting, and faith in the Word of God, Nehemiah led the people to complete the walls in 52 days (6:15). Great emphasis was placed upon hearing the Word, as well as understanding and applying it. This led to a revival among the people (8:2-3,7-8,12).

After the walls of Jerusalem were dedicated by Ezra and Nehemiah (12:27-43), Nehemiah continued in Jerusalem as governor of Judah for about 12 years (5:14). He then returned to the Persian court for an indefinite period of time. During Nehemiah's absence from Jerusalem, the Word of God was once again disregarded, and corruption and immorality gained acceptance (13:6). He again obtained leave from Persia and returned to Jerusalem. With great fervor, he turned the nation from its sins, reestablished its Covenant relationship with God, and restored the people to true worship (13:7-31).

JUNE 6 — Read Nehemiah 1 – 3

Highlights: Nehemiah sits weeping about the decay of Jerusalem (Neh. 1:1-4). God recognizes each person that goes up to rebuild the city (2:1-8). The enemy grieves (2:9-10,19). The Altar is set up; the foundation of the Temple is laid (3:1-13).

When Nehemiah's relative Hanani arrived in Persia from Jerusalem, he told Nehemiah of the pitiful conditions that existed there. Nehemiah said: ***When I heard these words . . . I sat down and wept, and mourned certain days, and fasted, and prayed before the God of heaven. . . . both I and my father's house have sinned. . . . and have not kept the Commandments*** (Neh. 1:4,6-7). Over a period of about four months, he continued to pray.

When King Artaxerxes asked why he was so sad, Nehemiah told him that it was because ***the city, the place of my fathers' sepulchres*** (tombs)***, lieth waste*** (2:1-3). The king graciously responded by appointing him governor over Judah and commissioning him to rebuild the walls of Jerusalem. The king even provided some of the needed materials (2:6-8).

Three basic characteristics made Nehemiah's efforts a success. First, he desired to do the will of God (1:4-11). This led him to leave the luxury and security of living in the king's palace in Persia and to endure the hardships in Jerusalem in order to restore the city of God. Second, he not only ***fasted and prayed***, but he confessed: ***We. . . . have not kept the Commandments*** (1:4-11). He identified with his people and recognized that obedience to the Word of God is essential to answered prayer. Third, he was determined to persuade his people to join him in rebuilding the walls, regardless of opposition.

Sanballat, a Gentile, and his crowd expressed their hostility to Nehemiah: ***They laughed us to scorn, and despised us***. Their ridicule then turned to slander: ***Will ye rebel against the king*** (2:19)? In addition, Judah's ***nobles put not their necks to the work of their lord*** (supervisor) (3:5).

Nehemiah refused to become discouraged and give up. Accomplishing the will of God is dependent upon remembering that He is Sovereign over the affairs of our lives. ***Be content with such things as ye have: for He hath said, I will never leave thee, nor forsake thee. So that we may boldly say, The Lord is my Helper, and I will not fear what man shall do unto me*** (Heb. 13:5-6).

Thought for Today: Much can be accomplished when Christians work together, ***for the body is not one member, but many*** (I Cor. 12:14).

Christ Revealed: Through Nehemiah's prayer for his people (Neh. 1:4-11). Christ also prayed for His own throughout the ages which includes us today (John 17:20).

JUNE 7 — Read Nehemiah 4 – 6

Highlights: Three lessons: 1) Expect attacks designed to keep us from building walls of protection against **the lust of the flesh, and the lust of the eyes, and the pride of life** (I John 2:15-17); 2) A righteous leader defends the oppressed (Neh. 5); and 3) Stay alert and stand firm against the lies, threats, and schemes of the enemy. It takes 52 days, but they win (chap. 6)!

Nehemiah determined to rebuild the walls around Jerusalem even though there was fierce opposition. He armed workers **with their swords, their spears, and their bows** (Neh. 4:13). He told them: **Be not ye afraid of them: remember the LORD, which is great and terrible** (to be reverenced). **. . . our God shall fight for us. So we laboured in the work: and half of them held the spears from the rising of the morning till the stars appeared** (4:14,20-21; Num. 14:9; Ex. 14:13-14). Working about 12 hours a day left little time for anything else. The Israelite's faith had been strengthened through the reading of the Word of God.

Sanballat again attempted to stop their work, saying: **Come, let us meet together in . . . one of the villages in the plain of Ono** (about 28 miles from Jerusalem) (Neh. 6:2). Nehemiah replied: **I am doing a great work, so that I cannot come down: why should the work cease, whilst I leave it, and come down to you** (6:3)? After five attempts, Sanballat accused Nehemiah of rebelling against the king (6:5-7). He then hired a prophet to foretell Nehemiah's death.

Eleven times it is recorded that Nehemiah prayed (1:4-11; 2:4; 4:4-5,9; 5:19; 6:9,14; 13:14,22,29,31). When taunted by his enemies, he simply replied: **The God of heaven, He will prosper us** (2:19-20). And He did, for Nehemiah records: **So built we the wall . . . for the people had a mind to work** (4:6). Because of his faithfulness and encouragement, it was completed **in fifty and two days** (6:15).

Once we recognize that **the battle is the LORD's** (I Sam. 17:47), and that God is the One who allows the opposition, we will not panic. Instead, we will seek to learn what the Lord expects of us in order to qualify to have our prayers answered. People of faith will always find a way to accomplish the will of God. It is human nature to procrastinate; but, like the Israelites, we can choose to use what we have available to get the job done for the Lord. Jesus said: **I must work the works of Him that sent Me, while it is day: the night cometh, when no man can work** (John 9:4).

Thought for Today: Prayerless Christians weaken their effectiveness.

Christ Portrayed: By Nehemiah and other Jews who had bought back (redeemed) some Jews who had been sold to the heathen as slaves while in Persia (Neh. 5:8). We, **which He hath purchased with His own blood** (Acts 20:28), were redeemed when we accepted Jesus as our Lord and Savior.

JUNE 8   **Read Nehemiah 7 – 8**

Highlights: Nehemiah's ministry in Jerusalem is finished (Neh. 7:1-2). The ever-important genealogy registry is consulted to determine who are genuine children of Israel (7:6-66). Ezra reads the Law (8:1-8). ***The joy of the LORD is your strength*** (8:10,12). Through their study, they discover a forgotten Law about the Feast of Booths (Tabernacles), and they fulfill it (8:14-18). Praise the Lord.

The ultimate purpose of God for His people was more than the restoration of His Temple and the walls of Jerusalem. These manmade structures were powerless to protect the Israelites from their enemies unless they knew and obeyed His Word. The Hebrew language in which ***the Book of the Law*** (Neh. 8:3) was written was no longer the common language of the people. During their captivity, they spoke Aramaic, which was the international trade language used by the Aramaeans, Persians, and Babylonians at that time. ***So they read in the Book in the Law of God distinctly, and gave the sense, and caused them to understand the reading*** (8:8).

This resulted in a renewal of the Covenant relationship of the Israelites with God and the restoration of scriptural worship. A revival then took place, ***for all the people wept, when they heard the words of the Law*** (8:9).

One of the most pressing needs is for Christians to read all of the Bible and obey it. The Word of God is ***a discerner*** (judge) ***of the thoughts and intents of the heart*** (Heb. 4:12). As we read the Word of God, His Holy Spirit brings to our minds the various acts of disobedience that we have committed – whether by choosing not to do right or through ignorance. This realization of sin should lead us to confess our sins and ask for forgiveness and cleansing. We will then become ***doers of the Word, and not hearers only*** (James 1:22).

Once we have confessed our sins and repented of them, we are also freed from the guilt of those sins. We dare not dig up sins that have been confessed and forgiven – whether they are our sins or the sins of others. Instead, we should rejoice in the merciful, forgiving love of God through Christ our Savior. ***It is of the LORD's mercies that we are not consumed, because His compassions fail not. They are new every morning: great is Thy faithfulness*** (Lam. 3:22-23).

Thought for Today: Obeying the Word of God prepares our hearts for the Holy Spirit to work in and through us.

Christ Revealed: Through the names required to be registered for priestly service (Neh. 7:64). Christ, our Great ***High Priest*** (Heb. 3:1), will soon return wearing His Name, ***KING OF KINGS, AND LORD OF LORDS*** (Rev. 19:16).

JUNE 9 — Read Nehemiah 9 – 10

Highlights: What a wonderful worship service! The reading of the Word of God leads the people to confess their sins, revival, and worship (Neh. 9). They renew their Covenant with God to follow His Word. Notice who signs it (9:38-10:39).

The completion of the wall provided protection from the surrounding enemies and provided peace of mind to hear what God had to say. It was symbolic of our necessity to **have no fellowship with the unfruitful works of darkness, but rather reprove them. . . . See then that ye walk circumspectly** (watchful of various dangers, hidden or visible)**. . . . understanding . . . the will of the Lord** (Eph. 5:11,15,17).

Ezra stands out as a godly man who led the people to "understand the will of the Lord." Ezra and other Levites **read in the Book of the Law of God distinctly, and gave the sense** (meaning)**, and caused them to understand the reading** (Neh. 8:8). The teaching of the Word of God was of such grave importance that it is mentioned seven times in one chapter (8:2,3,7,8,9,12,13). This points out how essential it is to read all the Bible from Genesis to Revelation.

On the 24th day of Tishri (September/October), **the children of Israel were assembled with fasting** (9:1). There was a movement of the Holy Spirit following the reading of the Scriptures. **They stood up in their place, and read in the Book of the Law of the LORD their God one fourth part of the day; and another fourth part they confessed, and worshipped the LORD their God** (9:2-3). The Levites were led to say to the people: **Stand up and bless the LORD your God for ever and ever: and blessed be Thy glorious Name, which is exalted above all blessing and praise** (9:5).

The priests revealed how God, in **manifold** (great) **mercies** (9:19), had provided His **good Spirit to instruct them . . . they lacked nothing** (9:20-21). The Holy Spirit still guides believers, as Jesus promised: **He will reprove** (convict) **the world of sin. . . . when He, the Spirit of Truth, is come, He will guide you into all Truth** (John 16:8,13). The Holy Spirit enlightens our minds, imparts conviction of sin, and empowers us to live a sanctified (holy) life (I Cor. 2:16; 6:11).

For this cause I bow my knees unto the Father . . . That He would grant you, according to . . . His glory, to be strengthened with might by His Spirit in the inner man (Eph. 3:14,16).

Thought for Today: If we live by faith, we never need to worry regardless of circumstances.

Christ Revealed: As the Creator (Neh. 9:6). **All things were created by Him, and for Him** (Col. 1:16).

JUNE 10   Read Nehemiah 11 – 12

Highlights: Jerusalem – the Holy City, the political capital of the kingdom, the city of David, the center of Worship – is nearly empty. Only the leaders live there (Neh. 11:1). Lots are cast to repopulate the city. See the list of "Who's Who" in Jerusalem (chap. 11); the returning priests and Levites (chap. 12).

Ordinary people, although not skilled in building walls, had willingly gone to work under Nehemiah's leadership and done the best they could to rebuild the walls around Jerusalem.

Only a minority of the people who left Persia to rebuild Jerusalem actually lived inside the city's walls. Most of the Jews lived in suburbs where they could grow crops, pasture their animals, and make a living more easily. Because of this, there were not enough people living in Jerusalem to maintain and protect it. **And the rulers of the people dwelt at Jerusalem: the rest of the people also cast lots, to bring one of ten to dwell in Jerusalem the holy city** (Neh. 11:1).

The Israelites could now assemble within the rebuilt walls of Jerusalem and worship without fear of their enemies. **At the dedication of the wall of Jerusalem they sought the Levites out of all their places, to bring them to Jerusalem, to keep** (observe) **the dedication with gladness, both with thanksgivings, and with singing. . . . Also that day they offered great sacrifices, and rejoiced: for God had made them rejoice with great joy . . . the joy of Jerusalem was heard even afar off** (12:27,43).

The Israelites' worship demonstrated a heartfelt commitment to the Lord in their renewed relationship to Him. Although all true Christians love the Lord, not all are willing to give up personal interests and financial security to do what is needed to accomplish His purposes.

It is important for followers of Christ to consider "the walls" which may need to be rebuilt in their own lives where worldly interests have broken through and devastated their zeal for the Lord.

In our Christian walk, we need to be on guard against anything, including good, wholesome activities, which may tempt us to divert our time or our money from their usefulness to God.

We all want to hear our Lord say what the earthly master said in the parable of the talents: **Well done . . . good and faithful servant: thou hast been faithful over a few things, I will make thee ruler over many things: enter . . . into the joy of thy lord** (Matt. 25:21).

Thought for Today: God can use the least servant to fulfill His needs.

Christ Portrayed: By the priests and Levites who purified (sanctified) themselves and the people (Neh. 12:30). Christ our High Priest, through His perfect sacrifice, purified His believers by His Word. **Now ye are clean through the Word which I have spoken unto you** (John 15:3; 17:17).

JUNE 11   **Read Nehemiah 13**

Highlights: It's amazing how reading the Word of God opens our eyes to see how He would have us live. The people conform to His will (Neh. 13:1-3). Nehemiah brings about reform when even the priests allow sin (13:4-7,10-13,15-28,30-31). As the Temple of the Lord, the people of God must take spiritual inventory to be sure there is no hidden sin in our hearts.

During Nehemiah's absence, the Israelites neglected to worship God or to observe the Sabbath. Nehemiah again **obtained... leave** (permission) **of the king: And... came to Jerusalem** (Neh. 13:6-7). He was grieved over the people's disregard of the Law and took firm action to return the nation to God. **On that day they read in the Book of Moses... therein was found written, that the Ammonite and the Moabite should not come into the congregation of God for ever** (13:1).

The greatest evils were committed by those who held the highest positions of spiritual leadership. **Eliashib the priest... was allied unto Tobiah** (through marriage)**.... And one of the sons of Joiada, the son of Eliashib the high priest, was son in law to Sanballat the Horonite** (13:4,28). Other priests had intermarried with the idol-worshipping, Canaanite women.

Nehemiah **understood** (learned) **of the evil that Eliashib did for Tobiah, in preparing him a chamber** (room) **in the courts of the House** (Temple) **of God** (13:7). This was not only forbidden by God (Deut. 23:3-4), but Tobiah formerly had opposed Nehemiah's work in rebuilding the walls around Jerusalem (Neh. 2:10,19; 4:3-8; 6:17-19). Nehemiah **cast forth all the household stuff of Tobiah out of the chamber** (room)**.... contended... with the rulers, and said, Why is the House** (Temple) **of God forsaken** (13:8-9,11)**?**

The reason was obvious. The nobles of Judah had violated the Law by marrying heathen women and, consequently, **defiled the priesthood** (13:29). Nehemiah warned the people: **Ye shall not give your daughters unto their sons, nor take their daughters unto your sons.... Did not Solomon king of Israel sin by these things? ... him did outlandish** (unbelieving) **women cause to sin** (13:25-26). Nehemiah was mightily used of God because he knew the Scriptures and refused to compromise. **Draw nigh to God.... ye sinners; and purify your hearts, ye double minded** (doubters) (James 4:8).

Thought for Today: Give all praise to the Lord for all your achievements. *I can do all things through Christ which strengtheneth me* (Phil. 4:13).

Christ Portrayed: By Nehemiah who cleansed the priests and Levites and defined their duties (Neh. 13:30). Christ cleanses us from all our sins when we confess them (I John 1:9). Through Him we have been made *a royal priesthood* to serve the Lord (I Pet. 2:9).

Introduction To The Book Of ESTHER

The Book of Esther centers around the descendants of the Israelites who remained in Persia after the 70-year captivity and around the Hebrew maiden Hadassah, who was given the Persian name Esther. The events in this book probably took place in the time period between chapters six and seven of the Book of Ezra, occurring about 40 years after the Temple had been rebuilt (Ezra 3:10; 5:14-15), but about 30 years before the walls of Jerusalem were rebuilt (Neh. 6:15). It is quite possible that Esther, who was by then the queen mother, was used of God to prepare the way for her fellow Israelite Nehemiah to become the cupbearer to her Persian stepson King Artaxerxes I. This trusted position and relationship with the king was probably the basis for Nehemiah to receive the king's support for rebuilding the walls in Jerusalem.

Ahasuerus is the Hebrew name and Xerxes the Greek name, of Khshayarsha, king of Persia. He ruled **from India even unto Ethiopia, over an hundred and seven and twenty provinces** (Esth. 1:1). It is assumed that, at the banquet which opens the Book of Esther, he was planning a battle against Greece which eventually led to his defeat. Ahasuerus reigned in Shushan (Susa) which was located in modern Iran near the eastern border of Iraq. The rule of his son Artaxerxes I is recorded in Ezra 7 – 10 and Nehemiah 1 – 13.

The Book of Esther, as well as the Books of Ezra and Nehemiah, confirm that our Creator can accomplish His perfect will through a helpless minority of faithful servants, even when they are ruled by evil men (Jer. 32:27).

Comfort

But the Comforter, Who is the Holy Ghost **(Spirit)** *. . . shall teach you all things* (John 14:26).

These things have I spoken to you, that My joy might remain in you, and that your joy might be full (John 15:11).

Blessed be God . . . Who comforteth us in all our tribulation, that we may be able to comfort them which are in trouble, by the comfort wherewith we ourselves are comforted of God (I Cor. 1:3-4).

This is my comfort in my affliction: for Your Word has quickened me (given me life) (Ps. 119:50).

My soul melts (weeps) *for heaviness* (sorrow): *strengthen me according to Your Word* (Ps. 119:28).

JUNE 12   **Read Esther 1 – 3**

Highlights: God implements His plan to preserve His chosen people. Queen Vashti is deposed. Esther, from an exiled Jewish family, is chosen to replace her (Esth. 1 – 2). Mordecai finds favor with the king (2:21-23). Haman, the king's chief advisor, plots to kill the entire Jewish population in Persia (3:7-15).

Hadassah was the Hebrew name for the Jewish orphan whose Persian name was Esther (Star). She was taken to the king's palace along with other maidens, either to be made queen or to become a part of the king's harem. Esther found herself in a situation over which she had no control. She and her faithful, older cousin Mordecai, who had adopted her (Esth. 2:7,15), could only trust God for direction and protection. To complicate their situation, the man given power to enforce the king's commands was the evil, self-serving Haman (3:10,15), an Amalekite descendant of Esau (3:1; Gen. 36:12; I Sam. 15:2-3,32-33), who hated all Jews (Deut. 25:17-19).

When **Mordecai bowed not, nor did him reverance** (Esth. 3:2), Haman was determined to use his authority to destroy him and all the Jews in the kingdom. Haman's plan was declared law with the king's approval and the lot **(Pur)** was cast to determine the best day to execute all the Jews (3:7-13). However, Mordecai and Esther used every legal means to defend the people of God, even risking their own lives.

God expects us to do all we can to resolve our own problems. However, we should never doubt that God is in ultimate control to do what we can't do for ourselves. He never errs, is never partial, and never overlooks His children. We should not give in to self-pity and defeat but should remain faithful and look to the Lord and His Word for guidance and strength. Like Mordecai, we must not bow down to the Hamans of this world who seek to destroy our loyalty to Christ.

Like Esther, you may feel hopelessly trapped in your situation and may long for the time when you will be free of it. But Jesus explained the importance of doing your best with what you have when He told the parable of a man with **two talents . . .** (who) **said** (to his master)**, Lord, thou deliveredst unto me two talents: behold, I have gained two other talents beside them. His lord said unto him, Well done, good and faithful servant; thou hast been faithful over a few things, I will make thee ruler over many things** (Matt. 25:22-23).

Thought for Today: God does hear and answer your prayers.

Christ Portrayed: By Mordecai, who adopted Esther (Esth. 2:15). We are adopted into the family of God by Jesus Christ (Eph. 1:5; I John 3:1). **For ye are all the children of God by faith in Christ Jesus** (Gal. 3:26).

JUNE 13   **Read Esther 4 – 7**

Highlights: Esther is faced with the question: ***Who knoweth whether thou art come to the kingdom for such time as this*** (Esth. 4:13-14)***?*** She can avoid getting involved. But, because she is a devout Jew, Esther is led of God to reveal Haman's intentions to the king (5:1-12; 6:14 – 7:10). In spite of Haman's evil plan and hatred of Mordecai (5:9,13-14), God protects His own people and the Messianic line in a miraculous way (6:1-13; 7:10).

About five years after Esther became queen, Haman was promoted ***above all the princes that were with him*** (Esth. 3:1-7). When Haman's decree was proclaimed that all Jews would be destroyed, Mordecai urged Esther to ***go in unto the king, to make supplication unto him, and to make request before him for her people*** (4:8). No one on the king's staff knew that Esther was a Jew because Mordecai had forbidden her to reveal her nationality. Persian law stated that anyone who approached the king uninvited could be put to death. Esther's risk was real, for she had ***not been called to come in unto the king these thirty days*** (4:11). She could have reasoned: "If the king has lost interest in me or discovers that I am a Jew, how could I favorably influence him?" But she believed that the risk of losing her prestige, as Queen Vashti had done, or even her own life, was not as important as doing what she could to save her people.

After three days of fasting, Queen Esther ***stood in the inner court of the king's house*** (5:1) and waited on the king's decision. He king welcomed her and accepted her request: ***If it seem good unto the king, let the king and Haman come this day unto the banquet that I have prepared for him*** (5:4). Then, at a second banquet, he again asked Esther what her request might be. He was shocked to hear her plead for her her life: ***O king . . . let my life be given me. . . . For we are sold, I and my people, to be destroyed. . . . The adversary*** (foe) ***and enemy is this wicked Haman*** (7:3-6). Angrily, ***the king said, Hang him. . . . So they hanged Haman on the gallows that he had prepared for Mordecai*** (7:9-10).

Esther encourages us to use whatever God-given abilities we gave been blessed with to tell a lost world that our King gave His life to save them from eternal hell. ***For whosoever will save his life shall lose it; but whosoever shall lose his life for My*** (the Lord Jesus Christ's) ***sake and the Gospel's, the same shall save it*** (Mark 8:35).

Thought for Today: Throughout the ages, Satan has tried to destroy witnesses of God, but the Lord guards His children who seek His guidance.

Christ Portrayed: By Esther, who went before the king's court willing to die for her people (Esth. 3:6-14; 4:16). Jesus was also willing to die for His people – ***I lay down My life for the sheep*** (John 10:15,17-18); I John 2:2).1

JUNE 14   Read Esther 8 – 10

Highlights: A decree to save the Jews is issued (Esth. 8) and God brings victory to His people (9:1-19). The Festival of Purim is established and is to be observed annually (9:19-32). King Ahasuerus proclaims Mordecai prime minister, second only to the king (chap. 10).

The king had promoted Haman and decreed that others bow to him in respect; but Mordecai, a devout Jew, refused. This so angered Haman that he wanted all Jews **destroyed**. He told the king about those who refused to obey the king's laws – laws that once decreed – even the king himself could not nullify. The king granted permission for this group of lawbreakers to be eradicated from his kingdom, just as Haman desired (Esth. 3:1-9).

Haman's "wise counselors" **had cast Pur** (the lot) to determine the most favorable time to execute all Jews. His "lucky day" fell on the 13th day of the 12th month (Esth. 3:7-13; 9:1,24) so that he would have plenty of time to prepare his evil plans.

The fixed day of execution, which came to be known as Purim (Lots), was turned from death to deliverance. Haman did not realize that Mordecai's God is <u>always</u> in control of <u>all</u> the affairs of His children. Even though **the lot is cast into the lap . . . the whole disposing thereof is of the LORD** (Prov. 16:33).

Following Haman's execution, the king allowed Mordecai to write a new decree giving the Jews the right to defend themselves. **In the day that the enemies of the Jews hoped to have power over them, (though it was turned to the contrary, that the Jews had rule over them that hated them;) . . . the fear of them fell upon all people** (Esth. 9:1-2). Although the name of God is not mentioned in it, the Book of Esther illustrates how God uses faithful servants to change world affairs in order to fulfill His Word.

Esther is testimony to the fact that, even in a secular society dominated by a heathen power, God can protect His people. But He expects us to respond courageously in faith to the threats of the Hamans of this world. Even though God is not seen, His followers are never out of His sight. He is infallible and guides and provides for His faithful servants. The peace and security ultimately enjoyed by Mor-decai and Esther can be experienced by those who remember that God **hath said, I will never leave thee, nor forsake thee** (Heb. 13:5).

Thought for Today: No sin works more deceitfully than pride.

Christ Revealed: By Mordecai's exaltation from servanthood to a position of honor and glory next to the king (Esth. 8:2,15; 10:3). Christ came to earth as a servant and was exalted to **the right hand of God** (Phil. 2:5-11; Mark 16:19).

Introduction To The Book Of JOB

The Book of Job opens with a brief history of a godly, praying man named Job, **the greatest of all the men of the east** (Job 1:3). In the first two chapters, we read of Satan's accusations against Job and the ordeal God permitted him to experience to prove his faith. Job showed that God could trust him to be faithful even through life's most painful experiences.

God said: **There was a man in the land of Uz, whose name was Job** (1:1). Uz was a descendant of Noah's third son Shem, through whom the Messiah would come (Gen. 10:22-23). The location of **the land of Uz** is not specifically identified, but it was situated in the area of the tribes of the Temanites, the Shuhites, and the Naamathites, as well as the Buzites (Job 2:11; 32:2; Gen. 22:20-22). It also would have been within raiding distance of the Sabeans and Chaldeans (Job 1:15,17). Jeremiah wrote of **all the kings of the land of Uz, and all the kings of the land of the Philistines** (Jer. 25:20). Most of these are well-documented places.

It appears that Uz was located in Edom, just below the Dead Sea: **O daughter of Edom, that dwellest in the land of Uz** (Lam. 4:21). The exact location is unimportant, but the spiritual insight concerning how we should understand and accept our circumstances and suffering is of utmost importance – relevant and applicable to every age.

In the Book of Job we see the reasonings of God, Job, his wife, his three friends, Elihu the Buzite, and Satan who is exposed as the instigator of all suffering. As you read through each chapter, carefully distinguish between the wisdom of godly Job and the well-meaning, but inaccurate, half-truths and misleading humanistic arguments of his friends. God highly complimented Job as being **perfect** (blameless) **and upright** (Job 1:1,8) for having spoken the truth.

Job's friends and Elihu reveal how deceptive and unreliable human reasoning can be. The only satisfying answers to the needs of all of us are found in the only infallible, Holy Word of God.

In each day's reading, note the intensifying of Job's suffering but also the development of his spiritual insight. In the final chapter, God once again removes all doubt concerning Job's righteousness and truthfulness when the Lord said to Eliphaz: **My wrath is kindled against thee, and against thy two friends: for ye have not spoken of Me the thing that is right, as My servant Job hath** (Job 42:7).

JUNE 15 — Read Job 1 – 4

Highlights: A great godly example, Job acknowledges God as his source of wealth and family (Job 1:1-5). God allows Satan to attack Job (1:12 – 2:9). In pain, Job curses the day he was born (chap. 3), while his friends offer "advice" (chap. 4).

Who can understand the heartache and sorrow of Job – the servant of the Lord who was stripped of family, possessions, reputation, and health? This suffering was not a misfortune or bad luck; nor was it punishment from God, as Job's friends mistakenly assumed. All of Job's sufferings were the attacks of Satan, but God allowed them in order to bring Job into a closer relationship with Himself.

Without the Holy Scriptures, we would never understand the reason for suffering. Our Creator, who knows the innermost thoughts of all mankind, declared that Job *was perfect and upright, and one that feared* (revered) *God, and eschewed* (shunned) *evil* (Job 1:1).

Behind all the world's evil is Satan, *going to and fro in the earth ... walking up and down in it* (1:7) in his continuous effort to destroy all that is good. But Satan is under the constant surveillance of God.

Satan assumed that, like every self-serving person, Job was faithful only because God would reward him. During his intense suffering and testing, Job's wife even suggested that he *curse* (renounce) *God, and die* (2:9). She too had suffered loss, but it seems that her greatest loss was her faith in God. Job realized he was not the owner of all he possessed, not even of his children; he was merely the Lord's manager of things entrusted to his care. From there, it was just one more step of faith for Job to accept that God, in His wisdom, had the right to reclaim His possessions anytime He chose. Instead of cursing God, Job worshiped Him, saying: *The Lord gave, and the Lord hath taken away; blessed be the Name of the Lord* (1:21).

Spiritual victories do not just happen; they are dependent upon one's faith in God, for *faith cometh by hearing, and hearing by the Word of God* (Rom. 10:17). Apart from the indwelling power of His Spirit and His Word, all efforts to live a victorious Christian life are doomed to failure.

God, our Master Planner, is still in full control. *Jesus Christ the same yesterday, and to day, and for ever* (Heb. 13:8).

Thought for Today: It is good to praise the Lord, to sing praise to His Name (Ps. 92:1).

Christ Revealed: In the conversation between Satan and God Almighty (Job 1:6-12). We can see the meaning of Christ's statement to Peter that Satan wanted to sift him *as wheat* (Luke 22:31). It is comforting to know that Satan cannot test us beyond the will of God.

JUNE 16   Read Job 5 – 8

Highlights: Job's friends don't understand what happened (Job. 5 & 8); Job responds with the wisdom of God (chap. 6) and then prays to Him (7:16-21).

After one full week of silent contemplation about Job's suffering, Eliphaz, his oldest friend, spoke first (Job 4:1). He tried to convince Job to confess his secret sin, saying: **Happy is the man whom God correcteth: therefore despise not... the chastening of the Almighty** (5:17). Eliphaz then elaborated on the blessings Job could expect if he would only confess his sin, and he confidently concluded: **Lo... we have searched it, so it is; hear it, and know thou it for thy good** (5:27).

In addition to Job's physical sufferings, his financial loss, the death of his children, and his wife's bitterness toward God, all three of his friends misjudged his integrity and continued to unmercifully attack him day after day. Job felt the bitter sting of Eliphaz's condemnation and his insinuation that Job was a hypocrite. Job did not understand why God had not come to his defense. Even worse, it seemed to him that he had even been struck down by **the arrows of the Almighty** (6:4).

However, through Job's sufferings we see how the Lord was bringing to light deeper spiritual insight, when Job said: **What is man, that Thou shouldest magnify him? and that Thou shouldest set Thine heart upon him? And that Thou shouldest visit** (examine) **him every morning, and try** (test) **him every moment** (7:17-18)?

We too recognize our insignificance in comparison to the eternal, Holy, and Almighty God. Although He created us, by nature we are defiled by Adam's sin and deserve eternal punishment. But, through the miraculous new birth, we have the joy of living eternally with our loving Creator. All who reject Christ as personal Savior and Lord will be **cast into the lake of fire. This is the second death** (Rev. 20:14).

It is not our Heavenly Father's will **that any should perish, but that all should come to repentance** (II Pet. 3:9). However, God tries (proves) us – either with afflictions or with blessings. Through it all, He is seeking to develop in us a genuine love for and commitment to Him.

All that God does and allows is for our ultimate good. **For unto you it is given in the behalf of Christ, not only to believe on Him, but also to suffer for His sake** (Phil. 1:29).

Thought for Today: Every trial gives us an opportunity to draw closer to God and can make us more the person He wants us to become.

Christ Revealed: Through Job's sorrowful condition (Job 7:1-6). Christ was known as **a Man of sorrows... acquainted with grief** (Is. 53:3). On the cross separated from God in His humanity, Jesus felt that pain in addition to all our sins which He bore (Mark 15:34).

JUNE 17

Read Job 9 – 12

Highlights: Man needs a *Daysman* (Mediator) (Job 9:33). Jesus is ours (I Tim. 2:5). Learn the *truth* – both the wicked and the righteous suffer (Job 10). Zophar says misfortune is sent by God to punish sin (chap. 11). When innocent, Job's defense is our defense (12:4,9-10,13).

All of us will benefit by carefully reading the spiritual discernment of Job, whom God said *was perfect and upright, and one that feared God, and eschewed* (avoided) *evil* (Job 1:1).

This man of spiritual insight proclaimed with confidence: *Are not his* (man's) *days also like the days of a hireling* (hired worker)*? ... So am I made to possess months of vanity, and wearisome nights are appointed to me* (7:1,3). His friend Bildad incorrectly believed that God had appointed *wearisome nights* of suffering only for sinners, and his response to Job was critical and cynical: *How long wilt thou speak these things? ... If thou wert pure and upright; surely now He would awake* (rouse Himself) *for thee, and make the habitation of thy righteousness prosperous* (8:2,6).

Bildad concluded that those who enjoy good things in this life are righteous, and that all suffering is the result of sin. But, in a parable given by Jesus, the rich man who built bigger barns for "greater blessings" was not one who pleased the Lord (Luke 12:18,20). Another time, Jesus revealed that sin was not the reason a man was born blind (John 9:2-3).

Job's suffering led him to experience deep, spiritual maturity as he acknowledged that God was far superior to himself. He spoke with confidence, saying: *Remember ... that Thou hast made me as the clay. ... Thou hast granted me life and favour, and Thy visitation hath preserved my spirit* (Job 10:9,12). However, Job knew that he and God could not meet on the same level: *For He is not a man, as I am, that I should answer Him, and we should come together in judgment* (court)*. Neither is there any daysman* (arbitrator) *betwixt us* (9:32-33). Job expressed the desperate need for a mediator, someone who would stand in the gap between the Holy God and sinful man.

Our Lord Jesus Christ is that Mediator – the only One who can restore man's broken fellowship with God (Rom. 5:8-10). *For there is One God, and one Mediator between God and men, the Man Christ Jesus* (I Tim. 2:5).

Thought for Today: You will be blessed when you love the person whom you consider unlovely.

Christ Portrayed: Through the daysman (mediator) Job longs for (Job 9:33). Christ is the only *Mediator between God and* (sinful) *men* (I Tim. 2:5).

JUNE 18 — Read Job 13 – 16

Highlights: Job testifies that he is upright and has done nothing to deserve suffering (Job 13 – 14). He speaks directly to God (13:20 – 14:22). Eliphaz calls Job a windbag (15:2) and uses his own experiences to "show" how wrong Job is (15:17-35). Job's fifth speech calls his friends *miserable comforters* (16:2)

Satan prompted the attacks on Job by his wife and by his "devoted" friends in an attempt to substantiate his own accusation that Job would curse God if his many blessings were removed.

Job's suffering intensified with days and weeks of sleeplessness and painful, ulcerating boils that would only become more intense since he had no painkillers. It may appear that he wavered at times, but Job always ended his comments on a high note of praise. Job could say with utmost confidence: *Though He slay me, yet will I trust in Him. . . . I know that I shall be justified* (Job 13:15,18).

Although Job gave up hope of recovering his health, wealth, children, or high esteem among the people, he did not become bitter or resentful toward his accusers or toward God. Instead, he looked forward to being with the Lord after his death, saying: *If a man die, shall he live again? all the days of my appointed time will I wait, till my change come* (14:14), meaning: "After death, I shall *live again* and I will be changed."

How different Job's attitude was from many today who blame fate, circumstances, God, or others for what goes wrong in their lives! Some easily become dissatisfied, bitter, pessimistic, or engulfed in self-pity. Their self-image depends on others' reactions. When others praise them, their self-esteem rises; when they are criticized or their plans fail, they feel defeated. Job didn't need praise from people to maintain his faith; he retained his confidence in the wisdom and justice of his Creator.

Christians can thank God for the perfect Savior and great High Priest, who *ever liveth to make intercession for them* (us) (Heb. 7:25). Accepting Jesus as Savior and Lord of our lives, we should have a sincere desire to know His will by reading all of His Word.

Job's unshakable faith in God resulted from obedience to the revealed Word of God. He said: *Neither have I gone back from the Commandment of His lips; I have esteemed the words of His mouth more than my necessary food* (Job 23:12).

Thought for Today: Treasures laid up in heaven pay high dividends. *Lay up for yourselves treasures in heaven, where neither moth nor rust doth corrupt, and where thieves do not break through nor steal: For where your treasure is, there will your heart be also* (Matt. 6:19-21).

Christ Revealed: Through the smiting of Job (Job 16:10). Christ also was struck by those who ridiculed Him (Matt. 27:29-44; John 18:22-23).

JUNE 19   **Read Job 17 – 20**

Highlights: Job continues to defend himself (Job 17). Bildad jumps in using proverbs (chap. 18). Read what Job knows – one of the greatest expressions of faith in the Old Testament (19:23-27). Zophar expounds on what happens to the wicked (chap. 20).

Job assumed all hope of recovery was gone when he said: ***My breath*** (spirit) ***is corrupt, my days are extinct, the graves are ready for me. . . . all my members are as a shadow. . . . My days are past, my purposes are broken off*** (Job 17:1,7,11).

Bildad interrupted this suffering saint with scathing words that were even more cruel and critical than his first speech. He assumed that Job's sufferings exposed him as a sinful hypocrite who was hopelessly condemned: ***For he is cast into a net by his own feet. . . . He shall be driven from light into darkness, and chased out of the world*** (18:8,18). Bildad went on to say: ***Surely such are the dwellings of the wicked, and this is the place of him that knoweth not God*** (18:21). This mistaken accusation from Job's "friend" must have been a bitter blow. Not only was Job facing death, but to die being misjudged as a hypocrite when he knew his heart was right with God must have been heartbreaking.

Our hearts are deeply stirred with compassion as this pitiful, lonely, suffering saint looked beyond his "friends." With great spiritual discernment and assurance, Job said: ***I know that my Redeemer liveth, and that He shall stand at the latter day upon the earth . . . in my flesh shall I see God*** (19:25-26). This revelation of life after death is one of the greatest in the Old Testament. Through Job, God leads us to see that we have no valid excuse to complain.

According to the Law, a redeemer was the next of kin who was responsible for redeeming (buying back) an enslaved kinsman or his lost inheritance (Lev. 25:25). The kinsman-redeemer foreshadowed the coming of Jesus Christ, our Savior-Redeemer. Without Him, we would be hopeless, lost sinners condemned to die and to be cast into eternal hell. ***By the deeds of the Law there shall no flesh*** (body) ***be justified in His sight: for by the Law is the knowledge of sin. But now the righteousness of God without the Law is manifested. . . . by faith of Jesus Christ, unto all and upon all them that believe . . . Being justified freely by His grace through the redemption that is in Christ Jesus*** (Rom. 3:20-22,24).

Thought for Today: The Christian has a personal, living Savior to guide him.

Christ Revealed: As the ***Redeemer*** (Job 19:25). Jesus Christ is our Redeemer. By His death, He provided the required sacrifice for our sins (Acts 20:28; Eph. 1:13-14; Rev. 5:9). ***Our Savior Jesus Christ . . . gave Himself for us, that He might redeem us from all iniquity*** (Titus 2:13-14).

JUNE 20   Read Job 21 – 24

Highlights: As Job responds, the question arises: "Why do the wicked prosper and go unpunished?" Eliphaz speaks for the 3rd time, making Job sound like a liar (Job 22:1-30). Job's response: *I shall come forth as gold* (23:10)

The key to Job's singleness of heart and ultimate victory was his conviction that obedience to the Word of God was more important than life itself: *His way have I kept, and not declined. . . . I have esteemed the words of His mouth more than my necessary food* (Job 23:11-12).

It is as if Job had said: "In the midst of my suffering and sorrows, in faith I turned to and trusted whatever He chose for me. So great was my need for assurance, I seized upon it as a starving man for a meal. I devoured it and indeed my soul was comforted and I was strengthened. I turned from the husks of 'comfort' that my friends offered and can testify that only faith in God will satisfy."

Job further explained his confidence by saying: *Behold, I go forward, but He is not there; and backward, but I cannot perceive Him: On the left hand . . . I cannot behold Him . . . on the right hand . . . I cannot see Him* (23:8-9). Regardless of where Job turned, it seemed that God was nowhere to be found. Job's faith did not rest in his fears and feelings, but in the Word of God. Job's faith was unshakable because he could truthfully say: *I shall come forth as gold. . . .* (for) *His way have I kept* (23:10-11).

Some people assume they are Christians because they are members of a church, but they have not experienced the transforming power of the Word of God. Like Judas, they may talk like a Christian, but they do not desire Christ as Lord of their lives. Until they desire to know how God would have them live, the Bible will have little meaning for them. *As ye have therefore received Christ Jesus the Lord, so walk ye in Him. . . . Beware lest any man spoil* (rob) *you through philosophy and vain deceit, after the tradition of men, after the rudiments of the world, and not after Christ* (Col. 2:6,8).

Christians who live year after year, never reading through the Bible because they believe they have sufficent wisdom without it, are spiritually defeated. They have neither armor nor weapon for protection (Eph. 6:11-17). *Unless Thy Law had been my delights, I should then have perished in mine affliction* (Ps. 119:92).

Thought for Today: Strength from the Word of God on a day-to-day basis upholds our faith in Him in times of testing.

Christ Revealed: Through Job's faithfulness to God throughout his suffering (Job 23:10-12). Christ's faithfulness to the Father is seen as He prayed for the Father's will to be done (Luke 22:42).

JUNE 21 — Read Job 25 – 29

Highlights: Bildad and Job debate the greatness of God (Job 25 & 26). Job seems to be fighting a losing battle. Three chapters of mere words cannot defend or prove his innocence as long as God is silent (chap. 27 – 29). This is a true test from God.

Although Job had lost family, wealth, and health, and despite the accusations of his friends, he maintained his integrity. The Book of Job is the inspired Word of God. Job was not searching for answers when he said: ***But where shall wisdom be found? and where is the place of understanding? Man knoweth not the price thereof; neither is it found in the land of the living. . . . neither shall silver be weighed for the price thereof. . . . seeing it is hid from the eyes of all living*** (Job 28:12-13,15,20-21).

Job was never as concerned about knowing the answer to his problems as he was about having a right relationship with God. ***Unto man he said, Behold, the fear of the Lord, that is wisdom; and to depart from evil is understanding*** (28:28). The more we truly humble ourselves and die to pride, the less we will be affected by the criticism of others.

Job had the utmost confidence that God is the Author and Revealer of true wisdom. There is no substitute for reading all of His Word to understand His perfect plan for our lives. It is vital to read through every book of the Bible, from Genesis to Revelation, with a sincere desire to apply its instruction to our lives.

The Israelites complained about their circumstances instead of acknowledging that God was in control. We, too, can make unwise decisions when we allow ourselves to become frustrated. We may say to someone: "You make me angry." But the fact is, we choose to be. Or we may say: "I am depressed today." However, the sad truth is that we have failed to see God in the circumstances He has allowed to take place in our lives. Our Lord is far more concerned with our best interests than we are. ***Wherefore let them that suffer according to the will of God commit the keeping of their souls to Him in well doing, as unto a faithful Creator*** (I Pet. 4:19). We all have the choice to move above and beyond anger and disappointments by permitting the indwelling Christ to rule our lives. This is the key to experiencing ***the peace of God*** (Phil. 4:7). ***The entrance of Thy words giveth light; it giveth understanding unto the simple*** (Ps. 119:130).

Thought for Today: Our faith in God is revealed by the way we react to both our sorrows and our sufferings.

Christ Revealed: Through Job's compassion for others (Job 29:15-17,21-25). Jesus was moved to compassion when He saw great crowds in need of healing and feeding (Matt. 14:14; 15:30-39).

JUNE 22   Read Job 30 – 33

Highlights: The humiliation and anguish of Job's present state is outlined (Job 30 – 31). Job accepts the fact that wisdom begins with, resides in, and ends with God. Our innocent Savior suffered humiliation and anguish for us. The younger man, Elihu, angrily tells others what he thinks (chap. 32 – 33).

Other than Christ, no one suffered so much public humiliation and intense physical and emotional pain as Job did. He had held the chief administrative position in his country and had **dwelt as a king** (Job 29:25). *I delivered the poor that cried, and the father-less, and him that had none to help him.... I was eyes to the blind, and feet was I to the lame. I was a father to the poor: and the cause which I knew not I searched out* (29:12,15-16). In chapter 31 he listed 12 common sins that no one could accuse him of committing. Yet, in his time of need, no one expressed compassion or kindness.

For Job, there seemed to be no end to the cruelty of the people who encouraged his suffering: **They push away my feet.... Terrors are turned upon me: they pursue my soul as the wind: and my wel-fare passeth away as a cloud. And now my soul is poured out upon me; the days of affliction have taken hold upon me** (30:12-17). It seemed that God neither cared nor heard his prayers: *I cry unto Thee, and Thou dost not hear me* (30:20).

At such times when we are put to the test, we can **walk by faith** (II Cor. 5:7) because we are not dependent merely on things we can see. We can confidently trust the Lord and the promises of His Word. Faith does not originate with us; it is the gift of God (Eph. 2:8).

Job's three friends misjudged his relationship to God, but he did not allow them to destroy his faith. As we consider Job, whom God declared the most perfect man on earth (Job 1:8), is it surprising when we are falsely criticized? The most devoted Christian can suffer the worst indignities and humiliation from thoughtless, inconsiderate people – even those who profess to be Christians.

So that we ourselves glory in (speak proudly of) **you in the churches of God for your patience and faith in all your persecutions and tribulations** (afflictions) **that ye endure: Which is a manifest** (visible, evident) **token of the righteous judgment of God, that ye may be counted worthy of the Kingdom of God, for which ye also suffer** (II Thess. 1:4-5).

Thought for Today: If you are confronted with gossip, immediately turn the conversation to something commendable (Phil. 4:8).

Christ Revealed: Through the ridicule and affliction which Job suffered (Job 30:10-11). Christ was afflicted and spat upon. After Pilate delivered Jesus to the Roman soldiers, they flogged Him, hit HIm with an open hand and spat on Him (a sign of great contempt) – and then they crucified Him (Mark 15:15-20; Is. 50:6; 53:2-5; Matt. 27:26-30; John 18:22; 19:1-3).

JUNE 23   Read Job 34 – 37

Highlights: Elihu becomes critical and accuses Job of being arrogant (Job 34). Then, in case Job is forgetful, he reminds him of the justice of God (chap. 35). Elihu talks on and on and reminds Job of the power of God (chap. 36 – 37).

Elihu did not speak until Job's three friends had ended their accusations. Then he condemned them. But he expressed even greater hostility toward Job. Four times in five verses we read variations of the words, Elihu's **wrath was kindled** (Job 32:1-5).

This young egotist referred to himself by the words "me," "my," and "I" at least 55 times to inform Job that he was chosen to intercede on Job's behalf and was **according to thy** (Job's) **wish in God's stead** (32:6 – 33:33). Elihu's accusations against Job were, at best, half-truths and misinterpretations (33:8-13).

One of Elihu's accusations was that Job had claimed to be sinlessly perfect (34:5). The fact is, Job acknowledged his imperfection as sin (7:21; 13:26). However, the Lord proclaimed Job as **My servant . . . that there is none like him in the earth, a perfect and an upright man** (1:8). Elihu falsely stated that Job had **said, It profiteth a man nothing that he should delight himself with God** (34:9). Job never said that. Elihu continued his vicious attack on this dear, godly man, saying: **Job hath spoken without knowledge, and his words were without wisdom. My desire is that Job may be tried unto the end because of his answers for** (like) **wicked men. For he addeth rebellion unto his sin . . . and multiplieth his words against God** (34:35-37).

Elihu's conclusions contradicted the testimony of God, who said that Job had **spoken of Me the thing that is right** (42:7).

During times of personal afflictions, heartbreaking bereavement, persecution, or financial struggles, we may be tempted to become depressed and even fail to pray. That is when we need someone's loving comfort and assurance that our Lord ultimately controls every situation that comes into our lives. Regardless of how bad our situation may seem, He wants to use it for our good and for His glory (Rom. 8:28; also Gen. 50:20).

Have faith in the wisdom of God, **casting all your care** (anxiety) **upon Him; for He careth for you** (I Pet. 5:7).

Thought for Today: Enjoying fellowship with God, among other things, is dependent upon one's attitude toward others.

Christ Revealed: As the One who watches how we live and all we do (Job 34:21). The Lord keeps His eyes on the righteous (I Pet. 3:12).

JUNE 24 Read Job 38 – 40

Highlights: A quick replay when Satan challenges God: "Take away Your favor and watch Job curse You" (Job 1:11). Job, hurting and confused, cries to God. God is silent. God speaks with an avalanche of questions that no man can answer (chap. 38 – 40), reminding Job of man's limited knowledge and the infinite wisdom of God. Job doesn't know how to answer God (40:3-5)!

Is it any surprise that God interrupted Elihu's speech and **answered Job out of the whirlwind, and said, Who is this that darkeneth counsel by words without knowledge** (Job 38:1-2)**?**

For the first time since his suffering started, Job began hearing words of comfort rather than condemnation. When the God of love said: **Gird up now thy loins like a man** (38:3), He seemed to be saying: "Step out of the ashes; you have suffered long enough. You have proven Satan a liar. I'm not as far away from you as it seemed when you said: **I cannot perceive Him. . . . I cannot see Him** (23:8-9). I want you to see that I, and I alone, control the vast universe and yet am greatly concerned with even the smallest detail of your life."

The second statement of God to Job was equally comforting: **I will demand of thee, and answer thou Me** (38:3). The Lord was saying to Job: "You no longer have to listen to the insults of cruel men, for I am in control and will reveal to you the most amazing wisdom concerning the universe ever given to mankind." First, God wanted Job to consider the limitations of his own wisdom compared to the wisdom of the One who created the universe: **Canst thou bind the sweet influences** (cluster) **of Pleiades, or loose the bands** (belt) **of Orion** (38:31)**?** God asked Job about 60 questions in this first cycle of conversation (38:1 – 40:2), and over 80 questions altogether (38 – 41). The wisest astronomer can't explain or change one star in the marvelous array of Pleiades, one of the most beautiful clusters of stars.

The Mighty God who created the universe also created us and cares for us. He patiently listens to our prayers and provides us with what is best for us in the light of eternity. We need to see how unqualified we are to question His wisdom. Nothing is unforeseen and no one is overlooked by our Heavenly Father. He gives inner strength and sustains us by His indwelling Holy Spirit.

The Lord's words to the Apostle Paul were also for us: **My grace is sufficient for thee: for My strength is made perfect in** (your) **weakness** (II Cor. 12:9).

Thought for Today: The vastness of the universe reveals the unlimited resources and matchless wisdom of God.

Christ Revealed: As the One who **laid the foundations of the earth** (Job 38:4). By Christ, God created our universe (Heb. 1:1-2). **All things were made by Him; and without Him was not any thing made that was made** (John 1:1-3).

JUNE 25   **Read Job 41 – 42**

Highlights: God elaborates on the power and strength of just one of His creations (Job 41). In contrast, the powerlessness of man is evident to Job, who repents (42:1-6). God rebukes Job's friends for their errors. Read whose prayers God accepts (42:8-9). God rewards Job for his faithfulness! Check out his blessings (42:10-17).

Through a series of more than 80 questions, God revealed to Job many of the wonders of the universe, some of which have only recently been "discovered" by science. Because of his faith in God and his patience through suffering, Job acknowledged the supreme authority of God compared to how little is known by mankind. It is no surprise to read that Job confessed to God: *I know that Thou canst do every thing, and that no thought can be withholden from Thee.... I uttered that I understood not; things too wonderful for me, which I knew not* (Job 42:2-3). By this he meant: "Although I did not understand, I will never again question what God does or what He allows to happen, since His love and wisdom are perfect." All of us need to be reminded that our limited knowledge and ability to cope with life's problems should cause us to realize how foolish and sinful it is to question the wisdom and love of God for us. We need to accept, with submissive hearts, the circumstances He allows in our lives, which He will use to fulfill His loving, eternal purpose.

During his suffering, Job experienced glorious revelations of the incomparable greatness of God and His ways. Job's spiritual understanding continued to grow as he said: *I have heard of Thee by the hearing of the ear: but now mine eye seeth Thee. Wherefore I abhor* (despise) *myself, and repent in dust and ashes* (42:5-6). Those who simply trust in the Lord, as Job did, are not searching for the answers to all of life's problems, nor asking the questions: "Why?" or "Why me?" Our loving, all-wise Father always knows what we need and will give His best to those who trust Him.

Job's friends must have been astounded to hear the Voice from heaven say to Eliphaz: *My wrath is kindled against thee, and against thy two friends: for ye have not spoken of Me the thing that is right, as My servant Job hath* (42:7). Job could have become proud after God came to his defense. Instead, he humbly prayed for God to forgive his three friends who had so cruelly misjudged him. Jesus also set an example when He said: *Bless them that curse you, and pray for them which despitefully use you* (Luke 6:28).

Thought for Today: Can the Lord say to you: *Well done, thou good and faithful servant* (Matt. 25:21,23)?

Christ Revealed: Through Job's praying for his "friends" (Job 42:10). We are reminded of Christ's command: *Bless them that curse you, and pray for them which despitefully use you* (Luke 6:28).

INTRODUCTION TO THE BOOK OF PSALMS

The Book of Psalms includes songs of praise and thanksgiving. Each of the last five psalms (Ps. 146-150) begins and ends with the phrase: **Praise . . . the LORD**, which is the English translation of the Hebrew word **Hallelujah**, a universal word, the same in every language. It is impossible to be praising the Lord while being dissatisfied with our circumstances. The psalms teach us to forgive others as well as to thank God for His forgiving of our many sins and restoring us to fellowship with Him.

The psalms also include prayers for mercy and help while expressing confidence in God. Prominent in the Book of Psalms is the high esteem God gives to Scripture itself. He inspired the psalmist to write: **Blessed are they that keep His testimonies, and that seek Him with the whole heart. . . . Then shall I not be ashamed, when I have respect unto all Thy Commandments. . . . Thy Word have I hid in mine heart, that I might not sin against Thee** (Ps. 119: 2,6,11). The vital importance of the Scriptures is brought to our attention at least 170 times in Psalm 119. The psalmist was led to write: **I will . . . praise Thy Name for Thy lovingkindness and for Thy truth: for Thou hast magnified Thy Word above all Thy Name** (138:2). God has exalted His Word above all else, and the Scriptures are exceedingly important for the personal well-being of all mankind.

Although written about a thousand years before the birth of Jesus, many psalms refer to the coming of the Messiah – His birth, life, betrayal, crucifixion, resurrection, and ascension into heaven, as well as His return to reign on earth. In the New Testament, the following psalms are applied to Jesus Christ: 2; 8; 16; 22; 40; 41; 45; 68; 69; 72; 89; 102; 109; 110; 118; and 132. Psalm 2 refers to the Messiah, the Son of God, who is to be worshiped; Psalm 16:10-11 proclaims His resurrection; Psalm 22, His suffering; and Psalm 40, His sacrifice. "God" in Psalm 45:6 is the Messiah. In Psalm 89 He is the One promised to fulfill the Covenant of God with David. In Psalm 110 He is **the LORD** (vs 1), is **the Rod of Thy strength** (Ruler) (vs 2), is **a Priest for ever** (vs 4), **shall strike through** (shatter, be a Conqueror of) **kings** (vs 5), shall **Judge among the heathen** (nations) (vs 6).

After His resurrection, Jesus opened the eyes of two of His disciples: **And beginning at Moses and all the Prophets, He expounded** (explained) **unto them in all the Scriptures the things concerning Himself. . . . And He said unto them . . . all things must be fulfilled, which were written in the Law of Moses, and in the Prophets, and in the Psalms, concerning Me** (Luke 24:27,44).

JUNE 26 — Read Psalms 1 – 9

Highlights: A songbook of praise to God. Hearts soar, voices lift in prayer, the anguish of sin, the joy of salvation! Two ways to live: righteously or ungodly (Ps. 1). Whose Son is King (chap. 2)? The Lord our shield (3:3); our peace (4:8); our defender (5:11). The Lord hears and answers our prayers (6:8-10). The Lord our victory (chap. 9).

The key to receiving a blessing from God begins with three negative statements. The first is: **Blessed** (Divinely favored, Fortunate) *is the man that walketh not in the counsel of the ungodly* (Ps. 1:1). who may live acceptable lifestyles that conform to the basic moral standards of society, but live and act as though the Creator God does not exist. Therefore, they assume that any religion, or none at all, is equally acceptable. Consequently, they feel no accountability to God and see no need of a Savior.

The second negative statement is: **Nor standeth in the way of sinners** (1:1), who live to please themselves. They may appear Christian-like in the eyes of the majority of people. They may even believe there is a God and live a good, moral life. Consequently, they are deceived and see no need to repent because they do not think they are sinners. The Christian life is centered in God, but the sinner's life is centered on himself.

Now we see the third negative statement is: **Nor sitteth in the seat of the scornful** (1:1), who have a belittling, antagonistic attitude against God as Creator of all things and against worshiping Jesus Christ as God the Son – *the great God and our Savior Jesus Christ* (Titus 2:13). The **scornful**, for the most part, stand against the Bible and Jesus Christ as the only way to be saved and go to heaven.

The blessed person has an attitude of **delight . . . in the Law of the LORD; and in His Law doth he meditate day and night** (Ps. 1:2). As we meditate on the Word of God, we will delight in pleasing Jesus and will have a desire to be led by **the Spirit of Truth** (John 16:13). As we prayerfully meditate *in His Law*, the Holy Spirit of God speaks to our hearts, guiding us according to His Word.

One of the great blessings that is imparted to those who meditate upon the Word of God comes silently and unnoticed, **like a tree planted by the rivers of water, that bringeth forth his fruit in his season; his leaf also shall not wither; and whatsoever** (whatever) **he doeth shall prosper** (Ps. 1:3).

Thought for Today: Only to the extent that we love God will we enjoy obeying His Word.

Christ Revealed: As the Son of God (Ps. 2:7). *God so loved the world, that He gave His only begotten Son, that whosoever believeth in Him should not perish, but have everlasting life* (John 3:16; Acts 13:33, Heb. 1:5).

JUNE 27 — Read Psalms 10 – 17

Highlights: Helpless? *L̲o̲r̲d̲, thou hast heard the desire of the humble* (Ps. 10:17). Cry to God (chap. 10), He is our refuge (chap. 11). Protection from a lying generation (chap. 12). Sound familiar? *I will sing unto the L̲o̲r̲d̲, because He hath dealt bountifully with me* (13:6). We can rely on God (chap. 17).

David asked a question that has eternal consequences: *L̲o̲r̲d̲, who shall abide* (dwell) *in Thy Tabernacle* (Ps. 15:1)*?* David focused on two of the all-important issues of life when he asked: *Who shall abide?* or *who shall dwell? . . . and worketh righteousness, and speaketh the truth in his heart* (15:1-2). A person can work *righteousness* only after he becomes a child of God through faith in Christ. Jesus told Nicodemus : *Except a man be born of water and of the Spirit, he cannot enter into the Kingdom of God* (John 3:5).

The Book of Psalms foretells the resurrection of Christ. In addition, it offers assurance that all who believe in Him will also rise to share in His resurrection and life eternal. *For the Lord Himself shall descend from heaven . . . and the dead in Christ shall rise first* (I Thess. 4:16). How wonderful to look forward to living in the presence of our Lord forever! Like David, let us rejoice: *I have set the L̲o̲r̲d̲ always before me: because He is at my right hand, I shall not be moved. Therefore my heart is glad, and my glory rejoiceth: my flesh also shall rest in hope* (Ps.16:8-9). Christ the Messiah fulfilled the prophecy of David: *For Thou wilt not leave my soul in hell* (the grave) (16:10). Forty days after His resurrection, Jesus Christ ascended heavenward to take His place at the right hand of the Father as had been prophesied.

On the *Day of Pentecost*, Peter quoted from this psalm to proclaim to about 3,000 people that Jesus was the Christ of whom David had prophesied: *And it shall come to pass, that whosoever shall call on the Name of the Lord shall be saved. . . . For David speaketh concerning Him, I foresaw the Lord always before my face . . . Therefore did my heart rejoice. . . . He seeing this before spake of the resurrection of Christ* (Acts 2:21,25,26,31).

The risen Christ is the Good News of the Gospel upon which our faith is based. *As in Adam all die, even so in Christ shall all be made alive* (I Cor. 15:22).

Thought for Today: Christ died to reconcile you to Himself.

Christ Revealed: In the prophecy that God would not allow His Holy One to see decay (Ps. 16:10). This foretells of the resurrection of our Lord Jesus Christ (Acts 2:25-27; 13:35-39). When Jesus spoke the Revelation to John, He declared: *I am He that liveth, and was dead; and, behold, I am alive for evermore, Amen; and have the keys of hell and of death* (Rev. 1:18).

JUNE 28 — Read Psalms 18 – 22

Highlights: Saved from our enemies (Ps. 18:3). How to praise God (chap. 18). The Commandments of God (19:8), **the fear of the LORD** (19:9), and **the words of my mouth** (19:14). Help from the Lord (20:7). We should all love the Lord as King David loved Him (chap. 21). Psalm 22 is a Messianic psalm, foretelling the suffering and death of Christ.

The effects of the Word of God are beyond compare, for it was by His Word that the worlds were created and by which they are still upheld (Heb. 1:3). **The heavens declare** (are telling of) **the glory of God; and the firmament** (expanse) **sheweth His handywork** (Ps. 19:1). Most exciting is the transforming power of Jesus, the Word of God made flesh, upon all those who receive Him as Lord.

The first six verses of Psalm 19 refer to the works of God in the world; and the remaining eight verses refer to the marvelous influence of His Word on the lives of all who love and obey Him. In this short psalm, six terms are used to express the Word of God:

1. It is the **Law of the LORD** (and, as such) **is perfect** (complete), **converting the soul** (restoring the whole person) **... making wise the simple** (19:7). It is as far superior to the words of man as the heavens are above the earth. Then why should anyone settle for less than to **receive with meekness the engrafted** (implanted) **Word, which is able to save** (deliver, preserve) **your souls** (James 1:21)?

2. The **testimony of the LORD is sure** (never fails), **making wise the simple** (Ps. 19:7). The Apostle Paul confirmed this to Timothy, saying: **Thou hast known the Holy Scriptures, which are able to make thee wise unto salvation** (II Tim. 3:15).

3. It is the **statutes** (precepts) **of the LORD that** are **right** (Ps. 19:8), because they are founded solely on His righteousness.

4. The **Commandment of the LORD** (that) **is pure** (19:8). It expresses the holiness of God. His Commandments provide a new life free from sin's bondage.

5. It reveals the **fear of the LORD** (19:9), an admiration of His holiness and a reverent fear of offending the God of Heaven.

6. It is the **judgments of the LORD** (which) **are true and righteous altogether** (19:9).

Our feelings concerning the incomparable Word of God should be as the psalmist's: **More to be desired are they than gold, yea, than much fine gold: sweeter also than honey** (Ps. 19:10).

Thought for Today: Thank the Lord for His presence in your life today!

Christ Revealed: As the One to whom the psalms refer when they speak of the nails that pierced His hands and feet on the cross and the parting of His clothing (Ps. 22:16,18). **When they had crucified Him, they parted His garments, casting lots upon them, what every man should take** (Mark 15:24). See also Matt. 27:35; Luke 23:34; John 19:18.

JUNE 29 — Read Psalms 23 – 30

Highlights: *The L̲ord is my Shepherd* (He never fails to provide) (Ps. 23). *The earth is the L̲ord's* (He owns it all). . . . *He is King of Glory* (chap. 24). *The meek will He teach His way* (25:9). David's patience and faith (27:14); God expects us to pray (chap. 28); the mighty power of God is available (chap. 29). Praise to Him (chap. 30).

David, the old shepherd-king, knew from years of experience that he was like a sheep that needed to be led to what was best for his life. He was inspired by the Holy Spirit to write: *The L̲ord is my Shepherd; I shall not want* (lack anything). . . . *He leadeth me in the paths of righteousness for His Name's sake* (for my best interest). . . . *I will dwell in the house of the L̲ord* (in fellowship with Him) *for ever* (Ps. 23:1-6).

Left alone, sheep can easily become separated from the flock and lose their way. Of all domesticated animals, sheep are the most defenseless. By nature, like David, we are all "sheep." We can become so caught up in our own interests that we lose sight of the *Good Shepherd* (John 10:11,14) and find ourselves separated from Him.

The humble recognize the *Good Shepherd* who died for the Church. This is one of the key reasons that *the Church is subject unto Christ* (Eph. 5:24). The Church is not a building nor a denomination; it is composed of born-again believers. We are comforted and encouraged to know that our *Good Shepherd* is with us (Ps. 23:4). The Lord works through people in the Church to encourage us. He is the Head and each of us (no exception) represents a function in the body. Some may think they are "know-it-alls," but the Holy Spirit moves through true believers in the Church, often providing advice that we need. No teacher or pastor is "above" this basic principle.

Even *Thy rod and Thy staff they comfort me* (23:4). We know that *whom the Lord loveth He chasteneth* (disciplines) regardless of to whom He chooses to administer the rod (Heb. 12:6).

The utmost desire of every one of our Lord's sheep should daily be *bringing into captivity every thought* (of independence) *to the obedience of Christ* (II Cor. 10:5). *Trust in the L̲ord with all thine heart; and lean not unto thine own understanding. In all thy ways acknowledge Him, and He shall direct thy paths* (Prov. 3:5-6).

Thought for Today: Often the ways of God differ from our expectations! The Lord declared: *For as the heavens are higher than the earth, so are My ways higher than your ways, and My thoughts than your thoughts* (Is. 55:9).

Christ Revealed: As our *Shepherd* (Ps. 23). Christ called Himself *the Good Shepherd* (who) *giveth His life for the sheep* (John 10:11).

JUNE 30   **Read Psalms 31 – 35**

Highlights: David's life is filled with daily conversations with the Lord, just as ours should be. His psalms describe his dependence on the Lord for protection and deliverance from enemies (Ps. 31; 35); his admission of sin and of his desperate desire for forgiveness and restoration (chap. 32); his rejoicing in the mercy and love of the Lord (chap. 33 – 34).

What a privilege we have to join with David and the multitudes since his time, singing: *I will bless the Lord at all times: His praise shall continually be in my mouth* (Ps. 34:1)! *O magnify the Lord with me, and let us exalt His Name together. . . . This poor man cried, and the Lord heard him, and saved him out of all his troubles. The Angel of the Lord encampeth round about them that fear Him, and delivereth them* (34:3,6-7).

Praise at all times is good and right and fills our hearts with joy. But the psalmist went beyond the expected times of worship and praise because he was continually expressing love and devotion to the Lord. He wrote: *And my tongue shall speak of Thy righteousness and of Thy praise all the day long* (35:28).

Even when things seem to go wrong, we can praise the Lord. *And we know that all things* (always) *work together for good to them that love God* (Rom. 8:28). *Many are the afflictions of the righteous: but the* Lord *delivereth him out of them all* (Ps. 34:19).

Even the most unjust and cruel things which we experience, whether deserved or not, become part of the process by which the Lord is transforming our lives. David had many similar experiences which worked together to make him *a man after Mine* (His) *own heart* (Acts 13:22; I Sam. 13:14). David suffered numerous injustices at the hands of enemies of God. He could have become bitter. Instead, he confidently declared: *But I trusted in Thee, O Lord. . . . My times are in Thy hand* (Ps. 31:14-15).

All opposition, sufferings, and disappointments become opportunities for us to respond so that, little by little, our Lord is able to produce in us His own character. Only in yielding our lives to God will we find the assurance, peace, and security for which we long.

Often, we may not feel like praising God because of some satanic attack. But, with David we can *be glad in the Lord. . . shout for joy* (Ps. 32:11) – without hesitation, and regardless of circumstances.

Thought for Today: Unwavering confidence in God results in a spontaneous spirit of gratitude and praise regardless of circumstances.

Christ Revealed: In the prophecy that not one of His bones would be broken as recorded concerning His crucifixion (Ps. 34:20). *For these things were done, that the Scripture should be fulfilled, A bone of Him shall not be broken* (John 19:36).

JULY 1   Read Psalms 36 – 39

Highlights: We are reminded of our sinfulness but then we hear of the perfection of God. Note how ***those that wait upon the Lord . . . shall inherit the earth*** (Ps. 37:9). Every day is precious and fleeting; let us be thankful and not waste our time on mere earthly pleasures and material things (39:1-6).

David sat watching a fire burning and recorded: ***While I was musing*** (meditating) ***the fire burned*** (Ps. 39:3); its bright flames slowly turned to ashes. He was reminded of how the most satisfying life soon fades and ends in death. This is a reminder to all of us that life will soon end. David then prayed: ***Lord, make me to know . . . the measure*** (brevity) ***of my days*** (life) (39:4). David realized how easy it is to get so caught up with material achievements that we fail to do the most important things in life. Opportunities for fulfilling the will of God will soon ***be no more*** (39:13). David's prayer points out that the brevity of life is an issue everyone should consider, not just senior citizens. Yet, strangely enough, it is easy to be so involved with daily activities that we do not take seriously the fact that we are just one breath away from death. How could we forget that the breath of life is the gift of God to each one of us! He can and will take it away when it is our time to finish this life.

In our brief journey on earth, we may sometimes retrace our steps or repeat a task; but wasted time can never be recovered. This points out that we need to seriously consider how we can be more effective and take advantage of every opportunity to wholeheartedly serve the Lord. ***See then that ye walk circumspectly, not as fools, but as wise . . . understanding what the will of the Lord is*** (Eph. 5:15-17). Only as we read through the Bible will we fully know what God expects of us and how we should serve Him.

Many make the mistake of waiting too long for a "convenient time" to serve the Lord. Just as the sun rises in the east, it will soon set in the west, and another day brings us that much closer to eternity. For the majority of us, death will come unexpectedly, and much sooner than we think.

It is of utmost importance that we reconsider our secular goals. Do they rob us of opportunities to ***seek . . . first the Kingdom of God, and His righteousness*** (Matt. 6:33)?

Thought for Today: Side by side with special privileges are temptations to test our willingness to sacrifice in order to gain the Lord's best for us.

Christ Revealed: As *the Fountain of Life* (and the) *Light* (Ps. 36:9). *In Him was Life; and the Life was the Light of men. . . . That was the True Light, which lighteth every man that cometh into the world* (John 1:4-9; 4:10,14; Rev. 22:1).

JULY 2   Read Psalms 40 – 45

Highlights: In today's reading learn more about Jesus and the glories of the Messiah and His Bride, the Church (born-again believers in Chris, the Savior and Lord of their lives). See the similarities between David's trusted adviser Ahithophel (II Sam. 15:12) and Judas, one of the 12 apostles (Matt. 26:25).

The psalmist foretold that the Messiah, our wonderful Lord Jesus Christ who is King of kings, would always uphold **truth... meekness and righteousness** (Ps. 45:4) in His reign. In contrast, earthly kings are known for being ruthless and oppressive. Because the Lord Jesus is the only begotten sinless Son of God, David was inspired to write: **Thy throne, O God, is for ever and ever: the sceptre of Thy Kingdom is a right** (true) **sceptre** (symbol of the divine right to rule) (45:6). The Father had anointed Jesus and poured out abundantly on Him **the oil of gladness** (45:7) far above all others. After His resurrection, Jesus told His disciples: **All things must be fulfilled, which were written in the Law of Moses, and in the Prophets, and in the Psalms, concerning Me** (Luke 24:44).

The Apostle Paul quoted from Psalm 45 concerning Jesus as the Son of God, saying: **Thy throne, O God, is for ever and ever: a sceptre of righteousness is the sceptre of Thy Kingdom.... God... hath anointed Thee with... oil** (Heb. 1:8-9). One of the numerous attributes of Christ is His love for what is right and His hatred of all that is wrong. Although we often fall short, those who have received Jesus Christ as Lord and Savior desire to express these same virtues.

Since Christians are the Bride of Christ, we desire to express the characteristics of the One we represent. The King sees only beauty in His Bride and we, in turn, recognize Him as our glorious Lord and worship Him (Ps. 45:11).

In the midst of trying circumstances, the Lord assures us of His loving care. No Christian needs to fear what the future may bring. The Lord tells us to trust Him for today's necessities **and seek not... what ye shall eat, or what ye shall drink.... For all these things do the nations of the world seek after: and your Father knoweth that ye have need of these things. But rather seek** (desire) **ye the Kingdom of God; and all these things shall be added unto you** (Luke 12:29-31). Jesus taught us to pray: **Our Father.... Give us day by day our daily bread** (whatever is needed for today) (Luke 11:2-3).

Thought for Today: Why worry? God knows what is best, so trust Him.

Christ Revealed: As One who will do the will of God (Ps. 40:6-8). Jesus said that His purpose on earth was **to do the will of Him that sent Me, and to finish His work** (John 4:34; Heb. 10:7-9).

JULY 3 — Read Psalms 46 – 51

Highlights: Confirmation that reliability and safety are found only in God; reminder to be still and listen to God instead of worrying or being fearful; encouragement to worship and praise the Lord because He is in control and will not withhold any good thing *from them that walk uprightly* (Ps. 84:11); our Lord – the true Ruler of the earth.

David disobeyed the Word of God by lusting after the beautiful wife of his neighbor, Uriah the Hittite, one of his mighty men. While Uriah was at war, David committed adultery with Uriah's wife. Through a planned military maneuver initiated by David, Uriah was killed. David then legally married Bathsheba. It appeared to be a happy ending for David and Bathsheba until Nathan, the fearless prophet of God, appeared and denounced David's selfish and wicked sins. Nathan asked: "Why did you despise the Word of God by killing Uriah the Hittite with the sword and then taking his wife to be your wife?" (II Sam. 12:9). Both acts were forbidden under the Law. David deserved to die and he knew it (Ex. 20:13; Lev. 20:10). He cast himself on the mercy of God as a brokenhearted sinner and humbly prayed: *Have mercy upon me, O God, according to Thy loving-kindness. . . . cleanse me from my sin. . . . Create in me a clean heart, O God; and renew a right spirit within me* (Ps. 51:1-2,10).

The Holy Spirit inspired David to record his own cry of sorrow and repentance. God is merciful to all repentant sinners. In answer to David's sincere prayers, God forgave him. But the result of his sin was personal shame and suffering for the rest of his life.

We wish that this blight upon David's life had not happened. But it was recorded, not only to reveal the deception and endless devastation of lust, but to let us know that God forgives our sins when we repent and pray. This gives hope to the sinner who truly repents that he can experience the mercy and forgiving love of God. It also teaches the inescapable consequences of sin. David's prayer for mercy is a prayer for release from the presence and power of sin. He prayed: *Blot out my transgressions. Wash me throughly from mine iniquity, and cleanse me from my sin* (51:1-2). To *blot out* illustrates the way a debt would be erased or forgiven. *Wash* and *cleanse me* illustrates the same way that dirty clothes would be washed.

If we walk in the light, as He is in the light . . . the blood of Jesus Christ His Son cleanseth us from all sin (I John 1:7).

Thought for Today: God does not overlook the sin of anyone. No one is above the Law of God.

Christ Revealed: As the One who will *judge His people* (Ps. 50:4). *The Lord Jesus Christ . . . shall judge the quick* (living) *and the dead at His appearing* (II Tim. 4:1).

JULY 4   Read Psalms 52 – 59

Highlights: In these Psalms David contemplates some discouraging times in his life. The end of the wicked is contrasted with the peace of the godly. Then he speaks of the folly of the godless and longs for Israel to be restored. These are followed by prayers for deliverance from adversaries, the treachery of "friends," and relief from tormentors. He finishes with a plea for judgment of the wicked and then offers praise to the Lord for His protection.

God must judge all unconfessed sin. It is fitting that David, the **man after His** (the Lord's) **own heart** (I Sam. 13:14), expressed the exceeding hatred God has for the evil which corrupts His creation. Included in Psalm 59 is David's prayer: **O my God: defend me from them that rise up against me** (Ps. 59:1). He also prayed that God would not be merciful to his enemies, since God cannot be merciful to any sinner who does not repent of his sins (59:5,13).

David recognized that sinful acts are rebellion against God as well as against others. He identified himself with God, who hates sin, and declared that he too hated those enemies who rebel against God. For David it was the expression of a king who loved the Lord and His ways and recognized that he was the anointed representative of God on earth and, therefore, should administer justice on the Lord's behalf.

A day of reckoning is coming when God **will render to every man according to his deeds: To them who by patient continuance in well doing seek for glory and honour and immortality, eternal life: But unto them that . . . do not obey the truth, but obey unrighteousness, indignation and wrath, Tribulation** (Distress) **and anguish,** (will be) **upon every soul of man that doeth evil** (Rom. 2:6-9). You can be among those who look forward to Christ's return if you repent and forsake your sins. Let Christ be Lord of your life; read His Word in order to fulfill His will. **Behold, now is the accepted time; behold, now is the day of salvation** (II Cor. 6:2).

Though Jesus first came as the "Suffering Servant," when He returns it will be as the "Conquering King" who will make war against the forces of Satan and will judge all mankind by His righteousness. The sharp sword that will go forth out of His mouth is the Word of God. Jesus said: **He that rejecteth Me, and receiveth not My words, hath One that judgeth him: the Word that I have spoken, the same shall judge him in the last day** (John 12:48).

Thought for Today: Obedience to Jesus insures where you spend eternity.

Christ Revealed: As the One who saves those who will call on Him (Ps. 55:16-17). *And it shall come to pass, that whosoever shall call on the Name of the Lord shall be saved* (Acts 2:21; Rom. 10:13).

JULY 5 — Read Psalms 60 – 66

Highlights: The reason for praise to our faithful God is revealed in these seven psalms. They begin with thanksgiving for restored fellowship. Today's reading will put in your heart a desire to give praise and more praise to our marvelous Creator.

Because of Saul's relentless efforts to kill him, David was forced to flee to a desolate area outside the promised land. Exiled from his loved ones, he prayed: ***Hear my cry, O God; attend*** (listen) ***unto my prayer. From the end of the earth will I cry unto Thee, when my heart is overwhelmed: lead me to the Rock that is higher than I. For Thou hast been a shelter for me, and a strong tower from the enemy*** (Ps. 61:1-3).

David was overwhelmed with sorrow and loneliness, even as anyone of us would be. He prayed intensely, asking God to hear his prayer. But more than confessing his distress, he expressed his confidence in God as ***the Rock that is higher than I. . . . a shelter . . . and a strong tower from the enemy***. Although his desolate situation seemed like the end of the earth, David was confident that his True Source of protection and safety from his enemies was the living God Himself, who was like a great ***tower*** of protection. Making God our ***strong tower*** means recognizing that His followers are in the protective care of the invincible God. Depression and frustration need not exist in the life of one who believes that God is the ***strong tower*** in the face of evil forces. We have His assurance that ***no good thing will He withhold from them that walk uprightly*** (84:11). Like David, we can depend upon the Lord for protection and provision. Regardless of how hopeless our circumstances may seem, the Lord has assured us: ***Behold, I am the Lord, the God of all flesh: is there any thing too hard for Me*** (Jer. 32:27)?

Although David was forced to endure difficult circumstances for many years, he continued to trust in the Lord: ***Truly my soul waiteth upon God. . . . He only is my Rock and my Salvation*** (Ps. 62:1-2). David then thought of others who faced difficulties, and encouraged all of us to ***trust in Him at all times . . . pour out your heart before Him: God is a Refuge for us*** (62:8). It is sobering to know that everything we face in life is used of the Lord to prepare us for eternity. In every situation, it is always safe to trust the Lord. We are reminded that nothing ***shall separate us from the love of Christ*** (Rom. 8:35).

Thought for Today: Our confidence in the Lord's power and protection will be increased as we daily read the Word of God.

Christ Revealed: As ***the Rock*** – the unmovable, eternal, unchanging Savior (Ps. 61:2; 62:2,6-7). Jesus is the Rock of our salvation and ***that spiritual Rock*** (Petras) ***that followed*** (accompanied) ***them*** (Israelites) (I Cor. 10:4).

JULY 6   **Read Psalms 67 – 71**

Highlights: A mixture of worship, giving glory to God, and pleas for deliverance for Israel from its adversaries. A Messianic prophecy is made (Ps. 68:18) and its fulfillment given in Ephesians 4:8. Today's reading ends with a testimony of praise to the *Holy One of Israel* (Ps. 71:9,22-23) for his redemption.

The psalmist encourages everyone to rejoice *and sing for joy* (Ps. 67:4). Singing and giving praise to the Lord bring satisfaction and peace of mind. While we await Jesus' return from heaven, the psalmist reminds us to rejoice: *Let the righteous be glad; let them rejoice before God: yea, let them exceedingly rejoice. Sing unto God, sing praises to His Name: extol* (praise) *Him that rideth upon the heavens by His Name JAH, and rejoice before Him* (68:3-4). *JAH* is short for the Name of Jehovah (Yahweh), who is ever in the present.

Let us join with the psalmist in praising and adoring Jesus Christ, our wonderful Savior and Lord, who generously pours out His blessings upon us. *Let the people praise Thee, O God; let all the people praise Thee* (67:3).

The psalmist also foretold the resurrection of Christ. A numerous host of people will proclaim the glorious news of His victory. All the kingdoms of the earth will *sing praises unto the LORD* (68:32) as they express their heartfelt worship for Jesus, who *ascended on high ... (and) led captivity captive* (68:18). The Apostle Paul quoted this verse in the New Testament referring to Christ (Eph. 4:8). This means that Jesus conquered death and Satan, who had held mankind in bondage (Heb. 2:15). Christ chose certain people for the ministry – apostles, prophets, evangelists, pastors, and teachers – to equip the people of God to do His work and to help them mature and grow in the likeness of Christ (Eph. 4:11-12).

Verily, verily, I say unto you, He that heareth My Word, and believeth on Him that sent Me, hath everlasting life, and shall not come into condemnation; but is passed from death unto life. ... Marvel not at this ... all that are in the graves shall hear His voice, And shall come forth; they that have done good, unto the resurrection of life; and they that have done evil, unto the resurrection of damnation (John 5:24,28-29).

Thought for Today: Life is like the uncontrollable sea until we turn to the Lord who imparts His perfect peace.

Christ Revealed: As the One who *led captivity captive* (Ps. 68:18). With His resurrection power, Jesus broke the captive power of Satan. When He led the Old Testament saints from paradise into heaven, *He led captivity captive* (Eph. 4:8; Gal. 5:1; Rev. 1:18).

JULY 7 — Read Psalms 72 – 77

Highlights: The end comes for mighty King David's reign. Old, feeble, and near death, he prays his last prayer (Ps. 72:20) for the one put over the people of God. Psalms attributed to Asaph, David's song leader, follows. He laments as he sees the wicked prosper. Then he praises God that the righteous triumph. Learn a lesson from Asaph. In his trouble he chooses to remember **who is so great a God as our God** (77:13)?

The psalmist praised the Lord for the assurance that no effort against the faithful people of God, regardless of how powerful, can prevent Him from protecting and blessing those who are obedient to His Word. **For promotion cometh neither from the east, nor from the west, nor from the south. But God is the judge: He putteth down one, and setteth up another** (Ps. 75:6-7). God controls both the present and the future of His people. His judgment is impartial and righteous.

As we face problems, we need to praise our Almighty God, who **hath said, I will never leave thee, nor forsake thee** (Heb. 13:5). However, the psalmist also revealed that the proud and self-willed who love to boast will be judged (Ps. 75:4-5).

To illustrate this fact, God is referred to as **the God of Jacob** (75:9); God wonderfully blessed Jacob. Esau had threatened to murder his brother Jacob over the birthright that God foretold belonged to Jacob, although Esau was the firstborn. God knew Esau would despise the birthright and Jacob would cherish the Covenant blessing promised to Abraham and Isaac (Gen. 25:21-23).

When Esau threatened to kill him, Jacob left home to live with his uncle Laban more than 500 miles north. Twenty years later, when he received word that Jacob was returning home, Esau went out to meet him with 400 of his servants (32:6). It appeared that Esau could regain his birthright by killing Jacob. This threat led Jacob to pray all night, after which God marvelously blessed him and gave this man of God a new name, Israel. He is referred to and praised far more times than any other men in Old Testament history (32:24-29).

Now that we have seen how God blessed Jacob, who wrestled all night in prayer, we should take this lesson to heart and spend more time in prayer. God assures us: **The wicked also will I cut off; but the horns** (strength) **of the righteous shall be exalted** (Ps. 75:10).

Thought for Today: Set your heart on being one of the few, even though **strait** (according to His Word without compromise) **is the gate, and narrow is the way, which leadeth unto life, and few there be that find it** (Matt. 7:14).

Christ Revealed: As the Righteous Judge who will crush **the oppressor** (Ps. 72:2-4). Psalm 75:8 describes the judgment of God upon those who refuse to accept the salvation so freely offered by Jesus, **the Lamb of God** (John 1:29,34-36; II Thess. 1:8-9).

JULY 8

Read Psalms 78 – 80

Highlights: Oh how quickly we forget! This could be describing us today. The people find themselves in trouble. They cry out to God, are saved, are restored, and promise to stay faithful! How often have we heard or said that (Ps. 78:34-42)?

God had chosen Israel to be His witness to the world. As His people, they were to be examples of how He would bless all who honor Him and His Word; but they failed miserably, and the glorious City of God was destroyed. Think of the heartbreak and horror felt by the Israelites following the destruction of the Temple and Jerusalem! They had assumed that, as the chosen Covenant people of God, they were secure even though they had disobeyed His Covenant and Commandments. The awful consequences of sin are inevitable. The psalmist cried out: **O God, the heathen** (nations) **are come into Thine inheritance; Thy holy Temple have they defiled; they have laid Jerusalem on heaps** (in ruins) (Ps. 79:1).

The few remaining faithful Israelites pleaded: **Help us, O God of our salvation, for the glory of Thy Name: and deliver us, and purge away our sins, for Thy Name's sake** (79:9).

Since Jerusalem's destruction in A.D. 70, there has been no Ark of the Covenant, Mercy Seat, Temple, Brazen Altar, Laver, Golden Candlestick, Table of Showbread, and Altar of Incense to scripturally observe any sacrifice as commanded by God through Moses. God allowed all these things to be destroyed because all of Israel's sacrifices and feasts were symbols created by Him to foreshadow the redemption that was to be accomplished by Jesus the Messiah.

After the crucifixion, death, and resurrection of Christ, all of the Old Testament sacrifices for sins were made obsolete. The blood sacrifices of animals only temporarily atoned for (covered) sins of the Israelites. **How much more shall the blood of Christ . . . purge** (cleanse) **your conscience from dead works to serve the living God** (Heb. 9:14)**?**

The sacrifice of Christ on the cross made it possible for sinful Jews and Gentiles, who truly repent, and receive Jesus as their Savior, to be forgiven of their sins. **For as many of you as have been baptized into Christ have put on Christ. There is neither Jew nor Greek, there is neither bond nor free, there is neither male nor female: for ye are all one in Christ Jesus** (Gal. 3:27-28).

Thought for Today: True success in life depends on living in accordance with the Word of God – not on our own well-laid plans.

Christ Revealed: As the true **Shepherd** (Ps. 80:1). Christ is **the Good Shepherd** and **the Door** through which one must enter to be saved. He alone is The Way to heaven (John 10:9,11).

JULY 9 — Read Psalms 81 – 87

Highlights: How sad! God, the Creator, speaks; then He waits for His indifferent servants: *I am the LORD thy God, which brought thee out of the land of Egypt. . . . But My people would not hearken to My voice. . . . they walked in their own counsels* (Ps. 81:10-12). However, in times of trouble, the people pray for protection. Then our merciful Father forgives and the exiles return. The love of God is clearly expressed: *No good thing will He withhold from them that walk uprightly* (84:11).

The Holy Spirit guided David to unite the only two weapons of our spiritual warfare – prayer and the inspired Word of God. Psalm 86 expresses the power we have when these become our way of life. When David prayed: *Bow down Thine ear, O LORD, hear me: for I am poor and needy* (Ps. 86:1), he was acknowledging his dependence on God (86:2). He continued to pray: *Be merciful unto me, O Lord: for I cry unto Thee daily* (86:3). Although David was the king of Israel he recognized the lordship of God over his life (86:4). He often spoke of himself as the *servant* of the Lord.

David continued in worship to confess the mercy of God and His readiness to forgive. He expressed with utmost confidence that God listens to His people's prayers and delivers them from harm (86:5,7,13,15). The godly person does not depend upon previous learning for a day-by-day walk in the way of truth, but upon daily guidance of God through His Word. Instruction is much more than just information; it reveals His will and the means to be obedient, for it carries the thought of correction (86:11). The child of God never graduates from His school of instruction; we all need to daily read His Word.

A commitment to Christ as the Lord of your life is essential. The Apostle Peter recognized this when he admonished us to diligently build upon our *faith virtue* (moral excellence), then *knowledge*, then *temperance* (self-control), then *patience*, then *godliness*, then *brotherly kindness*, which will produce in us genuine *charity* (love) to do the will of God (II Pet. 1:5-8). The God who created us has made everything which pertains to life and godliness available to us. The Holy Spirit is our Enabler as we read His Word, *for the Word of God is quick* (living and active), *and powerful* (Heb. 4:12). We must be faithful day-by-day and take the initiative. *Faith cometh by hearing, and hearing by the Word of God* (Rom. 10:17).

Thought for Today: The grace of God is sufficient for you.

Christ Revealed: By Jerusalem, from where the psalmist declared all of the *springs* (sources) of joy and happiness emanate (Ps. 87:7). Jesus is the source of our joy as the angel announced at His birth (Luke 2:10). Jesus also declared: *These things have I spoken unto you, that My joy might remain in you, and that your joy might be full* (John 15:11).

JULY 10 — Read Psalms 88 – 91

Highlights: Have you ever despaired in the long hours of night, calling out to God in your darkest hours like the psalmist in today's reading? Or, have you experienced the answer of God breaking forth in the dawn bringing light through His wonderful mercy as in this magnificent Psalm 89? Don't miss the 91st, one of the best-loved psalms, which pledges amazing promises of blessings.

He *that dwelleth in the secret place of the Most High shall abide under the shadow of the Almighty* (Ps. 91:1). This is one who is set on being obedient to the Lord. To *abide under the shadow of the Almighty* we must *draw nigh to God, and He will draw nigh to you. Cleanse your hands, ye sinners; and purify your hearts, ye double minded* (James 4:8); *abstain from all appearance of evil* (I Thess. 5:22).

The psalmist expressed the utmost confidence in the loving care of God when he said: *Thou shalt not be afraid for the terror by night; nor for the arrow that flieth by day* (Ps. 91:5). The psalmist then assured the faithful, saying: *Because thou hast made the LORD ... thy habitation* (dwelling place); *There shall no evil befall thee. ... For He shall give His angels charge over thee, to keep thee in all thy ways* (91:9-11).

Satan, a fallen angel, quoted these verses to Jesus after His 40-day fast in an attempt to persuade Jesus to leap off the pinnacle of the Temple. Satan said: *If Thou be the Son of God* (meaning: Since [or to prove] You are the Son of God), *cast Thyself down: for it is written, He shall give His angels charge concerning Thee: and in their hands they shall bear Thee up, lest at any time Thou dash Thy foot against a stone* (Matt. 4:6; Ps. 91:11-12). Our Lord set the example by quoting Scripture: *It is written again, Thou shalt not tempt* (test) *the Lord thy God* (Matt. 4:7; Deut. 6:16). We have no assurance that the Lord's angels will keep us if we choose to serve self and misapply His Word.

Satan deceives many by saying: "Your situation is an exception" or "Just this once," "Everyone is doing it," or "Religious people do these things, so why shouldn't you?" We must continually be *casting down imaginations, and every high thing that exalteth itself against the knowledge of God, and bringing into captivity every thought to the obedience of Christ* (II Cor. 10:5).

Thought for Today: *Wherefore be ye not unwise, but understanding what the will of the Lord is* (Eph. 5:17).

Christ Revealed: By the seed (descendants) of David (Ps. 89:3-4). *Concerning His Son Jesus Christ our Lord, which was made of the seed of David according to the flesh* (Rom. 1:3; Matt. 1:1; Luke 3:31-32).

JULY 11

Read Psalms 92–100

Highlights: The Holy Spirit leads the writer to walk and talk with God, and then tells everyone why and how to worship Him. God has made us and our God reigns. Give glory to His Name. Sing praise to the Lord for His holiness, love, faithfulness, and long-suffering. Praise Him for our salvation. What a mighty and marvelous God we serve!

Inspired of the Holy Spirit, the psalmist invites the faithful to *come, let us sing unto the LORD: let us make a joyful noise to the Rock of our salvation. . . . O come, let us worship and bow down: let us kneel before the LORD our Maker. For He is our God; and we are the people of His pasture, and the sheep of His hand* (Ps. 95:1,6-7). Praying with a heart of praise and *thanksgiving* (95:2) is a vital part of worship. Singing joyfully expresses devotion to our Lord.

Praise to the Lord will lift worship beyond the level of personal needs to the higher plane of love and adoration as we honor the Heavenly Father, the Son, and the Holy Spirit. A self-occupied person sometimes assumes the "worship" service was meant for his personal satisfaction. Consequently, they may say: "I didn't get much out of the service." The reason is clear – they didn't put much into it.

Worship is not a "time" set aside for personal satisfaction or for listening to a "sermon." Worship should be a heartfelt expression of prayer, praise, and adoration for our Heavenly Father and our Savior Jesus Christ. Following this, all else, including the sermon, becomes more meaningful.

Some lack spiritual fulfillment because they have chosen to reflect the mood and attitude of unbelievers when confronted with adverse circumstances, such as the loss of a job, the death of a loved one, a divorce, the betrayal of a friend, or some other painful experience. By choosing to be unhappy and dissatisfied, they deprive themselves of the joy of an abundant, peaceful life. The Lord has said: *The joy of the LORD is your strength* (Neh. 8:10).

When we think of all our Lord has done for us, and all He has promised to us for all eternity, we cannot help but praise, worship, and *serve the LORD with gladness: come before His presence with singing* (Ps. 100:2). Our *gladness* will be proportional to our faith in His unfailing presence and promises. *For the LORD is good; His mercy is everlasting; and His truth endureth to all generations* (Ps. 100:5).

Thought for Today: How much of Christ will others see in you today?

Christ Revealed: As the Creator: *It is He that hath made us* (Ps. 100:3) *All things were made by Him; and without Him was not any thing made that was made* (John 1:3; Eph. 3:9; Col. 1:16; Rev. 4:11).

JULY 12 — Read Psalms 101 – 105

Highlights: Let your spirit soar as you join King David in humility and glory, singing and worshiping God the Righteous King. The reading closes with a historical retrospect and celebration of the Exodus from Egypt.

David was inspired by the Holy Spirit to prophesy of Jesus' glorious coming kingdom reign when He will administer equal justice for all the world. Because of this, David declared: ***I will walk within my house with a perfect heart. I will set no wicked thing before mine eyes*** (Ps. 101:2-3). To maintain this attitude, David chose his friends wisely, saying: ***A froward*** (deceitful, perverted) ***heart shall depart from me: I will not know*** (have anything to do with) ***a wicked person*** (101:4). The influence of a wicked person will infect all those who associate with him.

A few of the many reasons for praising the Lord are given in Psalm 103, but it is our loving Lord Himself who merits our highest praise. First, we praise Him for who He is – the all-powerful, all-wise, righteous Creator – and then for His forgiving love and mercy. The psalmist reminds us to praise Him because ***He hath not dealt with us after our sins; nor rewarded us according to our iniquities. For as the heaven is high above the earth, so great is His mercy toward them that fear Him*** (103:10-11).

Just think, His forgiving love toward those who fear Him is as high as heaven itself. Therefore, it is an act of unbelief on our part, a deception of Satan, and contrary to the nature of our loving Lord, for us to bring up former sins – either ours or those of others. Forgiven means no longer remembered, not only by God, but by us as well (I John 1:9; II Pet. 1:9). Forgiveness must not depend on our emotions; rather, it is a decision that the Lord expects of us. As you begin praying, always remember to forgive anyone you feel has wronged you. When you do that, your Father will forgive your evil deeds; but, if you do not forgive others, your Father will not forgive you nor answer your prayers (Ps. 66:18; Matt. 6:14-15).

Unlimited forgiveness should characterize every true follower of Christ, for He said: ***When ye stand praying, forgive, if ye have ought against any: that your Father also which is in heaven may forgive you your trespasses. But if ye do not forgive, neither will your Father . . . forgive your trespasses*** (Mark 11:25-26).

Thought for Today: God often overrules our wishes and plans in order to accomplish His highest purpose in and for our lives.

Christ Revealed: As the One ***who forgiveth all thine iniquities; who healeth all thy diseases*** (Ps. 103:3). Forgiveness of sin and the healing power of God describe the ministry of our Lord Jesus, who was sent ***to preach deliverance to the captives, and recovering of sight to the blind, to set at liberty them that are bruised, To preach the acceptable year of the Lord*** (Luke 4:18-19; Matt. 9:6).

JULY 13   **Read Psalms 106 – 107**

Highlights: Want to take a 40-year trip? Travel with God's people as they relive their desert wanderings. They confess their sins, including when they **lusted** (Ps. 106:14), **murmured** (106:25), **mingled among the heathen** (106:35), and **shed innocent blood** (106:38). Finally, they praise God for their deliverance (note 107:19-20). There is a refrain in verses 8, 15, 21, 31.

Although God greatly blessed Israel, miraculously delivered them from Egyptian slavery, provided the promised land, and gave them victory over the Canaanites, **they soon forgat His works; they waited not for His counsel... and tempted God in the desert** (Ps. 106:13-14). Israel's unfaithfulness and numerous sins are recounted. **They made a calf in Horeb, and worshiped the molten image** (vs 19); **forgat God their Saviour** (vs 21); **despised the pleasant land, they believed not His Word** (vs 24); **murmured in their tents** (vs 25); **did not destroy the nations, concerning whom the LORD commanded them** (vs 34); **But** (they) **were mingled among the heathen, and. . . . served their idols** (vss 35-36).

The psalmist then pointed out the inevitable consequences of sin: **Therefore was the wrath of the LORD kindled against His people, insomuch that He abhorred His own inheritance. And He gave them into the hand of the heathen** (nations)**; and they that hated them ruled over them** (vss 40-41). But, the Lord's judgment on Israel was mingled with His mercy. When **they cried unto the LORD in their trouble... He delivered them out of their distresses. . . . He sent His Word, and healed them** (107:6,20).

Note carefully that Israel's means of deliverance is the same for everyone today: **He sent His Word, and healed them**. The psalmist chose to say: **He sent His Word, and healed them**. His Word is Jesus come in the flesh as well as His Written Word: **In the beginning was the Word, and the Word was with God, and the Word was God** (John 1:1). His Written Word, when believed and acted upon, is the means God has chosen to supply and satisfy man's every need.

Oh that men would praise the LORD for His goodness, and for His wonderful works to the children of men!... Whoso is wise, and will observe these things, even they shall understand the loving-kindness of the LORD (Ps. 107:8,15,21,31,43).

Thought for Today: How much of the Word do you make available for God to use in your life?

Christ Revealed: As the One who **maketh the storm a calm** (Ps. 107:2-9). When Jesus calmed the storm, His awestruck disciples exclaimed: **What manner of Man is this, that even the winds and the sea obey Him** (Matt. 8:27)! Jesus offers to calm the storms of our lives and give us His peace (John 14:8:27).

JULY 14   **Read Psalms 108 – 118**

Highlights: Picture David's mighty army as they go forth to battle singing Psalm 108! David prophetically speaks of Christ in His deity as King-Priest in Psalm 110. Let's rejoice with the psalmist in the hallelujah psalms (Ps. 111-113). Israel's God is contrasted with idols (115). *The LORD preserveth the simple* (sincere) (116:6). Exalt the Messiah with us – Psalm 118 – *for His mercy endureth for ever.*

Jesus quoted this psalm as referring to Himself (Mark 12:36): *The LORD* (God the Father) *said unto my LORD* (God the Son)*, Sit Thou at My right hand, until I make Thine enemies Thy footstool* (Ps. 110:1).

Israel, as a nation, rejected their Messiah-King. But *the Stone* (Christ) *which the builders refused is become the Head Stone* (Christ) *of the corner. This is the LORD's doing; it is marvellous in our eyes. . . . God is the LORD, which hath shewed us light.* David gives praise to God: *Thou art my God, and I will praise Thee: Thou art my God, I will exalt Thee. O give thanks unto the LORD . . . for His mercy endureth for ever* (Ps. 118:22-23,27-29).

Jesus quoted Psalm 118:22, saying: *What is this then that is written, The Stone which the builders rejected . . . is become the Head of the corner? Whosoever shall fall upon that Stone shall be broken; but on whomsoever It shall fall, It will grind him to powder* (Luke 20:17-18; Mark 12:10-11).

Paul quoted this psalm to the Ephesians: *Now therefore ye are no more strangers and foreigners, but fellow citizens with the saints* (believers) *. . . built upon the foundation of the apostles and prophets, Jesus Christ Himself being the chief Corner Stone; In whom all the building . . . groweth unto an holy temple in the Lord* (Eph. 2:19-21).

After a miracle of healing, *Peter, filled with the Holy Ghost* (Spirit)*, said . . . Ye rulers of the people, and elders of Israel . . . Be it known unto you all . . . that by the Name of Jesus Christ of Nazareth, whom ye crucified, whom God raised from the dead, even by Him doth this man stand here before you whole* (well). Peter then quoted Psalm 118: *This is the Stone . . . which is become the Head of the corner. Neither is there salvation in any other: for there is none other Name under heaven given among men, whereby we must be saved* (Acts 4:8,10-12).

Thought for Today: Fears vanish as we daily trust God.

Christ Revealed: Christ quoted Psalm 118:22: *The Stone which the builders refused* (rejected) – to the chief priests and the Pharisees when they willfully rejected Him as the Messiah (Matt. 21:42-45).

JULY 15   **Read Psalm 119**

Highlights: In this psalm the Word of God is exalted. Every verse in this magnificent psalm magnifies the Word of God. ***In the beginning was the Word, and the Word was with God, and the Word was God.... All things were made by Him; and without Him was not any thing made that was made. In Him was Life; and the Life was the Light of men*** (John 1:1-4), and He (Jesus Christ) brings the Light of Understanding (the Written Word) to all who trust Him.

The longest chapter in the Bible emphasizes that the Word is the only infallible Guide to Life given by our Creator. In it, God makes known what He plans for us to be and how to accomplish His purpose for creating us. It emphasizes how indispensable it is to know our Creator, Savior, and soon-coming Messiah-King. The chapter opens with: ***Blessed*** (Divinely favored) ***are the undefiled*** (blameless, conduct beyond reproach) ***in the way, who walk in the Law of the Lord.... and that seek Him with the whole heart*** (Ps. 119:1-2). ***The undefiled*** means much more than mechanically obeying rules and laws. We are specially blessed as we seek to please God ***with the whole heart***.

Like David, all who seek God will pray: ***With my whole heart have I sought Thee: O let me not wander from Thy Commandments. Thy Word have I hid in mine heart, that I might not sin against Thee*** (vss 10-11). It is by taking daily delight in the Word of God, ***as much as in all riches*** (vs 14), that our fellowship with the Lord is assured. The psalmist continues: ***I will not forget Thy Word*** (vs 16). This kind of forgetting is more than a momentary memory lapse. It means drifting away and neglecting the things of God by becoming too involved in other interests.

Daily we need to pray: ***Make me to go in the path of Thy Commandments ... unto Thy testimonies, and not to covetousness*** (vss 33-35). Many can also say: ***Before I was afflicted I went astray: but now have I kept Thy Word*** (vs 67).

Though he had been afflicted, the psalmist did not find fault with God. Often we painfully recognize that our past wrong choices have led to unwholesome consequences. In such circumstances we realize that the Bible is priceless, for it alone reveals life's true values and prepares us for eternity. All who love the Lord can say: ***I rejoice at Thy Word, as one that findeth great spoil*** (Ps. 119:162).

Thought for Today: Spiritual growth is dependant on the time we spend with the Lord letting Him speak to us through His Word.

Christ Revealed: By the psalmist who delighted in the Commandments of God (Ps. 119:47). Christ said: ***I came down from heaven, not to do Mine own will, but the will of Him that sent Me*** (John 6:38; 15:10).

JULY 16   **Read Psalms 120 – 131**

Highlights: Just as we pray in our hearts for help for our needs and protection from our enemies, or give joyful praise to God, the Israelites sang these psalms as they journeyed to Jerusalem for the sacred feasts. These are special verses in today's reading.

The Law required all male Jews physically able and ceremonially clean to go to Jerusalem three times a year to participate in the seven Feasts (Festivals) to make sacrifices and to worship (Ex. 23:14-17; Deut. 16:16). As they traveled toward Jerusalem, they sang psalms, confidently trusting the Lord to protect them on their journey and to protect their homes and possessions in their absence. *I will lift up mine eyes unto the hills* (beyond all human dependence). *. . . My help cometh from the LORD . . . The LORD shall preserve thee from all evil . . . for evermore* (Ps. 112:1-2,7-8).

Even though some may have traveled as long as three weeks to get there, they were journeys of great joy as the people trusted their Lord. **Behold, He that keepeth Israel shall neither slumber nor sleep** (121:4). Above all else, the psalmist proclaimed: **In His Word do I hope. . . . with Him is plenteous redemption** (130:5,7). We too can trust in the Lord for provisions and protection, as well as for forgiveness of our sins.

David was inspired to foresee that glorious time in the future when the Messiah will reign in Jerusalem, when **the kingdoms of this world are become the kingdoms of our Lord** (Rev. 11:15).

This prophecy foretells the reign of Christ: **Many people shall go and say, Come ye, and let us go . . . to the House of the God of Jacob . . . and He will teach us of His ways, and we will walk in His paths: for out of Zion shall go forth the Law, and the Word of the LORD from Jerusalem** (Is. 2:3). Centuries have passed since this prophecy was first given, but the day will soon arrive when Israel's throne will be occupied by Jesus Christ, the Messiah, the promised descendant of David.

Let all believers praise our loving Heavenly Father and echo the words of the Apostle Paul: **Blessed be the God and Father of our Lord Jesus Christ, who hath blessed us with all spiritual blessings . . . that we should be holy and without blame before Him in love . . . by Jesus Christ. . . . In whom we have redemption through His blood, the forgiveness of sins** (Eph. 1:3-5,7).

Thought for Today: Being satisfied is the key to praising the Lord. *I have learned, in whatsoever state I am, therewith to be content* (Phil. 4:11).

Christ Revealed: As our Protector – the One who **shall preserve thy going out and thy coming in** (Ps. 121:8). **By Me if any man enter in, he shall be saved, and shall go in and out, and find pasture** (John. 10:9). **And the Lord shall deliver me from every evil work, and will preserve me unto His heavenly kingdom: to whom be glory for ever and ever. Amen** (II Tim. 4:18).

JULY 17   Read Psalms 132 – 138

Highlights: Can we even count the number of times the Lord rescued David? And he never lost a war. The first five chapters in today's reading are full of trust and love for the Lord as David recalls the blessings. He then contrasts the One True God with worthless idols. Do we qualify as the Lord's *peculiar* (very special) *treasure* (Ps. 135:4; Ex. 19:5; Titus 2:14; I Pet. 2:9)? Psalm 136 is called The Great Hallel and was sung during Passover.

The psalmist reminds us of *how good and how pleasant it is for brethren to dwell together in unity! It is like the precious ointment upon the head, that ran down upon the beard, even Aaron's beard: that went down to the skirts of his garments* (Ps. 133:1-2; Ex. 30:25,30; Lev. 8:12). The oil that was poured upon the head of Aaron, the first high priest, symbolized the Holy Spirit who, in love, permeates the lives of those who have submitted themselves to Him. The same Holy Spirit lives within all true Christians (I John 2:27). Therefore, in a spirit of love, we should express our oneness as believers without partiality, and regardless of race, nationality, education, or wealth – for we *are the Body of Christ* (I Cor. 12:27).

The key to true unity is to *let nothing be done through strife or vainglory* (empty conceit or petty ambition); *but in lowliness of mind let each esteem other better than themselves* (Phil. 2:3). Our fallen (sin) nature is ever prone to distort unwelcome encounters with others, and our emotions can create a crisis out of unimportant incidents. Added to this, we all too often selfishly demand our own rights and blame our frustrations on others. Pride, self-will, and an independent spirit are all enemies of the Spirit-filled life. It is Christlike to accept personal offense with patience rather than to react to someone's rudeness. God permits difficult people to come into our lives to give us an opportunity to express His love and patience toward them – just as our Lord has made known His love and mercy toward us.

The unity of believers can be compared to a great orchestra with many instruments creating beautiful harmony. To maintain that harmony, we each must stay in tune by following the Master Conductor. *With all lowliness and meekness, with long-suffering, forbearing one another in love; Endeavouring* (making every effort) *to keep the unity of the Spirit in the bond of peace* (Eph. 4:2-3).

Thought for Today: All true Christians are members of the Body of Christ (Rom. 12:4-5; I Cor. 12:12-13).

Christ Revealed: As the descendant of David, who would sit upon David's throne (Ps. 132:11). *He shall be great, and shall be called the Son of the Highest: and the Lord God shall give unto Him the throne of His father David* (Luke 1:32; Acts 2:29-30).

JULY 18   **Read Psalms 139 – 143**

Highlights: Psalm 139 proclaims the universal presence and infinite knowledge of God. He knows our every thought, word, and deed. This could be any of us speaking to God. The closing prayer is one of the most needed prayers in the whole Bible. The last four psalms in today's reading reflect David's heartfelt pleas for protection.

Our Creator inspired David to write: *O LORD, Thou. . . . art acquainted with all my ways* (from the time I was conceived to this very day). . . . *Such knowledge is too wonderful for me* (beyond my understanding). . . . *For Thou hast possessed my reins* (formed my inward spirit and heart): *Thou hast covered me in my mother's womb. . . . when I was made in secret. . . . Thine eyes did see my substance . . . when as yet there was none* (Ps. 139:1-16). God reveals that, at conception, David became a person, a living soul. Although, as an unborn infant, he was hidden from human view, as if buried in the earth, his body was no mystery to his Creator, who was skillfully preparing him for his God-ordained destiny on earth.

God led Isaiah to prophesy concerning Christ as a Person even before He was conceived: *The LORD hath called Me from the womb; from the bowels* (body, internal parts) *of My mother hath He made mention of My Name. . . . in the shadow of His hand hath He hid Me. . . . And now, saith the LORD that formed Me from the womb to be His servant. . . . I will also give Thee for a Light to the Gentiles* (Is. 49:1-6).

The Holy Spirit also inspired the beloved physician Luke to record what the Angel Gabriel announced to the Virgin Mary: *Behold, thou shalt conceive in thy womb, and bring forth a son, and shalt call His Name JESUS* (Luke 1:31). Note that the Lord Jesus Christ was announced as a Person at conception.

God not only gives life but also determines that it will begin at conception. He revealed to Jeremiah: *Before I formed thee in the belly I knew thee; and before thou camest forth out of the womb I sanctified thee, and I ordained thee a prophet unto the nations* (Jer. 1:5). If the mothers of David, Isaiah, or Jeremiah had aborted them, they would have murdered great men of God. Life is sacred and is given by the Creator for His own purposes.

Jesus said, Suffer (Permit) *little children . . . to come unto Me: for of such is the Kingdom of Heaven* (Matt. 19:14).

Thought for Today: Wisdom declares: *Whoso findeth Me findeth life* (Prov. 8:35).

Christ Revealed: As the One who deals bountifully with us (Ps. 142:7). *I am come that they might have life, and that they might have it more abundantly* (John 10:10; Eph. 3:20).

JULY 19   **Read Psalms 144 – 150**

Highlights: We open with one of David's battle songs sung by his men as he marches forth to war (Ps. 144). The second (145) may have been sung by David's soldiers after victory in battle. The last five psalms are a grand outburst of Hallelujah songs to the majesty of our Lord. God reigns; let all Creation praise the One True Triune God; let the angels praise God; let the saints Praise God.

The psalmist begins and ends each of the last five psalms with the four words: ***Praise ye the L****ORD*****. . . . *While I live will I praise the* L*ORD: I will sing praises unto my God while I have any being.*** We ***praise the*** L*ORD* that we can look to Him for our needs. ***Happy is he that hath the God of Jacob for his help, whose hope is in the*** L*ORD* ***his God . . . Praise ye the*** L*ORD* (Ps. 146:1-2,5,10).

The psalmist continues by saying: ***Praise ye the*** L*ORD* **. . .** ***He healeth the broken in heart, and bindeth up their wounds. . . . He sendeth forth His Commandment upon earth: His Word runneth very swiftly*** (147:1,3,15). ***Kings of the earth, and all people . . . let them praise the Name of the*** L*ORD:* ***for His Name alone is excellent*** (148:11,13).

The psalms reveal that nothing comes into our lives by accident. Everything God permits is to develop His highest good in us.

We have a loving, Heavenly Father who desires the best for His children. He has provided His Word as the One True Guide that reveals how we should live to please Him and His Church as a place to share our testimonies, and receive instruction and inspiration from spiritual leaders. God does not intend for Christians to be self-sufficient, independent loners, but responsible members of His Church. Christ is ***the Head . . . From whom the whole body fitly joined together and compacted*** (held together) ***by that which every joint supplieth*** (Eph. 4:15-16).

As we purpose to truly put Christ first in our lives, we will experience interruptions which demand our time and attention. Even "good things" can keep us from "the best" that God would give us. The loss of "good things" may test us to see if, like Job, we can say: ***He knoweth the way that I take: when He hath tried me, I shall come forth as gold*** (Job 23:10).

The Book of Psalms concludes by proclaiming: ***Let every thing that hath breath praise the*** L*ORD.* ***Praise ye the*** L*ORD* (Ps. 150:6).

Thought for Today: Trusting in the Lord's unsearchable ways is better than hoping in man's predictable, fallible ways.

Christ Revealed: As the One who gives sight to the blind (Ps. 146:8). Jesus Christ opened blind eyes. ***Then He touched their eyes. . . . And their eyes were opened*** (Matt. 9:27-30; Mark 10:46-52; John 9:1-41).

Introduction To The Book Of PROVERBS

Solomon spoke **three thousand proverbs: and his songs were a thousand and five** (I Kin. 4:32), but the wisdom revealed to and through him was inspired by God. Solomon also collected many of the proverbs written by others (Prov. 30:1; 31:1).

The Book of Proverbs begins by stating its purpose: **To know wisdom and instruction; to perceive the words of understanding** (1:2). Then it clearly states that **the fear of the Lord is the beginning of knowledge; but fools despise wisdom and instruction** (1:7). Wisdom is an attribute of our Creator as revealed in His Word. We need His wisdom to gain the most in life.

Our Lord quoted frequently from Proverbs. He often said in a positive way what Proverbs say in a negative way. Compare Proverbs 4:19 with John 12:35; Proverbs 5:23 with John 8:24; Proverbs 8:35 with John 6:47; Proverbs 14:31 with Matthew 25:31-46; Proverbs 18:21 with Matthew 12:37; and Proverbs 23:7 with Matthew 12:34.

The Proverbs focus primarily on the daily conduct of the "wise" in contrast to the fool. Worldly achievements are worthless vanity compared to the eternal values to be gained by knowing His will: **For the Lord giveth wisdom: out of His mouth cometh knowledge and understanding** (Prov. 2:6). God gives His people wisdom for daily direction. Wisdom is more than knowledge; it is a distinct representation and application of Christ in all areas of our lives (8:12-36).

Every word of God is pure; He is a shield to them that put their trust in Him (30:5). **He that turneth away his ear from hearing the Law, even his prayer shall be abomination** (28:9).

The Heart of Our Government:
"In God We Trust"

The Bible is the Rock on which our republic stands.

General Andrew Jackson,
7th President of the United States 1829-1837

An entry in his diary states that he read three to five chapters of the Bible daily.

JULY 20   **Read Proverbs 1 – 3**

Highlights: Wisdom is the theme of Proverbs (compare Matt. 7:24-27). "Knowledge is the acquiring of facts; "wisdom" is the ability to rightfully apply those facts (Prov. 2:1-6). The **simple**, **fools**, and **scorners** (1:4,7; 3:34) pay a price (1:24-28).

Solomon, along with approximately 40 other writers of the Bible, was inspired by God to record exactly what God wanted us to know in order to be the person He created us to become. Consequently, we read: **Receive My** (God's) **words, and hide** (treasure) **My Commandments with thee; So that thou incline thine ear unto wisdom, and apply thine heart to understanding; Yea, if thou criest** (seek) **after knowledge, and liftest up thy voice for understanding; If thou seekest her as silver, and searchest for her as for hid treasures; Then shalt thou understand the fear of the LORD, and find the knowledge of God** (Prov. 2:1-5).

Speaking through Solomon, God is saying: **Understand righteousness, and judgment, and equity; yea, every good path. When wisdom entereth into thine heart, and knowledge is pleasant unto thy soul; Discretion shall preserve thee, understanding shall keep thee** (2:9-11).

Despite the Lord's urging, some people spend little or no time reading the Bible. The Apostle Paul said: **Study** (Be diligent) **to shew thyself approved unto God, a workman that needeth not to be ashamed, rightly dividing the Word of Truth** (II Tim. 2:15). Only a few ever pray for spiritual achievements so they may accomplish the purpose for which God created them. Discerning Christians will set their goals to **seek . . . first the Kingdom of God, and His righteousness** (Matt. 6:33) while making all secular goals secondary. **For our conversation** (citizenship) **is in heaven; from whence also we look for the Saviour, the Lord Jesus Christ** (Phil. 3:20).

Whom or what we will serve is of utmost importance, for it affects everything else in life. With the same intense energy by which many pursue worldly success, Christians should seek achievements of eternal value for the good of others and the glory of God.

One of life's most sobering thoughts is that **the Son of Man shall come in the glory of His Father with His angels; and then He shall reward every man according to his works** (deeds) (Matt. 16:27).

Thought for Today: Read the Word of God with an intense desire to accept His wisdom and reproof in order to mature spiritually.

Christ Revealed: As the Creator who **founded the earth . . . He established the heavens** (Prov. 3:19). **All things were created by Him, and for Him** (Col. 1:16; Eph. 2:9; Heb. 1:2-3).

JULY 21   **Read Proverbs 4 – 7**

Highlights: Have you heard someone say they wished they had known what they know now when they were young? Heeding **the instruction of a father** (Prov. 4:1) will spare a child much heartache and misery. The pitfalls of wicked living, bad company, immorality, and temptation vs. the wise way to live (4:18,20-22)! Know the **seven things** that **the Lord hates** (6:16-19). Again a **simple** person is pointed out and his destination predicted (7:7; 7:24-27).

Sexual sins are so deceptive and so destructive that more space is given in Proverbs to warnings of their wickedness than to any other sin. Sexual sin defiles the body which, for believers, **is the temple of the Holy Ghost** (Spirit) (I Cor. 6:19). The warnings against such sins are found in Proverbs in all of chapter 5; 6:23-35; all of chapter 7; 9:13-18; and 22:14. God reveals that the only sure way of safety is found **when wisdom entereth into thine heart . . .** then, **understanding shall . . . deliver thee from the strange woman . . . which flattereth with her words** (Prov. 2:10-11,16,19).

God warns that disastrous results are inevitable: **Whoso committeth adultery . . . lacketh understanding: he that doeth it destroyeth his own soul. . . . He goeth after her straightway, as an ox goeth to the slaughter** (6:32; 7:22). Some people assume that adultery is acceptable between consenting adults; but God says: **Be not deceived: neither fornicators, nor idolaters, nor adulterers, nor effeminate, nor abusers of themselves with mankind . . . shall inherit the Kingdom of God** (I Cor. 6:9-10). Satan can only tempt us, but we sin if we allow our thoughts to dwell upon the temptation and then yield to it. We win by obeying God's Word by **bringing into captivity every thought to the obedience of Christ** (II Cor. 10:5).

Anyone who has been drawn into sexual sins should genuinely repent of this evil and ask God for forgiveness, for **he that covereth his sins shall not prosper: but whoso confesseth and forsaketh them shall have mercy** (Prov. 28:13). **But this Man** (the Lord Jesus Christ)**, after** (when) **He had offered one sacrifice for sins for ever, sat down on the right hand of God. . . . For by one offering He hath perfected for ever them that are sanctified** (cleansed from sin, made holy)**. . . . And their sins and iniquities will I remember no more. Now where remission** (forgiveness) **of these is, there is no more offering** (sacrifice) **for sin** (Heb. 10:12,14,17-18).

Thought for Today: We are cautioned that as a man **thinketh in his heart, so he is** (Prov. 23:7).

Christ Revealed: By the teacher of **wisdom** (Prov. 4:7,11). Christ is the Teacher **in whom are hid all the treasures of wisdom and knowledge** (Col. 2:3).

JULY 22 — Read Proverbs 8 – 11

Highlights: We're admonished to praise wisdom and avoid folly (Prov. 9:10). Find a wealth of truth in Chapters 10 & 11 – God and righteousness vs. folly, sin, and wickedness.

Nothing in life is more to be treasured, more priceless, than knowing and obeying the Word of God. As Solomon spoke these proverbs to his "son," God also speaks to us as His "sons." ***All the words of my mouth are in righteousness; there is nothing froward*** (deceitful) ***or perverse*** (wrong) ***in them. They are all plain to him that understandeth. . . . Receive my instruction, and not silver; and knowledge rather than choice gold. For wisdom is better than rubies; and all the things that may be desired are not to be compared to it*** (Prov. 8:8-11).

Is it any surprise that Satan seeks so relentlessly to keep Christians from reading what God has written, the only sure Guide to knowing right from wrong?

The fear of the Lord is the beginning of wisdom: and the knowledge of the holy is understanding (9:10). This wisdom and understanding cover every aspect of life: ***The fear of the Lord is to hate evil: pride, and arrogancy, and the evil way, and the froward*** (perverted) ***mouth, do I hate. Counsel is Mine, and sound wisdom: I am understanding; I have strength. . . . I love them that love Me; and those that seek Me early shall find Me. . . . For whoso findeth Me findeth life, and shall obtain favour of the Lord. But he that sinneth against Me wrongeth his own soul: all they that hate Me*** (God's Word) ***love death*** (8:13-14,17,35-36).

The basic difference between the wise and the foolish – in addition to their acceptance or rejection of Christ as Savior – is the use of their time, talents, and possessions. When we rely on God and His Word, we will love and obey Him (3:5-6).

We all are on one of two roads in our journey through life. The road followed by the truly wise person is more narrow and difficult, but it brings happiness, satisfaction, peace, and eternal life. However, the broad road of the foolish (including the unsaved) inevitably leads to vanity (a life of self-interest) and, ultimately, into the eternal lake of fire. ***Death and hell were cast into the lake of fire. This is the second death. And whosoever was not found written in the Book of Life was cast into the lake of fire*** (Rev. 20:14-15).

Thought for Today: Failure to give help to others is motivated by selfishness.

Christ Revealed: As the Creator who ***prepared the heavens*** (Prov. 8:27-31). ***The heavens are the works of Thine hands*** (Heb. 1:10; John 1:3).

JULY 23   **Read Proverbs 12 – 15**

Highlights: Besides being a revelation of God to man, the Bible provides practical instruction that covers every aspect of life. Contrasts are used to illustrate the meanings. Check out Proverb 15:17! Eating a bowl of soup with someone you love is better than steak with someone you dislike!

God, in His infinite wisdom, has declared: ***He that spareth his rod hateth*** (has disregard for) ***his son: but he that loveth him chasteneth him betimes*** (diligently) (Prov. 13:24).

The greatest acts of love we can make to our children's future is to teach them obedience and respect – first to Christ as their personal Savior and Lord of their lives, then to their parents and all who are in authority, including schoolteachers and police officers (II Tim. 2:1-2). This obedience should also extend to the laws of our government (Matt. 22:21). As a prerequisite to teaching a child submission to authority, it is vital that parents themselves submit to authority.

The rod is the symbol of authority that God has committed to parents for training their children. To apply the rod means to exercise authority. The rod is to be used firmly yet lovingly. Using the rod of authority does not mean that parents should release their bottled-up frustrations by shouting demands, slapping faces, or severely spanking. These are examples of mental and physical abuse. Our children need the same loving-kindness and patience from us that we desire from our Heavenly Father. How often the Lord, with long-suffering love, has forgiven our sins and failures throughout the years.

Biblical discipline follows the example of our loving Father in heaven, who corrects and disciplines everyone whom He loves (Heb. 12:6). The psalmist declared: ***Before I was afflicted*** (disciplined) ***I went astray: but now have I kept Thy Word*** (Ps. 119:67).

We can develop our children's respect for God-ordained authority and, at the same time, provide them with an assurance of both our love and the love of God for them. It is important to spend time with our children, especially to encourage them to read the Bible and pray; to develop a concern for the things of God (Deut. 6:2-9; Prov. 22:6).

Children, obey your parents in the Lord: for this is right. Honour thy father and mother; (which is the first Commandment with promise;) That it may be well with thee (Eph. 6:1-3; Ex. 20:12).

Thought for Today: Prayerfully think before you act or speak.

Christ Revealed: As the One who hates *lying* (Prov. 12:22). ***He that sat upon the throne said. . . . all liars, shall have their part in the lake which burneth with fire and brimstone*** (Rev. 21;5,8).

JULY 24   **Read Proverbs 16 – 19**

Highlights: Proverbs 16 has a lot of *from the Lord*; *but the Lord*; *to the Lord*; or *in the Lord*. The rich, the poor, the wicked, the just, fools, wise, truth, or false – all are spoken of here. The lazy sleep so soundly they go hungry (Prov. 19:15), and some are so lazy they won't lift a finger to eat (19:24). We're told if we stop listening to instruction we've turned our back on knowledge (19:20,27).

No one is naturally humble. Our human nature is permeated with pride passed down from Adam; only the indwelling Christ can develop true humility in us. Humility will manifest itself in kindness toward the unkind, long-suffering toward those who annoy us, and love toward our enemies. How inconsistent to think we have "humbly given ourselves to Christ" if we react harshly to anyone.

The Lord leads us to see the end result of pride and false humility: ***Pride goeth before destruction, and an haughty spirit before a fall. Better it is to be of an humble spirit with the lowly, than to divide the spoil with the proud*** (Prov. 16:18-19).

It is natural to think of ourselves as humble, at least more humble than others. But humility, or a lack of it, is apparent by our attitude when someone irritates us. Personal views often create ill will. If our replies are expressed unkindly, either in our words or actions or in our thoughts, then our "humility" is not real; it is merely a pious mask.

Knowing the destructive power of pride, let us look upon the people who seem difficult to love as those chosen by God to provide us the opportunity to rid ourselves of self-righteousness, and to express Christlike humility and the love of God.

Humble people will feel no jealousy or envy when they are ignored while others are praised. God reminds us: ***Let nothing be done through strife or vainglory*** (pride, empty conceit); ***but in lowliness of mind let each esteem other better than themselves*** (Phil. 2:3).

The Christlike nature of a Christian enables him not to respond with a sharp, unfriendly attitude when differences of opinion exist. ***Be of the same mind one toward another. Mind not high things, but condescend to men of low estate. Be not wise in your own conceits*** (opinions) (Rom. 12:16).

To be Christlike is to be like Jesus and consider all people equally, regardless of their race, position, abilities, or wealth, for ***God is no respecter of persons*** (Acts 10:34).

Thought for Today: Avoid worldly-minded associates.

Christ Revealed: As the One who punishes the proud (Prov. 16:5). Jesus said: ***Whosoever exalteth himself shall be abased*** (humbled)***; and he that humbleth himself shall be exalted*** (Luke 14:11).As the ***Friend that sticketh closer than a brother*** (Prov. 18:24). Jesus is our Friend (John 15:14-15) and ***will never leave*** (us)***, nor forsake*** (us) (Heb. 13:5).

JULY 25 — Read Proverbs 20 – 22

Highlights: Integrity and a good reputation. Warning against alcoholic drink and its subtle, destructive addiction. How should we treat the less fortunate and our children? The writer gives us "thirty sayings of the wise."

Alcohol is amazingly deceptive. God has warned that ***wine is a mocker, strong drink is raging: and whosoever is deceived thereby is not wise*** (Prov. 20:1). The subtle "occasional" drink taken in moderation seems harmless and may even, at the moment, give the appearance of making life more enjoyable. But many a "social" drinker eventually discovers that he is an alcoholic and has exchanged a meaningful life for a degrading existence.

Many people who were once successful and influential have been reduced to poverty, and shame, because of alcohol. No words can express the pitiful consequences of alcohol abuse. Some are convinced that they can take it or leave it and stop drinking at any time.

Pity the person who tries to escape the pressures of life and relax with a "little" drink. God has said they are ***not wise***. God gives warning of alcohol's poisonous effects: ***At the last it biteth like a serpent, and stingeth like an adder*** (23:32).

Alcohol takes control of a person both chemically and emotionally, producing unavoidable, irreversible, and far-reaching physical and emotional disaster. Once a person is "hooked," dependence upon alcohol robs him of good judgment and, eventually, will keep him from realizing the Lord's purpose for his life.

The longer a person indulges in alcohol the more desensitized they become to their behavior and the consequences that follow. Gradually, millions have allowed themselves to be in direct violation of the Word of God. The only release from these tragic consequences is the mercy of God. When a person truly repents, the Holy Spirit becomes his source of strength to overcome sin. ***Wherefore be ye not unwise, but understanding what the will of the Lord is. And be not drunk with wine, wherein is excess; but be filled with*** (controlled by) ***the Spirit*** (Eph. 5:17-18).

Let us walk honestly (properly) ***. . . not in rioting*** (wild parties) ***and drunkenness, not in chambering*** (sexual indulgence) ***and wantonness*** (unbridled lust)***. . . . But put ye on the Lord Jesus Christ, and make not provision for the flesh*** (Rom. 13:13-14).

Thought for Today: Play it safe – ***Abstain from all appearances of evil*** (I Thess. 5:22).

Christ Revealed: As the King who sits on ***the throne of judgment*** (Prov. 20:8). ***For the Father judgeth no man, but hath committed all judgment unto the Son*** (John 5:22).

JULY 26   **Read Proverbs 23 – 26**

Highlights: "thirty sayings of the wise" continue. Woes of too much wine vividly outlined (Prov. 23:29-35). King Hezekiah's advisers compiled more proverbs of King Solomon (25:2 – 26:28).

It seems normal to stand up for our rights – to fight back against those who treat us unjustly or to get even with those who offend us. But it is a serious sin to be delighted when an enemy suffers and seems to reap what we think he deserves. It is even more serious to harbor a secret hatred and have a desire to bring about his downfall: ***Rejoice not when thine enemy falleth, and let not thine heart be glad when he stumbleth: Lest the L***ORD ***see it, and it displease Him, and He turn away His wrath from him*** (Prov. 24:17-18).

Attitudes of bitterness, revenge, hatred, or ill will toward another person are self-destructive and are indications that we are not living nearly as close to Christ as we should. ***Let us not love in word, neither in tongue*** (talk); ***but in deed*** (action) ***and in truth*** (I John 3:18). Since we were all created in the image of God, and since Christ died to save all mankind, let us pray that those whom we might consider "enemies" may become disciples of Christ and our brothers and sisters in Him.

No one is justified in taking revenge; nor qualified to be judge, jury, or executioner; nor to assume the position of God, who said: ***Dearly beloved, avenge not yourselves, but rather give place unto wrath*** (the wrath of God): ***for it is written, Vengeance is Mine; I will repay, saith the Lord*** (Rom. 12:19; Deut. 32:35; Heb. 10:30).

When unjustly treated, pray for your offender. Thoughts of hatred and revenge are temptations from Satan. The indwelling Holy Spirit can enable the Christian to reject those thoughts and be merciful and forgiving toward a wrongdoer. ***For if ye forgive men their trespasses, your Heavenly Father will also forgive you: But if ye forgive not men their trespasses, neither will your Father forgive your trespasses*** (Matt. 6:14-15).

Our reaction to unkind acts reveals whether we are controlled by the Holy Spirit or by our old sinful nature (Rom. 8:1-9). ***Blessed are the meek*** (submissive to the will of God): ***for they shall inherit the earth.... Blessed are they which are persecuted for righteousness' sake: for theirs is the Kingdom of Heaven*** (Matt. 5:5,10).

Thought for Today: To love the unlovely is an expression of Christ's love.

Christ Revealed: As the One who rewards those who repay evil with good (Prov. 25:21-22). ***If thine enemy hunger, feed him; if he thirst, give him drink*** (Rom. 12:20). Jesus commanded: ***Love your enemies*** (Matt. 5:44; Luke 6:27,35).

JULY 27   Read Proverbs 27 – 31

Highlights: Solomon is led by the Holy Spirit to present basic moral and spiritual principles to guide the young and old alike to avoid the treacheries and deceptive pitfalls of sin that they are confronted with throughout life. The Book ends by describing the **virtuous woman** (Prov. 31:10-31).

The admirable description of the **virtuous woman** (Prov. 31:10) sets a standard that most Christian wives and mothers pray they can live up to. The word **virtuous** means moral strength (of character), the meaning of which was used as Moses was searching for **able** (dependable and qualified) **men such as fear God, men of truth, hating covetousness** (Ex. 18:21). There is an underlying behavioral pattern here which outlines what God is looking for from all of us. In comparing the **virtuous woman** to **rubies** (Prov. 31:10), she is a "rare, precious gem." The Lord refers to the same basic quality of the godly man. **Help, Lord; for the godly man ceaseth; for the faithful** (no longer the majority) **fail from among the children of men** (Ps. 12:1).

The virtous women's spouse is honorable, a prominent leader in the land (Prov. 31:23). The godly woman takes pleasure in providing for her family – rises early, makes wise decisions, is diligent and industrious, realizes that success results from her labors, and reaps the fruits of hard work. We note that she often burned the 'midnight oil.'

A virtous woman is a crown to her husband (12:4). She is praised by those who know her best. The conclusion is that all of us, men and women alike, will be greatly blessed because he or she **feareth the Lord** (31:30).

Godly people are to have a heart of compassion and show it through deeds of mercy. **Wisdom . . . from above is . . . full of mercy** (James 3:17).

It is important to realize that in everything we do, we should honor the Lord. All of us – men and women alike – should be working to improve the traits of godliness and virtue. Then, when we finally lie down, in our sleep we will enjoy **the peace of God, which passeth all understanding** (Phil. 4:7).

Much is said in Proverbs 31 about clothing and coverings. Think of what Christ suffered that we might be clothed in splendor for all eternity (Is. 61:10)!

Thought for Today: Christ is the only Savior and the world needs to know.

Christ Revealed: As the One who descended from and ascended to heaven (Prov. 30:4). **Jesus came down from heaven, even the Son of Man which is** (now) **in heaven** (John 3:13).

Introduction To The Book Of ECCLESIASTES

The Book of Ecclesiastes is a confession of the worthlessness of all earthly treasures. While the tone of the book is largely negative and pessimistic, Ecclesiastes also offers us some important insights and wisdom. True enjoyment in life comes as we follow the guidelines of God and stay connected to Him (Eccl. 2:24-25); the timing of God is perfect (3:1-8); satisfaction is a gift from God (3:13); and all our days are in the hands of God (9:1). It is impossible to find lasting satisfaction apart from knowing the Word of God and living according to His will. Everything is indeed futile if Christ is not Lord of our lives. With insights like these, the Preacher ultimately concluded: **Fear God and keep His Commandments, for this is the whole duty of man** (12:13).

Solomon listed 27 achievements in his life and ended by saying: **Whatsoever my eyes desired I kept not from them, I withheld not my heart from any joy** (2:10). But he repeatedly used the expression: **All is vanity** (has no lasting satisfaction) (1:2).

Solomon violated all the commands given to kings in the Word of God. **He shall not multiply horses to himself, nor cause the people to return to Egypt** (to purchase horses). **. . . Neither shall he multiply wives to himself . . . neither shall he greatly multiply to himself silver and gold . . . he shall write him a copy of this Law in a book. . . . he shall read therein all the days of his life: that he may learn to fear** (revere) **the LORD his God, to keep all the words of this Law and these Statutes to do them** (Deut. 17:16-19).

After a lifetime of searching for satisfaction through wealth, women, and possessions, Solomon eventually recognized that man's true contentment lies only in full obedience to God. In the end, the Preacher observed that God alone is worthy of worship simply because of who He is. The lesson is clear: The pursuits of this world are empty without a vital and living relationship with God. He concluded by cautioning others: **Remember now your Creator in the days of your youth, while the evil days come not, nor the years draw near, when you shall say, I have no pleasure in them** (Eccl. 12:1).

The Heart of Our Government:
"In God We Trust"

Hold fast to the Bible as the anchor of your liberty; write its precepts in your hearts and practice them in your lives.

General Ulysses S. Grant,
18th President of the United States 1869-1877

JULY 28   Read Ecclesiastes 1 – 4

Highlights: Consider things in life that do not satisfy. Key words are **man**, **labour**, and **vanity**. Apart from God, **all is vanity** (Eccl. 1:2); seeking satisfaction, pleasures, or material riches do not satisfy the human spirit. Sounds hopeless? Read His wonderful answer!

It would be easy to be impressed by the achievements of Solomon. He wrote: ***I built me houses; I planted me vineyards: I made me gardens and orchards . . . I got me servants and maidens, and had servants born in my house; also I had great possessions of great and small cattle above all that were in Jerusalem before me: I gathered me also silver and gold . . . I gat me . . . delights of the sons of men. . . . So I was great, and increased more than all that were before me in Jerusalem. . . . And whatsoever mine eyes desired I kept not from them*** (Eccl. 2:4-10).

The key words here are "I" and "me." Solomon did all of these things for himself while finding less and less pleasure. Jesus declared the key to success in life: ***Seek ye first the Kingdom of God, and His righteousness; and all these things*** (material necessities) ***shall be added unto you*** (Matt. 6:33).

Solomon eventually concluded: ***I looked on all the works that my hands had wrought, and on the labour that I had laboured to do: and, behold, all was vanity and vexation of spirit*** (chasing after the wind)***, and there was no profit under the sun*** (Eccl. 2:11). Solomon was rightly troubled when he said: ***Therefore I hated*** (abhorred) ***life; because the work that is wrought under the sun is grievous unto me: for all is vanity and vexation of spirit*** (2:17). Sadly, many today are still trying to gain fulfillment with earthly pursuits while ignoring the will of God.

It is recorded that, when ***Solomon*** began his reign, he ***loved the Lord, walking in the statutes of David his father***. But Solomon's heart was divided; ***he sacrificed and burnt incense in high places*** (I Kin. 3:3). Consequently, his priorities became distorted and he gradually set his heart on material projects, wealth, and women.

Each of us needs to consider: "What is God's purpose for my brief life?" Can we expect to hear Jesus say: ***Well done, good and faithful servant; thou hast been faithful over a few things, I will make thee ruler over many things: enter . . . into the joy of thy Lord*** (Matt. 25:23)?

Thought for Today: Possessions and pleasures are worthless substitutes for the Person to whom we owe our supreme devotion – the Lord Jesus.

Christ Revealed: As God, the true source of ***wisdom, and knowledge, and joy*** – the One who truly satisfies (Eccl. 2:26). ***We have the mind of Christ*** which is wisdom, knowledge, and joy (I Cor. 2:16; Luke 21:15; John 15:11; Rom. 15:14).

JULY 29   Read Ecclesiastes 5 – 8

Highlights: More exhortations that tell why mere religious practices often conflict with the Word of God and thus cannot satisfy. There is no fulfillment in riches or a wasted life.

At Gibeon, the Lord appeared to Solomon in a dream in which Solomon asked for wisdom. Yet, we have no record that Solomon ever copied the Law in his own hand, as God had instructed Israel's kings to do, and he ignored all of the laws specifically given to kings (Deut. 17:14-20). As the years passed, he searched for satisfaction everywhere except from the Lord and His Word (Ps. 119:97-98). In his old age Solomon observed that rich and poor were equally obsessed with such fruitless endeavors.

Solomon's thoughts then turned from the secular to the religious life, and he noted that many attended the House of God, offering insincere prayers and making vows that they never kept. Speaking through him, the Holy Spirit warned: **Keep thy foot when thou goest to the House of God, and be more ready to hear, than to give the sacrifice of fools** (Eccl. 5:1). Hypocrisy is an insult to God, and is spiritually self-destructive. He further warned: **Be not rash with thy mouth** (5:2).

True worship requires a heart-inspired obedience to the Word of God. When we assemble to worship, we are to open our hearts to adore, praise, and exalt the Lord. Jesus defined worship when He said: **God is a Spirit: and they that worship Him must worship Him in spirit and in truth** (John 4:24). After creating Adam, God **breathed into his nostrils the breath of life; and man became a living soul** (Gen. 2:7). That eternal spirit and soul life is what must worship God; mere physical speech and religious ritual are not sufficient. The inner man, the eternal man, is what Jesus was saying must recognize and worship his Creator.

The place where we worship the Lord is not as important as how we worship Him. It may be a magnificent cathedral, a thatched hut, a disciple's home, or a cave, since **ye are the Temple of God, and ... the Spirit of God dwelleth in you** (I Cor. 3:16). There is no time or place where God is not with His children (John 14:16; Heb. 13:5). Because of this, we should always praise the Lord. **Let every thing** (and everyone) **that hath breath praise the Lord** (Ps. 150:6).

Thought for Today: Do not envy the wealth of evildoers – it is only temporary.

Christ Revealed: As the One who expects us to keep our vows made to Him (Eccl. 5;4). **So then every one of us shall give account of himself to God** (Rom. 14:12).

JULY 30   **Read Ecclesiastes 9 – 12**

Highlights: Our relationship to our Creator is stressed in today's reading. Study man's problems. Despite wisdom, death is certain. Beware of a little folly. Good advice for all mankind. Don't miss the conclusion (Eccl. 12:13-14).

Solomon was famous for his wisdom, but he was not clear when he said: *Rejoice, O young man, in thy youth; and let thy heart cheer thee in the days of thy youth, and walk in the ways of thine heart, and in the sight of thine eyes* (Eccl. 11:9). Stopping here would imply he was encouraging youth to let passion and pleasure go unchecked; but he continued: *But know thou, that for all these things God will bring thee into judgment.*

Solomon spent his lifetime searching for pleasure from every worldly source, but he used the word *vanity* (emptiness) over 30 times in the Book of Ecclesiastes. He concluded that, after living his life ignoring the Word of God, life was *vanity of vanities* (12:8). Before finishing his message, Solomon restated the basis for true wisdom: *Remember now thy Creator in the days of thy youth, while the evil days come not, nor the years draw nigh, when thou shalt say, I have no pleasure in them. . . . Let us hear the conclusion of the whole matter: Fear God, and keep His Commandments: for this is the whole duty of man* (12:1,13). Since the purposes of God apply to all of us, we should continue to seek opportunities to advance the Kingdom of God.

Satisfaction in life results from giving one's time, talents, and resources to doing the will of God. This is the only true source of happiness, peace of mind, and genuine enjoyment in life, for we were created to honor and glorify the Lord. *We are His workmanship, created in Christ Jesus unto good works, which God hath before ordained that we should walk in them* (Eph. 2:10).

Therefore, it is foolish to seek riches, security, power, popularity, or fleeting goals in life merely for earthly self-satisfaction. It is also vanity to give way to *the lust of the flesh* (gratification of the physical nature)*, and the lust of the eyes, and the pride of life* (I John 2:16).

Let no man deceive himself. If any man among you seemeth to be wise in this world, let him become a fool (put aside his wordly discernment)*, that he may be wise. For the wisdom of this world is foolishness with God* (I Cor. 3:18-19).

Thought for Today: The Word of God brings genuine joy. *These things have I spoken unto you, that My joy might remain in you, and that your joy might be full* (John 15:11).

Christ Revealed: In the statement: *For God shall bring every work into judgment* (Eccl. 12:14). Jesus will judge all, *for the Father* (God) *judgeth no man, but hath committed all judgment unto the Son* (Jesus) (John 5:22).

Introduction To The Book Of
THE SONG OF SOLOMON

The Song of Solomon is about a king's love for a maiden and her desire for everyone to admire him. It illustrates the relationship between Christ and those who will not be satisfied with anyone's love but His.

There are many difficulties in the spiritual interpretation of some of these passages, just as there are some difficulties in the interpretation of the Church as the Bride of Christ and Jesus as our Bridegroom.

Jewish rabbis regard this book as an illustration of the marriage relationship between God as Husband and Israel as His wife (Is. 54:4; Jer. 2:2; Ezek. 16:8-14; Hos. 2:16-20). Many Christian leaders believe that it expresses the love that exists between Christ and His Church. It expresses the longing of the Christian bride for the presence of the Heavenly Bridegroom (Jesus Christ, our Bridegroom, and the King of kings) and their precious union (Rev. 19:7-9,16; 21:9). This beautiful love story also expresses the love of a husband-and-wife marriage relationship as planned by the Creator.

The importance of this Song is recognized in two ways. First, the Creator who controls the king's heart led the compilers of Scripture to include **the song of songs, which is Solomon's** (Song 1:1). Second, through Paul, the Lord Himself said: **All Scripture is given by inspiration of God, and is profitable for doctrine** (teaching)**, for reproof, for correction, for instruction in righteousness: that the man of God may be perfect, throughly frunished unto all good works** (II Tim. 3:16-17). Because God inspired this book to be written, we should seek to know Him better through it.

The Heart of Our Government:
"In God We Trust"

Before all else, we seek, upon our common labor as a nation, the blessings of Almighty God.

**General Dwight D. Eisenhower,
34th President of the United States 1953-1961**

Eisenhower was very much influenced by the deep faith of his family. The Bible was read daily at family devotions as he grew up.

JULY 31   **Read The Song of Solomon 1 – 8**

Highlights: This beautiful love story shows the love of God for Israel and illustrates the love of Christ for His Church. It provides a model for the quality of love God desires to see between a man and his wife as well as our love for His Church. A handsome stranger wins the heart of a Shulamite maiden. He promises to return; when he does, he reveals himself as the mighty monarch.

This poem describes the wholesome enjoyment of married love between a man and a woman. It expresses the delight of the bridegroom in the bride and of the bride in her husband. The bride describes her wonderful memories as her bridegroom tarries. The whole narrative has a dreamlike quality. The longing, the wondering, and the searching represent the images of dreams. The bride is asleep on her bed, but her thoughts are about her beloved absent bridegroom. *By night on my bed I sought him whom my soul loveth: I sought him, but I found him not* (Song 3:1).

Every believer is assured that *my Beloved is mine, and I am His* (2:16), for Jesus Christ has entered into our very lives. Our love relationship continues to grow and deepen as we listen to Him speak to us as we read His Word and apply it to our lives. We become different people by virtue of our relationship with the coming Bridegroom. We too can say: *I live; yet not I, but Christ liveth in me: and the life which I now live in the flesh I live by the faith of the Son of God, who loved me, and gave Himself for me* (Gal. 2:20).

As Christians, sometimes we enjoy a very close sense of the presence of Christ. The hymn writer wrote: "He walks with me and He talks with me." But all too often His presence seems far away. Yet our love for Him continues to grow as we wait expectantly for that first glimpse of Him when He welcomes us home (John 3:29; Eph. 5:22-23; I Thess. 4:16-17).

As the bride, we wait with great anticipation for our Bridegroom Jesus when we too can say: *He brought me to the banqueting house, and His banner over me was love* (Song 2:4).

Let not your heart be troubled: ye believe in God, believe also in Me. In My Father's house are many mansions: if it were not so, I would have told you. I go to prepare a place for you. And if I go and prepare a place for you, I will come again, and receive you unto Myself; that where I am, there ye may be also (John 14:1-3).

Thought for Today: Be prepared for the Lord's return. *Heaven and earth shall pass away, but My words shall not pass away. But of that day and hour knoweth no man, no, not the angels of heaven, but My Father only. But as the days of Noe* (Noah) *were, so shall also the coming of the Son of Man be* (Matt. 24:35-37).

Christ Revealed: As *the chiefest* (outstanding) *among ten thousand* (Song 5:10). Jesus is the **KING OF KINGS, AND LORD OF LORDS** (Rev. 19:16)

Introduction To The Book Of ISAIAH

Isaiah's ministry spanned about 60 years during the reigns of Judah's kings Uzziah (Azariah), Jotham, Ahaz, and Hezekiah (II Kin. 14:21; Is. 1:1; II Chr. 26:22; 32:20-23). This was during the same period of time that Micah was prophesying in Judah, while Jonah, Amos, and Hosea were prophets to the Northern Kingdom of Israel.

The Book of Isaiah addresses the entire world: **Hear, O heavens, and give ear ... for the LORD hath spoken** (Is. 1:2). In its pages, we learn how God uses the nations of the world as His instruments for working out His perfect will for mankind. The message throughout the book is clear: **Hear the Word of the LORD** (1:10). This means not only to seriously read His Word but also to obey it and do His will.

The Lord made a wonderful promise, through Isaiah, for sinners. His invitation was: **Come now, and let us reason together, saith the LORD: though your sins be as scarlet, they shall be as white as snow** (1:18). It was an appeal for the Israelites to return to the Lord and once again live in obedience to His Word. He pleaded: **O house of Jacob, come ... and let us walk in the light of the LORD** (2:5). It is also a warning of judgment upon those who reject His Word (2:6 – 3:26). A severe warning of six woes is pronounced upon the faithless (5:8,11,18,20-22).

A glorious vision of the Lord God is described: **In the year that King Uzziah died I saw also the Lord sitting upon a throne, high and lifted up, and His train** (trailing edge of His robe) **filled the Temple. ... mine eyes have seen the King, the LORD of hosts** (6:1,5). Isaiah was blessed with the rare privilege of actually seeing the Creator sitting in His heavenly Temple. This book closes with the Lord's promises of comfort and peace for His children, as well as a warning that eternal punishment awaits those who reject Him (66:22-24).

Jesus Christ is the Supreme theme of this book. Isaiah prophesied the birth of Christ and His deity (7:14; 9:6-7), His ministry (42:1-7; 61:1-2), His sufferings and death (52:1-3; 53:1-12), His coming reign which will follow the great tribulation, and His triumph over the Antichrist (2:11; 9:7; 25:1 – 27:13; 42:4-7; 49:5-6; 52:13; 63:1-6). Isaiah frequently refers to God as **the Holy One of Israel** (1:4; 5:19,24; 10:20; 12:6; 17:7; 29:19,23; 30:11-12,15; 31:1; 37:23; 41:14,16,20; 43:3,14; 45:11; 47:4; 48:17; 49:7; 54:5; 55:5; 60:9,14).

Visions of **the** (coming judgment) **Day of the LORD of hosts**, sometimes simply called **that day**, are prominent (2:11-12,17,20; 3:7,18; 4:1-2; 5:30; 28:5; 29:18; 30:23; 31:7) with special attention given to it (10:20; 11:10-11; 12:1,4; 13:6,9,13; 14:3; 17:4,7,9; 19:16,18-19,21,23-24; 22:5,12,20,25).

Partial List of Names and Titles of Christ in Isaiah

Angel of His Presence 63:9	Lord, your Redeemer 43:14
Arm of the Lord 51:9-10	Man of Pains 53:3
Banner for the Peoples 11:10	Mighty God 9:6
Boy 7:16	Mighty One of Jacob 49:26
Branch of Jesse 11:1	Mighty to Save 63:1
Branch of the LORD 4:2	My Chosen,
Channels of Water 32:2	in Whom I Myself Delight 42:1
Child 9:6	My Messenger 42:19
Chosen One of the Lord 42:1	My Servant 49:3
Commander & Leader 55:4	Place to Hide; to Find Cover 32:2
Counseller 9:6	Polished Arrow 49:2
Covenant of the People 42:6	Precious Corner Stone 28:16
Creator of Israel 43:15	Prince of Peace 9:6
Crown/Diadem 28:5	Redeemer 59:20; 60:16
Eternal Father 9:6	Refuge from the Rain 25:4
Everlasting Rock 26.4	Righteous Servant 53:11
Everlasting Light 60:20	Rock of Israel 30:29
Glorious One 33:21	Rock to Trip Over 8:14
Glory of the Lord 40:5	Root of Jesse 11:10
God of Israel, Saviour 45:15	Salvation of
God of All the Earth 54:5	the Daughter of Zion 62:11
Great Light 9:2	Sanctuary 8:14
Heritage of Jacob 58:14	Saviour 19:20
Highway/Roadway/Pathway 35:8	Servant 42:1,19
Holy One of Israel 41:14; 49:7	Servant of Rulers 49:7
Husband 54:5	Shade from the Heat 25:4
Immanuel 7:14	Shadow of a Massive Rock 32:2
Israel 49:3	Sharp Sword 49:2
Lord 40:3	Shoot and Branch 11:1
King in His Beauty 33:17	Son given 9:6
King Lord of Hosts 6:5	Stone Laid in Zion 28:16
Lawgiver 33:22	Stone to Stumble Over 8:14
Light to the Nations 42:6	Stronghold for the Poor 25:4
Lord God [Jehovah] 40:10	Sure Foundation 28:16
Lord [Jehovah] of Hosts 6:3; 54:5	Witness to the Peoples 55:4
Lord, your Holy One 43:15	Wonderful 9:6

Christ In Isaiah

Incarnation (made in the flesh) 7:14-15; 9:6; 40:3-5
Lowliness & Youth in Nazareth 7:15; 11:1-2,10; 53:2
Descendant of Israel [Jacob] 49:3
Descendant of House of David 9:7; 11:1; 55:3-4
Relationship with the Father 42:1; 50:4-5; 53:1
Miracles 35:5-6
Message 61:1-2
Characteristics of His Life and Work .... 9:6; 11:1-9; 40:10-11; 42:1-7; 49:1-9; 50:4-11; 52:13-15; 53:1-12; 61:1; Anointed Preacher .... 61:1; Death destroyer .... 25:8; 26:19; Lamb of God .... 53:7; Saviour or Redeemer .... 53:4-6; 59:20; 62:11; 63:1; Mediator, Advocate, Intercessor .... 53:12; 59:16; 61:1; Servant of the Lord 42:1-7; 49:1-9; 52:13-15;53:1-12
Specific Ministry to the Gentiles 2:2-3; 9:1-2; 11:10; 42:1,6; 49:6; 55:4-5; 56:6; 60:3-5
Gracious Ministry to All 42:2-7; 53:4-6,12
Triumphal Entry into Jerusalem 62:11
Suffering and Death 50:6; 52:14; 53:1-12
Resurrection, Ascension, and Exaltation 52:13; 53:10-12
Millennial Reign 9:7; 11:3-5; 32:1-8; 33:22; 42:4-7; 49:1-12; 59:16-21; 61:1-3

AUGUST 1 — Read Isaiah 1 – 4

Highlights: God is angry! Why (Is. 1:4)? To disobey is to invite punishment (1:5). Genuine praise goes beyond praying and on to serving people (1:17). A vision of the Lord's future reign in the most important place on earth (2:2-3). God promises glorious restoration to Israel (4:2-6).

The God of Creation chose the Israelites to reveal Himself as the One True God and later as God in the flesh (Jesus Christ) (Jude 1:25) and to record the Written Word for all nations (John 1:1-14). It must have been with deep sorrow that God led Isaiah to say: **Hear . . . and give ear . . . for the LORD hath spoken, I have nourished and brought up children, and they have rebelled against Me. The ox knoweth his owner, and the ass his master's crib** (manger)**: but Israel doth not know. . . . they have provoked the Holy One of Israel unto anger, they are gone away backward** (turned away from Him) (Is. 1:2-4). Isaiah recorded how the Lord had chosen and provided for the Israelites, only to have them turn against Him by worshiping idols. The Lord lamented that even the animals He had created knew who their Master was, but the sinful Israelites refused to recognize their responsibility to their Creator as Master.

Like our Heavenly Father, many godly parents are heartbroken when they see their children turning from the Lord. They feel sorrow over children who are uncommitted to the Lord, to reading the Bible, or to regular worship in a local church. Whether or not our children succeed or fail in their earthly goals, by comparison, it is of little eternal consequence, for only their spiritual achievements will bring true success and eternal rewards.

The Lord has provided His Written Word which, through the guidance of the indwelling Holy Spirit, will teach us how to experience deliverance from guilt and the condemnation of sin, as well as the joy of forgiveness.

Isaiah prophesied of a coming King who would reign in righteousness and peace over children who had returned to Him. When the Messiah returns, **many people shall go and say, Come ye, and let us go up to the mountain of the LORD, to the House of the God of Jacob; and He will teach us of His ways, and we will walk in His paths: for out of Zion shall go forth the Law, and the Word of the LORD from Jerusalem** (Is. 2:3).

Thought for Today: Continued disobedience blinds one's eyes and hardens one's heart to the will of God.

Christ Revealed: As the One who will judge the nations (Is. 2:2-4). **The Lord Jesus Christ . . . shall judge the quick and the dead at His appearing** (II Tim. 4:1).

AUGUST 2   Read Isaiah 5 – 9

Highlights: God sings a love song to His beloved Israel (Is. 5:1-7). The brilliance of His holiness reveals the darkness of our sin (6:5). **Send me** (6:8). Will you go? A divine principle: God always leaves a seed (6:13)! A prophecy of Jesus, the Light of the World (7:14-16; 9:1-7). Whatever the circumstances, keep trusting God (8:20).

The prophet Isaiah foretold the judgment of God against the kingdom of Judah for the people's sins. Ahaz, king of Judah, was facing war. The prophet appealed to him, saying: **Ask thee a sign of the LORD** (Is. 7:11). Although Ahaz refused, Isaiah spoke a glorious prophecy of the true King of kings who was yet to come. The sign Isaiah offered was the declaration of a special Child: **A virgin shall conceive, and bear a Son, and shall call His Name Immanuel** (God with us) (7:14). Seven hundred years later, the Angel Gabriel confirmed to the Virgin Mary: **The Holy Ghost** (Spirit) **shall come upon thee, and the power of the Highest shall overshadow thee: therefore also that Holy Thing** (One) **which shall be born of thee shall be called the Son of God** (Luke 1:35). In fulfillment of Isaiah's prophecy, Jesus, the Son of God, was born. To reject the virgin birth and question either the deity or the humanity of Jesus is to miss the significance that He was both Holy God and sinless Man. Because He was the only sinless Man, only Jesus could qualify as the required Sacrificial Lamb to atone for our sins. Jesus redeemed what Adam had forfeited when he chose to disobey God in the Garden of Eden.

    The prophet Isaiah received another glorious revelation of the eternal King of kings of whom he foretold: **Unto us a Child** (Jesus Christ) **is born, unto us a Son is given: and the government shall be upon His shoulder: and His Name shall be called Wonderful, Counseller, The Mighty God, The Everlasting Father, The Prince of Peace** (Is. 9:6). We recognize the fulfillment of that prophecy in Jesus, who was born **of the virgin** and later crucified, by which He provided eternal life to all believers in His sacrificial death on the cross for our sins and triumphant resurrection from the dead. Not only was His first advent (coming) declared, but also His second.

    Jesus is the Second Person of the Godhead (God the Father, God the Son, and God the Holy Spirit). **The Same was in the beginning with God. All things were made by Him; and without Him was not any thing made that was made** (John 1:2-3; Heb. 1:3).

Thought for Today: All of our own righteousness is **as filthy rags** (Is. 64:6) before a Holy God. Self-righteous people assume they are "good enough" without the Savior.

Christ Revealed: Isaiah reveals that a Child shall be born; a Son shall be given; and that **the government shall be upon His shoulder** (Is. 9:6). **The kingdoms of this world are become the kingdoms of our Lord, and of His Christ; and He shall reign for ever and ever** (Rev. 11:15).

AUGUST 3 — Read Isaiah 10 – 14

Highlights: God allows evil kings to punish Israel, but He also punishes evil kings for harming Israel (Is. 10). A prophetic picture of Christ returning in glory (chap. 11), *the Holy One of Israel* (12:6), our salvation (12:2).

Concerning the coming return of Jesus to earth and His glorious millennial reign, Isaiah foretold: *The Spirit of the LORD shall rest upon Him, the Spirit of wisdom and understanding, the Spirit of counsel and might, the Spirit of knowledge and of the fear of the LORD . . . The earth shall be full of the knowledge of the LORD, as the waters cover the sea. And in that day there shall be a Root of Jesse, which shall stand for an ensign* (rallying flag) *of the people; to it* (Jesus) *shall the Gentiles seek: and His rest shall be glorious* (Is. 11:2,9-10).

The promise made by Isaiah concerning Jesus Christ, the Ruler who would come through King David, the Root of Jesse, is far-reaching as today we anticipate the millennial reign of Christ to be followed by the new heavens and the new earth. *In that day shall ye say, Praise the LORD, call upon His Name, declare His doings among the people, make mention that His Name is exalted. Sing unto the LORD; for He hath done excellent things: this is known in all the earth. Cry out and shout, thou inhabitant of Zion: for great is the Holy One of Israel in the midst of thee* (12:4-6).

Isaiah the prophet also looked beyond the defeat and captivity of Israel, the Northern Kingdom, by Assyria, to the future when Babylon would also capture the people of Judah. Surprisingly, about 180 years before it took place, he also foretold Babylon's defeat and destruction, saying: *Babylon, the glory of kingdoms, the beauty of the Chaldees' excellency, shall be as when God overthrew Sodom and Gomorrah* (13:19-20). In striking contrast, Isaiah prophesied Israel's future restoration: *The LORD will have mercy on Jacob, and will yet choose Israel, and set them in their own land: and the strangers shall be joined with them, and they shall cleave to the house of Jacob. And the people shall take them, and bring them to their place . . . and they shall rule over their oppressors* (14:1-2).

Until that day, let us proclaim to the world with Isaiah: *Behold, God is my salvation . . . the LORD JEHOVAH is my strength and my song; He also is become my salvation. Therefore with joy shall ye draw water out of the wells of salvation* (Is. 12:2-3).

Thought for Today: Our Lord's love is inexhaustible.

Christ Revealed: As the Descendant of Jesse, King David's father (Is. 11:1; Luke 3:31-32). Isaiah 11 reveals Christ's coming earthly rule of righteousness. One day soon Jesus will return to earth in all the fullness of His glory and accompanied by His angels. Then He will set up the millennial kingdom of His creation; this will be the beginning of His eternal rule (Matt. 25:31-46; Rev. 20 – 22).

AUGUST 4   Read Isaiah 15 – 21

Highlights: God warns: "You'll be sorry if you mess with My children!" (Gen. 12:3). Learn from His judgments against Moab (Is. 15 – 16); Damascus (Syria) (chap. 17); Ethiopia (chap. 18); Egypt (chap. 19 – 20); Babylon, Edom, Arabia (chap. 21). God sifts our lives to remove the chaff and draw us closer to Him (21:10).

The prophet Isaiah was led to turn his thoughts from the glorious future reign of the King of Peace to proclaim the judgment of God upon the unbelieving. First it was pronounced upon the idolatrous Northern Kingdom of Israel, saying: *The fortress also shall cease from Ephraim* (Is. 17:3). He then included Judah, saying: *In that day it shall come to pass, that the glory of Jacob shall be made thin . . . there shall be desolation. Because thou hast forgotten the God of thy salvation* (17:4,9-10).

The fortress of Ephraim refers to the ten-tribe Northern Kingdom, a symbol of wealth, power, and self-glory, which would be ruthlessly destroyed by Assyria. Surprisingly, he also prophesied that Judah, the *glory of Jacob,* would fade, a reminder that the Southern Kingdom and Jerusalem would eventually be destroyed because they too had become involved in worldly pursuits, numerous sins, and idolatry.

Nothing hides the will of God from view as deceptively as success and pride. Perhaps this is why our Savior cautioned: *Lay not up for yourselves treasures upon earth, where moth and rust doth corrupt* (destroy), *and where thieves break through and steal* (Matt. 6:19). Wealth accumulated for self-interest grows out of greed and can weaken faith, as James pointed out: *Hearken, my beloved brethren, Hath not God chosen the poor of this world rich in faith, and heirs of the kingdom which He hath promised to them that love Him* (James 2:5)*?* Covetousness leads to an endless pursuit of earthly possessions. Jesus warns: *Beware of covetousness* (greed)*: for a man's life consisteth not in the abundance of the things which he possesseth* (Luke 12:15).

The Lord desires to speak to each of our hearts personally as to how He would have us invest our lives in transforming others and fulfilling His Great Commission. Paul wrote to Timothy: *Charge* (Instruct) *them that are rich in this world, that they be not highminded* (conceited)*, nor trust in uncertain riches, but in the Living God, who giveth us richly all things to enjoy* (I Tim. 6:17; Deut. 8:18).

Thought for Today: Be vigilant and prepared for Jesus' return.

Christ Revealed: As the one who will sit on the throne of David (Is. 16:5). Gabriel told the Virgin Mary that *the Lord God shall give unto Him the throne of His father David* (Luke 1:32-33). Christ also was revealed as the Savior (Is. 19:20; Matt. 1:21; Luke 2:11).

AUGUST 5   Read Isaiah 22 – 26

Highlights: Isaiah weeps as God judges the unrepentant inhabitants of Jerusalem, who uncaringly eat and drink; then they are destroyed (Is. 22:1-14). Wicked leader deposed (22:15-25). Judgment and salvation promised (chap. 25). Our only deliverance from sin and its consequences (26:4).

Isaiah's prophecy was first directed to Judah, then to Israel, then to the surrounding Gentile nations, and finally to all the world. It foretold: *He will swallow up death in victory; and the Lord GOD will wipe away tears from off all faces . . . And it shall be said in that day, Lo, this is our God; we have waited for Him, and He will save us . . . we will be glad and rejoice in His salvation. . . . Thou wilt keep him in perfect peace, whose mind is stayed on Thee* (Is. 25:8-9; 26:3). His promises will come to pass without fail.

Just as surely as many of the prophecies were fulfilled in history, we can also expect that the Messiah (Jesus) will return as Christ the King. As *The Mighty God, The Everlasting Father, The Prince of Peace* (9:6), He will give eternal life to both Jews and Gentiles who have received Him as Savior.

Jesus has imparted His indwelling Holy Spirit into every true believer and has assured us: *Ye are of God, little children, and have overcome them* (spirits of Antichrist)*: because greater is He that is in you, than he* (Satan) *that is in the world* (I John 4:4). We need not live in slavery to Satan and our fleshly passions; we can *be strong in the Lord, and in the power of His might. Put on the whole armour of God, that ye may be able to stand against the wiles* (schemes, trickery) *of the Devil* (Eph. 6:10-11).

From the beginning, all are slaves to sin because we descended from Adam who chose to eat the fruit from the forbidden tree of the knowledge of good and evil (Gen. 2:17; Rom. 5:12). However, once we choose to obey God through receiving Jesus as our Savior, we no longer remain slaves to sin. The Word of God provides a simple revealing test: *Know ye not, that to whom ye yield yourselves servants to obey, his servants ye are to whom ye obey; whether of sin unto death, or of obedience unto righteousness? But God be thanked, that ye were the servants of sin, but ye have obeyed from the heart. . . . Being then made free from sin, ye became the servants of righteousness* (Rom. 6:16-18).

Thought for Today: Suffering, hardships, and handicaps have helped many come to know the will of God for their lives.

Christ Portrayed: By Eliakim, master of Hezekiah's household (Is. 22:20-22); what was said of him is true of Christ who is also Master over the household of faith. *Christ . . . a Son over His own house; whose house are we* (Heb. 3:6; Gal. 6:10).

AUGUST 6 — Read Isaiah 27 – 31

Highlights: God deals out "tough love" to Israel (Is. 27:11) and Judah (chap. 29 – 30). It is futile to rely on Egypt: ***Woe to them that go down to Egypt for help*** (31:1-3).

The magnificent Northern Kingdom was enjoying great prosperity when the Lord led Isaiah to prophesy its coming captivity by Assyria. He proclaimed: ***Woe to the crown of pride*** (Samaria, Israel's capital)***, to the drunkards of Ephraim, whose glorious beauty is a fading flower. . . . The crown of pride, the drunkards of Ephraim, shall be trodden under feet*** (Is. 28:1-3).

The people of Samaria were enjoying the luxury of summer and winter homes, ivory palaces, and a wealth of gardens. They were content in their affluence and unwilling to hear the Lord's prophet. With a heavy heart, Isaiah warned that all would soon be destroyed because, for many years they had rejected the Word of God and turned to idols. Samaria's ***beauty*** was likened to ***a fading flower*** that would soon disappear. ***Ephraim, shall be trodden under feet.*** Without God, the nation would be helpless to withstand the fierce Assyrians. Like most worldly-minded people today, Israel did not believe judgment would or could happen to them. ***The god of this world hath blinded the minds of them which believe not*** (II Cor. 4:4).

Isaiah also warned Judah that, since they also had refused to live in obedience to the Covenant of God, they too had made a covenant with death and would be attacked by Syria and eventually be taken captive by the Babylonians. They would pay the same price for their sins as the Northern Kingdom. ***Be not deceived; God is not mocked: for whatsoever a man soweth, that shall he also reap*** (Gal. 6:7).

Times and circumstances change; but all who will not receive Christ as their Savior are making an eternal ***covenant with death*** (that is, eternal separation from God) (Is. 28:15,18), whether knowingly or unknowingly. It is our responsibility to share the Good News with those who have not heard the Gospel and possess a Bible, and let them know what God has said.

We can praise the Lord that while there is life, there is still hope. ***The Lord is not slack*** (slow) ***concerning His promise, as some men count slackness; but is longsuffering to us-ward, not willing that any should perish, but that all should come to repentance*** (II Pet. 3:9).

Thought for Today: If it seems there is no hope, we are relying on human resources instead of the promises of the strength of God.

Christ Revealed: As the ***precious*** (Chief) ***Corner Stone, a sure foundation*** (Is. 28:16; Eph. 2:20-21; Matt. 21:42; Acts 4:10-12; Rom. 9:33; I Pet. 2:6-8).

AUGUST 7   Read Isaiah 32 – 37

Highlights: Be wary of nations which can't be trusted; they shall be destroyed. Hear the threats of God against ungodly nations (Is. 33:1,7-9; 34:1-17). The Lord promises victory (33:5-6,21-22; 34:8; 35:4,10; 37:5-7,22-38); just do as Hezekiah did (37:14-20).

I*n the fourteenth year of King Hezekiah... Sennacherib king of Assyria came up against all the defenced cities of Judah, and took them* (Is. 36:1). Even the walled cities were no match for Sennachcherib's mighty army. In one military campaign he quickly defeated 46 towns and villages of Judah. He carried away about 200,000 inhabitants, but he was not able to conquer Jerusalem. At that time, all of western Asia was under Assyria's control, including Babylonia, Media, Armenia, Syria, Phoenicia, Philistia, Edom, and most of the promised land.

Eventually, the king of Assyria demanded unconditional surrender and sent word to the people of Jerusalem: *Let not Hezekiah deceive you: for he shall not be able to deliver you. Neither let Hezekiah make you trust in the L*ORD*, saying, The L*ORD *will surely deliver us* (36:14-16). Upon hearing this, Hezekiah immediately did what we all should do when we receive bad news. *Hezekiah went up unto the House of the L*ORD *... And Hezekiah prayed... O L*ORD *of hosts, God of Israel... Thou art the God, even Thou alone, of all the kingdoms of the earth.... hear all the words of Sennacherib, which* (he) *hath sent to reproach the living God.... save us... that all the kingdoms of the earth may know that Thou art the L*ORD*, even Thou only* (37:14-17,20).

Isaiah sent a message to Hezekiah, saying: *Thus saith the L*ORD *God of Israel, Whereas* (Because) *thou hast prayed to Me against Sennacherib.... I will defend this city to save it for Mine own sake, and for My servant David's sake* (37:21,35). That night *the Angel of the L*ORD *went forth, and smote ... the Assyrians* (37:36), destroying 185,000 soldiers.

Like Hezekiah, it is important that we pray and trust the Lord for all of our needs. It is foolish to think we can *stand against the wiles* (schemes, trickery) *of the Devil* in our own might (Eph. 6:11).The Lord is still urging us: *Call unto Me, and I will answer thee, and shew thee great and mighty* (unsearchable) *things, which thou knowest not* (Jer. 33:3; also Eph. 3:20).

Thought for Today: You can depend on the promises of God; they cannot fail.

Christ Revealed: As the One who, in judgment, wields *the Sword of the L*ORD (Is. 34:6). *Out of His mouth goeth a sharp sword, that with it He should smite the nations* (Rev. 19:15).

AUGUST 8 — Read Isaiah 38 – 42

Highlights: Sickness, prayer, and healing (Is. 38; Ex. 15:26). Hezekiah's poem of praise (Is. 38:9-20). His poor judgment because of pride (chap. 39). Prophecy of the Deliverer and Savior (chap. 40).

About 13 years had passed since Isaiah brought Hezekiah news that his kingdom would be miraculously saved from Assyria. But this time Isaiah said to Hezekiah, who was gravely ill: **Thus saith the Lord, Set thine house in order: for thou shalt die, and not live** (Is. 38:1; II Kin. 20:1; II Chr. 32:24-26). With intense weeping, **Hezekiah turned his face toward the wall, and prayed unto the Lord, And said, Remember now, O Lord, I beseech** (beg) **Thee, how I have walked before Thee in truth and with a perfect** (sincere) **heart, and have done that which is good in Thy sight. And Hezekiah wept sore** (bitterly) (Is. 38:2-3; comp. 38:17).

Isaiah again heard the voice of God say: **Go, and say to Hezekiah... I have heard thy prayer... behold, I will add unto thy days fifteen years** (38:5). The additional years were due not only to Hezekiah's tears and prayer but also to his faithfulness during the previous 50+ years of his life.

Our Lord Jesus tells us: **Ask, and it shall be given you; seek, and ye shall find; knock, and it shall be opened unto you: For every one that asketh receiveth** (Matt. 7:7-8). We should never hesitate to ask, regardless of our circumstances. However, this does not mean that God always answers our prayer in the way we want nor according to our timing.

Since we often fall short in our desire to be like Jesus, we may be tempted to accept the condemnation of Satan that we are too unworthy for God to answer our prayers. Although it is right to assess our faults and confess our sins, it also magnifies the grace of God to recognize the good in our lives just as Hezekiah did. We can also remind the Lord of our sincere endeavors to live God-honoring lives. This only happens as we surrender to the power and inner working of the Holy Spirit.

Not by works of righteousness which we have done, but according to His mercy He saved us, by the washing of regeneration, and renewing of the Holy Ghost (Spirit) (Titus 3:5; James 5:16).

Thought for Today: Trusting in anything or anyone but the Lord for our eternal salvation is deception and will result in eternal death.

Christ Revealed: As the **Creator** (Is. 40:28; John 1:1-3); as the **Shepherd** (Is. 40:11; comp. John 10:11); as the **Redeemer** (Is. 41:14; comp. Gal. 3:13; I Pet. 1:18-19; Rev. 5:9).

AUGUST 9   Read Isaiah 43 – 46

Highlights: Here are powerful promises of the Lord's love and protection; prophecy of our Savior's redeeming work and Jerusalem's restoration. Cyrus introduced. Note the warning against false idols (Is. 46). Don't miss 46:13! What a promise!!

When Isaiah was a prophet, in spite of the people's unfaithfulness, they felt very secure in knowing that Jerusalem was the City of God and His presence dwelt there in its Temple. Because of their misplaced confidence, the people rejected Isaiah's prophecy concerning the "ruins" of Jerusalem.

Through Isaiah, God prophesied both the destruction and rebuilding of the Temple while the nation was still enjoying freedom and prosperity. He also prophesied: ***The cities of Judah . . . shall be built, and I will raise up the decayed places*** (ruins) (Is. 44:26).

At that time, Babylon, the capital city of the Chaldean dynasty, also thought it was invincible and that no one could successfully invade it. However, 50 years before it took place, Isaiah foretold that a man named Cyrus would conquer Babylon: ***Thus saith the L<small>ORD</small> . . . Cyrus . . . shall perform all My pleasure: even saying to Jerusalem, Thou shalt be built; and to the Temple, Thy foundation shall be laid*** (44:24,28).

Babylon thought itself invincible because of its 300-foot-high walls, as well as the great brass gates spanning the Euphrates River, which ran through its center. However, God declared exactly how the city would be taken by the armies of Cyrus. The river would dry up and the Lord would see that the gates across it would be left unlocked. And that is exactly what happened when, under the rule of Cyrus, Darius the Mede entered the city by channeling the river around it the same fateful night that King Belshazzar of Babylon saw the handwriting of God on the wall (Dan. 5:1-31).

Only God could have given Isaiah such remarkable details concerning the defeat of Babylon. At the end of the Kingdom of Judah's 70 years of captivity, this was fulfilled exactly as foretold. This prophetic fulfillment should dispel all doubt regarding the Lord's loving concern and care for His followers. It is a fact that even the ***king's heart is in the hand of the L<small>ORD</small>, as the rivers of water: He turneth it whithersoever He will*** (Prov. 21:1).

Thought for Today: God is not limited; He will keep His Word.

Christ Revealed: As the Redeemer (Is. 43:1; 44:22-24). Through His death on the cross, Christ has redeemed (bought back) all who trust Him as their Savior (I Cor. 6:20; Gal. 4:4-5; Titus 2:13-14; I Pet. 1:18-19).

AUGUST 10   Read Isaiah 47 – 51

Highlights: Prediction: Babylon will be destroyed for mistreating Israel (Is. 47:1-15; 49:25-26). The heartbroken Heavenly Father speaks to His unruly children (chap. 48). Warning (48:22)! The Servant officially commissioned as Savior (49:1-7). Whose hand holds you (49:16; 51:16)? Trust God (51:7-8,11,21-23).

We expect judgment upon the ungodly or upon the backslider, but many Christians do not understand why sincere believers experience so many critical situations. The prophet Isaiah encourages us to remain faithful, regardless of the circumstances, even though we cannot see why we face so many difficulties. *Who is among you that feareth* (reveres) *the LORD . . . that walketh in darkness, and hath no light? let him trust in the Name of the LORD, and stay* (rely) *upon his God* (Is. 50:10). God will bring blessings out of suffering and triumph out of tragedy for every child of God, just as He did for Job. Heartbreaking experiences test our faith, as well as develop greater faith. God said twice that Job was the most perfect man on earth (Job 1:1; 2:3), yet he suffered more than anyone in biblical history except Jesus, who died for the sins of the world.

Each of us can expect testing from the Lord, as well as temptation from the forces of evil; so do not be dismayed if your world crumbles and it seems the Lord has forgotten you. Then remember: *Can a woman forget her sucking child, that she should not have compassion on the son of her womb? yea, they may forget, yet will I not forget thee* (Is. 49:15).

The Apostle James, who later suffered martyrdom for his faith in Jesus Christ, encouraged believers: *Take . . . the prophets, who have spoken in the Name of the Lord, for an example of suffering affliction, and of patience* (James 5:10). Jesus explained to His disciples that, because the world hated Him, it would also hate them. Another time, He promised a hundredfold return to those who forsook home and family for Him (Mark 10:29-30), but also warned of persecution (John 15:18, 20-21).

Rejoice, inasmuch as ye are partakers of (share in) *Christ's sufferings; that, when His glory shall be revealed, ye may be glad also with exceeding joy* (I Pet. 4:13).

Let us express gratitude to *the God of all grace, who hath called us unto His eternal glory by Christ Jesus* (I Pet. 5:10).

Thought for Today: Regardless of circumstances, God is in control.

Christ Revealed: As the *Light to the Gentiles* (Is. 49:6; Luke 2:32; Acts 26:23). Jesus said: *I am the Light of the world* (John 8:12; 9:5).

AUGUST 11   Read Isaiah 52 – 57

Highlights: God reigns, Jerusalem redeemed (Is. 52:1-12); Weep over what your sins cost Jesus (52:13-15; chap. 53)! Israel, the restored wife (chap. 54). Note 54:17 & 55:8-9! Obedience rewarded (chap. 56); repentance and forgiveness (57:15-21).

God revealed to Isaiah that the Messiah, the King of kings, would first come as *My Servant . . .* (then) *He shall be exalted* (Is. 52:13). Jesus first came as the suffering *Servant* (Savior of God); but He will soon return and will be highly *exalted* as *KING OF KINGS AND LORD OF LORDS* (Rev. 19:16).

The first century religious leaders were looking for a warrior-king, like David, to deliver them from the oppression of Rome. However, Isaiah had foretold: *Surely He hath borne our griefs, and carried our sorrows* (Is. 53:4). He has provided for our emotional, spiritual, and physical needs of every kind. Although Isaiah was prophesying about the future, he wrote as if it had already happened: *He* (the Messiah) *was wounded for our transgressions, He was bruised for our iniquities: the chastisement of our peace was upon Him; and with His stripes* (lashes) *we are healed* (made whole) (53:5). Jesus' death on the cross provided the way for all repentant believers, Jew and Gentile alike, to receive eternal life and become acceptable to God when they receive Him as their Savior and Lord.

He was oppressed, and He was afflicted . . . He was taken from prison and from judgment . . . He was cut off out of the land of the living (He died)*: for the transgression of My people was He stricken. And He made His grave with the wicked, and with the rich in His death . . . Thou shalt make His soul an offering for sin* (53:7-10). Had they been in subjection to the Word of God, more of the first century Israelites would have recognized their Messiah who provided deliverance from sin and freedom from oppression. *He shall grow up before Him* (the Lord) *as a tender plant, and as a root out of a dry ground: He* (Jesus Christ, the Messiah) *hath no form nor comeliness; and when we shall see Him, there is no beauty that we should desire Him* (53:2).

Dry ground illustrates the spiritual condition of a world without Jesus. God alone provides eternal life. *For God so loved the world that He gave His only begotten Son, that whosoever believeth in Him should not perish, but have everlasting life* (John 3:16).

Thought for Today: Praise God today for His amazing grace.

Christ Revealed: As the One who was rejected by His own people (Is. 53:3; comp. Luke 23:18; John 1:11); remained silent when He was falsely accused (Is. 53:7; Mark 15:3-5); was buried with the rich (Is. 53:9; Matt. 27:57-60); and was crucified with sinners (Is. 53:12; Mark 15:27-28).

AUGUST 12   Read Isaiah 58 – 63

Highlights: Our sinful nature separates us from God (Is. 59:2-15). Solution: A Redeemer (59:16-21). The Light of the World (60:1,19-20). Jesus fulfills chapter 61 (Luke 4:16-29). The love of God, His mercy, pardon, and deliverance outlined in chapters 62 & 63.

During Isaiah's time, the Israelite leaders complained to God: *Wherefore have we fasted . . . and Thou seest not? Wherefore have we afflicted our soul, and Thou takest no knowledge* (Is. 58:3)? They accused Him of not paying attention to what they were doing, and they felt they had wasted their time. The Lord answered: *In the day of your fast ye find pleasure* (continue to seek selfish interests), *and exact* (exploit) *all your labours* (laborers). *. . . ye fast for* (continue your) *strife and debate, and to smite with the fist of wickedness* (58:3-4). God was saying: "Although you fast, you are contentious, demanding, overbearing, and stubborn."

Even more serious was their hypocrisy. The Lord said: *Is it such a fast that I have chosen? . . . is it to bow down his head as a bulrush, and to spread sackcloth and ashes under him* (to impress others with false humility) (58:5; Luke 18:10-14)? Through Isaiah, God reminded the Israelites that acceptable fasting was not for impressing the world of how religious they were, but it was to seek the will of God through intercession. The Lord said the fast He would accept would be preceded by acts of kindness: *Is not this the fast that I have chosen? to loose the bands* (bonds) *of wickedness, to undo the heavy burdens, and to let the oppressed go free . . . to deal* (divide) *thy bread to the hungry, and that thou bring the poor that are cast out* (wandering) *to thy house? when thou seest the naked, that thou cover him; and that thou hide not thyself from thine own flesh* (never neglect responsibility to family) (Is. 58:6-7)?

If we do something for the Lord or for someone else for the purpose of expecting something in return, our prayers and fasting will be futile. For our prayers to be truly effective, our attitude and our relationship with others should express the mercy and love of God.

When many people think of a Christian, they think of what that person does not do – smoke, drink, curse, commit adultery, steal, etc. But a Christian should be identified for who he is – a believer who loves the Lord and wants to please Him. *Let your light so shine before men, that they may see your good works, and glorify your Father which is in heaven* (Matt. 5:16).

Thought for Today: Graciously submit to the Lord's arrangements in your life, and under no circumstances grieve the Holy Spirit.

Christ Revealed: As the One anointed *to preach Good Tidings* (Is. 61:1). Jesus preached this passage to the rulers of the synagogue (Luke 4:16-22) but stopped before the completion of the second verse (Is. 61:2), thus showing that He fulfilled the first part but that the second part, the day of judgment, was yet to be fulfilled.

Isaiah & Jeremiah's Prophecies Concerning the Gentiles, Judah, and Israel

Isaiah's Prophecies Concerning The Gentiles

Babylon [13:17-22; 14:21-23] -- To be destroyed by the Medes; To become desolate
Assyria [14:24-27] -- To be crushed upon the mountains of Israel
Philistia [14:28-32] -- To suffer defeat [by Sargon, the Assyrian king]
Moab [15 – 16] -- Chief cities to be destroyed in one night [by Assyrians]
Damascus [Syria] [17] – To be defeated [by Assyrian king, Shalmaneser]
Ethiopia [18; 20:1-6] – To be taken captive by Assyria; Its dead to become food for wild animals
Egypt [19:4; 20:1-6] – To be cruelly ruled by its enemies; To be invaded within three years by Assyria
Edom (Dumah) [21:11-12] – To be overrun by the Babylonians
Arabia [21:13-17] – To have its armies scattered
Tyre [Phoenicia] [23:15] – To suffer a seventy-year Babylonian captivity

Isaiah's Prophecies Concerning Judah [Southern Kingdom]

1:1-31 – Condemnation and judgment of Judah pronounced
3:1-8; 5:26-30; 22:1-14; 39:5-7 – Babylonian captivity
7:4,16 – Judah would be saved from impending Syrian/Israelite invasion
8:7-8 – Assyria would invade Judah
10:20-21 – Judah to go into captivity with only a remnant to remain
29:1-24 – Woe to Ariel [Jerusalem]
30:1-33 – Woe to rebellious children [Judah]
31:1 – 32:20 – Woe to compromisers
37:33-35 – Jerusalem to be saved during Assyrian invasion
38:1 – 39:8 – Babylonian captivity
38:5 – Hezekiah's life extended by 15 years
41:2-3; 44:28; 45:1-4 – World conquests by a Persian king named Cyrus
44:28; 45:13 – Exiles to return to Jerusalem under Cyrus' decree
48:20 – Joy of returnees from Babylon

Isaiah's Prophecies Concerning Israel [Northern Kingdom]

5:1-30 – Charge against Israel
8:4; 17:1-14; 28:1-4 – Israel to be destroyed by Assyria
28:1-29 – Woe to Ephraim [Israel]

Jeremiah's Prophecies Concerning The Gentiles

Egypt [46:1-28] – Would be defeated by Nebuchadnezzar
Philistia [47:1-7] – Would be overrun by the Egyptians and its chief cities destroyed
Moab [48:1-47] – Would be overrun [by Nebuchadnezzar's armies]
Ammon [49:1-6] – Would be punished for occupying Israelite cities during their captivity and for worshiping the false god Milcom [Molech]

EDOM [49:7-22] – Its cities would become as desolate as Sodom and Gomorrah

DAMASCUS [SYRIA] [49:23-27] – Entire army would be destroyed in a single day

KEDAR AND HAZOR [49:28-33] – At God's command, these nomadic Arabic tribes [not the city of Hazor in Northern Israel] were to be destroyed by Nebuchadnezzar; Hazor never to be rebuilt

ELAM [49:34-39] – To be overrun and its people scattered to the four winds

BABYLON [50:1 – 51:64] – To be captured
by the Medes; Never to be inhabited again

JEREMIAH'S PROPHECIES CONCERNING JUDAH

1:13-16 – Great armies would march upon Jerusalem

2:18,36; 4:5-7 – Neither Assyria nor Egypt could help Judah against Babylon

4:1-31; 6:3-5 – Foe from north to invade; Jerusalem to be surrounded

4:31; 6:24; 13:21 – Her people will cry as a woman in travail [delivering a child]

6:6 – Jerusalem's trees would be used as battering rams against its own walls

7:14 – The Temple would be destroyed

7:15; 25:11; 29:10 – Thousands would be taken into a 70-year captivity in Babylon

7:32-33; 9:22; 12:8-9 – Judah's corpses would become food for wild animals

8:1-2 – Judah's graves would be desecrated

8:17 – Enemy troops would move among the people like poisonous snakes

13:24 – Some of her people would be scattered as chaff by the wind

15:3; 16:3-4; 21:9 – Many would die by the sword; by disease; by starvation

19:8; 22:8; 25:11 – The Gentiles would be astonished at the severity of Judah' punishment

21:3-7; 34:1-5; 37:5-10 – Zedekiah would be taken captive by Nebuchadnezzar

22:1-30 – Warnings for Judah's kings

25:1-38 – Babylonian invasion foretold

30:1 – 33:26 – Future Messianic kingdom

34:2 – Jerusalem would be burned

36:29-31 – Jehoiakim cursed; none of his lineage would sit upon the throne of David

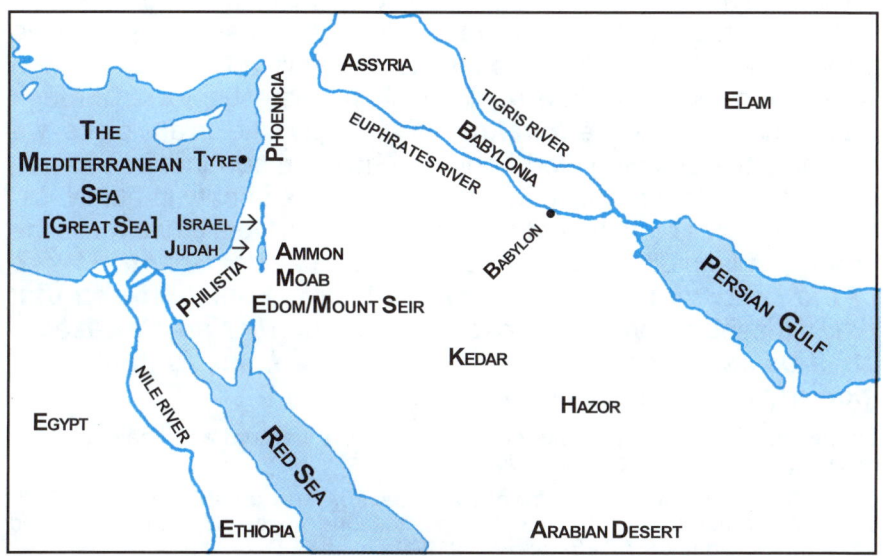

AUGUST 13 — Read Isaiah 64 – 66

Highlights: Included in these final chapters are prayers for mercy and forgiveness from God who is silent (Is. 64). Those pleading confess their sin and praise God for His deeds (64:4-7). God will spare His true servants (65:1-10). The rebirth of His nation and His promises (66:7-9,22).

Most of the people from the Northern Kingdom had been carried away captive by the Assyrians during the reign of wicked King Pekah (Is. 7:1; II Kin. 15:27-29). Hezekiah, king of the Southern Kingdom, witnessed the destruction of the Northern Kingdom before he became king. Undoubtedly, godly Hezekiah was greatly encouraged by the prophet Isaiah. Sadly, after Hezekiah's death, his son Manasseh became one of the most wicked kings in Judah's history (21:9).

During this time, the Word of God, as proclaimed by Isaiah, had been ignored; now a heartbroken God spoke through him these pitiful words: *I have spread out My hands all the day unto a rebellious people, which walketh in a way that was not good, after their own thoughts* (Is. 65:2). Although God had reached out to them, they had ignored and insulted Him. They had gone their own ways. The Lord continued: *I also will choose their delusions, and will bring their fears* (dread, terrors) *upon them; because when I called, none did answer; when I spake, they did not hear: but they did evil before Mine eyes, and chose that in which I delighted not* (66:4).

The Apostle Paul quoted from Isaiah 64:4 to encourage the Corinthian church: *It is written, Eye hath not seen, nor ear heard, neither have entered into the heart of man, the things which God hath prepared for them that love Him* (I Cor. 2:9). The magnificence of His wisdom and glory are now revealed to us as we read His Word. Paul went on to state that believers in Jesus as Messiah also receive the very thoughts of Christ through the written Word of God. Through Isaiah, God declared future things which were later bestowed through the Messiah upon those *that love Him*. At any time, in any place, we may pray to our loving God. While we have an opportunity to serve Him, we should determine to make His will the priority in our lives.

To the small minority who remained faithful then, as well as to the minority of faithful believers today, Isaiah is saying: *Hear the Word of the LORD, ye that tremble at His Word; Your brethren that hated* (despised) *you, that cast you out for My Name's sake . . . shall be ashamed. . . . For thus saith the LORD, Behold, I will extend peace to her like a river* (Is. 66:5,12).

Thought for Today: Sin breaks our fellowship with the Lord and keeps us from receiving His true peace and wisdom.

Christ Revealed: As the Creator of *new heavens and a new earth* (Is. 65:17; 66:22; comp. John 1:1-3; II Pet. 3:13). He is the One whose glory will be declared among the nations (Is. 66:18-19; Rev. 5:12-13).

INTRODUCTION TO THE BOOK OF JEREMIAH

Jeremiah prophesied during the last 40 years of the small Southern Kingdom of Judah. This was more than 100 years after the Assyrians destroyed the Northern Kingdom of Israel. As the years passed, the weakened Assyrian empire was overthrown by the Babylonians.

Jeremiah's public ministry began in the 13th year of the reign of godly King Josiah (Jer. 1:2), who ruled for 31 years (II Chr. 34:1). He continued his ministry through the reigns of the last four kings of Judah, all of whom were wicked: Jehoahaz (Shallum); followed by his brother Jehoiakim (Eliakim), *in his days Nebuchadnezzar* (was) *king of Babylon* (II Kin. 24:1); Jehoiachin (Coniah, Jeconiah); and Mattaniah (Zedekiah).

After Nebuchadnezzar defeated Egypt in the battle at Carchemish – the key city of northern Syria – the Southern Kingdom of Judah was then brought under his control. Seven years later, in the 11th year of Zedekiah's reign, Jerusalem and the Temple were destroyed by Nebuchadnezzar and his Babylonian armies who then controlled all of the area now known as the Middle East (25:2-21).

It was at this time in Judah's history that Jeremiah exposed their hypocrisy and declared: *From the least of them even unto the greatest of them every one is given to covetousness; and from prophet even unto the priest every one dealeth falsely* (Jer. 6:13). *The prophets prophesy falsely, and the priests bear rule by their means; and My people love to have it so* (5:31).

After most of the people were carried off into captivity by Nebuchadnezzar, the remaining people fled to Egypt and forced Jeremiah to accompany them. He faithfully continued to declare the Word of God to the unrepentant, defiant people (II Kin. 24:20 – 25:21; Jer. 39:1-10).

Although the Southern Kingdom of Judah was defeated and Jerusalem and the Temple were destroyed, as a nation the people were not finished. God had made a Covenant with Abraham, Isaac, and Jacob, and then with David, of a glorious future for His people. The God of mercy had also promised, through Jeremiah: *Again I will build thee, and thou shall be built... this shalt be the Covenant that I will make with the House of Israel; After those days, saith the L*ORD*, I will put My Law in their inward parts, and write it in their hearts; and will be their God, and they shall be My people* (31:4,33; Rom. 11:25-27).

The events in this book are not arranged in chronological order but by similar subjects to let us see more clearly the tragic results of sin.

AUGUST 14   **Read Jeremiah 1-3**

Highlights: God knew Jeremiah long before he was born (Jer. 1:4-5)! Is the Word of God in your mouth (1:9)? God reminds Judah of its blessings (2:1-7) and of the people forsaking Him (2:13) and worshiping false gods (2:10-12,26-28). Israel more righteous than Judah (3:6-11); Judah warned (3:14-17); national restoration promised (3:16-18). God speaks (3:22)!

God revealed to Jeremiah that He had a plan and purpose for each of us even before our birth: *The Word of the LORD came unto me, saying, Before I formed thee . . . I knew thee; and . . . I sanctified thee* (set you apart for God)*, and I ordained thee a prophet unto the nations* (Jer. 1:4-5). Through Jeremiah's revelation concerning the origin of human life, it is revealed that birth is not our real beginning, nor will death be our end. Since God is the Giver of Life, let us recognize the sanctity of all human life. Just think! God knew you and had a plan for your life even before you were conceived.

The Holy Spirit led King David to write: *I will praise Thee; for I am fearfully and wonderfully made: marvellous are Thy works; and that my soul knoweth right well. My substance was not hid from Thee, when I was made in secret* (Ps. 139:14-15). Both mother and father have the biblical responsibility to recognize that every unborn child, from the moment of conception, belongs to its Creator God. Both parents are responsible as faithful stewards of God to teach their children to know, love, and be obedient to Him.

Through the Apostle Paul, God revealed that *He* (God) *hath chosen us in Him* (Christ) *before the foundation* (beginning) *of the world, that we should be holy and without blame before Him in love . . . In whom* (Christ) *also we have obtained an inheritance . . . That . . . the Father of glory, may give unto you the spirit of wisdom and revelation in the knowledge of Him; The eyes of your understanding* (mind) *being enlightened; that ye may know what is the hope of His calling, and what the riches of the glory of His inheritance in the saints* (Eph. 1:4,11,17-18).

God has chosen each of us for His sacred purpose. He has also given us the freedom to choose whom we will serve. Jesus stated an often overlooked fact when He said that *no man can serve two masters: for either he will hate the one, and love the other; or else he will hold to the one, and despise the other* (Matt. 6:24).

Thought for Today: Without reading the Word of God we have no way of knowing the Truth of God and the standards He has set for His creation.

Christ Revealed: As *the Fountain of Living Waters* (Jer. 2:13). *Jesus stood and cried, saying, If any man thirst, let him come unto Me, and drink* (John 7:37; 4:1-26).

AUGUST 15   Read Jeremiah 4 – 6

Highlights: God warns Judah of impending destruction unless hearts and minds are cleansed (Jer. 4:3-4). The prophet grieves (4:19-22) over visions of Judah's coming judgment (4:23-31). Not one man *seeketh the truth* to save the city (5:1-9,19-25); last warning (6:1-9); Judah's constant rebellion results in rejection (6:10-30).

Jeremiah began his ministry during the reign of Josiah of Judah (Jer. 1:2). He exposed the Israelites' worldly, compromising lifestyle when he called them a *foolish people . . . without understanding; which have eyes, and see not; which have ears, and hear not . . . this people hath . . . a rebellious heart . . . your sins have with-holden good things from you* (5:21,23,25). The reason for their lack of understanding was clear; they were rebellious against God in their hearts. Jeremiah lamented: *The Word of the LORD is unto them a reproach; they have no delight in it. . . . every one is given to covetousness; and from the prophet even unto the priest every one dealeth falsely* (6:10,13).

Josiah's father Amon and grandfather Manasseh were wicked kings who had led the people to forsake God and had encouraged worship of false gods. However, young Josiah *did that which was right in the sight of the LORD, and walked in all the way of David his father* (ancestor)*, and turned not aside to the right hand or to the left* (II Kin. 22:2). No doubt, Jeremiah was a great encouragement and influence on Josiah. After *he had purged the land*, Josiah began repairing the Temple and restoring worship of the One True God (II Chr. 34:8-33). He then initiated a Passover Feast unequaled in Israel's history *from the days of the judges . . .* (and) *in all the days of the kings* (II Kin. 23:22).

Following Josiah's death (23:30-32), his son Jehoahaz reverted to the evil ways of both Amon and Manasseh. With deep concern, we see a parallel between Judah's false gods and immorality that led to its defeat, and America's growing false religions and moral decline.

The Apostle Paul was led by the Holy Spirit to warn us: *The time will come when they will not endure sound doctrine; but after their own lusts . . . they shall turn away their ears from the truth, and shall be turned unto fables* (false teachings) (II Tim. 4:3-5).

True Christianity teaches: *Keep yourselves in the love of God, looking for the mercy of our Lord . . . unto eternal life* (Jude 1:21).

Thought for Today: The more we read the Bible, the more the Lord's ways become our ways, and His thoughts our thoughts, and His actions our actions.

Christ Portrayed: By Jeremiah, whom God commissioned to reveal His Truth (Jer. 4:2). Jesus shall one day judge all mankind. *In the day when God shall judge the secrets of men by Jesus Christ. . . . Every man's work shall be made manifest* (known)*: for the day shall declare it, because it shall be revealed by fire; and the fire shall try* (test) *every man's work of what sort it is* (Rom. 2:16; I Cor. 3:13).

AUGUST 16   Read Jeremiah 7 – 10

Highlights: Judah, don't be fooled! **Hear the Word of the LORD** (Jer. 7:2,4-5; 9:20,24). Disobedient children experience complete disaster as a consequence of their sin. If the prophet of God is sorrowed, what do you think it does to the Heavenly Father's heart (8:18-22)? God, forgive our disobedience.

All adult men who were physically able were required by the Law to attend three major Feasts annually in Jerusalem. These occasions were to be joyful celebrations of praise to God for His provision and protection. But, on this occasion, Jeremiah did not give the crowd a warm welcome. Instead, he pronounced a harsh condemnation: **Hear the Word of the LORD, all ye of Judah, that enter in at these gates to worship the LORD. . . . Will ye steal, murder, and commit adultery, and swear falsely . . . and walk after other gods whom ye know not; And come and stand before Me in this House, which is called by My Name, and say, We are delivered to do all these abominations** (sinful things) (Jer. 7:2,9-10)?

The people considered Jeremiah's preaching far too narrow-minded, so they would not tolerate this prophet of God. They self-righteously declared: **We are wise, and the Law of the LORD is with us** (8:8). The physical presence of the Law and the Temple gave them a false sense of security. They were confident that God would never allow His chosen people to be destroyed. But the Lord's Covenants do not give His people license to sin or to ignore His Word.

Then, as now, people foolishly assume that each person should have the freedom to worship whomever or whatever he will, following his own conscience. But Jesus declared: **I am The Way, The Truth, and The Life: no man cometh unto the Father, but by Me** (John 14:6). Some today call themselves Christians but continue in secret sins. Jesus asks those who say they are Christians while still living sinful lives: **Why call ye Me, Lord, Lord, and do not the things which I say** (Luke 6:46)?

Jesus reminds us: **If ye continue in My Word, then are ye My disciples indeed; And ye shall know the Truth, and the Truth shall make you free. . . . Whosoever committeth sin is the servant of sin** (John 8:31-32,34). He also declared: **Not every one that saith unto Me, Lord, Lord, shall enter into the Kingdom of Heaven; but he that doeth the will of My Father** (Matt. 7:21).

Thought for Today: The best of religious accomplishments are never a substitute for godly living.

Christ Revealed: As the one who demanded a cleansed Temple (Jer. 7:1-11). Jesus said: **My House shall be called of all nations the house of prayer** (Mark 11:17).

AUGUST 17   Read Jeremiah 11 – 14

Highlights: Judah breaks a pledge (covenant) (Jer. 11:1-17). We should be men and women of integrity. Jeremiah's message meets with animosity. Men of Anathoth plot to kill Jeremiah but the Lord defends him (11:18-23). What is the significance of the marred belt (chap. 13)? A solemn warning (chap. 14).

All Israelites were called to be holy and to serve the Lord, as He said to Moses: *I am the LORD your God: ye shall therefore sanctify yourselves* (live in obedience to My Word)*, and ye shall be holy* (Lev. 11:44). And, in return, God promised to provide all their needs. Instead of obeying the Word of God, the majority forsook the Lord to worship idols. To expose their sin, the Lord told Jeremiah: *Get thee a linen girdle, and put it upon thy loins, and put it not in water* (do not wash it) (Jer. 13:1). Hebrew men wore long, loose, gown-like garments. They wore around their waist, a sash-like belt called a "girdle." The girdle represented the way the Israelites were bound to Jehovah (Yahweh).

Jeremiah reported that, eventually, *the Word of the LORD came unto me the second time, saying, Take the girdle . . . and . . . go to Euphrates, and hide it there in a hole of the rock. So I went, and hid it by Euphrates, as the LORD commanded me. And it came to pass after many days, that the LORD said unto me, Arise, go to Euphrates, and take the girdle from thence, which I commanded thee to hide there. Then I went to Euphrates, and digged, and took the girdle from the place where I had hid it: and, behold, the girdle was marred* (decomposed)*, it was profitable for nothing* (13:3-7). The girdle represented the spiritual condition of the Israelites. Then Jeremiah spoke: *Thus saith the LORD. . . . This evil people, which refuse to hear My words . . . and walk after other gods, to serve them, and to worship them, shall even be as this girdle, which is good for nothing* (13:9-10).

Like the Israelites, some today are intent on satisfying self-interests while rejecting their opportunities to serve the Lord. Many will discover too late that they have lost forever the opportunities given by God. The writer of Hebrews admonishes: *Let us lay aside every weight, and the sin which doth so easily beset us, and let us run with patience the race that is set before us, Looking unto Jesus the author and finisher of our faith* (Heb. 12:1-2).

Thought for Today: Wholeheartedly living for the Lord provides assurance that *all things work together for good to them that love God* (Rom. 8:28).

Christ Revealed: As *the Hope of Israel, the Saviour to them that love God* (Jer. 14:8). Christ is the only *Hope* of all mankind. *Looking for that blessed Hope, and the glorious appearing of the great God and our Saviour Jesus Christ* (Titus 2:13).

AUGUST 18   Read Jeremiah 15 – 18

Highlights: Although Jeremiah suffers much, he stays bold before man because he is broken before God (Jer. 15:10-21; 16:1-4,19-21; 17:11-18; 18:18-23). He tells Judah that punishment is inevitable (15:1-9; 16:5-13; 17:1-4), but that there's still hope (16:14-18) and wisdom (17:5-10,19-27). Fact: Our lives are in the hands of God (18:1-17)!

The LORD said, Verily (Truly) *... I will cause the enemy to entreat* (treat) *thee well in the time of evil and in the time of affliction* (Jer. 15:11). But, when the Israelites rejected God and His Word as their way of life, they forfeited His wonderful protective shield and tragically suffered both spiritual and physical loss.

To understand the Israelites' problems and their final outcome, Jeremiah was sent to the potter's house to see a live illustration of what God was about to do. God said to Jeremiah: ***Arise, and go down to the potter's house, and there I will cause thee to hear My words. Then I went down to the potter's house, and, behold, he wrought*** (was making) ***a work on the wheels. And the vessel that he made of clay was marred*** (ruined) ***in the hand of the potter: so he made it again another vessel, as seemed good to the potter to make it*** (18:2-4). Then the Lord said: ***O House of Israel ... as the clay is in the potter's hand, so are ye in Mine hand ... If it*** (a nation) ***do evil in My sight, that it obey not My voice, then I will repent of the good, wherewith I said I would benefit them*** (18:6,10).

When ***the vessel*** (the chosen people of God) ***was marred in the hand of the potter***, it was the hardness within the clay itself and not the potter's skills that made the vessel worthless. Israel had rejected the will of God and ***was marred*** (hardened) by its sin. Consequently, ***the vessel***, Israel, was broken and taken into captivity by Babylon, a nation used as the instrument of God to bring judgment. After 70 years of captivity (25:11), God made the ***clay*** into ***another vessel*** which was the small group (***remnant***) of Jews who willingly returned to Jerusalem to rebuild the Temple and worship Him.

God has a special plan for each of us to be a vessel for His use. When we yield ourselves to the Master Potter, with loving hands He will mold us again into ***another vessel,*** one better prepared to contain and express the Presence of Christ Himself. ***Therefore if any man be in Christ, he is a new creature: old things are passed away; behold, all things are become new*** (II Cor. 5:17).

Thought for Today: We were created for the glory of God.

Christ Revealed: By Jeremiah's words to God: ***Thy word was unto me the joy and rejoicing of mine heart*** (Jer. 15:16). Jesus said: ***The words that I speak unto you, they are Spirit, and they are Life*** (John 6:63).

AUGUST 19   Read Jeremiah 19 – 22

Highlights: God speaks to (1) Judah, that's us (Jer. 19:3-15); (2) Zedekiah and the rebellious people, Babylon wins (21:7-10); (3) the royal family, do right or else (21:11 – 22:5); (4) the palace, destroyed (22:6-9); (5) Jehoahaz (Shallum), you're gone (22:10-12); (6) Jehoiakim, you're dead and no one cares (22:13-23); (7) Jehoiachin (Coniah), exited, no heirs, nothing (22:24-30).

During the last days of the kingdom of Judah, Jeremiah courageously faced the son of the chief governor of the high priest and said: *Thus saith the LORD, Behold, I will make thee a terror to thyself, and to all thy friends: and they shall fall by the sword of their enemies... and I will give all Judah into the hand of the king of Babylon, and he shall carry them captive into Babylon, and shall slay them with the sword.... And thou, Pashur, and all that dwell in thine house shall go into captivity... to Babylon, and there thou shalt die... thou, and all thy friends, to whom thou hast prophesied lies* (Jer. 20:4,6).

Soon the people of Judah learned of the defeat of Assyria and Egypt. With Nebuchadnezzar's victory in the battle at Carchemish, Babylon emerged as the new dominant world power. This confirmed Isaiah's prophecy about 100 years earlier (Is. 39:6-7).

Even after being fully informed of the results of rejecting the Word of God, the religious leaders not only refused to repent, but they began a campaign to discredit Jeremiah before the king and the nation. In prison, Jeremiah was discouraged as he wrote: *I will not make mention of Him, nor speak any more in His Name. But His Word was in mine heart as a burning fire shut up in my bones, and... I could not stay* (hold it in) (Jer. 20:9). Jeremiah may have thought that he had failed to communicate the importance of obeying the Word of God; but, far beyond all his own expectations, he has been an inspiration to millions of the Lord's people for many centuries. God assures us: *My Word... shall not return unto Me void* (without result)*, but... it shall prosper in the thing whereto I sent it* (Is. 55:11).

Regardless of circumstances, everyone who is devoted to the Lord and to teaching the Word of God or who provides the money to make it possible for others to teach His Word is laying up *treasures in heaven* (Matt 6:20). Jesus promised: *For every tree is known by his own fruit.... A good man out of the good treasure of his heart bringeth forth that which is good* (Luke 6:44-45).

Thought for Today: Pray like Jesus: *Not My will, but Thine, be done* (Luke 22:42).

Christ Revealed: As the One who pronounces judgment upon those who refuse to obey His Word (Jer. 19:15). *For the Father... hath committed all judgment unto the Son* (John 5:22).

AUGUST 20   Read Jeremiah 23 – 25

Highlights: Are you a child of God? What a precious opportunity and responsibility to teach the Word of God (Jer. 23)! Christ, the **Righteous Branch** (23:5-8).

Only a few months remained before the Babylonians would destroy the kingdom of Judah. It was now too late to pray for Jerusalem or for the Temple to be saved from destruction for God had decreed judgment. The eyes of Judah's last king, Zedekiah, would be gouged out, and he would be taken in chains to Babylon (II Kin. 25:7).
These prophecies are all horrifying reminders that judgment is inevitable whenever the Word of God is disregarded.

Jeremiah's message turned from one of coming judgment to one of comfort. To illustrate, the Lord showed him that **one basket had very good figs, even like the figs that are first ripe: and the other basket had very naughty** (bad, rotten) **figs, which could not be eaten** (Jer. 24:2). Then the Lord said: **Like these good figs, so will I acknowledge** (regard) **them that are carried away captive of Judah, whom I have sent out of this place into the land of the Chaldeans for their good. For I will set Mine eyes upon them for good, and I will bring them again to this land** (24:5-6). There were three fig harvests – June, August, and November. The first figs, in June, were considered a great delicacy (Is. 28:4; Hos. 9:10; Mic. 7:1). Thus the Lord was lovingly sending the chosen "good figs" into captivity to correct them "for their own good." At times it may seem that circumstances are against us; but remember, the Lord says: **All things work together for good to them that love God** (Rom. 8:28).

Even while the armies of Babylon were besieging Jerusalem, Jeremiah assured those who were faithful to the Word of God: **Behold, the days come, saith the LORD, that I will raise unto David a Righteous Branch, and a King shall reign and prosper, and shall execute judgment and justice in the earth. In His days Judah shall be saved, and Israel shall dwell safely: and this is His Name whereby He shall be called: THE LORD OUR RIGHTEOUSNESS** (Jer. 23:5-6; 33:15-16).

We continue to look forward to the coming return of the Messiah Jesus, who is that **Righteous Branch**. **He** (God) **hath made Him** (Jesus) **to be sin for us, who knew no sin; that we might be made the righteousness of God in Him** (II Cor. 5:21).

Thought for Today: Give a friend **Bible Pathway** – a gift they'll use all year.

Christ Revealed: As *THE LORD OUR RIGHTEOUSNESS* (Jer. 23:5-8). *Of Him are ye in Christ Jesus, who of God is made unto us wisdom, and righteousness, and sanctification, and redemption* (I Cor. 1:30; II Cor. 5:21).

AUGUST 21

Read Jeremiah 26 – 28

Highlights: Sinners resist the Word of God and try to execute the messenger (Jer. 26:1-15). Only five more kings (27:3). The priests and the people are all warned: *Thus saith the LORD* (27:16). Check out the "yoke." Sin's "yoke" is heavy and leads to death (chap. 28) while the "yoke" of God is light and leads to abundant life (Matt. 11:28-30).

During the early part of Zedekiah's reign, God commanded Jeremiah to make a yoke and put it on his own neck, symbolizing the coming captivity of the kingdom of Judah. *Now have I given all these lands into the hand of Nebuchadnezzar the king of Babylon, My servant; and the beasts of the field have I given him also to serve him* (Jer. 27:6). Jeremiah proclaimed that, because of their sin, as well as the sins of Moab, Ammon, Tyre, and Sidon, God had appointed Nebuchadnezzar to be ruler over all these nations (27:2-11; Dan. 2:37-38). Sometime earlier, when Jeremiah had prophesied something similar, the priests were determined to kill him. *Then spake the priests and the prophets unto the princes and to all the people, saying, This man is worthy to die; for he hath prophesied against this city, as ye have heard with your ears* (Jer. 26:11).

When Jeremiah's prophecy was fulfilled and the Israelites were defeated by Nebuchadnezzar, it began *the times of the Gentiles* (Luke 21:24). We are nearing the end of that final generation when *the times of the Gentiles* (will) *be fulfilled*. God, in His sovereign power, has caused the Jews to return to Jerusalem and once again become a nation before the coming return of the Messiah, King Jesus – just as He declared centuries ago.

If we fail to tell others about the Lord, they will have less opportunity to receive Christ as their Savior and Lord and to escape eternal damnation, and we will have to answer to God for forfeited opportunities to bear fruit.

The grace of God that bringeth salvation hath appeared to all men, Teaching us that, denying ungodliness and worldly lusts, we should live soberly (sensibly), *righteously, and godly, in this present world; Looking for that blessed hope, and the glorious appearing of the great God and our Saviour Jesus Christ; Who gave Himself for us, that He might redeem us from all iniquity* (lawlessness)*, and purify unto Himself a peculiar* (special) *people, zealous of good works* (Titus 2:11-14).

Thought for Today: Speak boldly for the Lord; it will influence others.

Christ Portrayed: By Jeremiah, who was falsely accused by the priests and the false prophets (Jer. 26:8-9). Our Lord was threatened and falsely accused by the religious rulers of His day. *The elders . . . and the chief priests and the scribes. . . . began to accuse Him, saying, We found this fellow perverting* (misleading) *the nation, and forbidding to give tribute* (tax) *to Caesar, saying that He Himself is Christ a King* (Luke 22:66 – 23:2; John 8:48,59).

AUGUST 22 — Read Jeremiah 29 – 31

Highlights: As when He led the Israelites, God knows exactly where He is taking each of us. We are not to be fearful about the path He has chosen for us but bravely and faithfully trust in His Word (Jer. 29:10-13). God turns sadness into joy (31:13). A New Covenant is promised (31:27-40).

The destruction of the two powerful empires of Assyria and Babylon took place just as the Lord had foretold through Jeremiah. Jeremiah had also prophesied the destruction of Jerusalem and the captivity of the small kingdom of Judah. But God did not leave His people without hope. He said: **Thus saith the LORD; Behold, I will bring again the captivity of Jacob's tents, and have mercy on his dwellingplaces; and the city shall be builded upon her own heap** (ruin) (Jer. 30:18).

The Lord also revealed to Jeremiah that, at a future time, He would make a New Covenant: **I will put My Law in their inward parts, and write it in their hearts; and will be their God, and they shall be My people** (31:33). During their Babylonian captivity, through His prophet Jeremiah, the Lord taught the people to **seek the peace of the city whither I have caused you to be carried away captives, and pray unto the LORD for it: for in the peace thereof shall ye have peace** (29:7). This means they were to pray for, and be a blessing to, their captors; in turn, they would be blessed by God. The Lord reminds us also of the self-destructive results of unforgivingness when we are mistreated or faced with opposition.

Pity the person who, even though physically free, remains mentally trapped by dissatisfaction about his circumstances. Perhaps he is waiting for better opportunities, but he is always impatiently waiting for release from his present situation. A more serious example is the offended person who has quit attending church. Often such people are engulfed in bitter resentment and have made themselves prisoners of their own miserable attitudes (Heb. 13:5-6). They cannot be forgiven because of their own unforgiving spirit (see Matt. 6:14-15).

The Apostle Peter was led to write: **Gird up the loins of your mind... As obedient children, not fashioning** (conforming) **yourselves according to the former lusts in your ignorance: But as He which hath called you is holy, so be ye holy in all manner of conversation** (behavior); **Because it is written, Be ye holy: for I am holy** (I Pet. 1:13-16).

Thought for Today: Every reader of the Bible will be richly rewarded.

Christ Revealed: As the One who forgives sin (Jer. 31:34). **That ye may know that the Son of Man hath power** (authority) **on earth to forgive sins, (then saith He to the sick of the palsy,) Arise, take up thy bed, and go** (Matt. 9:6; John 8:10-11).

AUGUST 23   Read Jeremiah 32 – 33

Highlights: Do you get the point of Jeremiah purchasing land and receiving a legal deed to it (Jer. 32:9-15,40-44)? Eternal restoration of Israel is promised by God through Jesus Christ (33:14-26).

The king of Babylon's army besieged Jerusalem: and Jeremiah the prophet was shut up in the court of the prison, which was in the king of Judah's house (Jer. 32: 2). Yet, under such adverse circumstances when the destruction of the nation was imminent, the Lord told Jeremiah: **Buy thee the field for money, and take witnesses; for the city is given into the hand of the Chaldeans** (32:25). Without hesitation Jeremiah paid for the land, took receipts, registered the purchase, then handed over the documents in the presence of many witnesses (32:9-12).

This business transaction would have seemed ridiculous to those who had heard Jeremiah's repeated warnings of approaching destruction and captivity. But, Jeremiah had also proclaimed that the people would be restored to the land, and this purchase of land was evidence of his faith that the Sovereign God would faithfully fulfill His Word. Although Jeremiah could not see how God would accomplish this prophecy, he demonstrated his faith in the unfailing Word of God, who also said: **I am the Lord, the God of all flesh: is there any thing too hard for Me** (32:27)? God gave Jeremiah a fresh assurance concerning the future of Israel by saying: **I will gather them out of all countries, whither I have driven them . . . and I will bring them again unto this place . . . to dwell safely** (32:37).

How wonderful to know that, in the midst of the most difficult circumstances, we can rest assured that God is merciful and will protect and provide for the needs of His children! The Lord still invites us: **Call unto Me, and I will answer thee, and shew thee great and mighty things** (33:3).

Our faith in the Word of God can be measured by the influence we allow it to have upon our conduct. We should be thankful that: **It is of the Lord's mercies that we are not consumed, because His great compassions fail not. They are new every morning: great is Thy faithfulness. The Lord is my portion, saith my soul; therefore will I hope in Him. The Lord is good unto them that wait for Him, to the soul that seeketh Him** (Lam. 3:22-25).

Thought for Today: What occupies your thoughts most is a revelation of who or what is your god.

Christ Portrayed: By Jeremiah who acted as a kinsman-redeemer by purchasing the land of his cousin Hanameel even though Jeremiah was in prison (Jer. 32:6-14; Lev. 25:25,49; Ruth 2:20; 3:12-13). Jesus is our Kinsman-Redeemer who purchased our freedom from sin, hell, and the grave **with a price**; His own blood on Calvary (I Cor. 6:20; Gal. 4:4-5; Titus 2:13-14; Heb. 13:12).

AUGUST 24   Read Jeremiah 34 – 36

Highlights: In chapters 34 & 36, a very loving Heavenly Father warns His children of impending judgment so they may repent (Jer. 36:1-3). No matter how often the wicked try to destroy the Word of God, they cannot (36:32). The Rechabites are honored for their lifelong obedience (35:18-19).

More than three years after the Egyptians conquered Judah and appointed Jehoiakim as Judah's king, Nebuchadnezzar defeated Egypt and Jerusalem, and appointed Jehoiakim as his servant-king. Unlike his godly father Josiah, Jehoiakim was a ruthless, cruel, and wicked ruler.

At that time, Jeremiah instructed his secretary Baruch to record the judgment of God: **Take . . . a roll** (scroll) **of a book, and write therein all the words that I have spoken unto thee against Israel, and against Judah, and against all the nations** (Jer. 36:2).

Then **Jeremiah commanded Baruch . . . go . . . and read . . . the words of the LORD . . . in the LORD'S House . . .** (to) **all Judah. . . . It may be they will . . . return every one from his evil way** (36:5-7). The princes (leaders) were disturbed by the prophet's words and immediately informed the king, who **sent Jehudi to fetch the roll** (36:21). After **Jehudi had read three or four leaves** (of the scroll)**, he** (Jehoiakim) **cut it with the penknife, and cast it into the fire that was on the hearth, until all the roll was consumed in the fire** (36:23). Although Jehoiakim could easily cut up and burn the scroll, that was all he could do. It was beyond his power to destroy the Truth the scroll contained.

In the third year of the reign of Jehoiakim . . . came Nebuchadnezzar king of Babylon unto Jerusalem, and besieged it. And the LORD gave Jehoiakim . . . into his hand (Dan. 1:1-2).

Like Jehoiakim, some today seal their fate by refusing to read and believe the Truth that God considers necessary to fulfill His will. History records many Bible burnings. But although many people might not *burn* the Bible, some may ignore it – through negligence, unconcern, or busyness. In any case, leaving the Word of God out of one's life can result in that life not being changed by its illuminating Truth.

Without a doubt, godly believers suffer because of the sins of others; but, God is able to bless the faithful. Without exception, **all things work together for good to them that love God, to them who are the called according to His purpose** (Rom. 8:28).

Thought for Today: Those who seek counsel from the Lord through His Word will never be deceived.

Christ Revealed: As the One who desires liberty for all in bondage (Is. 61:1). Jesus said: **The Spirit of the Lord is upon Me . . . to preach deliverance to the captives** Luke 4:18-19).

AUGUST 25   Read Jeremiah 37 – 40

Highlights: See four kinds of people: The wicked, who hate and hurt those who stand for God and His Word (Jer. 37:11-16; 38:1-6); the disobedient, who want His blessings but will not repent of their sins (37:1-3,17; 38:14,20); Jeremiah, the faithful one who willingly suffers for God (40:1-6); and the compromiser, "puppet" governor (40:5-16).

During the 11th year of Zedekiah's evil reign, the armies of Nebuchadnezzar (sometimes spelled Nebuchadrezzar) surrounded Jerusalem, and Zedekiah frantically told Jeremiah: *Inquire... of the LORD for us; for Nebuchadrezzar... maketh war against us* (Jer. 21:2). But the Lord's answer was firm: *I have set My face against this city... the king of Babylon... shall burn it with fire* (21:10). Neither Zedekiah, *nor the people of the land,* listened to *the words of the LORD, which He spake by the prophet Jeremiah* (37:2).

In desperation Zedekiah sent his officials to Egypt to make an alliance, believing that Egypt could and would protect his subject kingdom from the Babylonians. Because it also seemed wise to show "good will" to the prophet, *Zedekiah the king sent...* (a) *priest to the Prophet Jeremiah, saying, Pray now unto the LORD our God for us* (37:3). Instead of praying, Jeremiah replied: *Thus saith the LORD; Deceive not yourselves, saying, The Chaldeans shall.... burn this city with fire* (37:9-10).

When the Chaldean army drew away from Jerusalem, the Israelites believed their alliance with Egypt had been successful without Jeremiah's prayers. Yet Zedekiah was uneasy. He removed Jeremiah from prison *and... asked him secretly in his house... Is there any word from the LORD? And Jeremiah said, There is... thou shalt be delivered into the hand of the king of Babylon* (37:17).

The city of Jerusalem held out for nearly a year and a half. During this time the people suffered the horrors of famine and pestilence, and even turned to cannibalism. When Zedekiah finally attempted to escape the city at night, he was captured near Jericho (39:5), where Joshua had victoriously begun the conquest of the promised land.

Zedekiah was blinded, taken to Babylon, and then imprisoned (39:7). He is an example of those who harden their hearts and refuse to seek the Lord's forgiveness for their sins. Regarding such, the Apostle Paul wrote: *The god of this world hath blinded the minds of them which believe not* (II Cor. 4:4).

Thought for Today: A person who rejects the Lord and His Word is blindly moving toward his own destruction.

Christ Portrayed: By Jeremiah, who stood as a faithful witness to the revealed will of God (Jer. 38:2-9). *Now the chief priests, and elders, and all the council, sought false witness* (testimony) *against Jesus, to put Him to death* (Matt. 26:59).

AUGUST 26 — Read Jeremiah 41 – 44

Highlights: A murderous plot is carried out as greed and betrayal change the course of the remnant (Jer. 41).

God allowed Nebuchadnezzar to defeat His rebellious people and fulfill His prophecy of the destruction of Jerusalem. ***The king of Babylon . . . made Gedaliah . . . governor in the land, and . . . committed unto him . . . them that were not carried away captive to Babylon*** (Jer. 40:7).

Gedaliah set up his government at Mizpah, about five miles north west of the ruins of Jerusalem. He then held a banquet in honor of Ishmael, a leader of an anti-Babylonian nationalist party. At this event, Ishmael and his ten companions murdered Gedaliah (II Kin. 25:25; Jer. 40:7 – 41:18). The Israelites who remained in the land were convinced that Nebuchadnezzar would retaliate, so they escaped to Egypt. When Jeremiah warned them not to go, he was accused of lying and was forced to go with them (chaps. 42 & 43).

In Egypt, Jeremiah watched the Israelites sink further into sin as they worshiped the Egyptian goddess Ashtoreth. When confronted with their sins, they ***answered Jeremiah, saying, As for the word that thou hast spoken unto us in the Name of the LORD, we will not hearken unto thee. . . . we will . . . burn incense*** (sacrifice, worship) ***unto the queen of heaven*** (female deity idol)***, and . . . pour out drink offerings unto her*** (44:15-17). Because of their refusal to heed the Word of God, they became totally disobedient to the Living God. They distorted the facts to fit their decision and said to Jeremiah: In Egypt ***had we plenty of victuals, and were well, and saw no evil. But since we left off to burn incense to the queen of heaven . . . we have wanted*** (lacked) ***all things*** (44:17-19).

Some would say the godly prophet Jeremiah surely deserved better treatment than this for his loyalty to the Lord. However, Jeremiah had nothing to fear. He knew his life was in the hands of the living God. Jeremiah never compromised. Regardless of how he was treated, he remained loyal to God. Centuries have passed and you can be sure that in heaven Jeremiah still has no regrets.

May it also be our desire to say with the Apostle Paul: ***I count all things but loss for the excellency of the knowledge of Christ Jesus my Lord: for whom I have suffered the loss of all things, and do count them but dung*** (rubbish), ***that I may win Christ*** (Phil. 3:8).

Thought for Today: Shed the Light of God on someone's path today.

Christ Revealed: By ***My servants the prophets*** (Jer. 44:4). God the Father called Jesus ***My Servant, whom I have chosen*** (Matt. 12:17-18).

AUGUST 27   Read Jeremiah 45 – 48

Highlights: Remember Genesis 12:3? Through Jeremiah, God sends a special word for the nations of Egypt (Jer. 46), Philistia (chap. 47), and Moab (chap. 48).

Among all the prophecies of Jeremiah, the Lord included a personal message to just one man, Baruch, Jeremiah's discontented assistant. ***Thus saith the Lord . . . unto thee, O Baruch; Thou didst say, Woe is me now! for the Lord hath added grief to my sorrow; I fainted in my sighing, and I find no rest*** (Jer. 45:2-3). Although he could not have known how the people would respond to Jeremiah's message, perhaps Baruch had hoped that his service as a scribe would be a means of achieving self-serving goals. Baruch's grandfather Maaseiah had been governor of Jerusalem during Josiah's reign (32:12; II Chr. 34:8). Did Baruch secretly think he was "over-qualified" to be a mere scribe to an unpopular prophet?

Instead of rewards for his frustrations, Baruch received a strong rebuke from the Lord: ***Seekest thou great things for thyself? seek them not: for, behold, I will bring evil upon all flesh, saith the Lord: but thy life will I give unto thee for a prey in all places whither thou goest*** (Jer. 45:5).

Baruch expressed no grief over the impending destruction of Jerusalem and the Temple of God nor the loss of freedom and the pitiful slavery of his people, as Jeremiah had foretold. He only expressed sorrow over his own lack of personal fulfillment.

Although Baruch was recording the Word of God spoken through Jeremiah, he did not have the spiritual concern nor insight of the prophet. Jeremiah was deeply concerned for the wayward people of God, desiring that they repent and avoid the coming judgment and destruction. Baruch should have considered it a great privilege to be a coworker in Jeremiah's ministry.

Our time and talents are precious treasures invested in us by the God of all creation to accomplish His will through us. True fulfillment comes only when we recognize God and willingly submit to His arrangement of the circumstances in our lives. Baruch is typical of those who are dissatisfied with their circumstances or their position of having less esteem than they think they deserve. In contrast are those whom God can use because they realize that ***godliness with contentment is great gain*** (I Tim. 6:6; also Heb. 13:5-6).

Thought for Today: Look at the birds of the sky: they down't sow or reap or gather into barns, ***yet your Heavenly Father feedeth them*** (Matt. 6:26).

Christ Revealed: As the One who corrects His people (Jer. 46:28). ***Whom the Lord loveth He chasteneth*** (disciplines)***, and scourgeth*** (whips) ***every son whom He receiveth*** (Heb. 12:6).

AUGUST 28   **Read Jeremiah 49 – 50**

Highlights: Jeremiah delivers a prophecy concerning Ammon (Jer. 49:1-6), Edom (49:7-22), Damascus (49:23-27), Kedar and the kingdoms of Hazor (49:28-33), and Elam (49:34-39). Next, a prophecy of judgment on Babylon and hope for Israel, Judah, and the remnant (chap. 50). The Good Shepherd speaks of His sheep and their wayward shepherds (50:6).

Jeremiah prophesied that the Ammonites, descendants of Lot who were historically hostile to the Israelites, would be destroyed (Jer. 27:3-6; also II Chr. 20:1-3; II Kin. 24:1-2). **Rabbah of the Ammonites ... shall be a desolate heap, and her daughters** (villages) **shall be burned with fire** (Jer. 49:2). The Lord then turned to Moab, saying: **Behold, I will bring a fear** (terror) **upon thee, saith the Lord God of hosts ... and ye shall be driven out** (49:5).

Our attention is turned to Edom, a nation that descended from Jacob's twin brother Esau. The Edomites had always been jealous enemies of Jacob's descendants and had joined with Nebuchadnezzar in plundering Jerusalem. They even expanded their territory by occupying part of southern Judah, inhabiting an area later called Idumea. Because of their antagonistic actions toward Israel, Edom's fate was foretold by the prophet: **I have made Esau bare** (49:10-12).

Judgment was then pronounced **against Babylon ... the land of the Chaldeans. ... there cometh up a nation against her, which shall make her land desolate** (50:1-3).

Jeremiah foretold that Israel would be released from captivity, and also that they will eventually repent and accept their Messiah Jesus **in a perpetual Covenant that shall not be forgotten** (50:4-5).

We can expect the forces of evil to discourage us in an effort to destroy our faith in God. However, we must keep our eyes on the promises of God, who has never failed. When we do, we will not allow the pressures and problems of life to depress or frustrate us and cause us to become despondent. **Count it all joy when ye fall into divers temptations** (various trials); **Knowing this, that the trying of your faith worketh patience. But let patience have her perfect work, that ye may be perfect and entire, wanting** (lacking) **nothing. ... Blessed is the man that endureth temptation: for when he is tried, he shall receive the crown of life, which the Lord hath promised to them that love Him** (James 1:2-4,12).

Thought for Today: God will hear the prayer of any repentant sinner.

Christ Revealed: As the Redeemer who pleads our cause (Jer. 50:34). **Blessed** (praised and extolled and thanked) **be the Lord God of Israel; for He hath visited and redeemed His people** (Luke 1:68). **It is Christ ... who is even at the right hand of God, who also maketh intercession for us** (Rom. 8:34).

AUGUST 29   Read Jeremiah 51 – 52

Highlights: Let's sum it up! Jeremiah wrote of the pitiful results of sins, the horrifying details of the destruction of the sacred city of Jerusalem, the **burned ... House of the LORD** (Jer. 52:13), and **the army of the Chaldeans ...** (who) **brake down all the walls of Jerusalem** (52:14). Note: Babylon was in modern-day Iraq!

The spectacular empire of the Chaldeans surpassed anything the world had ever known. Its capital Babylon appeared invincible, with high walls wide enough for chariots to be driven on them side by side. The empire was enjoying absolute rule over all the nations when Jeremiah declared that **Babylon is suddenly fallen. ... thine end is come. ... Babylon shall become heaps** (ruins) **... without an inhabitant** (Jer. 51:8,13,37).

As foretold by the prophet, the Babylonian capital "suddenly fell." This was fulfilled on the night that **Belshazzar the king. ... saw the part of the hand that wrote** (on the wall of his palace) **. ... God hath numbered thy kingdom, and finished it** (Dan. 5:1,5,26). After the fall of Babylon, Cyrus, the conquering king of the Persian Empire, issued a decree urging the Jews to rebuild the Temple in Jerusalem.

The unwillingness of the majority of the Jews to forsake the luxuries of Babylon for the poverty and hardships they would experience in returning to Jerusalem has a modern-day parallel. How accurately this describes those who love the pleasures of the world and will not respond to the invitation of Christ, who said: **If any man will come after Me, let him deny himself, and take up his cross daily, and follow Me** (Luke 9:23).

Many who seemingly consent to be "followers" of Christ drop out when things become difficult. Jesus illustrated this in His parable concerning the seed sown in stony places and among thorns. He likened such people to those who, **when tribulation or persecution ariseth because of the Word, by and by he is offended. ... and the care of this world, and the deceitfulness of riches, choke the Word** (Matt. 13:21-22). If a person truly is taking up his cross, he will devote his time, tithes, and talents to the Lord on a day-by-day basis.

Jesus promised: **There is no man that hath left house, or brethren ... for My sake, and the Gospel's, But he shall receive an hundredfold now in this time ... with persecutions; and in the world to come eternal life** (Mark 10:29-30).

Thought for Today: We are to live in the world but not by its standards.

Christ Revealed: As the Creator of the universe (Jer. 51:15). **All things were created by Him, and for Him** (Col. 1:16).

Introduction To The Book Of LAMENTATIONS

The Book of Lamentations is an expression of Jeremiah's deep sorrow over the sins of his people that eventually resulted in the destruction of the Temple of God and the kingdom of Judah. Jeremiah knew the inevitable consequences of Judah's disobedience: **Jerusalem has grievously sinned; therefore she is removed** (Lam. 1:8).

Jerusalem is the place God had chosen for His people to make sacrifices to Him. It was **the city of the great King** (Ps. 48:2) and His presence in the Temple gave the people a false sense of security. Ignoring the Word of God had resulted in sin; and for those sins the Israelites were subjected to the horrors of deprivation, disease, suffering, starvation and finally, the destruction of Jerusalem. Even more pathetic than the destruction of the city was the destruction of the sacred Temple where God dwelt. **The LORD hath ... poured out His fierce anger. ... For the sins of her prophets, and the iniquities of her priests** (Lam. 4:11,13; 2:3-7; Ex. 25:22; II Chr. 7:1-2).

> No time, no time to study
> to meditate and pray,
> And yet much time for doing
> In a fleshly, worldly way;
> No time for things eternal,
> But much for things of earth;
> The things of God are set aside
> For things of little worth.
> Some things, tis true, are needful,
> But first things must come first;
> And what displaces God's own Word
> Of God it shall be cursed.
> —M.E.H.

WISDOM

Let the Word of Christ dwell in you richly in all wisdom; teaching and admonishing (urging) *one another in psalms and hymns and spiritual songs, singing with grace in your hearts to the Lord* (Colossians 3:16).

And that from a child thou hast known the Holy Scriptures, which are able to make thee wise unto salvation through faith which is in Christ Jesus (II Timothy 3:15).

AUGUST 30 — Read Lamentations 1 – 2

Highlights: Jeremiah's intense burden for Jerusalem reflects the love and sorrow God has for His wayward children (yes, and even every one of us) (Matt. 23:37-38). God sent prophets to plead for obedience! In prosperity there are many places to turn, but in adversity only one – the Lord!

Jeremiah was deeply grieved that the Holy City of Jerusalem had *become as a widow! she that was great among the nations, and princess among the provinces, how is she become tributary! She weepeth sore* (bitterly) *in the night . . . she hath none to comfort her: all her friends . . . are become her enemies. Judah is gone into captivity* (Lam. 1:1-3). Jeremiah tells us why Jerusalem was reduced to such deplorable destruction: *The LORD hath afflicted her for the multitude of her transgressions* (1:5).

Jeremiah compared the once-affluent Israelites to a widow who had lost her husband. The loving Lord provided for and protected Israel, but the people rejected Him for heathen idols (Jer. 3:20). As a widow, Jerusalem was now destroyed, its remaining few people were left mourning, with no one to comfort them. *Jerusalem hath grievously sinned* (Lam. 1:8). The Covenant of God with Israel was designed to be a blessing, but spiritual neglect eventually led the Israelites to lose not only their prosperity and liberty but also the precious privilege of letting the world know that the One True God expects them to reject their idols and worship Him, their Creator.

We too have one supreme reason for living, and it is not for self-satisfaction. The question that needs to be addressed is: Will we read His Guidebook (the Bible) to learn how to gain His best for our lives, or will we have to suffer the consequences for neglecting His Word? Pity the people who waste their few short years of life chasing social and economic goals, but fail to achieve the purpose for which God created them! Jesus asked a sobering question: *Why call ye Me, Lord, Lord, and do not the things which I say* (Luke 6:46)? We can't do something we don't know, so, He calls upon each of us to learn of Him through the Scriptures, His Guide for our lives.

We must all appear before the judgment seat of Christ; that every one may receive the things done in his body, according to that he hath done, whether it be good or bad. Knowing therefore the terror of the Lord, we persuade men (II Cor. 5:10-11).

Thought for Today: *I will say of the LORD, He is my Refuge and my Fortress: my God; in Him will I trust* (Ps. 91:2).

Christ Revealed: As the one who will judge the nations (Is. 2:2-4). *The Lord Jesus Christ . . . shall judge the quick and the dead at His appearing* (II Tim. 4:1).

AUGUST 31 — Read Lamentations 3 – 5

Highlights: The loving compassion of God never fails (Lam. 3:23). By faith we seek Him (3:25-26); He always hears (3:55-57)! In worship, discipline is needed (3:27). He's our inheritance (3:24), Lawyer (3:58), and Judge (3:59). He is forever the same (5:19).

Jeremiah was one of the greatest prophets in biblical history; only a few have suffered so much public humiliation, rejection, and hostility. For more than 40 years, he warned the Israelites to follow the Lord, and obey His Law or else face the judgment of God for their sins. Because they failed to repent, they faced the inevitable destruction of their glorious Temple and Jerusalem, the City of God.

When God has to discipline His children, He often permits them to suffer in various ways. But this suffering has a twofold purpose: first, as judgment upon sin, and, second, to allow the offenders the opportunity to repent and commit their lives to Him. Jeremiah assures us: **Though He cause grief, yet will He have compassion according to the multitude of His mercies** (Lam. 3:32).

After the destruction of the Temple, the Israelites came to realize the awfulness of their sin and the consequences of disregarding His Word. They had assumed that the Covenant promise of God would continue even though they ignored their Covenant responsibility. Jeremiah called for a national confession of sin, repentance, and obedience to His Word. The prophet pleaded: **Let us search** (examine) **and try our ways, and turn again to the Lord** (3:40).

The once-powerful, proud kingdom of Judah was now subjected to every form of humiliation. Its people had to beg for bread from foreigners, pay for drinking water, and helplessly stand by and watch their children being taken as slaves into heavy, forced labor, knowing that these heathen soldiers had **ravished the women in Zion, and the maids in the cities of Judah** (5:11). Can we feel the heartbreak of the weeping prophet as he expresses his sorrow? **The crown is fallen from our head: woe unto us, that we have sinned** (5:16)!

The righteous suffer along with sinners in a wicked nation; but, for the Christian, suffering should help us see the true values of life. **We have had fathers ... which corrected us. ... they verily** (truly) **for a few days chastened us after their own pleasure** (judgment)**; but He** (God) **for our profit, that we might be partakers of His holiness** (Heb. 12:9-10).

Thought for Today: The Word of God imparts insight into true values.

Christ Revealed: As the merciful Savior (Lam. 3:22). **Keep yourselves in the love of God, looking for the mercy of our Lord Jesus Christ unto eternal life** (Jude 1:21).

Introduction To The Book Of EZEKIEL

Ezekiel lived in Jerusalem during the great reformation period that followed the discovery of the Law in the Temple. This was during the reign of Josiah, the last godly king of Judah (II Kin. 22:8-20; 23:1-29). After Josiah's death, the people chose his fourth son Jehoahaz as their king. Just three months later, Pharaoh-necho took him in chains to Egypt and set up Josiah's second son Eliakim as king over Judah (II Kin. 23:31-34; II Chr. 36:1-4). Pharaoh changed Eliakim's name to Jehoiakim (II Kin. 23:34-36). He was subject to Pharaoh-necho for about four years (Jer. 46:2); then Nebuchadnezzar defeated the Egyptians.

In the same year that he defeated Egypt, Nebuchadnezzar seized control of Jerusalem, stripped the capital and the Temple of its treasures and most of its golden vessels, and took many of the young royalty of Judah as captives to Babylon. Among them were Daniel and his three friends (Dan. 1:1-3,6; also Ezek. 33:21).

Nebuchadnezzar left Jehoiakim to be his puppet-ruler. Jehoiachin, Jehoiakim's 18-year-old son (also known as Jeconiah and Coniah), succeeded him and continued his father's evil policies (II Kin. 24:8-9). After only 3 months, Jehoiachin was also taken captive to Babylon, along with Ezekiel and 10,000 influential leaders and craftsmen.

Ezekiel's captivity began about eight years after Daniel was taken to Babylon. Ezekiel was placed at Tel-Abib near the Chebar River, an irrigation canal which routed water from the Euphrates in a large semi-circle through the countryside until it rejoined the Euphrates. Ezekiel prophesied for about 22 years (Ezek. 1:2; 29:17).

Nebuchadnezzar then appointed Mattaniah, the 3rd son of Josiah, to govern Judah and renamed him Zedekiah (II Kin. 24:17; I Chr. 3:15). During this time, Ezekiel's message was directed to his fellow captives as well as to the people remaining in the promised land. Both groups rejected Ezekiel's message. He eventually foretold the destruction of Jerusalem. After about 10 years, Zedekiah rebelled against the king and, as foretold by Ezekiel, Nebuchadnezzar once again attacked Jerusalem, broke down its walls and, this time, he destroyed the Temple built by Solomon. **None remained, save the poorest sort of the people of the land** (II Kin. 24:8-16,18 – 25:21; II Chr. 36:11-21).

The key thought in this book is the heart cry of our Creator, revealing the personal nature of His love for His creation! **They shall know that I am the Lord their God** (Ezek. 28:26; 39:22,28).

SEPTEMBER 1 — Read Ezekiel 1 – 4

Highlights: Ezekial 1:1 sets the stage: Ezekiel is a captive in Babylon when God calls him! No one can stand in the presence of God (Ezek. 1:26-28). The message to the people of Israel is also for us (2:8 – 3:17). Check our responsibility **carefully** (3:18-21)! Ezekiel acts out the messages of God (chap. 4).

As a captive of the most powerful nation on earth, Ezekiel was forced to live far from the promised land. But to Ezekiel's great joy, **the Word of the LORD came expressly unto Ezekiel the priest . . . in the land of the Chaldeans by the river Chebar; and the hand of the LORD was there upon him** (Ezek. 1:3).

In Ezekiel's first vision, **a whirlwind came out of the north, a great cloud, and a fire infolding itself** (flashing forth), **and a brightness was about it. . . . Also out of the midst thereof came the likeness of four living creatures. And . . . they had the likeness of a man** (1:4-5). The cherubim (angelic beings) were fulfilling the perfect will of God. Since the cherubim faced all directions simultaneously, it implied they were prepared to instantly obey the will of God in every situation (1:9,12,17).

Ezekiel remained a faithful servant of God even though he was forced from Jerusalem to live under the rule of heathens. In striking contrast, a multitude of "believers" today readily accept the standards of their secular surroundings, live like the world, and ignore taking responsibility in the Church which Christ died to establish. Jesus still must ask: **Why call ye Me, Lord, Lord, and do not the things which I say** (Luke 6:46)? He also warns: **Whosoever heareth these sayings of Mine, and doeth them, I will liken him unto a wise man . . . And every one that heareth these sayings of mine, and doeth them not, shall be likened unto a foolish man** (Matt. 7:24-26). **Not every one that saith unto Me, Lord, Lord, shall enter into the Kingdom of heaven; but he that doeth the will of My Father which is in heaven** (7:21).

To **believe on . . . Christ and . . . be saved** (Acts 16:31) is to forsake sin and live in obedience to His Word. **The devils also believe** (James 2:19) but, obviously, "don't do" the will of God. A true believer will **take up his cross daily, and follow** Jesus as Lord of his life (Luke 9:23). The Lord will protect and direct anyone who will **seek . . . first the Kingdom of God, and His righteousness** (Matt. 6:33).

Thought for Today: Regardless of our circumstances, we should trust the Lord and expect a good outcome.

Christ Revealed: In a *likeness as the appearance of a Man*, who sat upon the throne (Ezek. 1:26-28). This foreshadowed God appearing as a Man, **The Man Christ Jesus** (I Tlm. 2:5).

SEPTEMBER 2　　　　　　　　　　　Read Ezekiel 5 – 9

Highlights: What a haircut (Ezek. 5:1-4)! The reaction of God to disobedience (5:5-17) plus His prophesied consequences against Israel as the "End" nears (chap. 6, 7,9)! *They shall know that I am the LORD* (7:27).

Fourteen years after Nebuchadnezzar's initial conquest of the kingdom of Judah, life in Jerusalem seemed to have returned to normal. Consequently, its people would not believe Ezekiel when he prophesied concerning Jerusalem: *Your altars shall be desolate. . . . the cities shall be laid waste* (Ezek. 6:4,6). Even the Israelites who were captive in Babylon were sure that God would protect Jerusalem and the only Temple on earth where His Presence dwelt and sacrifices were made to Him. But Ezekiel continued to warn them: *He that is in the field shall die with the sword; and he that is in the city, famine and pestilence shall devour him* (7:15).

Fourteen months after his first vision (1:1-2), Ezekiel reported: *The Spirit . . . brought me in the visions of God to Jerusalem* (8:1-3). His visions revealed *the great abominations* (detestable things) *that the house of Israel committeth. . . . wicked abominations. . . . there sat women weeping for Tammuz* (the Babylonian god of fertility). *. . . men, with their backs toward the Temple of the LORD, and . . . they worshipped the sun* (8:6,9,14,16). As a result of their disobedience to the Word of God, the Israelites had *filled the land with violence* (8:17).

The people also would not believe his second vision that showed the reason for the horrifying judgment that was to come upon them. Jesus said: *It is written, Man shall not live by bread alone, but by every Word that proceedeth out of the mouth of God* (Matt. 4:4). Some believers are out of His will because of their overemphasis on material success. They place a low priority on reading His Word to learn why He created us and how He expects us to live.

Wealth was never meant to be selfishly accumulated or to be lavished on ourselves. God entrusts people with wealth, *that ye, always having all sufficiency in all things, may abound to every good work* (II Cor. 9:8). Having a right attitude of the heart is all-important since both rich and poor can lust after more possessions. The Holy Spirit warns: *They that will be rich fall into temptation and a snare* (trap), *and into many foolish and hurtful lusts, which drown men in destruction and perdition* (damnation) (I Tim. 6:9).

Thought for Today: *Godliness with contentment is great gain* (I Tim. 6:6).

Christ Portrayed: The man clothed in linen (Ezek. 9:2-11) represents Christ as High Priest, marking His people to be spared from the flaming sword of vengeance. *Seeing then that we have a great High Priest, that is passed into the heavens, Jesus the Son of God, let us hold fast* (firmly) *our profession* (confession) (Heb. 4:14; Rev. 7:2-3).

SEPTEMBER 3   Read Ezekiel 10 – 13

Highlights: Ezekiel foretold that our Creator God is **Jesus Christ the same yesterday, and today, and for ever** (Heb. 13:8). He has provided a new spirit within you. It is the only way for God to correct us (Ezek. 11:19-20). False prophets *that follow their own spirit* (not the Holy Spirit) are warned (13:3).

Ezekiel's vision revealed the dispatching of seven men – one to spare the faithful minority and six to slay the idolatrous majority of Israelites. **One man ... clothed with linen** marked the foreheads of all who remained faithful to the Lord (Ezek. 9:2-7). **Then the glory of the LORD departed from off the threshold of the House, and stood over the cherubims. And the cherubims lifted up their wings, and mounted up from the earth ... and every one stood at the door of the east gate of the LORD's House** (10:18-19).

Ezekiel observed the leaders of Jerusalem who, it seemed, were being blessed and called upon to remain in charge as the favored people, while so many others had been taken captive. But in reality, many of the deprived captives in Babylon eventually learned, through suffering, to repent of their pagan idolatry and trust in the Lord God of Israel. God promised a great future to those who were committed to Him. In Ezekiel's vision, as he prepared to leave the Temple, he saw the Presence of the Lord, who rested just above the Mercy Seat of the Ark of the Covenant in the Holy of Holies, slowly leaving the place where He had once chosen to dwell (Ex. 25:22).

As **the glory of the LORD went up from the midst of the city** (Ezek. 11:23), it reluctantly left **the city which the LORD did choose out of all the tribes of Israel, to put His Name there** (I Kin. 14:21).

It appears the Israelites were so involved in their idolatrous activities they were not even aware that God had forsaken them.

The Lord again gave Ezekiel a prophecy that reached far into the future: **I will put a new Spirit within you; and I will take the stony heart out of their flesh, and will give them an heart of flesh: That they may walk in My statutes** (decrees), **and keep Mine ordinances** (commands), **and do them: and they shall be My people, and I will be their God** (Ezek. 11:19-20; also 36:26-27).

Likewise, the Apostle Paul wrote: **Know ye not that ye are the Temple of God, and that the Spirit of God dwelleth in you** (I Cor. 3:16)**? Ye are ... of the household of God** (Eph. 2:19-20).

Thought for Today: True satisfaction and purpose are found only in Christ – never in material things.

Christ Revealed: As the One who gives *a new Spirit* (Ezek. 11:19). This is the promise fulfilled when we accept Jesus as our Savior and Lord of our lives. **God hath sent forth the Spirit of His Son into your hearts** (Gal. 4:4-7).

SEPTEMBER 4 — Read Ezekiel 14 – 16

Highlights: Each person is clearly accountable for his or her own choice to be saved (Ezek. 14:12-23). A breathtaking, tragic account of the love and faithfulness of God to Judah and her inconsiderate attitude (chap. 16). We must guard against spiritual adultery.

Although the Israelites regularly offered sacrifices to God, they also worshiped the idols of heathen nations. As judgment for their idolatry, they were brought under the control of Nebuchadnezzar, who took thousands captive. Once again, certain **elders of Israel** (Ezek. 14:1) came to consult Ezekiel, as if they desired to know the will of God. But the Lord revealed their hypocrisy to Ezekiel, saying: **These men have set up their idols in their heart. . . . Thus saith the Lord GOD; Repent, and turn yourselves from your idols; and turn away your faces from all your abominations** (detestable practices)**. . . . That the house of Israel . . . may be My people, and I may be their God** (14:3,6,11).

To illustrate their one purpose as the people of God, the Lord presented a parable to Ezekiel: **Is the vine tree** (the grapevine which was often used by God to symbolize the Israelites) **more than any tree . . . of the forest? Shall wood be taken thereof to do any work? or will men take a pin** (stake) **of it to hang any vessel thereon? Behold, it is cast into the fire for fuel** (15:2-4; Gen. 49:22; Deut. 32:32; Ps. 80:8-11; Jer. 2:21; Hos. 10:1). Every Israelite knew that the grapevine was valued only for its fruit and was worthless for making anything useful or of lasting value.

The vineyard of the LORD of hosts is the house of Israel (Is. 5:7), a nation that was chosen by God to let the world know there was only One True God. But **the vine** had failed to produce fruit; consequently it was to be uprooted and **cast into the fire** (Ezek. 15:4,7). This was a word picture of the Israelites being uprooted from the promised land and forced to live in Babylon.

The righteous judgment of God upon those in Jerusalem had to be consistent with the great privileges they had willfully misused. The principles of His Word are still true today. **No whoremonger, nor unclean person, nor covetous man, who is an idolater, hath any inheritance in the Kingdom . . . of God. Let no man deceive you with vain words: for because of these things cometh the wrath of God upon the children of disobedience** (Eph. 5:5-6).

Thought for Today: Consider your priorities today. Are they wrapped up in the things of the world or committed to serving the Lord?

Christ Revealed: In the **everlasting Covenant** (Ezek. 16:60). **He is the Mediator of a better Covenant** (Agreement) (Heb. 8:6).

SEPTEMBER 5 — Read Ezekiel 17 – 19

Highlights: Two eagles, symbolic of Babylon and Egypt, and three kings. The last two kings of Israel are removed by the Lord Himself (Ezek. 17:22-24; Is. 11:1). A just God deals with sinners (18:19-24). Turn and live (18:31-32; 19:14).

Ezekiel was given another parable: *A great eagle* (Nebuchadnezzar) *with great wings ... full of feathers, which had divers* (many) *colours, came unto Lebanon, and took the highest branch of the cedar: He cropped off the top of his* (its) *young twigs, and carried it into a land of traffick* (traders); *he set it in a city of merchants* (Ezek. 17:3-4).

This parable illustrates the vast extent of Nebuchadnezzar's dominion. The eagle's feathers represent the great number of nations he had conquered. Removing *the highest branch* symbolized Jehoiachin, king of Judah, and *a city of merchants* was Babylon, where Jehoiachin would be taken captive.

There was also another great eagle with great wings and many feathers (Egypt): *and, behold, this vine did bend her roots toward him* (17:7). The Lord God told Ezekiel to tell the people: *Thus saith the Lord GOD; Shall it prosper? shall he not pull up the roots thereof ... that it wither* (17:9)? The purpose of this important prophecy was to warn King Zedekiah not to betray his oath of submission to Nebuchadnezzar by forming an alliance with Egypt. The vow made to Nebuchadnezzar and sworn to in the Name of God was binding (Num. 30:2, II Chr. 36:13). Zedekiah foolishly chose to disobey the instruction of God.

In the ninth year of his reign, King Zedekiah made a military treaty with Egypt. As a consequence, Nebuchadnezzar besieged Jerusalem, and the people suffered many months of famine and pestilence before the city and Temple were captured and utterly destroyed.

Nebuchadnezzar's invasion of Judah could have been averted if Zedekiah kept his vow. We, too, are obligated to keep promises, even those made with the unsaved (Ps. 15:4) . There are always consequences when we break our promises whether it be a marriage vow or a business transaction. *If a man vow a vow* (a promise) *unto the LORD, or swear an oath to bind his soul* (obligate himself) *with a bond; he shall not break his word* (Num. 30:2).

When thou vowest a vow unto God ... pay it; for He hath no pleasure in fools: pay that which thou hast vowed (Ecc. 5:4).

Thought for Today: All who love the Lord will keep His Commandments.

Christ Revealed: As the One whose forgiveness provides life everlasting (Ezek. 18:20-22). *For God so loved* (the people of) *the world, that He gave His only begotten Son* (Jesus)*, that whosoever believeth in Him should not perish, but have everlasting life* (John 3:16).

SEPTEMBER 6 — Read Ezekiel 20 – 21

Highlights: Israel's leaders refuse to listen to the prophets of God. The consequences are inevitable (Ezek. chap. 20). God guides Babylon to fulfill His judgment against Israel (21:3). A fork in the road. Babylon heads for Judah (21:18-23). God accuses the people of open sin with no shame (21:24).

The king and the religious leaders of Judah had expressed growing hatred for Ezekiel because of his messages of judgment against them. When a person or nation continually ignores or rejects His Word, there may come a time when God will say: **Then shall they call upon Me, but I will not answer** (Prov. 1:28). This was the case with Jerusalem. It was too late for them to ask God to spare them from destruction. However, Ezekiel records: **Certain of the elders of Israel came to inquire** (ask for guidance) **of the LORD** (Ezek. 20:1). Then God gave Ezekiel the following message for them: **I will not be inquired of by you . . . . I chose Israel. . . . But they rebelled against Me. . . . they despised My judgments . . . for their heart went after their idols** (20: 3,5,8,16).

Following this, Ezekiel received a terrifying message from the Lord for Israel: **I am against thee, and will draw forth My sword. . . . to give it into the hand of the slayer** (21:3,11).

Ezekiel's prophecy of the sharpened sword was a message of impending destruction. King Zedekiah, the **profane wicked prince of Israel** (21:25), and the people would soon be captured. Jerusalem and the Temple would be destroyed by Nebuchadnezzar. But, he was unknowingly being used to fulfill the judgment of God upon His rebellious people. This is a reminder that **the lot is cast into the lap; but the whole disposing thereof is of the LORD** (Prov. 16:33). Again and again God orchestrates events, people, and circumstances to fulfill His righteous purposes.

No king has been anointed to sit on David's throne in Israel for the past 2,500 years. As Ezekiel foretold: **Thus saith the Lord GOD; Remove the diadem** (turban), **and take off the crown. . . . I will overturn, overturn, overturn, it: and it shall be no more, until He come whose right it is; and I will give it** (to) **Him** (Ezek. 21:26-27).

According to the purpose and prophetic Word of God, the promised land will continue to exist without a king until the return of Jesus Christ as **King of kings, and Lord of lords** (I Tim. 6:15).

Thought for Today: God is full of compassion toward all who hear His call, repent, and turn to Him "today" – tomorrow could be too late.

Christ Revealed: As the One who will gather His people from all nations and **will purge out** the false from the true (Ezek. 20:34-38). **When the Son of Man shall come . . . then shall He sit upon the throne of His glory: And before Him shall be gathered all nations: and He shall separate them one from another. . . . And these shall go away into everlasting punishment: but the righteous into life eternal** (Matt. 25:31-46; also 3:12).

SEPTEMBER 7 — Read Ezekiel 22 – 24

Highlights: Ezekiel's mission: Denounce Judah's terrible deeds in public (Ezek. 22). Who will save them (22:30)? Tale of two sisters who betray God and cause destruction (23:2-3,30,46-49). Who are they (23:4)? The Israelites' complete corruption in a boiling pot (24:3); judgment follows (24:6-14). Did you get the message when Ezekiel's wife died (24:15-24)?

On the very day that God revealed to Ezekiel that his precious wife, **the desire** (delight) **of thine eyes**, was to die, God also said: **Yet neither shalt thou mourn nor weep, neither shall thy tears run down** (Ezek. 24:16). Ezekiel was told by the Lord to refrain from all the conventional signs of mourning. It was not that he was to be insensitive to his wife's death, but his own personal grief was to give way to the far greater heartbreak over the people of God and the coming destruction of His Temple. **Thus saith the Lord G**OD**; I will bring up a company upon them, and will give them to be removed and spoiled** (plundered). **And the company ... shall slay their sons and their daughters ... and ye shall bear the sins of your idols: and ye shall know that I am the Lord G**OD (23:46-47,49).

News of Ezekiel's unusual reaction to his wife's death must have spread quickly, for the people asked: **Wilt thou not tell us what these things are to us** (24:19)**?** Then came the tragic news from Ezekiel: **Thus saith the Lord G**OD**; Behold, I will profane My Sanctuary ... and your sons and your daughters whom ye have left shall fall by the sword. ... when this cometh, ye shall know that I am the Lord G**OD (24:21-24).

Eventually, an escapee from Jerusalem arrived in Babylon to report the city's destruction (33:21). The Israelites' acceptance of false gods and their indifference to the True God had brought about the destruction of Jerusalem and the death of their own sons and daughters, just as they had been forewarned by Jeremiah in Jerusalem and by Ezekiel in Babylonia (Gal. 6:7-8).

Jesus told His disciples not to be preoccupied with earthly things, not even our daily needs: **For all these things do the nations** (heathen) **of the world seek after: and your Father knoweth that ye have need of these things. ... But seek ye first the Kingdom of God, and His righteousness; and all these** (material and otherwise) **things shall be added unto you** (Luke 12:30; Matt. 6:33).

Thought for Today: Allow Christ to truly be Lord of your life.

Christ Revealed: In the denunciation of Israel's false prophets (Ezek. 22:25-28). Compare them with those Christ spoke against, the scribes and the Pharisees. **Woe unto you, scribes and Pharisees** (Matt. 23:13-36).

SEPTEMBER 8   Read Ezekiel 25 – 28

Highlights: Six of Judah's enemies are warned of their destruction by the Lord. Can you name them and tell what they did against God? (See Ezek. 25:1,3,8,12,15; 26:2; 28:2, 21,24.)

Tyre was situated on the Mediterranean Sea and was one of the richest cities of the world. Its wealth was not gained from war, like that of Babylon, but from commercial business. Its fleet of ships was the greatest of all nations. Ezekiel prophesied: ***The Word of the Lord came unto me . . . I am against thee, O Tyrus*** (Ezek. 26:1,3). God foretold that Tyre would be destroyed, not only because of its immoral idolatry but also because it was rejoicing over the downfall of Jerusalem because its economic competition no longer existed. It was saying: ***Aha, she is broken . . . I shall be replenished*** (grow rich), ***now*** (that) ***she is laid waste*** (26:2).

Only God, could have known what would happen to the city. ***They shall destroy the walls of Tyrus, and break down her towers: I will also scrape her dust from her, and make her like the top of a rock. It shall be a place for the spreading of nets in the midst of the sea*** (26:4-5). Nebuchadnezzar later destroyed the mainland city. During that long siege, Tyre's administration and wealth was moved to the offshore island section of the city. More than two centuries later, Alexander the Great besieged Tyre, which was then just an island city nearly half a mile from the mainland. Since he had no ships, his men used the stones from the walls of the ancient mainland city to build a causeway to reach the island and destroy it, exactly as prophesied.

Knowing that God sees all things, the attitude of Tyre should be a warning to those who rejoice when their competition goes bankrupt, or to the "Christian" who resents the success of his "rivals" in church or in the marketplace. Christians have much to repent of here. Gossip does more damage than we can imagine when we rejoice over the so-called "failures" of others.

It is good to remember: ***These six things doth the Lord hate: yea, seven are an abomination unto Him: A proud look, a lying tongue, and hands that shed innocent blood, An heart that deviseth wicked imaginations, feet that be swift in running to mischief, A false witness that speaketh lies, and he that soweth discord among brethren*** (Prov. 6:16-19).

Thought for Today: When tempted, determine in your heart to remain faithful to God.

Christ Revealed: As the One who will rule over the destruction of Satan at the end of time: ***Therefore will I bring forth a fire . . . it shall devour thee*** (Ezej, 28:18-19). As Jesus reigns following the Great White Throne Judgment, ***the Devil*** (Satan ***. . . was cast into the lake of fire*** (Rev. 20:1-10,14).

SEPTEMBER 9   Read Ezekiel 29 – 32

Highlights: Another enemy and its destiny (Ezek. 29:3,13-15)! How quickly we forget the days of slavery (29:16)! A sad day for Egypt and its allies (30:2-8). Egypt, a prideful and arrogant nation (chap. 31). Look who God uses to defeat the Egyptians (32:11). Read the list of others who were judged by God (32:17-31).

About a year after the Babylonians surrounded Jerusalem, planning to starve them into submission, Ezekiel foretold the end of Egypt as a great nation. God said: **Son of man, set thy face against Pharaoh king of Egypt, and prophesy against him, and against all Egypt. . . . because they have been a staff of reed** (worthless support) **to the house of Israel. . . . Behold, I will bring a sword upon thee, and cut off man and beast out of thee. And the land of Egypt shall be desolate and waste. . . . neither shall it be inhabited forty years** (Ezek. 29:2-11). Although Egypt would no longer be a great power in the world, it would not be utterly destroyed as Babylon would be. Ezekiel foretold: **At the end of forty years will I gather the Egyptians . . . into the land of their habitation** (origin); **and they shall be there a base** (lowly) **kingdom. . . . neither shall it exalt itself any more above the nations: for I will diminish them, that they shall no more rule over the nations** (29:13-15). Over the centuries, Egypt has never regained the status of a world empire. It remains a witness to the supreme authority of God.

God brought judgment upon Israel, Judah, Tyre, Sidon, Egypt, and other nations to cause them to realize **that I am the Lord** (Self Existent God) (29:9). This phrase is mentioned 66 times in this book alone to point out the importance of obeying the Word of God.

An as yet future time of redemption and restoration was also foretold: **In that day will I cause the horn** (strength) **of the house of Israel to bud forth** (29:21). The horn is a symbol of power (I Sam. 2:10; Ps. 92:10). As prophesied, the people of God, both Jew and Gentile, have a future destiny of glory with Jesus as their Messiah. **God . . . hath. . . . given Him** (Jesus) **a Name which is above every name: That at the Name of Jesus every knee should bow, of things in heaven, and things in earth, and things under the earth; And that every tongue should confess that Jesus Christ is Lord, to the glory of God the Father** (Phil. 2:9-11).

Thought for Today: Regardless of our circumstances, we should trust the Lord and expect a good outcome.

Christ Revealed: In a *likeness as the appearance of a Man*, who sat upon the throne (Ezek. 1:26-28). This foreshadowed God appearing as a Man, **The Man Christ Jesus** (I Tim. 2:5).

SEPTEMBER 10   **Read Ezekiel 33 – 36**

Highlights: Our responsibility and judgment as watchmen (Ezek. 33:8-17). What is self accountability (33:20)? The Good Shepherd (34:11-20). The Covenant of Peace (34:25-31). Don't slander Israel (chap. 35)! Although God disciplines us, He's our hope (36:9,22-30).

God addressed Ezekiel as *a watchman unto the house of Israel*; and said to him: *Therefore thou shalt hear the Word at My mouth, and warn them from Me* (Ezek. 33:7). The Israelites disregarded Ezekiel's warnings that God would destroy Jerusalem if they refused to repent. The Jews in Babylon complained that the death of their kindred and the destruction of their homeland were inconsistent with the promise of the Covenant of God. Then the Lord said to Ezekiel: *Thy people say, The way of the LORD is not equal* (right): *but. . . . When the righteous turneth from his righteousness, and committeth iniquity* (sin), *he shall . . . die. . . . But if the wicked turn from his wickedness . . . he shall live* (33:17-19).

When the inevitable judgment had taken place as foretold by Ezekiel: *It came to pass in the twelfth year of our captivity . . . one that had escaped out of Jerusalem came unto me, saying, The city is smitten* (33:21). Then the Lord told him to say: *Ye . . . lift up your eyes toward your idols, and shed blood: and shall ye possess the land? . . . ye work abomination* (do detestable sins). *. . . As I live, surely they . . . shall fall by the sword, and . . . die of the pestilence. For I will lay the land most desolate. . . . Then shall they know that I am the LORD* (33:25-29).

Ezekiel proclaimed that holy living was the Israelites' responsibility in their Covenant relationship with God. This was rejected by those who were unwilling to forsake their sins. Times have not changed; living a godly life is equally unpopular today with many "professing Christians" who love what the world can offer for the gratification of the sinful human nature (I John 2:15-17).

Like the Israelites, many people today talk about the love of God while ignoring His command to live righteously. *As ye have yielded your members* (body parts) *servants to uncleanness and to iniquity unto iniquity* (sins leading to more sins); *even so now yield your members servants to righteousness unto holiness* (sanctification). *. . . for the end of those things* (sin) *is death* (Rom. 6:19,21).

Thought for Today: Sinful conduct cannot bring lasting satisfaction.

Christ Revealed: As the Shepherd (Ezek. 34:23). Jesus said: *I am the Good Shepherd, and know My sheep* (John:14).

SEPTEMBER 11 — Read Ezekiel 37 – 39

Highlights: All of us are just dry, dead bones – **dead in trespasses and sin** (Eph. 2:1) – until God fills us with eternal life (Ezek. 37:13-14). Like Job, the latter end of Israel will be far greater than its beginning (37:24-28). You need to know verses 38:23 and 39:25.

After Nebuchadnezzar destroyed Jerusalem in 586 BC, most of the Israelites who survived were scattered throughout Babylonia among exiles from many heathen nations. Since the Temple and the City of God were destroyed, the people abandoned hope for its restoration. It was at this time of national hopelessness that Ezekiel was given a new vision: **The hand of the LORD was upon me, and carried me out in the Spirit of the LORD, and set me down in the midst of the valley which was full of bones** (Ezek. 37:1).

The bones were dry and bleached by the sun, having been there for a long time. **And He said unto me, Son of man, can these bones live? And I answered, O Lord GOD, Thou knowest. Again He said unto me, Prophesy upon these bones, and say unto them: O ye dry bones, hear the Word of the LORD. Thus saith the Lord GOD unto these bones; Behold, I will cause breath to enter into you, and ye shall live** (37:3-5).

As a nation, Israel was spiritually dead. However, like the dry bones, it was not buried. Ezekiel continued to prophesy: **There was a noise, and behold a shaking, and the bones came together, bone to his bone** (37:7). Ezekiel proclaimed the Word of God: **And the breath came into them, and they lived, and stood up upon their feet, an exceeding great army** (37:10).

Ezekiel then was commanded to proclaim the good news: **I am the LORD ... And shall put My Spirit in you, and ye shall live, and I shall place you in your own land** (37:13-14). After more than 2,500 years, Israel is a nation within the promised land, and God will soon fulfill His promise to King David. Israel's Messiah-King, Jesus Christ, will rule the world from Jerusalem (Is. 2:1-4).

Dry bones also describe our sinful human nature, apart from the transforming, life-giving power of the Holy Spirit. Eternal life is made possible only when we confess and repent of our sins and invite Jesus to be Savior and Lord of our lives.

Salvation is freely offered to all **for by grace are ye saved through faith; and that not of yourselves: it is the gift of God: Not of works, lest any man should boast** (Eph. 2:8-9).

Thought for Today: Jesus is coming soon! What a great and glorious day that will be!

Christ Revealed: As the One who made possible the resurrection from the grave (Ezek. 37:12). **For the Lord Himself shall descend from heaven with a shout ... and the dead in Christ shall rise first** (I Thess. 4:13-18; John 11:25; Rev. 1:18).

SEPTEMBER 12   Read Ezekiel 40 – 42

Highlights: A spectacular Temple in which Jesus can dwell when He returns to earth to reign for 1,000 years is outlined in today's chapters.

A few years after the vision of dry bones, Ezekiel received another vision. *In the five and twentieth year of our captivity . . . in the fourteenth year after that the city was smitten, in the selfsame day the hand of the L*ORD *was upon me. . . . In the visions of God brought He me into the land of Israel, and set me upon a very high mountain* (Ezel. 40:1-2). This vision looked far into the future where Ezekiel beheld a glorious Temple, far more magnificent than the one Solomon built.

Only measurements of the grounds and the many details concerning the building and its unusual architectural design were given to Ezekiel. In striking contrast, God gave Moses detailed instructions for building the Tabernacle and even the names of the craftsmen who were to build it in the wilderness (Ex. 25:9; 31:1-11). But Zechariah foretold: *Thus speaketh the L*ORD *of hosts . . . Behold the man whose Name is The BRANCH* (Jesus Christ) *. . . He shall grow up out of His place, and He shall build the Temple of the L*ORD*: Even He shall build the Temple of the L*ORD*; and He shall bear the glory, and shall sit and rule upon His throne; and He shall be a priest upon His throne: and the counsel of peace shall be between them both* (Zech. 6:12-13).

Almost 2,000 years have passed since the Romans destroyed the Temple, with no recovery of the Brazen Altar, Laver of Brass, Pure Gold Candlestick and Mercy Seat, Table of Showbread, or Altar of Incense. The Ark of the Covenant disappeared in 586 BC, when Nebuchadnezzar destroyed Jerusalem.

The altar and the priests offering sacrifices for the sins of the people had all foreshadowed Jesus Christ, His atonement for our sins and our relationship with Him through His sacrifice on the cross. Through the Romans who destroyed Herod's temple, God removed the opportunity for the Jews to offer further sacrifices.

These laws were *imposed on them until the time of reformation. But Christ being come an High Priest . . . by a greater and more perfect Tabernacle . . . by His own blood He entered in once into the Holy Place, having obtained eternal redemption for us* (Heb. 9:10-12; comp. John 4:21-24; Gal. 3:23-25; Col. 2:17).

Thought for Today: We always seek first after what our hearts treasure most – whether it is the Lord or things of the world – it can't be both.

Christ Revealed: Through the Temple (Ezek. 40). Christ indwells His people who have become temples of God (I Cor. 6:10-20; II Cor. 6:16-17),

SEPTEMBER 13 — Read Ezekiel 43 – 45

Highlights: God is back! His glory fills the Temple once again (Ezek. 43:5)! The Holy Altar. Pay attention to the rules of God (chap 44). God expects us to support His ministry (chap 45). Note the keeping of the Passover pointing to Christ's death on the cross (45:21-24).

In a vision, Ezekiel had witnessed the departure of ***the glory of the God of Israel*** from the Temple and Jerusalem (Ezek. 9:3; 10:4,18-19; 11:22-23). Jerusalem and the once-glorious kingdom of Israel were only memories. The Israelites had chosen pagan practices and actually worshiped idols, the sun, and all sorts of creatures in the Temple that had been dedicated to God alone (8:5-17).

As judgment for their idolatry, the majority of Israelites were enslaved in a heathen land. Again Ezekiel received a vision of a future Temple, far greater than Solomon's, where the glory of the Lord would return to dwell. Ezekiel was ***brought . . . to the gate . . . that looketh toward the east: And, behold, the glory of the God of Israel came from the way of the east: and His voice was like a noise of many waters: and the earth shined with His glory. . . . And the glory of the LORD came into the House by the way of the gate whose prospect*** (face) ***is toward the east. So the Spirit took me up, and brought me into the inner court; and, behold, the glory of the LORD filled the House*** (43:1-2,4-5).

In this vision, the Lord of Glory entered His new Temple the same way through which He had departed from the former Temple (10:19; 11:22-23). The Eastern Gate led straight to the Temple entrance of the eternal King, who said: ***I will dwell in the midst of the children of Israel for ever, and My Holy Name, shall the house of Israel no more defile*** (43:7).

The physical Temple had foreshadowed the life and ministry of Christ. In the millennium there will be no need for types or symbols because God the Father and Jesus Christ, whom the symbols represented, will be present. Our preoccupation should not be with how and when the prophecies will be fulfilled; but above all else we should be concerned that we are prepared for the Lord's return.

Until then, ***know . . . that ye are the Temple of God, and that the Spirit of God dwelleth in you . . . If any man defile the Temple of God, him shall God destroy; for the Temple of God is holy, which Temple ye are*** (I Cor. 3:16-17).

Thought for Today: Determine that today others will see Christ in you.

Christ Revealed: As *the glory of the LORD* (Ezek. 1:26-28). Jesus is *the brightness of His* (God) *glory, and the express image of His Person* (Heb. 1:3).

SEPTEMBER 14 — Read Ezekiel 46 – 48

Highlights: Reminders of our Lord Jesus Christ. We see the Prince of Peace (Ezek. 46), the River of Healing (chap. 47), the land (chap. 48) with the Temple in the center (48:8), and *the LORD is there* (48:35).

The first part of Ezekiel's final vision from God described the **Temple** (Ezek. 40 – 43); the second part described the worship and the character of the worshipers (44 – 46). The final part tells us of life-giving waters that **issued out from under the threshold** (doorway) **of the house eastward** (47 – 48) and of the boundaries and divisions of the land. The further this water flowed, the deeper it became. Among other things, it symbolizes our continued walk with the Lord, for as we experience more and more the all-sufficiency of His provision, we come to realize that His supply for all of our needs is abundant and unlimited.

This is a vision anticipating the glorious future that all believers in Jesus as the Messiah will experience. All who know and love Him as their Savior will enjoy the new promised land during the millennial reign of our Lord Jesus Christ.

Ezekiel was led by his guide to the front of the Temple. The water apparently emerged from under the Eastern Gate as a small stream that flowed *a thousand cubits,* a little less than one-third of a mile. Ezekiel then records: **The man ... brought me through the waters** (47:2-3). Ezekiel states that it was ankle-deep. The same process was repeated at a second and at a third time, each distance measuring *a thousand cubits*. At these locations, the water was found to be **to the knees** and then **to the loins** (47:4). At a fourth distance of *a thousand* cubits (47:5), the water had become *a river that could not be passed over* because of its depth.

Water provides life for the trees which bear wholesome fruit (47:9,12). This is what the Holy Spirit does in the lives of those who yield to Him. We begin to experience His gracious supply as a small stream which flows out from Christ the Fountainhead, and continues to increase in preciousness as we daily walk in the light of His Word.

Our loving Father has prepared for His people *a pure river of water of life, clear as crystal, proceeding* (flowing) *out of the throne of God and of the Lamb,* the Lord Jesus Christ. ... *And whosoever will, let him take the water of life freely* (Rev. 22:1,17).

Thought for Today: The living water is available to all who *thirst after righteousness* (Matt. 5:6).

Christ Revealed: Through the river of living waters and in *the name of the city*, one of the names of God, *Jehovah (Yahweh)-Shammah* meaning: *The LORD is there* (Ezek. 47:1-12;48:35; Rev. 21 – 22).

INTRODUCTION TO THE BOOK OF DANIEL

The first chapter of Daniel is written in Hebrew, but chapters 2 – 7 are in Aramaic, the common language of the Israelites during their stay in Babylon as well as the common language spoken when Jesus was on earth. Chapters 1 – 7 describe Daniel and some of his fellow exiles who remained faithful to God despite life-threatening pressures. These **children of Israel, and of the king's seed** (royal family), **and of the princes** were among the first captives taken to Babylon (Dan. 1:1-17).

In chapters 8 – 12, Daniel writes in Hebrew of some events that are still future. Daniel's ministry covered the entire period of Judah's Baby-lonian captivity. He served as an official in the courts of both the Chaldean and Medo-Persian dynasties. He wrote during a time when the Jews were suffering great sorrow over the loss of life and of all their possessions in Jerusalem. The Book of Daniel gave comfort to the exiles and assurance of Israel's eventual triumph over its enemies. His writings were probably the basis for the wise men who, hundreds of years later, entered Jerusalem, saying: **Where is He that is born King of the Jews? for we have seen His star in the east, and are come to worship Him** (Matt. 2:2).

Only Daniel, through his God-given ability, could interpret the meaning of the giant image in Nebuchadnezzar's dream. God used this to move him into a position of administrative prominence. Nebuchadnezzar's dream image in chapter 2 and the first of Daniel's visions in chapter 7 both give similar outlines of the empires of Babylon, Medo-Persia, Greece, and Rome. These were nations that would successively rule the world. Near the end of this present age, the Antichrist will make **war with the saints** (Dan. 7:21), the faithful followers of the One True God. Then Jesus Christ will return and establish His Kingdom, **which shall never be destroyed** (2:44). The Stone cut without hands, which ultimately **became a great mountain, and filled the whole earth** (2:34-35), refers to Jesus Christ.

This book reveals the sovereignty of God over the affairs of man. Soon His Kingdom will fill **the whole earth**. Although it is far easier to get excited over details of future events, obedience is clearly the central theme and of primary importance in this great book. Jesus quoted Daniel when He spoke of the **abomination of desolation** (Matt. 24:15; Mark 13:14; compare Dan. 9:27; 11:31; 12:11) and of the **great tribulation** (Matt. 24:21; Dan. 12:1).

Two Views Of Governments That Rule During "The Times Of The Gentiles"

Nebuchadnezzar's Dream (DANIEL 2:31-45)
Daniel's Visions (DANIEL 7:1-14; 8:1-14)

Babylon is represented by *this image's head... of fine gold* (2:31-32,37-38; 7:4,17). The head of gold in Nebuchadnezzar's dream was seen in Daniel's vision as a lion with eagle's wings. Both the head of gold and the lion represent Nebuchadnezzar, the king who conquered Israel, which represents the earthly Kingdom of God.

Medo-Persia is represented in Nebuchadnezzar's dream by *his breast and his arms of silver* (2:32,39; 7:5,17; 8:3-4; 11:1-2). But, in Daniel's vision, they were seen as a bear with three ribs in its mouth. The bear and the ram with two horns represented Medo-Persia.

Greece is represented in Nebuchadnezzar's dream by *his belly and his thighs of brass* (2:32,39; 7:6,17; 8:5-8,21-22; 11:3-20). In Daniel's vision, the stomach and thighs of brass were seen instead as a leopard with four wings of a bird on its back. Like a leopard, Greece was swift in conquering the known world under the youthful Alexander the Great. In Daniel's second vision, he saw a ram and a he-goat (8:5-8). The one-horned goat (Greece) trampled the ram (Medo-Persia) to pieces. After his death, Alexander's kingdom was divided among his four generals, represented by the four heads of the leopard.

Rome is represented by *his legs of iron* (2:33,40-44; 7:7-8,23-24), **which Daniel interpreted from Nebuchadnezzar's dream** (2:33,40-43). They were the two great divisions of Rome. They are seen in Daniel's vision as a dreadful beast with iron teeth, ten big horns and one little horn. After defeating Greece, Rome (the beast) was the fourth great empire to rule the world.

Revived from Rome (The New World Order) *(10 toes... part of iron, and part of clay)* (2:40-44; 7:7-8,23-24). This confederacy will consist of 10 kings. In his intent to destroy Christianity and rule the world, one day soon the Antichrist (the **little horn** of 7:8,24; 8:9) will defeat 3 of the 10 kingdoms of this confederation. Ultimately, the New World Order will be destroyed by Jesus Christ (**the Stone** of 2:45) who will then set up His 1000 year earthly kingdom for all of His true followers.

A Stone was cut out without hands, which smote the image... and brake them to pieces
Daniel 2:34,44-45

THE WORLD'S POINT OF VIEW

A dazzling giant to be admired and achieved at any price: *The lust of the flesh, and the lust of the eyes, and the pride of life (one's lifestyle)* [I John 2:15-17].

FROM THE POINT OF VIEW OF GOD

The world system is full of pride, selfishness, greed, and cruelty, but is only temporary: *The world passeth away, and the lust thereof: but he that doeth the will of God abideth for ever* [I John 2:15-17].

SEPTEMBER 15   Read Daniel 1 – 3

Highlights: Daniel's faith is a prime example of the importance of teaching young people. Even as a teenage captive (Dan. 1:1-3), he would not defile himself (1:8-16). He declares that wisdom is from God (2:19-28).

Soon after their capture, Daniel and other selected Israelite captives were assigned new names which would identify them as citizens of Babylon. This was an attempt to remove their identities as children of God and be taught to think and live like Babylonians. Daniel's name means "God is Judge," but his Babylonian name Belteshazzar means "Prince of Baal."

As Daniel heard his new name called daily, it was intended to remind him that the comfort, esteem, and high position he enjoyed in his new society were all the result of his being the "Prince of Baal."

Nebuchadnezzar dreamed dreams, wherewith his spirit was troubled.... The king commanded to call ... the Chaldeans, for to shew the king his dreams.... The Chaldeans answered before the king, and said, There is not a man upon the earth that can shew the king's matter (Dan. 2:1-2,10). But, after Daniel and his friends prayed, the secret was revealed to **Daniel in a night vision**, and he proclaimed to the king that **there is a God in heaven that revealeth secrets, and maketh known to the King Nebuchadnezzar what shall be in the latter days** (2:19,28).

Daniel revealed to Nebuchadnezzar that the giant image in his dream represented successive kingdoms that would rule the world. The **head was of fine gold** and represented Nebuchadnezzar. **His breast and his arms of silver** symbolized the Medo-Persian Empire, which would become the next dominating world power. The Grecian Empire, represented by **his belly and his thighs of brass** came next. The fourth empire, with **his legs of iron, his feet part of iron and part of clay** (2:32-33), depicted the Roman Empire.

The Roman Empire will be revived as a one-world government in the end times. But it will be destroyed at the return of Christ, whose kingdom **shall never be destroyed** (2:44). The exact details may not be clear, but it is vitally important to be prepared for the soon coming of our King. **For now we see through a glass, darkly; but then face to face: now I know in part; but then shall I know even as also I am known** (I Cor. 13:12; comp. Acts 1:7).

Thought for Today: Jesus holds today and all your tomorrows.

Christ Revealed: As *the Stone that smote the image* (Dan. 2:35). *The Stone* is Jesus Christ (Acts 4:11; Eph. 2:20; I Pet. 2:4-8).

SEPTEMBER 16   Read Daniel 4 – 6

Highlights: Nebuchadnezzar's response to the interpretation of his dream (Dan. 4:34-37). Writing on the wall. The importance of the Holiness of God (5:23-24). Jealousy brings attack on Daniel (6:6-9), who trusts God and is honored (6:10,22,28). God punishes (6:24). God praised (6:26-27).

Belshazzar ruled Babylon near the end of the 70-year Jewish captivity. On the night the Medo-Persian army invaded Babylon and executed Belshazzar, he was celebrating a great feast with *a thousand of his lords . . . they brought the golden vessels that were taken out of the Temple . . . at Jerusalem; and . . . drank in them. . . . and praised the gods of gold, and of silver* (Dan. 5:1-4).

Suddenly the *fingers of a man's hand* (5:5) appeared and wrote on the wall. With great fear, Belshazzar panicked *and his knees smote* (struck) *one against another* (5:6). To his dismay, his astrologers and soothsayers were unable to interpret the message.

In desperation, Belshazzar summoned Daniel who boldly revealed the meaning of the handwriting: *This is the interpretation . . . God hath numbered thy kingdom, and finished it* (5:26). That night *Darius . . . took the kingdom* (5:31).

Darius decided *to set over the kingdom an hundred and twenty princes . . . over the whole kingdom; And over these, three presidents; of whom Daniel was first.* Because of envy, the other presidents and princes said to the king: *All . . . have consulted together to establish a royal statute . . . that whosoever shall ask a petition of any God or man for thirty days, save of thee, O king, he shall be cast into the den of lions* (6:1-2,7-8). Without realizing its real purpose, the king signed the decree.

Now when Daniel knew that the writing was signed, he went into his house; and his windows being open in his chamber (room) *toward Jerusalem, he kneeled upon his knees three times a day, and prayed, and gave thanks before his God, as he did aforetime* (6:10). We need to ask ourselves: "If a similar decree were issued today, would it make a difference if we were told by government officials that we could not worship in church on the Lord's Day?" Yes, Daniel ended up in *the den of lions* but, afterwards he was able to testify to the king: *My God hath sent His angel, and hath shut the lions' mouths* (Dan. 6:22).

Thought for Today: Pride blinds the mind to the will of God.

Christ Portrayed: By Daniel – a stone was rolled across the mouth of the den of lions and set with the king's seal (Dan. 6:16-17). There was a stone rolled across the mouth of the cave where Jesus was buried and it too was set with an official seal (Matt. 27:63-66). As Daniel came forth unscathed, so Jesus came forth from the dead proclaiming the saving power of God (Rev. 1:18).

SEPTEMBER 17 Read Daniel 7 – 9

Highlights: God reveals to Daniel what will happen in the future (Dan. 7:1-14)! His first vision explained (7:15-28). His second vision explained (8:19-27). A loving Creator provides understanding (9:22-27).

After the awesome grandeur of Nebuchadnezzar's dream of world governments is described (Dan. 2:19-45), the Lord reveals, through Daniel, another dream that exposes man's selfish ambition and use of cruel, savage power. Daniel said: *I saw in my vision ... and, behold, the four winds of the heaven strove upon the great sea* (7:2). *The great sea* represents fallen humanity. The *four winds* illustrate the impact of selfish ambition and greed.

Four great beasts came up from the sea, diverse (different) *one from another* (7:3). The beasts correspond to the kingdoms of Babylon, Medo-Persia, Greece, and Rome. *The first* (beast – Babylon) *was like a lion, and had eagle's wings* (7:4). Since the head of the great image in Nebuchadnezzar's dream was gold, it was fitting that a lion (king among animals) represent King Nebuchadnezzar. *And behold another beast* (Medo-Persia) *... like to a bear* (7:5), represented the empire which later would conquer Babylon. The third beast, *like a leopard, which had upon the back of it four wings of a fowl* (7:6), represented the Grecian Empire. The *four wings* illustrate the speed with which Alexander the Great would conquer the ancient world.

The *fourth beast . . . was diverse from all the beasts that were before it; and it had ten horns* (the ten nations of the revived Roman Empire). This final beast was *dreadful and terrible* (terrifying)*, and strong exceedingly; and it had great iron teeth: it devoured and brake in pieces, and stamped the residue with the feet of it* (7:7).

The *ten horns* (7:24) correspond to the ten *toes of the feet* (2:42) of Nebuchadnezzar's *great image* (2:31) and represent a confederation of ten future world rulers, followed by *another little horn* (king) (7:8). This *little horn* represents the Antichrist who *shall speak ... against the Most High, and shall wear out* (oppress) *the saints* (believers) (7:25). But he will be destroyed by "the Stone" (2:35,44-45), Christ, who *shall come to be glorified in His saints* (Christians), *and to be admired in all them that believe* (II Thess. 1:10). What a glorious time that will be!

Thought for Today: Living for Jesus provides satisfaction beyond compare.

Christ Revealed: As the *Son of Man* (Dan. 7:13-14). The truth of this vision was confirmed by our Lord as He spoke of His promised return. *They shall see the Son of Man coming in the clouds of heaven with power and great glory* (Matt. 24:30).

SEPTEMBER 18   Read Daniel 10 – 12

Highlights: A heavenly being revealed to Daniel that the prince of Persia (a demonic being) had hindered the answer to Daniel's prayers for 21 days. It's war and every child of God is in it (Dan. 10:11-13). The march of the kings, 1,2,3 (chap. 11). At the end, Michael the archangel appears and a time of great anguish follows. But read the promise to those whose names are written in the Book of Life (12:1).

The kingdoms of this world eventually will erupt into open hostility toward God and His people. Daniel foretold that during the period of the yet-to-come revived Roman Empire, terrible persecution will take place. The Antichrist ***shall ... magnify himself above every god, and shall speak marvellous things*** (blasphemies) ***against the God of gods, and shall prosper till the indignation*** (wrath) ***be accomplished*** (Dan. 11:36). Jesus spoke of the ***abomination of desolation, spoken of by Daniel the prophet*** (Mark 13:14).

There have been ***many antichrists*** over the past 2,000 years, as the Apostle John foretold (I John 2:18); and the ultimate goal of all antichrists is to destroy the Kingdom of God. ***There shall be a time of trouble, such as never was since there was a nation ... and at that time thy people shall be delivered, every one that shall be found written in the book*** (Dan. 12:1).

But Daniel also said: ***I heard, but I understood not: then said I, O my LORD, what shall be the end of these things? And He said, Go thy way, Daniel: for the words are closed up and sealed*** (kept secret) ***till the time of the end*** (12:8-9). Daniel admitted that he did not understand some of his prophecy, yet he faithfully recorded it.

Daniel's prophecy reminds us to be prepared for the soon return of Christ, when He shall reign and rule over all the world. ***Let no man deceive you by any means: for that day shall not come, except there come a falling away first, and that man of sin*** (antichrist) ***be revealed*** (II Thess. 2:3). The time will come when it seems that the wicked one has triumphed. ***And then shall that Wicked be revealed, whom the Lord shall consume with the Spirit of His mouth, and shall destroy with the brightness of His coming: Even him*** (antichrist)***, whose coming is after the work of Satan with all power and signs and lying wonders*** (II Thess. 2:8-9). ***... Now our Lord Jesus Christ Himself ... Comfort your hearts, and stablish you in every good word and work*** (II Thess. 2:8,16-17).

Thought for Today: There is no need to fear since our Creator loves us.

Christ Revealed: As the One *that liveth for ever* (Dan. 12:7). As One of the Three expressed Persons of the Trinity, Jesus Christ always has been and always will be. *Jesus said unto them, Verily, verily* (Truly, truly)*, I say unto you, Before Abraham was, I am* (John 8:58). *I* (Christ) *am ... Alpha and Omega, the Beginning and the Ending, saith the Lord, which is, and which was, and which is to come, the Almighty* (Rev. 1:8; 4:8).

Introduction To The Book Of HOSEA

Hosea lived in the Northern Kingdom of Israel and prophesied for about 50 years – during the reigns of **Uzziah, Jotham, Ahaz, and Hezekiah, kings of Judah, and ... Jeroboam the son of Joash, king of Israel** (Hosea 1:1).

It appears that, during Hosea's ministry, the Northern Kingdom was experiencing material prosperity and an expansion of its territory. This was primarily due to the decline of its enemies Syria and Moab, which resulted in the Northern Kingdom gaining control of the major east-west trade routes in the region. In the meantime, the golden calf worship centers, erected many years earlier in the cities of Bethel and Dan, had prepared the way for the immoral worship of Baal and Ashtoreth, resulting in Israel's further spiritual corruption and decline (I Kin. 12:28-32; Hos. 2:13; 10:5-6; 13:2).

Hosea endured deep humiliation because of his unfaithful wife Gomer. Her harlotry illustrated how Israel had broken her covenant relationship with God, just as an adulterous wife who chooses other lovers is unfaithful to her mate in the marriage covenant (2:7-13). Hosea's forgiving love toward his unfaithful wife and the restoration of their marriage was an example to Israel of how God, in His mercy, would restore His blessings upon the nation, if only they would return to Him and be faithful (2:8,15-16; 10:12; 11:8-9; 12:6; 14:1,4).

Some today, who call themselves "Christians," are like Israel, guilty of spiritual hypocrisy (4:1-2), adultery (4:2,11; 7:4), false dealings (10:4; 12:7), idolatry (4:12-13; 8:5; 10:1,5; 13:2), and drunkenness (4:11; 7:5) as a result of ignoring the Word of God (4:4,10; 8:14). The history of Israel should serve as a warning that the righteous judgment of God will fall upon those who are guilty of compromise and who allow wordly pressures to cause them to follow the ways of the world.

The Holy Word of God has surely been
Inspired of God and not of men;
No power or eloquence of men could ere
conceive the wondrous plan of God.
Withstanding all the tests of time,
It stands unchanged, unique, sublime;
Proving to every tongue and race,
The wisdom, mercy, love, and grace of God.
So hammer on, ye hostile hands;
Your hammers break, the anvil of God stands.

—M.E.H.

SEPTEMBER 19 — Read Hosea 1 – 6

Highlights: The faithfulness of God versus people's unfaithfulness. Who wins (Hos. 1:2)? Redemption (2:14). Charges against a sinful nation (chap. 4). God withdraws (chap. 5). Repent (chap 6)!

Jeroboam II was king of the Northern Kingdom. The moral and spiritual level of the Israelites had become so low as to embrace **sodomites** (male prostitutes) **. . . and . . . all the abominations** (detestable practices) **of the nations which the LORD cast out** (I Kin. 14:24). Not one of the 19 kings of the Northern Kingdom of Israel attempted to lead the people to worship in Jerusalem as God had instructed. It was under these circumstances that **the Word of the LORD . . . came unto Hosea . . . in the days of Jeroboam . . . king of Israel. . . . I will break the bow of Israel. . . . God said . . . I will no more have mercy upon the house of Israel** (Hos. 1:1-6).

As a demonstration of His own relationship to a rebellious people, God told Hosea to find and marry a prostitute. Her unfaithfulness to him pictured the nation of Israel and its unfaithfulness to God.

The Lord spoke against His people through Hosea **because there is no truth, nor mercy, nor knowledge of God in the land. By swearing, and lying, and killing, and stealing, and committing adultery, they break out** (with no restraint) (4:1-2). God revealed the consequences of Israel's sin, saying: **Because thou hast rejected knowledge, I will also reject thee, that thou shalt be no priest to Me: seeing thou hast forgotten the Law of thy God, I will also forget thy children** (4:6).

Israel's kings, as well as its political and religious leadership blatantly disregarded the importance of obedience to the Word of God. Jesus Christ set the example of how important the Old Testament should be to us. After 40 days of fasting, He was tempted of the Devil, who said: **If Thou be** (Since You are) **the Son of God, command that these stones be made bread. But He answered and said, It is written, Man shall not live by bread alone** (physical necessities)**, but by every Word that proceedeth out of the mouth of God** (spiritual necessities) (Matt. 4:3-4; compare Deut. 8:3). By quoting this Old Testament Scripture, our Lord revealed the "Key to Victory" over satanic deceptions. We can have that same victory over Satan when we allow **every Word that proceedeth out of the mouth of God** to become a vital part of our daily lives (Matt. 4:4).

Thought for Today: Love for the Lord is expressed when we forgive others.

Christ Revealed: Through Hosea's love for his unworthy, sinful wife (Hos. 3:1-5). Our Lord Jesus not only loved us **while we were yet sinners**, but He also died the death of shame for us on Calvary so that all He possessed might become ours (Rom. 5:8; 8:32; II Pet. 1:3). **I will betroth thee unto Me for ever** (Hos. 2:19).

SEPTEMBER 20   Read Hosea 7 – 14

Highlights: Israel seeks help from Egypt and Assyria (Hos. 7). They worship golden calves (chap. 8). Finally, a cry of repentance (8:2); reaping what you sow (8:7); punishment promised (chap. 9); the call of God to worship Him (10:12); the Lord's love for Israel (chap. 11); His anger at Israel (chap. 13); healing and the sacrifice of praise (chap. 14).

The Northern Kingdom did **not return to the LORD their God, nor seek Him . . . Ephraim also is like a silly dove without heart: they call to Egypt, they go to Assyria** (Hos. 7:10-11), seeking national security rather than trusting the Lord. Israel's leaders had **gone up to Assyria. . . . Israel hath forgotten his Maker. . . . They have deeply corrupted themselves. . . . their glory shall fly away like a bird. . . . they shall be wanderers among the nations** (8:9,14; 9:9,11,17). The Lord gave a heartrending plea for Israel to return to Him before they were destroyed: **It is time to seek the LORD** (10:12). Feel God's heartbreak as He says: **I drew them with . . . bands of love** (11:4). He lovingly pleaded: **O Israel, return unto the LORD thy God; for thou hast fallen by thine iniquity** (sin) (14:1).

Israel had foolishly put its trust in heathen nations, false gods (5:13; 7:11; 8:9-10), and in its own ability to manipulate peace and security (12:8) rather than in the One who is the only true source of peace and security. Still, we see the willingness of the Lord to show mercy, as He always does to any repentant sinner, when He said: **I will heal their backsliding, I will love them freely** (14:4). The final words of Hosea before the Israelites were conquered and carried away by the Assyrians are a reminder to all of us: **The ways of the LORD are right, and the just shall walk in them: but the transgressors shall fall therein** (14:9). When we receive Jesus as our Savior, repent of our sins, and let the indwelling Holy Spirit control our lives, we are freed from Satan's power, sin, and spiritual death.

If we say that we have fellowship with Him, and walk in darkness, we lie, and do (practice) **not the truth. . . . these things write I unto you, that ye sin not. And if any man sin, we have an Advocate** (Defender, Defense Attorney) **with the Father, Jesus Christ the righteous: And He is the propitiation** (appeasement, legal satisfaction) **for our sins: and not for ours only, but also for the sins of the whole world** (I John 1:6; 2:1-2).

Thought for Today: Those who rejoice in the Lord can rejoice in tribulation.

Christ Revealed: In the son who was called **out of Egypt** (Hos. 11:1). This prophecy is twofold: one is a historical reference pertaining to Israel (Ex. 4:22-23); and the other is prophetic, looking to the sojourn of Christ as a child in Egypt (Matt. 2:14-15).

Introduction To The Book Of JOEL

The future end-time ***day of the Lord*** is mentioned five times (Joel 1:15; 2:1,11,31; 3:14). Judah is mentioned six times (3:1,6,8,18-20) but, since the Northern Kingdom is not mentioned, we assume that it had already been destroyed by the Assyrians.

Joel prophesied a warning to Jerusalem of a coming national disaster, a result of the nation's departure from the Word of God. Joel likened this ***day of the Lord*** to an invasion of locusts sweeping through the country, devouring crops and stripping trees, leading to famine. Some scholars believe this refers to real locusts. Others believe it illustrates invading armies. Probably it was both. The fact is, Judah faced certain destruction. Joel foretold of ***a nation*** (the Babylonians) ***... strong, and without number.... He hath laid My vine waste, and barked*** (cut the bark from) ***My fig tree: he hath made it clean*** (completely) ***bare, and cast it away; the branches*** (people) ***thereof are made white*** (like the dry bones of Ezekiel's vision) (1:6-7). The vine and the fig tree were valuable crops. The destruction of the trees, which demanded years of patient labor, was a national calamity, as productiveness was a token of peace and Divine favor. The vine was the emblem of prosperity and peace (Ps. 80:8; Is. 5:1-5).

Joel prophesied of invaders that were ***a great people and a strong; there hath not been ever the like*** (Joel 2:2). They would invade the land and leave ***behind them a desolate wilderness; yea, and nothing shall escape them*** (2:3). Because of the impending doom, the Lord appealed to the Israelites to repent and ***turn ... even to Me with all your heart*** (2:12). Joel also foretold of a future ***day of the Lord*** (2:11) when God would pour out His ***Spirit upon all flesh*** (people) (2:28).

We are now living in the ***last days,*** which began on the Day of Pentecost when ***they were all filled with the Holy Ghost*** (Spirit). The Apostle Peter clearly declared: ***This is that which was spoken by the prophet Joel*** (Acts 2:4,16-17). Joel's prophecy also foretells the time of the Lord's judgment, saying: ***I will also gather all nations, and will bring them down into the valley of Jehoshaphat*** (Joel 3:2). Many scholars believe that this ***valley*** is located on the eastern side of Jerusalem and is known as the Kidron (meaning Gloomy) Valley, as well as ***the valley of decision*** (judgment) (3:14).

Soon, the nations that oppose God will assemble for war; but it will be their day of judgment. ***Then shall Jerusalem be holy*** (set apart), ***and there shall no strangers pass through her any more. ... for the Lord dwelleth in Zion*** (3:17,21).

SEPTEMBER 21   Read Joel 1 – 3

Highlights: Joel's message: destruction (Joel 1:15). The sun and moon grow dark (2:2,9-10). Turn, give me your heart (2:12-13). Worship through prayers of intercession and repentance (2:17) and by rejoicing (2:23); be saved (2:32); dwell with God (3:17).

Joel warned of the impending destruction of Jerusalem: ***The Word of the LORD . . . came to Joel . . . . Blow . . . the trumpet in Zion, and sound an alarm in My holy mountain*** (Joel 1:1; 2:1). The trumpet was often used to announce solemn days and feasts, and by watchmen to warn of approaching danger (Num. 10:1-10). But, the sins of the Israelites were even more serious than the approaching enemies. Because of their sins, God could not bless them or protect them. ***The day of the LORD cometh . . . nothing shall escape them. . . . Therefore . . . turn . . . to Me with all your heart, and with fasting, and with weeping, and with mourning*** (Joel 2:1-12).

The one condition for forgiveness and acceptance by the Lord is genuine repentance. True repentance is threefold. First, it is a sorrow for one's sins against God, as well as against others; second, it is a turning to the Lord, asking His forgiveness for all sins; and third, it is a forsaking of sin to live a life pleasing to Jesus Christ as Savior and Lord. Praise the Lord for His mercy (forgiving love) which makes salvation available to any and all sinners who are willing to admit their guilt and ask for His forgiveness.

On the Day of Pentecost, the Apostle Peter preached the prophetic meaning of Joel's words, saying: ***Whosoever shall call on the Name of the Lord shall be saved*** (Acts 2:21). He concluded his message by saying: ***Repent, and be baptized every one of you in the Name of Jesus Christ for the remission of sins, and ye shall receive the gift of the Holy Ghost*** (Spirit). ***For the promise is unto you, and to your children, and to all that are afar off*** (2:38-39). Believers today live among those ***that are afar off***.

Joel also foretold of the final ***day of the LORD*** that is yet to take place: ***Alas for the day! for the day of the LORD is at hand, and as a destruction from the Almighty shall it come*** (Joel 1:15). It will terminate the miserable rule of sinful mankind, and usher in the glorious reign of Jesus Christ, the righteous King. Jesus foretold when ***all the tribes of the earth . . . shall see the Son of Man coming in the clouds of heaven with power and great glory*** (Matt. 24:30).

Thought for Today: The Holy Spirit works in our lives to the extent that we yield to His will as revealed in His Word.

Christ Revealed: As the One who said: *I will pour out My Spirit upon all flesh* (people) (Joel 2:28) – fulfilled in part on the Day of Pentecost and still being fulfilled today (Acts 2:16-18).

INTRODUCTION TO THE BOOKS OF AMOS & OBADIAH

Amos was not a priest, nor was he schooled as a prophet; he was merely a shepherd and a caretaker of sycamore (fig) trees near the small mountain village of Tekoa. But, in obedience to God, he became a prophet (Amos 1:1; 7:14). Tekoa was located about 10 miles south of Jerusalem, in the area known as the wilderness of Judea, in Judah. God called Amos to preach in the Northern Kingdom (1:1; 3:9; 7:7-17). Amos traveled north about 22 miles to Bethel, the southern location of golden calf worship. He then boldly denounced their religious idolatry and social evils (2:6-8; 3:9-10; 4:1-5).

Amos told them that if they continued to disregard God's Word, the destruction of the kingdom would be inevitable. During this time, Uzziah was king of Judah; Jeroboam II was king of Israel, and the prophets Micah, Isaiah, Hosea, and Jonah were prominent. Both kingdoms were prospering (II Kin. 14:23,25; II Chr. 26:1-16) and nothing looked more unlikely to be fullfilled than the warnings of this simple country herdsman. The Israelites' prosperity and success only led to more immorality and injustice. But, according to the prophetic Word of God, about 30 years later, in 722 BC, the Northern Kingdom of Israel was invaded and destroyed by the Assyrians.

Obadiah is the shortest book in the Old Testament, but it has a profound message. Its twofold subject is the punishment of God upon Edom and the ultimate establishment of the Kingdom of God on earth.

The territory of Edom was located south and east of Judah, below the Dead Sea, and along the Arabah (a desert plain). The land of Edom was also called Mount Seir because of the rugged range of mountains that dominated it, chief of which was Mount Seir. Edom's capital was the illustrious red-rock city of Sela, or Petra, which was situated securely in the midst of limestone mountain peaks. It was considered very secure because of the narrow passageway through the rocky mountain that led into Petra. Edom's fortified cities were located on an important caravan route between Egypt in the south and Syria, Assyria, and others in the north.

Obadiah foretold the destruction of the Edomites, who had followed their ancestor Esau's example of disregard for godly values and intense hatred toward Jacob's descendants. The Edomites had aided Nebuchadnezzar in destroying Jerusalem when they should have shown compassion and protected the Israelites, since both were descendants of Abraham and Isaac (Obad. 1:10; Deut. 23:7).

SEPTEMBER 22   Read Amos 1 – 5

Highlights: God uses Amos, a lowly herdsman, who is burdened over Israel's sins (Amos 1:1-2). First a prophecy against their neighbors (1:3 – 2:3). then, against Judah and Israel (2:4-16). Why (3:2,10)? An enemy is coming (3:11). The people talk the talk but don't walk the walk. God wants a river of righteous living (5:23-24).

Amos was only a farm laborer from the village of Tekoa in Judah, but he was willing to speak for God against sin even beyond the borders of the Southern Kingdom. He delivered his prophecy of impending judgment in Bethel. Since the people of Israel were proud of their prosperity, it must have seemed ridiculous to hear this "outsider" shout: **Hear this word that the LORD hath spoken against you, O children of Israel . . . I will punish you for all your iniquities** (sins). **. . . . An adversary there shall be even round about the land; and he shall bring down thy strength from thee, and thy palaces shall be spoiled** (plundered) (Amos 3:1-2,11). Amos' message concerning the coming judgment of God was completely ignored (2:6-8; 5:11-12).

Amaziah, the non-Levitical paid priest of King Jeroboam II, was quick to get word to the king about this disagreeable prophet from the Southern Kingdom. He interpreted the words of Amos to mean that Jeroboam would die by the sword; but the prophet had only stated what God had said: **I will rise against the house of Jeroboam with the sword. . . . Amaziah said unto Amos . . . go, flee . . . into the land of Judah** (7:9-12). The prophecy **against the house of Jeroboam** was fulfilled when Zachariah, Jeroboam's son, was assassinated by Shallum after reigning only six months. Shallum took his place, but he only reigned for one month before he, in turn, was murdered by Menahem (II Kin. 15:8-10,13-14).

God often uses ordinary people like Amos to proclaim His message. It is not what we possess in talents, nor how popular we may be, but how obedient we are that qualifies us to be used by the Lord. One of the greatest abilities we can offer to God is our availability.

For ye see your calling, brethren, how that not many wise men after the flesh, not many mighty, not many noble, are called: But God hath chosen the foolish things of the world . . . base things . . . which are despised . . . That no flesh should glory in His presence (I Cor. 1:26-29).

Thought for Today: The Holy Spirit will provide His strength in anyone who willingly yields to Him.

Christ Revealed: As the Creator of the universe (Amos 5:8). **By His Son . . . He made the worlds** (Heb. 1:2-3; Rev. 4:11).

SEPTEMBER 23   Read Amos 6 – 9 and Obadiah

Highlights: Five visions: (1) Locusts – an invading army (Amos 7:1-3); (2) Fire – consumed by (7:4-6); (3) A plumbline – measuring correctness, Israel defective (7:7-9); (4) Ripe fruit – the end is coming (8:1-14); (5) God at the altar – Israel to be destroyed (9:1-10). The promise of God to David kept (9:11-15). God speaks to Edom (Obad. 1:4,15-18, 20-21).

The Edomites had been hostile to the Israelites for centuries – from the time Esau (Edom) sold his family birthright to his brother Jacob (Israel) for a bowl of soup (Gen. 25:29-34). The prophet Obadiah foretold the eventual triumph of Israel, as well as the complete destruction of Edom: ***For thy violence against thy brother Jacob shame shall cover thee, and thou shalt be cut off for ever. . . . for the LORD hath spoken it*** (Obad. 1:10,18).

Esau had moved to Mount Seir where the Edomites, his descendants, felt secure by building for themselves a mountain fortress. Their self-sufficiency and disinterest in the will of God deluded them and caused them to ignore Obadiah's warning.

The Edomites conspired with Ammon and Moab against Judah and took Israelites captive. They also raided Judah in the days of King Ahaz to take even more captives as slaves (II Kin. 8:20-22; II Chr. 28:16-17). When Jerusalem was destroyed by the Babylonian army, some of the Jewish escapees tried to flee out of the land; but the Edomites blocked roads, robbed them, and delivered them to the Babylonians (Obad. 1:12-14). Because of their treachery, God foretold that Edom would be utterly destroyed (1:9-10,18).

About 4 years after Jerusalem's fall, Nebuchadnezzar's army swept through Ammon, Moab, and Edom. Edomite refugees fled to the western area of southern Judah. They then made raids northward into Judah, taking part of a territory later known as Idumaea, from which came Herod, the Roman-appointed puppet king who sought to kill the Child Jesus. Eventually, the Edomites disappeared from history, just as Obadiah had earlier foretold. Unlike Amos' prophecy against the Edomites (Amos 9:11-15), Obadiah foretold that Judah would recover and finally ***possess their possessions*** (1:15-17).

The absolute justice of God and our assurance of His faithfulness encourage us. Jesus expressed the inevitable spiritual law of the Kingdom of God: ***As ye would that men should do to you, do ye also to them likewise*** (Luke 6:31).

Thought for Today: Give God the credit for your accomplishments, a safeguard against pride.

Christ Revealed: As the ***Plumbline*** (Amos 7:7-8). A plumbline is an instrument used in measuring an absolutely straight vertical line. Christ alone is qualified to walk amidst His people; measuring good and bad, true and false (Rev. 2 – 3).

Introduction To The Book Of JONAH

Jonah was a prominent prophet in the Northern Kingdom of Israel during the prosperous but evil reign of King Jeroboam II. He foretold the Jeroboam's great military success over the Syrians (II Kin. 4:25).

The Book of Jonah is the historical account of the prophet's mission to Nineveh, the capital of Assyria and Israel's great enemy. Because of this, Jonah at first failed to comply when God commanded him to prophesy of Nineveh's coming destruction as a result of their great wickedness. Undoubtedly, Jonah was delighted that God would destroy them. But, after a series of personally horrifying events, he obeyed. Then he was unhappy when the king and the people of Nineveh repented and God, in His great mercy, withdrew His judgment from them for a time. This book reveals **that God is no respecter of persons** (Acts 10:34) and no sinner is beyond the reach of His grace. His compassion still extends toward all who will repent, turn from their sins, put their trust in Jesus as Lord and Savior and worship Him.

The Book of Jonah reveals that God is concerned about Gentiles just as He is about Jews. Both are eternally lost apart from having faith in Jesus Christ as their Savior, for He proclaimed: *I am The Way, The Truth, and The Life: no one cometh unto the Father, but by Me* (John 14:6).

Not what I do, Lord, nor what I say,
But what I am, Lord, matters today.
Busy with nothing we fill up the years,
Hurrying, worrying, gathering tears.

Why can't I learn, Lord, that power is within,
Why can't I see, Lord, the waste of my sin?
If I could be, Lord, growing in soul,
Seeing each day, Lord, more clearly the goal.

If I could live, Lord, discerning Thy face,
Ever more strongly held by Thy grace;
So take and mold, Lord, this heart of mine,
Till it shall be, Lord, like unto Thine!

—M.E.H.

SEPTEMBER 24 — Read Jonah 1 – 4

Highlights: Learn a lesson from Jonah who learns firsthand what it means to hit rock bottom spiritually and emotionally. He cries to God who answers (Jon. 2:2,7). The enemy humbly prays for mercy (3:6-10). Jonah gets angry because God does not destroy them (4:1-2).

The Lord commanded Jonah: *Arise, go to Nineveh, that great city, and cry* (preach) *against it; for their wickedness is come up before Me. But Jonah rose up to flee unto Tarshish from the presence of the LORD* (Jon. 1:2-3). Jonah was probably delighted with the good news that the judgment of God would soon fall upon Nineveh. He did not want God to show mercy and love to Israel's enemies. So, he decided not to be a missionary to Nineveh. He must have felt fortunate when, on the very day he arrived in Joppa, he discovered a ship sailing to Tarshish, the most remote of the Phoenician trading places, and in the opposite direction from Nineveh.

For a while, events seemed to favor Jonah's "vacation plan" and gave him such peace of mind that he was soon *fast asleep* on the ship (1:5). However, favorable circumstances when avoiding the will of God are only temporary, and they never lead to a pleasant end. The sailors became fearful when a great storm arose. Then, when they heard that Jonah was fleeing from God, at Jonah's urging they made an effort to appease God. Jonah was thrown overboard, only to be swallowed by a *great fish* (1:17). After three days of soul searching, a repentant Jonah was vomited onto dry land in answer to his prayers. He then became the greatest evangelist of his day, and saw the entire city of Nineveh repent of its wickedness. God could have chosen another prophet and let Jonah sink to the bottom of the sea, but God was merciful, demonstrating His love toward both the reluctant prophet and the repentant people in Nineveh. The willingness of God to forgive even the greatest of sinners who repent was made known when Nineveh's king and people repented.

Jesus confirmed the historic truth concerning Jonah when He proclaimed: *As Jonas* (Jonah) *was three days and three nights in the whale's* (great fish's) *belly; so shall the Son of Man be three days and three nights in the heart of the earth. The men of Nineveh shall rise in judgment with this generation, and shall condemn it: because they repented at the preaching of Jonas; and, behold, a greater than Jonas is here* (Matt. 12:40-41).

Thought for Today: The one thing gained by ignoring God is trouble.

Christ Revealed: By Jonah's experience in the great fish (Jon. 1:7-2:10). Jesus used this historical event as an illustration to tell of His death, burial, and resurrection when the Pharisees demanded a sign from Him to prove who He was (Matt. 12:39-41; I Cor. 15:4).

Introduction To The Book Of MICAH

Micah was just a country man who lived in a small village in Judea, about 20 miles southwest of Jerusalem near Gath (Mic. 1:14). He prophesied during the reigns of kings Jotham, Ahaz, and Hezekiah of Judah and at the same time that Isaiah was a prominent prophet in Jerusalem. Micah exposed the sins of both the kingdoms of Judah and Israel, and boldly proclaimed the destruction of Israel (1:6-7), as well as of Jerusalem and the Temple (3:12). He also foretold Judah's restoration. Undoubtedly, King Hezekiah was greatly comforted by the prophecies of both Isaiah and Micah about the Israelites' promised restoration (Is. 1:1; 62:1-12; Mic. 1:1; 7:11-20). Micah also gave his most remarkable and best known prophecy, not only that the Messiah would be born in **Bethlehem** but also concerning His eternal existence (5:2).

In his prophecy of the millenial reign of Jesus, Micah declared: ***But in the last days it shall come to pass, that the mountain of the House of the Lord shall be established in the top of the mountains, and it shall be exalted above the hills; and people shall flow into it. And many nations shall come, and say, Come, and let us go up to the mountain of the Lord, and to the House of the God of Jacob; and He will teach us of His ways, and we will walk in His paths: for the Law shall go forth of Zion, and the Word of the Lord from Jerusalem*** (4:1-2).

The Book of Micah closes with a message of hope, declaring the last fulfillment of the covenant blessing God had promised to Abraham (7:20). Micah's prophecy confirms that without exception God requires obedience to His Word: ***He hath shewed thee, O man, what is good; and what doth the Lord require of thee, but to do justly, and to love mercy, and to walk humbly with thy God*** (Mic. 6:8)?

When Things Go Wrong

ROMANS 8:28 *And we know that all things work together for good to them that love God, to them who are the called according to His purpose.*

I THESSALONIANS 5:18 *In every thing give thanks: for this is the will of God in Christ Jesus concerning you.*

MATTHEW 6:33 *But seek ye first the Kingdom of God, and His righteousness; and all these things shall be added unto you.*

I JOHN 4:4 *Ye are of God, little children, and have overcome them: because greater is He that is in you, than he that is in the world.*

PHILLIPPIANS 4:13 *I can do all things through Christ which strengtheneth me.*

SEPTEMBER 25 — Read Micah 1 – 7

Highlights: Micah details the astonishing power of God (Mic. 1:3-4), who alone is worthy of our praise and worship (7:7-20). Predicted judgment breaks the Father's heart. He sheds tears (1:8). Jesus' first (5:2) and second (2:13; 5:2,4) comings foretold. Persecution will come but God has a plan (4:11-12). Check out the bottom line (6:8).

After David, who was born in Bethlehem, all the kings of Judah were born in Jerusalem – the City of God. But 700 years before Jesus was born, the prophet Micah was led to prophesy: **Thou, Bethlehem Ephratah, though thou be little among the thousands of Judah, yet out of thee shall He come forth unto Me that is to be ruler in Israel** (Mic. 5:2).

At the God-appointed time, **there went out a decree from Caesar Augustus, that all the world should be taxed. . . . Joseph** (the legal, but not actual father of Jesus) **also went up from Galilee . . . unto the city of David, which is called Bethlehem** (Luke 2:1,4). As a descendant of King David, Joseph had to go to David's hometown to register. When issuing his command from Rome, Caesar could have thought only of his own kingdom. But, God directed this heathen emperor's proclamation to fulfill His prophecy through Micah.

Perhaps the most significant statement of Micah's prophecy is: **Whose goings forth have been from of old, from everlasting** (Mic. 5:2). This proclaims both the deity and eternal existence of Jesus. The angel Gabriel later announced to Mary: **Thou shalt conceive in thy womb, and bring forth a Son, and shalt call His Name JESUS. He shall be great, and shall be called the Son of the Highest . . . and of His Kingdom there shall be no end. Then said Mary unto the angel, How shall this be, seeing I know not a man? And the angel answered and said unto her, The Holy Ghost** (Spirit) **shall come upon thee, and the power of the Highest shall overshadow thee: therefore also that Holy Thing** (Holy One) **which shall be born of thee shall be called the Son of God** (Luke 1:31-35).

Jesus could not have been qualified to be the Savior of mankind and give His life for the sins of the world if He had inherited Adam's sinful nature through man. Because of this, Jesus the Son of God, was born of the Virgin Mary without a human father. **By one man's** (Adam's) **disobedience many were made sinners, so by the obedience of One** (Jesus) **shall many be made righteous** (Rom. 5:19).

Thought for Today: Wise men seek Jesus regardless of what others do.

Christ Revealed: As the **Ruler in Israel** (Mic. 5:2) who was to be born in Bethlehem. Jesus Christ was born in Bethlehem as **the Son of the Highest: and the Lord God shall give unto Him the throne of His Father David** (Luke 1:32-33; 2:4-6).

Introduction To The Books Of
NAHUM & HABAKKUK

Nahum probably lived just before the defeat of Assyria, possibly during the same period as the prophet Zephaniah. Both prophesied after Isaiah, toward the end of the reign of Judah's sinful King Jehoiakim (II Kin. 23:34 – 24:5; Jer. 22:17). Both prophets foretold the destruction of Nineveh as a result of its cruelties, oppressions, adulteries, and witchcraft (Nah. 1:1-14; Zeph. 2:13-15). Its destruction had been delayed about 150 years because of its repentance following Jonah's message of judgment (Jon. 3:5-10), but, eventually, the people reverted to their sinful ways.

The Assyrian Empire destroyed the Northern Kingdom of Israel in 722 BC; but, in turn, Assyria was conquered by the Babylonians. About 100 years after Nahum's prophecy, the Assyrian empire was destroyed.

Habakkuk lived during the time when Nebuchadnezzar was conquering the world. He probably prophesied in Judah during the later years of Josiah's rule and into the reign of King Jehoiakim. Unlike his godly father Josiah, Jehoiakim **did that which was evil in the sight of the Lord** (II Kin. 23:37). Habakkuk cried out against the moral corruption of idolatrous Judah which prevailed in his day. He foretold how God would use the ruthless Babylonians to bring His judgment on Judah. During those horrifying times **the just shall live by his faith** became the watchword of the faithful (Hab. 2:4). It later became the major theme of Romans 1:16-17; Galatians 3:11; Hebrews 10:38.

The Book of Habakkuk encourages all believers to accept by faith that righteousness and justice will ultimately triumph according to the righteous judgment of the One True God.

> *Live out Thy life, Oh Christ, each day*
> *In this poor body made of clay,*
> *Reveal again, through me, dear Lord*
> *The mighty power of Thine own Word.*
> —M.E.H.

God's Word Ignored
Whoso despiseth the Word shall be destroyed: but he that feareth (respects) *the Commandment shall be rewarded* (Proverbs 13:13).

Guide
Thy Word is a lamp unto my feet, and a light unto my path (Psalm 119:105).

SEPTEMBER 26   Read Nahum 1 – Habakkuk 3

Highlights: Nahum writes with strong imagery, a sense of suspense and vivid language, a word of hope for the Covenant people of God (Nah. chap. 1 – 3). Habakkuk, a poet and prophet, hated sin (Hab. 1:2-4). His sense of judgment challenges the plan of God (1:12 – 2:1). His beautiful poem of praise (3:1-19).

About 150 years had passed since the revival of Jonah's day when all of Nineveh repented and fasted (Jon. 3:5-10). However, as the years passed, several generations of Ninevites failed to teach their children about the One True God who had spared their lives, so they reverted to their sinful behavior. The time had now come for God to judge them. Judah was oppressed by Assyria, but the prophet Nahum foretold its freedom if Judah remained faithful to God. He appealed to them: *O Judah . . . perform thy vows: for the wicked shall no more pass through thee; he is utterly cut off* (destroyed) (Nah. 1:15).

Assyria was probably the most brutal of all the ancient heathen nations, and its capital Nineveh had greatly enriched itself by wars. Through Nahum, God forewarned: *Woe to the bloody city! it is all full of lies and robbery. . . . Nineveh is laid waste. . . . the sword shall cut thee off* (3:1,7,15). Nineveh was destroyed exactly as foretold. That once-mighty city is still *laid waste* as a witness to the accuracy of the Word of God.

Habakkuk foretold that judgment from God would come on His idol-worshiping people to punish them. He also foretold the judgment on Babylon for destroying Judah: *O LORD, Thou hast ordained them* (Judah) *for judgment; and, O mighty God, Thou hast established* (ordained) *them for correction* (Hab. 1:12; II Cor. 4:17).

Like Habakkuk, we should trust in the *Holy One* (Hab. 1:12). God is just as uncompromising toward sin today as He was then. Yet the Lord also always forgives even the most sinful person who truly repents and turns to and receives Christ as Savior and Lord. All mankind will one day realize that the justice and mercy of *the LORD is good, a strong hold* (refuge) *in the day of trouble; and He knoweth* (loves) *them that trust in Him* (Nah. 1:7). We expectantly look forward to that day when *the earth shall be filled with the knowledge of the glory of the LORD* (Hab. 2:14; Rom. 1:17; Gal, 3:11; Heb. 10:38; 11:1-6).

Thought for Today: Religious activity is no substitute for godly living.

Christ Revealed: As the One whom even the sea obeys (Nah. 1:4). Jesus *rebuked the winds and the sea* (Matt. 8:26-27).

Introduction To The Books Of
ZEPHANIAH, HAGGAI, & ZECHARIAH

Zephaniah probably influenced King Josiah in his godly reformation, which began in the 8th year of Josiah's reign in Judah (II Chr. 34:3-7).

Zephaniah foretold the fall of Jerusalem perhaps 35 years before it took place (Zeph. 1:4-13). He warned of *a day of wrath* (anger), *a day of trouble and distress, a day of wasteness and desolation. . . . because they have sinned against the* L<small>ORD</small> (1:15,17). The prophet then appealed to the kingdom of Judah to repent: *Seek ye the* L<small>ORD</small>, *all ye meek* (humble) *of the earth, which have wrought* (carried out) *His judgment* (2:3). God assured them that He would, in His time, graciously restore the nation.

Zephaniah also prophesied that Christ would come in power and glory. Known as *the great day of the* L<small>ORD</small> (1:7,14), that end-time event is referred to 13 times in these three chapters. The *day of the* L<small>ORD</small> will be *a day of wrath* (1:15,18) upon all evildoers but a blessed "homecoming" for the faithful (3:14,17).

Zephaniah, Nahum, Habakkuk, and Jeremiah prophesied at the same time. They were among the last prophets who spoke for God before the 70-year Babylonian captivity.

Both **Haggai** and **Zechariah** were born in Babylon during the exile and went to Jerusalem some time after King Cyrus of Medo-Persia gave the decree to return and rebuild the Temple. Haggai and Zechariah began preaching in Jerusalem about 15 years after that decree.

Zechariah joined Haggai in encouraging the Jews to give first priority to their spiritual responsibility to rebuild the Temple: *The elders of the Jews builded, and they prospered through the prophesying of Haggai the prophet and Zechariah. . . . they builded, and finished it* in about four years (Ezra 6:14-15; Hag. 1:1). It was the preaching of the Word of God that turned the Israelites from their attitude of indifference toward spiritual needs to a willingness to carry out the will of God. A major turning point in anyone's life comes when he realizes the power of God's Word and appropriates it into his daily decisions and actions.

The Angel of the Lord is prominent in this book (Zech. 1:11-12; 3:1,5-6; 12:8). The second coming of Christ is foretold in 6:12 and 14:3-21. Zechariah foretold more about Christ than any other prophet except Isaiah. (Note 3:8; 9:9,16; 11:11-13; 12:10; 13:1,6.)

SEPTEMBER 27   Read Zephaniah 1 – Haggai 2

Highlights: *The Day of the LORD* – will be a day of wrath (Zeph. 2:11; 3:9). Rejoice, God is with you (3:14-20). Worship: Results of ignoring (Hag. 1:9-11). The presence of God and blessing promised (1:13;2:4-5,19).

The Israelites who had returned from Persia with Zerubbabel started to rebuild the Temple in Jerusalem with great enthusiasm. But, when their Samaritan enemies greatly opposed them, they began working on their own homes and fields. Personal interests contributed to their failure to put God first in their lives. No doubt, "legitimate" excuses were given for halting construction of the Temple.

As the people built their houses and developed their businesses, time to rebuild the Temple looked very elusive. Zerubbabel probably was discouraged as he thought of how much there was to do. Few workers were willing to help, and the opposition was threatening. For about 15 years, nothing more was accomplished for the Lord.

Then God moved upon the prophet Haggai to proclaim *the Word of the LORD* (Hag. 1:3-11, Ezra 5:1). Two months later, Zechariah also spoke *the Word of the LORD* (Zech. 1:1).

Haggai first announced: *Thus speaketh the LORD of hosts, saying, This people say, The time is not come, the time that the LORD's House should be built. Then came the Word of the LORD by Haggai the prophet, saying, Is it time . . . to dwell in your cieled* (paneled) *houses, and this House lie waste* (remain in ruins)? *. . . Consider your ways* (Hag. 1:2-5).

Upon hearing *the Word of the LORD*, the people renewed their commitment to rebuild the Temple, the one place designated by God for His people to worship Him. This time they ignored the threats of their enemies and *prospered through the prophesying of Haggai the prophet and Zechariah . . . And they builded, and finished it, according to the Commandment of the God of Israel* (Ezra 6:14). The Temple was completed in just four years.

Without *the Word of the LORD* as our standard, we also can fall prey to deception, but reading the Word of God imparts the spiritual strength needed to put Him first. Jesus promised: *The Comforter, which is the Holy Ghost* (Spirit), *whom the Father will send in My Name, He shall teach you all things, and bring all things to your remembrance, whatsoever I have said unto you* (John 14:26).

Thought for Today: Today, I will speak to someone about the Lord and how He has changed MY life.

Christ Revealed: As *King of Israel, even the LORD* (Zeph. 3:15; John 1:49)..

SEPTEMBER 28   Read Zechariah 1 – 7

Highlights: The future Jerusalem comforted (Zech. 1:16-17) and restored (2:10). Satan ever accusing (3:1-2). Joshua, the High Priest, a foreshadow of Jesus, the BRANCH, the Source of all our spiritual blessings (3:8). Ten visions each interpreted by Scripture (chap. 4 – 6). False fast (7:5-6), true fast (7:8-10).

Zechariah foretold the glorious promise of the presence of God when the Israelites will be inspired to ***sing and rejoice ... for, lo, I come, and I will dwell in the midst of thee, saith the LORD*** (Zech. 2:10). The Lord spoke through Zechariah who prophesied the restoration of the Jewish nation. He also declared: ***Many nations*** (people of every nationality) ***shall be joined to the LORD in that day, and shall be My people: and I will dwell in the midst of thee*** (2:11). The Israelites learned the futility of trusting in themselves or their abilities. They realized that only by trusting the Lord could they receive His blessings. It was at just such a time that an angel said to Zechariah: ***This is the Word of the LORD unto Zerubbabel, saying, Not by might, nor by power, but by My Spirit, saith the LORD of hosts. Who art thou, O great mountain*** (authority)***? before Zerubbabel thou shalt become a plain*** (4:6-7).

The work of God is not accomplished ***by might, nor by power*** (meaning, not merely by human intelligence, zeal, or finances)***, but by My Spirit, saith the LORD of hosts*** (4:6). Zechariah foretells the coming of our Lord: ***The Man whose Name is The BRANCH*** (Jesus Christ) ***... Even He ... shall sit and rule upon His throne; and He shall be a priest upon His throne: and the counsel of peace shall be between them both. ... And they that are far off shall come and build in the Temple of the LORD, and ye shall know that the LORD of hosts hath sent Me unto you. And this shall come to pass, if ye will diligently obey the voice of the LORD your God*** (6:12-13,15).

Today, the indwelling presence of the Holy Spirit enables believers to live a true Christian life and accomplish the will of God. Until the time Jesus rules on earth, we can take comfort knowing that ***He hath said, I will never leave thee, nor forsake thee. So that we may boldly say, The Lord is my helper, and I will not fear what man shall do unto me*** (Heb. 13;5-6).

Thought for Today: Jesus will return ***to be admired in*** (by) ***all*** (II Thess. 1:10).

Christ Revealed: ***As My Servant the BRANCH*** (Zech. 3:8). Christ was brought into the world in ***the fulness of the time*** (Gal. 4:4), and ***took upon Him the form of a servant*** (Phil. 2:7). But He will soon return as the ***righteous Branch*** to reign as King (Jer. 23:5).

SEPTEMBER 29   Read Zechariah 8 – 14

Highlights: God speaks to His people (Zech. 8:8; 10:6-12). Hear the prophets (8:9). Revelations of Jesus hundreds of years before His birth: (9:9; 11:12-13; 12:10;13:7). Refined like silver (13:9). The Lord Jesus' soon coming triumphant return to earth (14:4-9).

Although his message would not be fulfilled for centuries later, Zechariah proclaimed: *Rejoice greatly ... shout, O daughter of Jerusalem: behold, thy King cometh unto thee: He is just, and having salvation; lowly, and riding upon ... a colt the foal of an ass* (Zechariah 9:9). It was fulfilled as Jesus entered Jerusalem during the last week before His crucifixion. *A very great multitude. ... cried, saying, Hosanna to the Son of David: Blessed is He that cometh in the Name of the Lord; Hosanna in the highest* (Matt. 21:8-9). The people's cry of *Hosanna* (meaning "Save us!") was rejected by the jealous religious leaders who, instead, insisted that Jesus be crucified (Mark 14:1; 15:13).

Zechariah also foretold details concerning Judas, Jesus' betrayer, and his transactions with the religious leaders, saying: *I said unto them, If ye think good, give me my price* (wages, reward)*; and if not, forbear. So they weighed for my price thirty pieces of silver* (Zech. 11:12). Jesus was betrayed for a mere *30 pieces of silver* – the price of a mere slave (Ex. 21:32; Matt. 26:15).

Israel will soon recognize its Messiah as Zechariah foretold: *I will pour upon the house of David, and upon the inhabitants of Jerusalem, the Spirit of grace and of supplications: and they shall look upon Me whom they have pierced, and they shall mourn ... as one that is in bitterness for his firstborn* (Zech. 12:10; Rom. 11:26-27).

Zechariah warned: *Behold, the day of the Lord cometh. ... I will gather all the nations against Jerusalem to battle. ... Then shall the Lord go forth, and fight against those nations. ... And the LORD shall be King over all the earth* (Zech. 14:1-4,9).

Many believers waste time speculating on future events, forgetting what Jesus said to His disciples when asked: *Lord, wilt Thou at this time restore again the kingdom to Israel? And He said ... It is not for you to know the times or the seasons, which the Father hath put in His own power. But ye shall ... be witnesses unto Me ... unto the uttermost part of the earth* (Acts 1:6-8).

Thought for Today: Where God guides He provides.

Christ Revealed: As King (Zech. 9:9); as a Servant sold for *30 pieces of silver* (11:12). *They covenanted with him for thirty pieces of silver* (Matt. 26:15).

Introduction To The Book Of MALACHI

It is unknown at what time Malachi prophesied; but it is certain that Malachi's desire was for the Israelites to renew their covenant relationship with God. A spirit of worldliness prevailed among the Israelites just as it does in our communities today. Malachi pointed out the sins that separated the Israelites from experiencing the blessings of God and he appealed to them to repent (Mal. 3:7).

In chapter 1, Malachi first pleaded with Israel to return in full repentance to the Lord who loved them. Then, in chapter 2, he appealed to the priests, pointing out their hypocrisy. And, in chapter 3, he prophesied of both the coming Messiah and John the Baptist, probably 400 years before the Christian era: **Behold, I will send My messenger, and he shall prepare the way before Me: and the Lord, whom ye seek, shall suddenly come** (3:1; Luke 7:27). Finally, like other prophets before him, Malachi foretold **the coming of the great and dreadful day of the Lord** (Mal. 4:5) when **all the proud . . . and all that do wickedly** will be destroyed. To those who look for Him a different promise is made: **But unto you that fear** (reverence) **My Name shall the Sun of Righteousness arise with healing in His wings** (4:1-2).

Perhaps you've wondered why
Sore trials come your way,
Or murmured when dark clouds of grief
Obscured the light of the day.

God says the trial of your faith
More precious is than gold;
And He'll reward His servants true
With blessings manifold.

So trust in Him, His Word is sure
And infinite His love;
Oh, child of God, press on in faith –
Your Father reigns Above.

—*M.E.H.*

Helmet

And take the helmet of salvation, and the sword of the Spirit, which is the Word of God (**Ephesians 6:17**).

SEPTEMBER 30 — Read Malachi 1 – 4

Highlights: The people's worship is sloppy, the priests neglect the commands of God and offer unworthy sacrifices which indicate a lack of honor or respect for God (Mal. 1:7-10,12-14). The Messiah is worthy of pure offerings (3:2-3). Repent (3:6-9). Support the work of the Lord (3:10-12). Get ready! Judgment cometh (4:1-6)!

The first generation of Israelites that had returned to Jerusalem to rebuild the Temple had died, and following generations had lost sight of the purpose God had for them as His people. Malachi declared that God must be honored and His Word heard and followed or a curse would be brought upon the people, saying: *If ye will not hear, and if ye will not lay it to heart . . . saith the LORD of hosts, I will even send a curse upon you* (Mal. 2:2).

Malachi left no room for excuses when he declared that the Israelites were thieves. He boldly asked: *Will a man rob God? Yet ye have robbed Me. . . . In tithes and offerings* (3:8). He then pronounced the inevitable judgment: *Ye are cursed with a curse: for ye have robbed Me, even this whole nation* (3:9).

The seriousness of this sin can be seen in the severity of the famine that Israel was experiencing. The tithes belonged to God for the spiritual needs of the people and the support of the priesthood. The people of God are commanded to *honour the LORD with thy substance, and with the firstfruits of all thine increase* (Prov. 3:9; Ex. 22:29; II Chr. 31:5).

More than 500 years before the Law was given, tithing was demonstrated by Abraham, *the father of all them that believe* (Rom. 4:11). He gave a tenth of everything to *the priest of the Most High God* (Gen. 14:18). Giving one-tenth of all our *increase* to God expresses our faith that all we are and all we have belong to our Lord, and as caretakers, we return to Him a portion acknowledging that. Tithing demonstrates our love and gratitude to Him.

When we refuse to return *unto God the things that are God's* (Matt. 22:21), we keep for ourselves what God has said is for proclaiming the Gospel of Christ. Is it greed, selfishness, indifference, or just a stubborn refusal to be obedient to what the Word of God clearly states?

The Christian is to give *not grudgingly, or of necessity* (under compulsion): *for God loveth a cheerful giver* (II Cor. 9:7).

Thought for Today: Faith is demonstrated by obedience to the Word of God.

Christ Revealed: *The Lord, whom ye seek, shall suddenly come to His Temple* (Mal. 3:1; Mark 11:15-17), which meant that Jesus was the promised Messiah.

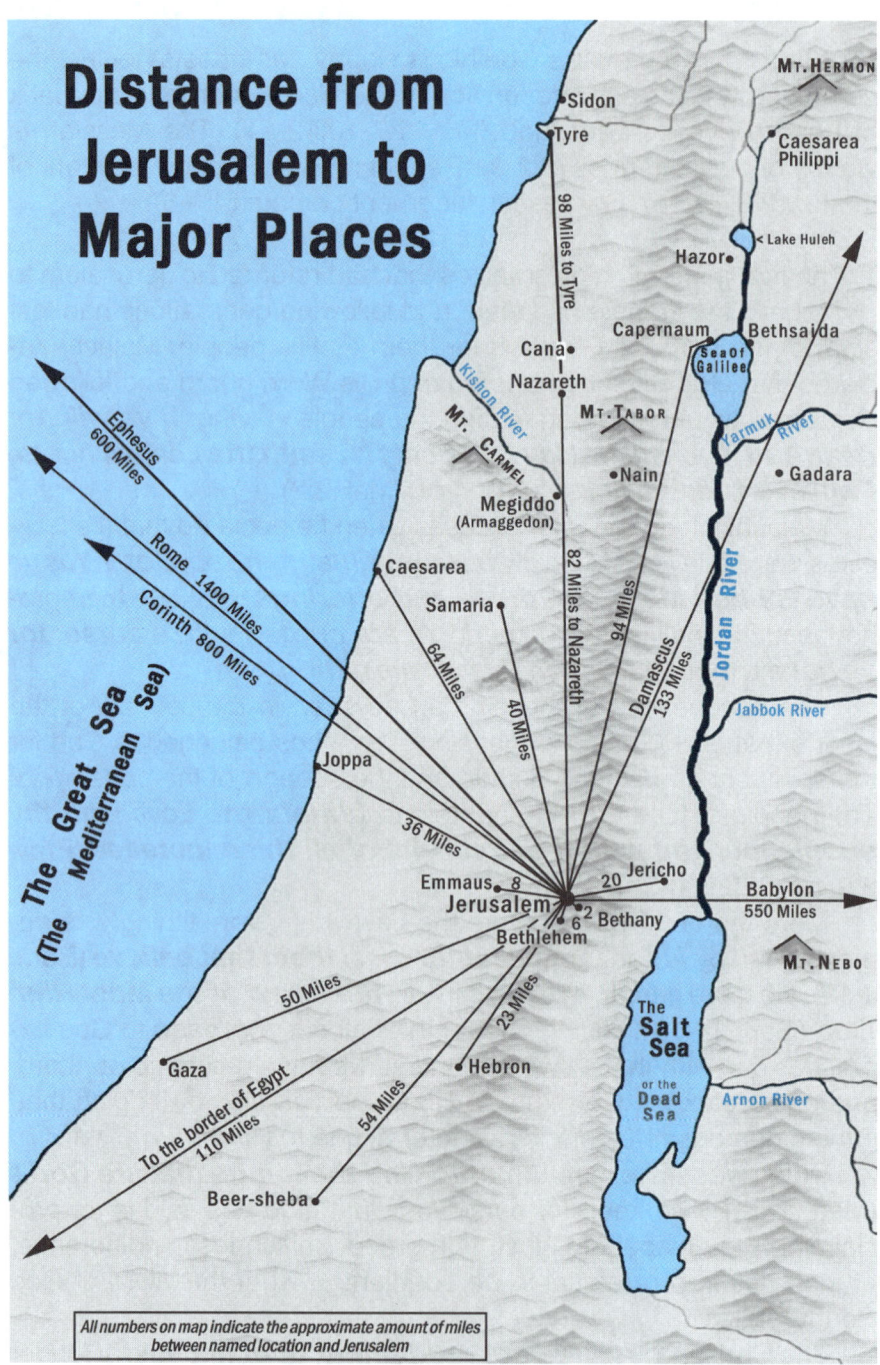

You will be My witnesses in Jerusalem, in all Judea and Samaria, and to the ends of the earth (Acts 1:8)

Intro To The Book of MATTHEW

The Gospel of Matthew was written by a Jew who was also known as Levi. He was a despised tax collector who worked for the Roman government (Matt. 10:3; Mark 2:14; Luke 5:27). Matthew presents Jesus as the fulfillment of all Messianic prophecy. In the opening sentence, we read: **The book of the generation of Jesus Christ, the Son of David, the Son of Abraham** (Matt. 1:1).

As the **Son of Abraham**, Matthew associates Jesus with the Covenant God had made with Abraham: **In thee shall all families of the earth be blessed** (Gen. 12:3; 17:7; II Sam. 7:8-17). **All families** includes both Jew and Gentile.

Since the focus of Old Testament Scripture is on the coming of the promised Messiah (Anointed One) and His Kingdom, Matthew used the phrase **Kingdom of Heaven** more than 30 times, **Son of David** 10 times, and **that it might be fulfilled which was spoken** at least 9 times. As confirmation that Jesus is the Messiah, the Holy Spirit led Matthew to record more than 20 of His miracles and more than 100 references to His parables. 10 contain the phrase: **The Kingdom of Heaven is likened** (Matt. 13:24,31,33,44-45,47,52; 20:1; 22:2; 25:1,14).

The Sanhedrin, religious high council, kept complete genealogical archives of the descendants of Abraham and David. They never questioned Jesus' ancestry. Both Joseph's and Mary's genealogies are the same from Abraham to David. Then Joseph's genealogy follows through David's son Solomon while Mary's traces from Nathan, another of David's sons.

To remove all doubt as to who Jesus is, Matthew records that, when Jesus was baptized, there was **a voice from heaven, saying, This is My beloved Son, in whom I am well pleased** (3:17). Later, Matthew also records the spectacular transfiguration of Christ during His conversation with Moses and Elijah, when again **a voice out of the cloud ... said, This is My beloved Son, in whom I am well pleased; hear ... Him** (17:2-5). The transfiguration completed Jesus' Galilean ministry. He then traveled south toward Jerusalem where He knew He would be crucified, **and the third day ... rise again** (20:19).

On the Mount of Olives (Luke 24:50), 40 days after His resurrection from the dead, Jesus told His disciples: **Go ... teach** (disciple) **all nations, baptizing them in the Name of the Father, and of the Son, and of the Holy Ghost** (Spirit): **Teaching them to observe all things whatsoever I have commanded you** (Matt. 28:19-20).

OCTOBER 1   Read Matthew 1 – 3

Highlights: Jesus' miraculous birth (Matt. 1:8-25) fulfills prophecies concerning the promised Messiah who would also be a descendant of Abraham and David (1:1-16). Herod is troubled by the news of the Wise Men (2:1-3). The enemy attempts to destroy the Lord's plan of salvation (2:13-18).

The birth of Jesus Christ was on this wise: When as His mother Mary was espoused to Joseph, before they came together, she was found with child of the Holy Ghost (Spirit) (Matt. 1:18). The amazing *wise men from the east*, perhaps from Babylon, were led by a star *to Jerusalem*, where they inquired: *Where is He that is born King of the Jews? for we have seen His star in the east, and are come to worship Him* (2:1-2). It is probable that these men had studied the prophecies of Daniel who, during the captivity, gave a detailed explanation of the number of years before the Messiah would be born (Dan. 9:25-26).

It must have taken the *wise men* some length of time after the birth of Christ to arrive in Bethlehem, since we read: *When they were come into the house, they saw the young Child with Mary His mother, and fell down, and worshipped Him* (Matt. 2:11). Finding the prophesied King in the house as a *young Child* rather than as a babe in the manger indicates He had grown out of infancy.

As a part of their worship they presented to Jesus three gifts (2:11). First, they offered *gold*, a fitting gift for *the King of kings, and Lord of lords* (I Tim. 6:15). Then, they offered *frankincense*, a sweet perfume used on the Altar of Incense in the Temple, symbolic of prayer ascending to God. It was an appropriate gift for a priest, for this King would become our *High Priest* (Heb. 4:14), *who also maketh intercession for us* (Rom. 8:34) before God. They also offered *myrrh,* which signified in advance that He was destined to die; myrrh was used as a burial spice (John 19:39).

In the providence of God, their gifts also provided adequate resources for Joseph and Mary's journey and stay in Egypt, where they remained *until the death of Herod: that it might be fulfilled which was spoken of the Lord by the prophet, saying, Out of Egypt have I called My Son* (Matt. 2:15; Hosea 11:1). Then they *dwelt in . . . Nazareth* where Jesus lived until He was about 30 years old (Matt. 2:23; Luke 3:23).

Thought for Today: Genuine love is expressed when we willingly give our time and tithes to the Lord.

Cross References: For **Matt. 1:23:** See Is. 7:14. **Matt. 2:6:** See Mic. 5:2. **Matt. 2:15:** See Hos. 11:1. **Matt. 2:18:** See Jer. 31:15. **Matt. 3:3:** See Is. 40:3.

OCTOBER 2   Read Matthew 4 – 6

Highlights: *Jesus . . . tempted of the devil* (Matt. 4:1-11). Christians are heirs of the Kingdom of God. The Christian's true spiritual food includes *every word that proceedeth out of the mouth of God* (4:4; Deut. 8:3). In the Sermon on the Mount, Jesus described the character of the children of God because of His new-birth nature they received at salvation (5:13-6:34). How to pray and fast (6:5-18).

Following His baptism in the Jordan River, Jesus was *led up of the Spirit into the wilderness to be tempted of the Devil* (Matt. 4:1). First, the Devil suggested an easy, self-serving way in which Jesus might satisfy His hunger (appealing to the lust of the flesh) (4:2-3). But Jesus, knowing that submission to the will of God must be the basis for all decisions, quoted Scripture, saying: *It is written, Man shall not live by bread alone, but by every word that proceedeth out of the mouth of God* (4:4).

Satan's second temptation came in *the Holy City . . . on a pinnacle* (highest point) *of the Temple* (4:5). Satan suggested that Jesus should leap down into the midst of the people and present Himself as a super-human Messiah (appealing to the pride of life). Satan quoted Scripture, saying: *He shall give His angels charge concerning Thee. . . lest at any time Thou dash Thy foot against a stone* (4:6; Ps. 91:11-12). The devil frequently appears religious by quoting Scripture, but only the portions which fit his scheme. Jesus responded: *It is written again, Thou shalt not tempt* (test) *the Lord thy God* (4:7). God often allows such testing as a necessary part of the believer's life because it reveals one's true character.

In Satan's final attempt to seduce Jesus to sin, he *sheweth Him all the kingdoms of the world . . . And saith . . . All these things will I give Thee, if Thou wilt fall down and worship me* (4:8-9). The devil suggested an easy way by which Jesus might avoid all pain and suffering of the cross and still rule *all the kingdoms of the world*. But even one exception would make Jesus a sinner. Jesus said: *Get thee hence* (away)*, Satan . . . it is written, Thou shalt worship the Lord thy God, and Him only shalt thou serve* (4:10). Then the devil left Jesus, and angels came and ministered to Him. *From that time Jesus began to preach, and to say, Repent: for the kingdom of heaven is at hand.* To Simon Peter and Andrew He said: *Follow Me, and I will make you fishers of men* (Matt. 4:17-19).

Thought for Today: The poor in spirit are rich in spiritual blessings.

Cross References: For **Matt. 4:4:** See Deut. 8:3. **Matt. 4:6:** See Ps. 91:11-12. **Matt. 4:7:** See Deut. 6:16. **Matt. 4:10:** See Deut. 6:13. **Matt. 4:15-16:** See Is. 9:1-2. **Matt. 5:21:** See Ex. 20:13. **Matt. 5:27:** See Ex. 20:14. **Matt. 5:31:** Deut. 24:1. **Matt. 5:33:** See Num. 30:2. **Matt. 5:38:** See Ex. 21:24. **Matt. 5:43:** See Lev. 19:18.

Old Testament Quoted by Christ — Partial List

Matthew	Old Testament Passage	Occasion
4:4	Deut. 8:3	40-Day Temptation
4:7	Deut. 6:16	
4:10	Deut. 6:13	
5:21	Ex. 20:13; Deut. 5:17	Sermon on the Mount
5:27	Ex. 20:14; Deut. 5:18	
5:31	Deut. 24:1	
5:33	Lev. 19:12; Num. 30:2; Deut. 23:21	
5:38	Ex. 21:24; Lev. 24:20; Deut. 19:21	
5:43	Lev. 19:18; Deut. 23:6; 25:19	
9:13	Hos. 6:6	Response to His Critics
11:10	Mal. 3:1	Concerning John
12:7	Hos. 6:6	Response to His Critics
13:14-15	Isa. 6:9-10	Why Speaks in Parables
15:4	Ex. 20:12; 21:17; Lev. 20:9; Deut. 5:16	Response to His Critics
15:7-9	Isa. 29:13	Response to His Critics
19:4-5	Gen. 1:27; 2:24	Sacredness of Marriage; Response to His Critics
21:16	Ps. 8:2	Triumphal Entry
21:42,44	Ps. 118:22-23	Stone Rejected by Builders
27:46	Ps. 22:1	On the Cross

Mark	Old Testament Passage	Occasion
7:6-7	Isa 29:13	Sermon on the Mount
7:10	Ex. 20:12; 21:17; Lev. 20:9; Deut. 5:16	
10:6	Gen. 1:27	Response to His Critics
10:7-8	Gen. 2:24	Response to His Critics
12:29-30	Deut. 6:4-5	Response to His Critics
12:36	Ps. 110:1	Teaching Concerning David's Son

Luke	Old Testament Passage	Occasion
4:4	Deut. 8:3	40-Day Temptation
4:8	Deut. 6:13	
4:12	Deut. 6:16	
4:18-19	Isa. 61:1-2	Nazareth Synagogue
7:27	Mal. 3:1	Concerning John
19:46	Isa. 56:7	The Temple Cleansing
23:46	Ps. 31:5	On the Cross

John	Old Testament Passage	Occasion
6:45	Isa. 54:13	Response to His Critics
8:17	Deut. 17:6	Response to His Critics
10:34	Ps. 82:6	Response to His Critics
15:25	Ps. 35:19; 69:4	Last Supper

OCTOBER 3   Read Matthew 7 – 9

Highlights: Jesus teaches how Christians should live (Matt. 7). Don't miss the Golden Rule and the narrow gate (7:12-14). Jesus emphasizes the power of faith (chap. 8 – 9). Like sheep, people need a shepherd. The harvest is great; *the labourers are few* (9:36-38).

Jesus warned: ***Beware of false prophets . . . in sheep's clothing*** (Matt. 7:15). Without a doubt, eternal life is a free gift from God – ***not of works, lest any man should boast*** (Eph. 2:9). But it is also true ***that faith without works is dead*** (James 2:20). To clarify one difference between true prophets and false prophets, He said: ***Not every one that saith unto Me, Lord, Lord, shall enter into the Kingdom of Heaven; but he that doeth the will of My Father which is in heaven*** (Matt. 7:21). However, the evidence of being a true Christian is not proved by doing great things but by being obedient to the Lord Jesus Christ.

Our Lord spoke a parable: ***Whosoever heareth these sayings of Mine, and doeth them, I will liken*** (compare) ***him unto a wise man, which built his house upon a rock . . . and the floods came, and the winds blew, and beat upon that house; and it fell not: for it was founded upon a rock. And every one that heareth these sayings of Mine, and doeth them not, shall be likened*** (compared) ***unto a foolish man, which built his house upon the sand . . . and the floods came, and the winds blew, and beat upon that house; and it fell: and great was the fall of it*** (7:24-27).

Obedience to Christ is twofold: First, one ***heareth these sayings*** and then one acts on them. When our desire is to please Christ, His Word will be the supreme rule of our life and will lead us to avoid the snares of ***the lust of the flesh, and the lust of the eyes, and the pride of life. . . . he that doeth the will of God abideth forever*** (I John 2:16-17). Through His Word, the Holy Spirit guides and enables us to live each day doing the will of God.

It is impossible to relive wasted years, but it is always possible to turn from sinking sand to build upon the eternal rock. ***For other foundation can no man lay than that is laid, which is Jesus Christ. Now if any man build upon this foundation . . . Every man's work shall be made manifest*** (known) ***. . . because it shall be revealed by fire; and the fire shall try*** (test) ***every man's work of what sort it is*** (I Cor. 3:11-13).

Thought for Today: Having the mind of Christ purifies our thoughts (Phil. 2:5).

Cross References: For **Matt. 7:23:** See Ps. 6:8. **Matt. 8:4:** See Lev. 13:49; 14:2. **Matt. 8:17:** See Is. 53:4. **Matt. 9:13:** Hos. 6:6.

OCTOBER 4 — Read Matthew 10 – 11

Highlights: Thank God for Jesus' promise: ***Whosoever therefore shall confess Me before men, him will I confess also before My Father which is in heaven*** (Matt. 10:32). John the Baptist is about to be beheaded, but he made the right choice (10:28). Jesus praised him as His messenger (11:1-15). Unbelievers' actions and judgment (11:16-24). Life's greatest invitation: ***Come unto Me*** (11:28-30).

When He saw the multitudes, He was moved with compassion on them, because they fainted, and were scattered abroad, as sheep having no shepherd. Then saith He unto His disciples, The harvest truly is plenteous (plentiful), ***but the labourers are few; Pray . . . the Lord of the harvest, that He will send forth labourers into His harvest*** (Matt. 9:36-38). In answer to this need, Jesus chose just 12 ordinary men whom He taught, saying: ***I send you forth as sheep in the midst of wolves: be . . . wise as serpents, and harmless as doves*** (10:16).

Persecution, often in the form of pressure to compromise, tests a Christian's sincerity. Times of peace often cause the ***sheep*** (followers of Christ) to be indifferent but, during persecution and temptation, the ***sheep*** discover they must depend on the Shepherd. Wolves are the natural enemy of sheep and ***wolves*** (false prophets) in human form often appear as ***sheep*** (7:15), quoting only the few verses of Scripture that support their agenda.

The Christian is given a "sheep-like" nature – symbolic of innocence and dependence, not of cowardice. Sheep, by their very nature, are in need of a shepherd or they will wander off and easily become prey to many enemies. Still worse, if one wanders, the entire flock may aimlessly follow. There is never safety in numbers for sheep; a shepherd is always necessary. ***All we like sheep have gone astray*** (Is. 53:6) and need ***the*** (Holy) ***Spirit . . . He will guide you*** (us) ***into all Truth*** each day (John 16:13).

Christians can boldly face the fiercest enemy for Jesus said: ***Fear not them which kill the body, but are not able to kill the soul*** (Matt. 10:28). The Christian has every reason not to expect kindness from a hostile world. Jesus said to His followers: ***Because ye are not of the world, but I have chosen you out of the world, therefore the world hateth you. . . . they will also persecute you*** (John 15:19-20).

Thought for Today: The meek are patient when faced with difficulties (Matt. 5:5).

Cross References: For **Matt. 10:11, 35-36:** See Mic. 7:6. **Matt. 11:5:** See Is. 35:5; 61:1. **Matt. 11:10:** See Mal. 3:1. **Matt. 11:23:** See Ezek. 26:20; 31:14; 32:18,24. **Matt. 11:29:** See Jer. 6:16.

OCTOBER 5   Read Matthew 12

Highlights: Who is Lord of the Sabbath (Matt. 12:1-14)? The true family of Jesus (12:46-50).

Jesus was confronted by the Pharisees who criticized His disciples, saying: ***Behold, Thy disciples do that which is not lawful to do upon the Sabbath day*** (Matt. 12:2). Jesus responded: ***I say unto you. . . . the Son of Man is Lord even of the Sabbath day*** (12:6,8). The Old Testament worship system foreshadowed the life and ministry of Jesus Christ. The Old Testament Israelite had been commanded to keep the last day of the week, the Sabbath, as a day of rest to commemorate the Lord's **work of creation** in six days (Ex. 20:9-11). But Jesus said He is not only far superior to the Temple, but to the Sabbath day of rest, and is to be worshiped far above all else.

The weekly Sabbath, as well as all Jewish worship days, which were also Sabbaths or holy convocations, were merely ***a shadow of things to come*** (Col. 2:17). The early Church recognized this and, in commemoration of Christ's resurrection, ***upon the first day of the week . . . the disciples came together to break bread*** (Acts 20:7). The Apostle Paul was led to write: ***Upon the first day of the week*** (no longer on the day of rest) ***let every one of you lay by him in store, as God hath prospered him, that there be no gatherings*** (of tithes and freewill offerings) ***when I come*** (I Cor. 16:2).

Most Christians today assemble to worship the Lord on the first day of the week. In this way, we honor Him as Lord of our lives by putting Him first in every week. In today's fast-paced world where some people work two or even three jobs, attend many weekly meetings, and are involved in multiple family activities, it is often hard to rest from one's labor. The rest God speaks of is needed for both physical and spiritual refreshment and to allow time to meditate on the Word of God and to commune with Him. Under the New Testament (Covenant) Jesus made, every day is considered holy as Paul wrote to the Colossians: ***Let no man therefore judge you in . . . respect of an holyday . . . or of the Sabbath days: Which are a shadow of things to come*** (Col. 2:16-17). Whatever day of rest one chooses, it is important to ***remember the Sabbath day, to keep it holy*** (pure, sanctified, set apart) (Ex. 20:8). The original plan of God is always the best.

Thought for Today: *The fear of the LORD is the beginning of wisdom* (Prov. 9:10).

Cross References: For **Matt. 12:7:** See Hos. 6:6. **Matt. 12:18-21:** See Is. 42:1-4. **Matt. 12:40:** See Jon. 1:17.

OCTOBER 6   Read Matthew 13 – 14

Highlights: The Word of God is the seed. We're just told to plant and let it grow. God provides the fruit (Matt. 13:1-23). Mustard seed, yeast, and hidden treasure. The pearl of great price (13:45-46). Jesus miraculously feeds 5,000 when there is only a little food (14:13-21); Jesus walks on water (14:25-27).

In the first parable of Jesus that Matthew recorded, Jesus described four kinds of responses from those who hear His Word. His true disciple is represented by the **good ground** that receives seed, which in turn brings forth fruit even to **an hundredfold** (Matt. 13:8-23). His second parable was of **tares** (weeds) that grew in the same field with wheat but could not produce fruit (13:24-30).

Tares look identical to wheat as they grow. In their young stages, only an expert can tell the difference. But, when these weeds reach maturity there is no head, exposing their lack of value. Jesus declared: **Let both grow together until the harvest** (13:30). Jesus explained that **the field is the world; the good seed are the children of the kingdom** (13:38).

The **tares** represent those who outwardly appear to believe in Christ, but who have never truly received Jesus as Savior and Lord of their lives. They may join a church, give their tithes, and deceive members of the church, but not Christ. It may seem startling to read that **the Son of Man shall send forth His angels, and they shall gather out of His Kingdom all . . . which do iniquity; And shall cast them into a furnace of fire: there shall be wailing and gnashing of teeth** (13:41-42).

No one expects to be hurled into **outer darkness** where there is weeping, **wailing and gnashing of teeth** forever (8:12). But Jesus warned: **Narrow is the way, which leadeth unto life, and few there be that find it. Beware of false prophets** (7:14-15).

These **few** who find eternal life have characteristics that are not true of the majority of people. They recognized that they were sinners and needed a Savior, and they asked the Lord to forgive them of their sins and to be Lord of their lives.

To **believe on the Lord Jesus Christ, and . . . be saved** (Acts 16:31) means much more than a mental assent to the fact; it's their way of life. They **continue in the faith grounded and settled, and be** (are) **not moved away from the hope of the Gospel** (Col. 1:23).

Thought for Today: Our faith is strengthened as we obey the Word of God – the *Source* of faith.

Cross References: For **Matt. 13:14-15:** See Is. 6:9-10. **Matt. 13:32:** See Ps. 104:12; Ezek. 17:23; 31:6; Dan. 4:12. **Matt. 13:35:** See Ps. 78:2. **Matt. 13:41:** See Zeph. 1:3. **Matt. 13:43:** See Dan. 12:3.

OCTOBER 7 — Read Matthew 15 – 17

Highlights: Jesus rebukes the ***hypocrites . . . saying, This people draweth nigh unto Me with their mouth, and honoureth Me with their lips; but their heart is far from Me*** (Matt. 15:7-8). Jesus' first mention of His ***Church*** (16:18). Disciples receive "faith builders" in viewing the transfiguration (17:1-13). The healing of the demon-possessed boy (17:14-18).

Caesarea Philippi was a center of worship for Pan, Greek god representative of all gods of paganism, as well as the Baal god, considered to be a "lord of heaven and earth." It was located about 25 miles north of the Sea of Galilee at the foot of the southern slope of Mount Hermon, with its snow-capped peak 9,000 feet above sea level, the "highest mountain" in the promised land (Matt. 17:2). Many believe that the transfiguration of Christ took place there.

Amid a large number of idol worshipers in Caesarea Philippi, Jesus asked His disciples: ***Whom do men say that I the Son of Man am?*** In response to His question, the disciples answered: ***Some say that Thou art John the Baptist: some, Elias; and others, Jeremias, or one of the prophets.*** But when He asked: ***But whom say ye that I am?*** – without hesitation, Peter said: ***Thou art the Christ, the Son of the Living God*** (16:13-16).

Our Lord then introduced the word Church for the first time (16:18). Christ is the Head of the Church which is composed of all people redeemed by His blood. The redeemed recognize their responsibility to help one another in living their covenant relationship with Christ since the Church is ***the Body of Christ*** (I Cor. 12:27). The local "church" is a community of caring brothers and sisters in fellowship with one another, seeking to ***be witnesses unto Me*** (Christ) ***. . . and unto the uttermost part of the earth*** (Acts 1:8).

Some who claim to be Christians disregard fellowship with other believers in worship. Unknown to them, their spiritual strength is weakened along with their influence and testimony.

In striking contrast, ***Christ also loved the*** (True) ***Church, and gave Himself for it; That He might sanctify and cleanse it with the washing of water by the Word, That He might present it to Himself a glorious Church, not having spot, or wrinkle, or any such thing; but that it should be holy and without blemish*** (Eph. 5:25-27; also I Cor. 1:10).

Thought for Today: Our worship is never in vain when we worship our Lord as God.

Cross References: For **Matt. 15:4:** See Ex. 20:12; 21:17; Lev. 20:9; Deut. 5:16. **Matt. 15:8-9:** See Is. 29:13. **Matt. 16:27:** See Ps. 62:12; Prov. 24:12.

OCTOBER 8 — Read Matthew 18 – 20

Highlights: The importance of helping and not hindering children (Matt. 18:3-10); Jesus' purpose in life: ***To save that which was lost*** (18:11-14); the importance of forgiving all offenses (18:21-35); Christ and divorce (19:3-12); the difficulty of being rich and entering heaven (19:16-30). By faith, we follow our King. With Jesus ***all things are possible*** (19:26). Laborers in His Kingdom (20:1-16). Jesus foretells His death and resurrection (20:17-19). Conduct of His followers; two blind men receive sight (20:17-34).

Peter asked a far more important question than he realized when he inquired of Jesus: ***Lord, how oft shall my brother sin against me, and I forgive him? till seven times? Jesus saith unto him, I say not unto thee, Until seven times: but, Until seventy times seven*** (Matt. 18:21-22). Peter thought he was being generous in suggesting ***seven times***. This was twice as many times as required by the traditions of the scribes, plus one more.

Unwillingness to forgive others while, at the same time, expecting Christ to forgive us is a sin. He warned of the horrifying consequences of an unforgiving attitude: ***If ye forgive not men their trespasses, neither will your Father forgive your trespasses*** (6:15).

The Lord gives an illustration of a servant who owed ***ten thousand talents*** to his king (18:24). This huge debt was impossible to repay even in a lifetime. The servant pleaded: ***Lord, have patience with me, and I will pay thee all. Then the lord ... forgave him the debt. But the same servant went out, and found one of his fellowservants, which owed him an hundred pence*** (mere pennies compared to 10,000 talents): ***and he laid hands on him ... saying, Pay me that thou owest. And his fellowservant fell down at his feet, and besought him, saying, Have patience with me, and I will pay thee all. And he would not: but went and cast him into prison*** (18:26-30). When his lord was made aware of what took place, he ***was wroth*** (angry), ***and delivered him to the tormentors, till he should pay all that was due unto him. So likewise shall My Heavenly Father do also unto you, if ye from your hearts forgive not every one his brother their trespasses*** (18:34-35).

Paul urged believers: ***Be ye kind one to another, tenderhearted, forgiving one another, even as God for Christ's sake hath forgiven you*** (Eph. 4:31-32; also Matt. 6:14-15).

Thought for Today: Live for the Lord now and you will enjoy eternity with Him.

Cross References: For **Matt. 18:16:** See Deut. 19:15. **Matt. 19:4:** See Gen. 1:27; 5:2. **Matt. 19:5:** See Gen. 2:24. **Matt. 19:7:** See Deut. 24:1-4. **Matt. 19:18:** See Ex. 20:13-16; Deut. 5:17-20. **Matt. 19:19:** See Ex. 20:12; Lev. 19:18; Deut. 5:16.

OCTOBER 9   Read Matthew 21 – 22

Highlights: Prophecy fulfilled of Jesus' triumphant entry to Jerusalem (Matt. 21:1-11); defiled Temple, cleansing, His miracles (21:12-15); fig tree cursed (21:18-22); authority of Jesus (21:23); a heavenly parable: The King's invitation is rejected; His parables expected fruit; marriage feast; importance of knowing Scripture; the Great Commandment (22:37-40).

On Monday before His crucifixion, and the day after His triumphant entry into Jerusalem, *Jesus went into the Temple of God, and cast out all them that sold and bought . . . And said unto them, It is written, My House shall be called the house of prayer; but ye have made it a den of thieves* (Matt. 21:12-13; Is. 56:7).

The chief priests were outraged. They dispatched a delegation to interrupt Jesus *as He was teaching, and said* (to Him)*, By what authority doest Thou these things* (Matt. 21:23)*?* They were referring to His accepting all the praise that the multitude had given him as the Messiah and in dismissing their money changers. They were infuriated and conspired to kill Him (26:4).

The Temple belonged to God, who was supposed to be there in their midst. Jesus' cleansing of the Temple illustrates how He alone cleanses us through His atoning blood (26:28; I John 1:7; Rev. 1:5).

After declaring: *The Kingdom of God shall be taken from you. . . . Jesus . . . spake unto them again by parables, and said, The Kingdom of Heaven is like unto a certain king, which made a marriage for his son. . . . Then saith he to his servants, The wedding is ready. . . . Go . . . therefore into the highways, and as many as ye shall find, bid to the marriage. . . . And when the king came in to see the guests, he saw there a man which had not on a wedding garment. . . . Then said the king to the servants . . . cast him into outer darkness; there shall be weeping and gnashing of teeth* (Matt. 21:43; 22:1-2, 8-13).

Hell is eternal separation from God and Jesus said more about the horrifying torments of it than all the writers of the New Testament combined. In this parable, Jesus exposes all who assume they are good enough for heaven. The Apostle Paul said: *There are many unruly and vain talkers and deceivers. . . . They profess that they know God; but in works they deny Him, being . . . disobedient, and unto every good work reprobate* (Titus 1:10,16).

Thought for Today: True humility includes an attitude of gentleness with others.

Cross References: For **Matt. 21:5:** See Is. 62:11; Zech. 9:9. **Matt. 21:9:** See Ps. 118:26. **Matt. 21:13:** See Is. 56:7; Jer. 7:11. **Matt. 21:16:** See Ps. 8:2. **Matt. 21:33:** See Ps. 80:8; Is. 5:1-2. **Matt. 21:42:** See Ps. 118:22-23. **Matt. 22:24:** See Deut. 25:5. **Matt. 22:32:** See Ex. 3:6. **Matt. 22:37:** See Deut. 6:5. **Matt. 22:39:** See Lev. 19:18. **Matt. 22:44:** See Ps. 110:1.

OCTOBER 10   Read Matthew 23–24

Highlights: Jesus announces the horrible fate of hypocritical religious leaders (Matt. 23:1-36)! Jesus deeply grieves over Jerusalem (23:37-39). Only God knows the day (24:36)!

Following the cleansing of the Temple and the denouncing of the religious leaders as hypocrites, the Lord sat with His disciples on the Mount of Olives and foretold: *Many false prophets shall rise, and shall deceive many. And because iniquity* (lawlessness) *shall abound, the love of many shall wax* (become) *cold. But he that shall endure unto the end, the same shall be saved. And this Gospel of the Kingdom shall be preached in all the world for a witness unto all nations; and then shall the end come. . . . Heaven and earth shall pass away, but My words shall not pass away* (Matt. 24:11-14,35). Like the Pharisees of old, the *false prophets* today substitute contemporary opinions and situational ethics as a contradiction to the authority of the Word of God.

On the Mount of Olives, just three days before His crucifixion, our Lord foretold the destruction of the Temple. It was destroyed according to His Word about 40 years after His resurrection. He also described to His disciples, His future return from heaven, saying: *Of that day and hour knoweth no man, no, not the angels of heaven, but My Father only* (24:36). He also warned: *Watch therefore: for ye know not what hour your Lord doth come. . . . Therefore be . . . ready: for in such an hour as ye think not the Son of Man cometh* (24:42,44).

Jesus made no attempt to give details concerning the soon destruction of Jerusalem, nor the more distant end of the age. But these words from the King emphasized the importance of always being prepared. The parable of two servants also emphasizes this importance: *Who then is a faithful and wise servant, whom his lord hath made ruler over his household, to give them meat in due season? Blessed is that servant, whom his lord when he cometh shall find so doing. . . . But . . . if that evil servant shall say in his heart, My lord delayeth his coming; And shall begin to smite* (beat) *his fellowservants, and to eat and drink with the drunken; The lord of that servant shall come in a day when . . . he is not aware of . . . and appoint him his portion with the hypocrites: there shall be weeping and gnashing of teeth* (Matt. 24:45-51).

Thought for Today: God is concerned about the inward condition of the heart as well as our daily conversation and attitudes.

Cross References: For **Matt. 23:39:** See Ps. 118:26. **Matt. 24:15:** See Dan. 9:27; 11:31; 12:11. **Matt. 24:29:** See Is. 13:10; 24:23; 34:4; Ezek. 32:7; Joel 2:10,31; 3:15; Zeph. 1:15. **Matt. 24:30:** See Dan. 7:13. **Matt. 24:31:** See Deut. 30:4; Is. 27:13; Zech. 2:6. **Matt. 24:38:** See Gen. 6:3-5; 7:7.

OCTOBER 11 — Read Matthew 25 – 26

Highlights: When the Lord returns, servants will be evaluated (Matt. 25:1-13). Wait faithfully. Share His Word (25:14-30,46). Last Supper – Jesus' New Covenant sealed in His blood (26:26-28). His betrayal (26:47-50).

Jesus spoke about Himself in a parable, saying: **The Kingdom of Heaven is as a man travelling into a far country, who called his own servants, and delivered unto them his goods. And unto one he gave five talents, to another two, and to another one; to every man according to his several** (own) **ability; and straightway took his journey** (Matt. 25:14-15). These talents did not belong to the servants, but remained the property of their master. The servants were to be his managers (stewards) of the **goods** entrusted to them. The **goods** of this parable represent the opportunities and abilities that God has given to us and expects us to use for His Kingdom.

The servant who received **five talents** recognized that what he had received was the property of his master. On the day of judgment he said: **Lord, thou deliveredst unto me five talents: behold, I have gained beside them five talents more** (25:20).

And likewise he that had received two, he also gained other two (25:17). He was not expected to gain five since he had been given according to his own ability. Both faithfully doubled their talents and both were equally commended.

The third servant had received **one** talent. He put forth no effort for his master. Instead, he **went and digged in the earth, and hid his lord's** (master's) **money** (25:18). His laziness and judgmental attitude were inexcusable, not unlike those today who shirk their responsibilities and pass judgment on others, thinking they are justified in their actions. The consequences of neglecting the opportunities to serve his master were irreversible; there was no second chance to relive his life. The master declared: **Cast ye the unprofitable servant into outer darkness: there shall be weeping and gnashing of teeth** (25:30; compare 8:12; 22:13; 24:51).

We can choose to ignore our opportunities to serve the Lord, withhold our tithes, and desecrate the Lord's Day; but, **every one of us shall give account of himself to God** (Rom. 14:12). **Ye are not your own ... ye are bought with a price: therefore glorify God in your body, and in your spirit, which are God's** (I Cor. 6:19-20).

Thought for Today: Christians receive and enjoy a spiritual experience as they help others (Titus 3:8).

Cross References: For **Matt. 26:31:** See Zech. 13:7. **Matt. 26:64:** See Ps. 110:1; Dan. 7:13.

OCTOBER 12   Read Matthew 27 – 28

Highlights: Pilate's question; what will <u>you</u> do with Jesus (Matt. 27:22)? The horrifying crucifixion of our Lord, His death (27:32-65), and His resurrection (28:1-15). ***Go ... teach ... them to observe all things*** (28:18-20).

The resurrection of Jesus gave His disciples the key to understanding that their King and His Kingdom were both eternal. ***Jesus came and spake unto them saying, All power*** (authority) ***is given unto Me in heaven and in earth. Go ... therefore, and teach all nations, baptizing them in the Name of the Father, and of the Son, and of the Holy Ghost: Teaching them to observe all things whatsoever I have commanded you*** (Matt. 28:18-20).

When we are baptized ***in the Name of the Father, and of the Son, and of the Holy Ghost*** (Spirit), we proclaim the fullness of the Godhead. Thus, by public baptism, we confess to the world that God is our **Heavenly Father**. The phrase **and of the Son** is our witness to the world that Jesus is now Savior and Lord of our lives. Upon our confession, **the Holy Ghost** becomes our indwelling Sanctifier, Comforter, and Guide throughout life (John 14:26; 16:13). By this we confirm and bear witness of the Triune nature of the Godhead and proclaim One God expressed in Three Persons.

Being **born again** (3:3,7) by His Spirit is a supernatural experience which changes the heart. Like **newborn babes,** (we are to) ***desire the sincere milk of the Word, that ye*** (we) ***may grow thereby*** (I Pet. 2:2). The Lord's only inspired Guide – the Bible – transforms our lives to one of daily worship and service to Him. His Holy Spirit teaches us how to live and what He expects us to do. Titus was guided by the Holy Spirit, to teach ***us that, denying ungodliness and worldly lusts, we should live soberly, righteously, and godly, in this present world; Looking for that blessed hope, and the glorious appearing of the great God and our Saviour Jesus Christ; Who gave Himself for us, that He might redeem us from all iniquity*** (lawlessness), ***and purify unto Himself a peculiar*** (special) ***people, zealous of good works*** (Titus 2:12-15). We all at times fail the Lord, but let us say with Paul: ***Forgetting those things which are behind, and reaching forth unto those things which are before, I press toward the mark*** (goal) ***for the prize of the high calling of God in Christ Jesus*** (Phil. 3:13-14).

Thought for Today: If God is your partner, you had better have BIG plans.

Cross References: For **Matt. 27:5-10:** See Zech. 11:12-13. **Matt. 27:34:** See Ps. 69:21. **Matt. 27:35:** See Ps. 22:18. **Matt. 27:39:** See Job 16:4; Ps. 109:25; Lam. 2:15. **Matt. 27:43:** See Ps. 22:8. **Matt. 27:46:** See Ps. 22:1.

Introduction To The Book of MARK

The Holy Spirit directed Mark to emphasize the deity of Jesus who also was the perfect Servant of God. Five times He is called either **Son of God, Son of the Most High God,** or **Christ, the Son of the Blessed** (Mark 1:1; 3:11; 5:7; 14:61; 15:39). The first verse of the Book of Mark reads: **The beginning of the Gospel of Jesus Christ, the Son of God** (1:1). To confirm Jesus as **the Son of God**, Mark records about 20 of His miracles, demonstrating Jesus' authority over demons, nature, disease, and death (1:21-28; 1:29-31; 1:32-34; 1:40-45; 2:3-12; 3:1-6; 4:35-41; 5:1-20; 5:25-34; 5:22-24,35-43; 6:31-44; 6:45-50; 6:51-54; 7:24-30; 7:31-37; 8:1-9; 8:22-26; 9:2-10; 9:14-29; 10:46-52; 11:12-14,20-26; 16:1-11; 16:19-20).

Mark also describes Jesus as **the Son of Man** (who) **came ... to give His life a ransom for many** (10:45); the Faithful Servant of God; a Man of action – always busy doing and working – using such terms as **immediately** (at once), **straightway,** and **forthwith** (shortly), which Mark used over 40 times. His servanthood is portrayed in such passages as: **The Son of Man came not to be ministered unto** (served)**, but to minister** (serve) (10:45). The Holy Spirit also led Mark to record 9 parables (2:21; 2:22; 4:1-20; 4:21-22; 4:26-29; 4:30-32; 12:1-12; 13:28-31; 13:32-37).

Only in Mark are the hands of Jesus so prominent. Only Mark records that His town folk said: **Even such mighty works are wrought by His hands** (6:2). All these are symbolic of the work of a servant. None of the other Gospels refer to Jesus' hands as in the following Scriptures: Mark 1:31; 8:23,25; 9:27; 7:33.

There is no genealogy of Jesus, no mention of His birth, or the wise men, and nothing about His childhood or youth, since none of these are of interest in the account of a servant's life.

Only the Gospel of Mark describes Jesus taking **a child ... in His arms** (9:36).

Mark also refers to Jesus as **Master** (Teacher, Rabbi) 15 times (4:38; 5:35; 9:5,17,38; 10:17,20,35; 11:21; 12:14,19,32; 13:1; 14:14,45).

Mark was appealing to Gentiles, so he was led to explain many Jewish customs and teachings about which non-Jewish readers might not be familiar (2:18; 7:3-4; 14:12; 15:42). Mark also explained Judean geographic names and plants (1:13; 11:13; 13:3) and the value of Jewish coins in Roman money (12:42).

OCTOBER 13

Read Mark 1 – 3

Highlights: The King who rules by serving others and loving the unlovable. Jesus teaches and heals, and reveals His power over evil spirits. Jesus, Lord of the Sabbath (Mark 2:28). Invitation to be united with God and a fisher of men (1:17; 3:31-35).

God had directed Moses to **command the children of Israel, that they put out of the camp every leper.... that they defile not their camps, in the midst whereof I dwell** (Num. 5:2-3). No disease occupies so much space in the Scriptures as leprosy. It first appears as just a white, then pink, spot. Eventually, a leper loses sensitivity to pain, flesh decays, and fingers and toes rot off. This loathsome disease often results in death. That it why it is used as an illustration of sin which may start small but eventually causes one to become insensitive to sin's decay.

For centuries, lepers were incurable and they were considered the untouchables of society. One of these pitiful outcasts boldly made his way to Jesus, **beseeching** (begging) **Him, and kneeling down to Him, and saying unto Him, If Thou wilt, Thou canst make me clean** (Mark 1:40). When the leper said: **If Thou wilt,** he knew Jesus could heal. But he doubted His willingness to do so since leprosy was more than just a hopeless disease; it made him unclean before God. It was not "Could He?" but "Would He?" **Jesus, moved with compassion, put forth His hand, and touched him, and saith unto him, I will; be ... clean** (1:41).

Matthew records that this leper **worshipped Him** (Matt. 8:2), and Luke said that he **fell on his face** before Him (Luke 5:12). Only Mark tells us that Jesus was **moved with compassion** and that His loving hand reached out to this defiled leper and **touched him**. Both Jesus' touch and the Word he spoke expressed compassion: **Be ... clean** (Mark 1:41; Luke 5:13).

Today Jesus says: **Now ye are clean through the Word which I have spoken unto you** (John 15:3). Faith in God comes through hearing His Word (Rom. 10:17). Once saved, like the cleansed leper who **began to publish it much** (Mark 1:45), we will want to tell others what Jesus has done for us. As we see how sin is devastating the spiritual lives of people, we need to tell them that **the Lord is ... longsuffering ... not willing that any should perish, but that all should come to repentance** (II Pet. 3:9).

Thought for Today: The greater the pressures, the more time we must give to prayer.

Cross References: For **Mark 1:2:** See Mal. 3:1. **Mark 1:3:** Is. 40:3.

OCTOBER 14   Read Mark 4 – 5

Highlights: Jesus is in a boat just offshore, teaching a crowd about spiritual growth and the Kingdom of God (Mark 4:1-34). At **even** (4:35) He calms the sea (4:39). Jesus rebukes demons, heals an issue of blood, and raises the dead (4:35 – 5:1-43)!

Jesus described in a parable four kinds of responses from those who hear His Word: *Behold, there went out a sower to sow ... some* (seed) *fell by the way side, and the fowls of the air came and devoured it* (Mark 4:3-4). This means that some people respond to the Gospel with total disinterest. They represent the hearer who expresses no concern for spiritual values but seeks after pleasures and self-indulgence. *Satan cometh immediately, and taketh away the Word that was sown in their hearts* (4:15).

Others who hear His Word are like seed sown *on stony ground* (4:5). At first they are receptive but soon lose interest. *And have no root in themselves, and so endure but for a time: afterward, when affliction or persecution ariseth for* (because of) *the Word's sake, immediately they are offended* (4:16-17). "Stony ground" means solid rock beneath a shallow covering of soil. These "converts" appear promising and full of life until they are faced with persecution because of the Word of God; then they immediately quit.

Other "converts" are like seed *sown among thorns; such as hear the Word, And the cares of this world, and the deceitfulness of riches, and the lusts of other things entering in, choke the Word, and it becometh unfruitful* (4:18-19). Such people seem to recognize the true worth of Christ and eternal life, but never break from their past. By not weeding out the things of the world that keep them from being devoted to the Lord, these things gradually take control of their hearts and spiritual interests are eventually crowded out.

But a more serious group of people who hear the Word of God are like seed *sown on good ground; such as hear the Word, and receive it, and bring forth fruit, some thirtyfold, some sixty, and some an hundred* (4:20). By faith, these people break up their *stony* places, removing the things that hinder spiritual growth. They root out the weeds and thorns of mixed motives, and they bear much fruit.

Jesus has said to all: *I am the Vine, ye are the branches: He that abideth in Me, and I in him, the same bringeth forth much fruit* (John 15:5).

Thought for Today: It is not *what* a person possesses that is important, but *who* possesses him.

Cross References: For **Mark 4:12:** See Is. 6:9-10; Jer. 5:21; Ezek. 12:2.

OCTOBER 15 — Read Mark 6 – 7

Highlights: Like the disciples, we're all on a mission (Mark 6:7-13). Follow Jesus as He feeds the multitudes, walks on water, teaches inner holiness (6:30-7:23; Heb. 12:14). Even the *crumbs* of faith are rewarded (7:25-30).

The Pharisees insisted the Law be observed as the scribes interpreted it. They believed in the Old Testament Scriptures, but followed *the tradition of the elders* more than the Scriptures (Mark 7:3). They believed that Jesus' disciples were defiled because they did not ceremonially wash before eating as prescribed by former scribes in *the tradition of the elders*. It should have been a wake-up call when Jesus said: *Well hath Esaias* (Isaiah) *prophesied of you hypocrites... This people honoureth Me with their lips, but their heart is far from Me.... teaching for doctrines the commandments of men.... Making the Word of God of none effect through ... tradition* (7:6-7,13).

Later, Jesus explained to His disciples: *Whatsoever thing from without* (outside the body) *entereth into the man, it cannot defile him; Because it entereth not into his heart.... For from within, out of the heart of men, proceed evil thoughts, adulteries, fornications, murders, Thefts, covetousness, wickedness, deceit, lasciviousness* (sensuality), *an evil eye, blasphemy* (slander), *pride, foolishness: All these evil things ... defile the man* (7:18-19, 21-23).

Satan often suggests evil thoughts, but they only become sin when we accept them and dwell upon them. We are deceived if we assume there is no harm in dwelling upon sinful thoughts as long as they are never verbalized or physically carried out.

Christians have the responsibility – and the ability, because of the indwelling Holy Spirit – to be overcomers of sinful thoughts: *Casting down imaginations, and every high* (proud) *thing that exalteth itself against the knowledge of God, and bringing into captivity every thought to the obedience of Christ* (II Cor. 10:4-5). A commitment to read through the Word of God with a desire to please the Lord will produce inward changes in attitudes that will affect our outward conduct, witness and ministry in all that we say and do. *This I say then, Walk in the Spirit, and ye shall not fulfil the lust of the flesh* (Gal 5:16).

Thought for Today: Our unspoken thoughts express the true desires of our hearts.

Cross References: For **Mark 7:6-7:** See Is. 29:13. **Mark 7:10:** See Ex. 20:12; 21:17; Lev. 20:9; Deut. 5:16.

OCTOBER 16   **Read Mark 8 – 9**

Highlights: Who is Jesus to you (Mark 8:29)? Jesus foretells His suffering and death (8:31-38; 9:30-32). Transfiguration (9:2-13). *All things are possible to him that believeth* (9:23).

Jesus and His disciples had been in the famous idol-worshiping town of **Caesarea Philippi** (Mark 8:27 – 9:1). It was here that Jesus **asked His disciples . . . Whom do men say that I am? And they answered, John the Baptist: but some say, Elias** (Elijah)*; and others, One of the prophets. And He saith unto them, But whom say ye that I am? And Peter answereth . . . Thou art the Christ* (8:27-29).

A short time later, Jesus invited the people to follow Him, but with certain qualifications, saying: **Whosoever will come after Me, let him deny himself, and take up his cross, and follow Me. For whosoever will save his life shall lose it; but whosoever shall lose his life for My sake and the Gospel's, the same shall save it. For what shall it profit** (benefit) **a man, if he shall gain the whole world, and lose his own soul? Or what shall a man give in exchange for his soul? Whosoever therefore shall be ashamed of Me and of My words in this adulterous and sinful generation; of him also shall the Son of Man be ashamed** (8:34-38).

In this same region, six days later, Jesus and three of His disciples went up on a **high mountain . . . and He was transfigured before them. . . . And there appeared unto them Elias with Moses: and they were talking with Jesus** (9:2,4). Moses and Elijah were now in the presence of their Messiah. At this momentous event, the two Old Testament prophets spoke with Jesus about **His decease** (dying) **which He should accomplish at Jerusalem** (Luke 9:31). Moses (representing the Law) and Elijah (representing the prophets) appeared and honored Jesus prior to His suffering, death on the cross, and physical resurrection.

Peter suggested they **make three tabernacles; one for Thee, and one for Moses, and one for Elias. For he wist** (knew) **not what to say** (Mark 9:5-6). Unknowingly, he was suggesting that Moses and Elijah were equal with Jesus. Christ who, as the Only Begotten Son of God, alone is worthy of our worship and obedience (Rev. 4:9-11). After Peter's **three tabernacles** suggestion, **a Voice came out of the cloud, saying, This is my beloved Son: hear Him** (Mark 9:7).

Thought for Today: The worship, love, and loyalty that is due Christ is not to be shared with anyone else.

Cross References: For **Mark 8:18:** See Ezek. 12:2. **Mark 9:44,46,48:** See Is. 66:24.

OCTOBER 17   Read Mark 10 – 11

Highlights: Jesus' wise guidelines for "human relationships" (Mark 10:1-16,35-45). Joy for those who receive Jesus as Messiah (11:1-10), who said: ***My House shall be called . . . the House of Prayer*** (11:17).

King Herod arrested John the Baptist, ***and bound him, and put him in prison for Herodias' sake, his brother Philip's wife. For John said unto him, It is not lawful for thee to have her. . . . And he sent, and beheaded John in the prison*** (Matt. 14:3-4,10). Later, in an effort to have Jesus arrested and, hopefully, executed by Herod, the Pharisees asked Jesus: ***Is it lawful for a man to put away his wife*** (Mark 10:2)? Jesus was not intimidated, but quoted the Word of God, saying: ***From the beginning of the creation God made them male and female. For this cause shall a man leave his father and mother, and cleave to his wife; And they twain*** (two) ***shall be one flesh: so then they are no more twain, but one flesh. What therefore God hath joined together, let not man put asunder*** (divorce) (Mark 10:6-9; Gen. 2:24).

Scripture is clear in the husband's responsibility in the marriage relationship: ***Husbands, love your wives, even as Christ also loved the Church, and gave Himself for it. . . . So ought men to love their wives as their own bodies. He that loveth his wife loveth himself. For no man ever yet hated his own flesh; but nourisheth and cherisheth it, even as the Lord the Church*** (Eph. 5:25,28-29). Although numerous imperfections exist within the Church, Jesus does not give up on it. Furthermore, Jesus doesn't force anyone to be in submission to Him. The husband's conduct toward, and compassion for, his wife need to be like that of Christ for His Church. Christ leads the way and sets the perfect example in compassion, kindness, and forgiveness.

When a man is in submission to Christ, he prepares the way for his wife to desire to be in submission to him. ***Therefore as the Church is subject unto Christ, so let the wives be to their own husbands in every thing*** (5:24). It is imperative that a wife feel secure in her husband's love. It is his responsibility to let her know by word and action how very important she is to him.

Husband and wife are a team and should be: ***Submitting yourselves one to another in the fear of God*** (Eph. 5:21).

Thought for Today: A helpmate is a working partner who provides support.

Cross References: For **Mark 10:6:** See Gen. 1:27; 5:2. **Mark 10:7-8:** See Gen. 2:24. **Mark 10:19:** See Ex. 20:12-16; Deut. 5:16-20. **Mark 11:9:** See Ps. 118:26. **Mark 11:17:** See Is. 56:7; Jer. 7:11.

OCTOBER 18   Read Mark 12 – 13

Highlights: Jesus skillfully deals with the Herodians (Mark 12:13-17), Sadducees (12:18-27), and Pharisees (12:28-44). We are to **watch and pray** (13:33).

Jesus was questioned by a scribe: **Which is the first** (foremost) **Commandment of all** (Mark 12:28)? Jesus answered him by quoting Deuteronomy 6:4-5. **The first of all the Commandments is, Hear, O Israel; The Lord our God is One Lord: And thou shalt love the Lord thy God with all thy heart, and with all thy soul, and with all thy mind, and with all thy strength** (Mark 12:29-30). Jesus then quoted Leviticus 19:18: **And the second is like** (it)**, namely this, Thou shalt love thy neighbour as thyself. There is none other Commandment greater than these** (Mark 12:31).

The Hebrew word **Elohenu** is translated in English as **our God**. However, God chose to use the plural form, **Elohim** (meaning **Gods**) 2,500 times in reference to Himself as the Self-Existent, One True God. This, then, is what the sacred proclamation to Israel literally says: **Hear, O Israel; The Lord our Gods is One Lord**. Furthermore, the Hebrew word for **One** used here literally means "united" and is also a solemn declaration that the Lord is a plurality in unity. **One** (**'echad**) is a word which expresses **one** in the collective sense. It signifies a compound unity – not an absolute unity. For example, God said: **Man . . . and . . . wife . . . shall be one flesh** (Gen. 2:24). There is a Hebrew word for **one** in the sense of an absolute one; it is the word **yacheed**. But this word is never used to express the Godhead, although it is used many other times in Scripture.

This truth of One God expressed in Three Persons exposes the foolishness of those who have not yet recognized Jesus as the One True God and Creator of all things. The Holy Spirit guided the Apostle Paul to write of Jesus: **For by Him were all things created, that are in heaven, and that are in earth** (Col. 1:16). Those who reject Jesus as God and the Holy Spirit as the One who **will guide you into all truth** (John 16:13) are, in fact, rejecting the revelation of God Himself as God the Father, God the Son, and God the Holy Spirit. Jesus left no doubt as to who He was when He said: **I and My Father are One** (John 10:30; also 5:18; 12:45; 14:9-11,20).

     Search the Scriptures; for in them ye think ye have eternal life: and they are they which testify of Me (John 5:39).

Thought for Today: Pray today for those in authority.

Cross References: For **Mark 12:1:** See Is. 5:2. **Mark 12:10-11:** See Ps. 118:22-23. **Mark 12:19:** See Deut. 25:5. **Mark 12:26:** See Ex. 3:3-6. **Mark 12:29:** See Deut. 6:4. **Mark 12:30:** See Deut. 6:5. **Mark 12:31:** See Lev. 19:18. **Mark 12:32:** See Deut. 4:35. **Mark 12:33:** See Deut. 6:5; Hos. 6:6. **Mark 12:36:** See Ps. 110:1. **Mark 13:14:** See Dan. 9:27; 11:31; 12:11. **Mark 13:24:** See Is. 13:10. **Mark 13:26:** See Dan. 7:13. **Mark 13:27:** See Deut. 30:4; Zech. 2:6.

OCTOBER 19　　　　　　　　　　Read Mark 14 – 16

Highlights: Two days until Passover with Jesus as the ultimate Sacrificial Lamb (Mark 14:1). His prayer (14:36); betrayal; arrest; Peter's denial (14:10-11,43-72). *Go . . . tell. . . . all the world* (16:7,15).

Simon, a leper who had been healed by Jesus, lived in Bethany, a small town less than two miles south of Jerusalem on the slope of the Mount of Olives. Just a few days before Jesus was crucified, Simon invited Him and the apostles to his home for supper. As they sat eating, *there came a woman having an alabaster box of ointment of spikenard* (perfume) *very precious* (costly); *and she brake the box, and poured it on His head* (Mark 14:3; also Matt. 26:6-13; John 12:1-8).

This *ointment of spikenard* was valued at *more than 300 pence* – about a year's wages for a common laborer (Mark 14:5; Matt. 20:2). *Some . . . had indignation within themselves, and said, Why was this waste of the ointment made* (Mark 14:4)? John records that it was Judas who spoke up, saying: *Why was not this ointment sold . . . and given to the poor? This he said, not that he cared for the poor; but because he was a thief, and had the bag* (money purse), *and bare what was put therein* (John 12:5-6). To Judas, anything that was poured out upon Jesus was wasted; he coveted the money that the ointment might have brought. Jesus replied: *Let her alone. . . . she hath wrought a good work on Me. . . . She hath done what she could* (Mark 14:6,8).

The lost opportunity to sell the ointment and pocket the money, coupled with the strong rebuke from Jesus and the great honor bestowed upon Mary, probably angered Judas, who *went unto the chief priests* (14:10). Judas revealed his heart's condition when he said to the chief priests: *What will ye give me, and I will deliver Him unto you* (Matt. 26:15-16)? *When they heard it, they were glad, and promised to give him money* (Mark 14:11). The betrayal, and even the amount paid to Judas, had been foretold by Zechariah 600 years earlier: *I said unto them . . . give Me My price . . . So they weighed for My price thirty pieces of silver* (Zech. 11:12).

Every person must make the personal choice whether to accept or to reject Jesus as Savior and Lord of their lives. The question asked by Pilate must still be answered: *What shall I do then with Jesus which is called Christ* (Matt. 27:22)?

Thought for Today: What you decide to do with Jesus determines your eternal destiny.

Cross References: For **Mark 14:27:** See Zech. 13:7. **Mark 14:62:** See Ps. 110:1; Dan. 7:13. **Mark 15:24:** See Ps. 22:18. **Mark 15:28:** See Is. 53:12. **Mark 15:29:** See Ps. 22:7-8. **Mark 15:34:** See Ps. 22:1. **Mark 16:19:** See Ps. 110:1.

INTRODUCTION TO THE BOOK OF LUKE

Luke, the beloved physician (Col. 4:14), was a Gentile. He addressed this Book, as well as the Book of Acts, to Theophilus, which means "friend of God." He proclaimed a Gospel to everyone who will be called a "friend of God" when he recorded the angel's message to the shepherds at the time of Christ's birth: **Behold, I bring you good tidings of great joy, which shall be to all people** (Luke 2:10). Luke revealed that the purpose for Jesus leaving heaven was **to seek and to save that which was lost** (19:10; 1:68; 2:11,38; 24:21).

Luke emphasizes the divinity of Christ even in His perfect humanity. The perfect humanity of Jesus is revealed as Luke presents Jesus as the Son of Man. The phrase **Son of Man** is mentioned 25 times in this book. Luke also proclaimed the full deity of Jesus as the virgin-born Son of God as he traced the genealogy of Jesus through His mother Mary back to the creation of the first man, Adam. Through the actual, physical genealogy of Mary, Christ is linked with all mankind.

No other Gospel provides as many details of the humanity of Jesus as does the Book of Luke. He tells us about the parents and the birth of John the Baptist, Jesus' cousin who was just 6 months older than Jesus (Luke 1:36). He also gives the details of the journey of Mary and Joseph to Bethlehem where Jesus was born (2:1-7). Only Luke records that Jesus was **laid . . . in a manger** (2:7); was presented for circumcision in the Temple (2:21-24); conversed with the teachers (rabbinic scholars) at the age of 12 (2:42-46); and that **Jesus increased in wisdom and stature, and in favour with God and man** (2:52).

Luke also reveals the human dependence of Jesus upon His Heavenly Father in prayer (3:21; 5:16; 6:12; 9:16,18,28-29; 10:21; 11:1; 22:17,19; 23:46; 24:30). This points out the vital importance for all of His followers to realize how dependent upon God we are to accomplish His will through prayer. Only Luke records that **one of His disciples said unto Him, Lord, teach us to pray** (11:1), or Jesus teaching **that men ought always to pray, and not to faint** (lose heart) (18:1). The parable of the unjust judge and the widow (18:2-8), and the parable of the midnight appeal: **Friend, lend me three loaves** (11:5-13) are found only in Luke. All of these teach the importance of continuing to pray until the need is met.

Luke demonstrates that the Gospel is for everyone – anyone can be saved by trusting in Jesus. As we obey Him, he gets the **glory** (Luke 17:11-19).

OCTOBER 20   Read Luke 1

Highlights: Luke lays groundwork for non-Jews to understand the truth about Jesus (Luke 1:4). Birth of John the Baptist foretold (1:5-25); birth of Jesus foretold (1:26-45); John born (1:57-66); his mission (1:67-79); his growth (1:80). Angel declares Jesus *Son of the Highest* and *Son of God* (1:32,35). Mary divinely blessed (1:46-48).

Jesus would have had the sinful nature of Adam if Joseph had been His biological father for it passed from the father. This would have made Jesus a sinner like all mankind and, thus, unable to be the sinless substitute sacrifice for our sins. But Gabriel, the angelic messenger of Good News, had come to Mary and said: *Hail, thou that art highly favoured, the Lord is with thee. . . . behold, thou shalt conceive in thy womb, and bring forth a Son, and shalt call His Name JESUS. He shall be great, and shall be called the Son of the Highest . . . the power of the Highest shall overshadow thee . . . that Holy Thing* (One) *which shall be born of thee shall be called the Son of God* (Luke 1:28,31-32,35).

Luke records that Mary was deeply *troubled at his saying* (1:29). Matthew records that Joseph also was troubled when he learned Mary was pregnant and contemplated a private divorce. *The angel of the Lord appeared unto him in a dream, saying, Joseph, thou son of David, fear not to take unto thee Mary thy wife: for that which is conceived in her is of the Holy Ghost. And she shall bring forth a Son, and thou shalt call His Name JESUS: for He shall save His people from their sins* (Matt. 1:20-21). "Jesus" in Hebrew is the same as "Joshua," meaning, "Jehovah (Yahweh) is salvation. How comforting it must have been to Mary! Instead of living under suspicion, there was a miraculous confirmation to Joseph of her virginity.

Jesus' birth revealed His unique nature as both God and Man. About 700 years before, Isaiah foretold: *Behold, a virgin shall conceive, and bear a Son, and shall call His Name Immanuel* (God With Us). *. . . . unto us a Child is born . . . the government shall be upon His shoulder: and His Name shall be called Wonderful, Counseller, The Mighty God, The Everlasting Father, The Prince of Peace* (Is. 7:14; 9:6).

Thought for Today: *We beheld His glory . . . full of grace and truth* (John 1:14).

Cross References: For **Luke 1:17:** See Mal. 4:5-6. **Luke 1:50:** See Ps.103:17. **Luke 1:53:** See Ps. 107:9. **Luke 1:71:** See Ps. 106:10. **Luke 1:76:** See Mal 3:1. **Luke 1:79:** See Is. 9:1-2; 59:8.

OCTOBER 21   Read Luke 2 – 3

Highlights: Angels declare the heavenly birth (Luke 2:9-14). Jesus is presented in the Temple (2:21-24). Jesus is the plan of God to rescue mankind from eternal damnation (2:25-30). Jesus speaks (2:41-52). John prepares the way (3:1-22).

The Passover brought Mary and Joseph to Jerusalem every year. The year Jesus was twelve years old, in the busy preparation for returning home after the feast, Mary and Joseph, **supposing Him to have been in the company** (group), **went a day's journey; and they sought Him among their kinsfolk** (relatives) **and acquaintance. And when they found Him not, they turned back again to Jerusalem, seeking Him. And it came to pass, that after three days they found Him in the Temple, sitting in the midst of the doctors** (teachers), **both hearing them, and asking them questions** (Luke 2:44-46).

After finding Him in the Temple, Mary said: **Son, why hast Thou thus dealt with us? behold, Thy father and I have sought Thee sorrowing** (2:48). Jesus calmly explained to them His reason for being in the Temple, saying: **How is it that ye sought Me? wist** (knew) **ye not that I must be about <u>My Father's</u> business** (2:49)? Jesus clearly acknowledged that God was His real Father. Devotion to His Heavenly Father's interests drew Him to the Temple; but His submission to the will of His Father also caused Him to return to Nazareth where He **was subject** (obedient) **unto them** (2:51).

In this age of rebellion, many young people are not taught to be in subjection to their parents or to anyone else. Honoring and obeying God-ordained parental authority **is the first commandment with promise** (Eph. 6:2; Ex. 20:12). Parents who are in submission to God have a responsibility to their children to spiritually train them – especially by personal example, through daily devotions, and by regular attendance in a Bible-teaching church on the Lord's Day.

But God has said: **Let every soul** (person) **be subject** (submit) **unto the higher powers** (of government authorities)**. For there is no power but of God: the powers that be are ordained of** (established by) **God. Whosoever therefore resisteth the power** (authority)**, resisteth** (sets himself in opposition to the appointments of God) **the ordinance of God: and they that resist shall receive to themselves damnation** (condemnation) (Rom. 13:1-2).

Thought for Today: The certainty that all of the Word of God will be fulfilled is the foundation of our Christian faith.

Cross References: For **Luke 2:23:** See Ex. 13:2,12. **Luke 2:24:** See Lev. 12:8. **Luke 2:32:** See Is. 9:2; 42:6; 49:6. **Luke 3:4-6:** See Is. 40:3-5.

OCTOBER 22   Read Luke 4 – 5

Highlights: Note, the devil attacks when and where we're weakest. Read how Jesus overcame His temptation (Luke 4:1-13). Jesus says He is the "Messiah" of Isaiah 61:1-3, but the religious leaders reject Him. Why? (Luke 4:18-30). Miracles happen when Jesus is in the boat (5:1-11).

Jesus recognized the need to honor God by regularly attending worship services. We read that **He taught in their synagogues** while in Galilee (Luke 4:15). **And He came to Nazareth, where He had been brought up: and, as His custom was, He went into the synagogue on the Sabbath day** (4:16). Jesus was invited to read the Scriptures. **And there was delivered unto Him the Book of the prophet Esaias** (Isaiah). **And ... He found the place where it was written, The Spirit of the Lord is upon Me, because He hath anointed Me to preach the Gospel to the poor; He hath sent Me to heal the brokenhearted, to preach deliverance to the captives, and recovering of sight to the blind, to set at liberty them that are bruised. ... And He closed the Book, and He gave it again to the minister** (4:17-20; Is. 61:1-2).

The Scripture Jesus read, Isaiah 61:1-2, contained a clear mention of all three Persons of the Trinity – the Holy Spirit, the Father, and the Anointed One (Messiah).

The people were amazed. **And He began to say unto them, This day is this Scripture fulfilled in your ears** (Luke 4:21). They marveled at His **gracious words** (4:22), but knew He clearly referred to Himself as the Messiah who had been foretold by Isaiah and other prophets beginning with Genesis 3:15. You can imagine how startled they were when Jesus said that He whom they assumed to be **the son of Joseph** (Luke 3:23) was really their long-awaited Messiah.

The congregation listening to Jesus was so infuriated at His equating Himself with God that they disrupted the worship service, seized Jesus, and attempted to put Him to death by pushing Him over a rocky precipice for speaking blasphemy. **But He passing through the midst of them went His way** (4:28-30). Luke emphasized that Christ is God (the Messiah).

In contrast to the Jews of Nazareth, the Jews in Berea later **received the Word with all readiness of mind, and searched the Scriptures daily, whether those things were so** (Acts 17:11).

Thought for Today: Just think! You have the privilege to work for your Creator.

Cross References: For **Luke 4:4:** See Deut. 8:3. **Luke 4:8:** See Deut. 6:13. **Luke 4:10-11:** See Ps. 91:11-12. **Luke 4:12:** See Deut. 6:16. **Luke 4:18-19:** See Is. 61:1-2. **Luke 5:14:** See Lev. 13:1-3.

OCTOBER 23   Read Luke 6 – 7

Highlights: *The Son of Man is Lord also of the Sabbath* (Luke 6:5). The Twelve Chosen (6:12-16). The Sermon on the Mount (6:20-49). Note why (6:46)? Foundation for life (6:47-49). Jesus heals the sick (7:1-10); raises the dead (7:11-18). *Her sins, which are many, are forgiven* (7:47).

We all have sinned far beyond our ability to count, and we should be deeply thankful that our Savior *said to the woman, Thy faith hath saved thee; go in peace* (Luke 7:50). If we are truly grateful, we will deal with everyone who sins against us with the same mercy and compassion that we receive from the Lord. Jesus, who knows how the human heart tends to be hypocritical, warned: *Thou hypocrite, cast out first the beam out of thine own eye, and then shalt thou see clearly to pull out the mote that is in thy brother's eye* (6:41-42). It is our responsibility to recognize *the mote* (evil) for what it is, but we must first recognize our own *beam* (negative attitudes and criticism towards others, among other things). Only then are we qualified to help others with their needs.

A heart of compassion and a concern to help others is in striking contrast to those who overlook or excuse their own faults and failures, but who rarely miss an opportunity to gossip about someone else's conduct or failures. It is human nature to judge ourselves by our good intentions and to judge others by their mistakes. Thankfully, God is a merciful God who fully forgives us when we repent of our sins. Since we expect the mercy of God toward us, it makes a vital demand upon us to extend that same mercy to others. *If ye forgive not men their trespasses, neither will your Father forgive your trespasses* (Matt. 6:15).

Criticism is often an act of self-righteousness in an attempt to build up one's own self-esteem by putting down others. Judgmental people, who wish to belittle another person, thrive on finding fault with things that person has said or done. It is these acts of self-righteousness that Jesus spoke of when He said: *Cast out first the beam out of thine own eye*. Then the love of Christ can be expressed through us.

If anyone is *overtaken in a fault* (sin), *ye which are spiritual, restore such an one in the spirit of meekness; considering thyself, lest thou also be tempted* (Gal. 6:1).

Thought for Today: It is unjust to criticize anyone – even those whose efforts fall short of what we expect. We answer to Christ for our own lives.

Cross References: For **Luke 7:22:** See Is. 61:1. **Luke 7:27:** See Mal. 3:1.

OCTOBER 24   Read Luke 8 – 9

Highlights: Women *healed of evil spirits and infirmities* (Luke 8:1-3). Parable of the Sower (8:4-15). Our new relationship with the Lord. *My mother and my brethren are these which hear the Word of God, and do it* (8:19-21). He stills the storms (8:22-25), defeats demons (8:26-40), heals the sick (8:43-48), and feeds the hungry (9:12-17). Cost of discipleship (9:23,57-62).

Jesus put the sincerity of would-be disciples to the test when *a certain man said unto Him, Lord, I will follow Thee whithersoever Thou goest. And Jesus said unto him, Foxes have holes, and birds of the air have nests; but the Son of Man hath not where to lay His head* (no place to sleep) (Luke 9:57-58). Jesus pointed out that, if he chose to follow Him, he could expect hardships. Jesus was also saying that He was not attached to earthly possessions, nor could His followers expect any guarantee of resources.

And another also said, Lord, I will follow Thee; but let me first go bid them farewell, which are at home at my house. And Jesus said unto him, No man, having put his hand to the plough, and looking back, is fit for the Kingdom of God (9:61-62). Our Lord did not welcome volunteers who were only willing to join Him on their own terms; serving Christ requires a lifetime commitment. Love dictates that there be no compromise in following Him.

Some people are often misled by believing there will be a more convenient time to follow the Lord. Their excuses reveal divided hearts. Some lack the "single eye" of devotion to Christ where, by comparison, all else in this world is of little importance. Others fail to put Christ first in their daily decisions; yet, all who put Him first will discover that the satisfaction of self-denial far exceeds fleeting earthly rewards. Each of us needs to consider whether there is someone in our life or something in our heart that is keeping us from giving Christ, His Word, and His will, first place in our lives.

Jesus warned: *The Kingdom of God is nigh* (near) *at hand. Verily* (Truly) *I say unto you. . . . Heaven and earth shall pass away: but My words shall not pass away. And take heed to yourselves, lest at any time your hearts be overcharged with surfeiting* (self-indulgence), *and drunkenness, and cares of this life, and so that day come upon you unawares* (suddenly) (Luke 21:31-34).

Thought for Today: Worldly ambitions fade into insignificance when we devote ourselves to knowing the Lord by reading His Word.

Cross References: For **Luke 8:10:** See Is. 6:9.

OCTOBER 25 — Read Luke 10 – 11

Highlights: Importance of witnessing (Luke 10:1-19). Most important Commandment (10:27) and question (10:29). How to pray (11:1-13)! Let your light shine (11:33-36). Insincere, self-righteous life condemned by Jesus (11:42-54).

A scribe (lawyer) was an official interpreter of both the Mosaic law and the traditions of the elders (those who came before them). One of them ***stood up, and tempted Him, saying, Master, what shall I do to inherit eternal life*** (Luke 10:25)***?*** Jesus replied: ***What is written in the Law?*** He answered: ***Thou shalt love the Lord thy God with all thy heart, and with all thy soul, and with all thy strength, and with all thy mind; and thy neighbour as thyself.*** And Jesus said: ***Thou hast answered right: this do, and thou shalt live. But he, willing to justify himself, said unto Jesus, And who is my neighbour*** (10:26-29)***?***

Jesus illustrated the answer by saying: ***A certain man went down from Jerusalem to Jericho, and fell among thieves, which stripped him of his raiment*** (clothing), ***and wounded him, and departed, leaving him half dead. And by chance there came down a certain priest that way: and when he saw him, he passed by on the other side. And likewise a Levite, when he was at the place, came and looked on him, and passed by on the other side. But a certain Samaritan, as he journeyed . . . when he saw him, he had compassion on him . . . and bound up his wounds . . . and brought him to an inn, and took care of him. . . . Which now of these three . . . was neighbour unto him that fell among the thieves? And he said, He that shewed mercy on him. Then said Jesus unto him, Go, and do thou likewise*** (10:30-37).

A ***neighbour*** is anyone who needs our compassion and care. It does not matter what his position, race, or religion may be. As Jesus taught: ***And as ye would that men should do to you, do ye also to them likewise*** (6:31).

All of us need to be reminded of our Lord's answer to the lawyer's question: ***What shall I do to inherit eternal life*** (10:25)***?*** Furthermore, Jesus said: ***A new commandment I give unto you, That ye love one another; as I have loved you, that ye also love one another. By this shall all men know that ye are My disciples, if ye have love one to*** (for) ***another*** (John 13:34-35).

Thought for Today: It is one thing to serve God, but quite another to show compassion to those who are less fortunate than we are.

Cross References: For **Luke 10:27:** See Lev. 19:18. **Luke 10:28:** See Lev. 18:5.

OCTOBER 26

Read Luke 12 – 13

Highlights: Jesus denounces scribes and Pharisees as hypocrites (Luke 12:1-12). Verses to heed (12:4-5,8-10). Learn of greed, money, possessions (12:13-15). Don't be a fool (12:19-20). Repent, be prepared for the Master, don't be left out (12:35-48; 13:1-5,22-30)! Jesus, Lord of the Sabbath (13:10-17). Jesus grieves for us too (13:31-35).

The Lord illustrated the self-deception of covetousness by telling this parable: *The ground of a certain rich man brought forth plentifully: And he thought within himself, saying, What shall I do, because I have no room where to bestow* (store) *my fruits? ... I will pull down my barns, and build greater* (larger); *and there will I bestow all my fruits and my goods. And I will say to my soul, Soul, thou hast much goods laid up for many years; take thine ease, eat, drink, and be merry. But God said unto him, Thou fool, this night thy soul shall be required of thee: then whose shall those things be, which thou hast provided* (Luke 12:16-20)*?*

By hard work in the highly-respected occupation of farming, this man had become wealthy. His sin was that he spent his lifetime in selfish gratification. God called him a *fool*, and then added: *So is he that layeth up treasure for himself, and is not rich toward God* (12:20-21).

Christians should not allow material desires to distract ourselves from doing the will of God. As important as food, clothing, and shelter are to maintaining life, our first priority should always be to *seek ... first the Kingdom of God, and His righteousness* (Matt. 6:33).

How we use our time and talents is an expression of our Christian faith. Christ taught that life is truly fulfilling by loving, serving, and giving to extend the Good News to a lost world. Regardless of how much or how little talent or possessions we may have or acquire, as good stewards we should prayerfully consider what Jesus would have us do with them. He knows you and your circumstances and has chosen you to be His representative in the area in which you live.

Thou, O man of God ... follow after righteousness, godliness, faith, love, patience, meekness (gentleness). *Fight the good fight of faith, lay* (take) *hold on eternal life, whereunto thou art also called, and hast professed a good profession* (confession) *before many witnesses* (I Tim. 6:11-12).

Thought for Today: If we are truly concerned about the interests of God, He will take care of ours.

Cross References: For **Luke 13:27:** See Ps. 6:8. **Luke 13:35:** See Ps. 118:26.

OCTOBER 27   Read Luke 14 – 16

Highlights: Don't miss the call of God (Luke 14:15-24). Consider the true devotion of discipleship (14:26-35). Together with Jesus, seek the lost (note: 15:7). Parable of the shrewd steward. No one **can serve two masters** (16:10-13). Rich man and Lazarus (16:19-31).

Our Lord illustrates two of life's choices. The first is a self-centered son who demanded freedom from his father's authority and then **took his journey into a far country, and there wasted his substance** (inheritance) **with riotous living. And when he had spent all . . . he began to be in want** (faced starvation) (Luke 15:13-16). Then this prodigal son made a wise choice when **he said . . . I perish** (die) **with hunger! I will arise and go to my father, and will say unto him, Father, I have sinned against heaven, and before thee** (15:17-18).

The word "prodigal" means "a waster." This young man had wasted his inheritance. After he repented, his father rejoiced saying: **This my son was dead, and is alive again; he was lost, and is found** (15:24).

Just as the prodigal son discovered that his father's love was far greater than he had previously realized, so too will every repentant sinner discover that the Heavenly Father is waiting with great compassion to forgive all who come to Him.

The second choice Jesus describes was of a rich man who never recognized that he had "wasted" his life, even though he had become "very successful." But, **in hell . . . being in torments. . . . he cried . . . I am tormented in this flame** (16:23-24). Only then did he discover that hell was eternal and that, between him and Abraham, there was **a great gulf fixed** (16:26). The rich man's preoccupation with earthly treasures had blinded him to heavenly purposes.

Our foremost purpose is to prepare for an endless eternity while using our brief life on earth to provide spiritual food for others.

Since the believer's true **conversation** (citizenship) **is in heaven** (Phil. 3:20), we dare not make secular goals, material gain, and physical satisfactions our priorities. Jesus made it very clear: All mankind, rich or poor, has one thing in common – physical death will open the door to either the joy of eternal life or the horrors of eternal hell. **Therefore we ought to give the more earnest heed to the things which we have heard. . . . How shall we escape, if we neglect so great salvation** (Heb. 2:1,3)?

Thought for Today: Are you a prodigal? The Father is lovingly awaiting to welcome you.

Cross References: For **Luke 16:15:** See Prov. 21:2.

OCTOBER 28   **Read Luke 17 – 18**

Highlights: Forgiveness and mustard seed faith (Luke 17:1-10). Signs that the end is near (17:20-37). Lessons from an evil judge (18:1-8); self-righteous Pharisee and humble tax collector who both pray (18:9-14); warning for those with riches (18:18-28); assurance of *life everlasting* (18:29-30); a blind man who would not give up (18:35-43).

No one question could be of greater importance than that of *a certain ruler* (Luke 18:18) who *came ... running, and kneeled to Him* (Jesus) (Mark 10:17). This *young man* (Matt. 19:20, 22) possessed great wealth. He asked: *Good Master, what shall I do to inherit eternal life? And Jesus said unto him. ... Do not commit adultery, Do not kill, Do not steal, Do not bear false witness, Honour thy father and thy mother* (Luke 18:18-20; also Matt. 19:16-30; Mark 10:17-31). Three Gospels report that he recognized Jesus as more than just another Teacher, but as the *Good Master* (Teacher). He knew that he wanted to prepare for eternal life.

In response to his most vital question: *What shall I do ... ?* Jesus told him: *Yet lackest thou one thing: sell all that thou hast, and distribute unto the poor, and thou shalt have treasure in heaven: and come, follow Me. And when he heard this, he was very sorrowful: for he was very rich* (Luke 18:22-23). Jesus' reply should not be twisted to suggest that eternal life can be earned by self-effort or sacrificial giving. Eternal life can only come from Him who *loved us, and washed us from our sins in His own blood* (Rev. 1:5). The young man was unwilling to give up the benefits his wealth provided to let Jesus be Lord of his life. He was a good man and very religious but, sadly, he was lost.

We must *charge* (instruct) *them that are rich in this world, that they be not highminded* (conceited), *nor trust in uncertain riches, but in the living God, who giveth us richly all things to enjoy; That they do good, that they be rich in good works, ready to distribute, willing to communicate* (share)*; Laying up in store for themselves a good foundation against the time to come, that they may lay hold on eternal life* (I Tim. 6:17-19).

Your lifestyle and daily decisions reveal who you are really living for. The young ruler illustrates why Jesus said: *Narrow is the way, which leadeth unto life, and few there be that find it* (Matt. 7:14).

Thought for Today: Read His Word. *He shall direct thy paths* (Prov. 3:6).

Cross References: For **Luke 18:20:** See Ex. 20:12-16; Deut. 5:16-20.

OCTOBER 29   Read Luke 19 – 20

Highlights: The real reason why Jesus came (Luke 19:10). We are to occupy until Christ returns (19:13). Jesus answers questions concerning the resurrection (20:27-40).

The Pharisees conspired against Jesus with the cooperation of the nonreligious political party called the Herodians, supporters of King Herod (Matt. 22:16). These opposite-thinking groups of people hypocritically sent an investigative committee from the Sanhedrin, pretending to be interested in following Jesus. They said to Him: ***Master, we know that Thou sayest and ... teachest the way of God truly: Is it lawful for us to give tribute*** (taxes) ***unto Caesar, or no*** (Luke 20:21-22)***?*** Since the Jews deeply resented paying taxes to Rome, they were sure the crowd would quickly turn against Jesus if He said "Yes." And the Pharisees could also say He was not the Messiah if He taught subjection to a Gentile government. But, if He said "No," the Herodian party could then accuse Him of conspiracy against the Roman government and Pilate could have Him arrested for treason.

But He perceived their craftiness, and said unto them, Why tempt ye Me? Shew me a penny (a Roman coin that was an accepted currency among Jews)***. Whose image and superscription*** (inscription) ***hath it? They answered ... Caesar's. And He said unto them, Render*** (Give) ***therefore unto Caesar the things which be Caesar's.*** The rest of His comment came as a stinging rebuke to their hypocrisy when He added ***and unto God the things which be God's*** (20:23-25). It is common knowledge that the image on a coin is representative of governmental authority, but added to that we must also submit to the highest authority (God) because we are created ***in the image of God*** (Gen. 1:26-27).

    The words of Jesus for us to tithe remain just as true today. Some misguided citizens accept the benefits of government but avoid paying taxes. They ignore the two reasons for paying them. Christians are to pay required taxes and obey the law, but they also pay them as a requirement to please God. We simply cannot ignore His clear command: ***Submit yourselves to every ordinance of man for the Lord's sake: whether it be to the king, as supreme; Or unto governors, as unto them that are sent by him for the punishment of evildoers*** (I Pet. 2:13-14).

Thought for Today: Oh, to hear Jesus say, "Well done!"

Cross References: For **Luke 19:38:** See Ps. 118:26. **Luke 19:46:** See Is.56:7; Jer. 7:11. **Luke 20:17:** See Ps. 118:22. **Luke 20:28:** See Deut. 25:5. **Luke 20:37:** See Ex. 3:6. **Luke 20:42-43:** See Ps. 110:1.

OCTOBER 30   Read Luke 21 – 22

Highlights: When the end will come (Luke 21:6-7) ; *signs* preceding the end (21:8-36). Judas' cruel betrayal (22:1-6,47-53). The Passover meal (22:7-30). Peter's denial (22:31-36; 22:54-62). Agonizing prayer of Jesus; an angel ministers to Him (22:39-46).

The Israelites' annual Passover meal was a reminder that the blood of an innocent lamb and obedience to the Word of God had redeemed their ancestors from death and Egyptian slavery.

On the evening of the Passover, Jesus *took bread, and gave thanks, and brake it, and gave unto them* (His 12 disciples), *saying, This is My body which is given for you: this do in remembrance of Me. Likewise also the cup after supper, saying, This cup is the New Testament* (Covenant) *in My blood, which is shed for you* (Luke 22:19-20). At this Passover, our Lord identified Himself with the sacrificial Passover lamb.

The Lord's Supper is a reminder that Jesus' death on the cross delivered us from Satan and set us free from the condemnation for our sins to receive eternal life. This ordinance is so sacred that the Holy Spirit emphasized its importance through the Apostle Paul who wrote: *This do ye, as oft as ye drink it, in remembrance of Me. For as often as ye eat this bread, and drink this cup, ye do shew the Lord's death till He come* (I Cor. 11:23-26). It is of the utmost importance that we consider carefully that our Lord said: *This do in remembrance of Me*. He did not make a suggestion but a command. Jesus reminds all who call themselves His followers: *Why call ye Me, Lord, Lord, and do not the things which I say* (Luke 6:46)?

The Lord wanted us to know that His death on the cross made the difference for us between spending eternity in *the lake of fire* (Rev. 20:14-15) or in heaven with Him (John 3:16; 14:2-3). The Lord's Supper is a continuing reminder that there is forgiveness for all who, by faith, accept Jesus' atoning sacrifice as the only means of receiving eternal life. It is also a time to confess and forsake attitudes of ill will toward others, revenge, lust, and all other sins. The Lord's Table is a reminder that *whosoever shall eat this bread, and drink this cup of the Lord, unworthily* (in a way that is unworthy of Him), *shall be guilty of* (sinning against) *the body and blood of the Lord. But let a man examine himself, and so let him eat of that* (the) *bread, and drink of that* (the) *cup* (I Cor. 11:27-28).

Thought for Today: We need to express forgiving love in our hearts toward all offenders.

Cross References: For **Luke 21:27:** See Dan. 7:13. **Luke 22:37:** See Is. 53:12. **Luke 22:69:** See Ps. 110:1.

OCTOBER 31   Read Luke 23 – 24

Highlights: The mock trials, crucifixion, death, burial, and resurrection of Jesus. Don't miss a word of this soul-stirring description of how Jesus carried all our shame and sin that He might save us. Praise the Lord for His great love! (Luke 24:46-47).

Some of the women who were followers of Jesus watched as He died on the cross, and then watched as the body of their beloved Lord was hastily laid in the rock-hewn tomb of Joseph of Arimathea. *That day was the preparation. . . . And the women. . . . returned, and prepared spices and ointments; and rested the Sabbath day according to the Commandment* (Luke 23:54-56). *Now upon the first day of the week, very early in the morning* (24:1), on their way to the tomb, these women were greatly concerned about *Who shall roll . . . away the stone from the door of the sepulchre* (tomb)*? . . . the stone . . . was very great* (large) (Mark 16:3-4). They soon discovered that an angel had taken care of their concern.

The Roman soldiers who guarded the tomb, were frightened when *the angel of the Lord descended from heaven, and . . . rolled back the stone from the door, and sat upon it* (Matt. 28:2,4). When the women came to the tomb to complete the burial procedures, *they entered in, and. . . . behold, two men stood by them in shining garments: And . . . said unto them, Why seek ye the living among the dead? He is not here: but is risen: remember how He spake unto you . . . Saying, The Son of Man must be delivered into the hands of sinful men, and be crucified, and the third day rise again* (Luke 24:3-7). The women rushed to tell the others.

These women had no thought of deserting their Lord in death. Neither the women nor the apostles were expecting such a glorious experience on that resurrection morning. God always has better things in store for us than we think possible. *That He would grant you, according to the riches of His glory, to be strengthened with might by His Spirit in the inner man . . . And to know the love of Christ, which passeth knowledge, that ye might be filled with all the fulness of God. Now unto Him that is able to do exceeding abundantly above all that we ask or think, according to the power that worketh in us, Unto Him be glory in the Church by Christ Jesus throughout all ages, world without end. Amen* (Eph. 3:16,19-21).

Thought for Today: God is merciful to all who ask.

Cross References: For **Luke 23:30:** See Hos. 10:8. **Luke 23:34:** See Ps. 22:18.

Introduction To The Book Of JOHN

The Holy Spirit guided the Apostle John to reveal the true nature and purpose of Jesus Christ, both as perfect man and as deity, One with God the Father in the creation of all things; to foster faith in the Lord Jesus Christ as the Son of God. The Gospel of John begins by declaring: **In the beginning was the Word, and the Word was with God, and the Word was God. The Same was in the beginning with God. All things were made by Him; and without Him was not any thing made that was made** (John 1:1-3). God further revealed Himself when **the Word was made flesh, and dwelt among us, (and we beheld His glory, the glory as of the Only Begotten of the Father,) full of grace and truth** (1:14).

John revealed Jesus as the prophesied, sinless **Lamb of God, which taketh away the sin of the world** (1:29; Is. 53:7). The religious leaders **sought the more to kill Him, because He ... said ...** (1) **that God was His Father, making Himself equal with God** (John 5:18); (2) that He knew **all things** (5:20); (3) that **the Father ... hath committed all judgment unto the Son** (5:22); (4) He received honor **even as they honour the Father** (5:23); (5) He imparted **everlasting life** (5:24-25); (6) He is self-existent, **as the Father hath life in Himself; so hath He given to the Son to have life in Himself** (5:26); and (7) that He gives life: **the Son quickeneth** (makes alive) **whom He will** (5:21,28-29).

Jesus declared: **I and My Father are One.... he that hath seen Me hath seen the Father** (10:30; 14:9). He spoke of **the glory** which He had with the Father **before the world was** (17:5). Jesus also revealed Himself as the eternal **I AM** of the Old Testament (Ex. 3:14) with eight **I am** statements: **I am the Bread of Life** (John 6:35); **Before Abraham was, I am** (8:58); **I am the Light of the world** (8:12); **I am the Door: by Me if any man enter in, he shall be saved** (10:9); **I am the Good Shepherd** (10:11); **I am the Resurrection, and the Life** (11:25); **I am The Way, The Truth, and The Life: no man cometh unto the Father, but by Me** (14:6); and **I am the True Vine.... If a man abide not in Me, he is cast forth as a branch, and is withered; and men gather them, and cast them into the fire** (15:1-2,6).

The purpose of John is clear. **These are written, that ye might believe that Jesus is the Christ, the Son of God; and that believing ye might have life through His Name** (20:31).

NOVEMBER 1 — Read John 1 – 3

Highlights: Jesus Christ is the Living Word, the only virgin-born **Son of God** (John 1:1-5,14,34,48-51; 2:1-11) who proclaimed: ***I am The Way*** (14:6) to get to heaven (3:1-18).

There was a man of the Pharisees, named Nicodemus, a ruler of the Jews: The same came to Jesus by night (John 3:1-2). This prominent rabbi was a member of the Sanhedrin, the council which controlled the religious life of Israel; yet, he confessed to Jesus: ***Rabbi, we know that Thou art a teacher come from God*** (3:2).

Jesus said to Nicodemus: ***Except a man be born of water and of the Spirit, he cannot enter into the Kingdom of God. That which is born of the flesh*** (human parents) ***is flesh; and that which is born of the Spirit is spirit. . . . Ye must be born again*** (3:5-7). Peter writes: ***Ye have purified your souls . . . Being born again . . . by the Word of God*** (I Pet. 1:22-23).

To illustrate how essential it is to be ***born again*** (receive eternal life), Jesus reminded Nicodemus of the Israelites who, near the end of their 40 years of wilderness wandering, once again complained about their circumstances. Consequently, they removed themselves from the protection and authority of God. Thousands of the Israelites were bitten by fiery serpents and died in the desert (wilderness). When the people cried out to the Lord, God mercifully commanded Moses to make ***a serpent of brass*** (Num. 5:9) and lift it up on a pole. The people were healed by looking up at the brazen serpent (21:5-9). That serpent was made of brass, since brass is a biblical symbol of judgment.

Jesus told Nicodemus: ***As Moses lifted up the serpent in the wilderness, even so must the Son of Man be lifted up: That whosoever believeth in Him should not perish, but have eternal life*** (John 3:14-15). ***He that believeth on Him is not condemned*** (judged): ***but he that believeth not is condemned already, because he hath not believed in the Name of the Only Begotten Son of God*** (3:18).

When we were born physically, we received the sinful nature which we inherited from Adam. When we are ***born again*** into the family of God, we receive Christ's divine nature and will ***walk*** (live) ***as children of light: (For the fruit of the Spirit is in all goodness and righteousness and truth;) Proving what is acceptable unto the Lord*** (Eph. 5:8-10).

Thought for Today: The most insignificant person by the world's standards is precious in the eyes of God.

Cross References: For **John 1:23:** See Is. 40:3; Mal. 3:1. **John 2:17:** See Ps. 69:9.

NOVEMBER 2

Read John 4 – 5

Highlights: Jesus of Nazareth is The Living Water (John 4:5-14); The Great Physician (4:46 – 5:16); **equal with God** (5:18). Jesus was confirmed by many witnesses: (1) John the Baptist (5:33-35); (2) His works (5:36); (3) The Father (5:37-38); (4) Scripture (5:39-47). Worship Him **in Spirit and in Truth** (4:23-24).

The sheep gate where lambs were bought for sacrifice was located at the northeast area of the Temple court in Jerusalem. Nearby was **a pool, which is called . . . Bethesda, having five porches. In these lay a great multitude of impotent folk. . . . For an angel went down at a certain season . . . and troubled the water: whosoever then first . . . stepped in was made whole** (John 5:2-4). At this pool **lay a great multitude of impotent** (sick, invalid, and physically disabled) **folk** (5:3). It was believed by some that the first to enter the pool of water after **an angel** stirred it up would be cured (5:4). Jesus, the Great Physician, approached this crowd of sufferers, but no one recognized Him.

In this crowd of helpless people was **a certain man . . . which had an infirmity thirty and eight years** (5:5). Who would care if he were ever healed? When this man expressed his hopelessness, Jesus looked beyond the man's problem and asked him to do something about it, saying: **Rise, take up thy bed, and walk. And immediately the man was made whole, and took up his bed, and walked** (5:8-9).

Like this man, you and I once were spiritually helpless. We should be eternally grateful that Jesus did not pass us by but revealed through a person, the Bible itself, or other means, that He gave us an opportunity to be made whole. Jesus cares for even the most hopeless sinner and desires that all trust in Him as their personal Savior.

The sheep gate points to Jesus, **the Lamb of God, which taketh away the sin of the world** (1:29). **Bethesda** means "house of mercy or grace." It is only through the compassion of Christ that lost sinners, without exception, can find mercy and grace by accepting His sacrifice on the cross for their sins.

The Apostle Paul reminds us that we once were **children of wrath**, but we have been cleansed from our sins and given a new nature with the privilege to **put on the new man, which after God is created in righteousness and true holiness** (Eph. 2:3; 4:24).

Thought for Today: Temporal "satisfactions" may "quench our thirst" momentarily, but only Jesus can provide the "water of life."

NOVEMBER 3 Read John 6 – 8

Highlights: Jesus: the Bread of Life (John 6:1-14,22-51); the Light of the World (8:12). During all the storms of life, Jesus still says: *Be not afraid* (6:18-20).

Jesus entered *into the Temple* (court), *and all the people came unto Him; and He sat down, and taught them* (John 8:2). Jesus was interrupted by *the scribes and Pharisees* who *brought unto Him a woman. . . . They say unto Him, Master, this woman was taken in adultery, in the very act. Now Moses in the Law commanded us, that such should be stoned: but what sayest Thou* (8:3-5)? Their reason for bringing this woman to Jesus was not because their hearts were grieved that the Law of God had been broken, but *that they might have* (a reason) *to accuse Him* (8:6). If He said: "Let her go," they would have accused Him of compromising with sin and breaking the Mosaic Law. If He had said: "Stone her," He would have broken Roman law and been accountable to Rome.

Jesus brought conviction to each of her accusers when He said: *He that is without sin among you, let him first cast a stone at her* (8:7). *And they which heard it . . . went out one by one, beginning at the eldest . . . and Jesus was left alone, and the woman standing in the midst* (8:9). Then He said to her: *Woman, where are . . . thine accusers? hath no man condemned thee? She said, No man, Lord. And Jesus said unto her, Neither do I condemn thee: go, and sin no more* (8:10-11). Jesus resumed His teaching, saying: *I am the Light of the world: he that followeth Me shall not walk in darkness, but shall have the Light of life* (8:12).

Like the scribes and Pharisees, many people are quick to "point the finger" at others who sin, not stopping to consider that they, too, are guilty of sinning against the Lord. *Being filled with all unrighteousness . . . fornication, wickedness, covetousness, maliciousness; full of envy. . . . debate, deceit . . . whisperers, backbiters . . . despiteful, proud, boasters* (Rom. 1:29-30). *But as many as received Him, to them gave He power to become the sons of God, even to them that believe on His Name: Which were born, not of blood, nor of the will of the flesh, nor of the will of man, but of God* (John 1:12-13). *Whoso keepeth His Word, in him verily* (truly) *is the love of God perfected: hereby know we that we are in Him* (I John 2:5).

Thought for Today: To know what is right and not live it is sin.

Cross References: For **John 6:31:** See Ex. 16:4; Ps. 78:24. **John 6:45:** See Is. 54:13.

NOVEMBER 4   Read John 9 – 10

Highlights: The power of a changed life vs. spiritual blindness (John 9:1-41). ***The Good Shepherd*** and His ***sheep*** (10:11). Jesus, the Father, the sheep, and eternal life (10:23-30). False accusations against Jesus; the enemy seeks to kill Him (10:31-42).

The religious leaders in Israel were considered the shepherds of Israel; but they were self-serving, as Ezekiel had foretold: ***Woe be to the shepherds of Israel that do feed themselves! should not the shepherds feed the flocks*** (Ezek. 34:2)? Ezekiel then revealed the True Shepherd: ***I will set up one Shepherd over them, and He shall feed them, even My servant David . . . And I the L***ORD ***will be their God, and My servant David a prince among them . . . I will make with them a Covenant of Peace*** (34:23-25).

Jesus identified Himself as the fulfillment of Ezekiel's prophecy when He said: ***I am the Good Shepherd: the Good Shepherd giveth His life for the sheep. But . . . an hireling . . . seeth the wolf coming, and leaveth the sheep, and fleeth: and the wolf catcheth them, and scattereth the sheep. . . . I am the Good Shepherd. . . . I lay down My life for the sheep*** (John 10:11-15).

One of the distinguishing marks of a Christian is that he recognizes the need for guidance and desires to follow the Good Shepherd. ***The sheep follow Him: for they know His voice. And a stranger will they not follow, but will flee from him*** (10:4-5).

The Holy Spirit led the Apostle Paul to write: ***Now the God of peace, that brought again from the dead our Lord Jesus, that Great Shepherd of the sheep, through the blood of the everlasting Covenant, Make you perfect in every good work to do His will, working in you that which is wellpleasing in His sight, through Jesus Christ; to whom be glory for ever and ever*** (Heb. 13:20-21).

Jesus also said: ***I give unto them eternal life; and they shall never perish, neither shall any man pluck them out of My hand. My Father, which gave them*** (to) ***Me, is greater than all*** (John 10:28-29). How comforting it is to be assured that we have Jesus the Good Shepherd caring for us!

The Apostle Peter foretold: ***When the Chief Shepherd*** (Christ) ***shall appear, ye shall receive a crown of glory that fadeth not away*** (I Pet. 5:4).

Thought for Today: Christians, like sheep, need to stay near the Shepherd in order to be protected from the deceptions of the world.

Cross References: For **John 10:34:** See Ps. 82:6.

NOVEMBER 5   Read John 11 – 12

Highlights: Inevitably death enters all of our homes, but there is hope because believers in Jesus pass from death unto life eternal (John 11:25-26). Power of the Word and prayer (11:38-44).

Throughout the years of Jesus' ministry, He often withdrew from public notice and bid **His disciples that they should tell no man that He was Jesus the Christ** (Messiah) (Matt. 16:20). When He raised the daughter of Jairus, **He charged them straitly** (strictly) **that no man should know it** (Mark 5:43). When they came down from the Mount of Transfiguration, He instructed His disciples **that they should tell no man what things they had seen, till the Son of Man were risen from the dead** (9:9). The reason for this can be seen when the 5,000, who were miraculously fed by two fish and five loaves of bread, intended **to make Him a king, He departed again into a mountain Himself alone** (John 6:15). When His unbelieving brethren urged Him to **shew Thyself to the world. . . . Jesus said unto them, My time is not yet come** (7:4,6).

Some time later, as Passover approached, Jerusalem was crowded with worshipers who had come from Judea, Samaria, Galilee, and as far away as Greece. They came several days ahead in order that they might be ceremonially qualified to partake of the feast: **The Jews' Passover was nigh at hand: and many went out of the country up to Jerusalem . . . to purify** (cleanse) **themselves** (11:55), as well as to see Jesus.

As Jesus made His public entry into Jerusalem, the religious leaders were overwhelmed by the immense crowd that followed Him. They said: **Behold, the world is** (has) **gone after Him** (12:19).

The prophet Zechariah had foretold almost 500 years earlier: **Rejoice greatly, O daughter of Zion; shout, O daughter of Jerusalem: behold, thy King cometh unto thee . . . having salvation; lowly, and riding upon an ass, and upon a colt the foal of an ass** (Zech. 9:9).

Finally, at the God-appointed time, Israel's True King openly presented Himself as fulfilling that prophecy. **Many believed on Him; but because of the Pharisees they did not confess Him, lest they should be put out of the synagogue: For they loved the praise of men more than the praise of God** (John 12:42-43).

Thought for Today: We should live so others can see Christ living in us.

Cross References: For **John 12:13:** See Ps. 118:26. **John 12:15:** See Zech. 9:9. **John 12:38:** Is. 53:1. **John 12:40:** See Is. 6:9-10; Ex. 4:21.

NOVEMBER 6   Read John 13 – 16

Highlights: The defiled cannot enter the Kingdom of God, BUT Jesus can and will cleanse them (John 13:4-17). Are we guilty of betrayal or denial (13:18-38)? The Comforter promised (14:16-17; 15:26; 16:7-15). New relationship (14:20-21;15:12-21) described (15:1-11). Jesus overcomes sorrow and trials with joy and peace (16:16-33).

Eleven of the apostles were convinced that Jesus was the Messiah. Along with the multitudes, they too had joined in shouting: ***Hosanna: Blessed is the King of Israel*** (John 12:13). But Jesus had said earlier that He must ***suffer many things of the elders and chief priests and scribes, and be killed*** (Matt. 16:21). Now, as they celebrated the Passover, the apostles were perplexed because Jesus had said He was leaving them (John 13:33) and troubled that He had said that one of the apostles would betray Him (13:21-22).

Some of the most comforting words Jesus spoke were at the time that the religious leaders were planning to kill Him and He knew it. With the utmost calmness He said: ***Let not your heart be troubled: ye believe in God, believe also in Me. . . . I go to prepare a place for you. . . . I will come again, and receive you unto Myself; that where I am, there ye may be also. . . . Peace I leave with you, My peace I give unto you: not as the world giveth, give I unto you. Let not your heart be troubled, neither let it be afraid*** (14:1-3,27).

The picture is much clearer to us 2,000 years later, as we read the full story. However, like the disciples, occasionally, each of us is faced with fears of what tomorrow may bring. When we are facing financial loss, divorce, disease, handicaps, or other "things" that happen to those who love the Lord, we need to remember that the Lord knows how to take care of our tomorrows. Along with the disciples, we too can have the utmost confidence in our Lord's comforting words: ***Let not your heart be troubled: ye believe in God, believe also in Me*** (14:1). We make the choice whether we will or will not allow our hearts to be troubled. With every disappointment the Lord provides an opportunity to overcome stress, fear, and depression, and to develop patience and faith in Him.

Beloved, think it not strange concerning the fiery trial (painful ordeal) ***which is to try*** (test) ***you, as though some strange thing happened unto you: But rejoice, inasmuch as ye are partakers*** (sharers) ***of Christ's sufferings*** (I Pet. 4:12-13).

Thought for Today: We need to be thankful for the ministry of the Holy Spirit in and through us.

Cross References: For **John 13:18:** See Ps. 41:9. **John 15:25:** See Ps. 35:19; 69:4.

NOVEMBER 7   Read John 17 – 18

Highlights: Looking beyond the cross and the tomb, Jesus asks the Father for seven things (John 17:1,5,11,15,17,21-24). He prays for Himself (17:1-5); His disciples (17:6-19), and us (17:20-26). The love-gift of God to the world is Jesus (3:16).

After the Passover meal, Jesus began praying: **Father, the hour is come; glorify** (honor) **Thy Son.... I have glorified** (honored) **Thee on the earth.... I have manifested** (made known) **Thy Name unto the men which Thou gavest Me ... and they have kept Thy Word** (John 17:1,4-6). All true believers should unite in glorifying the **Father** and Christ our Lord and in keeping His Word.

Jesus continued praying for all who would ever believe in Him, **that they may be one, even as We are One** (17:20-22). Jesus and eleven of the disciples then went to the Mount of Olives. Jesus knew that Judas would soon arrive with the religious leaders who would lead a hostile mob and Roman military to crucify Him. Soon, all of Jesus' followers forsook Him.

Satan is **the accuser of our brethren** (Rev. 12:10); but it is comforting to know that Jesus sees far more in His followers than we see in ourselves or in each other. He knew His disciples would leave Him; but He loved them and forgave them and they became even more loyal.

The difference between the weakest Christians and the worldly, unsaved person is revealed in Jesus' prayer: **I have given unto them the words which Thou gavest Me; and they have received them** (John 17:8). Notice the order: You gave Me the words; I gave the words to them; and They received the words. This emphasizes that **faith cometh by hearing, and hearing by the Word of God** (Rom. 10:17). Faith and spiritual discernment are imparted when we pray: **Shew me Thy ways, O LORD; teach me Thy paths. Lead me in Thy truth ... for Thou art the God of my salvation** (Ps. 25:4-5).

Jesus also prayed: **Keep through Thine own Name those whom Thou hast given Me** (John 17:11). His prayer included every one of us as He prayed: **I have given them Thy Word.... They are not of the world, even as I am not of the world. Sanctify** (Keep holy for God's service) **them through Thy truth: Thy Word is Truth. ... Neither pray I for these alone, but for them also which shall believe on Me through their word** (John 17:14,17-20).

Thought for Today: In fulfillment of the Prayer of the Lord Jesus as saints, we should be likeminded, having the same love, being of one accord, of one mind (Phil. 2:2).

Cross References: For **John 17:12:** See Ps. 41:9.

APPEARANCES OF JESUS AFTER HIS RESURRECTION

Seen By	Where	When	Reference
Mary Magdalene	In the garden outside the tomb	Early Sunday Morning	Mark 16:9-11; John 20:11-18
Mary the mother of James, Joanna, and Salome	On the road after leaving the tomb	Early Sunday morning	Matt. 28:1-10; Mark 16:1-8; Luke 24:1-12; John 20:1-9
Peter	Jerusalem	Sunday	Luke 24:12, 24, 34; I Cor. 15:5
Two disciples	Road to Emmaus	Midday Sunday	Luke 24:13-32; Mark 16:12-13
Ten Apostles and those who were with them	Upper room in Jerusalem	Sunday evening	Mark 16:14; Luke 24:33-43; John 20:19-25
The 11 Apostles including Thomas	Upper room in Jerusalem	After 8 days	John 20:26-31; I Cor. 15:5
Seven Apostles	Fishing in Galilee	Dawn	John 21:1-14
Eleven Apostles, 500 disciples	Galilee, on a mountain	Much later	Matt. 28:16-20; Mark 16:15-18
James, the brother of Jesus, then all the Apostles	Unknown	Unknown	I Cor. 15:7
Mary the mother of Jesus, devoted women, Jesus' brothers, and other disciples	Mount of Olives	40 days after His resurrection at His ascension	Luke 24:44-53; Acts 1:3-14
Saul of Tarsus (Hebrew name) Apostle Paul (Roman name)	Road to Damascus	Midday, time unknown	Acts 9:1-9; 22:1-8; 26:12-18; I Cor. 15:8

NOVEMBER 8 — Read John 19 – 21

Highlights: The cross. Cruelty of soldiers (John 19:1-3). Jesus' death, burial and His resurrection (19:28-42; 20:1-29; 21:14). Why John wrote this Book (20:30-31). A threefold emphasis, not just to Peter, but to all of us: *Feed My sheep* (21:15-17).

Judas had led a mob and Roman soldiers to arrest Jesus. After His arrest, they *led Him away to Annas first . . . father in law to Caiaphas, which was the high priest that same year* (John 18:13).

According to the Word of God, the *high priest* was to be a direct descendant of Aaron and was to retain his office until death (Ex. 40:15; Num. 35:25). However, Rome appointed a new *high priest* every year. Annas was the true *high priest* through Aaronic succession but had been replaced by his son-in-law Caiaphas, who was appointed by Rome.

Jesus, the prophesied *Lamb of God, which taketh away the sin of the world* (John 1:29), was led first to the Jewish and then the Gentile-appointed high priests. With Caiaphas were the scribes, the elders, the chief priests *and all the council* (Matt. 26:57,59). In response to the question by the high priest regarding His deity, Jesus said: *Hereafter shall ye see the Son of Man sitting on the right hand of power, and coming in the clouds of heaven* (26:64). Understanding that Jesus was claiming to be coequal with God, Caiaphas ripped his robe of authority as a sign of righteous indignation and shouted: *What further need have we of witnesses? behold, now ye have heard His blasphemy* (26:65). Caiaphas had ignored God's promise of a Prophet like Moses to whom they were to hearken (Deut. 18:15). Jesus, that Prophet stood before him.

When they had bound Him, they . . . delivered Him to Pontius Pilate the governor (Matt. 27:2). Pilate knew Jesus was innocent and said: *I find in Him no fault at all* (John 18:38). But the religious leaders cried out violently: *Crucify Him, crucify Him. . . . He ought to die, because He made Himself the Son of God. . . . If thou let this Man go, thou art not Caesar's friend* (19:6-7,12). Pilate had to choose between Jesus *the Son of God* and the angry religious crowd; he chose the crowd. When a person compromises what is right in God's sight, he has taken a huge step away from the Lord. Jesus said: *No servant can serve two masters* (Luke 16:13).

Thought for Today: Every Christian is responsible to tell of the forgiving love of God.

Cross References: For **John 19:24:** See Ps. 22:18. **John 19:36:** See Ex. 12:46; Ps. 34:20. **John 19:37:** See Zech. 12:10.

INTRODUCTION TO THE BOOK OF ACTS

The Gospel of Luke ends with the Ascension (Luke 24:51-53), while the Book of Acts begins with it. It includes 10 recorded appearances of Christ during the 40 days following His physical resurrection. His parting words to His disciples before **He was taken up. . . . into heaven** (Acts 1:9-11) are of utmost importance: **Ye shall receive power, after that the Holy Ghost** (Spirit) **is come upon you: and ye shall be witnesses unto Me . . . unto the uttermost** (farthest) **part of the earth** (1:8).

Throughout the first 30 years of the Church, on every occasion, a believer was baptized following a confession of Jesus as Lord and Savior (Matt. 28:18-20; Mark 16:16; Acts 2:38,41; 8:12-13,36,38; 9:18; 10:47-48; 16:15,33; 18:8; 19:5).

The first 12 chapters of this book focus on the Apostle Peter and the first local church in Jerusalem concluding with his experiences among believing Gentiles in Samaria.

Beginning with the stoning of Stephen, intense persecution began against the Church (7:59 – 8:4). Saul of Tarsus was one of the chief leaders of the persecution of all who accepted Jesus as the prophesied Messiah (the Anointed One). These believers would later be called Christians (followers of Christ) (11:26).

After his remarkable conversion, Saul – who was both a Jew and a Roman citizen by birth – dedicated his life to Christ for worldwide evangelism. He became known as the Apostle Paul, his Roman name, as he ministered to a Gentile world. His headquarters in Antioch of Syria, a Gentile city, became the center of world evangelism. Acts 13:1 through 21:26 describe the events of Paul's three missionary journeys.

From Acts 21:27 to the end of the book, we have details of Paul's arrest and his transfer to Rome to appear before Emperor Nero. The book ends with Paul still under house arrest in Rome after two years (28:30). Prominent throughout this book is "the Word," which refers to the recorded Scriptures (2:41; 4:4,29,31; 6:2,4,7; 8:4,14,25; 10:36-37,44; 11:1,16,19; 12:24; 13:5,7,26, 44,46,48-49; 14:3,25; 15:7,35-36; 16:6,32; 17:11,13; 18:11; 19:10,20; 20:32). The Holy Spirit is referred to more than 40 times as He fills, guides, and sustains Christians. Prayer is mentioned over 30 times. This book demonstrates how vital the Word of God, prayer, and the Holy Spirit are in the life of every believer and in the collective Body of Christ, His Church.

NOVEMBER 9 Read Acts 1 – 3

Highlights: Purpose of the Church (Acts 1:8). Unite together and pray (1:13-14). The power of the Holy Spirit (2:1-21). Peter preaches Jesus: crucified, risen, exalted as Lord and Christ (2:22-36); Results – the 1st Church (2:41-47) became witnesses (3:18-26).

The Feast (Festival) of Unleavened Bread portrayed the sinless Savior, who is the **Bread of Life** (John 6:35,48) and was celebrated in conjunction with the Passover. The lamb without blemish offered as a sacrifice at Passover also typified Jesus, the perfect **Lamb of God** (1:29,36). The third observance of Passover week was Firstfruits. It was celebrated on the Sunday (Lev. 23:11) following the Passover observance. It was on the day of Firstfruits that Jesus arose: **Now is Christ risen from the dead, and become the Firstfruits of them that slept** (died) (I Cor. 15:20).

The second major feast for which every male was to appear annually before God was 50 days later, **the morrow after the seventh Sabbath** (rest day) following Firstfruits (Lev. 23:15-16). It celebrated the first ingathering of the spring harvest. This festival became known to Christians as Pentecost (Greek: pent'kost') from the Greek word for 50 (pent'konta). On that day, being filled with the Holy Spirit and quoting the prophetic Scriptures (Joel 2:28-29), Peter boldly proclaimed **that God hath made . . . Jesus, whom ye have crucified, both Lord and Christ** (Acts 2:36). Then the crowd said to Peter and the apostles: **Brethren, what shall we do? Then Peter said unto them, Repent, and be baptized every one of you in the Name of Jesus Christ for the remission of sins, and ye shall receive the gift of the Holy Ghost** (Spirit). **For the promise is unto you, and to your children, and to all that are afar off, even as many as the Lord our God shall call** (to be saved) (2:37-39).

The required offering on Pentecost consisted of two loaves of leavened bread (Lev. 23:17). These two loaves foreshadowed both Jewish and Gentile believers, and included leaven, symbolizing sin, since everyone except Jesus has sinned. The separate identities of the ground grains, blended into a oneness, symbolize all believers who lose their individual identities to become the Bride of Christ – His Church (Eph. 5:21-32; I Cor. 12:27). The Apostle Paul later declared: **There is neither Greek nor Jew . . . but Christ is all, and in all** (Col. 3:11).

Thought for Today: We need to tell others about the joy of Christian fellowship.

Cross References: For **Acts 1:20:** See Ps. 69:25; 109:8. **Acts 2:17-21:** See Joel 2:28-32. **Acts 2:25-28:** See Ps. 16:8-11. **Acts 2:34-35:** See Ps. 110:1. **Acts 3:22-23:** See Deut. 18:15,18-19. **Acts 3:25:** See Gen. 12:3; 22:18.

NOVEMBER 10   Read Acts 4 – 6

Highlights: Faithfulness in persecution (Acts 4:1-12). Disciples warned not to preach (4:13-18). How to combat threats (4:19-20,23-31; 5:29-32). Death because of lying to Holy Spirit (5:1-11). Results of ***prayer, and . . . the ministry of the Word*** (6:4). A deacon full of faith and the Holy Spirit (6:1-6).

Loyalty to the Lord and love for one another permeated the first Church. ***The multitude of them that believed were of one heart and of one soul: neither said any of them that ought*** (any) ***of the things which he possessed was his own; but they had all things common. . . . as many as were possessors of lands or houses sold them, and brought the prices of the things that were sold, and laid them down at the apostles' feet: and distribution was made unto every man according as he had need*** (Acts 4:32,34-35). Undoubtedly, this was a great encouragement to the congregation because most Jews who confessed Jesus as the Messiah had probably lost their jobs.

Ananias and his wife Sapphira also sold a piece of property; but gave only a part of the proceeds to the Church while implying they were giving all (5:1-2). The property was theirs to do as they pleased. All giving was voluntary (5:4). No one was required to sell his property or to share his wealth, but the "generous gift" of Ananias and Sapphira was a lie ***to the Holy Ghost*** (Spirit) (5:3; Rev. 21:8; Jer. 17:9).

Christians today also have a serious problem – perhaps not of lying to the Holy Spirit, but of stealing from God (Mal. 3:8-10). Many refuse to give even a tithe (10%) of their income, the minimum that God requires for the ministry of His Word. Tithing is not an option; it is a debt we owe. God rightfully owns all that He created, but He only requires us to return to Him one-tenth of what He has entrusted to us, thereby acknowledging that we are only stewards (managers) of His property.

This principle was demonstrated by Abraham over 500 years before the Law was given (Gen. 14:20; Heb. 7:1-2). Later, the Law stated: ***All the tithe*** (tenth portion) ***of the land, whether of the seed of the land, or of the fruit of the tree, is the L***ORD***'s: it is holy*** (sacred, set apart) ***unto the L***ORD (Lev. 27:30).

Thought for Today: Nothing is impossible. Put your trust in God (Phil. 4:13).
Cross References: For **Acts 4:11:** See Ps. 118:22. **Acts 4:25-26:** See Ps. 2:1-2.

NOVEMBER 11   Read Acts 7 – 8

Highlights: Stephen speaks up (Acts 7:1-53). This first Christian martyr gives us a glimpse of heaven (7:54-60). The Lord's plan: (1) Allows persecution (8:1-3); (2) Believers scatter, sharing the Word as they go (8:4); (3) Individuals hear Word and believe (8:12,27-38); (4) Preaching continues *in all the cities* (8:40).

Stephen was a deacon in the church at Jerusalem. He knew the Old Testament Scriptures well, and boldly reminded the unbelieving authorities: *Ye do always resist the Holy Ghost* (Spirit): *as your fathers did, so do ye. Which of the prophets have not your fathers persecuted? and they have slain them which shewed before of the coming of the Just One; of whom ye have been now the betrayers and murderers* (Acts 7:51-52).

With the same hatred of those who had crucified Christ, the angry authorities dragged Stephen *out of the city, and stoned him.* As he was dying, *he . . . cried with a loud voice, Lord, lay not this sin to their charge* (7:58,60). Stephen could have avoided death by saying nothing, but he made it clear that the religious authorities were responsible for crucifying Jesus, *the Just One*. Stephen's faith and forgiving attitude in the face of death was the same as his Savior's on the cross, and it surely must have made a powerful impression on those who witnessed Stephen's love toward his murderers. In the same spirit of love, we too need to pray for those who treat us *despitefully* (Matt. 5:44; Luke 6:28). Those who seem to be our enemies today may someday be saved if we express the love of Christ to them as Stephen did to his persecutors.

At that time there was a great persecution against the church which was at Jerusalem (8:1). Instead of discouraging believers, this resulted in a great missionary movement as Jesus' followers dispersed throughout the region. Philip, who was also a deacon in the first church, was led by the Holy Spirit to meet an Ethiopian official who was reading the Book of Isaiah on his way home. God led Philip to explain to him how the prophecy of Isaiah 53:7-8 had been fulfilled in Jesus of Nazareth. On learning that Jesus was the Messiah (Savior), the Ethiopian asked to be *baptized*. Philip told him: *If thou believest with all thine heart, thou mayest. And he answered and said, I believe that Jesus Christ is the Son of God. . . . and they went down both into the water . . . Philip and the eunuch; and he baptized him.* Then the man *went on his way rejoicing* (8:36-39).

Thought for Today: Christ desires to control all of your thoughts every day.

Cross References: For **Acts 7:3:** See Gen. 12:1. **Acts 7:27-28:** See Ex. 2:14. **Acts 7:32:** See Ex. 3:6. **Acts 7:33-34:** See Ex.. 3:5,7-8,10. **Acts 7:37:** See Deut. 18:15. **Acts 7:40:** See Ex. 3:21. **Acts 7:42-43:** See Amos 5:25-27. **Acts 7:49-50:** See Is. 66:1-2. **Acts 8:32-33:** See Is. 53:7-8.

NOVEMBER 12 — Read Acts 9 – 10

Highlights: Saul seeks to destroy Jesus' followers (Acts 9:1-2). Never underestimate our Lord's power to change a heart (9:3-18). The Church strengthened (9:19-31). Miraculous healings; many believe (9:32-42). Christ also died for the Gentiles (chap. 10).

Saul of Tarsus was a sincere Pharisee determined to stamp out Jesus' followers, whom he considered blasphemers. So he obtained letters from the high priest to go to Damascus in Syria to arrest those who had fled there. He stated *that if he found any of this Way* (followers of Jesus), *whether they were men or women, he might bring them . . . unto Jerusalem* (Acts 9:2); for trial and execution.

As he neared Damascus, *suddenly there shined round about him a light from heaven: And he fell to the earth, and heard a voice saying unto him, Saul, Saul, why persecutest . . . Me? And he said, Who art Thou, Lord? And the Lord said, I am Jesus whom thou persecutest* (9:3-5). Three days later, the Lord spoke to Ananias, a disciple of Christ who lived in Damascus, saying to him: *Arise, and go into the street which is called Straight, and inquire . . . for one called Saul, of Tarsus: for, behold, he prayeth, And hath seen in a vision a man named Ananias* (9:11-12). Ananias replied to the Lord: *I have heard . . . how much evil he hath done to Thy saints* (followers) *at Jerusalem . . . But the Lord said . . . he is a chosen vessel unto Me, to bear My Name before the Gentiles . . . and the children of Israel: For I will shew him how great* (many) *things he must suffer for My Name's sake. And Ananias . . . entered into the house; and putting his hands on him said, Brother Saul, the Lord, even Jesus . . . hath sent me, that thou mightest receive thy sight, and be filled with the Holy Ghost* (Spirit). *. . . and he* (Paul – 13:9) *received sight forthwith, and arose, and was baptized* (9:13-18).

At about the same time, Peter also had a vision which caused him to realize *that God is no respecter of persons* (10:34). Speaking to Gentiles at the home of Cornelius, Peter declared: *To Him give all the prophets witness, that through His Name whosoever believeth in Him shall receive remission of sins. While Peter yet spake these words, the Holy Ghost* (Spirit) *fell on all them which heard the Word* (10:43-44). *By one Spirit are we all baptized into one Body* (I Cor. 12:13).

Thought for Today: LIve for God and He will give you His best.

NOVEMBER 13   Read Acts 11 – 13

Highlights: Jesus died for all, even those who do not receive Him as Savior and Lord (Acts 11:1-18). Peter's defense: "God said it" (11:17). Persecution spreads the Gospel (11:19-26;12:24). James martyred (12:1-2); Peter lives (12:6-19). Paul's first mission trip (chap. 13).

Saul's family, it seems, had considerable wealth. Following the prescribed study of the Scriptures in Tarsus, Saul was selected for further rabbinic studies in Jerusalem as a student of the famous Rabbi Gamaliel (22:3). He later shared with the Galatian Christians that he was *exceedingly zealous of the traditions of my fathers* (oral teachings of past religious leaders considered as authoritative) (Gal. 1:14).

After he accepted Jesus as the Messiah, he changed his Hebrew name Saul to his Roman (Gentile) name Paul to identify himself better with Gentiles. On his first missionary journey, *Paul and his company loosed* (departed) *from Paphos . . . to Perga. . . . to Antioch in Pisidia*, a Roman province of Galatia in what is now Turkey. They *went into the synagogue on the Sabbath day, and sat down. And after the reading of the Law and the prophets* (Acts 13:13-15), they were invited to speak. Paul chose prophetic Scriptures to prove that Jesus was the long-awaited Messiah. He began with a review of how *the God of . . . Israel chose our fathers. . . . raised up unto them David to be their king. . . . Of this man's seed* (offspring) *hath God according to His promise raised unto Israel a Saviour, Jesus. . . . their rulers, because they knew Him not. . . . desired* (requested from) *. . . Pilate that He should be slain. And when they had fulfilled all that was written of Him, they took Him down from the tree, and laid Him in a sepulchre* (tomb). *But God raised Him from the dead* (13:17,22-23,27-30).

Through Christ's death and resurrection, we receive eternal life. But, being saved and *justified from all things* is far more than just choosing a better way of life. First, it is realizing the awfulness of sin as an offense against God, having real sorrow for our sins and a sincere desire to be delivered from those sins. This is followed by a decision to live life by avoiding and resisting sin through the power of the Holy Spirit. Paul declared: *By Him all that believe are justified* (acquitted) *from all things, from which ye could not be justified by the Law of Moses* (Acts 13:39).

Thought for Today: Share what Jesus means to you with someone today (Mark 8:38).

Cross References: For **Acts 13:22:** See I Sam. 13:14; Ps. 89:20. **Acts 13:33:** See Ps. 2:7. **Acts 13:34:** See Is. 55:3. **Acts 13:35:** See Ps. 16:10. **Acts 13:41:** See Hab. 1:5. **Acts 13:47:** See Is. 49:6.

Devotions continued on page 391

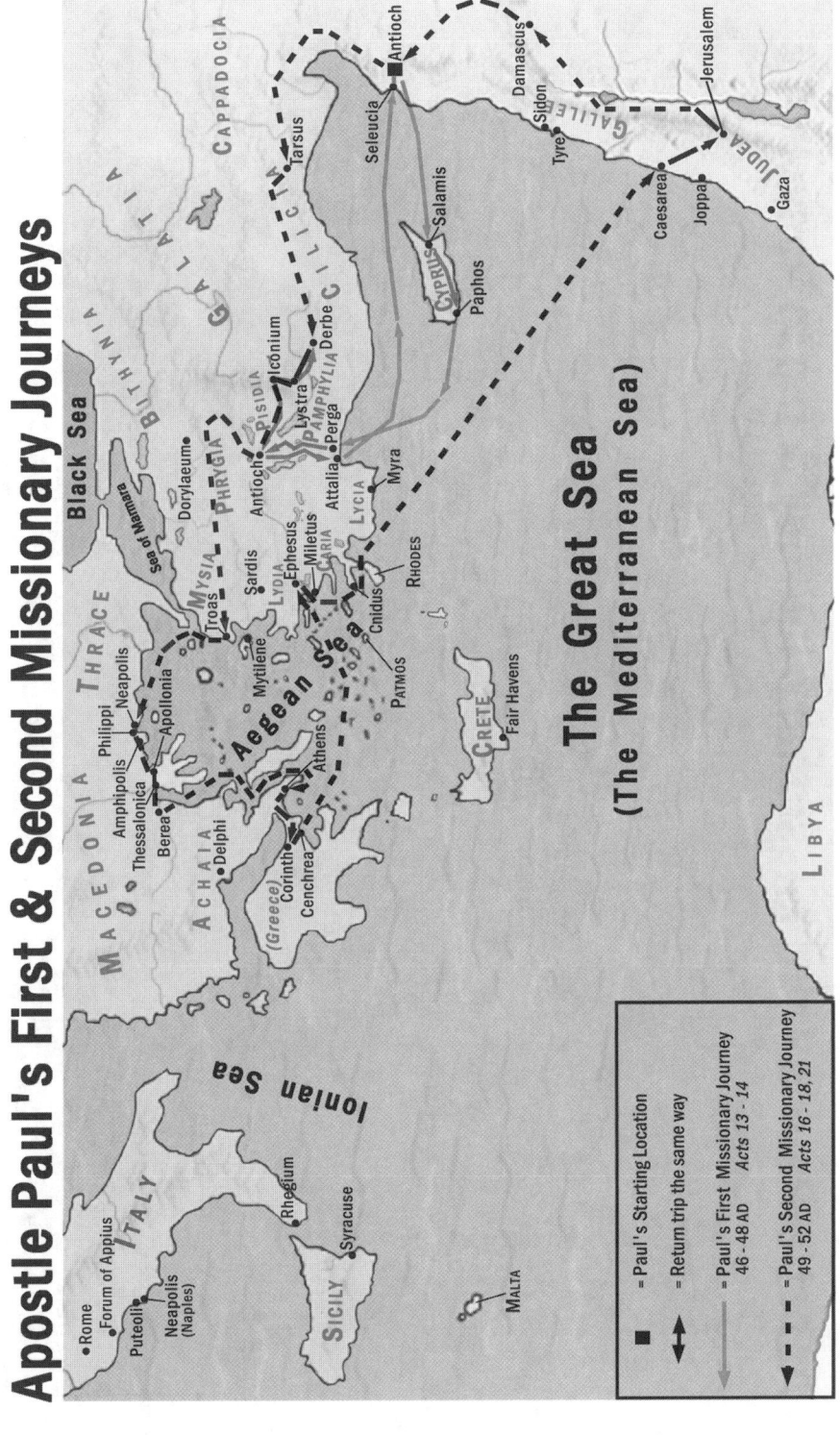

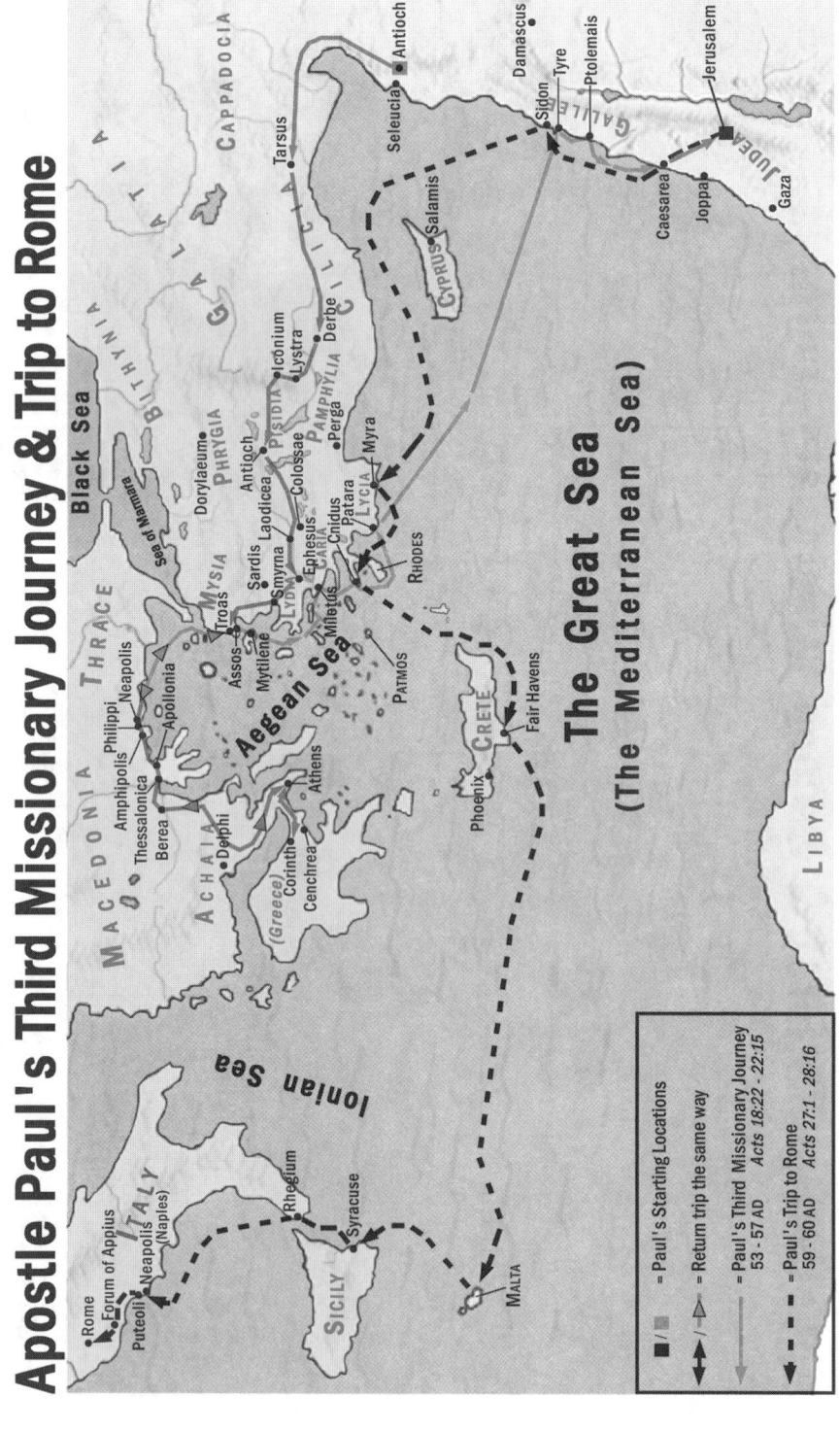

EVENTS IN THE LIFE OF THE APOSTLE PAUL

TARSUS – The capital of Cilicia was the birthplace of Paul (the Roman name for Saul). He was a devout Jew, but also a Roman citizen by birthright (Acts 16:37-38; 22:3-29). He grew up in the Hellenistic (Greek) culture of Tarsus, which also had Hebrew tradition. Located in the province of Cilicia in Asia Minor, Tarsus had one of the three greatest universities in the world comparable to Athens of the eastern Mediterranean and Alexandria in Egypt. **JERUSALEM** – Paul received his Old Testament education in Jerusalem from Gamaliel, the greatest Hebrew intellectual educator of the time, *according to the perfect manner of the Law of the fathers* (22:3; comp. 5:34-40). The first mention of Paul in the New Testament was at the stoning of Stephen, when *Saul was consenting unto his death* (7:58 – 8:1). He persistently persecuted Christians and *made havock of the Church* (8:3; 9:1).

CONVERSION TO CHRIST – Saul obtained a commission from the high priest to go to Damascus and persecute believers in Jesus. On the way, blinded by a brilliant light, Saul *heard a voice saying unto him, Saul, Saul, why persecutest thou Me? . . . I am Jesus* (9:4-5). After Saul received Christ, he was *filled with the Holy Ghost* (Spirit). *. . . and was baptized* (9:17-18). **ARABIA** – He *immediately . . . went into Arabia* (possibly near Mount Sinai), *and returned again unto Damascus* (Gal. 1:16-17). *Then was Saul certain days with the disciples which were at Damascus. And straightway he preached Christ in the synagogues, that He is the Son of God. . . . proving that this* (Jesus) *is* (the) *very Christ* (Acts 9:19-20,22). **JERUSALEM** – *After three years* (Gal. 1:18) certain Jews of Damascus determined to kill Saul, but he escaped (Acts 9:25) and went to Jerusalem (about 133 miles from Damascus) where he saw Peter and James (Gal. 1:18-19) and *spake boldly in the Name of the Lord Jesus . . . but they* (the Jews) *went about to slay him. . . . when the brethren knew, they brought him down to Caesarea, and sent him forth to Tarsus* (Acts 9:26,29-30). **TARSUS** – Later, Barnabas, knowing how Paul had preached boldly in the Name of Jesus, both in Damascus and Jerusalem – went to Tarsus and brought Paul to Antioch (about 100 miles southeast of Tarsus) (11:25-26).

ANTIOCH – Paul joined *Barnabas, and Simeon that was called Niger, and Lucius of Cyrene, and Manaen* (13:1). A famine was prophesied *throughout all the world* (11:28) and the disciples sent Barnabas and Saul with money for their brethren *in Judaea* (11:27-30). In Jerusalem, Paul met with *James, Cephas, and John, who seemed to be pillars* in the Church (Gal. 2:1-20) – possibly 14 years after Paul's first journey to the church in Jerusalem. On their return from Jerusalem to Antioch, they brought with them John Mark, a cousin of Barnabas (Acts 12:25). **ANTIOCH** – In Syria (13:1-3), Paul and Barnabas were set apart by the church at Antioch, as commanded by the Holy Spirit, for missionary work among the Gentiles. Antioch was the starting point for all three of Paul's great missionary journeys. Barnabas and Saul were *sent forth by the Holy Ghost* (Spirit) (13:4). They took John Mark with them, and departed for Seleucia and then for Cyprus. **CYPRUS** (13:1-4) – The native land of Barnabas (4:36), an island in the Mediterranean Sea about 60 miles from Syria. **SALAMIS** (13:5) – Paul preached in the synagogues in this eastern port. He and Barnabas traveled through the island (about 100 miles) to Paphos.

PAPHOS (13:6-7) – Sergius Paulus, the Roman *deputy* (governor) became a believer (13:12). *Paul and his company* then sailed to Perga. **PERGA** (13:13) – The capital of the province of Pamphylia was about 180 miles north of Paphos. John Mark deserted them and returned to Jerusalem. Paul and Barnabas proceeded on to Antioch. **ANTIOCH** (13:14-41) – This Antioch was located in Pisidia, about 120 miles north of Perga. Here *the Word of the Lord was published throughout all the region* (13:49). But the unbelieving Jews *raised persecution against Paul and Barnabas, and expelled them out of their coasts* (13:50). The Apostles then followed the Roman Road about 100 miles to Iconium. **ICONIUM** (13:51) – Iconium was the capital of Lyconia where *a great multitude both of the Jews and also of the Greeks believed* (14:1). Paul and Barnabas stayed a *long time* (14:3), until a mob attempted to stone them, then fled about 20 miles to Lystra.

LYSTRA (14:6) – Lystra was a small rural town of Lycaonia where Timothy lived and *there they preached the Gospel* (14:7). Soon, hostile Jews from Antioch in Pisidia and Iconium arrived and raised such opposition to Paul's preaching that the people stoned him, dragged him out of the city, and left him for dead (14:19); but Paul revived. Timothy probably witnessed Paul's preaching and the cruel stoning. The next day Paul and Barnabas went to the small town of Derbe. **DERBE** (14:20-21) – Derbe, where *they had preached the Gospel*, was about 30 miles to the southeast. They then returned through Lystra, Iconium, and Antioch in Pisidia where they appointed elders in every church (14:21-23). Paul and Barnabas then returned to Perga.

PERGA (14:25) – Paul and Barnabas preached the Word of God; then went to Attalia and sailed to Antioch in Syria, completing Paul's first missionary journey. **ANTIOCH** in Syria (14:26) – Paul and Barnabas remained here several years. **JERUSALEM** – The church at Antioch sent Paul and Barnabas with other believers to Jerusalem where they testified how God had saved the Gentiles.

ANTIOCH – Paul and Barnabas returned to Antioch, *teaching and preaching the Word of the Lord* (15:22,35). Barnabas left and sailed home to Cyprus (15:39). Paul then chose Silas to accompany him to the places where he had preached the Word on his first journey (15:40).

~SECOND MISSIONARY JOURNEY~

SYRIA AND CILICIA – *Being recommended by the brethren*, they left Antioch and journeyed by land *through Syria and Cilicia* (15:40-41). Here Paul strengthened the faith of the churches. **DERBE THEN LYSTRA** (16:1-3) – Here Timothy joined them *as they went through the cities. . . . so were the churches established in the faith* (16:4-5). **PHRYGIA AND GALATIA** (16:6) – As they continued through these territories, they *were forbidden of* (by) *the Holy Ghost* (Spirit) *to preach the Word in Asia* (16:6). They moved on toward Mysia. **MYSIA** (16:7-8) – Once again, being forbidden by the Spirit to continue the intended journey to Bithynia, they passed by Mysia and came to Troas.

TROAS (16:8) – Here Luke joined them (16:10). Paul had a vision of a man asking him to come to Macedonia. Immediately they boarded a ship and sailed *to Samothracia, and the next day to Neapolis*. **NEAPOLIS** (16:11 – Modern Kavalla)

From there they went 10 miles inland to the Macedonian city of Philippi. **PHILIPPI** (16:12) – Lydia of Thyatira – a businesswoman, *a seller of purple* – was baptized, along with her family (16:13-15). These were the first converts in Europe. Soon afterward, Paul and Silas were severely beaten, imprisoned, and miraculously released at night (16:16-26). The jailer was converted and baptized, along with his household (16:22-34). Luke remained in Philippi while Paul, Silas, and Timothy went on *to Thessalonica, where* (there) *was a synagogue of the Jews* (17:1). **THESSALONICA** (17:1 – Capital of Macedonia, about 100 miles away) – *Paul . . . went in unto them, and three Sabbath days reasoned with them out of the Scriptures. . . . And some of them believed* (17:2,4). Then a mob *set all the city on an uproar. . . . And the brethren immediately sent away Paul and Silas by night unto Berea* (17:5-10), about 50 miles away.

BEREA (17:10) – The people *received the Word with all readiness of mind, and. . . . many of them believed* (17:11-12). But radical opposition incited by those from Thessalonica caused Paul to immediately depart (17:14). Paul and the others went to Athens while Silas and Timothy remained in Berea. **ATHENS** (17:15) – This was one of the great learning centers in the ancient world. Seeing widespread idolatry throughout the city, Paul *disputed . . . in the synagogue . . . and in the market daily. . . . Then certain philosophers* took him to *Mars' Hill* (Areopagus) where he urged them to *seek the Lord . . .* (who) *now commandeth all men every where to repent* (17:17-32). A few believed. Paul then went to Corinth.

CORINTH (18:1) – Corinth was a great seaport city where Paul met Aquila and his wife Priscilla. Silas and Timothy soon joined him, and *Paul was pressed in the Spirit, and testified to the Jews that Jesus was Christ* (18:5). *Crispus, the chief ruler of the synagogue, believed on the Lord . . . and many of the Corinthians hearing believed, and were baptized* (18:8). Paul remained in Corinth for more than a year and a half (18:11); then sailed with Aquila and Priscilla to Ephesus. **EPHESUS** (18:19) – This magnificent city had a population of over 225,000. After a short ministry in the synagogue, Aquila and Priscilla remained there, but Paul left by sea and *landed at Caesarea*, going on to Jerusalem to keep the *feast* (18:18-22). He then returned to Antioch. **ANTIOCH IN SYRIA** (18:22) – Paul had been gone for three or four years. He remained *some time* (18:23), perhaps a year. He then left on his third missionary journey with Timothy as his coworker.

~THIRD MISSIONARY JOURNEY~

GALATIA AND PHRYGIA (18:23) – Leaving Antioch they traveled through all the country of Galatia and Phrygia and came to Ephesus. **EPHESUS** (19:1) – Paul taught daily for about two years in the school of Tyrannus (19:9-10). *Mightily grew the Word of God and prevailed* (19:20). Paul sent Timothy and Erastus to Macedonia, but he remained in Ephesus until Demetrius, a silversmith, caused a riot (19:23-41). Paul then left for Macedonia. **MACEDONIA** (20:1) – Paul encouraged the believers in the places he visited on his former journey. He then went on to Greece. **GREECE** (20:2) – Paul stayed three months, probably visiting the churches on the way to Corinth. He intended to sail from there to Syria, but learned of a plot to kill him (20:3). So he went back through Macedonia to Philippi.

PHILIPPI (20:6) – There he was joined by Luke. They sailed together and, in five days, came to Troas. **TROAS** (20:6) – Paul and Luke remained here seven days, then departed – Paul on foot, but sending the others by ship to Assos where he joined them to sail on to Miletus (20:13-15). **MILETUS** (20:15) – Here the elders of the church at Ephesus met with him (20:17-38). Paul then sailed past Rhodes to Patara. **PATARA** (21:1) – Here they changed ships, embarking on one going directly to Phenicia (21:2). Passing to the south of Cyprus, they landed at Tyre.

TYRE (21:3) – The disciples here warned Paul not to go on to Jerusalem (21:4). But, after praying with them, he boarded a ship and continued on to Ptolemais. **PTOLEMAIS** (21:7) – They stayed here for a day and had fellowship with other believers. The next day they went on to Caesarea. **CAESAREA** (21:8) – They stayed with Philip, the evangelist. Agabus foretold that Paul would be imprisoned if he went to Jerusalem (21:10-11). **JERUSALEM** – Paul was welcomed by the brethren (21:15-17). But he was seized by a mob because of mistaken identity (21:29,38), beaten, arrested, bound with chains (21:32-33), and imprisoned. The Lord appeared to him, saying: *Be of good cheer . . . must thou bear witness* (of Me) *at Rome* (23:11). After Paul's nephew overheard a plot to kill him (23:12-30), Paul was taken to the Roman governor Felix at Caesarea (23:32-33).

CAESAREA (24:1 – 26:29) – Paul's accusers were Ananias the high priest with the elders and an orator named Tertullus (24:1-26). Paul remained a prisoner in Caesarea for two years (24:27). The high priest appealed to Festus, the successor of Felix, for a hearing in Jerusalem (25:1-9); but Paul appealed to *stand at Caesar's judgment seat* (25:10-11) so Festus had him present his defense before King Agrippa who was visiting (25:13,22 – 26:29). Both Festus and Agrippa agreed that Paul *doeth nothing worthy of death*, but, because he had appealed to Caesar, Paul was transported by ship to Rome (26:30-32).

ENROUTE TO ROME (27:1 – 28:11) – The ship sailed south of Crete and passed Salmone *unto a place which is called The Fair Havens* (27:7-8). After *they sailed close by Crete. . . . there arose against it a tempestuous wind* (27:13-14). During the storm, Paul had a vision of an *angel of God* (27:23-24) and was told that the ship would *be cast upon a certain island*; and, as the ship broke up during the storm, *they escaped all safe to land* (27:26-44). On the island of Melita, Paul was bitten by a deadly viper, but *he shook off the beast into the fire, and felt no harm* (28:3-5). While there, Paul also *healed the father of Publius* (28:8-9). *After three months we departed in a ship of Alexandria. . . . and so we went toward Rome* (28:11-14).

ROME (28:16-31) – Though Paul was still a prisoner, as a Roman citizen he was granted permission to dwell in his own rented house and continued to preach for two years. During that time, he probably wrote Ephesians, Philippians, Colossians, and Philemon. Since there is no clear statement in Scripture that he was freed, we assume his trial took place and Nero had him placed in the Mamertine Prison where he wrote the second letter to Timothy, saying: *The time of my departure is at hand. I have fought a good fight, I have finished my course, I have kept the faith: Henceforth there is laid up for me a crown of righteousness, which the Lord, the Righteous Judge, shall give me at that day: and not to me only, but unto all them also that love His appearing* (II Tim. 4:6-8).

Continued from page 384

NOVEMBER 14 — Read Acts 14 – 16

Highlights: First mission trip ends (Acts 14:27-28). Paul's second mission trip (Acts 16). A call from Macedonia (16:6-10). Peace and joy in prison (16:22-25). Miraculous victory in Jesus (16:26-40).

Almost everywhere Paul and Barnabas traveled, **an assault was made... to use them despitefully** (wrongfully), **and to stone them** (Acts 14:5). In Iconium, violent opposition again erupted when Paul told **the unbelieving Jews** that Jesus was the Messiah who was foretold by the prophets (14:2). He fled about 20 miles to Lystra where his attention was drawn to a crippled man. **Paul... stedfastly beholding him, and perceiving that he had faith to be healed, Said with a loud voice, Stand upright on thy feet. And he leaped and walked** (14:9-10). Upon seeing this miraculous healing, the people said: **The gods are** (have) **come down to us in the likeness of men** (14:11). Paul and Barnabas strongly objected to being made objects of idolatrous worship and shared their faith in Christ with these idolators (14:12-18).

Following this event, **certain Jews from Antioch and Iconium, who persuaded the people, and, having stoned Paul, drew him out of the city, supposing he had been dead. Howbeit, as the disciples stood round about him, he rose up, and came into the city: and the next day he departed with Barnabas to Derbe,** where they made many disciples (14:19-21).

Later, Paul made a brief reference to his sufferings for Christ, saying: **We must through much tribulation enter into the Kingdom of God** (14:22; also 9:16). Whenever there is a true spiritual awakening and people are being saved, without exception, Satan will seek to disrupt, discourage, and destroy the results. So, we too should not be surprised that, following our best efforts to serve the Lord, Satan will seek to discourage us through hardships and even disappointments from the very ones we should have expected to receive encouragement. Paul, the man God chose to write most of our New Testament, faced many dangers; but still he could testify: **I know both how to be abased** (made low), **and I know how to abound** (have abundance)**: every where and in all things I am instructed both to be full and to be hungry, both to abound and to suffer need. I can do all things through Christ which strengtheneth me** (Phil. 4:12-13).

Thought for Today: To be guided into all truth, we must read and obey all the Truth.

Cross References: For **Acts 15:16-17:** See Amos 9:11-12.

NOVEMBER 15 — Read Acts 17 – 19

Highlights: Preaching Jesus, Paul challenges the Greek worship of idols (Acts 17:16-17), false gods and philosophers (17:18-34). He leaves Greece, returns to Syria, and then begins his third mission trip, sailing for Ephesus (present-day Turkey) (chap. 19). After 2 years, **all they which dwelt in Asia heard the Word of the Lord** (19:10). Wicked people cause a riot (19:21-41)!

Paul and Silas were tried and beaten in Philippi, then put into prison. However, through a miracle of God, they were freed the next day. **When they had seen the brethren, they comforted them, and departed. . . . to Thessalonica** (Acts 16:40 – 17:1). **Paul, as his manner was, went in unto them, and three Sabbath** (Rest) **days reasoned with them out of the Scriptures . . . alleging** (giving evidence), **that Christ must needs** (of necessity) **have suffered, and risen again from the dead; and that this Jesus . . . is Christ. And some of them believed** (17:2-4).

When the unbelieving religious leaders learned of these conversions, they were angry and started a riot. Paul immediately left by night and traveled southwest to Berea. Upon arrival, they **went into the synagogue of the Jews. These were more noble than those in Thessalonica, in that they received the Word with all readiness of mind, and searched the Scriptures daily, whether those things were so. Therefore many of them believed** (17:10-12). Confessing Jesus as their Messiah affected everyone in their lives. Their seeking after the truth should encourage Christians to study all the Scriptures with a sincere desire to know the Truth it reveals.

Our Creator has allotted to each of us only one lifetime to prepare for our eternal destiny. We have a responsibility to become the person He wants us to be in order to accomplish the purposes for which He created us. Think how embarrassed we will be, when we stand before the Lord, if we have wasted our few short years achieving only material, social, and financial goals for self-gratification. God has provided one perfect Guidebook – His Word.

The times of this ignorance God winked at (overlooked); **but now commandeth all men every where to repent: Because He hath appointed a day, in the which He will judge the world in righteousness** (Acts 17:30-31).

Thought for Today: Praise the Lord! His ways are always best.

NOVEMBER 16   Read Acts 20 – 22

Highlights: One message (Acts 20:20-21). One destination (20:22). Our part (20:28). Lift up the poor and weak; remember what Jesus said (20:35). Jerusalem and the brethren (21:15-25). People riot – Paul arrested (21:26-36). Paul's defense (21:39; 22:1-29).

The Apostle Paul met with the Ephesian elders at Miletus, saying: ***I go bound in the spirit unto Jerusalem, not knowing the things that shall befall*** (happen to) ***me there: Save*** (Except) ***that the Holy Ghost*** (Spirit) ***witnesseth in every city, saying that bonds and afflictions abide*** (await) ***me. But ... neither count I my life dear unto myself, so that I might finish my course with joy, and the ministry, which I have received of the Lord Jesus, to testify*** (solemnly affirm) ***the Gospel of the grace of God*** (Acts 20:22-24).

The indwelling Holy Spirit will strengthen us to withstand our trials and temptations as He did for Paul. Jesus promised believers: ***I will pray the Father, and He shall give you another Comforter, that He may abide*** (remain) ***with you for ever*** (John 14:16). We have not been left alone in our trials; we are ***strengthened with might by His Spirit in the inner man*** (Eph. 3:16). With the Holy Spirit, we can face the future with certainty. This enables us to enjoy a deep, inward peace that comes from God alone (John 14:27). We experience a contentment that ***passeth all understanding*** (Phil. 4:7), one that outward circumstances cannot affect. Because God is within us, we can respond to others with love and mercy that sweeps away prejudice, jealousy, hate, and envy. Though we have not always permitted Christ to rule our hearts, we can say: "Thanks to Christ, I'm becoming what I was meant to be."

Spiritual growth takes place as we give our love, forgiveness, and understanding. As we do this, we become more like Jesus. Paul never denounced the evil Roman Emperor Nero, but he prayed for him. Even as a prisoner in Rome, Paul wrote: ***I exhort therefore, that, first of all ... prayers, intercessions, and giving of thanks, be made for all men; For kings, and for all that are in authority; that we may lead a quiet and peaceable life in all godliness and honesty. For this is good and acceptable in the sight of God our Saviour; Who will have all men to be saved, and to come unto the knowledge of the Truth*** (I Tim. 2:1-4).

Thought for Today: Our willingness to die daily to self-interest will increase our spiritual growth as we follow in the Master's footsteps.

NOVEMBER 17   Read Acts 23 – 25

Highlights: Paul before a divided Jewish High Council (Acts 23:1-11). Kill the man of God (23:12-24). Jews demand his death before Roman rulers: (1) Felix, Roman governor (24:1-27); (2) Festus, new Roman governor (25:1-12); (3) King Agrippa, Roman ruler of Galilee (25:23-27).

When Paul arrived in Jerusalem following his third missionary journey, the religious leaders **stirred up all the people** with false accusations against him: **This is the man, that teacheth . . . against the people, and the Law, and this place** (Acts 21:27-28). An angry mob then seized Paul and tried to kill him, but he was rescued by Roman soldiers. He was then allowed to speak to the angry Jews in his own defense. But when Paul mentioned his commission by Jesus to go to the Gentiles, they immediately considered him a traitor to their religion, and angrily shouted: **Away with such a fellow from the earth: for it is not fit that he should live** (22:22).

After the Sanhedrin authorities tried Paul and failed to convict him, religious zealots decided to take the law into their own hands and murder him (23:12-15). **Paul's sister's son** overheard their wicked plan to murder Paul and told the Roman captain, who then arranged for Paul to be secretly transferred by night to Felix, the Roman governor of Judea residing at Caesarea (23:16-35).

During his years of confinement in Caesarea, Paul was tried before three Roman rulers who listened to what he had to say about his faith in Jesus Christ. He faithfully **reasoned of righteousness, temperance** (self-control), **and judgment to come** (24:25). Each of his judges had a different reaction as Paul spoke of the **judgment to come**. His first judge Felix **trembled** (24:25), but he only heard him from time to time. Later, his second judge Festus exposed his indifference when he exclaimed in a **loud voice, Paul, thou art beside thyself** (out of your mind) (26:24). And, for whatever he may have meant, his third judge Agrippa said: **Almost thou persuadest me to be a Christian** (26:28). Whether Agrippa's words were sincere or sarcastic is not important – the outcome was the same. As far as we know, none of these men received Christ as Savior and Lord of their lives and, consequently, all were eternally lost.

God invites all to repent and receive Christ as their Savior and Lord: **Behold, now is the day of salvation** (II Cor. 6:2).

Thought for Today: Christ gave His all for us; let's give Him our all that He might live His life through us.

Cross References: For **Acts 23:5:** See Ex. 22:28.

NOVEMBER 18

Read Acts 26 – 28

Highlights: Paul warns of danger but is ignored; shipwreck follows (Acts chap. 27). Paul: Shipwrecked on Malta (28:1-10); his witness in Rome (28:17-31).

When Paul confessed his faith in Jesus as the risen Savior and Messiah, Festus, the new Roman governor of Judea, thought he was *mad* (insane) (Acts 26:24-25).

After Paul, as a Roman citizen, had appealed his case to Caesar, Festus placed him in the custody of *one named Julius, a centurion of Augustus' band* (27:1). Julius' responsibility was to take Paul safely to Rome to stand trial before Nero, the Roman Emperor. They set sail and, after a brief docking at Sidon, continued along the northern coast of Cyprus. Stormy winds kept them from making much progress. On reaching *The fair havens* in Crete (27:8), Paul urged them to stay there during the winter months. He warned: *I perceive that this voyage will be with hurt* (danger) *and much damage, not only of the lading* (cargo) *and ship, but also of our lives*. But the majority of the people on board urged Julius to continue on to *Phenice, and there to winter; which is an haven* (harbor) *of Crete* (27:10-12).

While they were attempting to reach Phenice, furious hurricane-force winds beat upon them. After two stormy weeks, their ship began to sink off the coast of Melita. *Paul stood forth in the midst of them, and said, Sirs. . . . be of good cheer: for there shall be no loss of any man's life among you, but of the ship. For there stood by me this night the* (an) *angel of God . . . whom I serve, Saying, Fear not, Paul; thou must be brought before Caesar: and, lo, God hath given thee all them that sail with thee* (27:21-24). From this experience we learn that our judgment is only as good as our source of information.

Our life's voyage, like Paul's, may also be filled with violent storms. We may experience physical, financial, or emotional "shipwreck" and *all hope that we should be saved* may appear to be gone (27:20). But there will come a day when the tempests we have weathered will seem insignificant compared to what God has accomplished through our faithfulness. Because of Christ, Paul could confidently say: *I take pleasure in infirmities, in reproaches, in necessities, in persecutions, in distresses for Christ's sake: for when I am weak, then am I strong* (II Cor. 12:10; Rom. 5:1-5).

Thought for Today: There is no guarantee that you can accept Christ tomorrow because you may not have tomorrow.

Cross References: For **Acts 28:26-27:** See Is. 6:9-10.

INTRODUCTION TO THE BOOK OF ROMANS

The Book of Romans is progressively the Christian life. Its main theme is **the Gospel of Christ: for it is the power of God unto salvation to every one that believeth... For therein is the righteousness of God revealed from faith to faith: as it is written, The just shall live by faith** (Rom. 1:16-17; Hab. 2:4).

Chapters 1 – 3 establish three facts: (1) **The wrath of God is revealed from heaven against all ungodliness and unrighteousness** (Rom. 1:18); (2) **Both Jews and Gentiles... are all under sin** (3:9-11); (3) **By the deeds of the Law there shall no flesh** (person) **be justified** (3:20).

Chapters 4 – 5 explain that the righteous God has provided the only way of forgiveness of sins: **Jesus our Lord... was delivered** (put to death) **for our offences, and was raised again for our justification** (4:24-25).

Chapter 6 explains the meaning and importance of believer's baptism: **Know ye not, that so many of us as were baptized into Jesus Christ were baptized into His death? Therefore we are buried with Him by baptism into death: that like as Christ was raised up from the dead by the glory of the Father, even so we also should walk in newness of life** (6:3-4).

Chapters 7 – 8 reveal the conflict between the believer's new spiritual nature and the old fleshly (sinful) nature. Victory is also revealed: **If Christ be in you, the body is dead because of sin; but the Spirit is life because of righteousness.... For if ye live after the flesh, ye shall die: but if ye through the Spirit do mortify** (put to death) **the deeds of the body, ye shall live** (8:10,12-13).

Chapters 9 – 11 declares: **There is no difference between the Jew and the Greek.... For whosoever shall call upon the Name of the Lord shall be saved** (10:12-13).

Chapters 12 – 16 contain guidelines for spiritual growth and insight: (1) **Present your bodies a living sacrifice... unto God**; (2) **Be not conformed to this world**; (3) **Be ye transformed by the renewing of your mind, that ye may prove** (discern) **what is that good, and acceptable, and perfect, will of God** (12:1-2).

The Old Testament is important to an understanding of the nature of God and of the Christian life: **For whatsoever things were written aforetime were written for our learning** (15:4).

NOVEMBER 19   Read Romans 1 – 3

Highlights: Paul's mission to preach the *Gospel* to the Romans (Rom. 1:15-17). *The wrath of God is . . . against all . . . unrighteousness of men, who hold the Truth in unrighteousness* (1:18). God judges it (2:1-16). Jews and the Law (2:17-29). No one is righteous; all have sinned (3:10,23). Redeemed through Jesus (3:22,24).

Satan and all unbelievers will one day be cast into the eternal *lake of fire* (Rev. 20:10,13,15). *The wrath of God is . . . against all . . . unrighteousness of men, who hold* (suppress) *the truth . . . so that they are without excuse: Because . . . when they knew God, they glorified Him not as God . . . their foolish heart was darkened. . . . they . . . changed the glory of the uncorruptible God into an image made like to corruptible man. . . . Wherefore God also gave them up to uncleanness through the lusts of their own hearts* (Rom. 1:18-24).

Three times we read that *God . . . gave them up* to their degrading passions (1:24,26,28). There are some who view sex as no more than a physical appetite to be satisfied. But Christ said: *The fearful, and unbelieving, and the abominable, and murderers, and whoremongers . . . shall have their part in the lake which burneth with fire* (Rev. 21:8). Sex is a gift from God which can only bring lasting satisfaction and fulfillment within the marriage relationship of one man with one woman. There is no victory over sexual perversion until it is seen for what it really is – not as sickness or as an alternative lifestyle but as a repulsive and abominable sin against our Creator God.

There is a disturbing and growing ignorance of the Bible – the only Book that reveals sin for what it is. Regardless of what man may say or what kind of sin we might be involved in, ultimately, sin is rebellion against God. As Creator, He alone has the right to set the standard for righteousness. Have you also noticed there is a growing neglect of the Church and a tendency to use the Lord's Day and His tithe for self-centered pleasures? Doing so usually leads to *leanness* of the soul (Ps. 106:12-15).

The Good News is that, *now we are delivered from the Law, that being dead wherein we were held; that we should serve in newness of Spirit, and not in the oldness of the letter* (Rom. 7:6).

Thought for Today: God desires to take care of your life. Trust Him.

Cross References: For **Rom. 1:17:** See Hab. 2:4. **Rom. 2:24:** See Is. 52:5. **Rom. 3:4:** See Ps. 51:4. **Rom. 3:10:** See Ps. 14:1. **Rom. 3:11:** See Ps. 14:2. **Rom. 3:12:** See Ps. 14. **Rom. 3:13:** See Ps. 5:9. **Rom. 3:14:** See Ps. 10:7. **Rom. 3:15:** See Is. 59:7. **Rom. 3;16-17:** See Is. 59:7-8. **Rom. 13:18:** See Ps. 36:1.

NOVEMBER 20 — Read Romans 4 – 7

Highlights: Before we can "do right," we have to "be right" with the Lord (Rom. 4:16-25). Faith brings joy (5:1-2). Jesus transforms us from *enemies* to family and friends, from death to life (5:10,17). With sin's power broken (6:1-14), we are free to obey God (6:15-23).The battle between the flesh and the spirit (7:7-25).

The more we understand the suffering and death of Jesus and the glory and power of His resurrection, the more we will desire to *walk in newness of life*, daily expressing the life of Christ within us. *For if we have been planted together in the likeness of His death, we shall be also in the likeness of His resurrection: Knowing this, that our old man* (nature) *is crucified with Him, that the body of sin might be destroyed, that henceforth we should not serve sin* (Rom. 6:4-6).

Our Lord pays attention to everything we say. He said: *By thy words thou shalt be justified, and by thy words thou shalt be condemned* (Matt. 12:35-37). As Christians we need to recognize the seriousness of questionable "jokes." The Word of God warns: *Let no corrupt communication proceed out of your mouth, but that which is good to the use of edifiying, that it may minister grace unto the hearers* (Eph. 4:29).

Paul was primarily referring to improper joking concerning sexual, evil, or questionable matters when the Holy Spirit led him to write: *But fornication, and all uncleanness, or covetousness, let it not be once named among you, as becometh saints; Neither filthiness, nor foolish talking, nor jesting, which are not convenient: but rather giving of thanks. For this ye know, that no whoremonger, nor unclean person, nor covetous man, who is an idolator, hath any inheritance in the kingdom of Christ and of God* (5:3-6).

It is *the Spirit of Him that raised up Jesus from the dead . . . that dwelleth in you* (Rom. 8:11) which not only frees us from sin's control but also daily inspires us to *walk in newness of life*. Followers of Christ are *dead indeed unto sin. . . . Let not sin therefore reign in your mortal body, that ye should obey it in the lusts thereof* (6:4,11-12).

Our old "natural" man is still capable of yielding to the sinful desires of the flesh. But, Christ has made it possible to be *more than conquerors through Him* (8:37).

Thought for Today: Sin only has power over us when we allow it.

Cross References: For **Rom. 4:3:** See Gen. 15:6. **Rom. 4:7-8:** See Ps. 32:1-2. **Rom. 4:17:** See Gen. 17:415. **Rom. 4:18:** See Gen. 15:5. **Rom. 7:7:** See Ex. 20:17; Deut. 5:21.

NOVEMBER 21

Read Romans 8 – 10

Highlights: *The Spirit of life in Christ* has freed us from the old sin nature and death (Rom. 8:1-17). Nothing that Satan can do can *separate us from the love of God* (8:31-39). Gentiles also are *called the children of the Living God* (9:23-26,30). *Whosoever shall call upon the Name of the Lord shall be saved* (10:9-10,13).

When we accept Christ as Savior and Lord of our lives, we receive the spiritual nature of God and sincerely commit ourselves to a new way of life, *that the righteousness of the Law might be fulfilled in us, who walk not after the flesh, but after the Spirit. For they that are after the flesh do mind the things of the flesh.... Because the carnal* (fleshly) *mind is enmity* (hostile) *against God: for it is not subject to the Law of God* (Rom. 8:4-5,7). Praise God, we don't have to be ruled by our carnal nature! *If ye live after the flesh, ye shall die: but if ye through the Spirit do mortify* (put to death) *the deeds of the body (the lust of the flesh, and the lust of the eyes, and the pride of life* – I John 2:16*), ye shall live* (8:13).

True repentance results in a change of heart. Sharing the Good News that Jesus saves (Matt. 1:21), supporting missions, and being involved in a local church when physically able. Sadly, some people join a church and assume that their good works are sufficient for entrance into heaven. However, they may only be expressing *a form of godliness, but denying the power thereof* (II Tim. 3:5). God is concerned first with what we <u>are</u>, then with what we <u>do</u> for Him.

Set your affection (heart) *on things above, not on things on the earth.... Mortify* (Put to death) *therefore your members which are upon the earth; fornication, uncleanness, inordinate* (unnatural) *affection, evil concupiscence* (desire), *and covetousness... For which things' sake the wrath of God cometh on the children of disobedience: In the which ye also walked some time* (once)*, when ye lived in them. But now ye also put off all these; anger, wrath, malice, blasphemy* (slanderous statements against God), *filthy* (immoral) *communication out of your mouth. Lie not to one another, seeing that ye have put off the old man with his deeds; And have put on the new man, which is renewed in knowledge after the image of Him that created him* (Col. 3:2,5-10).

Thought for Today: Without the transforming power of the Holy Spirit – as revealed in the Word of God – no one can ever be saved.

Cross References: For **Rom. 8:36:** See Ps. 44:22. **Rom. 9:7:** See Gen. 21:12. **Rom. 9:9:** See Gen. 18:10. **Rom. 9:12:** See Gen. 25:23. **Rom. 9:13:** See Mal. 1:2-3. **Rom. 9:15:** See Ex. 33:9. **Rom. 9:17:** See Ex. 9:16. **Rom. 9:25:** See Hos. 2:23. **Rom. 9:26:** See Hos. 1:10. **Rom. 9:27-28:** See Is. 10:22-23. **Rom. 9:29:** See Is. 1:9. **Rom. 9:33:** See Is. 28:16. **Rom. 10:5:** See Lev. 18:5. **Rom. 10:6-7:** See Deut. 30:12-13. **Rom. 10:8:** See Deut. 30:14. **Rom. 10:11:** See Is. 49:23. **Rom 10:13:** See Joel 2:32. **Rom. 10:15:** See Is. 52:7. **Rom. 10:16:** See Is. 53:1. **Rom. 10:18:** See Ps. 19:4. **Rom. 10:19:** See Deut. 32:21. **Rom. 10:20:** See Is. 65:1. **Rom. 20:21:** See Is. 65:2.

NOVEMBER 22   Read Romans 11 – 13

Highlights: The mercy of God on Israel (Rom. 11:1-24); for everyone (11:25-32). A living sacrifice – just think, our hands, our feet, our mouth used for the Lord (12:1-2). Do things the way God says. It's always best (12:19-21). Respect authority, obey laws of the land, pay taxes, pay debts; love fulfills all requirements of God (chap. 13).

To be a Christian is to receive a new nature – the nature of God. **Ye must be born again** (John 3:7). Then the indwelling Holy Spirit enables us to follow Christ's example. It is only reasonable that we should live each day demonstrating that we now live for Christ. The Apostle Paul wrote: **Present your bodies a living sacrifice, holy, acceptable unto God, which is your reasonable service. And be not conformed to this world: but be ye transformed by the renewing of your mind** (and thoughts)**, that ye may prove what is that good, and acceptable, and perfect, will of God** (Rom. 12:1-2).

As we read through and obey the Bible, God's Word becomes our spiritual food and our source of strength and spiritual insight to accomplish His will. Just as physical food is assimilated into our bodies to provide good health and physical strength, so the indwelling Holy Spirit strengthens our spiritual lives through His Word. The Holy Spirit alone can **guide you into all Truth** (John 16:13). However, He will not guide us into **all Truth** if we refuse to read **all Truth** (all the Bible) from Genesis to Revelation. We are either slaves to sin and under the influence of Satan or children of God with a desire for Him to control our lives. The Word of God enlightens and then empowers us to overcome our former way of life. This is true freedom. **Know The Truth, and The Truth shall make you free** (8:32).

We daily live in the midst of many voices calling for our attention. We will always be tempted to satisfy our self-serving, fleshly desires. We also need to daily be on guard against allowing "good things," or even "good people," to occupy our time and keep us from the best God has for us. Life is far too short to allow material possessions and the desire for worldly accomplishments to dominate our lives. Our opportunities to serve the Lord and to be prepared to meet Him will soon end. **See then that ye walk circumspectly** (with great concern for how you live), **not as fools, but as wise, Redeeming the time** (making the most out of every opportunity), **because the days are evil** (Eph. 5:15-16).

Thought for Today: When we are controlled by the indwelling Holy Spirit we are pleasing to God.

Cross References: For **Rom. 11:3:** See I Kin. 19:10,14. **Rom. 11:4:** See I Kin. 19:18. **Rom. 11:8:** See Is. 29:10. **Rom. 11:9-10:** See Ps. 60:22-23. **Rom. 11:26-27:** See Is. 59:20-21; Jer. 31:33. **Rom. 11:34:** See Is. 40:13. **Rom. 11:35:** See Job. 41:11. **Rom. 12:19:** See Deut. 32:35. **Rom. 12:20:** See Prov. 25:21-22. **Rom. 13:9:** See Ex. 20:13-17; Lev. 19:18.

NOVEMBER 23   Read Romans 14 – 16

Highlights: Dangers of criticism; don't condemn others (Rom. chap. 14). Live in harmony, giving praise and glory to the Lord (15:1-6). Paul's ambition should also be part of ours (15:20-21). Christians in one area took up a collection for believers in need (15:26-28).

Not one person in history, except Jesus, has lived without sinning. Since we cannot know the heart of another person, we are warned: *Who art thou that judgest another man's servant? to his own master he standeth or falleth. Yea, he shall be holden up: for God is able to make him stand* (Rom. 14:4).

We then that are strong ought to bear the infirmities (imperfections) *of the weak, and not to please ourselves. Let every one of us please his neighbour for his good to edification* (spiritual development). *For even Christ pleased not Himself* (15:1-3). The perfect example of how we are to live our lives is Jesus Christ, who unselfishly took all our sins upon Himself, suffering insult, persecution, and a cruel physical death on the cross for our sakes. His personal sacrifice demonstrated the Christian way to deal with people for their good and for the glory of God. Even now, Christ makes intercession on our behalf because of our weaknesses and temptations (Heb. 7:25; Rom. 16:25-27).

The Word of God instructs the "stronger" brother to willingly put aside his personal desires and lovingly consider how to strengthen his "weaker" brother without passing judgment, so as not to give Satan a foothold through a critical spirit or self-righteousness.

When we allow Christ to be Lord of our lives, it results in a sincere, compassionate concern for others, not only for a weaker brother or sister in Christ, but for the lost as well. Spiritual discernment leads us to be understanding of others and their situations. The admonition *to bear the infirmities* of others requires compassion on the part of mature Christians, making ourselves available to help others.

While it is true that God judges sin, His Word makes it clear that pastors and church leaders must *reprove* (correct), *rebuke, exhort* (encourage) *with all longsuffering* (expressing Christ's love) *and doctrine* (teaching) (II Tim. 4:2). Our loving Lord is also saying to those who represent Him: *Be . . . merciful, as your Father also is merciful* (Luke 6:36). *By this shall all men know that ye are My disciples, if ye have love one to* (for) *another* (John 13:35).

Thought for Today: Giving – not getting – is the key to receiving blessings from God.

Cross References: For **Rom. 14:11:** See Is. 45:23. **Rom. 15:3:** See Ps. 69:9. **Rom. 15:9:** See Ps. 18:49. **Rom. 15:10:** See Deut. 32:43. **Rom. 15:11:** See Ps. 117:1. **Rom. 15:12:** See Is. 11:1,10. **Rom. 15:21:** See Is. 52:15.

Introduction To The Books Of I & II CORINTHIANS

Corinth was the capitol of the Roman province of Achaia. This seaport community was one of the most prominent cities in Greece, having an estimated population of 400,000 or more.

Paul stayed in Corinth for more than a year and a half on his second missionary journey. During that time, Priscilla and Aquila helped him established a church. Silas and Timothy also helped Paul in the ministry. After Paul left Corinth, Apollos became a leader there (see Acts 18:1-28; I Cor. 3:5-6).

Paul's purpose for writing the first letter to the church at Corinth was to correct problems that existed among its members. The church was divided (1:10-4:21), and some of its members were involved in sins that greatly hindered the spiritual life of the church (5:1-13).

The finest definition of love ever written is recorded in chapter 13, and the best explanation of the resurrection of Christ, as well as the believer, is given in chapter 15.

Soon after Paul had written I Corinthians, he almost lost his life in the great riot at Ephesus (see Acts 19). Paul left Ephesus and went to Macedonia on his way to Corinth. At Macedonia, in the midst of many anxieties and sufferings, he met with Titus, who was returning from Corinth with word that Paul's letter to the Corinthian church had accomplished much good. Paul gave Titus another letter to the Corinthian church and indicated that he himself planned to go to Corinth soon.

The major theme of the Book of II Corinthians is the ministry of reconciliation. Christians have the responsibility to make every effort to bring about peacable solutions to their family problems, as well as personal conficts with others. This book also shows the importance of sharing one's resources with the needy.

In II Corinthians, Paul commended the church for correcting its moral problems. He pointed out the necessity to resolve divisions within the church and the importance of a generous offering for the church in Jerusalem.

NOVEMBER 24 — Read I Corinthians 1 – 4

Highlights: Called by God to be His (I Cor. 1:2). Stay focused on His mission (1:10-31). *The foolishness of God is wiser than men* (1:23-25).This is "too" good to overlook (2:9)! God has revealed His wisdom to His people (2:10-14). Learn this Truth (3:6-7). Responsibilities of leadership (4:1-4,15-16, 20-21).

The church at Corinth was divided over who was the most spiritual leader. To correct them Paul wrote: *Who then is Paul, and who is Apollos, but ministers by whom ye believed, even as the Lord gave to every man* (I Cor. 3:5)? Christians are not to be competitors but *labourers together with God* (3:9).

As Christians, we are members of the Body of Christ. Our foremost concern should be that we *be perfectly joined together in the same mind and in the same judgment. . . . Is Christ divided* (I Cor. 1:10,13)? All of us need each other, so that together we can fulfill the Lord's will in the Body of Christ through our prayers, tithes, gifts, talents, and witness to others. No one should feel either indispensable nor inadequate, for all *are one* (3:8) serving the Lord.

It takes every Christian to make up the Body of Christ, which is the Church; without exception, everyone is needed: *We being many are . . . one Body: for we are all partakers of that one Bread* (10:17), and *we are labourers together with God* (3:9). This leaves no room for envying another person's ability or usefulness, nor for being puffed up with pride as if we had done anything of ourselves. Both jealousy and pride dishonor Christ and hinder the spirit of unity. The source of the problems these two sins cause is often not addressed because it is not recognized.

Just as devastating are words that impart suggestions of smut or thoughts of immoral sex. In contrast words can be a powerful healing tool when used with the love of Christ to uplift, inspire, and encourage others to be more like Jesus. You can choose to make a difference every day and change the course of a life.

It is important to recognize that Paul was not expecting uniformity of views but oneness of Spirit in the midst of differences. *The wisdom that is from above is first pure, then peaceable, gentle, and easy to be intreated, full of mercy and good fruits, without partiality, and without hypocrisy. And the fruit of righteousness is sown in peace of them that make peace* (James 3:17-18).

Thought for Today: Don't find fault with the gifts God has bestowed on others.

Cross References: For **I Cor. 1:19:** See Is. 29:14. **I Cor. 1:31:** See Jer. 9:24. **I Cor. 2:16:** See Is. 40:13. **I Cor. 3:19:** See Job 5:13. **I Cor. 3:20:** See Ps. 94:11.

NOVEMBER 25   Read I Corinthians 5 – 9

Highlights: Refrain from spiritual pride and open sin (I Cor. chap. 5 – 6). Power in the Blood (5:7)! Marriage "101" (chap. 7). Our conversation weakens or strengthens others (8:8-13); the Lord's anointed ones are due reasonable support (9:9-14). Run to win (9:24).

It was reported to Paul that one member of the church was committing fornication or adultery with **his father's wife** (I Cor. 5:1), which seems to mean that he had an ongoing sexual relationship with his stepmother. This was also forbidden in the Old Testament Law that stated: **The nakedness of thy father's wife shalt thou not uncover** (Lev. 18:8). It is assumed that his father was still alive. Paul admonished them to immediately excommunicate the offending member **in the Name of our Lord Jesus Christ ... To deliver such an one unto Satan for the destruction of the flesh, that the spirit may be saved in the day of the Lord Jesus** (I Cor. 5:4-5).

    Our concern should be not only how our lives affect our relationship with God but perhaps, equally important, how they affect our church, families, and Christian friends. Many people who were once diligent to guard their mouths are becoming more worldly, condoning and even indulging in questionable conversations. **But fornication, and all uncleanness, or covetousness, let it not be once named among you, as becometh saints; Neither filthiness, nor foolish talking, nor jesting, which are not convenient: but rather giving of thanks** (Eph. 5:3-4).

    When leaders of a church body overlook and allow obvious ongoing sin among its members, it encourages those members who are sinning to continue their sins. This, in turn, has a corrupting influence on others to follow their immoral lifestyle.

    If we believe what God has said in His Word about sin, we will realize that the sinner must be held accountable for his sins. Consequently, the decision to say or do nothing, merely in the interest of "harmony," is in opposition to the will of God: **If any man that is called a brother be a fornicator, or covetous, or an idolater, or a railer** (reviler), **or a drunkard, or an extortioner; with such an one no not to eat. ... put away from among yourselves that wicked person** (5:11-13). **And such were some of you.** The key word here is WERE because all who have truly received Christ as Savior and Lord have been **washed ... sanctified** and **justified** (6:11).

Thought for Today: To neglect the Word of God is to neglect God Himself.

Cross References: For **I Cor. 6:16:** See Gen. 2:24. **I Cor. 9:9:** See Deut. 25:4.

NOVEMBER 26   Read I Corinthians 10 – 13

Highlights: We will have temptations. God will provide a way (I Cor. 10:13). We should glorify God in all we do (10:31-33). The Church working together wins (chap. 12)! Love defined (chap. 13).

Surprising as it may seem to the world, from the point of view of God, it is more important to be known for your loving-kindness, thoughtfulness, and consideration of others than for being a famous evangelist, preacher, or teacher. **Though I speak with the tongues of men and of angels, and have not charity** (love)**, I am become as sounding brass, or a tinkling cymbal** (I Cor. 13:1).

It is also more important to be known as one who loves, just as God loves, than for being the most prominent prophetic speaker in the world. Paul went on to describe this God-given ability to love: **Though I have the gift of prophecy** (forth or foretelling)**, and understand all mysteries, and all knowledge; and though I have all faith, so that I could remove mountains, and have not charity** (love)**, I am nothing** – worthless to God (13:2).

Charity suffereth long, and is kind (13:4). It **vaunteth not itself** (does not brag with inflated ideas of its own importance), meaning, it does not insist on its own way and is not rude to anyone. Neither is it self-seeking, quick to take offense, or resentful. Love does not think evil of anyone. This God-kind of love is very patient – never envious or boastful.

Another dimension of love is that it **doth not behave itself unseemly, seeketh not her own, is not easily provoked, thinketh no evil** (13:5), meaning, it is tactful; it gives love without expecting love in return; and it is willing to forgive. Love has a way of making us more concerned for the feelings and rights of others and less preoccupied with our own. The love that God gives keeps us from always trying to grab the best for ourselves or taking advantage of others.

Love also has a way of helping us decline listening to people who are anxious to pass on the latest gossip about the faults and failures of other brothers or sisters in Christ.

Love **beareth all things . . . endureth all things** (13:7) without getting frustrated or angry. **Charity** (love) **never faileth** (13:8), regardless of whether it is for friends, difficult people, or strangers. **Every one that loveth is born of God, and knoweth God. He that loveth not knoweth not God; for God is love** (I John 4:7-8).

Thought for Today: When you love the Lord, love for others will be its natural overflow.

Cross References: For **I Cor. 10:7:** See Ex. 32:6. **I Cor. 10:26:** See Ps. 24:1.

NOVEMBER 27   Read I Corinthians 14 – 16

Highlights: Spiritual gifts (I Cor. 14:22-40; Jesus resurrected (15:1-12) – first of many raised to life again (15:20); our resurrected bodies (15:38); total victory (15:54-58); offerings for others on every Lord's Day (16:1-3).

It is a triumphant fact **that Christ died for our sins according to the Scriptures; And that He was buried, and that He rose again the third day according to the Scriptures** (I Cor. 15:3-4). For the Christian, death is not the end of life; nor is it a tragedy. It is the beginning of our magnificent, eternal future in the glorious presence of our wonderful Lord. **We shall all be changed, In a moment, in the twinkling of an eye, at the last trump: for the trumpet shall sound, and the dead shall be raised incorruptible, and we shall be changed** (15:51-52). Paul concluded his glorious thoughts on the return of the Lord Jesus by saying: **Therefore, my beloved brethren, be ye stedfast, unmoveable, always abounding in the work of the Lord, forasmuch as ye know that your labour is not in vain in the Lord** (it is always profitable) (15:58).

While Paul wrote of a joyful eternity with Christ, the Apostle John wrote of the dreadful coming judgment for all unbelievers. **I saw a great white throne, and Him that sat on it . . . And I saw the dead, small and great, stand before God; and the books were opened: and another book was opened, which is the Book of Life: and the dead were judged out of those things which were written in the books, according to their works. . . . And whosoever was not found written in the Book of Life was cast into the lake of fire** (Rev. 20:11-12,15).

Christians have the utmost confidence that, **if the Spirit of Him that raised up Jesus from the dead dwell in you, He that raised up Christ from the dead shall also quicken** (make alive) **your mortal bodies by His Spirit that dwelleth in you** (Rom. 8:11).

Our threefold purpose for living is first to become the person that God planned for us to be. Second, we need to be committed to doing what He wants us to do. Then we can look forward to the splendor of heaven. Concerning heaven, the words of Jesus have brought precious comfort to millions when He said: **Let not your heart be troubled. . . . I go to prepare a place for you. And . . . I will come again, and receive you unto Myself** (John 14:1-3).

Thought for Today: Christians will live with Christ forever. What a precious assurance!

Cross References: For **I Cor. 14:21:** See Is. 28:11-12. **I Cor. 15:3-4:** See Hos. 6:2. **I Cor. 15:25:** See Ps. 110:1. **I Cor. 15:27:** See Ps. 8:6. **I Cor. 15:32:** See Is. 22:13. **I Cor. 15:45:** See Gen. 2:7. **I Cor. 15:54:** See Is. 25:8. **I Cor. 15:55:** See Hos. 13:14.

NOVEMBER 28   Read II Corinthians 1 – 4

Highlights: The Lord expects us to comfort others with the comfort He has given us (II Cor. 1:3-7). Holy Spirit seals us (1:21-22). ***The letter*** (of the Law) ***killeth, but the Spirit giveth life*** (3:6). Ministry is tough; Paul says: "Don't give up" (4:1). Present troubles are short-lived, but glory with the Savior is forever (4:16-18).

Earthen vessels (clay pots) have very little value of their own. Their essential worth depends upon what they contain. If they are left empty, they have no purpose for existence. However, if they are filled with gold, their value increases dramatically. The body of a Christian is compared to an ordinary clay pot. The precious treasure it contains is ***Christ in you, the hope of glory*** (Col. 1:27). ***We have this treasure in earthen vessels*** (II Cor. 4:7); we are precious to God and responsible to Him to let others see Jesus in us. The Corinthian Christians were responsible to God, not to Paul, just as any Christian is only responsible to God in matters of faith.

Being accountable to God for the treasure in us includes how we respond to difficulties common to many of God's children: ***We are troubled on every side, yet not distressed; we are perplexed*** (puzzled), ***but not in despair; Persecuted, but not forsaken; cast down, but not destroyed; Always bearing about in the body the dying of the Lord Jesus, that the life also of Jesus might be made manifest*** (known) ***in our body*** (4:8-10). Since the Holy Spirit dwells in every Christian and gives each of us His power to overcome, we are expected to express His characteristics during every trial and suffering. We can also face trials and suffering with the confidence that our Lord is lovingly working out what is best for our eternal good.

Trials and troubles, in whatever form, are necessary for spiritual growth; without them, we would not exercise our faith or develop spiritual insight and strength (Acts 14:22; I Pet. 1:6-7). Just as it was necessary for Jesus to die, we too must die to self-interests and become willing partakers of His sufferings.

Our light affliction (trouble), ***which is but for a moment, worketh for us a far more exceeding and eternal weight of glory; While we look not at the things which are seen, but at the things which are not seen: for the things which are seen are temporal*** (temporary); ***but the things which are not seen are eternal*** (II Cor. 4:17-18).

Thought for Today: We are called to be ***partakers of Christ's sufferings*** (I Pet. 4:13).

Cross References: For **II Cor. 3:13:** See Ex. 34:33. **II Cor. 4:13:** See Ps. 116:10.

NOVEMBER 29   Read II Corinthians 5 – 8

Highlights: *Absent from the body . . . present with the Lord* (II Cor. 5:8). We represent Christ; our privilege is to bring others to Him (5:18-21). We are the Temple of the Living God and are to be cleansed and separated from sin (chap. 6). Worship, dedication, humility (8:5); a call to generous giving (8:1-15).

No one would deny that we are living in a day of deception and compromise; and, unfortunately, Christians are tempted to search for satisfaction through what the world has to offer. To provide answers for this problem, Paul earnestly asked five questions that deserve our prayerful consideration because they have eternal consequences for us. *Be ye not unequally yoked together with unbelievers: for what fellowship hath righteousness with unrighteousness? and what communion hath light with darkness? And what concord* (harmony) *hath Christ with Belial* (Satan)*? or what part hath he that believeth with an infidel* (unbeliever)*? And what agreement hath the Temple of God with idols? for ye are the Temple of the Living God* (II Cor. 6:14-16).

Since there is a real danger of being caught up with world views that press upon us daily, James was led to warn us that *whosoever therefore will be a friend of the world is the enemy of God* (James 4:4). This is important to remember, since the believer and the unbeliever each have a different master. Any time a Christian yields to worldly temptation, he is serving his old master. Paul wrote: *If ye then be risen with Christ, seek those things which are above, where Christ sitteth on the right hand of God. Set your affection* (mind and emotions) *on things above, not on things on the earth* (Col. 3:1-2).

The Christian's call is to *come out from among them, and be ye separate, saith the Lord, and touch not the unclean* (morally impure) *thing . . . and ye shall be My sons and daughters, saith the Lord Almighty* (II Cor. 6:17-18). To *come out from* means, among other things, that we should avoid becoming involved with unbelieving friends or joining in activities that keep us from being our best for Christ and His Church.

Paul went on to say: *Having therefore these promises, dearly beloved, let us cleanse ourselves from all filthiness of the flesh and spirit, perfecting holiness in the fear of God* (II Cor. 7:1).

Thought for Today: It is only by the grace of God that we *are* anything or can *do* anything of eternal value.

Cross References: For **II Cor. 6:2:** See Is. 49:8. **II Cor. 6:16:** See Lev. 26:11; Ezek. 37:27. **II Cor. 6:17:** See Is. 52:11. **II Cor. 8:15:** See Ex 16:18.

NOVEMBER 30   Read II Corinthians 9 – 13

Highlights: A harvest of generosity (II Cor. chap. 9). Use the weapons of God against the Devil (10:4-6). Jesus said that without Him, we can do nothing of spiritual worth (see John 15:5). Guard against false teachers (II Cor. 11:1-15). Guard against pride (12:7). We are weak but God is strong (12:9). Focused on Jesus (13:5).

Paul often faced rejection from hostile enemies of Christ and occasionally from believers. He recalled: *Of the Jews five times received I forty stripes* (lashes) *save one. Thrice was I beaten with rods, once was I stoned, thrice I suffered shipwreck, a night and a day I have been in the deep; In journeyings often, in perils of waters, in perils of robbers, in perils by mine own countrymen, in perils by the heathen, in perils in the city, in perils in the wilderness, in perils in the sea, in perils among false brethren; In weariness and painfulness, in watchings* (sleepless nights) *often, in hunger and thirst, in fastings often, in cold and nakedness. Beside those things that are without* (outside)*, that which cometh upon me daily, the care* (concern) *of all the churches* (II Cor. 11:24-28).

After Paul's conversion, he had only one purpose – *to preach the Gospel in the regions beyond* (10:16). We too have the same high calling. Surely everyone should have the opportunity of hearing, at least once, that at death there are two destinations – eternal death in the lake of fire or eternal life in heaven. Our Creator Jesus Christ said: *I am The Way, The Truth, and The Life: no man cometh unto the Father, but by Me* (John 14:6). Have you ever seriously thought what it means for your friends or loved ones to die without being saved?

The dividing line between the saved and the lost rests upon one fact: *If thou shalt confess with thy mouth the Lord Jesus, and shalt believe in thine heart that God hath raised Him from the dead, thou shalt be saved* (Rom. 10:9).

We must consider our priorities. Do they bring us closer to the Lord and His purpose for our lives or take us further away from Him? *When the Son of Man shall come... before Him shall be gathered all nations: and He shall separate them... as a shepherd divideth his sheep from the goats.... Then shall the King say unto them on His right hand, Come... inherit the kingdom prepared for you from the foundation of the world* (Matt. 25:31-34).

Thought for Today: *Live in peace; and the God of love and peace shall be with you* (II Cor. 13:11).

Cross References: For **II Cor. 9:9:** See Ps. 112:9. **II Cor. 10:17:** See Jer. 9:24. **II Cor. 13:1:** See Deut. 19:5.

Introduction To The Book Of GALATIANS

The Apostle Paul wrote this letter **to the churches of Galatia** (Gal. 1:2). This group of churches included Pisidian Antioch, Iconium, Lystra, and Derbe. In various districts within the Roman province of Galatia. False teachers were persuading some Christians to believe that keeping the ceremonial laws that God had given through Moses were essential for Jew or Gentile to become Christians. **As many as desire to make a fair shew in the flesh, they constrain** (compel) **you to be circumcised; only lest they should suffer persecution for the cross of Christ. For neither they themselves who are circumcised keep** (obey) **the Law; but desire to have you circumcised, that they may glory** (boast) **in your flesh** (6:12-13).

Paul wrote this letter to refute false teachings regarding salvation. He called the teachings **another Gospel: which is not another** but an attempt to **pervert the Gospel of Christ** (1:6-7). Paul does not leave us in doubt as to the sinister nature of the Galatian deception. They were being drawn away to something which was essentially a different gospel.

Cults and others who teach a supposed "later revelation of Truth" still are deceiving many. It is so serious that the Holy Spirit led Paul to write: **Though we, or an angel** (messenger) **from heaven, preach any other Gospel unto you than that which we have preached unto you, let him be accursed** (condemned). **As we said before, so say I now again, If any man preach any other Gospel unto you than that ye have received, let him be accursed** (1:8-9).

DECEMBER 1   Read Galatians 1 – 3

Highlights: The greatest news in history – there is only one *Gospel* that calls us *into the grace of Christ* (Gal. 1:6-9)! The Lord sent Peter to Jews, Paul to Gentiles (2:8). We are not *justified by the works of the Law*. But did you know justification is by faith in Jesus Christ, that we *might live unto God* (2:16-21; Matt. 5:16; John 6:36)? *Christ liveth in me* (Gal. 2:19-20).

This letter, inspired by God, reveals among other important truths, two fundamental facts: (1) there is only one Gospel (Good News) and that is *the Gospel of Christ* (Rom. 1:10; 15:19.29; I Cor. 9:12,18; II Cor. 4:4; 9:13;10:14; Phil. 1:27; I Thess. 3:2); *of Christ crucified* (I Cor. 1:23) and *Christ risen* (I Cor. 15:20); (2) there is only one way of salvation and eternal life for Jews and Gentiles. We can only *be justified* (declared righteous) *by the faith of Christ, and not by the works of the Law: for by the works of the Law shall no flesh* (no one) *be justified* (2:16). *There is none righteous, no, not one ... For all have sinned* (Rom. 3:10,23). *Our Lord Jesus Christ ... gave Himself for our sins, that He might deliver us from this present evil world, according to the will of God* (Gal. 1:3-4).

The full meaning of the grace of God was revealed when Jesus told Nicodemus *God so loved the world, that He gave His only begotten Son, that whosoever believeth in Him should not perish, but have everlasting life* (John 3:16). Jesus, the only sinless, begotten Son of God, took our place and paid the penalty for our sin when He died on the cross so we could be delivered from our sins. Without His sacrificial death for our sins, we could never become righteous. But because of His loving-kindness (grace) toward us, we can be *born again* (3:5) and *become the sons of God* (1:12).

Because of our sinful nature, no one has the ability to keep all of the Law of God (James 2:10). *Christ hath redeemed us from the curse* (the righteous penalty of death) *of the Law, being made a curse* (undergoing death on the cross, the appointed penalty of the curse) *for us* (Gal. 3:13). These facts should cause all mankind to recognize their great need of a Savior.

As many of you as have been baptized into Christ have put on Christ.... And if ye be Christ's, then are ye Abraham's seed, and heirs according to the promise (Gal. 3:27-29).

Thought for Today: We fear men so much because we trust in God so little.

Cross References: For **Gal. 3:6:** See Gen. 15:6. **Gal. 3:8:** See Gen. 12:3, 22:18. **Gal. 3:10:** See Deut. 27:26. **Gal. 3:11:** See Hab. 2:4. **Gal. 3:12:** See Lev. 18:5. **Gal. 3:13:** See Deut. 21:23.

DECEMBER 2

Read Galatians 4 – 6

Highlights: *No more a servant, but a son . . . an heir . . . through Christ* (Gal. 4:1-7). Live in freedom through Jesus (5:1, 5-6, 13-14). The indwelling Spirit of God produces fruit (5:22-23).

The Apostle Paul recorded seventeen sins: *Now the works of the flesh are manifest* (evident), *which are these; Adultery, fornication, uncleanness, lasciviousness* (sensuality), *Idolatry, witchcraft, hatred, variance* (discord), *emulations* (jealousy), *wrath, strife, seditions* (dissensions), *heresies, Envyings, murders, drunkenness, revellings, and such like* (such like includes vile affections listed in Rom. 1:26-31): *of the which I tell you before, as I have also told you in time past, that they which do such things shall not inherit the Kingdom of God* (Gal. 5:19-21).

However, *the works of the flesh* also include everything that defiles a person's mind – such as sexually explicit magazines, watching ungodly movies and television programs, pornography, sexual predators, immoral jokes, and evil thoughts.

Idolatry could include money, an occupation, a person, a personal pleasure, or a habit. Though some of these are not evil in themselves, if they occupy the time and loyalty which only God deserves, they could be an idol to us. Often overlooked is *witchcraft*, which includes horoscopes, palm reading, hypnotism, seances, and other acts of the occult.

Also on the list are *hatred, variance, emulations* (jealousy), *wrath, strife, seditions, heresies* (5:20). *Strife* and *seditions* include rivalry and discord, while *envyings* include jealousy and wrong attitudes of the heart (Mark 7:20-23).

We are not without hope. *For it is God which worketh in you both to will and to do of His good pleasure. . . . That ye may be blameless and harmless, the sons of God, without rebuke, in the midst of a crooked and perverse nation, among whom ye shine as lights in the world* (Phil. 2:13,15).

We can thank God for His long-suffering and mercy that *they that are Christ's have crucified the flesh with the affections and lusts* (Gal. 5:24). We are no longer enslaved by the works of the flesh, but we are endowed with the Holy Spirit and can bear His fruit, which is *love, joy, peace, longsuffering, gentleness, goodness, faith, Meekness, temperance* (Gal. 5:22-23).

Thought for Today: Perhaps the failure we see in another person's life is a reflection of the hidden sin of self-righteousness in our own hearts.

Cross References: For **Gal. 4:27:** See Is. 54:1. **Gal. 4:30:** See Gen. 21:20. **Gal. 5:14:** See Lev. 19:18.

Introduction To The Book Of EPHESIANS

Beginning his third missionary journey, Paul returned to Ephesus and stayed there for about two years, preaching and teaching (Acts 19:1,8-10; 20:31). During this time, a great number of people renounced the false worship of Diana and became Christians. Paul focused attention on how God makes us alive in Christ Jesus. He reminds us: **You hath He quickened** (made alive), **who were dead in trespasses and sins; Wherein in time past ye walked according to the course of this world, according to the prince of the power of the air** (Satan)**, the spirit that now worketh in the children of disobedience . . . fulfilling the desires of the flesh and of the mind; and were by nature the children of wrath** (Eph. 2:1-3). All of us are to **be renewed in the spirit of your mind** (4:23).

In contrast to those who walk in newness of life in Christ are those who **walk . . . as other Gentiles** (non-Christians) **walk** (live), **in the vanity** (futility) **of their mind, Having the understanding darkened, being alienated from the life of God through the ignorance that is in them, because of the blindness of their heart** (4:17-18).

Ephesians teaches us to prepare for spiritual warfare, to **put on the whole armour of God, that ye may be able to stand against the wiles** (deceptions, schemes) **of the Devil. For we wrestle not against flesh and blood, but against principalities, against powers, against the rulers of the darkness of this world, against spiritual wickedness in high places. Wherefore take unto you the whole armour of God, that ye may be able to withstand in the evil day, and having done all, to stand. Stand therefore, having your loins girt** (belted) **about with truth, and having on the breastplate of righteousness; And your feet shod with the preparation of the Gospel of Peace; Above all, taking the shield of faith, wherewith ye shall be able to quench** (put out) **all the fiery darts of the wicked** (arrows, attempts of Satan to defeat the child of God)**. And take the helmet of salvation, and the sword of the Spirit, which is the Word of God** (6:11-17).

The Book of Ephesians leads us to see how powerful the Word of God is in guiding our minds and empowering us to overcome **the wiles of the Devil** (6:11). It is our protection from evil and also our offensive weapon. Jesus used only the Word of God to defeat the Devil (Matt. 4:4). Ephesians 4:1-16 is a magnificent explanation of what our Christian life is to be.

DECEMBER 3   Read Ephesians 1 – 3

Highlights: Spiritual blessings for believers (Eph. 1:3-8). ***We all ... were by nature the children of wrath*** but now ***we have redemption*** (Eph. 2:3-4,7). We are ***strengthened*** by the Spirit of God (3:16).

The God who created all mankind has chosen us to be His children. In fact, ***He hath chosen us in Him before the foundation*** (beginning) ***of the world, that we should be holy and without blame before Him. . . . In whom we have redemption through His blood, the forgiveness of sins, according to the riches of His grace*** (Eph. 1:4,7). We can confidently pray and depend upon the Holy Spirit to guide our lives, ***for we are His workmanship, created in Christ Jesus unto good works, which God hath before ordained that we should walk in them*** (2:10).

Before Christ came to earth, only the Jews had a Covenant relationship with God. Paul explained to the Ephesian believers: ***At that time ye were without Christ, being aliens from the commonwealth of Israel, and strangers from the Covenants of promise, having no hope, and without God in the world. But now in Christ Jesus ye . . . are made nigh*** (brought near) ***by the blood of Christ. For He is our peace*** (2:12-14). Jews and Gentiles alike who receive Christ as their Savior and Lord now have a Covenant relationship with God through ***the New Testament*** (Covenant) sealed with Christ's blood (Matt. 26:28; Mark 14:24; Luke 22:20; I Cor. 11:25). ***Through Him*** (Jesus) ***we both have access . . . unto the Father*** (Eph. 2:18).

In A.D. 70, God used the Roman general Titus to destroy the Temple, the Brazen Altar of Sacrifice, and thus the functions of the High Priest. These had merely foreshadowed Jesus, the Messiah, our ***Great High Priest*** (Heb. 4:14). ***We have boldness and access*** (to God) ***with confidence by the faith of Him*** (Eph. 3:12).

Is it any surprise that Satan will seek to keep us busy, even doing "good" things, in his effort to keep us from praying, by distracting us from reading and obeying the Word of God? Because of our love for the Lord, we should look forward to a daily dialog of prayer (talking to God) and reading His Word (God talking to us).

I pray ***that Christ may dwell in your hearts by faith; that ye, being rooted and grounded in love, May be able to . . . know the love of Christ, which passeth knowledge, that ye might be filled with all the fulness of God*** (Eph. 3:17-19).

Thought for Today: Prayer is a powerful force that goes beyond our limited human wisdom and strength.

Cross References: For **Eph. 1:22:** See Ps. 8:6. **Eph. 2:17:** See Is. 57:19.

DECEMBER 4

Read Ephesians 4 – 6

Highlights: As children of God, we need *to keep the unity of the Spirit in the bond of peace* (Eph. 4:3), to *grow up into Him* (4:15). We need *the whole Armour of God* (6:10-18).

When we let the love of Christ flow through us, we manifest His loving-kindness to everyone without discrimination. Because He forgives us without exception, we can enjoy and express His bountiful blessings. *Let all bitterness, and wrath, and anger, and clamour, and evil speaking, be put away from you, with all malice* (Eph. 4:31). Rather, *be ye kind one to another, tenderhearted, forgiving one another, even as God for Christ's sake hath forgiven you* (4:32).

Wrath and anger are often demonstrated in an outburst of abusive language as a reaction against someone who disagrees with our views and actions. Sadly, when some people are offended they are also unwilling to forgive. Another serious sin is slander (malicious report), one of the seven sins that God hates the most (Prov. 6:16-19).

The presence of any of these evils robs us of our peace of mind, grieves the Holy Spirit, and affects our relationship with God. However, as we allow the Holy Spirit to rule our hearts and lives, the fruit of the Holy Spirit – love, joy, peace, patience, gentleness, and kindness – will be manifest and will replace our feelings of anger.

Instead of letting our thoughts dwell on bitterness, revenge, and anger, we need to see difficult situations as opportunities to pray for those who wrong us. *Love your enemies, bless them that curse you, do good to them that hate you, and pray for them which despitefully use you, and persecute you* (Matt. 5:44). Consider Stephen, who prayed while he was being stoned to death. *He kneeled down, and cried with a loud voice, Lord, lay not this sin to their charge* (Acts 7:60).

Every Christian is a representative of Christ and is responsible to respond with the love of Jesus toward all others. It is of utmost importance that we realize how serious Jesus considers the sin of unforgiving: *But if ye do not forgive, neither will your Father which is in heaven forgive your trespasses* (Mark 11:26). Christ is the Head of His Body the Church and we are that Body. It is under His direction that we are to work in harmony. *Till we all come in the unity of the faith* (Eph. 4:13).

Thought for Today: Those who love the Lord keep His Commandments.

Cross References: For **Eph. 4:8:** See Ps. 68:18. **Eph. 4:25:** See Zech. 8:16. **Eph. 4:26:** See Ps. 4:4. **Eph. 5:31:** See Gen. 2:24. **Eph. 6:2-3:** See Ex. 20:12; Deut. 5:16.

VICTORY OVER SATAN ASSURED

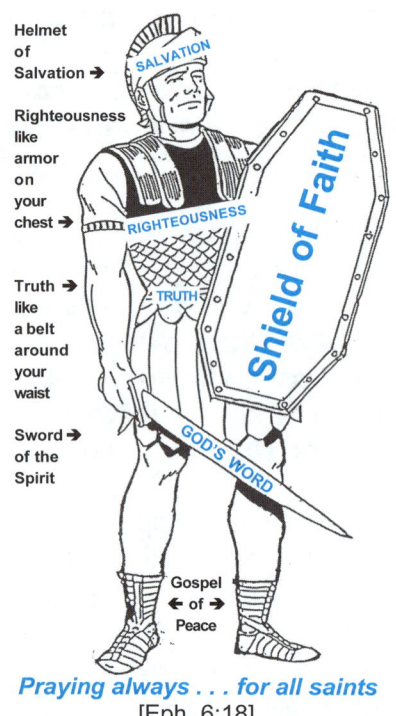

Praying always . . . for all saints
[Eph. 6:18]

Be strong in the Lord, and in the power of His might. Put on the whole armour of God, that ye may be able to (successfully) *stand against* (all) *the wiles* (strategies, strength, and deceits) *of the Devil. For we wrestle not against flesh and blood, but against principalities, against powers, against the rulers of the darkness of this world, against spiritual wickedness* (forces of evil) *in high places. Wherefore take unto you the whole armour of God, that ye may be able to withstand in the evil day* (when you are tempted)*, and having done all, to stand* (Eph. 6:10-13).

Jesus' victory over Satan during His 40 days in the wilderness was accomplished as He quoted Scripture. And He reminds us that *man shall not live* (victoriously) *by bread alone* (physical needs that supply physical strength), *but by every Word that proceedeth out of the mouth of God* (Matt.4:4). "Every Word" begins in Genesis.

Every piece of the *armour of God* illustrates the Word of God. Never is there a time when the Christian soldier can put aside his *armour* and say: "The battle is won." We are to *fight the good fight of faith* (I Tim. 6:12), and *faith cometh by hearing, and hearing by the Word of God* (Rom. 10:17). *The Word of God is quick* (living) *and powerful . . . a discerner* (judge) *of the thoughts and intents of the heart* (Heb. 4:12). *It is God* (through His Word) *who worketh in you both to will and to do of His good pleasure* (Phil. 2:13).

We overcome in the great conflict with worldliness as the soldier of Christ when we *put on the whole armour of God* (Eph. 6:11). Furthermore, there are no alternatives, no substitutes. College degrees, theology, and psychology are all powerless to prepare the soldier for spiritual warfare. It is futile to put on only half the *armour*, for Satan and his tactics are sure to aim his *fiery darts* (arrows) at the most vulnerable spot (6:16). We're all inclined to fortify ourselves against certain selected sins and neglect the areas in which we think of ourselves as most secure. But the Lord warns: *Wherefore let him that thinketh he standeth take heed* (care) *lest he fall* (I Cor. 10:12). God knows all the enemy forces that we face, and He knows our weaknesses and has provided full protection and complete armor for us to be victorious – *more than conquerors through Him that loved us* (Rom. 8:37).

Ephesians Verse 6:10: *Be strong in the Lord*

These are the same words that God spoke to Joshua: *Be strong*. Joshua was able to conquer the kings in the promised land in just seven years. His secret of strength is pointed out in Joshua 1:8: *This Book of the Law shall not depart out of thy mouth; but thou shalt meditate therein day and night, that thou mayest observe to do according to all that is written therein: for then thou shalt make thy way prosperous, and then thou shalt have good success*. The key to Joshua's conquest of the promised land is evident: *So did Joshua; he left noth-*

ing undone of all that the Lord commanded Moses (11:15). Israel's history illustrates that whenever there were failures, they were a direct result of ignoring the Word of God.

In the power of His might

To be overcome by sin is a faith failure, and *faith cometh by hearing, and hearing by the Word of God* (Rom. 10:17). Pray as David did: *Open . . . mine eyes, that I may behold wondrous things out of Thy Law* (Ps. 119:18).

Verse 11: *Put on the whole armour of God*

We cannot provide our *armour*, but we are merely required to put it on. Its effectiveness depends entirely upon the One who made it. And *the whole armour of God* is essential for a victorious Christian life.

Stand against the wiles of the Devil

The purpose of Satan (the Devil) is to destroy our relationship and loyalty to Christ and make us ineffective as His soldiers. Satan is real, and unseen satanic forces around us are seeking to discourage and then to defeat every Christian. The Devil is *seeking whom he may devour* (I Pet. 5:8). But, resist the Devil. He is only a big noise. God, through His Word, has made available to every Christian everything necessary to be an overcomer.

Verse 6:12: *For we wrestle not against flesh and blood*

Our conflict may appear to be with men, organizations, laws, and other obstacles that seek to hinder our Christian activities. But, in reality, behind all opposition to the Gospel is Satan – *against principalities, against powers, against the rulers of the darkness of this world*. This darkness is the result of satanic efforts to pervert the truth.

Christ (is) *. . . Far above all principality, and power, and might, and dominion* (Eph. 1:20-21) and *greater is He that is in you, than he* (Satan) *that is in the world* (I John 4:4). The normal Christian life is one of continual victory over satanic assaults. In the natural man, there is a desire for *the lust of the flesh, and the lust of the eyes, and the pride of life* (one's lifestyle) (I John 2:16). However, *if ye live after* (according to) *the flesh, ye shall die: but if ye through the Spirit do mortify* (put to death) *the deeds of the body, ye shall live* (Rom. 8:13).

Verse 6:13: *Take unto you the whole armour of God, that ye may be able to withstand in the evil day* (when you are tempted)

The evil day of temptation will come but at a time when we least expect it.

and having done all, to stand

Our reason for failure is *friendship of the world. . . . whosoever therefore will be a friend of the world is the enemy of God* (James 4:4). Jesus said: *No man can serve two masters* (Matthew 6:24). We must decide who and what we are living for. James wrote: *A double minded man is unstable in all his ways* (James 1:8). And Paul wrote: *Therefore, my beloved brethren, be ye stedfast, unmoveable, always abounding in the work of the Lord, forasmuch as ye know that your labour is not in vain in the Lord* (I Cor. 15:58).

Verse 6:14: *Having your loins girt* (belted) *about with truth*

The *belt* was often made of linen, wide enough for several folds that could carry valuables around the waist. Such is the Word of God, wrapped around us, encompassing our life, involving our whole being, preparing us to be effective.

The words *with truth* have a twofold meaning. One: it denotes the whole truth of God's Word in order to know His will and to accomplish His purposes.

The second meaning is personal integrity – honesty, sincerity, devotion, and determination – the opposite of hypocrisy, indifference, halfheartedness or selfishness.

Truth is our belt holding our valuables. Nothing short of the Truth of God is sufficient as we move into action against the *wiles of the Devil*.

Having on the breastplate of righteousness

The *breastplate* of the Roman soldier was worn to protect his heart – the source of physical life. The *armour* of the Christian is here called *righteousness*. *Righteousness* is an attribute of **THE LORD OUR RIGHTEOUSNESS** (Jer. 23:6; 33:16).

The *breastplate* covers the heart, the motives, the desires of our inmost being. Jesus prayed: *Sanctify them through Thy Truth: Thy Word is Truth* (John 17:17). His ultimate desire for every Christian is *that He might sanctify* (make us holy) *and cleanse* (us) *with the washing of water by the Word. . . . holy and without blemish* (blameless) (Eph. 5:26-27).

Verse 6:15: *Your feet shod with the preparation of the Gospel of peace*

The *feet* must be protected to *run with patience* (endurance) *the race* (Hebrews 12:1). To be *shod* (sandaled) has reference to the military sandals – a symbol *of the Gospel of peace*. The *Gospel of peace* keeps us moving forward in the never-ending goal to win lost souls for Christ.

Verse 6:16: *Taking the shield of faith*

The Roman soldier's *shield* was a large, oblong instrument covering most of his body. But it was his responsibility to hold it. The *shield* becomes our overall protection. *This is the victory that overcometh the world, even our faith* (I John 5:4-5). *Without faith it is impossible to please Him* (God) (Hebrews 11:6). This *shield of faith* affirms our faith in the Bible as the infallible Word of God. We believe in God the Father; Christ, our Redeemer; and the Holy Spirit to *guide* (us) *into all Truth* (John 16:13).

Ye shall be able to quench (extinguish) *all the fiery darts* (arrows) of the wicked

Fiery darts were tipped with flammable materials, like a fire brand, and shot through the air. They were intended to cripple or put out of service the enemy. The *fiery darts* are temptations of covetousness, lust, immorality, pride, love of money, revenge, hate, bitterness, and strife that will cripple the Christian and put him out of commission as an active, effective soldier of Jesus Christ.

Verse 6:17: *Take the helmet of salvation*

The helmet is the head covering. It is *the helmet* that protected the head and allowed the Roman soldier to hold his head high and face the enemy. And it is *salvation* – the new birth experience – *born of . . .* (His) *Spirit* (John 3:5) – that causes us to look up in faith, knowing that our salvation is *not by works of righteousness which we have done, but according to His mercy He saved us* (Titus 3:5).

Furthermore, having accepted Christ as our Savior, as did the believers who listened to Peter on the Day of Pentecost, we *gladly received His Word and are baptized* (Acts 2:41). His Word not only has the solution for gaining eternal life but gives direction to overcome all of life's problems.

And the Sword of the Spirit

The Sword of the Spirit is the Word of God. That Word makes us aware of the *wiles* (schemes, trickery) *of the Devil*. It is the soldier's weapon of offense against unbelief, covetousness, pride, hatred, and worldliness. The secret to spiritual effectiveness is determined by how much of the Word of God is a living reality in our lives. We need to ask ourselves: "How big is our *Sword*?" Is it the size of a toothpick – a few verses here and there?

Just as the good soldier does not make up his mind whether or not to fight or in which direction to move, so the good soldier of Christ must be familiar with and trained to use his *Sword* under the authority of the Holy Spirit.

This same indwelling Holy Spirit *will guide you into all Truth* (John 16:13). But He cannot guide us into the truth that we have refused to read. There is no substitute for the Word of God. That is why the Holy Spirit led David to write: *I will . . . praise* (give thanks to) *Thy Name for . . . Thou hast magnified Thy Word above all Thy Name* (Ps. 138:2). Only the Word of God is said to be the source of our new birth, *being born again* (I Pet. 1:23; James 1:18). Only the Word of God is said to be the source of our spiritual growth. *Desire the sincere* (unadulterated, pure) *milk of the Word, that ye may grow thereby* (I Pet. 2:2).

The church world has a thousand imitation swords -- one for every problem. You name it and someone has written a book about it. One of the greatest victories of Satan is keeping Christians busy reading "good" books that keep them from reading THE BOOK. The Bible was created for your profit, for *all Scripture . . . is profitable* (II Tim. 3:16).

Verse 6:18: *Praying always with all prayer and supplication in the Spirit, and watching thereunto with all perseverance and supplication*

It becomes evident that the Christian soldier is not left defenseless. *The weapons of our warfare are not carnal* (fleshly)*, but mighty through God to the pulling down of strong holds* (II Cor. 10:4). As the Word of God becomes our way of life, our prayers are answered. Satan will do everything in his power to distract us from reading the Word of God, living the Word of God, and praying according to the Word of God. *He that turneth away his ear from hearing the Law* (the Word of God)*, even his prayer shall be abomination* (Prov. 28:9).

The Christian's *warfare* never ends. It's 365 days of every year. There is no leave of absence, no vacation, no time off. It is a continual fight against *the lust of the flesh, and the lust of the eyes, and the pride of life* (one's lifestyle) (I John 2:16).

for all saints

The Christian soldier is a volunteer in the King of kings' army – not for self-interests – but *for all saints* (Eph. 6:18). It is of utmost importance that we pray for the leadership, pastors, evangelists, missionaries, our church, and heads of ministries. But it is of equal importance to pray for the weakest saint – the one who may have offended us. Difficulty in forgiving others indicates an inadequate view of our need of forgiveness from God. Jesus warned: *If ye forgive not men for their trespasses* (from your heart)*, neither will your Father forgive your trespasses* (Matt. 6:15; comp. 18:21-35).

This points out the importance of heartfelt earnestness in prayer. When Jesus prayed: *I pray for them . . . which Thou hast given Me; for they are Thine. . . . that they might have My joy fulfilled in themselves. I have given them Thy Word. . . . They are not of the world, even as I am not of the world. Sanctify them through Thy Truth: Thy Word is Truth. As Thou hast sent Me into the world, even so have I also sent them into the world. . . . That they all may be one. . . . That the love wherewith Thou hast loved Me may be in them, and I in them* (John 17:9,13-14,16-18,21,26). Oh, how we need to recognize the importance of heartfelt praying *for ALL saints*!

Continued from Page 415

Introduction To The Books Of
PHILIPPIANS & COLOSSIANS

The Apostle Paul was in Troas, in Asia Minor, on his second missionary journey when he received the call, in a vision, to carry the Good News into Macedonia, ***to Philippi, which is the chief*** (leading) ***city of that part of Macedonia... and we were in that city abiding certain days*** (Acts 16:12). The first church established in Europe grew out of his ministry in Philippi.

As he wrote this letter to the Philippian Christians, Paul was a prisoner in the custody of the Roman Emperor Nero, but he called himself a ***prisoner of Jesus Christ***. Like Paul, we need to remember who is in control of our lives (Eph. 3:1; 4:1; II Tim. 1:8; Phil. 1:1,9). He assured the Philippians that Christ is the never-failing source of strength during adverse circumstances, saying: ***I can do all things through Christ which strengtheneth me*** (Phil. 4:13). The key thought of this letter is: ***Rejoice in the Lord alway: and again I say, Rejoice*** (4:4). The words ***joy, rejoice,*** and ***rejoiced*** occur a total of 21 times in this short book (1:4,18,25-26; 2:2,16-18,28; 3:1,3; 4:1,4,10).

The city of Colossae was located in the Roman province of Asia Minor on the east/west trade route that ran from Ephesus to Tarsus, and then to Syria. In the brief letter of Colossians, Paul focused on the fundamental doctrines of our faith in God the Father ***who hath delivered us from the power of darkness, and hath translated us into the kingdom of His dear Son: In whom we have redemption through His blood, even the forgiveness of sins*** (Col. 1:13-14).

Paul also combated false teachings by confirming the deity of Christ Jesus, ***Who, being in the form of God, thought it not robbery to be equal with God*** (Phi. 2:5-6).

Out of Touch

Only a day, yes, only a day
But ah! could you guess my friend,
Where the influence reaches
And where it will end

Of the hours you have frittered away?
The Master's command is, "Abide in Me."
And fruitless and vain will your service be
If you are out of touch with your Lord.

—M.E.H.

DECEMBER 5   Read Philippians 1 – 4

Highlights: Expressions of Christ-like love. ***In lowliness of mind let each esteem other better than themselves*** (Phil. 2:3). We are encouraged to: ***Rejoice.... by prayer... with thanksgiving... and*** then experience ***the peace of God*** (4:1-8).

Near the city of Philippi, Paul went to a place of prayer ***by a river side, where prayer was wont*** (accustomed) ***to be made*** (Acts 16:13). There, he met Lydia, a businesswoman from Thyatira, who was saved along with a few others and there Paul founded the first church in Europe. It also was here that Paul and Silas were scourged and put in prison for preaching the Gospel (16:13-24).

Paul's imprisonment gave him the opportunity to share the Good News about Jesus with the elite guards of the Roman Empire. There was a change of guard three or four times a day; this gave Paul a great opportunity to tell many about Jesus the Messiah, who was foretold in the Hebrew Scriptures. He wrote: ***The things which happened unto me have fallen*** (turned) ***out rather unto the furtherance of the Gospel; so that my bonds in Christ are manifest*** (known) ***in all the palace*** (military headquarters), ***and in all other places*** (Phil. 1:12-13). Paul encouraged the Philippian Christians to hold ***forth the Word of Life; that I may rejoice in the day of Christ, that I have not run in vain, neither laboured in vain*** (2:16).

Our occupation in life may be in politics, the military, business, education, manual labor, or homemaking; but our primary concern should always be to share the Gospel.

We all have a natural desire for physical comforts, security, and material things. However, our first consideration and loyalty should be to Christ. There is a storehouse of spiritual wealth and peace in Him that surpasses all earthly possessions.

Paul had renounced a prominent religious and political career in Jerusalem for a life of unceasing hardship and persecution that was destined to end in a violent death by the enemies of Christ. Knowing what the future held, he purposed: ***According to my earnest expectation... Christ shall be magnified in my body, whether it be by life, or by death. For to me to live is Christ, and to die is gain*** (1:20-21). We too should be able to say with Paul: ***I count all things but loss for the excellency*** (superiority) ***of the knowledge of*** (a personal relationship with) ***Christ Jesus my Lord*** (Phil. 3:8).

Thought for Today: Happiness cannot result from an act of sin.

DECEMBER 6 — Read Colossians 1 – 4

Highlights: Christ is Supreme (Col. 1:15-20). Once enemies, now friends (1:21-22). Paul instructed to reveal *the mystery which hath been hid* (1:26). Before, *dead in . . . sins*, now, alive in Christ (chap. 2). Live the new life in Christ (3:1-17). What is a Christian household (3:18-25)? We are encouraged to: *Continue in prayer* (4:1-4).

As we continue reading the Word of God with a desire to please Him in all of our decisions, the Holy Spirit guides us into a deeper revelation of Himself and His ways. Unlimited understanding, strength, and endurance are made available to every Christian. Christ alone, through His Word, can reveal and meet all of our spiritual needs. To help us grasp the importance of this, the Holy Spirit led Paul to write: *We . . . do not cease to pray for you, and to desire that ye might be filled with the knowledge of His will in all wisdom and spiritual understanding; That ye might walk worthy of the Lord unto all pleasing, being fruitful in every good work, and increasing in the knowledge of God; Strengthened with all might, according to His glorious power, unto all patience and longsuffering with joyfulness; Giving thanks unto the Father, which hath made us meet* (qualified) *to be partakers of the inheritance of the saints* (believers) (Col. 1:9-12). Notice how often the word *all* is used – *all wisdom . . . all pleasing . . . all might. . . all patience*, which means that the Lord is sufficient to meet our every need.

What follows is the practical expression of the new life in Christ for all believers. *Buried with Him in baptism, wherein also ye are risen with Him through the faith of the operation of God, who hath raised Him from the dead. And you, being dead in your sins . . . hath He quickened* (made alive) *together with Him, having forgiven you all trespasses* (2:12-13).

As evidence of this new life as Christians, Paul encouraged the new believers to *mortify* (treat as dead) *therefore your members* (physical nature) *which are upon the earth; fornication, uncleanness* (sexual immorality), *inordinate affection* (lust), *evil concupiscence* (desire), *and covetousness, which is idolatry: For which things' sake the wrath of God cometh on the children of disobedience* (3:5-6).

The key to fulfilling the will of God is letting *the Word of Christ dwell in you richly in all wisdom* (Col. 3:16).

Thought for Today: The prayers of the upright are the Lord's delight.

Introduction To The Books Of
I & II THESSALONIANS

After being beaten and jailed in Philippi along with Silas, and then being miraculously delivered, the Apostle Paul arrived in Thessalonica on his second missionary journey (Acts 17:1). It was the capital of Macedonia (northern Greece) and its chief seaport and commercial center. Some Jews, and many Greeks, accepted Jesus during this time and a church was established. Paul wrote: **For this cause also we thank God without ceasing, because, when ye received the Word of God which ye heard of us, ye received it not as the word of men, but as it is in Truth, the Word of God** (I Thess. 2:13).

Forced to leave Thessalonica because of violent opposition to the Gospel message, Paul journeyed to Berea, where he was well received. Within a short time, fanatical Jews came from Thessalonica and again fiercely opposed him. He then went on to Athens, where he faced the indifference of the intellectuals with little success (Acts 17:15-33; I Thess. 3:1). From there he went to Corinth (Acts 18:1).

In this first letter to the Thessalonians, Paul alludes five times to the return of Christ (1:10; 2:19; 3:13; 4:15-16; 5:2-3). He earnestly urged them to prepare for Christ's return and prayed for them, saying: **The very God of peace sanctify you wholly; and I pray God your whole spirit and soul and body be preserved** (kept) **blameless unto the coming of our Lord Jesus Christ** (I Thess. 5:23).

In Paul's second letter to the Thessalonians, he foretold that **the Lord Jesus shall be revealed from heaven with His mighty angels, In flaming fire taking vengeance on them that know not God, and that obey not the Gospel of our Lord Jesus Christ** (II Thess. 1:7-8). Before Christ returns to earth, evil will become more intense under **that man of sin**, the Antichrist (2:3; also Dan. 7:25). During that time there will be intense opposition to the Truth. Paul also warned that false teaching will cause a great falling away from the faith. **Let no man deceive you by any means: for that day shall not come, except there come a falling away first, and that man of sin be revealed, the son of perdition. . . . whose coming is after the working of Satan with all power and signs and lying wonders, And with all deceivableness** (deception) **of unrighteousness in them that perish; because they received not the love of the Truth, that they might be saved** (II Thess. 2:3,9-10). Christ's return is referred to more than 20 times in the 8 short chapters of these letters.

DECEMBER 7   Read I Thessalonians 1 – 5

Highlights: *Our Gospel came not . . . in Word only, but also in power* (I Thess. 1:5). We are children of Light; be ready for the Day of the Lord (5:4-5,11). It is of utmost importance *to know them which . . . are <u>over you</u> in the Lord, and admonish you; And <u>to esteem them</u> very highly in love for their work's sake. And <u>be at peace</u> among yourselves* (5:12-13). We, and all we possess, belong to Jesus (5:18).

The return of Christ will be the greatest event in history since His ascension when, *while they beheld, He was taken up; and a cloud received Him out of their sight* (Acts 1:9). Prior to His ascension, Jesus had assured His disciples: *I go to prepare a place for you. And if I go and prepare a place for you, I will come again, and receive you unto Myself; that where I am, there ye may be also* (John 14:2-3). His impending return was also confirmed at His ascension by two angelic witnesses from heaven: *This same Jesus, which is taken up from you into heaven, shall so come in like manner as ye have seen Him go into heaven* (Acts 1:11).

There are no words to adequately describe the glorious return of our Lord Jesus Christ who will make all things *in perfect peace* (Is. 26:3). All of history is reduced to just two ages: the present age that began with Adam, and the age to come. You *know perfectly* (full well) *that the day of the Lord so cometh as a thief in the night* (I Thess. 5:2). This is the joyous anticipation of every Christian who is faithfully preparing and waiting for the triumphant return of our Redeemer.

The certainty of the believer's eternal life with Christ is assured by His physical resurrection (I Cor. 15:20-23). Paul wrote: *If we believe that Jesus died and rose again, even so them also which sleep* (die) *in Jesus will God bring with Him. For this we say unto you by the Word of the Lord, that we which are alive and remain unto the coming of the Lord shall not prevent* (precede) *them which are asleep* (have died). *For the Lord Himself shall descend from heaven with a shout, with the voice of the archangel, and with the trump of God: and the dead in Christ shall rise first: Then we which are alive and remain shall be caught up together with them in the clouds, to meet the Lord in the air: and so shall we ever be with the Lord. Wherefore comfort* (encourage) *one another with these words* (I Thess. 4:14-18).

Thought for Today: Security is found in Christ, not in the abundance of material things.

Cross References: For **I Thess. 5:4:** See Is. 35:4.

DECEMBER 8   Read II Thessalonians 1 – 3

Highlights: Jesus is coming! Prepare to meet your Creator (II Thess. 1:3-12). The Bible reveals the difference between false claims and true (2:2-12). Stand firm; our comfort, hope, and strength are in the Lord (2:16-17). ***Occupy*** until Jesus comes (3:6-15; Luke 19:13).

The majority of mankind is blindly rushing toward the eternal lake of fire, either ignoring or not knowing the Word of God. ***When the Lord Jesus shall be revealed from heaven with His mighty angels, In flaming fire taking vengeance on them that know not God, and that obey not the Gospel of our Lord Jesus Christ: Who shall be punished with everlasting destruction from the presence of the Lord, and from the glory of His power; When He shall come to be glorified in His saints, and to be admired in all them that believe (because our testimony among you was believed)*** (II Thess. 1:7-10).

Jesus Himself said there is a ***broad . . . way, that leadeth to destruction*** (Matt. 7:13). Many have their hearts set on worldly activities and goals with little, if any, concern that they are ignoring the plan of God for their lives. That is why the Word of God states: ***Love not the world, neither the things that are in the world. . . . For all that is in the world, the lust of the flesh, and the lust of the eyes, and the pride of life, is not of the Father, but is of the world*** (I John 2:15-16). One day soon those who have accepted Christ will hear Him say: ***Come . . . inherit the Kingdom prepared for you*** (Matt. 25:34). ***And every man that hath this hope in Him purifieth himself, even as He is pure*** (I John 3:3).

It was Jesus Himself who revealed the final destination of all who refuse to trust Him as Savior:***Depart from Me, ye cursed, into everlasting fire, prepared for the Devil and his angels*** (Matt. 25:41). One chooses in this life to trust Christ in salvation and spend eternity with God in heaven or to ignore Christ who died to save them from eternal hell. When Jesus returns to the earth, He will be ***glorified in His saints***, and ***admired*** (adored) ***in all them that believe*** (II Thess. 1:10). What a glorious future for each of us who has chosen to trust Christ as Savior and to live for Jesus!

We pray always for you, that our God would count you worthy of this calling . . . That the Name of our Lord Jesus Christ may be glorified in you, and ye in Him (II Thess. 1:11-12).

Thought for Today: Jesus Christ is coming soon! It could be today. Are you ready?

Cross References: For **II Thess. 1:8:** See Is. 1:28. **II Thess. 2:3:** See Dan. 7:25. **II Thess. 2:4:** See Ezek. 28:2.

Introduction To The Books Of
I & II TIMOTHY

In these two letters to Timothy, Paul emphasized that knowing the Scriptures was vital, both for living to please the Lord and for defeating the Devil. Paul stressed the importance of being **a good minister** (servant) **of Jesus Christ, nourished up** (educated) **in the words of faith and of good doctrine** (biblical teaching). **. . . . If any man teach otherwise, and consent not to wholesome words, even the words of our Lord Jesus Christ, and to the doctrine which is according to godliness; he is proud, knowing nothing** (I Tim. 4:6; 6:3-4). Because of ignorance of the Word of God, many people do not know **the doctrine which is according to godliness.** Consequently, far too few are aware that, without holiness, **no man shall see the Lord** (Heb. 12:14). Christians have been instructed to be **obedient children, not fashioning yourselves according to the former lusts in your ignorance: But as He which hath called you is holy, so be ye holy in all manner of conversation** (conduct) (I Pet. 1:14-15).

In this first letter to Timothy, Paul clearly states: **There is One God, and One Mediator** (Arbitrator) **between God and men, the Man Christ Jesus** (I Tim. 2:5).

Shortly before his martyrdom in Rome, Paul wrote his second letter to Timothy, which was also his last letter to anyone (II Tim. 4:6-7). Paul again urged Timothy to **be strong in the grace that is in Christ Jesus** (2:1). He warned that failure to thoroughly study all the Scriptures would ultimately result in facing God **ashamed**. He encouraged Timothy to **study** (be diligent) **to shew thyself approved unto God, a workman that needeth not to be ashamed, rightly dividing the Word of Truth** (2:15).

The Word of God alone provides His wisdom to instruct us to know and do His will (3:15). Deceptions result from a mixture of truth and error. Paul declared Scriptures to be the standard by which all Truth is measured. We must **preach the Word; be instant** (ready) **in season, out of season; reprove, rebuke, exhort** (encourage) **with all longsuffering and doctrine. For the time will come when they will not endure sound doctrine; but after their own lusts shall they heap to themselves teachers, having itching ears; And they shall turn away their ears from the Truth, and shall be turned unto fables** (popular contemporary views) (II Tim. 4:1-4).

DECEMBER 9   Read I Timothy 1 – 6

Highlights: Truth. All Christians need to take this seriously (I Tim. 1:8-10). ***There is One God and One Mediator between God and men, the Man Christ Jesus*** (2:5). We are ***the Church of the Living God*** (3:15). You can't go wrong when you ***keep this Commandment without spot*** (6:14).

The Roman emperor Nero was ruthlessly persecuting Christians and condemning many of them to death. Yet, Paul emphasized the importance of Christians praying for those who are in authority. He wrote: ***I exhort therefore, that, first of all, supplications, prayers, intercessions, and giving of thanks, be made for all men; For kings, and for all that are in authority; that we may lead a quiet and peaceable life in all godliness and honesty*** (I Tim. 2:1-2). The Bible reminds us: ***The king's heart is in the hand of the LORD, as the rivers of water: He turneth it withersoever He will*** (Prov. 21:1). Only eternity will reveal what impact our prayers have had.

Christians should faithfully witness to the truth as revealed by Christ in His Word, even when speaking the truth could mean imprisonment or death. While many ***shall turn away their ears from the Truth***, we must remain faithful ***in all things, endure afflictions*** (II Tim. 4:4-5; see also Matt. 10:28). The number of those ***suffering affliction*** (James 5:10) and being martyred for their faith in Christ continues to grow in many countries.

The Apostle Peter emphasized the responsibility for Christians to be law-abiding citizens: ***Submit yourselves to every ordinance of man for the Lord's sake: whether it be to the king, as supreme; Or unto governors, as unto them that are sent by him for the punishment of evildoers, and for the praise of them that do well*** (I Pet. 2:13-14).

Luke recorded the one exception because it reveals our highest authority. Peter was willing to defend his faith in Christ when he was confronted by the religious Jewish Sanhedrin who warned him that he ***should not teach in this Name and, behold, ye have filled Jerusalem with your doctrine, and intend to bring this Man's blood upon us. Then Peter and the other apostles answered and said, We ought to obey God rather than men*** (Acts 5:28-29).

Thought for Today: Christians enjoy the peace of God regardless of circumstances.

Cross References: For **I Tim. 5:8:** See Deut. 25:4.

DECEMBER 10 — Read II Timothy 1 – 4

Highlights: *Be not... ashamed of the testimony of our Lord* (II Tim. 1:8). *Flee also youthful lusts: but follow righteousness* (2:22). All the Bible is given as our Guide to gain the Lord's best for our lives (3:16-17).

Paul reminds Timothy that his mother and grandmother had faithfully taught him that *the holy Scriptures ... are able to make thee wise unto salvation through faith which is in Christ Jesus.* He encouraged Timothy to remember that: *All Scripture is given by inspiration of God, and is profitable for doctrine, for reproof, for correction, for instruction in righteousness: That the man of God may be perfect* (lack nothing)*, throughly furnished* (equipped) *unto all good works* (II Tim. 3:15-17). This means God expects us to read it *all.* Jesus never once implied that some Scripture was inspired and other portions were not inspired. *All Scripture* obviously means every verse in the Bible. This fact is of vital importance. Both the Old and New Testaments warn against adding to or taking from the inspired Word of God (Deut. 4:2; Prov. 30:6; Rev. 22:18-19).

Paul wrote: *But though we, or an angel from heaven, preach any other Gospel unto you than that which we have preached ... let him be accursed.... If any man preach any other Gospel unto you than that ye have received, let him be accursed* (Gal. 1:8-9). *Beginning at Moses* (the first five Books of the Bible) *and all the prophets, He* (Jesus) *expounded unto them* (two of His followers) *in all the Scriptures the things concerning Himself* (Luke 24:27; comp. 24:44). We are to *preach* (teach) *the Word ... in season,* and *out of season* (II Tim. 4:2). Nothing is as essential as knowing the Word of God. No options or alternatives can replace it.

Paul also spoke of some who have *a form of godliness, but* (are) *denying the power thereof* (3:5). The Word of God has no genuine effect upon their heart, thoughts, or conduct because they deny the power of God. *All Scripture is ... profitable* for discipline *in righteousness,* giving direction for growing in grace. This means all Scripture teaches us to be all that God would have us to be in order to fulfill His perfect will for our lives. Surely the Holy Spirit is still saying: *Study to shew thyself approved unto God, a workman that needeth not to be ashamed, rightly dividing the Word of Truth* (II Tim. 2:15).

Thought for Today: The will of God does not lead where the grace of God does not provide.

Cross References: For **II Tim. 2:19:** See Num. 16:5.

INTRODUCTION TO THE BOOKS OF
TITUS & PHILEMON

Paul had left Titus on the island of Crete to continue the ministry there. He later sent this letter to Titus and instructed him to **set in order the things that are wanting, and ordain elders in every city, as I had appointed thee** (Titus 1:5). Through Paul, the Holy Spirit clearly set forth qualifications for bishops or elders – an excellent guideline for all church leaders (1:6-9).

While a prisoner in Rome, Paul wrote a personal letter to a man named Philemon, who may have been an influential Christian in Colossae and was possibly one of Paul's converts. It appears that Onesimus, a slave who belonged to Philemon, had run away and perhaps later also had become a convert to Jesus Christ through Paul's ministry. It is assumed that, after becoming a Christian, Onesimus agreed to return to his master in Colossae. This gracious letter urged Philemon to receive Onesimus, not as a runaway slave but as a beloved brother in the Lord, just as he would have received Paul himself (Philem. 1:16-17). This is of great value in the teaching of practical righteousness, Christian brotherhood, Christian courtesy, and the law of love.

---

*We all have sinned against the Lord
And stand condemned by His own Word,
No prayer or plea of ours could win
free forgiveness of God for all our sin.*

*But Jesus came and took our place
That He might save us by His grace;
He bore our sins – so great and wide –
That we, through Him, be justified.*

*And as we plead Christ's work complete
Upon the Cross – where He did meet
Each claim of the most righteous Law of God –
God wipes away each sin and flaw.*

*He speaks His peace within the heart
And bids all guilt and fear depart,
Counts us accepted in His Son
And sees the life of faith begun.*

*May we, in gratitude and love,
Seek e'er those things that are Above
And let Christ live His life anew
Through all who love His will to do.*

–M.E.H.

DECEMBER 11   Read Titus 1 – 3 and Philemon

Highlights: Witness and live your faith with enthusiasm (Titus chap. 1–2). Qualifications of elders and bishops (1:5-9). **Sound doctrine** for **the aged men ... the aged women. ... the young men**, and the **servants** (2:1-9). The coming of our **great God and our Saviour Jesus Christ** (2:13-14). **Speak evil of no man ... but be gentle** (3:2). A beautiful portrayal of a sinner facing God with Christ the Intercessor (Philem. 1:1-25).

The churches on the island of Crete needed spiritual leadership. Paul left Titus in Crete to set in order what was lacking, instructing him to ordain elders in every city. Such men were to **be blameless** (above reproach), **the husband of one wife** (married but once), **having faithful** (believing) **children. ... For a bishop must be blameless, as the steward** (manager) **of God; not selfwilled, not soon angry, not given to wine, no striker** (not violent), **not given to filthy lucre** (not greedy for financial gain); **But a lover of hospitality ... sober, just, holy, temperate** (disciplined); **Holding fast the faithful Word ... that he may be able by sound doctrine both to exhort and to convince the gainsayers** (opposition) (Titus 1:6-9). The Church belongs to Christ and is His Body on earth. Therefore, the spiritual leaders must be blameless in their personal and family lives.

Paul gave instructions that older men and women should teach the younger men and women to forsake evil passions and worldly ambitions, and to live honorably for the Lord. **The grace of God that bringeth salvation hath appeared to all men, Teaching us that, denying ungodliness and worldly lusts, we should live soberly** (sensibly), **righteously, and godly, in this present world; Looking for that blessed hope, and the glorious appearing of the great God and our Saviour Jesus Christ; Who gave Himself for us, that He might redeem us from all iniquity** (lawlessness), **and purify unto Himself a peculiar** (special) **people, zealous of good works** (2:11-14).

Although Paul was imprisoned in Rome, he knew who his real Master was. He identified himself as simply **a prisoner of Jesus Christ** (Philem. 1:1) in his letter to Philemon. Recognizing this freed him to pray for others: **I thank my God, making mention of thee always in my prayers, Hearing of thy love and faith, which thou hast toward the Lord Jesus, and toward all saints** (Philem. 1:4-5).

Thought for Today: Attitudes of superiority or that another is inferior are evil.

Introduction To The Book Of HEBREWS

The authorship of this book is uncertain, but many Bible scholars believe that Paul wrote it while *in his own hired house* in Rome (Acts 28:30). However, the true Author of every book in the Bible is the Holy Spirit. The Jews had the only true revelation of the One True God and the only divinely-appointed city and Temple for over a thousand years. Following the persecution mentioned in Acts 8, hostility against Jesus' followers intensified. Some Christians were attempting to add Christianity to Judaism, and some were in doubt about what to believe. Consequently, there are about 30 direct quotations and 50 allusions to the Old Testament in the Book of Hebrews to instruct Jewish believers about how the Old Covenant had been fulfilled by Jesus, the Messiah, as had been foretold by the prophets.

The superiority of Christ, His High Priesthood, and His New Covenant are the themes of this book. **God, who at sundry times and in divers** (various) **manners spake in time past unto the fathers by the prophets, Hath in these last days spoken unto us by His Son, whom He hath appointed Heir of all things, by whom also He made the worlds.... Therefore we ought to give the more earnest heed to the things which we have heard, lest at any time we should let them slip** (drift away) (Heb. 1:1-2; 2:1; also 3:3; 7:21-27).

The Book of Hebrews declares that the **Word of God is quick** (living), **and powerful, and sharper than any twoedged sword, piercing even to the dividing asunder** (in two) **of soul and spirit, and of the joints and marrow, and is a discerner of the thoughts and intents of the heart** (4:12).

The word **better** (superior) is one of the key words in Hebrews. **For the Law made nothing perfect, but the bringing in of a better hope did; by the which we draw nigh unto God.... Jesus** was **made a surety of a better Testament** (Covenant). **... now hath He obtained a more excellent** (superior) **ministry... He is the Mediator of a better Covenant, which was established upon better promises** (7:19,22; 8:6).

The Ten Commandments were written by the finger of God on tablets of stone, but Christ's new Covenant is written in the **hearts** of His disciples (8:10). The Old Covenant, with its endless animal sacrifices, is in striking contrast to the New Covenant which required only One Sacrifice, the perfect Lamb of God (John 1:29). By His blood He cleanses us from sin (Heb. 9:12; 10:1-14).

DECEMBER 12   Read Hebrews 1 – 4

Highlights: Jesus, the Son and Heir, is greater than the angels (Heb. chap. 1). Jesus, the Man (2:17; 3:6), overcame all temptations (4:15). Jesus is greater than Moses (chap. 3). Jesus, the Word, cuts deeply and truly (4:12; see John 1:1-5). Jesus provides His mercy and grace every day (4:16).

It was angels who delivered Lot out of Sodom (Gen. 19:1-26); angels ministered to Jesus following His 40-day fast (Matt. 4:11); and an angel delivered Peter from prison (Acts 12:7-11). And for us today angels are **ministering spirits, sent forth to minister for them who shall be heirs of salvation** (Heb. 1:14). **Heirs of salvation** includes those of us today who have trusted Christ as Savior!

While God has His angels who minister to us, Satan has his fallen angels (demons) who do his bidding. And Paul warned us: **Satan himself is transformed into an angel of light** (II Cor. 11:14). John recorded: **Believe not every spirit, but try** (test) **the spirits whether they are of God** (I John 4:1).

The importance of angels does not compare to the superiority of Christ. **For unto which of the angels said He at any time, Thou art My Son**? (1:5). Yet, regardless of His eternal superiority as Creator of angels and because of His great love for us, Jesus willingly **was made a little lower than the angels for the suffering of death ... that He by the grace of God should taste death for every man. For it became** (was proper for) **Him ... to make the Captain** (Author, Source) **of their salvation perfect through sufferings. . . . For verily** (truly) **He took not on Him the nature of angels; but He took on Him the seed** (offspring) **of Abraham. Wherefore in all things it behoved** (was best for) **Him to be made like unto His brethren, that He might be a merciful and faithful High Priest ... to make reconciliation for the sins of the people** (2:9-10,16-17).

We do not worship angels, as some do today; angels are created beings. We are to worship the Creator, not the creation. The Apostle John records in Revelation: **When I had heard and seen, I fell down to worship before the feet of the angel which shewed me these things. Then saith he unto me, See thou do it not: for I am thy fellowservant ... worship God** (Rev. 22:8-9).

Thought for Today: When Christ, the Prince of Peace rules our hearts, we will not insist on having things our way.

Cross References: For **Heb. 1:3:** See Ps. 110:1. **Heb. 1:5:** See Ps. 2:7; II Sam. 7:14. **Heb. 1:6:** See Ps. 97:7. **Heb. 1:7:** See Ps. 104:4. **Heb. 1:8-9:** See Ps. 45:6-7. **Heb. 1:10-12:** See Ps. 102:25-27. **Heb. 1:13:** See Ps. 110:1. **Heb. 2:6-8:** See Ps. 8:4-6. **Heb. 2:12:** See Ps. 22:22. **Heb. 2:13:** See Is. 8:18. **Heb. 3:7-11:** See Ps. 95:7-11. **Heb. 4:3:** See Ps. 95:11. **Heb. 4:4:** See Gen. 2:3.

DECEMBER 13   Read Hebrews 5 – 7

Highlights: Jesus *called of* (by) God *an High Priest* (Heb. 5:1-10). *He* (Jesus) *became the Author of eternal salvation unto all them that obey Him* (5:9; Rom. 6:23).

How thankful we are that mercy is an attribute of God, for it is one of our greatest daily needs! Mercy is an expression of His desire to forgive sinners and deliver them from eternal hell. Mercy involves love and is a practical demonstration of compassion.

Because God is also holy, He must enforce the penalty for sin *without respect of persons* (I Pet. 1:17), and *the wages of sin is death* (Rom. 6:23). In the Old Testament, a sinless (unblemished) animal took the place of an Israelite who slew it for his sin (Lev. 4:32). The devout Jew was continually reminded that *the life of the flesh is in the blood: and . . . it is the blood that maketh an atonement for the soul* (17:11). A blood sacrifice was required because taking the blood meant taking life, thus paying *the wages of sin*. But the need for numerous sacrifices ceased in the New Testament. *For such an High Priest became us, who is holy, harmless, undefiled, separate from sinners, and made higher than the heavens* (Heb. 7:26). Jesus, who had no sin, was qualified to die for our sins. He died on the cross for our sins and became *the Lamb of God, which taketh away the sin of the world* (John 1:29).

By His own blood He entered in once into the Holy Place, having obtained eternal redemption for us. For if the blood of bulls and of goats . . . sanctifieth . . . the flesh: How much more shall the blood of Christ, who through the eternal Spirit offered Himself without spot (defect) *to God, purge* (cleanse) *your conscience from dead works to serve the living God* (Heb. 9:12-14)?

It is the forgiving mercy of God that gives a Christian assurance of a continued relationship with Him, even though we sin and rightly deserve His judgment. In turn, the true believer will express mercy in his relationships with others because the Spirit of God dwells in his heart. He has assured us in His Word: *Blessed are the merciful: for they shall obtain mercy* (Matt. 5:7).

Put on therefore, as the elect (chosen) *of God, holy and beloved, bowels of mercies, kindness, humbleness of mind, meekness, longsuffering; Forbearing one another, and forgiving one another . . . even as Christ forgave you* (Col. 3:12-13).

Thought for Today: We can no more attain a worthwhile purpose in life apart from God than the clay can become a useful vessel apart from the potter.

Cross References: For **Heb. 5:5:** See Ps. 2:7. **Heb. 5:6:** See Ps. 110:4. **Heb. 6:14:** See Gen. 22:17.

DECEMBER 14 — Read Hebrews 8 – 10

Highlights: Jesus is seated at the right hand of God (Heb. 8:1-2). Jesus Christ is *the Mediator of a better Covenant, which was established upon better promises* (8:6). *For this is the Covenant that I will make... I will put My Laws in their mind, and write them in their hearts* (8:10). *The just shall live by faith* (10:38).

The Tabernacle and worship system for Israel were revealed by God to Moses on Mount Sinai. The system of worship consisted of numerous sacrifices. The sacrifices could not cleanse the worshiper from sins; they could only "cover" them temporarily until Jesus died on the cross. Every detail of this complex worship system was symbolic of the future single sacrifice of Christ on the cross. The Lord Jesus Christ replaced Israel's many priests as well as the high priest and all of the sacrificial worship system. God foretold through His prophet Jeremiah of a future Covenant: *I will make a New Covenant with the house of Israel, and with the house of Judah* (Jer. 31:31; comp. Heb. 8:6-13).

Under the Old Covenant (Testament) worship system, *the blood of goats and calves* (9:12,19), which were innocent animals, was offered daily for worshipers' sins. Under the New Covenant Christ shed His own blood *once for all* (10:10).

God led the writer of Hebrews to reveal that the Old Covenant had looked forward to *a greater and more perfect Tabernacle* (9:11). The words *more perfect Tabernacle* refer to the bodily manifestation of God the Son, since the Tabernacle's contents, as well as the Tabernacle itself, symbolized Christ, His life, ministry, and death, as did all of the sacrifices. Animal sacrifices are no longer acceptable because *Christ being come an High Priest of good things to come, by a greater and more perfect Tabernacle, not made with hands, that is to say, not of this building; Neither by the blood of goats and calves, but by His own blood He entered in once into the Holy Place, having obtained eternal redemption for us* (9:11-12).

As we publicly confess our faith in Christ, we acknowledge that we have renounced the world. Our confession shows we desire to remain loyal to our Lord and Savior Jesus Christ, who has done so much for us. *God commendeth His love toward us, in that, while we were yet sinners, Christ died for us* (Rom. 5:8).

Thought for Today: Yes, God is all-wise, all-powerful, and ever-present. How could we fear the future?

Cross References: For **Heb. 8:5:** See Ex. 25:40. **Heb. 8:8-12:** See Jer. 31:31-34. **Heb. 9:20-21:** See Ex. 24:8. **Heb. 10:5-7:** See Ps. 40:6-8. **Heb. 10:12-13:** See Ps. 110:1. **Heb. 10:16-17:** See Jer. 31:33-34. **Heb. 10:30:** See Deut. 32:35-36. **Heb. 10:37-38:** See Hab. 2:3-4.

DECEMBER 15   Read Hebrews 11 – 13

Highlights: What *faith* is and what it does. God gives the measure of faith. (Heb. 11; Rom. 10:17). Like a faithful parent, the Lord disciplines His children (Heb. 12:5-13), so listen and obey when He speaks (12:14-29). He is *the same yesterday, and to day, and for ever* (13:8) – never out of date.

The history of the people of God confirms that some endured hostile circumstances and intense suffering, yet they remained faithful and fulfilled His will. In the "Heroes of Faith Hall of Fame" (Heb. 11:1-38), we are given a review of some of these people. *By faith Abraham, when he was tried* (tested), *offered up Isaac . . . Accounting that God was able to raise him up, even from the dead . . . By faith Moses . . . refused to be called the son of Pharaoh's daughter; Choosing rather to suffer affliction with the people of God, than to enjoy the pleasures of sin for a season; Esteeming the reproach of Christ greater riches than the treasures in Egypt* (11:17-26). The Old Testament men and women listed in this chapter chose to remain faithful to God, regardless of discouraging circumstances, suffering, opposition, and even family members who hindered them.

Their faithfulness is a reminder of Jesus' willingness to suffer and die for our sins. And through His indwelling Holy Spirit, we are strengthened to *lay aside every weight, and the sin which doth so easily beset us, and . . . run with patience* (endurance) *the race that is set before us* (12:1) to live a life of faithfulness and obedience. The runners who win the race of life are *looking unto Jesus the Author and Finisher of our faith; who for the joy that was set before Him endured the cross, despising* (thinking little of) *the shame, and is set down at the right hand of the throne of God* (12:2). Every born-again Christian will *enter into the Kingdom of God* (John 3:3-5).

To follow Christ and live the Christian life demands self-denial, discipline, and wholehearted love for the Lord and His Word. These characteristics distinguish the true Christian from the self-indulgence practiced by the world. Are there worldly hindrances to our spiritual lives that need to be dealt with and eliminated?

Jesus *said . . . If any man will come after Me, let him deny himself, and take up his cross daily, and follow Me* (Luke 9:23).

Thought for Today: *Let thine heart keep My Commandments: For length of days, and long life, and peace, shall they add to thee* (Prov. 3:1-2).

Cross References: For **Heb. 11:8:** See Gen. 21:12. **Heb. 12:5-6:** See Prov. 3:11-12. **Heb. 12:12:** See Is. 35:3. **Heb. 12:26:** See Hag. 2:6. **Heb. 13:5:** See Josh. 1:5; Deut. 31:8. **Heb. 13:6:** See Ps. 118:6.

INTRODUCTION TO THE BOOK OF JAMES

The author of this book identifies himself as **James, a servant of God and of the Lord Jesus Christ** (James 1:1). He was not one of the original twelve apostles (Matt. 10:2-4) but appears to be the first presiding elder over the Jerusalem church (Acts 12:17; 15:13-21). Paul spoke of him as **James the Lord's brother** (Gal. 1:19; also Matt. 13:55; Mark 6:3).

James often quotes the Old Testament Scriptures, then proceeds to apply them to Christian living (James 2:8,23; 4:5-6). And he warns: **Whosoever therefore will be a friend of the world is the enemy of God** (4:4).

He presents a series of practical tests whereby we may recognize the genuineness of saving faith (2:14,17-18,20,22,24,26; 5:15). He admonished each believer **to keep himself unspotted from the world** (1:27).

He reminds us that we have become spiritual children of God by His Word of Truth, **which is able to save your souls** (1:21). **Of His own will begat He us with the Word of Truth, that we should be a kind of firstfruits of His creatures.... Wherefore lay apart** (rid yourselves of) **all filthiness and superfluity of naughtiness** (whatever wickedness still remains), **and receive with meekness the engrafted** (implanted) **Word, which is able to save your souls. But be ye doers of the Word, and not hearers only, deceiving your own selves** (1:18,21-22).

James also explains the great power of prayer by reminding us of Elijah. **The effectual fervent prayer of a righteous man availeth** (accomplishes) **much. Elias** (Elijah) **was a man subject to like** (the same) **passions as we are, and he prayed earnestly that it might not rain: and it rained not on the earth by the space of three years and six months. And he prayed again, and the heaven gave rain, and the earth brought forth her fruit** (5:16-18; I Kin. 17:1; 18:1,45).

PEACE

These things I have spoken unto you, that in Me ye might have peace. In the world ye shall have tribulation (oppression): *but be of good cheer; I have overcome the world* (John 16:33).

Being justified by faith, we have peace with God through our Lord Jesus Christ (Romans 5:1).

BE FAITHFUL

But whoso keepeth His Word, in him verily (truly) *is the love of God perfected: hereby know we that we are in Him* (I John 2:5).

DECEMBER 16   Read James 1 – 5

Highlights: *God is no respecter of persons.* He treats everyone, rich or poor, as equals – sinners that need to be saved (James 2:1-9; Acts 10:34). *Bridle* the tongue, control *the whole body* (3:2). *Envying and strife* are *earthly, sensual, devilish* (3:14-15). Real treasure. The importance of patience *for the coming of the Lord* (5:7-8). Prayer is powerful (5:13-18).

Some people are inclined to tell others about all their sufferings and sorrows with a "woe is me" attitude, hoping to receive sympathy. Others are prone to blame anyone, even God, for their problems. James' message may surprise you, because the Holy Spirit moved him to write: *My brethren, count it all joy when ye fall into divers temptations* (manifold trials); *Knowing this, that the trying* (testing) *of your faith worketh* (develops) *patience. But let patience have her perfect work, that ye may be perfect* (mature) *and entire* (complete), *wanting* (lacking) *nothing* (James 1:2-4).

Furthermore, James reminds us: *Blessed is the man that endureth temptation* (remains faithful): *for when he is tried* (approved)*, he shall receive the crown of life, which the Lord hath promised to them that love Him. Let no man say when he is tempted, I am tempted of God: for God cannot be tempted with* (by) *evil, neither tempteth He any man* (1:12-13). But trials can be used by the Lord as a great benefit in the lives of all who remain teachable and faithful. The fact is, *the trial of your faith, being* (is) *much more precious* (of far greater value) *than of gold* (I Pet. 1:7).

All of us need to be reminded: *Submit yourselves therefore to God. Resist the devil and he will flee from you. Draw nigh* (near) *to God, and He will draw nigh to you* (James 4:7-8). Pity the poor soul who believes that it is the devil who is responsible for and has a free hand in giving us a "hard time." In reality, we can be victorious over our trails and assaults by Satan when we resist him by claiming the promises of God through His Word.

We are to put on *the whole armour of God* so that *ye* (we) *may be able to stand against the wiles* (schemes, deception) *of the devil* (Eph. 6:11). The Holy Spirit led Paul to write words of encouragement to us: *Above all, taking the shield of faith, wherewith ye shall be able to quench all the fiery darts of the wicked. . . . and the Sword of the Spirit, which is the Word of God* (Eph. 6:16-17).

Thought for Today: Sinful things blight our lives, but good things result from prayer, Bible reading, and obeying the Word of God.

Cross References: For **James 2:8:** See Lev. 19:18. **James 2:11:** See Ex. 20:13-14. **James 2:23:** See Gen. 15:6. **James 4:6:** See Prov. 3:34.

INTRODUCTION TO THE BOOKS OF
I & II PETER

In writing these two letters, Peter obeyed two specific commands given to him by Jesus. *I have prayed for thee, that thy faith fail not: and when thou art converted, strengthen thy brethren* (Luke 22:32). Then Jesus said *unto him the third time, Simon. . . . Feed My sheep* (John 21:17). Peter called himself *an apostle of Jesus Christ* (I Pet. 1:1) and *an elder, and a witness of the sufferings of Christ, and also a partaker* (sharer) *of the glory that shall be revealed* (5:1). In this first letter, he encouraged Christians who had fled Israel due to persecution and now were *strangers scattered throughout Pontus, Galatia, Cappadocia, Asia, and Bithynia* (1:1).

Throughout the past 2,000 years, Christians have been subjected to much suffering just as Jesus foretold (John 15:18). Peter affirmed this by writing: *Hereunto were ye called: because Christ also suffered for us, leaving us an example, that ye should follow His steps* (I Pet. 2:21). The highlight of his first letter is the importance of the Word of God as the only Guide for living and growing in Christ: *Being born again, not of corruptible seed, but of incorruptible, by the Word of God, which liveth and abideth for ever* (1:23). He further encouraged: *As newborn babes, desire the sincere* (unadulterated) *milk of the Word, that ye may grow thereby* (2:2).

Later, Peter wrote to all *that have obtained like precious faith* (II Pet. 1:1). He warned of a critical situation of false teaching that still confronts the Church. To meet this growing need, he urged: *Giving all diligence, add to your faith virtue; and to virtue knowledge; And to knowledge temperance* (self-control); *and to temperance patience; and to patience godliness; And to godliness brotherly kindness; and to brotherly kindness charity* (love). *. . . He that lacketh these things is blind . . . and hath forgotten that he was purged from his old sins. . . . There were false prophets also among the people, even as there shall be false teachers among you, who privily* (craftily) *shall bring in damnable* (destructive) *heresies, even denying the Lord that bought them, and bring upon themselves swift destruction. And many shall follow their pernicious* (destructive) *ways; by reason of whom the way of Truth shall be evil spoken of* (1:5-7,9-10; 2:1-2). Although they would face persecution, false teachers, and deception, they were to keep their focus on the coming of Christ, looking *for new heavens and a new earth, wherein dwelleth righteousness* (3:13).

DECEMBER 17   Read I Peter 1 – 2

Highlights: Comfort and reassurance in *the trial of your faith* (I Pet. 1:1-25). *Being born again . . . by the Word of God* (1:22-23; James 1:18). *Submit* to the laws of your government (I Pet. 2:13-15).

Peter referred to Christians as *elect* (chosen by God). *. . . through sanctification of the Spirit, unto obedience and sprinkling of the blood of Jesus Christ* (I Pet. 1:2). "Sprinkling" alludes to the blood which was sprinkled on the Brazen Altar, symbolizing the people's obedience to God, as well as symbolizing His acceptance of them (Ex. 24:1-11).

As Christians, we look forward to *an inheritance incorruptible* (imperishable), *and undefiled . . . reserved in heaven for you, Who are kept* (protected) *by the power of God through faith unto salvation ready to be revealed in the last time* (I Pet. 1:4-5). Since Christians are given such a promise, Peter urged that as *strangers* (sojourners) *and pilgrims* (foreign residents) whose lifetime on earth is limited, we should *abstain from fleshly lusts, which war against the soul* (2:11).

Peter continued to remind us of the importance of living a holy life: *As obedient children, not fashioning* (conforming) *yourselves according to the former lusts in your ignorance: But as He which hath called you is holy, so be ye holy in all manner of conversation* (behavior). *. . . Seeing ye have purified your souls in obeying the truth through the Spirit . . . see that ye love one another with a pure heart fervently: Being born again, not of corruptible seed, but of incorruptible, by the Word of God, which liveth and abideth for ever* (1:14-15,22-23).

Since the Bible is our one complete source of guidance and strength, Peter urged believers: *As newborn babes* (new converts), *desire the sincere* (perfect) *milk* (spiritual food) *of the Word, that ye may grow thereby* (2:2). Peter points out that the nourishment of the Word is essential if we are to live *as obedient children* (1:14). Our desire to know the Bible in order to do the Lord's will is always in our best interest. *Seeing ye have purified your souls in obeying the truth through the Spirit* explains how surrender to the Lord's authority and the power of His Word transforms lives. Peter describes Christians as *a spiritual house, an holy priesthood, to offer up spiritual sacrifices, acceptable to God by Jesus Christ* (2:5).

Thoughts for Today: Can others see a difference between your life as a Christian and your former life as an unbeliever?

Cross References: For **I Pet. 1:16:** See Lev. 11:44-45. **I Pet. 1:24-25:** See Is. 40:6-8. **I Pet. 2:6-7:** See Is. 28:16; Ps. 118:22. **I Pet. 2:22:** See Is. 53:9. **I Pet. 2:24:** See Is. 53:4-5,12.

DECEMBER 18   Read I Peter 3 – 5

Highlights: A believer's lifestyle should be a testimony of what Jesus is like (I Pet. 3:1-5), so we should treat each other as joint heirs (3:7). ***Be good stewards of the manifold grace of God*** (4:1-11). Rejoice that we are partakers of Christ's sufferings (4:12-19). Pray for Church leaders to feed and strengthen their flocks (5:1-11).

The Bible is the One True and Complete Source of spiritual knowledge and strength. The Holy Spirit led the Apostle Peter to write: ***If any man speak, let him speak as the oracles*** (utterances) ***of God; if any man minister*** (serve), ***let him do it as of the ability which God giveth: that God in all things may be glorified through Jesus Christ, to whom be praise and dominion for ever and ever*** (I Pet. 4:11). In contrast to the Word of God are the opinions and traditions of men. We must not modify or ignore the only Guide to life that God has given as the standard by which we must live.

Jesus' parting words to Peter were: ***Simon, son of Jonas, lovest thou Me? . . . Peter was grieved because He said unto him the third time, Lovest thou Me? And he said unto Him, Lord . . . Thou knowest that I love Thee. Jesus saith unto him, Feed My sheep*** (John 21:15-17). ***Feed*** indicates Jesus wanted Peter to nourish His sheep by passing along all His words (Matt. 28:18-20). For His followers today ***feed My sheep*** means to teach them all of the Word of God, from Genesis through Revelation. The Word of God has the power to change lives. All of us can be involved. Some write, edit, and print, while others support the distribution of the teaching ministries for Jesus, who also commands us: ***Feed My sheep***.

The underlying principle of most worldly endeavors is: "How much is in it for me?" This spirit of greed, pride, and power permeates self-serving ambition. Because the Word of God is alive and never changes, the message the Holy Spirit led the Apostle Paul to write to Timothy is still applicable to us today: ***Before God, and the Lord Jesus Christ, who shall judge the quick*** (living) ***and the dead at His appearing and His Kingdom; Preach the Word; be instant*** (ready) ***in season, out of season; reprove, rebuke, exhort*** (encourage) ***with all longsuffering*** (patience) ***and doctrine*** (teaching) (II Tim. 4:1-2). ***The Lord is not slack concerning His promise . . . not willing that any should perish, but that all should come to repentance*** (II Pet. 3:9).

Thought for Today: Christian growth is evident when one finds satisfaction in helping others discover spiritual values.

Cross References: For **I Pet. 3:10-12:** See Ps. 34:12-16. **I Pet. 5:5:** See Prov. 3:34.

DECEMBER 19   Read II Peter 1 – 3

Highlights: Don't forget the promise of a glorious life in Jesus in contrast to life in a sinful world (II Pet. 1:3-12). The Holy Spirit gave the prophecy that Jesus is coming (1:16-21). Don't believe everyone; false prophets and teachers are everywhere (2:1-22).

Peter's second letter begins with one significant thought: ***God . . . hath given unto us all things that pertain unto life and godliness, through the knowledge of Him that hath called us to glory and virtue*** (II Pet. 1:2-3). The Holy Spirit led Peter to reveal how a life of godliness is made possible by applying to our lives the ***exceeding great and precious promises: that by these ye might be partakers of the divine nature, having escaped the corruption that is in the world through lust*** (covetousness). ***And beside this, giving all diligence*** (make every effort), ***add to your faith virtue*** (moral excellence); ***and to virtue knowledge; And to knowledge temperance*** (self-control); ***and to temperance patience*** (patient endurance); ***and to patience godliness; And to godliness brotherly kindness; and to brotherly kindness charity*** (Christian love). ***For if these things be in you, and abound, they make you that ye shall neither be barren nor unfruitful in the knowledge of our Lord Jesus Christ. But he that lacketh these things is blind, and cannot see afar off, and hath forgotten that he was purged*** (cleansed) ***from his old sins*** (II Pet. 1:4-9).

Spiritual maturity is an ongoing process that lasts a lifetime. It is dependent on our obedience and allowing the Holy Spirit to guide us through His Word.

God is concerned for His children's moral and spiritual health. Whatever is contrary in our lives to His Word brings about His loving correction. His holiness and His wrath against sin are inseparable. ***For if we would judge ourselves, we should not be judged. But when we are judged, we are chastened of the Lord, that we should not be condemned with the world*** (I Cor. 11:31-32).

God has given us the freedom to choose whether we will let His judgment work for us or against us. ***Beloved, seeing ye know these things before, beware lest ye also, being led away with the error of the wicked, fall from your own stedfastness. But grow in grace, and in the knowledge of our Lord and Savior Jesus Christ. To Him be glory both now and for ever. Amen*** (II Pet. 3:17-18).

Thought for Today: The Lord forgives all who repent of their sin and desire to live for Him.

Cross References: For **II Pet. 2:22:** See Prov. 26:11.

Introduction To The Book Of I JOHN

John said that he and others had seen with their own eyes the One (Jesus Christ) **which was from the beginning, which we have heard . . . which we have looked upon, and our hands have handled, of the Word of Life** (I John 1:1). **He that saith, I know Him, and keepeth not His Commandments, is a liar, and the truth is not in him. But whoso keepeth His Word, in him verily** (truly) **is the love of God perfected: hereby know we that we are in Him** (2:4-5).

John exposed the hypocrisy of "professing Christians" who continue to pursue **the lust of the flesh** (desire of the carnal nature)**, and the lust of the eyes, and the pride of life** (2:16).

We are also reminded that love is the distinguishing characteristic of a Christian. The word **love** appears about 46 times in these five short chapters. The indwelling love of God causes a remarkable transformation in the lives of Christians. It imparts a desire to live in full obedience to the will of God, as revealed in His Word.

Satan will do all he can through false teachers to divert an awareness in us that **every man that hath this hope in Him purifieth himself, even as He is pure** (3:3). Consequently, we are again warned against false preachers and teachers: **They are of the world: therefore speak they of the world, and the world heareth** (believes) **them** (4:5).

These things have I written unto you that believe on the Name of the Son of God; that ye may know (and not be deceived by false prophets) **that ye have eternal life** (5:13). Assurance of salvation and eternal life are prominent throughout the Book of I John (2:3,5,29; 3:14,19,24; 4:13,16; 5:15,18-20).

No time, no time to study
To meditate and pray,
And yet much time for doing
In a fleshly, worldly way;
No time for things eternal,
But much for things of earth;
The things of little worth.
Some things, tis true, are needful,
But first things come first;
And what displeases the Word of God
Of God it shall be cursed.

—M.E.H.

DECEMBER 20

Read I John 1 – 3

Highlights: Confession of sin brings cleansing from sin and all unrighteousness (I John 1:9). If we hate our Christian brother, we are in darkness (2:9-10). To love is to abide in the light. If we keep His Commandments we dwell in Him and He in us (3:22-24).

Our Heavenly Father has provided us with a Savior, Jesus Christ. What better way to live our lives than to turn from anything that hinders our relationship with Him! *If we say that we have fellowship with Him, and walk in darkness, we lie, and do not* (practice) *the truth: But if we walk in the light, as He is in the light, we have fellowship one with another* (I John 1:6-7).

There are some who assume they have a relationship with Christ but still **walk in darkness**. God directed John to write that darkness is associated with a heart that hates his brother. Walking in the Light is associated with a right relationship with our brother and leads to fellowship with one another. The spiritually minded who **walk in the Light, as He is in the Light**, are first and foremost concerned that Christ be exalted in their lives (II Cor. 10:5; Rom. 12:1-2).

Darkness is associated with those who have not seen the Light concerning Jesus. How do we know if we are in darkness? Spiritual darkness is the absence of Light – the Light of life. It appears in many forms such as adultery or fornication, hate or murder, a sensitive spirit that is easily offended, or a tendency to criticize or to be resentful when contradicted. Darkness is also manifested by jealousy, envy, or a tendencey to speak ill of others.

Some **walk in darkness** with a spirit of discouragement and self-pity and a determination to convey that spirit to everyone who will listen. Many of those people display an air of superiority by drawing attention to themselves and seeking to dominate conversations. Light exposes the darkness of anything that is unholy and unclean.

Even though our desire is to walk *in the Light* and *in fellowship with the Lord and with one another,* there are times when we will sin, because we still have our sin nature. When we sin though, let us remember *if any man sin, we have an Advocate with the Father, Jesus Christ the righteous* (I John 2:1). We can get discouraged when we fall into sin, but we can again walk in the Light with Him: *If we confess our sins, He is faithful and just to forgive us our sins, and to cleanse us from all unrighteousness* (I John 1:9).

Thought for Today: Those who harbor hatred do far more damage to themselves than they do to those whom they hate.

Cross References: For **I John 1:8:** See Eccl. 7:20. **I John 3:12:** See Gen. 4:8.

DECEMBER 21   Read I John 4 – 5

Highlights: *Try the spirits* (I John 4:1). Avoid false prophets (4:1-6). What is real love? (Compare 4:7-21 with I Cor. 13:1-12.) Assurance that Jesus is the Son of God (I John 5:1-12). The family of God; children of the living God (5:13-20). Don't let anything take the place of the will of God for your life (5:21).

The Holy Spirit directed the Apostle John to write: *Beloved, believe not every spirit, but try* (test) *the spirits whether they are of God: because many false prophets are gone out into the world* (I John 4:1). Doctrinal deception is widespread and difficult to discern. Jesus warned: *Not every one that saith unto Me, Lord, Lord, shall enter into the Kingdom of Heaven; but he that <u>doeth</u> the will of My Father which is in heaven* (Matt. 7:21).

Jesus warned that many who believe they are *the children of the Kingdom shall be cast out into outer darkness: there shall be weeping and gnashing* (grinding) *of teeth* (8:12). The consequence of being deceived is horrifying. The majority of "religious" people will be *cast . . . into a furnace of fire: there shall be wailing and gnashing of teeth* (13:42). Our loving Savior said it would happen.

As Christians read the Bible with a desire to know and do His will, the Holy Spirit of God bears witness with our spirit that we are among the *few there be that find* eternal life (Matt. 7:14). Since salvation through faith determines one's destiny for eternity, we are told: *Examine yourselves, whether ye be in the faith* (II Cor. 13:5). Jesus warned: *Take heed that ye be not deceived* (Luke 21:8). We are also warned: *Seducers* (imposters) *shall wax worse and worse* (progress from bad to worse)*, deceiving, and being deceived* (II Tim. 3:13). John said: *This is the love of God, that we keep His Commandments. . . . and this is the victory that overcometh the world, even our faith. Who is he that overcometh the world, but he that believeth that Jesus is the Son of God* (I John 5:3-5)*?*

Being *born of God* is far more than just becoming a member of a church or believing certain facts about Jesus Christ. The Holy Spirit brings conviction to our hearts as we read His Word, which leads us to repentance for our sins. The Word of God affects the whole life. It molds character and guides conduct. If we have genuinely put our faith in *Jesus* as *the Son of God* (4:15), we will have a desire to be obedient to His Commandments (I John 5:2).

Thought for Today: The sincerity of our love for Christ can be measured by the kindness that we show to others.

Introduction To The Books Of
II & III JOHN & JUDE

The writer of the Book of II John referred to himself as **the elder**, and the letter is addressed **unto the elect lady and her children, whom I love in the Truth; and not I only, but also all they that have known the Truth** (II John 1:1). While some believe the letter was addressed to an individual, others believe that, since persecution was so intense at the time it was written, the author was actually writing to the Church, the Bride of Christ, and its members, whom he addressed as **children, whom I love in the Truth**. He went on to say: **I rejoiced greatly that I found of thy children walking in Truth, as we have received a Commandment from the Father** (1:4). The importance of teaching the Word of God is emphasized. The word **Truth** is used five times in the first four verses of II John.

In **III John**, the word **Truth** is used 6 times in its 14 verses. Here we are introduced to three people: Demetrius, whom John praises; Gaius, a generous helper and co-laborer in the work of the Lord; and Diotrephes, a man with exceptional abilities but who was a hindrance to the ministry. These men are examples of many today who are either helping or hindering the ministry of Christ.

The writer of **Jude** identified himself as **Jude, the servant of Jesus Christ, and brother of James**. He wrote **to them that are sanctified by God the Father, and preserved in Jesus Christ** (Jude 1:1). Jude probably was the Judas of Matthew 13:55 and Mark 6:3 and, therefore, the half-brother of Jesus.

Jude's letter is devoted to exposing the fearful, deadly consequences of believing false doctrines and false teachers. **Certain men crept in unawares** (unnoticed), **who were before of old ordained to this condemnation, ungodly men, turning the grace of our God into lasciviousness** (unbridled lust), which is **denying the only Lord God, and our Lord Jesus Christ** (1:4). Since salvation is by grace and not of works, these religious leaders taught that Christians were not obligated to keep any Commandments even though Jesus said: **If ye love Me, keep My Commandments** (John 14:15). He also said: **Why call ye Me, Lord, Lord, and do not the things which I say** (Luke 6:46)**?** Peter quoted from Leviticus 11:44-45: **It is written, Be ye holy: for I am holy** (I Pet. 1:16). The Apostle Paul wrote to warn against such apostasy: **How shall we, that are dead to sin, live any longer therein** (Rom. 6:2)**?**

DECEMBER 22   Read II John, III John, Jude

Highlights: Be faithful to the teachings of Christ; be diligent; don't be deceived (II John). All believers in the world are the Family of God (III John). Beware of false worship; express mercy to all; rescue others from sin. The Bible is the Truth, the only way to eternal life. The Son – Lord of all (Jude).

In his brief but very important letter to all believers, Jude wrote: *It was needful for me to write unto you, and exhort* (urge) *you that ye should earnestly contend for the faith ... delivered unto the saints. For there are certain men crept in unawares ... ungodly men, turning the grace of our God into lasciviousness, and denying the only Lord God, and our Lord Jesus Christ* (Jude 1:3-4). To *earnestly contend for the faith* includes the necessity of believing that *all Scripture is given by inspiration of God* and it is the final Word on all doctrine (II Tim. 3:16).

Today there is a superficial and deceptive unity being promoted by some who have included religions that reject Jesus of Nazareth as *The Only Lord God, and our Lord Jesus Christ* (Jude 1:4).

Jude says such deceivers will be judged, *even as Sodom and Gomorrah ... are set forth for an example, suffering the vengeance of eternal fire. ... these filthy dreamers defile the flesh, despise dominion, and speak evil of dignities. ... they corrupt themselves. Woe unto them* (1:7-8,10-11)*!* Having been enlightened by the Word of God to recognize false doctrine, we can add a resounding "Praise the Lord" to Jude's statement.

Other religions deny either the total deity or the total humanity of Jesus. Some assume there is only One God but that He is called by various names. They ignorantly conclude that as long as people are sincere, it doesn't matter what they believe. But Jesus said: *I am The Way, The Truth, and The Life: no man cometh unto the Father, but by Me* (John 14:6). And Peter proclaimed: *Neither is there salvation in any other* (than Jesus Christ)*: for there is none other name under heaven given among men, whereby we must be saved* (Acts 4:12).

Now unto Him that is able to keep you from falling, and to present you faultless ... To the only wise God our Saviour, be glory and majesty, dominion and power, both now and ever (forever). *Amen* (Jude 1:24-25).

Thought for Today: Knowing and obeying the Word of God is the only safeguard against being deceived by false teachings

Introduction To The Book Of REVELATION

The aged Apostle John was imprisoned on Patmos (Rev. 1:9), a small, rocky island which lies about 35 miles off the southwest coast of Asia Minor (modern-day Turkey). During this imprisonment, John received **the Revelation of Jesus Christ, which God gave unto him, to shew unto His servants things which must shortly come to pass** (1:1). John was told: **What thou seest, write in a book, and send it unto the seven churches which are in Asia; unto Ephesus ... Smyrna ... Pergamos ... Thyatira ... Sardis ... Philadelphia ... Laodicea** (1:11). **.... from Jesus Christ, who is the Faithful Witness, and the First Begotten of the dead, and the Prince of the kings of the earth** (1:5; also 1:18; 2:8). This final message of Christ to His Church is exceedingly important. These seven churches represent the dangers that still confront Christians today. In addition, we learn the importance of being an "overcomer."

We may not understand everything but it is of utmost importance that we read this book: **Blessed is he that readeth, and they that hear the words of this prophecy, and keep those things which are written therein: for the time is at hand** (1:3). It should not be ignored for it contains some of the most important warnings and some of the most precious promises of all Scripture. Since we can't obey something we have never read, we need to study it carefully. There are more than 300 symbolic terms throughout the Book of Revelation which describe numerous events concerning Christ and His Church. By referring to their use in over 500 references in the Old Testament, the symbols can be understood.

Beware of a fascination with future events so that we fail to see that this book is the unveiling of the Person and purpose of Jesus Christ. His ultimate, glorious, and eternal reign is its primary theme. The key phrase is the book's first five words: **The Revelation of Jesus Christ**. We find the sacrificial title of Christ as the Lamb about 30 times in Revelation. Four aspects of Christ as the Lamb are seen in Revelation. In chapters 4 – 5, the worship of the Lamb is celebrated; in chapters 6 – 18, the wrath of the Lamb is detailed; the wedding of the Lamb as well as the great white throne judgment are revealed in chapters 19 – 20; and, in chapters 21 and 22, the wife of the Lamb is described.

The last glorious event involving Christ on earth was His ascension; the next great event will be His return!

The 7 Churches of Asia
(Revelation Chapters 2 & 3)

The Island of Patmos is situated in the SE Aegean Sea. It is a small, mountainous, almost barren island.

It served as a prison for the Roman government, since the prisoners needed no guards because they could not escape.

In the side of one of the mountains is a cave where it is assumed that the Apostle John recorded the Book of Revelation. John tells us that he *was in the isle that is called Patmos* (Revelation 1:9). He recorded *The Revelation of Jesus Christ* (1:1). John is the writer; Jesus Christ is the Author. Its purpose is not a revelation of the future but of a Person, Jesus Christ. It is our Savior's call to His Churches for repentance, obedience, and faithfulness. We are to be prepared for His coming (1:7).

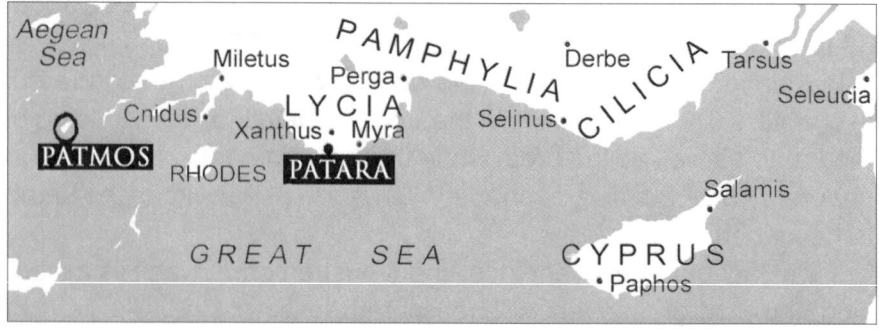

DECEMBER 23   Read Revelation 1 – 2

Highlights: Prayerfully consider the faults as well as the good of all seven churches as a guide for our conduct. A counterpart of each has existed in every generation to this day (Rev. 1:4,20).

The seven churches of Asia Minor each received a letter dictated by Christ and recorded by John while he was on the island of Patmos. Since Christians are similar in every generation, the messages are just as vital and applicable for us today.

Words of praise were given to the church at Ephesus for its sound doctrine. However, Christ said: **Thou hast left thy first love** (Rev. 2:4). Losing devotion to Christ can happen gradually, by becoming so involved in business, leisure activities, or church activity, that the worship of Christ becomes a mere formality. This charge is most serious: **Remember therefore from whence thou art fallen, and repent... or else I will come... and will remove thy candlestick** (the church, see 1:20) **... except thou repent** (2:5). Twice in one verse Jesus warned the church to **repent**.

The letter sent to the church at Smyrna acknowledged that they were suffering: **I know thy works, and tribulation, and poverty, (but thou art rich)** (2:9). This church appeared destitute of the comforts of life. Some would be cast into prison, others would suffer persecution. Because of their loyal devotion, the Lord promised: **Be thou faithful unto death, and I will give thee a crown of life.... He that overcometh shall not be hurt of** (by) **the second death** (2:10-11).

The letter sent to the church at Pergamos reminded them that they lived **where Satan's seat is: and thou holdest fast** (remain true to) **My Name** (2:13). However, some held **the doctrine of Balaam, who taught Balac to cast a stumblingblock before the children of Israel... to commit fornication** (2:14). Jesus warned: **Repent; or else I will come unto thee quickly, and will fight against them with the Sword of My mouth** (2:16).

And unto... the church in Thyatira.... hold fast till I come. And he that overcometh, and keepth My works unto the end... I will give him the Morning Star (2:18-28).

The Gospel must warn of hell and eternal punishment. In Paul's letter to the Galatians, we are warned of such dangers: **If any man preach any other gospel unto you than that ye have received, let him be accursed** (condemned) (Gal. 1:9).

Thought for Today: Our present burdens may often seem heavy, but the Lord always enables us to bear them.

Cross References: For **Rev. 1:5:** See Ps. 89:27. **Rev. 1:6:** See Ex. 19:6. **Rev. 1:7:** See Dan. 7:13; Zech. 12:10. **Rev. 2:7:** See Gen. 2:9. **Rev. 2:23:** See Jer. 17:10. **Rev. 2:27:** See Ps. 2:9.

DECEMBER 24   Read Revelation 3 – 5

Highlights: The Holy Spirit speaks to us through His Word (Rev. 1:3). The Lord admonishes the church in Sardis (3:1-3). Commendation is given to some in Sardis because they have not defiled their garments (3:4). The church in Philadelphia is rewarded (3:8-12). Warning is given to the lukewarm church in Laodicea (3:15-19). The Lord will come in to sup (provide spiritual food) and dine when we open our hearts to Him (3:20). Worship (4:1-11). The Lamb is worthy! The Chorus resounds! (5:4-14).

The church in Sardis boasted of not teaching false doctrines, but another serious sin existed. ***Unto ... the church in Sardis write ... I know thy works, that thou hast a name that thou livest, and art dead. Be watchful, and strengthen the things which remain, that are ready to die. ... repent*** (Rev. 3:1-3).

A few ... in Sardis ... have not defiled their garments; and they shall walk with Me in white: for they are worthy. <u>***He that overcometh ... I will not blot out his name out of the Book of Life***</u> (3:4-5). During the earthly ministry of our Lord, He said: ***If ye keep My Commandments, ye shall abide in My love*** (John 15:10; see 15:6).

Jesus commended the church in Philadelphia for their faithfulness, saying: ***Behold, I have set before thee an open door, and no man can shut it: for thou ... hast kept My Word. ... I also will keep thee from the hour of temptation, which shall come upon all the world*** (Rev. 3:8,10).

The church in Laodicea considered themselves a broad-minded church. They boasted of being rich and in need of nothing. The Lord told them that they were wretched, poor, blind, and naked. He strongly condemned their condition: ***So then because thou art lukewarm, and neither cold nor hot, I will spue*** (vomit) ***thee out of My mouth*** (3:16). Still, He appealed to them: ***Be zealous*** (diligent) ***therefore, and repent*** (3:19).

Jesus still knocks with words of encouragement: ***I stand at the door, and knock: if any man hear My voice, and open the door, I will come in to him, and will sup with him, and he with Me.*** Nothing can compare to the blessed fellowship we enjoy as we daily continue to read through His Word. ***To him that overcometh will I grant to sit with Me in My throne, even as I also overcame, and am set down with My Father in His throne*** (Rev. 3:20-21).

Thought for Today: No one on earth can steal your treasures in heaven.

Cross References: For **Rev. 3:5:** See Ex. 32:32. **Rev. 3:12:** See Is. 62:2. **Rev. 4:2-3:** See Ezek. 1:28. **Rev. 4:5:** See Zech. 4:2. **Rev. 4:6:** See Ezek. 1:22. **Rev. 4:7:** See Ezek. 1:10. **Rev. 4:8:** See Is. 6:2-3.

DECEMBER 25   Read Revelation 6 – 8

Highlights: A study of the first six seals (Rev. 6). The people of God preserved (chap. 7). Silence, as the 7th seal breaks (8:1-3)! Sweet smell (satisfaction) of prayer (8:4-5). The 1st four trumpets blow (8:6-12). If this is dreadful, read what's coming (8:13)!

The exile of John on Patmos and the suffering that took place in Smyrna (Rev. 2:8-10) are examples of the persecution that was intensifying against Christians throughout the Roman Empire. As it was then, so it is in much of the world today. The persecuted stand before the Lamb. *After this I beheld, and, lo, a great multitude, which no man could number, of all nations, and kindreds, and people, and tongues, stood before the throne, and before the Lamb* (Jesus Christ), *clothed with white robes, and palms in their hands; And cried with a loud voice, saying, Salvation to our God which sitteth upon the throne, and unto the Lamb* (7:9-10).

In heaven, multitudes of victorious overcomers stand in the presence of their Lord and Savior Jesus Christ. Throughout the centuries, this revelation has strengthened the faith of many Christians who have faced fierce opposition from a hostile world. In every generation, there are some who follow the Lord with their whole heart. The Lord tells us: *Narrow is the way which leadeth unto life, and few there be that find it* (Matt. 7:14). However, a minority of the world's population in many successive generations adds up. There will be *a great multitude, which no man could number.... which are arrayed in white robes.... He said to me, These are they which came out of great tribulation, and have washed their robes ... in the blood of the Lamb* (Rev. 7:9-14). These are the faithful who have followed Him through trials and sufferings and who see beyond sufferings to being in the presence of the King of kings and Lord of lords for all eternity.

Faithful Christians may not have much of earth's pleasures, but earthly life is exceedingly short compared to eternity. The trials we face now will seem insignificant compared to the glorious privilege of being in the presence of the Lord.

For the Lamb ... shall feed them, and shall lead them unto living fountains of waters: and God shall wipe away all tears from their eyes (7:17). *Thanks be to God, which giveth us the victory through our Lord Jesus Christ* (I Cor. 15:57).

Thought for Today: Every day "Praise the Lord" for who He is and what He has done for you!

Cross References: For **Rev. 6:12:** See Joel 2:31. **Rev. 6:13:** See Is. 34:4. **Rev. 6:17:** See Joel 2:11. **Rev. 7:3:** See Ezek. 9:4. **Rev. 7:17:** See Ezek. 34:23.

DECEMBER 26   Read Revelation 9 – 11

Highlights: The 5th trumpet is sounded, bringing five months of torment, as of a stinging scorpion. ***Men seek death . . . and death shall flee from them*** (Rev. 9:6). The 6th trumpet sounds and the third part of men on the earth are killed, ***yet*** those who remained ***repented not*** (9:20). ***The Holy City*** is trampled ***under foot forty and two months*** (11:2). The 7th trumpet sounds, ***and there were great voices in heaven, saying, The kingdoms of this world are become the kingdoms of our Lord, and of His Christ; and He shall reign for ever and ever*** (11:15).

A voice from heaven directed the Apostle John: ***Go and take the little book which is open in the hand of the angel which standeth upon the sea and upon the earth. And I went unto the angel, and said unto him, Give me the little Book. And he said unto me, Take it, and eat it up; and it shall make thy belly bitter, but it shall be in thy mouth sweet as honey. And I took the little Book out of the angel's hand, and ate it up; and it was in my mouth sweet as honey: and as soon as I had eaten it, my belly was bitter. And he said unto me, Thou must prophesy again before many peoples, and nations*** (Rev. 10:8-11).

John was first given a ***little Book,*** symbolic of the Word of God. Once it was digested, he was qualified to tell the world that the ***little Book*** has a message that is sweet to those who receive Christ as Savior. As we "eat" His Word, the Scriptures give us understanding for our daily lives. We can live by ***every word that proceedeth out of the mouth of God*** (Matt: 4:4).

Jesus said: ***I will give power unto My two witnesses*** (thought by some to be Moses and Elijah), ***and they shall prophesy a thousand two hundred and threescore*** (1260) ***days*** (Rev. 11:3). They will face fierce opposition. ***And when they shall have finished their testimony, the beast that ascendeth out of the bottomless pit shall make war against them . . . and kill them*** (11:7). These ***two witnesses*** cannot be martyred until they ***have finished their testimony.*** Then, and only then, the enemies of God ***shall . . . kill them.***

No matter how fearful our future, the Lord gives us His peace, as we trust His sovereign control. ***We give Thee thanks, O Lord God Almighty, which art, and wast, and art to come; because Thou hast taken to Thee Thy great power, and hast reigned*** (Rev. 11:17).

Thought for Today: Praise the Lord! Our work for the Lord cannot end until He allows it.

Cross References: For **Rev. 9:2:** See Joel 2:10. **Rev. 9:4:** See Ex. 12:2. **Rev. 9:6:** See Joel 2:4. **Rev. 9:7:** See Joel 1:6. **Rev. 10:6:** See Neh. 9:6. **Rev. 11:4:** See Zech. 4:12,14. **Rev. 11:11:** See Ezek. 37:5.

DECEMBER 27 Read Revelation 12 – 13

Highlights: *A great wonder in heaven* (Rev. 12:1-6). War in heaven – Michael defeats the dragon (12:7-8) known as Satan, the Devil (12:9). Weapons used against Satan (12:11). Beast of the sea and earth, number of man, satanically dominated world system, ruled by force, greed and evil pleasure (13:1-18; see 15:2).

There appeared a great wonder in heaven; a woman clothed with the sun, and the moon under her feet, and upon her head a crown of twelve stars: And she being with child cried, travailing in birth, and pained to be delivered. And there appeared another wonder in heaven; and behold a great red dragon, having seven heads and ten horns. . . . stood before the woman which was ready to be delivered, for to devour her Child as soon as It (He) *was born. And she brought forth a Man Child, who was to rule all nations . . . and her Child was caught up unto God* (Rev. 12:1-5). This refers to the birth and ascension of Christ.

The trial of the faithful people of God occurs in *the wilderness* (12:6) to illustrate the desert-like moral condition of this world ruled by the *great red dragon* (Satan) (12:3). In this desert there is a precious peace that comes by leaving the results in the hands of our Creator.

The great dragon . . . that old serpent, called the Devil, and Satan, which deceiveth the whole world (12:9), is always in opposition to the faithful people of God. There are four descriptive names given to Satan: *dragon* portrays his monstrous character as the enemy of God and His servants; *serpent* points out his deceptive character demonstrated in the Garden of Eden; *Devil* depicts him as a slanderer and a liar; and *Satan* means adversary. *Your adversary the Devil . . . walketh about, seeking whom he may devour* (I Pet. 5:8). But praise God *we are more than conquerors through Him that* (who) *loved us* (Rom. 8:37)! Even in difficult situations, Christians have peace because it comes from within (John 14:27). *He hath said, I will never leave thee, nor forsake thee* (Heb. 13:5-8). We know that all Christians are kept by His love and blessed beyond words to express, "His abiding presence is with me."

It can be said that Christians in every generation *overcame him* (Satan) *by the blood of the Lamb, and by the word of their testimony* (His Word that has become our way of life)*; and they loved not their lives unto the death* (Rev. 12:11).

Thought for Today: Satan thrives on the biblical ignorance of saints.

Cross References: For **Rev. 12:5:** See Is. 66:7. **Rev. 12:14:** See Ex. 19:4. **Rev. 13:1:** See Dan. 7:8,24. **Rev. 13:5:** See Dan. 7:8.

DECEMBER 28   Read Revelation 14 – 16

Highlights: The people of God sing a new song at the throne (Rev. 14:1-5; Ps. 96:1; 98:1; 149:1; Is. 42:10). A special offering of **firstfruits unto God and to the Lamb** (Rev. 14:4). What to preach and to whom (14:6-7). **The wrath of God** (14:9-20; 15:1,5-8; 16:1-21). Victory over evil (15:2-4). Be ready (16:15).

As a prisoner on Patmos, John is led to report good news. The *narrow ... way* (Matt. 7:14) is victorious beyond compare. The Christian discovers the fulness of the love of God who provided an escape from this sin-cursed, Satan-controlled world to the higher spirit world before the throne. John proclaims: **I looked, and, lo, a Lamb stood on the Mount Sion, and with Him an hundred forty and four thousand, having His Father's Name written in their foreheads. And I heard a voice from heaven ... as the voice of a great thunder: and I heard the voice of harpers ... And they sung as it were a new song before the throne, and before the four beasts** (living creatures), **and the elders: and no man could learn that song but the hundred and forty and four thousand, which were redeemed from the earth. These are they which were not defiled with women; for they are virgins. These are they which follow the Lamb whithersoever He goeth. These were redeemed ... being the firstfruits unto God and to the Lamb** (Rev. 14:1-4). **The Lamb** is the exalted Christ who will stand on Mount Zion with His redeemed sheep, whom Satan could not hold.

    Here is the patience of the saints (Christians) **... that keep the Commandments of God, and the faith of Jesus. And I heard a voice from heaven saying unto me, Write, Blessed are the dead which die in the Lord from henceforth. ... that they may rest from their labours; and their works do follow them** (14:12-13).

    The dead which die in the Lord can only mean those for whom Jesus prayed: **They have kept Thy Word. ... They are not of the world, even as I am not of the world** (John 17:6,16).

    The visions in Revelation reveal that God is not indifferent to suffering endured by the faithful. Judgment of the unbelieving is inevitable. The heavenly choir sings praise to God for His faithfulness. They praise God because Truth has won the battle over the deception of the Devil. **Alleluia; Salvation, and glory, and honour, and power, unto the Lord our God** (Rev. 19:1).

Thought for Today: The loving care of God for us is unlimited (Rom. 8:38-39).

Cross References: For **Rev. 14:7:** See Ps. 146:6. **Rev. 14:8:** See Is. 21:9. **Rev. 14:10:** See Jer. 25:15; 51:7. **Rev. 14:20:** See Joel 3:13. **Rev. 15:1:** See Lev. 26:21. **Rev. 15:4:** See Ps. 86:9; Is. 66:23; Jer. 10:7. **Rev. 15:8:** See I Kin. 8:10-11.

DECEMBER 29 — Read Revelation 17 – 18

Highlights: Prophecy of the judgment of **MYSTERY BABYLON**, who deceives multitudes and martyrs Christians who are united with the Lamb (Rev. chap. 17). Her horrifying fall (chap. 18).

The Apostle John reported that *he carried me away in the Spirit into the wilderness: and I saw a woman sit upon a scarlet coloured beast, full of names of blasphemy, having seven heads and ten horns. . . . having a golden cup in her hand full of abominations* (detestable sins, deception) *and filthiness of her fornication* (time devoted to wickedness and dishonoring God): *And upon her forehead was a name written: MYSTERY, BABYLON THE GREAT, THE MOTHER OF HARLOTS AND ABOMINATIONS OF THE EARTH* (Rev. 17:3-5). Babylon was the most magnificent capital city of that time. Its king, Nebuchadnezzar, controlled the world. He destroyed the kingdom of Judah, the Temple of God, and Jerusalem.

BABYLON THE GREAT, THE MOTHER (numerous things keep her followers occupied with activities that could have served to fulfill the will of God) *OF HARLOTS* illustrates God-defying forces in politics and religion that will soon control the world. The apostate federation of churches and world religions will give full support to the one-world political and economic system, the *scarlet coloured beast,* which will be ruled by the Antichrist.

THE MOTHER OF HARLOTS and the *beast* represent the close alliance that exists between the world government, called the beast, and Babylon, who pretends to be the true Church.

Eventually, they will fiercely oppose Jesus Christ as the only Way to obtain eternal life. The false superchurch will be based on social issues, humanitarian objectives, and lifeless formalism, and will demand the "equality of all religions" for all people (II Tim. 4:3-5; Gal. 1:8).

As we consider these prophecies, we need to set our hearts and minds on things above, knowing that the Lord will sustain all who trust Him. *By so much was Jesus made a surety of a better Testament. . . . He is able also to save them to the uttermost that come unto God by Him* (Heb. 7:22,25).

The forces of the world *shall make war with the Lamb, and the Lamb shall overcome them: for He is Lord of lords, and King of kings: and they that are with Him are called, and chosen, and faithful* (Rev. 17:14).

Thought for Today: Jesus of Nazareth, the King of Peace will soon return.

Cross References: For **Rev. 17:34:** See Jer. 51:7. **Rev. 17:12:** See Dan. 7:20-24. **Rev. 17:14:** See Dan. 2:47. **Rev. 18:2:** See Jer. 50:39; Is. 21:9. **Rev. 18:5:** See Jer. 51:9. **Rev. 18:7-8:** See Is. 47:7-8; Zeph. 2:15. **Rev. 18:22:** See Ezek. 26:13. **Rev. 18:24:** See Jer. 51:49.

DECEMBER 30 — Read Revelation 19 – 20

Highlights: The roar of the crowd; four great hallelujahs (Rev. 19:1-6). The Lamb and His bride (19:7-9). The Second Coming; the Word of God (19:11-16). Armageddon; doom of the beast; and false prophet (19:17-21). The thousand-year sentence (20:1-3). Martyrs resurrected (20:4-6). Satan defeated (20:7-10). The Book of Life and the final Judgment (20:11-15).

Think how joyous it will be for those who repent and accept Jesus Christ as Savior and Lord of their lives, to see again their loved ones and all the saints of the ages: Abraham, Jacob, Joseph, David, Paul, and others! *And I heard as it were the voice of a great multitude... and as the voice of mighty thunderings, saying, Alleluia: for the Lord God Omnipotent reigneth. Let us be glad and rejoice, and give honour to Him: for the marriage of the Lamb is come, and His wife hath made herself ready* (Rev. 19:6-7).

Another scene takes place: *And behold a white horse; and He that sat upon him was called Faithful and True* (Jesus Christ), *and in righteousness He doth judge and make war* (Rev. 19:11). *And I saw the beast* (the Antichrist), *and the kings of the earth, and their armies, gathered together to make war against Him ... and ... His army. And the beast was taken, and with him the false prophet that wrought miracles before him, with which he deceived them that had received the mark of the beast ... both were cast alive into a lake of fire burning with brimstone* (19:19-20).

I saw a great white throne, and Him that sat on it, from whose face the earth and the heaven fled away; and there was found no place for them. And I saw the dead, small and great, stand before God; and the books were opened ... and the dead were judged out of those things which were written ... And the sea ... and death and hell delivered up the dead which were in them: and they were judged every man according to their works. And death and hell were cast into the lake of fire. This is the second death (20:11-14). This is the final destination of Satan and all who reject Jesus Christ as Savior and Lord.

We are given a choice. Repentance is a redemptive experience which leads to forgiveness. *But as many as received Him, to them gave He power to become the sons of God, even to them that believe on His Name* (John 1:12).

Thought for Today: Satan distorts the facts, but the Word of God reveals the Truth.

Cross References: For **Rev. 19:2:** See Ps. 19:9; Deut. 32:43; II Kin. 9:7. **Rev. 19:5:** See Ps. 115:13. **Rev. 19:11:** See Ps. 96:13. **Rev. 19:16:** See Deut. 10:17. **Rev. 19:18:** See Ezek. 39:4. **Rev. 20:2:** See Is. 24:22. **Rev. 20:8:** See Ezek. 38:2,15. **Rev. 20:12:** See Dan. 7:10.

DECEMBER 31   Read Revelation 21 – 22

Highlights: *A new heaven and a new earth. . . . all things new* (Rev. 21:1-5). End of pain, sorrow, and death (21:4; 22:3). Do you know *The Lamb*? We will *see His face* (22:4). The Lamb and God are the Temple and the Light (21:22-23,25). Who can enter (21:27; 22:14)? The River of Life, the Tree of Life (22:1-2,14). Jesus is coming soon (22:20)!

Two thousand years ago *God so loved the world, that He gave His only begotten Son, that whosoever believeth in Him should not perish, but have everlasting life* (John 3:16). "To believe in Him" is much more than mentally believing the historical fact that Jesus died on the cross to save sinners. It means that I trust my eternal destiny to Him as Savior and Lord of my life. Jesus said: *He that hath My Commandments, and keepeth them, he it is that loveth Me: and he that loveth Me shall be loved of My Father, and I will love him, and will manifest Myself to him* (John 14:21).

There shall in no wise enter into it (the Holy City, new Jerusalem) *any thing that defileth . . .* (or) *worketh abomination* (detestable sins), *or maketh a lie: but they which are written in the Lamb's Book of Life* (Rev. 21:27) will be there.

The greatest story ever told is the story of our salvation! On the cross Jesus Christ died for you: *The Lord hath laid on Him the iniquity of us all* (Is. 53:6). God transferred your sins to Christ but that wonderful transfer takes place only when we ask for and receive it by faith (Eph. 2:8).

We have hope about what lies beyond the grave. All true followers of Christ will one day dwell in *a new heaven and a new earth* in the very presence of our glorious Lord. The Apostle John *saw the holy city, new Jerusalem, coming down from God out of heaven, prepared as a bride adorned for her husband. And . . . heard a great voice out of heaven saying, Behold, the Tabernacle of God is with men, and He will dwell with them, and they shall be His people* (Rev. 21:1-3).

Oh! the joy that awaits us. Our wonderful Lord will soon welcome us home. Praise the Lord! We close this glorious revelation of Jesus Christ, having completed the reading of the entire Bible: *And the Spirit and the bride say, Come. . . . And let him that is athirst come. And . . . let him take the water of life freely* (Rev. 22:17).

Thought for Today: Death promotes Christians into everlasting life.

Cross References: For **Rev. 21:35:** See Is. 25:8. **Rev. 21:23:** See Is. 29:33. **Rev. 21:25:** See Is. 60:11. **Rev. 21:27:** See Is. 52:1. **Rev. 22:2:** See Ezek. 47:12; Gen. 2:9. **Rev. 22:3:** See Zech. 14:11. **Rev. 22:12:** See Is. 40:10. **Rev. 22:13:** See Is. 44:6; 48:12. **Rev. 22:16:** See Is. 11:1. **Rev. 22:18:** See Deut. 12:32.

Dictionary of Archaic Words

abated - diminished; reduced
Abba - Father, an Aramaic Term
abhor - disregard, reject (Lev. 26:15); loathe, hate (Job 42:6; Is. 7:16)
abjects - slanderers (Ps. 35:15)
abominable/abominaton - defiled, unclean, detestable to God
abusers of themselves - sodomites
according to his months - every month
according to the manner - as prescribed by Law (Lev. 5:10)
accounted of - considered of value
accursed - devoted, set apart, as holy unto the Lord (Josh. 6:17-18)
activity - competence, skill (Gen. 47:6)
Adar - compares with Feb/Mar
addicted - devoted (1 Cor. 16:15)
adjure - solemnly put under oath
advertise - to inform (Ruth 4:4)
afflict your souls - humble yourselves, practice self-denial (Lev. 16:29)
affinity - an alliance (I Kin. 3:1)
after - according to (Gen. 10:20); committed to (II Sam. 15:13)
against - waiting to meet (Gen. 43:25; Ex. 7:15; Num. 10:21); opposite (Num. 8:2-3); before (II Kin. 16:11)
Aha, aha - an expression of scorn
Alpha and Omega - the first and last letters of the Greek alphabet. Christ is saying he is everything A to Z
ambassage - delegation; representatives
Amen - So be it; It is true
amerce - to punish with a fine (Deut. 22:19)
Anathema - accursed (1 Cor. 16:22)
ancients - elders (Is. 24:23; Ezek. 7:26)
angle - hooks (Is. 19:8)
Anointed - Messiah (Hebrew) and Christ (Greek) (Ps. 2:2)
anon - immediately (Matt. 13:20; Mar. 1:30)
answerable - corresponding (Ex. 38:18)
answereth - corresponds (Gal. 4:25)
Apollyn - Destroyer (Rev. 9:11)
apothecary - perfumer (Ex. 30:25)
apparently - clearly (Num. 12:8)
appertaineth - belongs (Lev. 6:5)
appoint - name (Gen. 30:28); comfort (Is. 61:3)
Areopagus - name of the Athenian court or council which met on Mars Hill
Ariel - the lion city of Jerusalem (Is. 29:1)
arm - family (I Sam. 2:31)

artificer - craftsman (Gen. 4:22)
artillery - small armor; weapons
asp - cobra (Is. 11:8)
assay - endeavor, attempt, venture (Deut. 4:34; Job 4:2; Acts 16:7; Heb. 11:29); be reluctant (I Sam. 17:39)
assuaged - subsided (Gen. 8:1)
asunder - in two halves; apart
atonement - blood sacrifice that becomes covering for sin, resulting in reconciliation with God (Lev. 4:20); reconciliation (Rom. 5:11)
augment - increase (Num. 32:14)
austere - stern, harsh, exacting
avenger of blood - the nearest relative of the person slain who should avenge his death by destroying the slayer
averse - returning (Mic. 2:8)
avouched - openly declared (Deut. 26:17)
Baale of Judah - refers to the town of Kirjath-jearim (II Sam. 6:2)
Baali - my lord and master (Hos. 2:16)
Baalim - idols of Baal (Judg. 3:7)
babbling - complaints (Prov. 23:29)
bade/badest - ordered/told
baldness - shaving their head as a sign of sorrow (Deut. 14:1)
band - a woven binding to keep it from tearing (Ex. 39:23); one of the ten divisions of the Ancient Roman Legion (Acts 10:1)
bands - painful diseases (Ps. 73:4); ensnared by deceit (Eccl. 7:26); punishment (Is. 28:22); unity (Zech. 11:7); ligaments (Col. 2:19; I Thes. 2:19)
bar - carrying frame (Num. 4:10)
barbarian/barbarous - foreigner/foreign
bare record - related what had happened
barked - broken, splintered (Joel 1:7)
bases - original foundation (Ezra 3:3)
battlement/s - guard railing/branches
be at charges with - pay the expenses of
beat off - handpick His "harvest" (Is. 27:12)
beauty - grace, good will (Zech. 11:7)
Beelzebub - the fly god idol of the Philistines meaning dung god or filth god, since the fly finds its food in refuse
Beer-sheba - well of oath (Gen. 26:33)
beeves - bullocks (Lev. 22:19)
begat - fathered
beguile - deceive, seduce
Belial, children/sons/daughter of - apostate evildoers (Deut. 13:13); sodomites

(Judg. 19:22); sinful woman (I Sam. 1:16)
belly - mind (Job 32:19)
beside ourselves - insane (II Cor. 5:13)
besom - broom (Is. 14:23)
besought - asked (John 19:31)
bestowed - stationed (I Kin. 10:26)
Bethel - House of God
bethink - think it over/learn a lesson
betimes - early in the morning (Gen. 26:31); diligently (Prov. 13:24)
betwixt - between (Gen. 30:36)
Beulah - married (Is. 62:4)
bewail - mourn (Deut. 21:13)
bewray - betray (Is. 16:3)
bier - coffin or stand for carrying a corpse
bishop - spiritual overseer (I Tim. 3:31)
blast - spirit of bad fortune (II Kin. 19:7)
blasting - blight; mildew (Hag. 2:17)
blaze - to make known (Mark 1:45)
blemish - defect; permanent injury
blindness of their hearts - closed minds
blood of Jerusalem - sins of Jerusalem of killing innocent prophets including Jesus Christ (Is. 4:4)
Bochim - weeping (Judg. 2:5)
bolled - in the bud (Ex. 9:31)
bolster - pillow; headplace (I Sam. 26:7)
bondman/bondservant - slave
bonnets - headpieces; turbans
booths - temporary shelters (Neh. 8:14)
borders - ornaments (Song. 1:11)
borrow - ask (Ex. 11:2)
bosses - thick layers (Job 15:26)
botch - boils or sores (Deut. 28:27)
bottles - made of animal skins (Josh. 9:4)
bound in the bundle of life - protected in the cave of the living (I Sam. 25:29)
bowed - swayed (II Sam. 19:14)
bowels - your own body (Gen. 15:4); body (Gen. 25:23); heart (Gen. 43:30; Song. 5:4); whole being (Is. 16:11); emotions (Jer. 4:19); affections (II Cor. 6:12); affection (Phil. 1:8)
bowels boiled - heart is troubled (Job 30:27)
bravery - beauty (Is. 3:18)
brawling - contentious (Prov. 21:9)
bray - beat (Prov. 27:22)
breaches - damaged places; gaps; breaks in the city wall (Amos 4:3)
bread - food (I Kin. 21:5)
Breaker - Messiah (Mic. 2:13)
breaking in - flood (Job 30:14)
breaking up - breaking in (Ex. 22:2)
breath - spirit (Job 17:1)

brigandine(s) - armor (Jer. 46:4; 51:3)
bright - sharp (Jer. 51:11)
brother - one of their own people (Deut. 22:1); uncle (II Chr. 36:10)
bruise - greatly injure or wound, literally break in pieces (Gen. 3:15)
bruit - report; rumor (Jer. 10:22; Nah. 3:19)
brutish - stupid (Prov. 12:1); cruel (Ezek. 21:31)
buckler - defender (II Sam. 22:31); shield (Prov. 2:7; Song. 4:4)
buffet - discipline; hit with the fist
builded against - besieged (Lam. 3:5)
Bul - compares with Oct/Nov
bunches - humps (Is. 30:6)
burden - mournful oracle or prophecy
burning - brand as a slave (Is. 3:24); public fire to honor (II Chr. 21:19; Jer. 34:5)
busybody - meddler, prying into
by and by - before long or soon
by their polls - each one individually
Cabul - unproductive wasteland
calves - calf idols (Hos. 10:5)
camphire - flowers (Song. 1:14)
candlestick - oil lamp; lampstand
cankered - corroded (James 5:3)
captivity - fortune (Job 42:10); captives (Hos. 6:11)
careful - concerned; anxious
carefulness - fearfulness and anxiety (Ezek. 12:18); diligence, seriousness (II Cor. 7:11)
carelessly - securely (Is. 47:8; Ezek. 39:6)
carriage(s) - baggage
cast - placed (Gen. 21:15)
cast a cord make boundaries (Mic. 2:5)
cast about - deserted (Jer. 41:14)
cast clouts - worn-out clothes (Jer. 38:12)
cast up - highway to life (Jer. 18:15)
casteth not - does not miscarry (Job 21:10)
castles - settlements or camps (Gen. 25:16); fortresses, strongholds (II Chr. 17:12)
caul - appendage on the liver (Ex. 29:22); lobe of fat (Lev. 3:4)
cauls, and their round tires - hairdos
celestial - heavenly (I Cor. 15:40)
certify - inform II Sam. 15:28; Ezra 5:10)
chafed - angered (II Sam. 17:8)
Chaldean - Babylonian
chambering - immorality (Rom. 13:13)
chamberlain/s - treasurer/officials
chambers - storerooms (Ezra 8:29); constellations (Job 9:9); dwelling place (Ps. 104:13)
champaign - flat open country
changed - scorched (Dan. 3:27)

chapiter - upper part, a cap which goes on top of a column (Jer. 52:22)
chapmen - merchant traders (II Chr. 9:14)
chapt - dried up, parched (Jer. 14:4)
charge - admonish (Ex. 19:21); to fix responsibility, to commission (Deut. 3:28); responsibility (1 Kin. 4:28)
chargeable - burdensome II Sam. 13:25)
charged - commanded (Gen. 28:1)
charger - large dish, platter, or tray
charity - love (I Cor. 13:1; Rev. 2:19)
chasten - humble (Dan. 10:12)
Chemarims - the priests in charge
cherish - attend, be of service as his nurse
chide/chode- find fault; quarrel/argued
chief - foremost men (II Sam. 23:13); masters (Lam. 1:5)
children - young men (Dan. 1:4)
Chinneroth - also called Sea of Galilee
choler - furious anger/rage
churl/ish - cruel crafty men/rough, uncouth
circumspect - careful, cautious
clave - split (Gen. 22:3; Num. 16:31; I Sam. 6:14; Ps. 78:15); was passionately attracted to (Gen. 34:3)
clean - ceremonially undefiled (Lev. 15; Num. 19:11); entirely (Isa. 24:19; Zech. 11:17)
cleave - be joined (Gen. 2:24); cut (Lev. 1:17); remain faithful (Josh. 23:8)
clift - hollow opening (Ex. 33:22)
cloke - covering (John 15:22)
close - aloof, concealed (I Chr. 12:1)
close places - fortresses or strongholds
clouted - patched (Josh. 9:5)
cloven - divided (Acts 2:3)
coast - territory border; surrounding region
cockatrice - viper (Is. 11:8)
cockle - weeds (Job 31:40)
cogitations - thoughts (Dan. 7:28)
collops of fat - figuratively speaking, bulging in prosperity (Job 15:27)
color - pretense (Acts 27:30)
come at - go near (Num. 6:6; Ezek. 44:25)
come without - go outside (Num. 35:26)
comely - lovely (Song. 2:14); proper (I Cor. 11:13)
comfortably - encouragingly (II Chr. 30:22); kindly and tenderly (Is. 40:2)
common - unholy (Acts 10:14)
commune - speak; discuss
communicate - meet the financial needs
communicate with - express your concern
compacted - true unity (Eph. 4:16)

companies - collection of idols (Is. 57:13)
compass - ledge (Ex. 27:5); go around (Num. 21:4); surround (II Sam. 22:6; II Kin. 11:8; Ps. 116:3; Rev. 20:9)
compassion - lovingkindness (Rom. 9:15)
concision - false circumcision (Phil. 3:2)
concubine - a servant/secondary wife
concupiscence - evil desires of lust
condemned - taxed; fined (II Chr. 36:3)
confounded - put to shame; disgraced
confusion - perversion (Lev. 18:23); dishonor, humiliation, shame (I Sam. 20:30; Is. 30:3; Dan. 9:7; Ezra 9:7)
consecration - ordination (Lev. 8:33)
constrain - try to compel (Gal. 6:12)
consulted shame - brought dishonor
consumption - destruction (Is. 10:22)
contemn - defy; despise (Ps. 10:13)
conversant - associated (I Sam. 25:15)
conversation - conduct (Ps. 50:23; Gal. 1:13; Eph. 4:22); citizenship (Phil. 3:20)
convey me - allow me to pass (Neh. 2:7)
convocation - holy/sacred assembly
coping - the top, the highest, coarse of stone on which the timber is laid
corn - grain
cornfloor - threshing floor (Hos. 9:1)
couchingplace - resting place (Ezek. 25:5)
council - Sanhedrin, the prosecuting body for both civil and religious crimes (John 11:47)
counsel - purpose, plan (Heb. 6:17)
countenance - be partial to (Ex. 23:3); face (Neh. 2:2)
countervail - justify, compensate
course - the assigned divisions of priests (Ezra 3:11); in turn (I Cor. 14:27)
cover his border - establish his territory
cover his feet - take a nap (I Sam. 24:3)
cover the ark - install the veil as a partition
cover with a covering - make an alliance
covering of the eyes - compensation
covert - protecting power (Ps. 61:4); shelter (Is. 32:2); hiding place (Jer. 25:38)
cracknels - cakes (I Kin. 14:3)
crisping pins - money bags (Is. 3:22)
crowned - officials, princes (Nah. 3:17)
cubit - about 18 inches
cumbrance - burden of complaints (Deut. 1:12)
cunning - skillful; skilled; skill
cunning women - women skilled at weeping and mourning (Jer. 9:17)
curious - artistic; skillfully made
current money - legal note (Gen. 23:16)

curtains - tent; Tabernacle (I Chr. 17:1)
cut down - silenced (Jer. 48:2)
cut off - excommunicated (Lev. 17:4); destroyed; put to death
dam - mother
daughter - people (Jer. 46:11)
daughters - cities and villages (Ps. 48:11; Jer. 49:2)
day - fate (Job 18:20)
day of the Lord - the time of judgment upon the ungodly as well as the time of rejoicing for the faithful (Is. 2:12)
days are determined - allotted time to live is set (Job 14:5)
dayspring - dawn (Job 38:12)
dead dog - worthless person (II Sam. 9:8)
dealt - distributed (II Sam. 6:19)
dealt hardly - treated harshly (Gen. 16:6)
dearth - famine; drought
debate - contention; quarreling (Is. 58:4)
decayed - giving way (Neh. 4:10)
deceitfully - negligently; halfheartedly (Jer. 48:10)
decline after many - yield to the evil majority (Ex. 23:2)
decree - boundary (Prov. 8:29)
defiled - raped and dishonored (Gen. 34:2)
defraud - deprive (I Cor. 7:5)
degree - reputation (I Tim. 3:13)
delectable - cherished (Is. 44:9)
delicately - trembling with fear (I Sam. 15:32)
deputed - appointed judge (II Sam. 15:3)
derision - ridicule; laughingstock
describe - map out, survey (Josh. 18:6)
descry - spy out, keep a watch (Judg. 1:23)
desire of all nations - Christ, the Messiah
desolate - suffering for their guilt
device - scheme, plan, purpose, plot
devils - idols, demons (II Chr. 11:15)
diadem - turban or headdress (Job 29:14)
diet - regular allowance (Jer. 52:34)
dirt - dung (Judg. 3:22)
disallowed - rejected (I Pet. 2:4)
discomfited - defeated, caused to panic
discover - uncover
discover his father's skirt - commit adultery with his father's wife
discover itself - express itself (Prov. 18:2)
discover not a secret to another - do not betray another man's confidence
discover the face of his garment - strip off his outer garment (Job 41:13)
discreet - shrewd and discerning

disorderly - irresponsibly; undisciplined
dispensation - Divine Order (Eph. 1:10); special ministry (Eph. 3:2)
disposing - decision (Prov. 16:33)
dispossessed - drove out (Num. 32:39)
dissemble - act deceitfully (Josh. 7:11)
dissimulation - hypocrisy; insincerity
distress not - do not create a problem
ditch - reservoir (Is. 22:11)
divers - a double standard (Prov. 20:10); various (Heb. 13:9)
divide their tongues - bring confusion
divided by lot - assignment by drawing lots to determine the will of God (Prov. 16:33)
divination - wonder-working words of their own minds (Jer. 14:14)
divine - could discover by divination who stole it (Gen. 44:15); practice (Ezek. 13:23)
diviners - fortune-tellers (I Sam. 6:2)
doctors - scholars, the Rabbis (Luke 2:46)
doubtful disputations - passing judgment on his opinions (Rom. 14:1)
dragon - serpent or crocodile (Ps. 91:13); large sea animal (Ps. 148:7); jackal or wolf (Job 30:29; Is. 43:20)
draught - sewer (Matt. 15:17); catch (Luke 5:9)
dreadful - awesome; holy (Rom. 14:1)
dress - tend or cultivate (Gen. 2:15); prepare (Gen. 18:7)
dried away - dissatisfied and discouraged
drop thy word toward - preach against
dropping - irritation (Prov. 19:13)
drought - heat (Gen. 31:40)
drove - herd (Gen. 32:16)
dukes - chiefs (Gen. 36:15)
dung it - fertilized it (Luke 13:8)
dureth - continues (Matt. 13:21)
durst - dares to; dared
dust - descendants (Num. 23:10)
dwell deep - hide in deeply concealed places (Jer. 49:8)
ear - plow (I Sam. 8:12; Is. 30:24)
early - diligently; earnestly (Prov. 1:28)
earnest - pledge guarantee (Eph. 1:14)
ears ... opened - open to obedience
ears shall tingle - will be astonished with horror (II Kin. 21:12)
earth divided - people became separated (Gen. 10:25)
earth upon his head - a sign of grief or mourning (I Sam. 4:12)
Easter - a mistranslation of Passover
effect - fulfillment (Ezek. 12:23)

effectual - in its inworking, bringing the praying person to recognize the will of God (James 5:16)
effeminate - homosexual perversion
El-beth-el - the God of Bethel (Gen. 35:7)
emerods - tumors (Deut. 28:27; I Sam. 5:6)
eminent place - mound or high place for pagan shrine (Ezek. 16:31)
employed about - opposed to (Ezra 10:15)
emulation - jealousy (Rom. 11:14)
enchantment - fortune-telling or practice of witchcraft (Lev. 19:26)
engines of war - battering rams
enjoin - give orders; appoint (Job 36:23)
enlarged - filled with love (II Cor. 6:11)
enquire at her mouth - ask her personally
enquired early - sought diligently
ensign - tribal banner; signal to rally, flag
ensue - pursue, go after (I Pet. 3:11)
entreat - treat (Acts 7:6; I Thes. 2:2)
ephod - priestly garment (Ex. 39:2); shield or breastplate (Judg. 8:27)
Ephraim - Northern Kingdom (Jer. 7:15)
Ephratah - district in which Bethlehem was located
epistle - letter, message (Col. 4:16)
equal - compare (Lam. 2:13); fair (Ezek. 18:25)
equity - skill (Eccl. 2:21)
eschew - to shun, turn from (I Pet. 3:11)
Esh-baal - another name for Ish-bosheth
espied - saw (Gen. 42:27); searched out, selected (Ezek. 20:6)
espoused - betrothed or engaged
espy - watch (Jer. 48:19)
estate - council (Acts 22:5)
Ethiopian - Cushite (II Chr. 14:9)
even - twilight (Ex. 29:39)
evenings - desert wasteland (Jer. 5:6)
evidence - deed (Jer. 32:10)
evil - bad (Jer. 29:17); sinful (Matt. 6:23); wrong (John 18:23); **the evil** - Satan (John 17:15)
evil communications corrupt good manners - evil companions or associations ruin or defile good character (I Cor. 15:33)
evil entreateth - cruelly took advantage of
evil travail - misfortunes (Eccl. 5:14)
evilfavouredness - serious defect
exacted - assessed, taxed (II Kin. 15:20)
exacteth - demands (Job 11:6)
excellency - advantage (Eccl. 7:12); pride (Amos 6:8)
exchangers - bankers, moneylenders
exercise - concern (Ps. 131:1)

exorcists - claimed they could cast out evil spirits (Acts 19:13)
expected end - hopeful future (Jer. 29:11)
experiment - experience, proof, evidence
fain - desire to
faint - give up; lose courage; be distressed
fairs - wares (Ezek. 27:12)
fall (out) - turn out (Ruth 3:18; Phil. 1:12)
fall not out by the way - don't argue
fall (away) - desert (I Chr. 12:19; Jer. 37:13)
falleth - surrenders (Jer. 21:9)
fame - news (Gen. 45:16)
familiar - close (Job 19:14)
familiar spirit - medium, spiritualist, witch, or fortune-teller (I Sam. 28:7)
familiars - friends (Jer. 20:10)
famish - reduce to nothing (Zeph. 2:11)
fanners - destroyers (Jer. 51:2)
fast - securely (Judg. 16:11); firm (Prov. 4:13; I Cor. 16:13; I Thes. 3:8)
fast by - close by (Ruth 2:8)
fat - rich, good, the best (Gen. 49:20; I Chr. 4:40; Neh. 9:25; Ezek. 34:14); prosperous (Deu. 32:15); strong (Is. 58:11); well watered (Ezek. 45:15)
fat or lean - fertile or barren (Num. 13:20)
father - grandfather (Dan. 5:2)
fathers - ancestors (Deut. 11:21)
fear - includes deep respect, honor, devotion, reverential awe, an attitude of unconditional trust and submission (Prov. 9:10; Phil. 2:12; Rev. 14:7)
feign - pretend (II Sam. 14:2; I Kin. 14:5)
fell - died (II Sam. 21:9)
fell a lusting - was greedy for better things
fell unto me - came over and joined me
fell upon - murdered (I Sam. 22:18)
feller - tree cutter (Is. 14:8)
fellows - female virgin companions
fellowship - pledge of partnership (Lev. 6:2)
fenced - knit (Job 10:11); dug up (Is. 5:2); fortified (Dan. 11:15)
fens - marshes (Job 40:21)
fetch a compass - make a turn or circuit; circle around
fetch his pledge - carry off his collateral
filled with - controlled by (Eph. 5:18)
fillets - ornamental thin bands around the pillars (Ex. 27:10)
filthy - corrupt (Ps. 53:3); rebellious, defiant (Zeph. 3:1); immoral (II Pet. 2:7)
filthy lucre - financial gain (I Tim. 3:8)
fire - oppression (Is. 43:2)

fires - dawning light (Is. 24:15)
firebrands - torches of flax on fire
flagons - cakes of raisins or grapes (Song. 2:5); bottles or jars (Is. 22:24)
flay - skin (Lev. 1:6)
flow together - be enlightened (Is. 60:5)
follow - pursue (II Sam. 2:26; I Chr. 10:2)
folly - wicked conduct (Judg. 20:10)
for - instead of (Num. 8:18); have been like (Job 34:36)
forbear - refuse; neglect (Num. 9:13; Ezek. 2:5); do what you prefer (Jer. 40:4)
force of the Gentiles - wealth of the nations
forecast his devices - devise plans
forehead - attitude (Ezek. 3:8-9)
former - eastern (Dead Sea) (Zech. 14:8)
forswear - to swear falsely (Matt. 5:33)
forwardness - earnestness (II Cor. 8:8); willingness (II Cor. 9:2)
foundation - creation (Eph. 14:4)
foundations - principles of society based on the Word of God (Ps. 11:3); **out of course** - ignored (Ps. 82:5)
fourscore - 80
flowers - monthly period (Lev. 15:33)
frame - pronounce (Judg. 12:6); devise (Ps. 94:20); prepare (Jer. 18:11)
fray - frighten; terrorize; drive away
free born - born a Roman citizen (Acts 22:28)
fretted - provoked to anger (Ezek. 16:43)
fretteth - is resentful (Prov. 19:3)
fretting - contagious, spreading
frontlets - memorial symbol (Ex. 13:16)
froward - perverse (II Sam. 22:27); cunning (Job 5:13); unfavorable; opposed (Ps. 18:26, second use); wrongful and false (Prov. 2:12; 8:8); obstinate and evil (Ps. 101:4); deceitful (Prov. 4:24)
frowardly - rebelliously (Is. 57:17)
fruit depart - miscarry (Ex. 21:22)
fuller - to bleach, make white, to clean
furbish - polish (Jer. 46:4; Ezek. 21:9)
furniture - saddle (Gen. 31:34); utensils, vessels (Ex. 35:14)
gainsay - speak against; contradict; faultfind
gall - bitter afflictions (Jer. 8:14)
gat him - returned (Num. 11:30)
gate - meeting place to transact legal or official business (Ruth 4:1)
gates - towns; **of hell** - the powers of Satan
gathering - obedience, respect (Gen. 49:10)
gazingstock - object of ridicule (Heb. 10:33)
ghost - spirit (Gen. 35:29)

gift - bribe (Ex. 23:8; Deut. 16:19)
gin - trap, snare (Job 18:9; Ps. 140:5)
gird up your loins - fasten the loose, flowing garments with a belt (II Kin. 4:29)
girdle - interlaced belt (Ex. 28:8); apron (II Kin. 1:8)
girt - clothed (II Kin. 1:8); put on (John 21:7); wrapped around (Rev. 1:13)
glass - mirror (Is. 3:23; I Cor. 13:12)
gleaned - killed (Judg. 20:45)
glory - wealth (Gen. 31:1)
glory over me - the honor is yours to tell me
go to - come; listen (Gen. 11:3; Is. 5:5)
goads - pointed rods used to prod an animal
goats - civic/political leaders (Zech. 10:3)
Godhead - the Trinity — God the Father, God the Son, God the Holy Spirit
gods - earthly rulers and judges (Ps. 82:1); My representatives (Ps. 82:6)
good speed - success (Gen. 24:12)
goodman - a male head of a household
government - authority (Is. 22:21)
grave - engrave, inscribe (Ex. 28:9)
graven images - carved idols (Deut. 7:25)
great sea - Mediterranean Sea (Num. 34:6)
grieved - annoyed, incensed (Acts 4:2)
grievous - severe (Ex. 9:3); cruel (I Kin. 12:4); harsh (Prov. 15:1); a hardship (Phil. 3:1)
grievousness - oppression (Is. 10:1)
grove - idol (Deut. 12:3); place of worship to the goddess Ashtaroth
guile - deceit; lie or deception
habergeon - sleeveless coat (Ex. 39:23)
haft - handle (Judg. 3:22)
hale - to take by force (Luke 12:58)
hallow - set apart, consecrate, sanctify (Ex. 40:9; I Kin. 8:64); cleanse (Lev. 16:19)
halt - limp (Gen. 32:31); waver (I Kin. 18:21); lame or crippled (Mark 9:45)
halting - downfall (Jer. 20:10)
hand(s) - word (Ezra 10:19; Ezek. 17:18); care (Ps. 95:7)
hap was to light - happened to come
hard by - near, close (Lev. 3:9)
hardened their neck - were stubborn
hardly bestead - sorely distressed
harness/ed - armor/in military order
harts - deer (Lam. 1:6)
hasty fruit - first ripe fig (Is. 28:4)
hated - unloved (Gen. 29:31; Deut. 21:15)
haunt - location; **haunt it** - dwell there
health - salvation (Ps. 42:11)
heap/s - failure/ruins (Is. 17:11/Ps. 79:1)

heart - human mind (Dan. 7:4)
heart smote - conscience accused
heat - anger (Ezek. 3:14)
heath - dry bush (Jer. 17:6)
heave offerings - implies willing offerings
heave shoulder - thigh (Lev. 10:14)
heaved - offered (Num. 18:30)
hell: Sheol - the grave (Job 26:6); Gehenna - eternal destiny of the lost; indescribable torment (Luke 16:24; Mark 9:48; Matt. 10:28)
Hephzibah - My delight is in her (Is. 62:4)
heresy - a belief that is not the true religion
hew - to cut stones (II Chr. 2:2)
hewn down - destroyed (Is. 33:9)
Hiddekel - Tigris (Gen. 2:14)
high - proud (Is. 10:12)
high arm - great power (Acts 13:17)
high day - early in the day (Gen. 29:7)
high hand - boldly (Ex. 14:8)
high heaps - road signs (pointing back to Israel) (Jer. 31:21)
high places - places/shrines for idol worship
hinder - western (Mediterranean Sea) (Zech. 14:8)
hindermost - last (Gen. 33:2; Jer. 50:12)
Hinnom - later called Gehenna, which Jesus used to illustrate the place of eternal punishment (II Chr. 28:3)
hires - earnings (Mic. 1:7)
hiss - scoff, ridicule, shame (I Kin. 9:8; Jer. 49:17; Jer. 25:9); signal (Zech. 10:8)
hoar - gray (I Kin. 2:6; Is. 46:4)
hold - stronghold, safe place (I Sam. 22:4)
holden - held fast (Job 36:8)
holes - sockets (Zech. 14:12)
hollow - socket (Gen. 32:25)
holpen - helped (Is. 31:3; Dan. 11:34)
holy - sanctified, set apart (Lev. 2:3)
Horeb - Sinai (I Kin. 19:8)
horn/s - esteem; strength/military power
hosen - tunic or undergarments (Dan. 3:21)
Hoshea - Joshua (Deut. 32:44)
host - camp (Gen. 32:2); army (II Sam. 17:25)
houghed - hamstrung, crippled (Josh. 11:9)
husbandmen - farmers (II Kin. 25:12)
husbandry - the soil (II Chr. 26:10)
hyssop - plant used for purging/cleansing
ignominy - dishonor (Prov. 18:3)
imagery - perverse idol imagination
images - household gods (Gen. 31:19); likenesses (I Sam. 6:5); incense altars (Ezek. 6:4)
Immanuel - God with us (Is. 7:14)
immutability - unchangeableness

imperious - shameless (Ezek. 16:30)
importunity - unwanted persistence
impotent - helpless, crippled (Acts 14:8)
impudent - stubborn (Ezek. 2:4)
impute sin - hold sin against him (Rom. 4:8)
in my hand - in danger (Ps. 119:109)
in the ear - ripening (Ex. 9:31)
inclosings - settings (Ex. 28:20)
incontinent - without self-control
instant - insistent or persistent (Luke 23:23)
instantly - earnestly (Acts 26:7)
instruments - furniture (Ex. 25:9); yokes (I Kin. 19:21); schemes (Is. 32:7)
inventions - deeds (Ps. 106:29); insight (Prov. 8:12)
inward/s - dearest, intimate/inner organs
Ishi - my husband (Hos. 2:16)
issue - offspring (Gen. 48:6); discharge (Lev. 15:2)
issues - escapes (Ps. 68:20)
JAH - an abbreviation of Jehovah — the Eternal, Self-Existent One — and corresponds to I AM THAT I AM
jangling - arguing (I Tim. 1:6)
jealous - zealous (I Kin. 19:14)
jealousy - fury (Is. 42:13); protective love (Zech. 8:2)
Jebus - Jerusalem (Judg. 19:11)
Jehovah-jireh - the Lord will provide
Jehovah-nissi - YHWH is my refuge
Jerubbaal - Gideon (I Sam. 12:11)
Jeshurun - Israel as complacent people
Jewry - the Judean region (John 7:1)
jubilee - every fiftieth year, when all debts were canceled (Lev. 25:10ff)
judgment - justice (Ps. 111:7)
keep the charge - obey the regulations (Lev. 8:35); assist in the duties and assignments (Num. 8:26)
keeper of mine head - captain of my bodyguard (I Sam. 28:2)
Kerioth - cities (Jer. 48:41)
kine - cattle; heifers
kine of Bashan - fat cows, raised in the best pasturelands — but here, it is used figuratively in referring to self-gratifying, sensual, influential women
know - rape and abuse (Gen. 19:5); have homosexual relations with (Judg. 19:22); have anything to do with (Ps. 101:4)
lade - load (Gen. 45:17; Luke 11:46)
laid waste - destroyed (Is. 64:11)
lament - commemorate (Judg. 11:40)

languisheth - wastes away, dies
lasciviousness - lustfulness (II Cor. 12:21)
laver - basin, bowl used for washing
lay - take (Eccl. 7:2)
league - peace treaty; covenant
leap on the threshhold - rush into houses to confiscate the property (Zeph. 1:9)
leasing - lies (Ps. 5:6)
leave - permission (Num. 22:13; John 19:38); forego (Neh. 10:31)
leaved gates - double doors (Is. 45:1)
lesser cattle - sheep (Is. 7:25)
let - rented (Mark 12:1); prevented (Rom. 1:13)
levy - forced labor (I Kin. 5:13; 9:15)
liberal - noble (Is. 32:5)
licence - opportunity (Acts 25:16)
liers - secret ambush (Judg. 20:29)
lieth out - extends (Neh. 3:25)
lift up the head - exalt themselves (Ps. 83:2); pardon (Jer. 52:31; 2 Kin. 25:27)
lifted up mine hand - promised, vowed
lighted upon - came to (Gen. 28:11); spoken against (Is. 9:8)
lightly - ignorantly (Gen. 26:10)
lightness - shameless behavior (Jer. 3:9); vain boasting (Jer. 23:32)
like - equal (Ex. 30:34; Deut. 18:8)
liking - in appearance (Dan. 1:10)
lintel - the crosspiece at the top of the door
list - choose, desire (Mark 9:13; James 3:4)
loins - waist (II Chr. 10:10; Ezek. 47:4)
loins girded - dressed for a journey
looked on - gloated over (Obad. 1:12)
loose the loins - weaken (Is. 45:1)
lucre - money (I Sam. 8:3)
lunatic - one affected by the moon, such as epilepsy (Matt. 17:15)
lusty - strong fighters (Judg. 3:29)
lying vanities - vain idols (Ps. 31:6); false worship (Jon. 2:8)
Magor-missabib - terror on every side
Mahanaim - two camps (Gen. 32:2)
make inquiry - reconsider (Prov. 20:25)
mammon - material things (Matt. 6:24)
mantle - robe (I Sam. 28:14; Ezra 9:3)
mar - ruin (Jer. 13:9)
Mara/h - bitter/bitterness
Maranatha - the Lord is coming!
mark - notice (Ruth 3:4; I Kin. 20:22); record (Ps. 130:3)
Massah (and sometimes) **Meribah** - tempted the Lord to slay them because of their faultfinding (Ex. 17:7)

matrix - womb (Ex. 13:12; Num. 3:12)
maw - stomach (Deut. 18:3)
mean - commoner (Is. 2:9); unimportant (Acts 21:39)
meat - food (Gen. 1:29; 9:3; Lev. 25:6; Joel 1:16; John 4:8); grain/cereal (Ezek. 45:24); a meal (Matt. 9:10)
meddle - associate (Prov. 20:19)
meet - qualified (Deut. 3:18); justly due (Prov. 11:24); right (Jer. 26:14; Phil. 1:7; 2 Thes. 1:3); worthy (I Cor. 15:9)
melt - test by affliction (Jer. 9:7); scatter (I Sam. 14:16); be weary from grief (Ps. 119:28)
menstealers - people who enslave (control) others (I Tim. 1:10)
mete - measure; parcel out
Midian - the descendants of Abraham through his second wife Keturah
Millo - mound of earth raised as a fortress
minish - make fewer in number (Ex. 5:19)
minister - servant (Matt. 20:26)
mischief - harm; evil intent; malice
mite - a very small unit of money
mitre - headdress, turban (Ex. 29:6)
mock - abuse (Jer. 38:19); deceive (Matt. 2:16)
moderation - humility and reputation for graciousness (Phil. 4:5)
mortify - put to death (Col. 3:5)
mote - small speck, dirt, dust or splinter
mother - grandmother (II Chr. 15:16)
motions of sins - sinful passions or cravings
mount - mound for fortification (Jer. 6:6)
mountain - power (Jer. 51:25)
mourneth - dries up (Is. 24:7)
murrain - pestilence or disease (Ex. 9:3)
mystery - hidden purpose of God (Eph. 3:3)
nail - secure hold (Ezra 9:8)
nail of the tent - large tent peg (Judg. 4:21)
naked - out of control (Ex. 32:25)
nakedness of the land - weak points of our defense (Gen. 42:9)
narrowly look upon - gaze at (Is. 14:16)
naturally - sincerely (Phil. 2:20)
navel - body (Prov. 3:8)
nephews - grandsons or other descendants
nether - lesser or bottom; lower
Nethinims - Temple attendants or servants
new moon - Passover Feast (Ps. 81:3)
ninth hour - 3 p.m.
nitre - a wound (Prov. 25:20); strong lye soap (Jer. 2:22)
No - the city of Thebes in Egypt
noise - report (Jer. 10:22; Mark 2:1)

Noph - Memphis, ancient capital of lower Egypt
notable - notorious (Matt. 27:16)
obeisance - bowing in respect
oblation - offering, gift (Lev. 7:14); Holy Place (Ezek. 45:7); contribution (Ezek. 45:13); sacred district (Ezek. 48:20)
occupy - use (Judg. 16:11); do business (Luke 19:13)
offend - be held guilty (Jer. 2:3); cause to sin (Matt. 18:6)
ofttimes - often (Matt. 17:15; John 18:2)
omnipotent - all-powerful
opened thy feet - played the harlot
oppress - cheat, defraud (Lev. 25:14)
oracle - inner room, Holy of Holies (I Kin. 6:5); Temple (Ps. 28:2)
oracles - the Scriptures (Rom. 3:2)
order the child - teach; train (Judg. 13:12)
order the lamps - tend to; keep burning
ouches - mountings or settings for precious stones (Ex. 28:11; 39:13)
ought - anything (Ex. 22:14; John 4:33); whatever (Lev. 19:6); sin (Num. 15:30)
out of hand - at once (Num. 11:15)
outlandish - foreign (Neh. 13:26)
outwent - went farther than or ahead of
over against - in front of; opposite
overcharge - be too severe (II Cor. 2:5)
overran - outran (II Sam. 18:23)
owls - ostriches (Is. 43:20)
Palestina - Philistia; Philistines
paps - breast (Luke 23:29); chest (Rev. 1:13)
passion - suffering and death (Acts 1:3)
patrimony - family property (Deut. 18:8)
peculiar - special (Ex. 19:5)
peeled - rubbed bare (Ezek. 29:18)
peep - whisper (Is. 8:19)
penury - poverty (Prov. 14:23; Luke 21:4)
peradventure - suppose; perhaps
perdition - destruction
perfect - blameless; mature; complete
Pharaoh - title of the monarchs of Egypt
phylacteries - small boxes containing Scripture texts worn by Jews as a reminder to keep the Law (Matt. 23:5)
pictures - carved figures that were objects of worship (Num. 33:52)
pilled - peeled (Gen. 30:37)
pillows - magic protective charms (Ezek 13:18,20)
pipes - flutes (I Kin. 1:40)
pit - cistern (Jer. 41:9)
pitched - encamped (Ex. 17:1)

pitiful - compassionate (Lam. 4:10)
place - settle, establish (Ezek. 37:26); trace (Dan. 2:35)
plagues wonderful - extraordinary afflictions (Deut. 28:59)
platted - shaped (John 19:2)
play - hold a contest (II Sam. 2:14); show joy (II Sam. 6:21)
play the men - show courage
played with his hand - played the harp
pleasant bread - desirable food (Dan. 10:3)
pleasant pictures - religious imagery
pleasant vessel - valuable vesesel
pledge - news (II Sam. 17:18)
polled - cut (II Sam. 14:26)
porter - gatekeeper; doorkeeper
portion - part or property; inheritance
possess the gate - overcome, be victorious
posts - couriers (Esth. 3:15; 8:10)
pots - sheepfolds (Ps. 68:13)
potsherd - piece of broken pottery (Job 2:8); earthen vessel (Prov. 26:23; Is. 45:9)
prating against - ridiculing (III John 1:10)
prating fool - self-sufficient know-it-all
prayed - urged (John 4:31)
precious - rare, scarce (Is. 13:12)
presbytery - the elders (I Tim. 4:14)
prevent - trap (2 Sam. 22:6); overtake (Job 30:27); go/come before (Ps. 59:10); speak before (Matt. 17:25)
prey - prize of war; prize (Jer. 21:9; 45:5)
prince of this world - Satan (John 12:31)
privily - unobserved; secretly
privy to - aware of in your own heart
profane - common (Ezek. 42:20); guilty of violating or breaking the law (Matt. 12:5)
prolong the perfection - reap the harvest
proper good - personal treasure
propitiation - atoning sacrifice, Mercy Seat
protest - warn (Gen. 43:3; I Kin. 2:42)
prove - test (Ex. 16:4; Judg. 3:4; II Chr. 9:1)
provender - straw and fodder (Judg. 19:19)
prudence - spiritual insight (Eph. 1:8)
publican - tax collector (Luke 5:27)
publisheth afflictions - announces disaster
puffeth - makes light (Ps. 10:5)
pulse - vegetables (Dan. 1:12)
purge - cut back (John 15:2); declare ceremonially clean (Mark 7:19)
purifying - religious cleansing ritual
purloining - stealing, pilfering, embezzling
purtenance - inner organs of an animal
push - drive (Deut. 33:17); gore (I Kin. 22:11)

put away - divorce (Ezek. 44:22)
putteth his mouth in the dust - speaks humbly (Lam. 3:29)
quarter - own way (Is. 47:15); a region (Mark 1:45)
quaternion - unit of four soldiers (Acts 12:4)
quicken - give life (Ps. 80:18; John 6:63)
quiet - strong (Nah. 1:12)
quit - guiltless (Ex. 21:28); no longer bound (Josh. 2:20); be courageous (I Sam. 4:9; I Cor. 16:13)
quite - completely (Ex. 23:24)
Rabsaris - the chief financial official
Rabshakeh - chief officer
Raca - worthless one, said in contempt
Rahab - poetic name for Egypt (Ps. 89:10)
rail (on) - belittle; denounce; insult; slander
raiment - clothing
raised - awakened (Song. 8:5)
ranges - hearth (Lev. 11:35)
ravening - viciousness, covetousness
ravished - delighted (Prov. 5:19)
receipt of custom - tax collector's office
recompence in the same - fair return
record - witness (Phil. 1:8)
redound - abound (II Cor. 4:15)
reins - inner self (Ps. 26:2); waist (Is. 11:5)
remission/remit - forgiveness/forgive
rend - to tear or pull apart
renowned - chosen representatives
rent - tore/torn (Gen. 37:34; II Sam. 1:2); split apart (I Kin. 13:3); rope (Is. 3:24)
repent - renunciation and sorrow for sin, turning to the Lord for forgiveness and a desire to obey the Lord (II Cor. 7:10); change to the opposite direction
reproach - disgrace; rebuke
reprobate - impure, rejected (Jer. 6:30)
reputation - high esteem (Phil. 2:29)
requite - repay (Deut. 32:6; II Sam. 2:6)
rereward (rearward) - rear guard
reserve - keep safe (Jer. 50:20)
residue - balance; remainder
resort - gather (Mark 10:1)
respect - approval (Gen. 4:4); concern (Ex. 2:25); obedience (Ps. 119:6)
rest - burial (Job 17:16)
sea - large bronze laver at which the priests ceremoniously cleansed their hands and feet before entering the Tabernacle (Jer. 27:19)
sea of the Philistines - Mediterranean Sea
sea of the plain - area of the Dead Sea
seed - descendants, offspring, children

seer - prophet (II Sam. 15:27)
seethe - boil (Deut. 14:21; Zech. 14:21)
Selah - the rock fortress city of Petra (just south of the Dead Sea) (II Kin. 14:7)
sepulchre - grave, tomb
served themselves of them - enslaved them
servile work - work at your occupations
set - take to (Ex. 7:23); expose (Hos. 2:3)
set at nought - reject; discredit; look down upon
set forward - oversee (Ezra 3:8)
set light - dishonor (Deut. 27:16)
setteth thee on - incited or influenced you
settle - ledge (Ezek. 43:14, 20)
settled his countenance - stared intensely
sever - set apart; select
several house - separated house
severally - individually (I Cor. 12:11)
shadow - protection (Gen. 19:8)
shadowing shroud - forest shade
shambles - meat market (I Cor. 10:25)
shamefacedness - modest behavior
Shebah - oath (Gen. 26:33)
sheepcote - pasturelands; protecting sheep
sheets - linen garments, like shirts
Sheshach - Babylon
shipping - boats (John 6:24)
shoot out the lip - ridicule, hurl insults
sick of love - lovesick (Song. 2:5)
sickness - menstrual period (Lev. 20:18)
signet - ring bearing a seal with which documents were stamped to officially give personal authority (Gen. 38:18)
signification - meaning (I Cor. 14:10)
Sihor - the Nile River (Jer. 2:18)
similitude - likeness; figure, shape, or form
simplicity - sincere faithfulness (II Cor. 11:3)
sincere - pure, without a mixture (I Pet. 2:2)
single - free from deceit; sincere
singular - special (Lev. 27:2)
Sitnah - enmity, anger (Gen. 26:21)
sixth hour - noon by Jewish time and 6 pm by Roman time
slack - negligent, lazy (Prov. 10:4); weak, powerless (Hab. 1:4; Zeph. 3:16)
sleep - be dead (Job 7:21)
sleep with his pledge - keep it overnight
slide - waver, fall (Ps. 26:1)
slideth back - stubborn (Hos. 4:16)
small cattle - sheep (2 Chr. 35:8; Is. 43:23)
smell - be pleased, take delight (Amos 5:21)
smite - defeat; crush (Deut. 7:2; Ps. 143:3)
smote - attacked; defeated; struck down; stabbed

snuffed - sneered (Mal. 1:13)
sober - of sound mind (II Cor. 5:13)
sod(den) - boiled (Ex. 12:9; II Chr. 35:13)
softly - slowly (Gen. 33:14)
sojourn - live temporarily (Gen. 12:10)
solace - delight (Prov. 7:18)
solemn(ity) - appointed (time) (Deut. 31:10)
solemn days - appointed Feasts, festivals
sometimes - formerly (Eph. 2:13)
son of perdition - Judas Iscariot (John 17:12)
sons - descendants (I Chr. 1:6)
soothsayer - fortune-teller (Josh. 13:22)
sorcery - witchcraft (Acts 8:9)
sore - afflictions (Ps. 38:11); severe(ly); fierce(ly); grievous(ly)
sore broken - severely crushed (Ps. 44:19)
sorrow(s) - pain, suffering (Gen. 3:16); toil, struggle to make a living (Gen. 3:17)
sottish - devoid of spiritual understanding
soul - person (Lev. 5:4); well-being (Prov. 29:10)
sounding - yearning affection (Is. 63:15)
span - about nine inches (Is. 40:12)
spikenard - perfume (Song. 1:12)
spirit of infirmity - disability (Luke 13:11)
spirits - motives (Prov. 16:2)
spoil - take the wealth of; plunder and rob
spoon - bowl (Num. 7:44)
sport - ridicule (Is. 57:4)
sporting with - caressing, expressing love to (Gen. 26:8)
sprinkle - purify by His blood (Is. 52:15)
squares - sides (Ezek. 43:17)
stablish - strengthen (II Thes. 2:17)
staff - supply (Ezek. 5:16)
staff of reed - false support (Ezek. 29:6)
stairs - cliffs, steep places (Song. 2:14)
stalled - fattened (Prov. 15:17)
stand against the blood - fail to help when a neighbor's life is in danger (Lev. 19:16)
standing - pools of (Ps. 114:8)
staves - carrying poles; sticks; clubs; staffs
stay - support (II Sam. 22:19); cease, do not move (II Sam. 24:16); help (Prov. 28:17); rely (Is. 10:20; 48:2); leading men (Is. 19:13)
stayed - persuaded, restrained (I Sam. 24:7); propped (I Kin. 22:35); ceased flowing (II Kin. 4:6); stopped (Ps. 106:30)
stays - armrests (I Kin. 10:19; II Chr. 9:18)
stealeth - kidnaps (Ex. 21:16)
stiffnecked - stubborn; hardened
stirs - shoutings (Is. 22:2)
stock/stone - idols (Jer. 2:27)

stomacher - rich robe (Is. 3:24)
store - number (Gen. 26:14); food supply (Lev. 26:10); kneading trough or bread bin (Deut. 28:5)
stout - arrogant; harsh (Mal. 3:13)
stouthearted - stubborn-minded
straightway - immediately, without delay
strait - distress (II Sam. 24:14); small (Is. 49:20); narrow, strict (Luke 13:24)
straitened - hindered (Prov. 4:12); limited (Mic. 2:7); restricted (Luke 12:50)
straitly - specifically (Gen. 43:7); strictly, definitely (I Sam. 14:28)
straitly charged - sternly warned
straits - where there was no way out
strakes - strips (Gen. 30:37); marks (Lev. 14:37)
strange - improper, unholy (Num. 26:61); foreign, false (I Sam. 7:3; I Kin. 11:1; Ezra 10:2; Ps. 137:4); alien (Job 19:3); repulsive (Job 19:17); adulterous (Prov. 5:3); awesome, unusual (Is. 28:21)
strange woman - harlot (Prov. 2:16)
strangers - foreigners (Neh. 13:30); exiles (I Pet. 1:1)
strawed - scattered; spread (Mark 11:8)
streets - fields (Ps. 144:13)
strength - normal depth (Ex. 14:27); ability to resist (Is. 23:10); refuge (Nah. 3:11)
strengthened the hand(s) - encouraged; assisted (I Sam. 23:16; Ezra 1:6)
strengtheneth - acts proudly (Job 15:25)
stretched out arm - mighty power
stricken - advanced (Gen. 24:1)
striketh hands - responsible for his neighbor (Prov. 17:18)
stripes - beatings; wounds
stripling - youth (I Sam. 17:56)
stroke - case of dispute (Deut. 21:5)
strove - quarreled; contended; disputed
suborned - bribed; persuaded; influenced to do wrong (Acts 6:11)
subscribe evidences - sign deeds
substance - property (Ezra 10:8)
subtil - cunning, clever, shrewd, crafty (Gen. 3:1; II Sam. 13:3); deceitful (Prov. 7:10); treacherous (Acts 7:19)
subtilty - insight (Prov. 1:4)
suburbs - pasturelands (Num. 35:5)
succor/succour - help; assist
suffer - allow, permit, tolerate
suffer them - let them remain (Esth. 3:8)
sufficeth - will satisfy (John 14:8)

sum - census (Num. 1:2; 26:2)
sundered - separated (Job 41:17)
sunrising - eastern border (Num. 21:11)
sup - take something to eat and/or to drink (Luke 17:8); share spiritual food and fellowship (Rev. 3:20)
superfluity of - what remains (James 1:21)
superfluous - deformed (Lev. 21:18; 22:23); unnecessary (II Cor. 9:1)
supplanted - taken the place of
suppliants - worshipers
sure - safe (Prov. 11:15)
sure house - lasting dynasty (I Sam. 25:28)
sureties for - responsible for (Prov. 22:26)
surfeiting - overindulgence (Luke 21:34)
swaddled - reared and cared for
swaddling - to wrap with cloth, implying special care is given to Him
swaddlingband - wrapping
swallowed up - without restraint (Job 6:3)
swear/sware - promise/d solemnly
swearing - the curse of God (Jer. 23:10)
swellings - pride; self-assertion
tabering - beating (Nah. 2:7)
tabernacles - tents (Job 11:14)
tabernacles of bribery - houses of the bribetaker (Job 15:34)
tablets - perfume boxes (Is. 3:20)
tabret - object of contempt, ridicule (Job 17:6); tamborine (Is. 5:12)
taches - devices for fastening two parts together (Ex. 26:6)
taken - caught (John 8:3)
tale - quota, number (Ex. 5:8)
tare - mauled or mangled (II Kin. 2:24)
tares - darnel; a weed (Matt. 13:25)
target - javelin (I Sam. 17:22)
tarry - continue; stay (Lev. 14:8; Ps. 101:7)
Tartan - title of Assyria's commander in chief (II Kin. 18:17)
tear themselves - prepare food, break bread
teareth him - violent convulsions
Tebeth - compares with Dec/Jan
tell - count (Gen. 15:5; Ps. 22:17; Ps. 147:4)
tempered - combined (I Cor. 12:24)
tempest - storm (Is. 32:2)
tempt - test, try (Gen. 22:1)
tender - weak; inexperienced
tenons - clasps (Ex. 26:19)
tenor - general idea (Gen. 43:7)
tenth hour - 4 p.m.
teraphim - household idols (Hos. 3:4)
terrestrial - earthly (I Cor. 15:40)

terrible - awesome; wonderful; fearful
terribleness - fierceness (Jer. 49:16)
testimony - Ark of the Covenant (Num. 17:10)
tetrarch - ruler of a fourth part or one of four rulers of a country or province
thankworthy - approved or acceptable
thigh - hip (Gen. 32:25)
thing - message (Dan. 10:1)
third hour - 9 a.m; **of the night** - 9 p.m
thitherward - toward (Jer. 50:5)
threescore - 60
throne of iniquity - workers of evil
thyine - scented wood (Rev. 18:12)
time no longer - no more waiting, delay
times - years (Dan. 4:16; 12:7); astrology (Lev. 19:26)
tire - turban (Ezek. 24:17)
Tirshatha - governor (Ezra 2:63; Neh. 10:1)
title - monument, grave marker (II Kin. 23:17)
token/s - sign/testimony and experience
told out - assigned (II Chr. 2:2)
torn him - thrown him into convulsions
touch a woman - have sexual relations
touching - concerning (Num. 8:26)
tow - straw or kindling to be burned
toward - near (Gen. 13:12); friendly/favorable to (Gen. 31:2; Jer. 15:1)
traffick - do business (Gen. 42:34)
train - royal attendants (I Kin. 10:2); trailing robe (Is. 6:1)
translate - transfer (II Sam. 3:10)
travail - give birth (Gen. 38:28; I Sam. 4:19); hardship (Ex. 18:8)
tributary - slave (Lam. 1:1)
tribute - an assessment; taxes (Num. 31:39; Rom. 13:6); forced labor (Josh. 17:13; I Kin. 4:6)
tried - proven true (II Sam. 22:31)
trimmest - scheme (Jer. 2:33)
troubled - made trouble for (Gen. 34:30); confused, panicked (Ex. 14:24)
trow - trust, think, give acceptance to
try - examine, test (Lam. 3:40)
tumult - uproar, riot, disorderly disturbance
turn - restore (Job 42:10; Ps. 80:3)
thitherward - in that direction
turning - corner (Neh. 3:19)
turning leaves - hinged panels
twain - two (Mark 15:38)
unawares - unintentionally (Num. 35:15)
uncircumcised - ceremoniously defiled and forbidden (Lev. 19:23); those without a covenant with God (I Chr. 10:4); heathen (Is.

52:1); unrepentant (Acts 7:51)
uncircumcised lips - poor speech
unclean - ceremonially defiled (Lev. 5:2)
undefiled - blameless (Ps. 119:1)
unfeigned - sincere; genuine; without hypocrisy (II Cor. 6:6; I Tim. 1:5)
ungirded - unloaded (Gen. 24:32)
unicorn - wild ox (Num. 23:22; Job 39:9)
unleavened - without yeast (Lev. 2:4)
unsearchable - beyond our understanding
unseemly - rudely (I Cor. 13:5)
untempered morter - whitewash
untimely - green, unripe (Rev. 6:13)
untimely birth - stillborn (Job 3:16)
untoward - sinful (Acts 2:40)
upbraid - rebuke, denounce, condemn
upholden - helped (Job 4:4)
Urim and Thummim - two objects kept in the high priest's breastplate and used for determining the will of God
usury - interest on money lent (Matt. 25:27)
utter - outer (Ezek. 47:2)
uttermost sea - Mediterranean Sea
vain - void of understanding (Prov. 12:11); morally misguided (Rom. 1:21); worthless
vainglory - boasting (Phil. 2:3)
vanities - worthless idolatry (I Kin. 16:13)
vanity - dishonesty (Prov. 13:11; 30:8)
variance - a state of disagreement
vaunteth not itself - is not boastful
vehemently - angrily (Luke 11:53)
vein - mine (Job 28:1)
verity - truth (Ps. 111:7)
vesture - clothing; robe; garment
vexed - afflicted; distressed; grieved; tormented
vial - container; bowl or cup
victuals - provisions; food
vigilant - self-controlled (I Tim. 3:2)
vile - undignified (2 Sam. 6:22); rotten (Jer. 29:17)
villany - disgraceful things (Jer. 29:23)
vine - Israel (Ps. 80:8)
viol/s - strings/harps (Is. 5:12/Amos 5:23)
virtue - healing power (Mark 5:30; Luke 6:19); power from a supernatural being (Luke 8:46)
visage - appearance (Is. 52:14)
visit - punish (Jer. 50:31); look after the needs (James 1:27)
wait (on) - serve, minister (in) (I Chr. 6:32)
wall - moat (Dan. 9:25)
want - lack; be without (Ps. 23:1; Jer. 35:19)
wanton - seductive (Is. 3:16)
ward - duty (Neh. 13:30); custody; guarded house; guard post
wave them - present with a waving motion
wax - become; grow (Ps. 102:26)
weaken the hands - discourage, frighten
wealth - well-being (Ezra 9:12)
weigh - make smooth and straight (Is. 26:7)
wench - maidservant (II Sam. 17:17)
whisperers - gossipers (Rom. 1:29)
whited wall - hypocrite (Acts 23:3)
wiles - treacherous/cunning deceit
will worship - self-inspired efforts at worship (Col. 2:23)
wimples - shawls (Is. 3:22)
winebibber - one who drinks wine
winked at - overlooked (Acts 17:30)
wise hearted - skillful, expert craftsman
wist - knew (Lev. 5:17; Mar. 14:40)
wit - see, know (Gen. 24:21; Ex. 2:4)
with - against (Gen. 14:9)
withs - small ropes (Judg. 16:7)
without - outside (Lev. 6:11; Ezra 10:13; John 18:16); independent of (I Cor. 11:11); beyond (II Cor. 10:13)
wonderful - horrible (Lam. 1:9; Dan. 8:24); mighty (I Sam. 6:6)
wont - accustomed (Matt. 27:15)
work - concern (Prov. 16:11)
wormwood - bitterness (Lam. 3:15)
wot - know (Gen. 21:26; 44:15; Num. 22:6)
wreathed - joined together (Lam. 1:14)
wreathen - woven, braided, twisted
wrest - pervert; distort (Deut. 16:19)
wroth - exceedingly angry; furious
wrought - committed (Neh. 9:18); acted (Ezek. 20:9); prepared (II Cor. 5:5)
yoke - burden (Acts 15:10)

Topical Reference Index
(Note: Numbers refer to pages)

Abomination: 37, 86, 122, 128, 144, 145, 174, 293, 313, 457
Abortion: 237
Accountability: 124, 215, 337, 404, 404
Accusations/false: 203, 207, 211
Adultery (see Fornication): 4, 29, 133, 222, 241, 312, 404, 412
Alcoholism: 245
Alliances/friendships/relationships: 4, 10, 25, 47, 50, 86, 96, 106, 110, 111, 125, 178, 179, 408
Altar of Incense/Golden Altar (see The Tabernacle pg 31): 35, 38, 303, 334
Angel of the LORD, the/Angel of God, the (Christ Pre-Incarnate): 14, 103, 262, 326
Anger/hatred/hostility: 4, 209, 246, 265, 280, 412, 415
Anointing: 221, 236, 355
Antichrist: 254, 306, 307, 310, 311, 423, 455, 456
Apostasy: 37, 102, 106
Ark of the Covenant/LORD/God/Testimony (see The Tabernacle pg 31): 30, 39, 40, 120, 132, 144, 170, 303
Assurance/confidence: 19, 127, 221, 224, 229, 235, 338, 424, 433, 442
Atonement (see also Salvation/redemption): 26, 39, 42, 43, 46, 49, 60, 66, 113, 266, 303, 373, 398, 399, 407, 411, 414, 431, 433, 434, 439, 453
Atonement, Day of: 26, 38, 39, 41, 49, 51, 72
Attitude/indifference: 12, 13, 111, 113, 230, 372, 399, 400, 403, 405, 412, 415, 425, 443, 449
Attitudes/motives (see also Motives): 62, 65, 86, 119, 165, 206, 209, 215, 244, 246, 250, 267, 280, 293
Authority, submission (see also Submission): 7, 65, 243, 358, 427, 439
Babylon: 455
Babylonian exile: 258, 264, 280, 284, 287, 306, 308, 325
Balaam: 68, 73
Baptism, water: 346, 379, 380, 382, 383, 396, 398, 411, 422
Baptism of Holy Spirit: 383
Betrayal/denial/rejection: 375, 376
Blessings/curses: 13, 19, 30, 54, 72, 79, 83, 85, 87, 89, 98, 100, 102, 124, 145, 147, 158, 170, 171, 188, 205, 208, 215, 226, 235, 280, 331, 415, 437, 451, 453, 454, 457
Booths, Feast of: 51, 72
Brazen Altar/Altar of Brass/Altar of Burnt Offering (see The Tabernacle pg 31): 32, 35, 303, 439
Burnt Offerings: 11, 37, 42, 44
Candlestick of Pure Gold/Lampstand (see The Tabernacle pg 31): 35, 36, 38, 53, 303
Capital punishment: 75
Captivity: 262, 268, 276, 278, 279, 280, 291
Census: 55, 71
Cherubim: 292
Chosen people (Israel): 227, 252, 256, 274, 276, 286
Christian walk/conversion/discipleship: 72, 86, 143, 215, 219, 231, 234, 244, 253, 260, 268, 274, 287, 379, 381, 383, 391, 393, 397, 399, 400, 403, 404, 406, 407, 408, 410, 415, 522, 427, 435, 439, 441, 442, 443, 446, 447, 449, 451, 453, 454

Church: 162, 221, 225, 227, 236, 238, 250, 253, 341, 353, 379, 380, 381, 397, 399, 403, 404, 415, 421, 430, 440, 447, 449, 450, 455

Church leadership/elder/bishop/minister (see also Leadership & Priest/minister, requirements of & Leadership/elder/bishop/minister): 15, 50, 57, 72, 197, 404, 426, 429, 430

Church/body of Christ/the bride of Christ: 94, 221, 252, 253, 379, 380, 403, 415, 430, 457

Circumcision/consecration/service: 94, 124, 125, 166, 182

Cities of Refuge: 75

Cleanness/purification/uncleanness: 15, 36, 47, 48, 50, 66, 351

Commandments: 29, 40, 54, 79, 81, 87, 89, 100, 103, 106, 354

Commitment/dedication/devotion/loyalty: 11, 42, 43, 58, 68, 71, 76, 77, 82, 87, 88, 91, 96, 98, 106, 110, 111, 115, 144, 151, 165, 169, 181, 188, 196, 199, 200, 208, 284, 368, 372, 379, 392, 398

Compassion/love/kindness: 16, 18, 29, 45, 54, 59, 67, 82, 85, 115, 127, 212, 342, 353, 362, 364, 368, 371, 372, 373, 375, 376, 381, 382, 393, 401, 402, 405, 409, 411, 414, 415, 432, 433, 440, 441

Compassion/love of God/Christ: 54, 59, 67, 77, 85, 114, 115, 195, 204, 312, 314, 320, 321, 371, 372, 373, 375, 376, 411, 414, 415, 432, 433, 439, 441, 450

Complaining/criticizing/faultfinding/murmuring: 24, 27, 28, 55, 56, 62, 63, 64, 67, 78, 91, 99, 167, 171, 182, 185, 207, 209

Compromise/lukewarmness: 8, 10, 25, 73, 74, 81, 99, 101, 102, 103, 106, 110, 123, 142, 147, 158, 177, 180, 197, 372, 373, 378, 397, 404, 408, 428, 446, 449, 450, 455

Confession/repentance (see also Repentance): 10, 18, 49, 54, 67, 106, 113, 133, 189, 194, 374, 379, 392, 395, 434

Consecration (see also Holiness/godliness/sanctification): 42, 43, 47, 50, 58, 99, 109, 110, 111

Conversion: 370

Covenants/promises/oaths/vows (see also Blessings/curses): 9, 10, 12, 14, 20, 43, 68, 77, 84, 85, 88, 94, 96, 109, 110, 111, 114, 119, 138, 160, 271, 274, 280, 289, 290, 301, 312, 414, 431, 434

Covetousness/greed (see also Greed/covetousness & Selfishness/self-seeking/self-sufficiency/self-centered/self-will/self-denial/greed): 3, 14, 62, 68, 73, 74, 86, 152, 259, 363

Creation/Creator (see also God/Christ: Creator/creation)

Cross/crucifixion (see also Jesus Christ: Crucifixion/death/resurrection): 67, 371, 375, 411, 434, 454

Day of the Lord: 254, 315, 316, 326, 329, 330, 424

Death: 3, 26, 48, 55, 67, 68, 73, 77, 127, 132, 206, 207, 298, 382, 383, 406, 407, 421, 422, 424, 449, 450, 454, 456, 457

Deception/lies/spiritual blindness: 18, 25, 86, 96, 108, 134, 152, 229, 245, 283372, 381, 394, 397, 408, 414, 425, 443, 444, 446, 450, 453, 454, 455

Dedication/devotion/loyalty (see Commitment/dedication)

Defeat/failure: 95, 159, 181

Defilement: 47, 60, 58, 66, 75, 197, 455, 457

Deliverance/destruction/restoration (see also Salvation/redemption): 5, 20, 26, 27, 60, 102, 108, 140, 156, 160, 183, 201, 319, 324

Dependence/independence: 7, 23, 28, 37

Determination: 193

Disappointment: 149, 208, 375, 391

Discernment: 12, 16, 17

Discipleship (see Christian walk): 402, 404
Discipline/correction: 243
Discontentment/discontent: 56, 65
Discouragement (see Encouragement/assurance)
Dishonesty: 86
Double-minded/instability:
Encouragement/assurance/discouragement: 126, 127, 149, 158, 166, 187, 212, 375, 391, 401, 405, 424
Envy/jealousy/pride: 4, 14, 62, 124, 125, 126, 299, 403, 405
Eternity/eternal life: 1, 19, 54, 67, 127, 162, 216, 220, 260, 261, 266, 279, 302, 362, 364, 365, 370, 372, 373, 384, 392, 398, 406, 407, 408, 409, 411, 424, 442, 444, 446, 451, 456
Evil alliances (see also Alliances): 150
Evil/wickedness/abomination (see also Abomination/wickedness): 397, 398, 406, 408, 412, 422, 427, 436, 450, 452
Faith/trust: 5, 8, 9, 11, 20, 27, 28, 55, 56, 63, 67, 78, 83, 91, 96, 97, 98, 99, 101, 107, 109, 119, 120, 148, 149, 158, 169, 173, 177, 182, 185, 187, 189, 193, 200, 201, 203, 206, 207, 208, 210, 213, 216, 224, 226, 262, 265, 281, 324, 370, 375, 376, 382, 384, 391, 392, 395, 398, 406, 407, 411, 414, 421, 424, 425, 435, 437, 444, 451, 454
Faithfulness/unfaithfulness: 8, 9, 11, 17, 19, 27, 71, 74, 76, 89, 91, 98, 99, 100, 110, 142, 144, 163, 165, 176, 177, 199, 200, 206, 268, 309, 363, 372, 381, 382, 394, 395, 421, 424, 427, 435, 437, 449
False teachers/teaching: 410, 423, 438, 442, 444, 445, 446, 449
Family (see also Parents/children): 15, 77, 79, 82
Fasting: 267
Fear of the Lord (see Reverence)
Fear/anxiety/depression/patience: 27, 98, 122, 124, 128, 153, 375, 378, 425
Feasts/Passover: 41, 51, 52, 60, 72, 182, 274
Fellowship/fellowship with God/communion: 43, 59, 74, 234, 236, 341, 415, 429, 443
First-fruits, Feast of: 51
Flood: 5
Fornication (see Adultery): 68, 241, 412
Forgiveness: 4, 18, 26, 38, 39, 43, 49, 54, 67, 89, 106, 113, 133, 159, 187, 194, 213, 221, 222, 227, 231, 283, 321, 342, 360, 364, 367, 371, 372, 376, 382, 384, 393, 396, 397, 405, 415, 429 433, 456
Friendship (see Alliances/friendships/relationships)
Gentiles, times of: 54, 279, 306, 315
Glorifying God: 47, **376, 401, 402, 440, 443**
Glory of the Lord (Shekinah glory): 144, 294, 304
God/Christ:
    All sufficiency of: 9, 24
    Care/provision/presence/protection of: 5, 14, 19, 27, 28, 30, 53, 59, 64, 74, 83, 88, 89, 91, 114, 115, 153, 185, 193, 201, 218, 224, 229, 276, 281, 289, 373
    Creator/creation: 1, 3, 54, 88, 212, 217, 228, 237, 246, 256, 268, 272, 381, 392, 414, 431, 432, 453
    Glory of: 294, 457
    Goodness of: 64, 156
    Guidance of: 13, 28, 60, 61, 73, 78, 108
    Kingdom of: 84
    Lordship of: 54, 131, 228

Love/Care of: 27, 54, 64, 89, 114, 115, 178
One True: 26, 80, 88, 148, 256, 300
Power of: 24, 108, 120, 148
Presence/protection/providence of: 11, 18, 19, 27, 28, 30, 31, 39, 40, 53, 64, 72, 74, 78, 79, 83, 88, 91, 97, 99, 114, 106, 115, 120, 155, 170, 451
Promises of: 8, 9, 14, 24, 79, 90, 94, 101
Purpose/will of (see also Service/ministry & Stewardship/serving God/devotion & Tithes/offerings)**:** 13, 17, 18, 19, 22, 23, 25, 28, 36, 58, 59, 60, 61, 76, 78, 85, 87, 91, 98, 106, 119, 124, 130, 131, 139, 156, 162, 170, 172, 188, 192, 193, 198, 204, 208, 209, 211, 212, 213, 220, 238, 240, 251, 259, 272, 276, 285, 318, 392, 393, 400, 406, 407, 409, 414, 422, 426, 428, 432, 435, 442, 447
Rejection of: 181, 247, 276
Relationship with: 45, 46, 54
Sovereignty of: 1, 9, 13, 17, 18, 19, 22, 25, 48, 83, 108, 115, 135, 139, 155, 162, 185, 193, 199, 201, 203, 208, 209, 212, 213, 254, 264, 265, 279, 281, 297, 299, 306, 420, 427, 432, 437, 452, 453
What God hates: 86, 229
Wrath of: 88, 139, 145, 159
Godliness/holiness/sanctification: 15, 26, 29, 30, 35, 41, 47, 50, 52, 58, 66, 275, 301
Godliness/ungodliness: 12, 158, 160, 178
Good Samaritan: 85, 362
Gossip: 130
Grace (see also Mercy)**:** 30, 35, 39, 67, 91, 106, 153, 159, 187, 194, 212, 231, 245, 314, 321, 371, 393, 396, 411, 428, 432, 446
Grain Offering (see also Meat or Meal Offering)**:** 43, 44
Gratitude/thanksgiving (see also Thanksgiving/gratitude)**:** 27, 59, 83, 225, 230, 371, 451
Great Commission: 259, 333, 346
Greed/covetousness (see also Covetousness/greed & Selfishness/self-seeking/self-sufficiency/self-centered/self-will/self-denial/greed)**:** 68, 73, 74, 86, 99, 123, 128, 133, 135, 136, 412, 440, 449
Guidance/seeking God: 60, 61, 73, 78, 95, 96, 108, 128, 142, 166, 195, 217, 228, 240, 247, 267, 373, 438, 439, 440
Happiness/contentment: 89
Hardness of heart: 25, 28
Hardships/difficulties (see also Sorrow/burdens/grief/misery/suffering & Suffering/grief/hardship/misery/sorrow)**:** 22, 24, 56, 78, 87, 107
Heaven, eternal: 127, 137, 367, 406, 409, 411, 424, 432, 444, 454, 456, 457
Hell, eternal/everlasting: 73, 279, 343, 364, 367, 378, 394, 397, 399, 406, 409, 411, 425, 432, 433, 444, 446, 456
Holiness/godliness/sanctification (see also Godliness/holiness/sanctification)**:** 30, 35, 41, 47, 50, 52, 58, 66, 89, 100, 109, 195, 397, 399, 401, 403, 404, 408, 422, 426, 433, 436, 439, 441
Holiness/sanctification (see Godliness/holiness/sanctification)
Holy Spirit/Spirit of God: 23, 33, 36, 143, 165, 195, 215, 222, 233, 236, 245, 246, 250, 256, 260, 263, 276, 294, 302, 305, 351, 357, 379, 380, 382, 383, 384, 393, 399, 400, 407, 412, 414, 415, 435, 439, 440
Holy Spirit, gifts of: 402
Holy Spirit/Trinity: 1, 23, 33, 36, 40, 53, 60, 61, 78, 80, 81
Homosexuality (see also Immorality/morality & Lust & Morality/immorality/homosexuality/lust)**:** 10, 112, 113

Honesty: 86
Honor/dishonor: 130
Honoring God: 83, 132
Humiliation:
Humility/meekness (see also Meekness): 23, 66, 71, 99, 107, 119, 167, 174, 213, 244
Hypocrisy: 37, 57, 135, 152, 154, 207, 250, 267, 360
Idolatry/witchcraft: 37, 54, 68, 73, 88, 101, 102, 103, 106, 109, 148, 150, 154, 156, 157, 159, 180, 181, 190, 256, 275, 412, 422
Immorality/morality (see also Morality/immorality/homosexuality/lust & Lust & Homosexuality): 37, 68, 112, 113, 215, 241, 273, 317, 372, 397, 399, 404, 412
Indifference (see also attitude): 12, 113
Ingathering, Feast of (see also Feast of Tabernacles): 51, 72
Infirmities/weaknesses: 371, 401, 407
Inheritance: 99, 100, 101, 103, 114, 115
Jealousy/envy/pride (see also Hatred/anger/hostility/murder & Envy/jealousy/pride & Murder/manslaughter/hatred): 4, 14, 62, 412, 440, 443, 450
Jesus Christ (see chart on page 255): 379, 383, 393, 411, 413, 430, 431, 434, 443, 454, 457
    Arrest/trial: 376, 378
    As the I Am: 369
    Ascension of: 233, 424, 453
    Atonement of: 26, 35, 39, 42, 43, 46, 49, 60, 66, 67, 101, 113
    Authority of: 343, 346
    Betrayal of: 355
    Birth/baptism/genealogy of (see also Jesus Christ: Genealogy of & Jesus Christ: Virgin birth & Jesus Christ: Messianic genealogy): 91, 114, 162, 161, 190, 254, 257, 322, 323, 333, 334, 356, 357, 453
    Blood of: 113
    Bread of Life: 33, 36, 52, 53
    Bridegroom, the: 252, 253
    Chief Cornerstone/headship (see Stone, the/Branch/the): 233, 306, 329
    Compassion/love of: 54, 349
    Creator: Genesis
    Crucifixion/death/resurrection: 11, 26, 41, 42, 43, 46, 53, 60, 66, 67, 94, 101, 216, 225, 226, 254, 266, 309, 368, 379, 380, 382, 384, 392, 396, 398, 400, 401, 402, 406, 407, 424, 433
    Death/resurrection of (see Jesus Christ: Crucifixion/death/resurrection)
    Deity/humanity/Son of God/Servant of God (see also Jesus Christ: Savior/Messiah/Servant & Suffering Servant): 1, 10, 14, 26, 39, 45, 52, 53, 54, 67, 80, 84; 101, 113, 221, 223, 246, 254, 257, 266, 348, 352, 354, 356, 357, 358, 369, 373, 376, 378, 420, 432, 434, 446
    Dominion: 225, 328
    Door, the: 30, 31
    Genealogy of (see Jesus Christ: Birth/baptism/genealogy of)
    Good Shepherd: 218, 338, 373
    High Priest, our: 32, 34, 38, 49, 303
    Humility of/meekness of: 66
    Incarnation: 255, 256, 257
    Intercessor, our: 34, 38
    Judge, the: 97, 278
    Lamb of God: 11, 26, 30, 32, 227, 367, 369, 371, 378, 380, 431, 433, 447, 454, 455

Light of the world: 33, 36
Living Word: 369
Lord/King/Savior (see Jesus Christ: Messiah/King/Lord/Savior)
Lord (see Jesus Christ: Messiah/ King/ Lord/ Savior)
Mediator/Intercessor (see Jesus Christ: Messiah/King/Lord/Savior)
Messiah/King/Lord/Savior/Redeemer (see also Jesus Christ: Deity/humanity/ Son of God/ Servant of God & Jesus Christ: Lord/King/Savior & Jesus Christ: Lord & Jesus Christ: Lord & Jesus Christ: Mediator/Intercessor & Jesus Christ: Savior/Messiah/Servant & Jesus Christ: Suffering Servant): 10, 14, 54, 67, 80, 84, 166, 173, 205, 206, 207, 214, 221, 260, 266, 329, 333, 334, 359, 365, 370, 371, 372, 374, 375, 378, 379, 380, 382, 383, 384, 384, 391, 392, 393, 394, 396, 399, 406, 409, 411, 414, 420, 421, 424, 431, 433, 434, 444, 446, 450, 451, 452, 456, 475
Millennial reign of: 231, 235, 254, 256, 258, 259, 302, 304, 305, 306, 328
Passover Lamb/Unleavened Bread: 26, 41, 60
Redeemer (see Jesus Christ: Messiah/King/Lord/Savior/Redeemer)
Relation with: 7, 76, 247, 252, 253, 341
Sacrifice of: 26, 35, 42, 266
Savior/Messiah/Servant (see Jesus Christ: Messiah/King/Lord/Savior/Redeemer)
Second coming: 5, 97, 260, 278, 302, 311
Sinless nature of/perfect/blameless/sinless: 26, 39, 45, 52, 53, 67, 323
Son of man/Abraham/David: 235, 258
Stone, the/Branch, the (see Jesus Christ: Cheif Cornerstone/headship)
Suffering Servant (see Jesus Christ: Messiah/King/Lord/Savior/Redeemer)
Transfiguration: 89, 352
Virgin birth/childhood of (see Jesus Christ: Birth/baptism/genealogy of)
Word, the: 217, 232
Joy/gladness (see also Rejoicing/joy & Praise/rejoicing/singing): 72, 230, 420, 421, 437, 457
Judgment/justice/judging/vengeance: 20, 24, 26, 35, 55, 57, 62, 67, 68 73, 75, 86, 87, 89, 95, 97, 101, 103, 106, 107, 113, 133, 138, 152, 154, 157, 180, 181, 183, 223, 231, 232, 240, 259, 261, 289, 293, 295, 298, 300, 301, 312, 315, 319, 324, 325, 340, 345, 364, 370, 394, 396, 397, 401, 406, 409, 411, 413, 425, 433, 441, 446, 454, 456
Justification (see Redemption/justification/restoration)
Kingdom of God/Christ/Heaven: 216, 311, 315, 317, 319
Kingdom, united/divided: 140
Kinsman redeemer: 114, 205, 207
Lamb, innocent (see also Sacrifices/offerings): 26
Laver of Brass/Brasen Sea (see **The Tabernacle** pg 31): 35, 36
Law, the (see also Word of God): 29, 39, 79, 89, 114, 195, 197
Leadership/elder/bishop/minister (see Church leadership/elder/bishop/minister)
Leadership (see Church leadership/elder/bishop/minister):
Leprosy: 48, 62, 152, 349
Long-suffering: 111
Lord's Supper/communion (see also Passover, Feast of/ Passover/communion) : 20, 26, 51, 52, 60, 94, 339, 367, 374, 376, 380, 402
Love: 253
Lust (see Immorality/morality & Morality/immorality/homosexuality/lust & Homosexuality): 133, 134
Marriage/intermarriage/divorce: 4, 47, 50, 76, 105, 179, 190, 197, 252, 253, 353, 397, 408

Materialism: 8, 15, 17, 73, 74, 145, 156, 163, 392, 400, 421, 425, 428, 453
Meat (meal) Offering: 43, 44
Meekness/humility (see also Humility/meekness): 23, 71, 107
Mercy (see also Grace): 64, 67, 91, 106, 111, 113, 231, 314, 342, 360, 371, 393, 396, 401, 433
Mercy Seat (see **The Tabernacle** page 31): 39, 120, 144, 294, 303
Messianic/geneology (see also Jesus Christ: Birth/baptism/genealogy or & Jesus Christ: Genealogy of & Jesus Christ: Virgin birth): 91, 97, 114, 115, 190
Morality/immorality/homosexuality/lust (see also Homosexuality & Immorality/morality & Lust): 10, 29, 37, 68, 112, 113, 133, 147, 412, 430, 436, 453
Motives (see also Attitudes/motives): 65, 86, 355
Murder/manslaughter : 75, 105, 125, 126, 134, 222, 237, 382
Nazarite vow: 58
Obedience/disobedience/rebellion (see also Rebellion/disobedience): 3, 5, 7, 20, 26, 29, 37, 40, 46, 50, 54, 55, 57, 61, 63, 64, 65, 67, 68, 71, 74, Dueteronomy, 79, 81, 82, 83, 84, 85, 87, 88, 89, 90, 94, 95, 96, 97, 98, 101, 102, 103, 106, 107, 122, 123, 135, 141, 142, 145, 147, 150, 153, 158, 176, 180, 181, 190, 192, 194, 206, 223, 227, 232, 247, 256, 276, 318, 322, 337, 350, 351, 352, 367, 383, 393, 397, 398, 399, 404, 409, 415, 433, 435, 436, 439, 442, 443, 444, 445, 450, 454
Offerings/sacrifices (see also Sacrifices/offerings): 42, 44, 45, 46, 57, 59, 60, 68, 83, 90, 100, 303
Oneness in Christ: 341
Opposition (see also Satan): 63, 65, 98, 187, 193, 338, 391, 393, 395, 401, 427, 449, 451, 452, 453, 455
Oppression/bondage: 24, 102, 107, 108, 225
Parables of Jesus: 340, 343, 348
Parents/children (see also Family): 77, 79, 82, 182, 256, 272
Passover, Feast of/ Passover/communion (see Lord's Supper/communion)
Patience/impatience: 28, 405, 428, 437
Peace/contentment: 28, 45, 54, 72, 185, 375, 343, 395, 406, 415, 421, 424, 452, 453
Peace Offering: 44, 45
Pentecost/prophecy: 51, 52, 77, 84, 216, 316
Persecution/cruelty/martyrdom: 210, 211, 311, 338, 379, 382, 383, 391, 392, 409, 421, 427, 449, 451, 452
Plagues: 25, 26, 300
Pleasing God: 13
Potter, the: 276
Power of God (see God, power of):
Praise/rejoicing/singing (see also Joy/gladness & Rejoicing/joy): 34, 53, 89, 167, 168, 171, 173, 214, 219, 230, 231, 374, 391, 420, 437, 451, 454, 456, 457
Prayer/intercession: 9, 14, 28, 34, 38, 43, 60, 66, 95, 96, 102, 106, 107, 113, 119, 128, 130, 132, 135, 136, 138, 144, 148, 159, 167, 168, 171, 173, 174, 214, 224, 226, 228, 231, 247, 262, 263, 268, 280, 297, 308, 309, 355, 376, 379, 382, 393, 403, 414, 415, 427, 436, 454
Pride/self sufficiency/over-confident (see also Selfishness/self-seeking/self-sufficiency): 7, 23, 62, 95, 99, 108, 110, 121, 136, 180, 236, 244, 259, 275, 440, 450
Priest/minister, requirements of (see also Church leadership/elder/bishop/minister & Leadership): 50
Priorities: 17, 82, 83, 99, 152, 163, 220, 249
Prodigal son: 364
Promises (see also Covenants/promises/oaths/vows & Vow/oaths/promises):

109, 138, 451
Prophecy: 257, 260, 261, 278, 281, 297, 306, 311,313, 317, 326, 329, 333, 334, 355, 357, 373, 374, 384, 392, 447
Prophecy, Messianic: 14, 30, 39, 43, 1, 77, 84, 214, 235, 254, 255, 256, 257, 258, 260, 278, 322, 223, 329, 330, 333, 334, 355, 357, 373, 384, 392
Prophecy/fulfilled: 43, 77, 84, 160, 163, 185, 233, 264, 271, 277, 280, 284, 286, 287, 298, 299, 300, 318, 322, 323, 326, 329, 330, 333, 334, 357, 373, 374, 384, 392
Prophets, true and false: 338, 344, 373
Prosperity/luxury/riches/wealth: 83, 87, 248, 249, 259, 289, 293, 298, 317, 363, 364, 365
Rape: 134
Reasoning, human: 96, 103
Rebellion/disobedience (see also Obedience/disobedience/rebellion): 223, 268, 273, 277, 284, 397, 446, 452, 455
Rebuke/reproof:
Reconciliation: 26, 35, 45, 46, 49, 54, 396, 402
Redemption/justification/restoration (see also Justification): 35, 39, 54, 66, 67, 227, 300, 302, 322, 328, 329, 384
Reformation: 160, 182
Rejoicing/joy (see also Praise/rejoicing/singing & Joy/gladness): 72
Relationships (see Alliances/friendships/relationships)
Repentance (of God): 276
Repentance (of man) (see also Salvation): 10, 25, 46, 48, 54, 67, 106, 113, 133, 159, 173, 174, 187, 194, 195, 222, 227, 290, 314, 316, 324, 364, 372, 380, 384, 399, 449, 450, 456
Resentment/bitterness/revenge: 124, 405
Respect: 79, 82
Responsibility: 76, 85, 88, 94, 137, 138, 165, 170, 223, 238, 256, 272, 341, 353, 360, 392, 415, 427
Restoration of Israel: 54, 271, 281, 302, 328
Resurrection (see Jesus Christ: Crucifixion/death/resurrection):
Resurrection of believers: 216
Revenge/vengeance (see also Vengeance/revenge):
Reverence: 79, 82, 167
Revival: 194
Righteousness: 143
Sabbath/Lord's Day: 64, 339
Sacrifices/offerings (see also Offerings/sacrifices): 4, 11, 20, 26, 35, 41, 42, 43, 44, 45, 46, 47, 49, 59, 60, 66, 83, 90, 109, 122, 144, 431, 434, 439
Salvation/redemption (see also Deliverance/destruction/restoration): 1, 5, 10, 26, 30, 31, 35, 38, 39, 48, 49, 60, 67, 101, 143, 162, 225, 227, 266, 302, 314, 357, 364, 370, 371, 382, 383, 384, 399, 400, 409, 411, 424, 432, 433, 439, 442, 446, 450, 451, 456
Satan/devil (see also Opposition): 1, 3, 56, 63, 76, 81, 110, 177, 202, 203, 209, 225, 229, 231, 241, 242, 260, 262, 263, 265, 286, 335, 338, 367, 376, 391, 397, 400, 401, 408, 414, 432, 453, 456
Satisfaction/dissatisfaction: 53, 56, 182, 230, 248, 251, 280, 285
Scapegoat: 42, 49
Security/safety: 5, 224, 229, 274, 376
Seeking the Lord: 176
Selfishness/self-seeking/self-sufficiency/self-centered/self-will/self-denial/

greed (see also Covetousness/greed & Greed/covetousness): 7, 12, 23, 63, 65, 74, 76, 86, 87, 95, 99, 110, 111, 121, 154, 169, 170, 172 215, 226, 251, 364, 435, 443, 454

Self-righteousness: 351

Separation (see also Nazarite): 47, 58, 106, 110

Serpents, fiery/plagues: 67

Service/ministry (see also God: Purpose/will of & Stewardship/serving God/ devotion & Tithes/offerings): 8, 25, 50, 59, 65, 99, 107, 151, 164, 165, 170, 391, 403

Silver trumpets: 61, 72, 73

Sin Offering: 32, 44, 46

Sin/consequences of: 1, 3, 4, 15, 26, 29, 30, 31, 35, 46, 47, 48, 49, 50, 53, 54, 55, 57, 62, 66, 67, 68, 71, 73, 78, 87, 88, 89, 95, 96, 101, 102, 103, 107, 110, 111, 112, 113, 120, 122, 123, 125, 128, 132, 133, 134, 138, 139, 141, 146, 147, 153, 156, 157, 159, 163, 179, 180, 181, 183, 215, 222, 223, 227, 232, 241, 245, 257, 259, 260, 261, 271, 274, 288, 293, 297, 298, 313, 316, 317, 318, 345, 349, 364, 370, 384, 396, 397, 398, 399, 404, 411, 412, 422, 432, 433, 434, 441, 444

Sincerity: 151

Sorrow/burdens/grief/misery/suffering (see also Hardships/difficulties & Suffering/grief/hardship/misery/sorrow): 17, 22, 24, 220, 222, 224, 234, 265, 276, 278, 288, 289, 290, 375, 391, 392, 393, 395, 407, 409, 4435, 437, 438, 441, 449

Sower/sowing: 287, 340

Spirit filled/led by (see also Holy Spirit): 215, 236, 245, 399

Spiritual gifts/growth/maturity: 16, 215, 225, 376, 392, 393, 396, 407

Spiritual influence: 50, 74

Spiritual warfare: 101, 228, 413, 425, 437

Stewardship/serving God/ devotion (see also Service/ministry & Tithes/offerings & God: Purpose/will of): 83, 85, 165, 170, 345, 381, 400, 403

Stewardship/serving God/devotion: 425, 449

Strange fire/unauthorized fire: 57

Strongholds: 131

Submission (see also Authority/submission & Submission/to authority & Submission/to God): 25, 42, 57, 61, 65, 71, 78, 95, 166, 213, 353

Submission/to authority (see also Authority/submission & Submission & Submission to God): 65, 71, 79, 358, 366

Submission/to God (see also Authority/submission & Submission & Submission/to authority): 25, 57, 61, 65, 71, 78, 79, 95, 361

Success/failure: 77, 79, 95, 102, 121, 122, 123, 128, 149, 180, 259, 364

Suffering/grief/hardship/misery/sorrow (see also Hardships/difficulties & Sorrow/burdens/grief/misery/suffering): 17, 22, 24, 78, 87, 106, 107, 110, 111, 124, 127, 130, 133, 134, 137, 153, 192, 203, 204, 205, 207, 213

Tabernacle, the: 30, 31-34, 35, 36, 38, 39, 40, 53, 59, 303, 375, 391, 392, 393, 395, 407, 409, 435, 437, 438, 441, 449

Tabernacles, festival of (see also Booths): 51, 72

Table of Showbread/Shewbread (see **The Tabernacle** pg 31): 35, 36, 53, 303

Taxes: 366

Temple, the: 143, 144, 165, 169, 182, 287, 288

Temple, cleansing of: 343

Temple/destruction: 184, 227, 287, 288, 303

Temple, future/millennial: 303, 304, 305

Thanksgiving/gratitude (see also Gratitude/thanksgiving): 27, 59, 83, 156, 167,

171, 371, 451
Throne of David: I & II Samuel
Tithes/offerings (see also Service/ministry & God: Purpose/will of & Stewardship/serving God/devotion): 59, 83, 100, 331, 366, 381, 403
Traditions: 351
Trespass Offering: 44
Trials/tests/temptations: 3, 9, 11, 15, 16, 17, 18, 19, 22, 24, 27, 28, 78, 81, 86, 87, 88, 95, 103, 106, 110, 111, 121, 122, 124, 126, 127, 133, 139, 192, 193, 199, 203, 204, 207, 208, 224, 234, 238, 335, 339, 365, 368, 375, 391, 393, 395, 400, 407, 421, 425, 435, 437, 449, 450, 451, 452, 453
Tribulation, Great: 254, 306, 311, 455
Trinity, the Godhead: 1, 80, 144, 257, 346, 354, 359
Trumpets, Feast of: 51, 61, 73, 316
Truth: 30, 57, 61, 73, 400, 413, 428, 445, 446, 454
Unbelief: 27, 28, 55, 56, 63, 64, 77, 78, 370, 408
Unity/fellowship (see also Fellowship/unity): 236, 376, 381, 403, 408
Unleavened Bread, Feast of: 51, 52
Vanity/emptiness: 248, 249, 250, 251
Vengeance/revenge (see also Revenge/vengeance): 246
Victory/overcoming: 81, 87, 95, 96, 97, 98, 101, 121, 123, 148, 422, 444, 450, 451, 452, 453, 454, 455
Violence: 126, 131
Vow/oaths/promises (see also Covenants/promises/oaths/vows & Vow/oaths/promises & Promises): 14, 58, 96, 109, 111, 296
Wealth/materialism (see also Prosperity): 83, 87, 156, 177
Weeks, Feast of (see also Pentecost): 52
Wickedness/evil: 147, 156, 159, 179, 181, 183
Willingness: 165
Wisdom/instruction/knowledge: 142, 172, 209, 212, 242, 426
Wise men: 334
Witch: 128
Witness/witnessing: 177, 382, 394, 404, 409, 421, 427, 452
Word of God: 5, 7, 20, 23, 24, 25, 29, 33, 35, 36, 40, 53, 54, 57, 60, 61, 76, 77, 78, 79, 81, 82, 83, 87, 88, 89, 90, 95, 100, 107, 126, 132, 138, 141, 142, 146, 148, 150, 155, 157, 158, 160, 168, 169, 172, 174, 188, 190, 193, 194, 195, 210, 214, 217, 234, 239, 240, 242, 247, 248, 251, 253, 268, 281, 288, 300, 313, 315, 335, 340, 344, 350, 351, 376, 379, 383, 392, 397, 400, 404, 407, 413, 414, 422, 430, 435, 437, 439, 440, 441, 450, 452
Works of the flesh: 412
World empires: 7, 196, 306, 307, 310, 364, 400, 408, 425, 430, 435, 436, 450, 453, 455
Worship/praise/rejoicing/singing: 167, 171, 173, 196, 230, 451, 454, 456
Worship, true/false: 5, 15, 25, 30, 37, 54, 80, 81, 82, 83, 88, 99, 106, 107, 181, 182, 250, 284, 352, 413, 434, 449